Learning disability

A life cycle approach

Second edition

*Edited by Gordon Grant, Paul Ramcharan,
Margaret Flynn and Malcolm Richardson*

Open University Press

Open University Press
McGraw-Hill Education
McGraw-Hill House
Shoppenhangers Road
Maidenhead
Berkshire
England
SL6 2QL

email: enquiries@openup.co.uk
world wide web: www.openup.co.uk

and Two Penn Plaza, New York, NY 10121-2289, USA

First published 2005
This edition published 2010

A catalogue record of this book is available from the British Library

ISBN-13: 9780335238439 (pb)
ISBN-10: 0335238432 (pb)

Library of Congress Cataloging-in-Publication Data
CIP data applied for

Typeset by RefineCatch Limited, Bungay, Suffolk
Printed in the UK by Bell and Bain Ltd, Glasgow

Mixed Sources
Product group from well-managed
forests and other controlled sources
www.fsc.org Cert no. TT-COC-002769
© 1996 Forest Stewardship Council
FSC

The **McGraw-Hill** Companies

For all the silenced voices of people with learning disabilities and their families

Contents

About the editors

Gordon Grant is Emeritus Professor, Centre for Health and Social Care Research, Sheffield Hallam University, UK, formerly having been Professor of Cognitive Disability at the University of Sheffield and Doncaster, Rotherham and South Humber NHS Foundation Trust. He has long-standing interests in the experiences and contributions of vulnerable groups, coping and resilience in families, the applications of participatory and emancipatory research, and evaluation of national policy for people with learning disabilities. With Paul Ramcharan he was co-ordinator of the Department of Health Learning Disability Research Initiative linked to the evaluation of *Valuing People*.

Paul Ramcharan is Co-ordinator of Research and Public Policy at the Australian Centre for Human Rights Education at RMIT University, Melbourne, Australia. Paul has been involved in research around learning disabilities for 20 years stretching back to the evaluation of aspects of the All Wales Strategy. He has maintained an interest in empowerment and people with learning disabilities, most recently in an Australian Research Council grant exploring the history of self-advocacy in Victoria, Australia. Together with Gordon Grant he has also acted as co-ordinator of the Learning Disability Research Initiative supporting research tied to the implementation of *Valuing People*.

Margaret Flynn is the Independent Chair of Lancashire County Council's Safeguarding Vulnerable Adults Partnership Board, a Senior Associate of CPEA Ltd and a Director of Flynn and Eley Associates Ltd. Her interests include the adult social care workforce, the experiences of family caregivers and safeguarding. She is a joint editor of the *Journal of Adult Protection*.

Malcolm Richardson is currently a Principal Lecturer at Sheffield Hallam University, UK, and was formerly Head of the Department of Mental Health and Learning Disabilities in the School of Nursing and Midwifery, University of Sheffield. His research interests are in the areas of disability, health, and social and political inclusion. His professional background is in learning disabilities nursing and nurse education.

Contributors

Dawn Adams, Research Fellow, Cerebra Centre for Neurodevelopmental Disorders, School of Psychology, University of Birmingham and Academic Tutor, Division of Clinical Psychology, University of Manchester

Kathryn Almack, Research Fellow, Sue Ryder Care Centre for Palliative and End of Life Studies, School of Nursing, Midwifery and Physiotherapy, University of Nottingham, Nottingham, UK

Dorothy Atkinson, Professor of Learning Disability, Faculty of Health and Social Care, Open University, Walton Hall, Milton Keynes, UK

Nigel Beail, Honorary Professor, University of Sheffield, Consultant Clinical Psychologist and Head of Psychology Services for Adults with Learning Disabilities, Psychological Health Care, Barnsley Learning Disability Service, Barnsley Primary Care Trust, Barnsley, UK

Christine Bigby, Professor and Director of Undergraduate Programmes, Department of Social Work and Social Policy, La Trobe University, Bundoora, Victoria, Australia

Alison Brammer, Senior Lecturer, Department of Law, University of Keele, Keele, Staffordshire, UK

Jacqui Brewster, Nursing Lecturer, Faculty of Health and Wellbeing, Sheffield Hallam University, Sheffield, UK

Hilary Brown, Professor and Consultant in Social Care, Social Care and Adult Protection, Salomans Centre, Kent, UK

Jennifer Clegg, Associate Professor, University of Nottingham; **Honorary Consultant Clinical Psychologist and Head of the Psychology Service** for the Community Learning Disability Directorate, Nottinghamshire Healthcare NHS Trust, Nottingham, UK

Lesley Cogher, Manager, Sheffield Speech and Language Therapy and Community Dieticians, Sheffield Primary Care Trust, Sheffield, UK

Helen Combes, Clinical Lecturer, Shropshire and Staffordshire Clinical Psychology Training Programme, Faculty of Health and Sciences, Staffordshire University, Mellor Building, College Road, Stoke-on-Trent, UK

Clare Connors, formerly Research Fellow at the University of Durham, currently studying homeopathy in the north east of England

Bronach Crawley, Parent and Clinical Psychologist

Eric Emerson, Professor of Clinical Psychology, Centre for Disability Research, Lancaster University, Lancaster, UK

Margaret Flynn, Consultant, Flynn and Eley Associates Ltd and CPEA Ltd UK and **Independent Chair**, Lancashire County Council Safeguarding Adults Board. She has a brother with a learning disability

Linda Gething, formerly **Divisional Head of Learning Disability Studies**, University of Huddersfield, Huddersfield, UK

Dan Goodley, Professor of Psychology, Research Institute for Health and Social Change, Manchester Metropolitan University, Manchester, UK

Peter Goward, Post-registration Academic Development Manager, Faculty of Health and Wellbeing, Sheffield Hallam University, Sheffield, UK

Gordon Grant, Emeritus Professor, Centre for Health and Social Care Research, Sheffield Hallam University, Sheffield, UK

Chris Hatton, Professor of Psychology, Health and Social Care, Centre for Disability Research, Lancaster University, Lancaster, UK

Sheila Hollins, Professor of Psychiatry of Learning Disability, Division of Mental Health, St George's, University of London, London, UK

Jane Hubert, Senior Research Fellow and Honorary Senior Lecturer in Social Anthropology, St George's, University of London, London, UK

Kelley Johnson, Professor and Director, Norah Fry Research Centre, University of Bristol, Bristol, UK

Gwynnyth Llewellyn, Professor and Dean, Faculty of Health Sciences, University of Sydney, Lidcombe, Australia

Heather McAlister, Child and Adolescent Learning Disability Psychiatrist, Chesterfield Royal Hospital NHS Foundation Trust, Chesterfield, UK

Michelle McCarthy, Senior Lecturer in Learning Disability, Tizard Centre, University of Kent at Canterbury, Canterbury, UK

Alex McClimens, Research Fellow, Centre for Health and Social Care Research, Sheffield Hallam University, Sheffield, UK

Roy McConkey, Professor of Learning Disability, School of Nursing, University of Ulster, Newtownabbey, Northern Ireland, UK

David McConnell, Professor, Department of Occupational Therapy, University of Alberta, Edmonton, Canada

Fiona Mackenzie, Consultant Psychiatrist, Sheffield Care Trust, Sheffield, UK

Keith McKinstrie, Service Manager (Social Care), Joint Learning Disabilities Service, Sheffield City Council, Sheffield, UK

Ghazala Mir, Senior Research Fellow and Head, Centre for Health and Social Care, University of Leeds, Leeds, UK

Ada Montgomery, Behavioural Nurse Specialist, Rotherham, Doncaster and South Humber NHS Foundation Trust, Doncaster, UK

Lesley Montisci, Assistant Director of Registered Care, Enable Group, Derbyshire, UK

Elizabeth Murphy, Professor of Sociology, Pro-Vice Chancellor and Head of the College of Social Science, University of Leicester, Leicester, UK

Chris Oliver, Professor of Neurodevelopmental Disorders, Cerebra Centre for Neurodevelopmental Disorders, School of Psychology, University of Birmingham, Birmingham, UK

Richard Parrott, Strategic Commissioning Manager, Learning Disabilities, Sheffield City Council, Sheffield, UK

Paul Ramcharan, Coordinator Research and Public Policy, Australian Centre for Human Rights Education, Royal Melbourne Institute of Technology, Melbourne, Australia

Malcolm Richardson, Principal Lecturer (Learning Disabilities), Nursing and Midwifery, Faculty of Health and Wellbeing, Sheffield Hallam University, Sheffield, UK

Bronwyn Roberts, Nursing Lecturer, University of Huddersfield, Huddersfield, UK

Dame Philippa Russell, OBE, Chair of the Standing Commission on Carers, and **Disability Policy Adviser** to the National Children's Bureau. She is the parent of an adult son with a learning disability, London, UK

Kirsten Stalker, Professor, Faculty of Education, University of Strathclyde, Glasgow, Scotland, UK

Martin Stevens, Research Fellow, Social Care Workforce Research Unit, Kings College, University of London, London, UK

John L. Taylor, Professor of Clinical Psychology, CHESs Research Centre, Northumbria University, Newcastle upon Tyne, UK

Irene Tuffrey-Wijne, Palliative Care Nurse Specialist, Division of Mental Health, St George's, University of London, London, UK

Sally Twist, Consultant Clinical Psychologist/Clinical Lead for Learning Disabilities, Pennine Care NHS Foundation Trust, Oldham Learning Disabilities/Vulnerable Adult Clinical Psychology Service, Oldham, UK

Jan Walmsley, Independent Consultant and Visiting Professor in the History of Learning Disability, Open University, UK

Kate Woodcock, Research Fellow, Cerebra Centre for Neurodevelopmental Disorders, School of Psychology, University of Birmingham, UK

Preface

This textbook is written primarily as a reader for students intending to work with people with learning disabilities in health and social care services, but also as a resource for professionally qualified practitioners. This second edition is refreshed and updated, and includes new chapters on aetiology, breaking news (about disability) and early intervention, transition to adulthood, the sexual lives of women, employment, personalization, and finally people with hidden identities.

In answer to the question, 'Why another textbook?' we were prompted to rise to this challenge for several reasons. First, we wanted to underline the importance of the voice of people with learning disabilities. We have therefore retained narrative chapters in the book that describe, in the words of people with learning disabilities themselves, their own accounts of their lives past and present, and their hopes for the future. We hope that these narrative chapters provide a more textured feel for the everyday lives of people with learning disabilities, helping to illuminate the part played by families, advocates and services in supporting them. In nearly all the chapters, contributing authors have in addition made extensive use of case studies or vignettes in order to bring theories, concepts and practice 'to life'.

Second, we wanted to acknowledge more fully something that is often overlooked in a lot of contemporary writing – namely, learning disability as a lifelong disability. It was this recognition that led us to structure the book around the idea of the life cycle. In this second edition of the book we have incorporated a new introduction posing the question 'Why the life cycle?' In answering this question we try to convey a sense of the textured connections between changing personal, social and environmental factors shaping people's life experiences as they grow and develop, thereby providing different kinds of lenses for making sense of people's everyday lives, their identities and aspirations.

A third reason for writing this book was to provide space for a critical discussion of the contested nature of 'disability' (learning disability in particular), what this means or implies, and how it has been represented historically and contemporaneously. The very title of this book implies a category, but we were keen to locate this within the contexts where people live out their lives, where a fuller sense of their identities as human beings can be appreciated. In doing so we therefore draw not only from medical models and constructions of learning disability, but also from legal and social models, each offering different accounts of how disability is produced, reproduced and understood.

The book comprises five sections, each beginning with an overview that introduces the themes and principal ideas covered. Respective sections are intended to take the reader on a journey through different life stages from childhood to adolescence and early adulthood, to adulthood and finally to later life. We have located chapters where we think they are most relevant to a particular life stage, but recognize many cut across the lifespan. However, the first part dwells upon different constructions of learning disability and how these have affected thinking and practice around about service models, approaches to quality assurance, quality of life and advocacy. We have deliberately positioned the narrative chapters at the beginning of each of the five sections of the book so as to provide a 'proper' place for people with learning disabilities to speak for themselves. The narrative chapters 'invite' readers to listen to what is being communicated, to reflect upon the ideas being articulated and to use these accounts as an interpretive device for subsequent chapters in the section. To further support learning, each chapter contains exercises.

With the growing importance of evidence-based practice we have endeavoured to summarize and critique relevant bodies of theoretical and empirical knowledge, and to be frank about where we think knowledge is still lacking. It will remain important to ask 'Whose knowledge?' and 'What knowledge counts?' and to remember that people with learning disabilities, and their families, are above all else most knowledgeable about themselves. Professional knowledge counts, but so does professional humility. This book does not provide cookbook recipes. Supporting people with complex or high support needs does not come so easily. Rather, the book seeks to encourage intending practitioners to think reflexively and to act in a principled way that respects the dignity and rights of people with learning disabilities and their families.

In bringing this volume together we have been fortunate to secure contributions from respected figures from a range of disciplines including nursing, midwifery, psychology, psychiatry, human communication sciences, social policy, social work, sociology, social anthropology, law, occupational therapy and management sciences. We hope this in its own way emphasizes the importance of inter-disciplinary thinking to the support of people with learning disabilities.

Finally, our rationale for revising the book's title arises from its proximity to English policy. Readers familiar with the first edition will be aware that we have dropped the term 'valuing people' from the sub-title. This has been done to avoid possible confusion that the book is a reader dedicated to the White Paper bearing the same title. In this book contributors do of course acknowledge key policy instruments that reinforce important values, organizational responsibilities and professional practices. It is hoped that, by bringing together both evidence and critique, the book will stimulate student readers to be trail-blazers in helping to improve the lives of people with learning disabilities and their families across the life cycle.

Gordon Grant, Paul Ramcharan, Margaret Flynn
and Malcolm Richardson

Acknowledgements

When as editors we began work on this second edition we were daunted by both its scope and scale. Having elected to emphasize the importance of both life cycle issues and also personal, social and environmental factors in the everyday lives of people with learning disabilities, it was clear that contributions from many people would be required. We were helped substantially in our task by our employers, Sheffield Hallam University, UK, and the Royal Melbourne Institute of Technology, Australia, who gave us the time and support to bring this text to fruition. The support of the universities has been equalled by the expertise and enormous goodwill of the contributors to the 35 chapters in this volume, many of whom have responded with patience and humour to our requests for editorial changes.

Many of the contributors have spent substantial amounts of time undertaking research with, providing services to and for, or looking after people with learning disabilities. Although many people with learning disabilities and their families, advocates, support workers and friends remain individually anonymous in this volume, we nevertheless hope that their voices can be heard throughout the text. We express our gratitude to them for sharing their knowledge and for their help and co-operation.

A project of this scale would not have been possible without the commitment and guidance of key people at the Open University Press/McGraw Hill Education. In this regard we are particularly indebted to Catriona Hoyle, Bryony Skelton, Julie Platt and Kiera Jamison who provided helpful, expert and friendly advice at all stages.

Introduction: why the life cycle?

When we first set out to structure this textbook we were drawn unhesitatingly to the idea of the life cycle. Though, as discussed in some detail in Part 1 of this book, learning disability is a contested construct, one thing more difficult to deny is that it is a lifelong condition. We think that this has been neglected both by policy and by practice; yet life cycle perspectives have much to offer in helping health and social care practitioners reflect upon important connections between the past lives of people with learning disabilities, their present circumstances and future prospects.

Too often, when a term like 'transition' is used in this context, it is applied to the singular and important transition between childhood and adulthood. Indeed one of the new chapters in this edition problematizes this particular transition and discusses how young people and families experience it. But people's lives are not devoid of other transitions, and it can be argued that the entire life cycle is characterized by challenges around definition, events and circumstances to which people have to adapt, develop and change.

We therefore take the reader on a journey through various life stages, Parts 2–5 of the book focusing on childhood and early parenting (Part 2), adolescence and transitions to adulthood (Part 3), adult identities and community inclusion (Part 4), and finally ageing and end-of-life issues (Part 5). Our hope is that this will help readers to anticipate change and discontinuity in people's lives and to think of strategies for support that are far more seamless and effective in enabling inclusion, control, independence and expression of rights over the life cycle.

Contributors to this edition raise many 'cradle to grave' issues. The life cycle debate now encompasses 'pre-cradle', because of the arrival of new challenges brought about by improved genetics, and 'post-grave', because of the voids that can be left in people's lives following the bereavement of either people with learning disabilities, their family members or significant others. However, we are not suggesting that there is a linear connection between chronological age and human development because this overlooks the important idea that life is culturally embedded and socially constructed (Priestley 2000). In this book, therefore, we try to illustrate how people's lives as individuals are shaped by social, cultural and environmental circumstances across the life cycle as much as by personal agency or capacity.

One way of understanding this rather more contingent notion of the life cycle is through the lenses of clocks and calendars. Most obvious, perhaps, is the internal clock of the individual, which can be divided into biological and psychological components. The *biological clock* is tied to the reasonably predictable circuit of the human body as it moves through its own physical timetable, and in this connection we begin to see associations between health, co-morbidities and survival. *Psychological readiness* is also claimed to be connected to human development but it is now more readily accepted that self-identity formation reflects the interplay between historical, cultural and social contexts (Giddens 1991). Several chapters in this book draw attention to tensions that can arise in people's lives between biological and psychological perspectives on development and the responses required from support workers.

Cultural and social time, however, are especially important in this edited text. In this view the norms, values and rules about the time at which life events are expected to occur and the meaning ascribed to temporality by different social groups or cultures play a significant role (Zerubavel 1981; Mills 2000). For many people with learning disabilities in post-industrial societies, for example, there is no wage earning life stage, retirement and old age are taken to occur at any age over 50 and retirement offers very little of shared experience with other retirees. Exploring how such norms and values play out has significant value in understanding continuities and discontinuities in the lives of people with learning disabilities and their families. Family caregiver stress, for example, has been linked to the idea that families of children with disabilities can over the years find themselves caring 'out of time', compared to other families, which can lead to predictable problems and adaptations. At the same time, the ageing of family caregivers does not lead to an inevitable decline in the physical and psychological status of these caregivers – time and experience have many compensations, not the least of which is knowledge and expertise. A sensitivity to temporal experiences in people's lives may therefore be just as important in challenging practitioners to question stereotypes.

But *institutional calendars* have a powerful influence on individual and collective human behaviour. There are for example the calendars of the family, religious, educational, work and civic institutions. For people with learning disabilities especially there is also the prospect of negotiating transitions between different services – health, education, housing and social care services for example – over the life course. This can be particularly difficult when these services operate with different, sometimes incompatible, schedules, values, philosophies and priorities. These externally sourced discontinuities can be hugely disruptive, as for example evidenced by people with learning disabilities facing 'out of area' placements as a result of a paucity of local joined-up services. This leads to important questions about how to create seamless partnerships between services, built upon the hopes and aspirations of people with learning disabilities and their families. It also calls into question the role of civil society in supporting them, in protecting and fulfilling their human rights and in ensuring that their well-being is at least comparable to other groups.

Many chapters in this volume bring together an understanding of how biological, psychological, cultural and institutional elements define historical events and policies. They shape the experiences and outcomes of their generation and have long-lasting effects – for example, the experience of institutionalization has left indelible marks on the lives of many adult and older men and women with learning disabilities, as several chapters in this book attest. But future cohorts will hopefully be enabled to avoid these experiences. *Historical time* is therefore an inescapable factor framing the conditions, practices and experiences of particular ages.

If there are macro-level changes that affect policy and practice, the experiences of parallel clocks and calendars also affect each individual. Taking account of these temporal factors in people's lives can help to inform why moments, periods or transitions are important to them, and why they may require careful decisions about ways to scaffold support in order to enable self-determination and adaptation. These clocks and calendars also have the potential to highlight asynchronous periods in the life cycle when time clocks are running counter to one another. These are likely to be difficult periods for people. For example, upon reaching adulthood many people with learning disabilities find themselves not engaging typical roles such as holding down a job, progressing their careers and therefore building up pensions. This would be an example of a major disjunction between physical or psychological clocks and the normative work calendar.

The connections between the experience of everyday life and the life cycle are elaborated in much greater detail throughout the book. The validity and authenticity of these connections stems from the fact that they can often be found in the narratives and talk of people with learning disabilities and families and, as such, the first chapter of each of the five parts of this book starts with those views as a primer to the following chapters.

References

Giddens, A. (1991) *Modernity and Self-Identity: Self and Society in the Late Modern Age*. Cambridge: Polity Press.

Mills, M. (2000) Providing space for time: the impact of temporality on life course research, *Time and Society*, 9(1): 91–127.

Priestley, M. (2000) Adults only: disability, social policy and the life course, *Journal of Social Policy*, 29(3): 421–39.

Zerubavel, E. (1981) *Hidden Rhythms: Schedules and Calendars in Social Life*. Berkeley, CA: University of California Press.

Part One
The construction of learning disability

At the start of each Part in this book, the editors provide a content guide to the section and, by reviewing the chapters individually, identify some of the main themes and learning outcomes. In Parts Two to Five the first chapter of each is a narrative account which places the voice of people with learning disabilities across the life cycle at the forefront of our interest in their lives. By hearing their voice at the head of each Part in Chapters 8, 15, 23 and 31, the chapters that follow can be read against their interests and experiences. These chapters seek to establish the evidence base in terms of contemporary knowledge, as well as providing practice-based knowledge, information and advice.

To identify our subject matter for this volume as 'people with learning disabilities' may seem unproblematic. It is not.

Over the past century and a half there have been huge changes in the labelling of those people we presently categorize as having learning disabilities. In social policy terms, they have been labelled as 'vagabonds', 'idiots', 'mentally subnormal', 'mentally handicapped', 'learning disabled' and 'people with learning difficulties' among other names. Each of these labels has been the product of 'warranted ascription' by others – i.e. labels applied by interests who hold the power to define others and who, through their power, claim the label to be warranted. Needless to say, the 'official' label at any one point in time has harnessed and supported the development and growth, at least since industrialization, of 'an industry of professionals' whose work has been based upon these varying definitions.

You will find in Part One that, historically, the separation of people with learning disabilities from the 'mainstream' (i.e. from everybody else) features among other things: placing them into the same category as other unemployable people who receive charity; seeing them as a threat to the national gene pool and hence placing them 'around the bend' (out of sight in institutions), separated by gender or sterilized to avoid procreation; medicalized and treated as 'cases' predominantly through biomedical interventions; viewing them as the focus of rehabilitation and social programmes; and only latterly defining them through their own efforts as 'people first' with the same rights as others; and, as in *Valuing People Now* (Department of Health 2009), making bold moves towards a personalization agenda which seeks to place them in control of their lives and services.

The history of people with learning disabilities has not always been a pleasant one and nor have their life experiences. Their place within various categories has changed across the ages but each 'warranted ascription', though superseded, has left within contemporary policy and practice a residue of the past. In making these points it is essential therefore to see present definitions and practice as occupying just one historical point in time. It is also necessary in these respects to ask ourselves what values are driving definitions and what effect this is likely to have on the people we now label as people with 'learning disabilities'.

It is the aim of the seven chapters in Part One of this book to review the varying constructions of learning disability historically and to help readers think about whether the contents of the following parts of the book themselves create our present history as a 'warranted ascription'.

In Chapter 1, Dorothy Atkinson establishes why life stories and narrative accounts by people with learning disabilities matter, how such accounts have come to be told and the practical and ethical dilemmas of such work. From uncovering history through people's personal experiences to the development of a personal identity that provides a means of reclaiming their lives and planning for the future, the chapter provides a voice of hope and of reason. The life story accounts in this chapter highlight humanity at its most sublime and instruct the reader to see:

- the ways in which people with learning disabilities as expert witnesses have related the rich variety of their experience and diversity of life histories;
- resilience in the face of seemingly insurmountable odds as well as liberation from institutional practices;
- the development and maintenance of meaningful and loving relationships in the face of exclusion;
- the development of a sense of identity through storytelling that liberates people from their past and produces in them hope for their future;
- the importance of storytelling and how it can be facilitated.

The history of people with learning disabilities stretches beyond those who can give living testimony and Chapters 2 and 5 provide historical evidence to fill this gap. In the first of these, Chapter 2, Alex McClimens and Malcolm Richardson consider how warranted ascriptions of people with learning disabilities have changed through time. They demonstrate how (learning) disability has been socially constructed through the ages from pre-history to the present day. They demonstrate how the mode of production and dominant values of any era influence the response of the public and of government and how these in turn reflect in the legitimacy of varying professional groups and the services they provide. The chapter demonstrates that:

- the varied history of how people with learning disabilities have been viewed makes us question the 'fact' of learning disability, helping us to see the term as socially constructed and each of us as contributing to the contemporary construction through our beliefs and actions;
- the growth of scientific thinking had a crucial effect on defining people with learning disabilities and, under such definitions, the appropriate professional inputs;
- science and definition are not value-free and the consequences whether intended or not can be harmful;
- contemporary services carry the ghosts of previous definitions and eugenic principles still operate in contemporary society.

Chapter 2 finishes at around the time when the medical hegemony in relation to the treatment of people with learning disabilities was at its height. The movement towards a social model of learning disabilities in the past 20 years or so often seeks to dismiss the biomedical model as creating the label 'learning disability' and as being a primary pathologizing source of exploitation. In Chapter 3, Fiona Mackenzie and Heather McAlister relate how a bio-psycho-social account is constructed within the medical profession. The source of different terminology in categorizing people with learning disabilities is outlined alongside the means through which diagnoses are made. A case study is used to establish how, by using the medical categorizations appropriately, in this case of Prader-Willi syndrome, it is possible to improve the health and life quality of those so labelled. In an age in which the social model seems to have an ascendancy, this chapter urges the reader to:

- see the importance to social inclusion of the bio-psycho-social model in recognizing medical and health care needs;
- understand limitations in common forms of medical classification and diagnostic criteria in classifying forms and levels of impairment;
- understand the struggles at different stages of the life cycle, from neonate to late adult life, of applying a diagnosis and developing an appropriate intervention;
- develop (in non-medical practitioners) an understanding of the ways in which the bio-psycho-social model can be used to improve health and life quality.

The chapters in Part One show substantial recent movement in the ways we think about people with learning disabilities and their place as citizens. In Chapter 4, Alison Brammer brings to our attention a significant raft of new legislation and case law since publication of the first edition of this volume. In particular the relevance of the Mental Capacity Act 2005 is explained in detail along with the relevance of the Human Rights Act 1998 and Britain being signatory to the UN Convention of the Rights of People with Disabilities. Updated legislation such as the Disability Discrimination Act 2005, the Sexual Offences Act 2007 and the Mental Health Act 2007 are covered and case studies are used to impose some clarity in terms of how the law operates. In this chapter the reader will:

- learn the exceptions to the rule that people with learning disabilities are treated no differently under the law;
- learn the definitions applied to people with learning disabilities for the purposes of the law;
- understand the importance of 'capacity' and how it is applied in decision-making under the 2005 Act;
- become conversant with human rights legislation and Conventions;
- learn about both different forms of abuse and the nature of sexual offences under recent legislation;
- seek to apply an understanding of the law to case studies.

The nature of service provision after the Second World War and, in particular, accommodation for those not living in a family home is the focus for Eric Emerson and Paul Ramcharan in Chapter 5. The chapter offers an account of the patchy and extreme conditions in which some people with learning disabilities were housed under the Poor Laws of the nineteenth century, the development of the 'educational' model within large institutions up to the 1960s and the incremental move towards deinstitutionalization, community care and normalization. This has culminated in the UK policy of closing all long-stay hospitals by 2006 and most recently the aim to shut down remaining cluster housing also. In reviewing empirical evidence about contemporary community residential options a note of caution is sounded about how we might best assess different community residential options, pointing to the contingent relation between service provision and outcome. The chapter notes that, while there are some residential options more likely to lead to better outcomes, the benefits are still a far cry from accomplishing the aspirations of present policy. In this chapter we are guided to:

- understand our present service delivery and residential options as products of a long history;
- explore the real degradation, exploitation and misery of many people with learning disabilities during the period of institutionalization;
- question, using the evidence, the assumptions we presently hold about how service design and delivery affect outcomes and impact;
- make judgements, on the basis of empirical data, about the relative merits of different residential

options for people with learning disabilities in contemporary society.

Taken consecutively the chapters in Part One demonstrate substantial changes to policy and services in the past 30 years. In Chapter 6, Lesley Montisci and Gordon Grant summarize the ways in which quality of services can be judged. The contemporary focus is on quality of life, the intended outcome, standards, equity and quality of service provision. These intentions are problematic and the authors usefully outline competing quality of life models and describe responsibility for monitoring and review of service quality in England. In this chapter the reader will:

- learn to use critically the concept of 'quality of life';
- see the ways in which government policy has led to a preoccupation with risk and with clinical governance;
- understand how services operationalize and measure service quality;
- learn how quality of life and service quality might be related to each other within practice settings.

In Chapter 1, Dorothy Atkinson made a strong case for hearing the voice of people with learning disabilities through narratives. Moving from narrative to 'voice' as a 'political' tool, Dan Goodley and Paul Ramcharan review in Chapter 7 the development of advocacy over the past 40 years. Identifying the different forms of advocacy and the limits of professional involvement in this arena, they argue that advocacy itself has a history that has increasingly moved from professional and service orientations towards one in which the voice of people with learning disabilities is fully reclaimed. This is best represented in the growing campaigning role that has, they argue, emerged over time out of the self-advocacy movement. Having read this chapter the reader will:

- be able to distinguish different forms of advocacy;
- understand the limits to professional involvement within advocacy;
- have a clear idea about how the historical development of advocacy demonstrates a consistent move towards people with learning disabilities reclaiming their voice as 'people first';

- understand how some of the contemporary issues around the government funding for advocacy can be viewed as a form of colonization on the one hand but, on the other, a powerful means of exerting pressure and establishing a joined-up approach by government departments to addressing the agenda of self-advocates;

- see how campaigning represents a relationship between interests shared by people with learning difficulties and other groups.

We hope you will enjoy Part One of this book. At the end you might ask yourself what values you feel underlie your view about people with learning disabilities and the extent to which the chapters have influenced that view.

You see things; and you say 'Why?'
But I dream things that never were; and I say 'Why not?'
(George Bernard Shaw, *Back to Methusela*, 1921)

1

Narratives and people with learning disabilities

Dorothy Atkinson

Introduction

Everyone has a story to tell. However, an *entire* life story is rarely told. Instead, it is recounted in a series of oral narratives, or stories, told throughout the life as it is lived (Linde 1993). Only rarely is the full account written down as a life story or autobiography, a preserve that remains largely for the rich and famous. And yet other lives matter too, especially where they shed light on otherwise neglected or hidden areas of social life. This chapter switches the focus away from celebrity stories to celebrating and understanding the life stories of people with learning disabilities.

Not surprisingly, perhaps, there are relatively few published life stories, or autobiographies, written or commissioned by people with learning disabilities. Examples include: *Tongue Tied* (1974) by Joey Deacon; *The World of Nigel Hunt* (1967); *A Price To Be Born* (1996) by David Barron; Mabel Cooper's life story (1997); and *Cold Stone Floors and Carbolic Soap* (2004) by John Able. In addition to the single life stories are the collected narratives and autobiographies in anthologies, such as *'Know Me As I Am'* (Atkinson and Williams 1990) and *Positive Tales* (Living Archive 1996). The anthology *'Know Me As I Am'* contained the life stories, many originally in oral form, of around 200 people with learning disabilities. It demonstrated through its unique size, scope and diversity that people with learning disabilities could, with support, tell their stories in their own words or images.

People with learning disabilities portrayed themselves in the anthology as fully rounded and complex human beings, with distinct personal histories and a wealth of experiences. Together, the anthology contributors brought out the differences and the commonalities between their lives and the lives of other people in society, including the ordinary, the everyday and the mundane as well as stories of loss, separation and segregation.

This chapter explores more fully why life stories matter, especially to people with learning disabilities. It also traces the influences that have come together to make life stories important now, and reviews the ways in which life stories come to be told. Finally, the chapter draws out some of the ethical and practical issues of life story work, and considers what implications they may have for practice.

> ### Exercise 1.1
>
> Think about times when you tell other people about your life. Why is that important to you? Why is it important to the people you are telling?

Why life stories matter

Life stories matter to everyone – they enable us to express our sense of self, conveying to others who we are and how we got that way (Linde 1993; Widdershoven 1993; Meininger 2006). Life stories, and the narratives that make them up, are oral stories, told to another person or audience at various points in time. They may be rehearsed and refined and, over time, may be revised. Life stories, and the opportunity to tell them, are particularly important for people with learning disabilities because often they have been silent, or silenced, while other people – families, practitioners, historians – have spoken on their behalf. Life stories begin to redress that balance as they become a means by which people with learning disabilities have a voice that is theirs.

The life story, when written down, conveys the author's sense of identity and becomes something to show other people, a point made by Mabel Cooper in reflecting on hers: 'You've got something to show for your life. You've got something so that you can say, "That's what happened to me". It will keep history in my mind for years to come, what's happened to me and a lot of others like me' (Atkinson 1998: 115). Mabel Cooper's life story is no 'ordinary' story; it takes its readers into a separate and segregated world of children's homes and long-stay institutions. The process of telling the story was important to Mabel in making sense of history – not just her own personal history ('what's happened to me') but the history of many thousands of people who, like her, were labelled and excluded from everyday life. The end product, the written story, is 'something to show' for a life lived to a large extent in a separate world.

It is, therefore, possible to suggest that the life stories of people with learning disabilities are important for a number of reasons. They:

- help us trace an otherwise hidden history;
- treat people as 'expert witnesses';
- enable people to represent themselves as fully rounded human beings;
- show the beginnings of a resistance movement;
- encourage historical awareness and reflexivity.

Each of these points will now be considered in turn.

Tracing a hidden history of learning disability

On the whole, people with learning disabilities were silent and invisible in the historical accounts of learning disability policy and practice (Ryan and Thomas 1981). Their very invisibility and silence meant that the degradation and inhumanity of their lives in the long-stay hospitals went unrecorded for many years (Oswin 1978; Ryan and Thomas 1981; Malacrida 2006). These were forgotten people, leading forgotten lives so that telling their stories became a social and historical imperative (Atkinson *et al.* 1997; Potts 1998).

The telling of history by historians relying on documentary sources has meant losing the 'richness and complexity' of lived historical experience as told through people's life stories (Rolph 1999). Without their own written accounts and, until recently, their own oral accounts, people with learning disabilities were seen as a people with 'no history' (Prins 1991). The development of methods that support people in the telling of their life stories (such as oral history techniques) has meant that 'more history' (new

insights into history) and 'anti-history' (another set of stories or understandings which challenge conventional perceptions) (Frisch 1990) can now be told and recorded.

Treating people as expert witnesses

Life stories can act as 'a counterbalance' to accounts (Williams 1993) which focus on pathological differences or deficits/defects and give a very limited view of people's lives. The life story, or autobiography, allows for a richer and more rounded account that can temper the professional orientation of normalization, for example, or 'the "victim" approach of many of the well-intentioned revelations of the worst aspects of institutional life' (Williams 1993: 57).

In public life more generally, people with learning disabilities are seen as people who have to be cared for – they are the disregarded and excluded, 'the other' (Walmsley 2000: 195). However, in telling their life stories, often in depth (Booth and Booth 1998), they become 'expert witnesses' in the matter of their own lives (Birren and Deutchman 1991; Bjornsdottir and Svensdottir 2008). They are not simply 'sources of data' for researchers' own narratives, but people with personal stories to tell (Booth and Booth 1996). Without the usual 'stock of stories' from family, friends and community, and the everyday documents, photographs and memorabilia of family life from which to draw in order to make sense of their lives, the need for people with learning disabilities to tell their own story becomes even more compelling and empowering (Gillman *et al.* 1997). What is needed is the time, space and support in which life stories can be told because that enables people to regain their past and 'also helps them towards a future' (Thompson 1988: 265).

Enabling people to represent themselves as fully rounded human beings

Where their own histories remain untold, people may be objectified, seen as members of a homogeneous group, and have identities imposed by others (Sutcliffe and Simons 1993; Gillman *et al.* 1997). By way of contrast, the life story that is initiated and told by the person concerned holds the greatest potential for self-representation. It allows people with learning disabilities to represent themselves as human beings; to develop their own accounts of family life, school-days, relationships and so on; and to be seen as a person rather than a 'case'. This enhances people's sense of personal identity, which is an empowering process. Those who have been involved attest to the positive affirmation of identity which this has given them: 'We are self-advocates who are running work-shops on "telling your life story" for people with learning disabilities. We have both been supported to write our own life stories and want to help others to do theirs' (Able and Cooper 2000: 7).

Beginning a resistance movement

There are two ways in which life stories can be part of a resistance movement. First, when telling their own stories, people can actually demonstrate their resilience in the face of adversity (Goodley 2000). Rather than portraying themselves solely as victims they see themselves as people who showed resistance against the forces of oppression (see Chapter 21). From their own accounts, they resisted, they fought back and they mocked the people, and the systems, which sought to control them (Potts and Fido 1991; Sibley 1995; Goodley 1996; Stuart 1998, 2002; Rolph 1999). Fighting back (see Chapter 7) is one way to become a 'border crosser' from a segregated life to an inclusive one in the mainstream of society (Ramcharan *et al.* 1997; Rolph 1999).

Second, people's life stories become part of a resistance movement when their individual and collective accounts connect to tell a different, and more complex, story of their lives (Gillman *et al.* 1997). Put together, life stories become historical documents, between them mapping the events of the twentieth century. In their accounts, authors emerge not only as victims of an oppressive system but as people who survived it, and were actors in their own lives (Stefansdottir 2006). They showed resistance in the face of adversity; agency in the shaping of their lives; and a capacity to reflect on how, and why, they survived (see Chapter 21 for further discussion of resilience).

Encouraging historical awareness and reflexivity

Life stories can bring with them a greater personal awareness of history and an understanding of how past policies and practices have shaped people's lives. This is because the telling of the life story allows the narrator to stand back and develop reflexivity, to begin to explicate his or her own history as part of the wider history of people with learning disabilities.

These are points echoed by Mabel Cooper in reflecting on the importance of her (written and published) life story:

> You've got something so that you can say, 'This is what happened to me.' Some of it hurts, some of it's sad, some of it I'd like to remember. My story means a lot to me because I can say, 'This is what happened to me', if anyone asks. So it's great, and I will keep it for the rest of my life. I will keep the book.
>
> (Atkinson *et al.* 1997: 11)

Working on her life story enabled Mabel to start to make sense of her life, and to put past events into perspective (life review). In addition, she is able to tell other people what it was like to live a separate and segregated life – to be a historical witness. The written word is important in this context: it is enduring, and it is 'something to show' for the life that has been led.

Exercise 1.2

Think of one or two people with learning disabilities with whom you work or have worked. What do you know of their history? From what sources does that history come? Is there anything else you might want to know that would help you in your support role?

Why life stories have come into prominence now

There are three key factors, in particular, that help explain how and why life stories have come into prominence as a late twentieth- and early twenty-first-century phenomenon: normalization, participatory research and self-advocacy. The people who were involved in the life story research that underpins this chapter have all, at some point in their lives, been labelled and segregated, often in long-stay hospitals. Normalization brought in its wake a pool of people with learning disabilities who were leaving the long-stay hospitals and who were more accessible as potential participants in research. Normalization also helped create the conditions in which 'speaking up' became possible (Walmsley 2001). 'Valued' research roles, such as respondent, interviewee, oral historian and so on, have been attributed to normalization's insistence on valued social roles. Similarly, the researcher in some post-normalization research is seen as an advocate, as well as a researcher, a development also attributed to the legacy of normalization (Walmsley 2001; Walmsley and Johnson 2003).

Subsequently, the development of participatory research in learning disability has also helped bring life stories to prominence. Life story work is by its very nature participatory, as it involves a person, or a group of people, in a very active process of storytelling. Participatory research lends itself well to engaging people in the various stages of the research process, and it changes the social relations of research, making it a partnership rather than a hierarchical relationship where people 'take charge' of their history (Westerman 1998: 230). Participatory research, in these terms, can be seen as part of the struggle of people with learning disabilities to name oppression and counter it; to develop a historical awareness of their situation and the situation of others (Freire 1986). The capacity of participatory research to encourage and support the empowerment of people with learning disabilities makes it an attractive option both for researchers and participants, and helps explain how it has become an important development for learning disability research (Chappell 2000). See also Chapter 35 in this volume.

Finally, it could be argued that self-advocacy was also a factor in the growth of interest in life stories, demonstrating to researchers both that people with learning disabilities *wanted* to 'speak up' and that they *could do so*. At the same time, it seems likely that self-advocacy influenced the people who were involved in it, showing them the value of research and giving them the confidence to take part.

It is through self-advocacy that people with learning disabilities have started to articulate their experience of being labelled, or categorized, as different. This trend has been accompanied by a steady stream of autobiographies (already referred to) which have challenged their negative portrayal by others, including the eugenicists, who saw them as the perpetrators of social ills (Abbot and Sapsford 1987; Williams 1989), and the normalization writers, who portrayed them as the victims of an oppressive system (Wolfensberger 1975).

How life stories come to be told

In essence, life stories are told through a 'mixed method' approach, drawing on the techniques of oral history, life history and narrative inquiry. They may be told on a one-to-one basis, with the interviewer/researcher being the audience – or told in a group setting where the researcher and the peer group form a combined audience. The development of oral history from the 1960s provided a means by which the accounts of ordinary people could be recorded and preserved as historical documents in their own right (Thompson 1988; Bornat 1989). Oral history involves people remembering and recalling past personal and social events. It enables people to 'put a stamp on the past' (Bornat 1994) and provides the means by which people in oppressed groups (e.g. women, black people and disabled people) can record, document and reclaim their individual and shared histories. The reclaiming of history in this way can be seen as a way of resisting the accounts and interpretations of others, and celebrating a distinctive identity (Walmsley 1998).

Alongside the growth in popularity of oral history has been the re-emergence of life history research, which seeks to draw out and compile individual auto/biographies. The life history/narrative tradition in sociology can be traced back to the work of the Chicago School in the US in the 1920s, in particular to the work of Thomas and Znaniecki (1918–20). The approach flourished in the 1920s and 1930s, then declined, but re-emerged in the 1980s and flourished again in the 1990s (Stanley 1992; Gillman et al. 1997; Rolph 1999). Plummer (1983) argued for the reinclusion of life history methods in sociological research, and Maines (1993: 17) noted that the 'narrative's moment' had arrived in social science methods of inquiry. This reflects a more general move towards what Booth and Booth (1996) have called the 'age of biography', including storytelling and narrative methods of research.

Life story research sheds light on history by making possible the telling of insider accounts by people on the 'fringes' or margins of society, accounts which are grounded in real-life human experience (Booth and Booth 1994). In learning disability research, however, researchers needed to overcome barriers such as 'inarticulateness, unresponsiveness, a concrete frame of reference and problems with time' (Booth and Booth 1996: 55). Although life stories tell the stories of individuals, they are part of a wider social, historical and political context; they form a bridge between the individual and society, showing up the structural features of people's social worlds (Booth and Booth 1998). Thus, life story methods allow for 'listening beyond' the words of the informant to the world around and beyond the person (Bertaux-Wiame 1981): to other people in similar situations, and to the networks of the wider society to which they belong. The common threads which emerge from life story research reveal how individual lives are shaped and constrained by the social world – and historical era – in which they are situated (Goodley 1996; Booth and Booth 1998).

Life story research (including both oral and life history methods) is now being used in the learning disability field. Literature is still relatively sparse, however, the slow take-up perhaps reflecting the fact that this approach was seen to require people who could articulate and reflect on their experiences (Plummer 1983; Thompson 1988). Only recently has it become apparent that barriers to life story research could be overcome (Booth and Booth 1994, 1996, 1998; Goodley 1996; Rolph 1999; Stuart 2002).

The role of the researcher is important in enabling people to tell history 'in their own words'. This, however, may be problematic as some people with learning disabilities may not easily find the words with which to recount their stories. What is emerging in the literature is the need sometimes to co-construct accounts with people where the words are hard to find, and where researchers have to listen to silences and proceed using 'creative guesswork' (Booth and Booth 1996) or the strategy of 'successive approximation' (Biklen and Moseley 1988). Instead, the challenge is to overcome the barriers to involvement through sensitivity and innovation on the part of the researcher (Ward 1997; Owen and Ledger 2006). 'Guided tours' of familiar places and 'guided conversations' using props such as photographs and drawings may be needed to dismantle the barriers (Stalker 1998; Ledger 2008).

Inclusive methods involve the researcher working closely with the oral or life historian to enable them to tell their story (see Chapter 35 for a discussion of inclusive research methods). A 'feeling human observer' (Booth and Booth 1994: 36) is needed not only to facilitate the proceedings, but also to observe the consistency and coherence of the stories as they emerge. The researcher needs to be reflexive and self-aware: to facilitate stories, not to take them over; to work with people, not to exploit them; and to 'listen beyond' words, not speak for people (Goodley 1996). Echoing this, Ristock and Pennell (1996) recommend constant self-monitoring by researchers as a safeguard against making and acting on unwarranted assumptions about research participants.

Exercise 1.3

Think about a person with learning disabilities who you work with. How would you enable that person to 'tell their story'? What approaches would you use? What places would you visit? Where else might you look for information?

Research roles can include acting as advocate, scribe or supporter as well as researcher. Similarly, where people with learning disabilities are unable to articulate or elaborate on their experiences, the researcher may become their interpreter or biographer (Goodley 1996). Close and prolonged involvement between researcher and participants can continue long after the research has ended (Booth 1998).

Compiling individual life stories

A classic approach to co-constructing a life story is to work directly with the person who wants to tell it. This applied to my work with Mabel Cooper, some of whose words have already been quoted in this chapter. Our work together started when Mabel asked me to help her write her life story. We met at her home where she talked to me about her childhood in children's homes, her subsequent move to St Lawrence's Hospital and her later life in the community, including her work in the self-advocacy movement. We tape-recorded our conversations and I later transcribed them word for word. From those question-and-answer transcripts, I prepared a more flowing and chronological account which I then read back to Mabel for confirmation or amendment. The readings triggered more memories which were themselves woven into the emerging story. The result was initially a private publication for Mabel and her friends, but subsequently the life story was published in a book (Cooper 1997) and placed on the internet.

As suggested above, the autobiographical process enabled Mabel to make sense of her life and to see it in a wider social context. In telling her life story, she was not only reclaiming her past, she was at the same time reflecting on the social history of learning disability in the second half of the twentieth century. The extract below combines personal history with period detail. Here, Mabel recalls how and why she came to leave the children's home in Bedford to move to St Lawrence's Hospital:

> I moved to St Lawrence's when I was seven, because they only took children what went to school in this home. And I never went to school, so I had to move. In them days they give you a test. You went to London or somewhere because they'd give you a test before they make you go anywhere. It used to be a big place, all full of offices and what-have-you. Because they said you should be able to read when you're seven or eight. I couldn't read, I hadn't been to school. That was 1952, I was seven years old . . . When I first went in there, even just getting out of the car you could hear the racket. You think you're going to a madhouse. When you first went there you could hear people screaming and shouting outside. It was very noisy but I think you do get used to them after a little while because it's like everywhere that's big. If there's a lot of people you get a lot of noise, and they had like big dormitories, didn't they?

(Cooper 1997: 22)

There seems little doubt that Mabel gained historical awareness and understanding through the process of compiling her life story – and also that the finished product brought with it a great sense of achievement. The experience of being an autobiographer has proved a rewarding one. Mabel is well aware of her role as a historical witness, a role which entails letting people know what life was like for her and others in the past. In one of our many subsequent conversations about the meaning and significance of her life story, Mabel pinpointed both the sense of personal achievement it brought for her and its importance as a historical record of the past:

> It's an achievement with me being in St Lawrence's for so many years, and not knowing anything else but St Lawrence's. I thought it would be nice to let people know what it was like, and to let people know how difficult it was for someone with a learning disability, and who was stuck away because of that. I thought that people outside should know these things because they're not aware of it at the moment and I think it would be nice.

(Atkinson et al. 1997: 9)

The compilation of Mabel's life story, initially from memory, pinpointed many gaps. She was left with unanswered questions such as: Who was she? Who were her parents? What had become of them? Mabel's need to know led her into a search for documentary evidence from her own case records and from the archived papers of the institutions where she had spent her childhood and much of her adult life. Such a quest seemed daunting at times, and some of the language of the past proved hurtful, but the need to know became a strong driving force. Consequently, we visited together the records of the Lifecare Trust, the London Metropolitan Archives and the Bedfordshire Record Office, in search of case notes, diaries, photographs, newspaper cuttings and any other documentary evidence of the time. The successful location and access to personal records for Mabel (and subsequently the four other people who later became involved in what is now known as the Life History Project) meant that many long-forgotten – or never known – areas of life were revealed. Since those early visits with Mabel, the life story process with other people with learning disabilities invariably includes whatever written accounts of the time can be unearthed, the aim being to confirm key dates, times, places and people. It is important to note, though, that these records are not simply 'there', waiting to be perused, they have to be searched for and then accessed, mediated and understood.

Mabel's involvement in the 'telling' of the history of learning disability owes much to the development of the self-advocacy movement, which has enabled her and other people to 'speak up' about themselves and their lives. She and others in the life story research were, or are, self-advocates; their capacity to 'speak up' in self-advocacy groups has enabled them to speak up in the telling of their life stories. Just as self-advocacy is about self-representation, so too is the recounting of the life story. It enables people to make sense of their own lives but also to understand their lives in relation to those of other people. This has proved to be, for Mabel and others, an empowering process.

Using group work for storytelling

An alternative to individual work is to invite people to join a group. This was an approach I used in what came to be known as the Past Times Project – an approach which aimed to capture, if possible, the richness of individual accounts but to do so within what I hoped would prove to be the more insightful and reflective mode of a group setting. The Past Times Project involved a group of people with learning disabilities recalling and reflecting on their past lives. The group consisted of nine people; seven men and two women. The age range was 57 to 77, with most participants being in their late sixties or early seventies. Potential group members were approached, and invited to join, via the staff of the special residential and day settings of which they were currently users. The group met over a two-year period, each meeting lasting an hour and, with permission, being tape-recorded and later transcribed. This is where oral history techniques proved invaluable as I was able to use reminiscence and recall to enable group members to talk about their past lives.

At the time, this was set up as a history project which would cover not only the history of difference (exclusion, separation and incarceration) but also the history of sameness. The research participants were, accordingly, invited to remember and share the ordinary and everyday experiences of their lives; to recall happy memories as well as sad ones and to see their lives as part of the unfolding and wider history of the twentieth century. Against this backdrop, of course, emerged the histories of difference, where people's lives diverged from the ordinary and the everyday.

The Past Times Project used a group setting in order to provide a supportive and friendly atmosphere where (sometimes) painful memories could be shared, and to provide a forum where one person's memories of past events would spark off memories in others. The group format in the end worked well in that the group eventually became that supportive-but-stimulating environment that I had anticipated. But it took time, practice and patience to reach that point. Early group meetings were characterized at times by silence and, at other times, by anarchic cross-talking and multiple side conversations. Some members loved to hold the floor and recount extended anecdotes whereas others seemed content to sit quietly, venturing little. Various memory triggers were used, ranging from the simple, 'Do you remember . . .?' to the use of professionally produced reminiscence slides and tapes, and our own authentic cigarette cards, photographs and other memorabilia of the time.

Running the group was never easy. There were problems of communication throughout our meetings, as it was often difficult for me to understand the words and content of many of the contributions, even when the tapes were replayed later at home. One or two staff members from the day and residential services, who knew group members well, helped where they could with translation and interpretation. Thus we struggled together to hear and be heard for the whole of the first year. At that point we took a break from meetings so that I could compile the numerous fragments and vignettes from the (by now) large pile of transcripts into a booklet which I entitled *Past Times*.

This booklet was, as it turned out, the first of a series of versions of 'our book' (as members preferred to call it). A series of readings from *Past Times* over a period of many weeks triggered off more and deeper memories. A second draft was compiled which incorporated these new accounts. Again, I proceeded on a series of readings from the expanded version and, again, more memories emerged. Thus a third and final version of *Past Times* was produced, reflecting the group's wish that we should produce a 'bigger and better' book rather than just a booklet (Atkinson 1993). Looking back, it seems as if the process of readings-and-amendments could have continued indefinitely with the book continuing to grow and grow. Certainly, at the time, group members were united in their wish to continue with the project rather than being persuaded to stop after two years.

As it was, the written account, *Past Times*, proved to be of immense importance to its contributors. As people with learning disabilities they had had restricted access to the written word. Yet they clearly recognized its value as a means of influencing opinion and shaping attitudes. They wanted their work to be in print because – like Mabel Cooper in another context – they wanted other people to know about them and their lives. They also saw the written word as authoritative. Their experiences were, it seemed, validated through being written down.

The book proved of interest to people beyond contributors, and their immediate circle of families and friends. Some accounts of childhood and schooldays were quite ordinary for their time and place; an example being Brian Sutcliffe's memory of his northern working-class childhood in the early/mid years of the twentieth century: 'We had a back-to-back house with a cellar and gas lights. We had a coal fire and a coal hole.'

In later years, Brian's life, and the lives of other contributors, turned out to be far from ordinary because, sooner or later, they became users of separate or segregated services. For some people, like Margaret Day, this happened in childhood, as the following extract illustrates: 'When I was a little girl I was put away. I was 14 and a half. I went to Cell Barnes to live because they said I was backward. My dad refused to sign the papers for me to go, but the police came and said he would go to prison if he didn't. I cried when I had to go with the Welfare Officer.'

In addition, *Past Times* also includes shared memories of hospital life. These afford us glimpses into a hidden world hitherto described primarily in formal documents. In the following extract, George Coley recalls a well-remembered character from years ago: 'I don't know if Bert still remembers Lewis? He was a Charge Nurse. He used to have three stripes on each arm and three pips on the top of his jacket. And

first thing in the morning you knew he was about. If you said anything, and he went like that [raises his arm], you knew what he meant. Bed!'

Overall, the stories told in the group had many classical 'narrative features' (Finnegan 1992: 172). They were clearly bounded and framed narratives, containing characters in addition to the narrator. They portrayed an event or episode, or a series of events and episodes, featuring a sequence of moves or actions, and were often spoken in different voices to indicate a dialogue. Sometimes the story also conveyed some sort of moral or message. In addition, the performance element of storytelling, and the audience effect, meant that the stories became more complex over time with increased exposure and practice.

Reviewing ethical and practical issues

There are, undoubtedly, important moral and ethical issues that arise in working with people with learning disabilities on their life stories. For example, the close involvement with 'vulnerable' or 'lonely' people over a period of time feeds into the debates in feminist and disability literature on the dangers of exploitation in participatory research (Gluck and Patai 1991; Finnegan 1992; Ristock and Pennell 1996; Oliver 1997; Stalker 1998; Rolph 1999). There are complex issues around ending research, and its aftermath – the sense of loss and betrayal which may be felt by ex-participants (Ward 1997; Booth 1998; Northway 2000) and in some participatory research the option of contact continuing beyond the life of the project is built into the process. Not all participants opt for this but it is considered by some researchers to be an important safeguard, especially for people with relatively few social networks (e.g. see Booth 1998; Northway 2000).

The 'telling' of life histories involves close personal contact over time between the 'feeling human observer' and the research participants (Booth and Booth 1994). This means that self-awareness, and the capacity to be self-critical and reflective, are vital attributes in oral and life history research. The importance of researcher awareness and reflexivity is echoed in the wider literature (Goodley 1996; Ristock and Pennell 1996). The process of recording and co-constructing life histories involves telling, recording, searching (through records), revising (through 'readings') and compiling the words and fragments into a coherent whole. The researcher's role also entails 'listening beyond' the words of each life story to pick up echoes of other people's stories; to tease out the common threads which have shaped their lives; and to see the links into the networks and structures of the wider society (Bertaux-Wiame 1981; Booth and Booth 1994; Goodley 1996).

Finally, what are the implications of life story work for practice? One thing to note in this context is that nurses, care workers, social workers, occupational therapists and other people at the front line of practice are uniquely placed to promote and support life story work, not only through their existing relationships with people with learning disabilities, but also through their access to documentary and family sources. Good practice in field work emulates good practice in research. Enabling people with learning disabilities to develop a life book or multi-media profile, for example, involves the same processes of spending time and working closely with potential authors; searches for, and interrogation of, docu-mentary sources; and the tracking down and inter-viewing, where appropriate, of family, friends and other significant people (Fitzgerald 1998). This is a labour-intensive process which, at its best, will feed into and influence person-centred planning (Chapter 25). It is important to note in this context, however, that life stories are not the same as case notes or case histories, as they are told (or compiled) from the point of view of the people most centrally concerned. Case notes/histories, on the other hand, are formal and more 'distant' accounts of the person, told by others.

Exercise 1.4

You can try out the difference between a life story and case notes by (a) writing a paragraph about yourself as if it is written by a professional who knows you (but not well) and (b) by writing a paragraph directly about yourself. Compare the two – they should look very different.

Conclusion

Life stories are not just a series of events in more or less chronological order but are narratives, shaped and structured by the author in the telling of the story. People tell their stories in order to make sense of their lives, to establish their identity, and to make connections with others (Gillman et al. 1997). This is where research emulates good practice in fieldwork. The telling of the story as part of historical research can be empowering – but so too can the constructing of a life story book by people with learning disabilities with a care worker, social worker or other practitioner. A life story book gives people an opportunity to 're-author' their life history, and to bring out those bits which have been repressed and silenced (Sutcliffe and Simons 1993; White 1993). The life story book becomes an alternative or counter document which can recount the person's resilience and struggle against discrimination and exclusion (Goodley 1996; Gillman et al. 1997). The success of narrative research in influencing practice still remains to be seen but it has the potential to strengthen self-advocacy through the emerging sense of a shared history among people with learning disabilities and to improve practice in both research and field work settings.

Life story research can harness the reflexivity of people with learning disabilities, and heighten their historical awareness. As research awareness grows, more people are likely to become involved in the telling of their personal histories and thus in the telling of history itself. Those accounts, separately and together, will help tell the history of learning disability in the twentieth and twenty-first centuries. The challenge that still remains is how that history is presented, and to whom – and how it properly becomes a history that is known and owned by people with learning disabilities themselves.

Exercise 1.5

If you want to follow up the possible ways of enabling people with learning disabilities to tell their stories, there are a number of things you can do next:

1 Discover more about oral history

Oral History – a journal
Consider joining the Oral History Society (which runs oral history conferences and training workshops
Tips on doing oral history: http://www.ohs.org.uk/advice/
Visit the national sound archives at the British Library, London

2 Find out about doing oral history interviews

Ritchie, D.A. (2003) *Doing Oral History: A Practical Guide,* 2nd edn. Oxford: Oxford University Press.
Thompson, P. (2000) *The Voice of the Past: Oral History,* 3rd edn. Oxford: Oxford University Press.
Yow, V. (2005) *Recording Oral History,* 2nd edn. Walnut Creek, CA: AltaMira Press.

3 Look at examples of life story work with people with learning disabilities

Ashby, I. and Lewis, K. (1996) *Real Lives: Memories of Older People with Learning Difficulties.* London: Elfrida Rathbone.
Atkinson, D. (1997) *An Auto/biographical Approach to Learning Disability Research.* Aldershot: Avebury.
Atkinson, D., McCarthy, M., Walmsley, J. *et al.* (2000) (eds) *Good Times, Bad Times: Women with Learning Difficulties Telling their Stories.* Kidderminster: BILD Publications.
Brigham, L., Atkinson, D., Jackson, M., Rolph, S. and Walmsley, J. (2000) *Crossing Boundaries. Change and Continuity in the History of Learning Disability.* Kidderminster: BILD Publications.
Manning, C. (2008) *Bye-Bye Charlie: Stories from the Vanishing World of Kew Cottages.* Sydney: University of New South Wales Press.
Traustadottir, R. and Johnson, K. (2000) *Women with Intellectual Disabilities: Finding a Place in the World.* London: Jessica Kingsley Publishers.

4 Consider using other resources to get you started

Gibson, F. (2006) *Reminiscence and Recall: A Practical Guide to Reminiscence Work,* 3rd revised edn. London: Age Concern Books.
Hewitt, H. (2006) *Life Story Books for People with Learning Disabilities.* Kidderminster: BILD Publications.
Looking Forward, Looking Back: Reminiscence with People with Learning Difficulties (1998). A training resource developed by Mary Stuart. Available from Pavilion Publications, Brighton.
The Open University's Social History of Learning Disability website contains examples of life stories: http://www.open.ac.uk/hsc/ldsite/
A group of story tellers with learning disabilities living in Somerset have a website about their work: http://www.openstorytellers.org.uk

References

Able, J. (2004) *Cold Stone Floors and Carbolic Soap.* Milton Keynes: Private publication.

Able, J. and Cooper, M. (2000) Mabel Cooper's and John Able's stories, in *Self Advocacy Stories.* London: Mencap.

Abbot, P. and Sapsford, R. (1987) *Community Care for Mentally Handicapped Children.* Milton Keynes: Open University Press.

Atkinson, D. (1993) *Past Times.* Milton Keynes: private publication.

Atkinson, D. (1998) Reclaiming our past: empowerment through oral history and personal stories, in L. Ward (ed.) *Innovations in Advocacy and Empowerment for People* with Intellectual Disabilities. Chorley: Lisieux Hall Publications.

Atkinson, D. and Williams, F. (1990) 'Know Me As I Am': An Anthology of Prose, Poetry and Art by People with Learning Difficulties. London: Hodder & Stoughton.

Atkinson, D., Jackson, M. and Walmsley, J. (1997) Forgotten Lives: Exploring the History of Learning Disability. Kidderminster: BILD Publications.

Barron, D. (1996) A Price To Be Born. Huddersfield: H. Charlesworth & Co. Ltd.

Bertaux-Wiame, I. (1981) The life history approach to the study of internal migration, in D. Bertaux (ed.) Biography and Society: The Life History Approach in the Social Sciences. Beverly Hills, CA: Sage.

Biklen, S. and Moseley, C. (1988) 'Are you retarded?' 'No, I'm Catholic': qualitative methods in the study of people with severe handicaps, Journal of the Association of Severe Handicaps, 13: 155–62.

Birren, J. and Deutchman, D. (1991) Guiding Autobiography Groups for Older Adults. London: Johns Hopkins University Press.

Bjornsdottir, K. and Svensdottir, A.S. (2008) Gambling for capital: learning disability, inclusive research and collaborative life histories, British Journal of Learning Disabilities, 36(4): 263–70.

Booth, T. and Booth, W. (1994) Parenting under Pressure: Mothers and Fathers with Learning Difficulties. Buckingham: Open University Press.

Booth, T. and Booth, W. (1996) Sounds of silence: narrative research with inarticulate subjects, Disability and Society, 11(1): 55–69.

Booth, T. and Booth, W. (1998) Growing Up With Parents Who Have Learning Difficulties. London: Routledge.

Booth, W. (1998) Doing research with lonely people, British Journal of Learning Disabilities, 26(4): 132–4.

Bornat, J. (1989) Oral history as a social movement, Oral History, 17(2): 16–24.

Bornat, J. (1994) Is oral history auto/biography? Auto/Biography, 3(1) and 3(2) (double issue).

Chappell, A.L. (2000) Emergence of participatory methodology in learning disability research: understanding the context, British Journal of Learning Disabilities, 28(1): 38–43.

Cooper, M. (1997) Mabel Cooper's life story, in D. Atkinson, M. Jackson and J. Walmsley (eds) Forgotten Lives: Exploring the History of Learning Disability. Kidderminster: BILD Publications.

Deacon, J. (1974) Tongue Tied. London: NSMHC.

Finnegan, R. (1992) Oral Traditions and the Verbal Arts: A Guide to Research Practice. London: Routledge.

Fitzgerald, J. (1998) It's never too late: empowerment for older people with learning difficulties, in L. Ward (ed.) Innovations in Advocacy and Empowerment for People with Intellectual Disabilities. Chorley: Lisieux Hall Publications.

Freire, P. (1986) Pedagogy of the Oppressed. Harmondsworth: Penguin.

Frisch, M. (1990) A Shared Authority: Essays on the Craft and Meaning of Oral History. New York: SUNY Press.

Gillman, M., Swain, J. and Heyman, B. (1997) Life history or 'case' history: the objectification of people with learning difficulties through the tyranny of professional discourses, Disability and Society, 12(5): 675–93.

Gluck, S.B. and Patai, D. (1991) Women's Words: The Feminist Practice of Oral History. London: Routledge.

Goodley, D. (1996) Tales of hidden lives: a critical examination of life history research with people who have learning difficulties, Disability and Society, 11(3): 333–48.

Goodley, D. (2000) Self-Advocacy in the Lives of People with Learning Difficulties: The Politics of Resilience. Buckingham: Open University Press.

Hunt, N. (1967) The World of Nigel Hunt. Beaconsfield: Darwen Finlayson.

Ledger, S. (2008) Developing a visual mapping method to support people with intellectual disabilities to tell their life story. Paper presented at 13th IASSID World Congress, Cape Town, 25 August.

Linde, C. (1993) Life Stories: The Creation of Coherence. Oxford: Oxford University Press.

Living Archive (1996) Positive Tales. Milton Keynes: Living Archive Press.

Maines, D.R. (1993) Narrative's moment and sociology's phenomena: toward a narrative sociology, The Sociological Quarterly, 34(1): 18–38.

Malacrida, C. (2006) Contested memories: efforts of the powerful to silence former inmates' histories of life in an institution for 'mental defectives', Disability and Society, 21(5): 397–410.

Meininger, H.P. (2006) Narrating, writing, reading: life story work as an aid to (self) advocacy, British Journal of Learning Disabilities, 34(3): 181–8.

Northway, R. (2000) Ending participatory research? Journal of Learning Disabilities, 4(1): 27–36.

Oliver, M. (1997) Emancipatory research: realistic goal or impossible dream?, in C. Barnes and G. Mercer (eds) Doing Disability Research. Leeds: The Disability Press.

Oswin, M. (1978) Children Living in Long Stay Hospitals. London: Heinemann.

Owen, K. and Ledger, S. (2006) People with learning disabilities: perspectives and experiences, in J. Welshman and J. Walmsley (eds) Community Care in Perspective: Care, Control and Citizenship. Basingstoke: Palgrave Macmillan.

Plummer, K. (1983) Documents of Life. London: Allen & Unwin.

Potts, M. and Fido, R. (1991) 'A Fit Person To Be Removed': Personal Accounts of Life in a Mental Deficiency Institution. Plymouth: Northcote House.

Potts, P. (1998) Knowledge is not enough: an exploration of what we can expect from enquiries which are social, in P. Clough and L. Barton (eds) Articulating with Difficulty: Research Voices in Inclusive Education. London: Paul Chapman Publishing.

Prins, G. (1991) Oral history, in P. Burke (ed.) New Perspectives on Historical Writing. Cambridge: Polity Press.

Ramcharan, P., Roberts, G., Grant, G. and Borland, J. (1997) Citizenship, empowerment and everyday life, in P. Ramcharan, G. Roberts, G. Grant and J. Borland (eds) *Empowerment in Everyday Life: Learning Disability*. London: Jessica Kingsley.

Ristock, J. and Pennell, J. (1996) *Community Research as Empowerment: Feminist Links, Postmodern Interruptions*. Oxford: Oxford University Press.

Rolph, S. (1999) *The history of community care for people with learning difficulties in Norfolk 1930–1980: the role of two hostels*. Unpublished PhD thesis, Milton Keynes, Open University.

Ryan, J. with Thomas, F. (1981) *The Politics of Mental Handicap*. Harmondsworth: Penguin.

Sibley, D. (1995) *Geographies of Exclusion*. London: Routledge.

Stalker, K. (1998) Some ethical and methodological issues in research with people with learning difficulties, *Disability and Society*, 13(1): 5–19.

Stanley, L. (1992) *The Auto/biographical I*. Manchester: Manchester University Press.

Stefansdottir, G. (2006) Resilience and resistance in the life histories of three women with learning difficulties in Iceland, in D. Mitchell *et al.* (eds) *Exploring Experiences of Advocacy by People with Learning Disabilities*. London: Jessica Kingsley.

Stuart, M. (1998) *Mothers, sisters and daughters: an investigation into convent homes for women labelled as having learning difficulties*. Unpublished PhD thesis, Milton Keynes, Open University.

Stuart, M. (2002) *Not Quite Sisters: Women with Learning Difficulties Living in Convent Homes*. Kidderminster: BILD Publications.

Sutcliffe, J. and Simons, K. (1993) *Self-advocacy and Adults with Learning Difficulties*. Leicester: NIACE.

Thomas, W.I. and Znaniecki, F. (1918–20) *The Polish Peasant in Europe and America* (5 vols). Chicago, IL: University of Chicago Press.

Thompson, P. (1988) *The Voice of the Past: Oral History*, 2nd edn. Oxford: Oxford University Press.

Walmsley, J. (1998) Life history interviews with people with learning disabilities, in R. Perks and A. Thompson (eds) *The Oral History Reader*. London: Routledge.

Walmsley, J. (2000) Caring: a place in the world? in K. Johnson and R. Traustadottir (eds) *Women with Intellectual Disabilities: Finding a Place in the World*. London: Jessica Kingsley.

Walmsley, J. (2001) Normalisation, emancipatory research and inclusive research in learning disability, *Disability and Society*, 16(2): 187–205.

Walmsley, J. and Johnson, K. (2003) *Inclusive Research with People with Learning Disabilities: Past, Present and Futures*. London: Jessica Kingsley.

Ward, L. (1997) *Seen and Heard: Involving Disabled Children and Young People in Research and Development Projects*. York: Joseph Rowntree Foundation.

Westerman, W. (1998) Central American refugee testimonies and performed life histories in the sanctuary movement, in R. Perks and A. Thomson (eds) *The Oral History Reader*. London: Routledge.

White, M. (1993) Deconstruction and therapy, in S. Gilligan and R. Price (eds) *Therapeutic Conversations*. New York: Norton.

Widdershoven, G. (1993) The story of life: hermeneutic perspectives on the relationship between narrative and life history, in R. Josselson and A. Lieblich (eds) *The Narrative Study of Lives*. London: Sage.

Williams, F. (1989) Mental handicap and oppression, in A. Brechin and J. Walmsley (eds) *Making Connections: Reflecting on the Experiences of People with Learning Difficulties*. London: Hodder & Stoughton.

Williams, F. (1993) *Social policy, social divisions and social change*. Unpublished PhD thesis, Milton Keynes, Open University.

Wolfensberger, W. (1975) *The Origin and Nature of our Institutional Models*. Syracuse, NY: Human Policy Press.

2

Social constructions and social models: disability explained?

Alex McClimens and Malcolm Richardson

Introduction

In this chapter we argue for a social constructionist understanding of learning disability and explain what this means. It is possible to understand disabilities from a number of perspectives. Here we acknowledge other perspectives, for example the biomedical perspective (Chapter 3). However, instead of asking to judge their validity by how such perspectives define disability we offer the reader an historical overview of the ways in which, over time, perspectives have changed and how understandings and definitions have themselves been constructed to reflect these historical contexts. By advocating a broader historical approach we locate lasting influences and most notably those of eugenics, the vestiges of which, we argue, continue to affect personal, policy and political thinking today.

One of the problems of an account based on ideas of social construction is that it recognizes multiple interpretations, making it difficult for any single account to be read as privileged or definitive. However, we show that responses by people in power and policy initiatives reflect how society at any historical juncture views people with disabilities. By understanding the interplay between structural, cultural and political influences and concurrent perspectives around disability it is possible to subject each account to scrutiny and criticism based less on its theoretical validity and more on its outcomes. When we consider that peculiar categorization of disability that has come to be known as learning disability we will demonstrate that socially constructed explanations, especially when understood in relation to the social model of disability, provide the most comprehensive account with implications for practitioners, family carers and people with disabilities alike. As a framework for examining changing constructions this chapter moves from descriptions of early attitudes to impairment and disability through to discussions on the influences

of Victorian values, before we end with some discussion on emergent models of disability and how, in prospect, these might influence future practice.

Social construction

In their seminal work on the social construction of reality Berger and Luckmann (1967) argue that:

> Every individual is born into an objective social structure within which he (sic) encounters the *significant others* who are *in charge* of his socialization. These significant others are *imposed* on him. Their definitions of his situation are posited for him as objective reality. He is thus born into not only an objective social structure but also an objective social world. The significant others who mediate this world to him modify it in the course of mediating it. They select aspects of it in accordance with their own location in the social structure, and also by virtue of their individual, biographically rooted idiosyncrasies.
>
> (Berger and Luckmann 1967: 151)

Put simply, those with power to define a person and his or her needs and to control a person act on the basis of their own definitions. Sometimes that power is one which has been conferred upon them to act in that way by society through its governments, social policies or functionaries such as health care professionals. So, for example, people who are classified by the medical professions as inhabiting the spectrum of learning disability are rendered liable to be treated in certain ways sanctioned by society (Burr 1995: 63–4). Thus medics exert power over access to education, through employment law and through the courts, significantly influencing the lives of many people with learning disabilities. How this came about will be explained below with reference to historical eras (presented in tabular form) and partly through an examination of what social construction offers us by way of understanding how knowledge, language and power manufacture the circumstances that created a separate social grouping of people with learning disability.

Reflection point: if you are a student, how are you classified, categorized and controlled by the institution you attend? Does the 'label' of student fit comfortably with you? How would it feel if you were constantly described and treated in a way that didn't correspond to how you saw yourself?

History and the social construction of disability:

Pre-history to the middle ages
In the UK most people probably think of community care as of recent origin in relation to people with learning disabilities, but care in the community is probably as old as human society. At Skhul, in Israel, the 95,000-year-old remains of an 11-year-old boy showing evidence of a healed cranial injury indicates that his community must have looked after him for a considerable time; at Shanidar cave in Northern Iraq, the 46,000-year-old skeleton of a 40-year-old man revealed a congenital underdevelopment of his right side, a right arm amputated at the elbow, arthritis and other injuries of such a nature that he would have needed support from his society throughout his life. These finds suggest that survival for some individuals with severe impairments was achieved only through support from society and community. Indeed, as will be shown, community living has historically been a majority experience for people with disabilities and not an invention of the modern era. What is shown in what follows, however, is that this community experience has by no means been comfortable (see Table 2.1).

But not all societies are the same and hence their responses to impairment differ. For example, at the Neolithic settlement of Catalhoyuk (c.10,000 BC) in Turkey, from the thousands of skeletons excavated only one was not afforded the traditional family burial, that of an individual with a hunched back which was discovered 'unceremoniously dumped on a rubbish tip, perhaps because he was . . . perceived as an outsider' (Rudgley 2000: 74). This might be one of the earliest evidences of someone with a physical impairment being excluded from society, a pattern repeated, as will be shown, even to the present day.

The varied examples in Table 2.1 indicate two extreme societal responses to people with disabilities: one extreme holds life-threatening exclusion, while the other extreme holds veneration. Examples of life-threatening exclusion cited by Heddell (1980) are exposure of an infant to the elements overnight to encourage the survival of healthy offspring practised in the ancient civilizations of Greece, Scandinavia and Sparta; and Roman law permitting infanticide of any unwanted infant. The frequency of such practices is a cause for debate (McLaren 1990; Bredberg 1999). Interestingly, Table 2.1 also shows a distinction between disabilities where, despite exposure of impaired babies, soldiers who acquired impairments in battle were treated with respect and honour. Clearly, however, in these societies an element of social stigma was attached to impaired infants and society sanctioned social exclusion as a policy response.

Arguably such patterns of discrimination may be attributed to the cultures existing in a dim and distant history. Yet Wolfensberger (1989) has argued that 'death-making', i.e. the higher incidence of death among those with learning disabilities, continues, a point most recently and graphically discussed by Mencap in their report *Death by Indifference* (2007). However, we are getting ahead of the story.

The contrasting view exemplified in Nordic and Celtic mythology points to physical exceptionalities (including impairments) being associated with the gift of supernatural capacities (Table 2.1) such as great wisdom, being a 'seer', having a memory for stories, poetry and so on (Bragg 1997; Bredberg 1999). The belief was that by giving up an attribute, such as speech, the use of a limb or sight, in a contract with the supernatural, the person became endowed with special powers. In contrast to this positive regard, the Malleus Maleficarum, published in 1486, significantly influenced ideas about people perceived to be different. Well into the sixteenth century in some parts of Europe, it resulted in the persecution and deaths of thousands who were deemed to be practising witchcraft or cavorting with the Devil (Hart 1971).

Era	Context and experience	Orientation of the public	Effects limiting the distribution of social networks
Pre-history	Skhul, in Israel, the 95,000-year-old remains of an 11-year-old boy showing evidence of a healed cranial injury	His community must have looked after him for a considerable time	
	At Shanidar cave in Northern Iraq, the 46,000-year-old skeleton of a 40-year-old man with significant impairments	He would have needed support from his society throughout his life	
Early history to pre-middle ages	Varied experiences: Nordic and Celtic mythology: physical exceptionalities (including impairments) associated with supernatural capacities	Veneration of 'gifted' individuals was mediated by a cautious respect for the supernatural	Varied but: Limited by resources
	Hard to sustain individuals with disabilities without economic or agricultural surplus	Greeks: High priority on care of soldiers injured in battle but advocated infanticide for sickly or deformed children	Care and support likely to be within the family if at all
Middle Ages	However, where there was agriculture and surplus, sedentary population arose and more people with disabilities were likely to survive	1325 (England) *De Praerogativa Regis* – land of 'idiots or natural fools' held for heirs. Protected the land-owning classes and title. No provision for 'village idiot'	Legal protection for the rich and titled with disabilities
			Family care for others. Since few people could read or write many with mild intellectual disabilities would have been able to work in the fields
		The Malleus Maleficarum 1486 to sixteenth century when many people perceived to be different were persecuted	Vilification among a wider amorphous group of morally disreputable, vagrants, criminals, and physically disabled

Table 2.1 From pre-historic times to the middle ages

From the above it should be apparent that the varied ways in which disability was once understood relied very much on who had the power to influence societies and communities and to shape their attitudes. Some of these responses may seem strange to our twenty-first-century sensibilities and it was only fairly recently, in the nineteenth century, that our present understanding of disability began to take more recognizable shape. The Victorian reforms of the early to mid-nineteenth century presaged the first attempts at what we might now recognize as a welfare system (Marcus 1981: 53), as shown in Table 2.2 and discussed further below.

Industrialization

Significant changes in the lot of people with learning disabilities came with eighteenth- and nineteenth-century industrialization, its associated land enclosures and the commercialization of agriculture. Prior to industrialization, working practices were largely rural. Gradually, work turned from small peasant labour or craftwork to village artisan or smallholder cottage industry (Hobsbawm 1962, 1968; Thompson 1968). For a period, the timing and pace of work continued to be largely self-determined and therefore favourable to people with impairments (Ryan and Thomas 1980). But with accelerating industrialization the pace and timing of work altered significantly and created further inequalities between an emergent minority bourgeoisie and the majority of labourers paid for the speed of production but not the full worth of their labour. This was typified by the motto 'every man for himself and the devil take the hindmost' (Hobsbawm 1962: 239).

Era	Context and experience	Orientation of the public	Effects limiting the distribution of social networks
Industrialization	Land enclosed; wage labour not ownership: families could not afford care Treatment in institutions Over time new classifications: lunatics vs 'defectives' (blind, deaf or lack of speech vs mentally subnormal: later in this period the rise of charitable institutions As industrialization moved to heavier physical work more people were institutionalized; the rise of science (e.g. Darwin 1859) and medicalization of mental disorder	Free movement of labour so parish poor houses became redundant; Poor Law Amendment Act 1834 – national uniformity, denial of relief outside institutions, deterrence ('less eligibility'); growth of workhouses and then asylums Move towards medicalized interventions over time	Those living away from industrial conurbations did not necessarily have disruptions to their support networks (see Walton 1980) But in industrial areas, families were broken up Workhouses and asylums were 'total institutions' – uniforms, regimented, no recreation and socialization forbidden during working hours

Table 2.2 Nineteenth-century history and industrialization

The threat of jail for workers who did not conform and low wages that forced workers into unremitting and uninterrupted toil in order to survive (Hobsbawm 1968) led to a volatile rise in vagrancy and an unprecedented increase in the social exclusion of people with physical or mental impairments (Scull 1979). Hobsbawm's (1962) analysis saw the capitalist system ascribing one's position in society according to one's individual attributes and capacity to work. Ervelles (1996) suggests a circular logic

> through invoking biological difference as the 'natural' cause of all inequality, thereby successfully justifying the social and economic inequality that maintains social hierarchies.
>
> (Ervelles 1996: 526)

In this context disability, seen as 'deviance', was a peculiarly nineteenth-century creation, arising out of the Poor Law Reforms of 1834 and the burgeoning medicalization and subsequent professionalization of health and social care. The amendments to the Poor Laws of 1834 were passed largely due to the far-reaching effects of the Industrial Revolution.

Exercise 2.1

Until the late nineteenth century there was no separate or specific name that distinguished people with what we now refer to as 'learning disability'. Would things have been any different if they had been described differently?

It was only during the latter part of the nineteenth century that the division between madness and developmental delay was being made with any certainty (Heddell 1980; Clarke 1983; Race 1995a; Miller 1996). By this time, however, the mesh of scientific discovery, of increasing industrialization, of medicine and political theory were all combining to alter the relations of the individual to the society they inhabited. Symonds and Kelly note that

> It was the passing of the Poor Law Amendment Act 1834 which acted as the spur to much of the work of the voluntary sector; it meant that a tripartite system of provision of social and health care was created: insti-

tutionalisation in the workhouse, relief by charitable organisations, and self-help.
>
> (Symonds and Kelly 1998:19)

The further sorting of social categories continued and was formalized by legislation such as the Lunacy Act (1845), the Lunatic Asylums Act (1853) and the Idiots Act (1886) (Pilgrim 1993: 168). It was against this background that the Victorian zeal for classification made itself felt within the medical system. To be unable to participate in the waged economy was to be isolated socially and, crucially, economically, leading to a corresponding separation of the individual on the grounds of pathology. Oliver (1990) summarizes the argument as follows:

> The idea of disability as individual pathology only becomes possible when we have an idea of individual able-bodiedness, which is itself related to the rise of capitalism and the development of wage labour. Prior to this, the individual's contribution had been to the family, the community, the band, in terms of labour, and while, of course differences in individual contributions were noted, and often sanctions applied, individuals did not, in the main, suffer exclusion.
>
> (Oliver 1990: 47)

The result of industrialization was an unprecedented rise in the building of houses of correction, jails and 'madhouses' (Scull 1979). Between 1720 and 1825, 150 hospitals were built in England to cater for the rising numbers of the sick poor (Baly 1973, 1995).

A concomitant was that for all but the few who might maintain familial relations largely outside of the industrial conurbations (Walton 1980), state intervention compounded the economic exclusion, a by-product of which was the charity and welfare systems, the remnants of which still exist. And for adults with learning disabilities a number of 'idiot' asylums were built. Heddell (1980) points to the opening, in 1847, of Park House at Highgate, by the philanthropist Andrew Reid. This was followed by Colchester, later to become the Royal Counties Hospital, and the Earlswood asylum, which opened with 500 beds in 1855 and was regarded as the model institution of its time. And in 1886 the Idiots Act allowed local authorities to build asylums for 'idiots' (Scull 1979).

Feeling threatened by the same exclusionary measures that they had introduced, the ruling classes instigated further controls to protect themselves. These included the so-called humanitarian reforms as exemplified by Quakers such as William Tuke, founder of the Retreat at York. Similarly, the Insanity Act of 1845 established new controls and, significantly, ensured that all asylums procured the safeguard of a medical superintendent (Scull 1979; Clarke 1983; Baly 1995).

The appointment of these medical superintendents hastened the medicalization of 'mental disorder' and emergence of psychiatry (Scull 1979; Potts and Fido 1991; Fennell 1996). The physicians regarded mental disorder rather as they did physical disease, as something located within the individual and potentially treatable. However, alongside treatment there is a darker, more final response to disease. For when disease is seen as threatening to the social order, eradication can appear as a measured reaction.

Exercise 2.2

'It's the economy, stupid'
We have seen how people with learning disability came to be separated out from mainstream society by a combination of economic, commercial and medical influences which led to segregation on an industrial scale.

How far has this situation been remedied today?

Eugenics: biological beginnings

At the same time as the building of asylums and the emergence of superintendents and psychiatry, Mendel (1822–84) and later Darwin were formulating the science of genetics and the idea of natural selection in which the most adaptable survived and passed on their genes. It was only with the work of Galton and the Eugenic Society in the early days of the twentieth century that the possibilities of genetics were grasped.

Galton, a cousin of Darwin, first used the term 'eugenics' in 1883 to describe his emergent ideas on selective breeding by which he hoped to 'improve' the quality of the human species. He then developed a particular focus on intelligence measurement and

testing. This aspect was taken up and developed elsewhere until the notion of the IQ or 'intelligence quotient' was formalized by Alfred Binet (1857–1911), who invented the first IQ test.

When combined with eugenic principles under the influence and power of medical science and a growing public concern over the sheer numbers of the asylum population, the policy and practice that emerged began to display increasing severity.

As founder of the Eugenic Society, Galton's work on the hereditary associations and measurement of intelligence had a massive influence on the way disability was viewed in both Europe and America. Social policy on both sides of the Atlantic was for decades driven by the segregationist principles that informed this perspective.

Eugenics was not some esoteric cult movement. It attracted interest and approval from the many of the 'great and good of society'. This interest waned significantly after the 1940s as the Nazi Party gave a graphic illustration of an extreme policy of eugenics with concentration camps and sterilization programmes to control the spread of unwanted genes from Jews, Gypsies, people with disabilities and others. And so, as the disabled joined the Jews and the Gypsies in the queues for the gas chambers, the civilized world turned away from eugenics. For the time being.

Exercise 2.3

Then, as now, public opinion could be influenced by the utterances of well-known figures. For example, H.G. Wells, D.H. Lawrence, Winston Churchill and Alexander Graham Bell all indicated some approval of eugenic principles. In contrast, some very public figures from very well-known families were on the receiving end of such policies. Prince John, the youngest child of George V, had epilepsy and autistic tendencies. He was never seen in public. Likewise, Rosemary Kennedy, sister of the late President J.F. Kennedy, lived most of her adult life in an institution following a lobotomy performed in her twenties.

What effect might a statement have, either for or against disability rights, coming from a twenty-first-century 'celebrity'?

Era	Context and experience	Orientation of the public	Effects limiting the distribution of social networks
Early 1900s UK – the eugenics movement	The science of psychology proposed intelligence was inherited. It was believed that people with disabilities were breeding faster than the general population; it was believed that there was a relationship between social problems and feeble-mindedness

Therefore a call to limit birth and procreation to protect the national gene pool | A battle around issues relating to sterilization though eugenicists lost this one; however, the eugenicists won over in relation to separating the sexes in institutions and trying to prevent procreation

Subhuman and diseased organism, menace to society and object of dread | The pinnacle of institutionalization with the emergence of the 'total institution'

Tens of thousands of people institutionalized in the UK alone |

Table 2.3 The influence of eugenics

Eugenics: statistical credibility

It can be argued that the correlate of the eugenics debate of a century ago is the Human Genome Project and contemporary tabloid-led debates on 'designer babies'. In the nineteenth century the social engineering tools were more blunt. Galton lent scientific credence to the eugenic project by adopting statistical techniques associated with the 'normal distribution'.

Sometimes known as the bell curve, for its shape, it is, put simply, the plotted line on a standard x–y axis of the distribution of almost any measurable naturally distributed variable. Height or income are two good examples. With a large enough sample the curve will be very smooth and peak around the mean.

Galton was well aware of the potential of the bell curve. He was influenced here by his cousin's work and by Malthu's (1766–1834) *Essay on the Principles of Population* ([1872] 1971). His main contention, however, was that any variation away from the mean, expressed as 'standard deviation', would, in purely statistical terms, be the same whether the deviation was to the left or to the right of the mean. Therefore, someone whose intelligence was rated as above average (see Figure 2.1) would deviate from the mean just as someone with lower than average intelligence

would deviate. It was here that Galton introduced his innovation. He divided the normal distribution curve into four sections called quartiles by dividing the space on either side of the mean (Figure 2.1). He then gave these a ranked order, starting at the left side with the lowest values working to the right side of the graph. Now the apparent arithmetical neutrality of the design had given way to a new moral order. Davis (1995) explains the significance of this.

> What these revisions by Galton signify is an attempt to redefine the concept of the 'ideal' in relation to the general population. First, the idea of the application of a norm to the human body creates the idea of deviance or a 'deviant' body. Second, the idea of a norm pushes the normal variation of the body through a stricter template guiding the way the body 'should' be. Third, the revision of the 'normal curve of distribution' into quartiles, ranked order, and so on, creates a new kind of 'ideal'. This statistical ideal is unlike the classical ideal which contains no imperative to be ideal. The new ideal of ranked order is powered by the imperative of the norm, and then is supplemented by the notion of progress, human

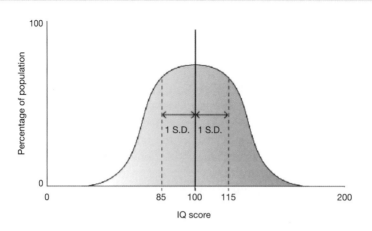

Figure 2.1 The natural distribution curve (courtesy of Luke Miller, Sheffield Hallam University)

perfectibility, and the elimination of deviance, to create a dominating, hegemonic vision of what the human body should be.

(Davis 1995: 34–5)

Furthermore, people with learning disability were deemed during this period not only to be polluting the gene pool but, according to Goddard, an American psychologist, they represented a danger to society. He said,

> For many generations we have recognized and pitied the idiot. Of late we have recognized a higher type of defective, the moron, and have discovered that he is a burden; that he is a menace of society and civilization; that he is responsible to a large degree for many, if not all, of our social problems.
>
> (Goddard 1915: passim 307–12)

This terminology was to prove useful to eugenic-inspired administrators in early twentieth-century England.

Eugenics: consequences

Wolfensberger (1972) demonstrates at least eight myths that support eugenic and segregationist ideologies within contemporary services to people with learning disabilities. These myths are the learning disabled person as subhuman organism, diseased organism, menace to society, unspeakable

object of dread, object of ridicule, object of pity, holy innocent and eternal child.

To prevent the populace from 'degenerating', the eugenicists persuaded many western nations, including the UK, to segregate thousands of people identified as 'feeble-minded within asylums or colonies in order to prevent them from multiplying' (Mittler 1979; Heddell 1980; Clarke 1983; Race 1995b). The eugenicists, led by Sir Francis Galton, pressured the Home Office to make special provision for people with learning disabilities, resulting in the 1913 Mental Deficiency Act. This Act created four categories: 'feeble-minded', 'idiots', 'imbeciles' and 'moral defectives'. The feeble-minded were given education but idiots and imbeciles were not (Beacock 1992). Moral defectives were those people whom society wished to exclude, such as unmarried mothers in receipt of poor relief. It is not surprising that the 1913 Act recognized 'feeble-mindedness' as a social rather than a medical issue. After all, the eugenic aims of the Act were, in effect, to 'clear the streets' of undesirables. Hence, so-called 'moral defectives' were caught under the Act, regardless of their IQ. The admission of patients as a medical case was a formal process with no scope for any to be admitted informally (Heddell 1980).

Borsay (1997) points out that the twentieth-century institutionalization of people with learning disabilities overwhelmed nineteenth-century notions of treatment. Instead, care and control mediated by costs became the order of the day. Effectively this meant placing resources under 'one roof'. Medical interest in the causes of crime, immorality and poverty ascribed blame to people with learning disabilities (Scull 1979; Heddell 1980). Mary Dendy, writing in 1920 on 'Feeblemindedness in children of school age', represented that view, writing that these children should be 'detained for the whole of their lives' in order to 'stem the great evil of feeblemindedness in our country' (cited in Potts and Fido 1991: 1).

So far we have discussed people with learning disabilities as if they were one homogeneous mass. This is just about permissible for argument's sake, but what are the effects on individuals when they are faced with the consequences of living outside society? In contradistinction to the absence of first person accounts from people with disabilities throughout history, such accounts are just within our reach. Pam, a lady now in her fifties, spent much of her life in an institution for people with learning disabilities. Speaking to a group of former institutional residents and one of the authors about her elder non-disabled sister who, unlike Pam, married and had children she says:

Pam: . . . my sister . . . she's grown-up and married. Got kids of her own. Nice house. Left school, she were only 14 then.

Writer: What happened when you got to 14, did you have to leave school?

Pam: Oh we left school at 14 years old. Monica was 14. My sister . . . she was 14. She fell in love with a young man . . . and they got happily married and have children of their own and a nice house.

Writer: What happened to you when you were 14? Did you leave school and get a job?

Pam: Er not exactly . . . When me mum was alive she brought us here [the institution] . . . because they couldn't cope. So me and Jane came here.

Writer: Where did you go to live?

Pam: Up at . . . I was on Field View.

Writer: . . . what was it like in those days?

Pam: Well it, staff were bossy and that.

Pam's account clearly indicates that the regime within the institution, built for eugenic purposes, was strict. Later, Pam told her story about some parts of her life; this is what she had to say:

It's true what I said, my life has been different to that of my sister Margaret. My mum and dad told me when I was younger that children and marriage were not for me. But I have never wanted children. I did enjoy my nephews when they were children and it is lovely to visit staff and see their children . . .

Like the vast majority of people with learning disabilities in Pam's generation, the idea that 'children and marriage are not for them' took a deep hold within their concept of self.

At the start of the twenty-first century, the continued practice of eugenics has been characterized as eugenics by stealth (Stanworth 1989; Swain 1989; Williams 1989). The approach differs but the result is the same. Hence the eugenic 'it's better to be dead than disabled' message invades the individual and group consciousness promoting eugenic abortion, euthanasia, voluntary euthanasia, sterilization, genetic screening and, perhaps for some, trips to Switzerland for assisted suicide. All of these aimed at eradicating people likely to be stigmatized for their difference. In summary, social policy within the early eugenic epoch stigmatized specific groups of individuals, and denied their basic human rights, in order to maintain the genetic 'purity' of the rest of society. Today it operates by more subtle means.

Social research: antidotes and social models

Emerging with the systems of categorization referred to above in the eighteenth and nineteenth centuries were the new medical professions and the recognition by successive governments of their power to treat. The medical sciences researched the medical roots and genetic causes of impairments and their treatment and hence the medical model came to determine the life courses of people with learning disabilities. Meanwhile some competing discourses emerged from educational and clinical psychologists who demonstrated the potential of people with severe learning disabilities to benefit from education and training for skills and employment (e.g. Tizard and O'Connor 1952; Clarke and Clarke 1954; Clarke and Hermelin 1955). This pointed to the importance of social and environmental factors in the creation of learning

The construction of learning disability

disabilities, as opposed to genetics or disease. One example, the Brooklands experiment (Tizard 1964), demonstrated the disabling effects of institutional care upon children, while also illuminating the clear advantages of child-centred practices in alternative community-based care environments. In the same period, Goffman's *Asylums* (1957) exposed the mechanisms of institutionalization and stigmatization. Morris's *Put Away* (1969) and Miller and Gwynne's *A Life Apart* (1972) further exposed the detrimental consequences of institutionalizing people with learning disabilities, and King *et al.* (1971) demonstrated how institutionalized patterns of care were detrimental to those living within them.

By 1959, public opinion had been sufficiently influenced to prompt a change in the law. The 1959 Mental Health Act was the first major revision since 1913. Under the new Act, degrading certification ended. 'Mental deficiency' was replaced by what many considered a more disablist term, 'mental subnormality'. Most patients were technically free to leave or remain in the hospitals as voluntary patients. Some left, mainly those who had worked as unpaid staff, but for most there was simply nowhere else to go (Clarke 1983; Potts and Fido 1991). Additionally, the hospital scandals of the 1960s and 1970s (DHSS 1969, 1971, 1978) revealed degrading conditions and abuses within institutions. These scandals helped spur government policy in the direction of community care for the 52,000 people with learning disabilities then in hospital. Peter Mittler (1978) summarized the situation:

> Anyone who looks at mental handicap hospitals today cannot fail to be struck by the discrepancy between the quality of life for the general population and that of mentally handicapped hospital residents. The physical conditions under which mentally handicapped people are expected to live and work for year after year have long been regarded as unacceptable for the rest of society. Wards of over 50 adults and over 30 children are not only unpleasant places in which to live but are totally incompatible with good standards of professional practice.
>
> (Mittler 1978: 1)

Listening to the voices of people with learning disabilities

The 1960s marked not only a move to deinstitutionalization but also a change in the focus of research (Whittlemore *et al.* 1986) with a focus on parents' and guardians' stress and coping and planning with professionals collaboratively over the life course of their relatives (Ryan and Thomas 1991; Race 1995a, 1995b; Atkinson and Walmsley 1999).

A much smaller literature reflecting the voices of people with learning disabilities has grown significantly since then (see Chapter 1). These accounts vividly convey the common humanity of people with learning disabilities trying to get by in their daily lives, much like the rest of society (Edgerton 1967; Hunt 1967; Edgerton and Bercovici 1976; Edgerton *et al.* 1984; Flynn 1986; Jahoda *et al.* 1988). Adults with learning disabilities generally prefer to live in the least restrictive places, usually separate from their parents (Flynn and Saleem 1986), in a hostel rather than hospital, in a group home rather than a hostel and in independent living rather than a group home (Passfield 1983; Conroy and Bradley 1985; Heal and Chadsey-Rush 1985; Richards 1985; Booth *et al.* 1990; Gold 1994); many are coping with impoverished circumstances in social positions without the rights, privileges or obligation of others. Despite being further accredited with the same emotional capacities as others (Flynn 1989; Potts and Fido 1991; Cambridge *et al.* 1994; Cheston 1994; Etherington and Stocker 1995; Collins 1996; Holland and Meddis 1997; Emerson *et al.* 2005) and despite these adversities, they are often making the best of community living, and complaining less than they might (Flynn 1989; McVilly 1995).

Their stories are, therefore, largely reflective of the resilience of the human spirit, revealing that people with learning disabilities, in contrast to eugenic assumptions, develop throughout their lifespan, adapting to changing circumstances much like the rest of people in society. They contribute to society in a variety of ways such as through their diverse social presence, the work they do and, in some cases, the way they provide for others. Too often their network of friendships and relationships is underdeveloped and the support and assistance to develop and maintain such relationships is lacking.

Human rights and normalization

The twentieth century was also marked by other major upheavals. The Holocaust and atrocities of the Second World War led in 1948 to the United Nations Universal Declaration of Human Rights. The 1971 *United Nations Declaration on the Rights of Mentally Retarded Persons* and more recently the Convention on the Rights of People with Disabilities adopted in 2006 point to a continued emphasis on promoting social justice and human rights at civil, political, social, cultural and economic levels. Humanist conceptions of person and being (e.g. Maslow 1943, 1954; Rogers 1951), combined with the principles of basic human rights, were beginning to influence the ideologies of a broad spectrum of professionals in health and educational fields. Beacock (1992) identifies how these were combined within the principles of normalization (Bank Mikkelsen 1969; Nirje 1972; Wolfensberger 1972, 1983; O'Brien and Tyne 1981).

Normalization began formally in the Danish Mental Retardation Act of 1959. It aimed to create normal living conditions for people with learning disabilities (Bank-Mikkelson 1969). Hence it stood in stark contrast to both eugenics and the medical model. Normalization influenced a generation of professionals, generating a mini-epoch of social policy. While it did not significantly influence government policy over the closures of the old 'mental handicap' hospitals, it did help to win hearts and minds in favour of deinstitutionalization (Race 1999).

Despite improvements in community services, eugenics has not gone away. For example, we have laws that make abortion possible up to the full term of pregnancy for impairments as 'trivial' as a club foot or cleft palate. And, although people are no longer hospitalized because of their learning disabilities, this is not to say that deprivation and institutional practices have disappeared. For example, Orchard Hill in London was the very last long-stay institution in the UK for people with learning disability to be closed down. And when it was closed it was in the wake of an investigation by the Healthcare Commission (2007) into institutionalized abuse. With no more long-stay institutions will there be no more scandals? This may be a naïve hope but at least with the recent appointment of Scott Watkin to the position of co-Tsar of learning disabilities for the Department of Health, people with learning disabilities have real claims to having a voice in policy-making (see Chapter 7).

And finally . . .

In this chapter it has been shown how across the ages the social construction of learning disability has led to widely divergent values, social structures, power relations and, consequently, outcomes. The arguments presented remind us that we are ourselves at a staging post in our own social constructions and policies. The present context of individualization (see Chapter 22), the trick of turning community presence to community inclusion and the protection and fulfilment of human rights are some of the challenges our society faces and spring from many of the values voiced within the chapters of this book.

This chapter has taken a social constructionist perspective on learning disability, adopting a long view that takes us from pre-history to the present day. It invites the reader to draw from the lessons of history, to be vigilant in the maintenance and upholding of human rights, watchful for the insidious hand of modern eugenics, respectful and inclusive towards the differences that make us all human. But as the philosopher and poet George Santayana has remarked, those who cannot learn from history are doomed to repeat it. If we can avoid this mistake then what might the future of learning disability look like? We outline some of our ideas in Table 2.4, which begins to categorize the contemporary lives of people with learning disabilities.

What do you think? What else should be placed in the chart?

Era	Context and experience	Orientation of the public	Effects limiting the distribution of social networks
Early twenty-first century, post-industrial, post-Fordist, post-economic crash	Higher profile of people with intellectual disability (ID) In the media. The 'Susan Boyle Award' for contribution to television is inaugurated	Increasing legislation (DDA) and emphasis on rights coupled with strengthened self-advocacy movement sees a realignment of public opinion towards positive acceptance	Proliferation of cheap and accessible web tools herald ID-specific dating sites, as blogs, Tweets and e-zines attract advertisers and begin to fund advocacy
	Mencap supports a person with LD to stand as a local councillor on an accessibility ticket	Court rulings reinforce discrimination policy with landmark judgments against top organizations – big cash payouts and exemplary fines	Increased uptake of personalized budgets leads to increased social mobility and independence
	Some media performers, athletes and public figures 'come out' as having ID and associated conditions	Backlash begins in right-wing press with letters and comments; graffiti makes a comeback	Home ownership rises as banks and building societies look for new markets
		PA sues LD employer for wrongful dismissal and sexual harassment	The first self-made LD millionaire is a partner in a law firm specializing in disability rights
Your views.			

Table 2.4 The future now

References

Atkinson, D. and Walmsley, J. (1999) Using autobiographical approaches with people with learning difficulties, *Disability and Society*, 14(2): 203–16.

Baly, M.E. (1973) *Nursing and Social Change*. London: Routledge.

Baly, M.E. (1995) *Nursing and Social Change*, 3rd edn. London: Routledge.

Bank-Mikkelson, N.E. (1969) A metropolitan area in Denmark: Copenhagen, in R. Krugel and W. Wolfensberger (eds) *Changing Patterns in Residential Services for the Mentally Retarded*. Washington, DC: President's Committee on Mental Retardation.

Beacock, C. (1992) Triggers for change, in T. Thompson and P. Mathias (eds) *Standards and Mental Handicap: Keys to Competence*. London: Bailliere Tindall.

Berger, P.L. and Luckmann, T. (1967) *The Social Construction of Reality: A Treatise in the Sociology of Knowledge*. Harmondsworth: Penguin.

Booth, T., Simons, K. and Booth, W. (1990) *Outward Bound: Relocation and Community Care for People with Learning Difficulties*. Buckingham: Open University Press.

Borsay, A. (1997) Review article – language and context issues in the historiography of mental impairments in America, c. 1800–1970, *Disability and Society*, 12(1): 133–41.

Bragg, L. (1997) From mute God to the lesser God: disability in medieval Celtic and Norse literature, *Disability and Society*, 12(2): 165–77.

Bredberg, E. (1999) Writing disability history: perspectives and sources, *Disability and Society*, 14(2): 189–201.

Burr, V. (1995) *An Introduction to Social Constructionism*. London: Routledge.

Cambridge, P., Hayes, L., Knapp, K., Gould, E. and Fenyo, A. (1994) *Care in the Community Five Years On: Life in the Community for People with Learning Disabilities*. Aldershot: Ashgate.

Cheston, R. (1994) The accounts of special education leavers, *Disability and Society*, 9(1): 59–69.

Clarke, A.D.B. and Clarke, A.M. (1954) Cognitive changes in the feeble-minded, *British Journal of Psychology*, 45: 173–9.

Clarke, A.M. and Hermelin, B.F. (1955) Adult imbeciles, their abilities and trainability, *Lancet*, 2: 337–9.

Clarke, D. (1983) *Mentally Handicapped People: Living and Learning*. London: Bailliere Tindall.

Collins, J. (1996) Housing, support and the rights of people with learning difficulties, *Social Care Research*, 81: March.

Conroy, J. and Bradley, V. (1985) *The Pennhurst Longitudinal Study: A Report of Five Years of Research and Analysis*. Philadelphia, PA: Temple University Developmental Disabilities Centre.

Davis, L.J. (1995) *Enforcing Normalcy: Disability, Deafness and the Body*. London: Verso.

DHSS (1969) *Report of the Committee of Inquiry into Allegations of Ill-treatment of Patients and Other Irregularities at the Ely Hospital, Cardiff*. Cmnd 3975. London: HMSO.

DHSS (1971) *Report of the Farleigh Hospital Committee of Inquiry*. Cmnd 4557. London: HMSO.

DHSS (1978) *Report of the Committee of Inquiry into Normansfield Hospital*. Cmnd 7357. London: HMSO.

Edgerton, R.B. (1967) *The Cloak of Competence: Stigma in the Lives of the Mentally Retarded*. Berkley, CA: University of California Press.

Edgerton, R.B. and Bercovici, S. (1976) The cloak of competence: years later, *American Journal of Mental Deficiency*, 80: 485–97.

Edgerton, R.B., Bollinger, M. and Hess, B. (1984) The cloak of competence after two decades, *American Journal of Mental Deficiency*, 88: 345–51.

Emerson, E., Robertson, J. and Wood, J. (2005) Emotional and behavioural needs of children and adolescents with intellectual disabilities in an urban conurbation, *Journal of Intellectual Disability Research*, 49(1): 16–24.

Ervelles, N. (1996) Disability and the dialectics of difference, *Disability and Society*, 11(4): 519–37.

Etherington, A. and Stocker, B. (1995) Moving from hospital into community: an evaluation by people with learning difficulties, *Social Care Research*, 64.

Fennell, P. (1996) *Treatment Without Consent: Law, Psychiatry and the Treatment of Mentally Disordered People Since 1845*. London: Routledge.

Flynn, M. (1986) *A Study of Prediction in the Community Placement of Adults who are Mentally Handicapped*. Final report to ESRC, Hester Adrian Research Centre, University of Manchester.

Flynn, M.C. (1989) *Independent Living for Adults with Mental Handicap: A Place of My Own*. London: Cassell.

Flynn, M. and Saleem, J. (1986) Adults who are mentally handicapped and living with their parents: satisfaction and perceptions regarding their lives and circumstances, *Journal of Mental Deficiency Research*, 30: 379–87.

Goddard, H.H. (1915) The possibilities of research as applied to the prevention of feeble-mindedness, *Proceedings of the National Conference on Charities and Corrections*, 307–12.

Goffman, E. (1957) *Asylums*. New York: Doubleday.

Gold, D. (1994) We don't call it a circle: the ethos of a support group, *Disability and Society*, 9(4): 165–9.

Hart, R. (1971) *Witchcraft*. London: Wayland.

Heal, L. and Chadsey-Rush, J. (1985) The Life Style Satisfaction Scale (LSS): assessing individual satisfaction with residence, community setting and associated services, *Applied Research in Mental Retardation*, 6: 475–90.

Healthcare Commission (2007) *Investigation into the service for people with learning disabilities provided by Sutton and Merton Primary Care Trust*, London.

Heddell, F. (1980) *Accident of Birth*. London: British Broadcasting Corporation.

Hobsbawm, E.J. (1962) *The Age of Revolution*. New York: Mentor.

Hobsbawm, E.J. (1968) *Industry and Empire*. Harmondsworth: Penguin.

Holland, A.C. and Meddis, R. (1997) People living in community houses: their views, *British Journal of Learning Disabilities*, 25(2): 68–72.

Hunt, N. (1967) *The World of Nigel Hunt*. Beaconsfield: Darwen Finlayson.

Jahoda, A., Markova, I. and Cattermole, M. (1988) Stigma and self concept of people with a mild mental handicap, *Journal of Mental Deficiency Research*, 32: 103–15.

King, J., Raynes., N.V. and Tizzard, J. (1971) *Patterns of Residential Care: Sociological Studies in Institutions for Handicapped Children*. London: Routledge and Kegan Paul.

McLaren, A. (1990) *A History of Contraception*. Oxford: Blackwell.

McVilly, K.R. (1995) Interviewing people with a learning disability about their residential service, *British Journal of Learning Disabilities*, 2(25): 138–42.

Malthus, T.R. ([1872] 1971) *An Essay on the Principle of Population*. New York: A.M. Kelley.

Marcus, S. (1981) Their brothers' keepers: an episode from English history, in W. Gaylin, I. Glasser, S. Marcus and D. Rothman (eds) *Doing Good: The Limits of Benevolence*. New York: Pantheon Books.

Maslow, A. (1943) A theory of human motivation, *Psychological Review*, (50): 370–96.

Maslow, A. (1954) *Motivation and Personality*. New York: Harper and Row.

Mencap (2007) *Death by Indifference*. London: Mencap.

Miller, A. and Gwynne, R. (1972) *A Life Apart*. London: Tavistock.

Miller, E. (1996) Idiocy in the nineteenth century, *History of Psychiatry*, 7: 361–73.

Mittler, P. (1978) *Helping Mentally Handicapped People in Hospital: A Report to the Secretary of State for Social Services*. London: DHSS.

Mittler, P. (1979) *People not Patients*. Cambridge: Methuen.

Morris, P. (1969) *Put Away*. London: Routledge and Kegan Paul.

Nirje, B. (1972) The right to self determination, in W. Wolfensberger (ed.) *The Principle of Normalization in Human Services*. Toronto: National Institute on Mental Retardation.

O'Brien, J. and Tyne, A. (1981) *The Principle of Normalisation: A Foundation for Effective Services*. London: Campaign for the Mentally Handicapped.

Oliver, M. (1990) *The Politics of Disablement*. London: Macmillan.

Passfield, D. (1983) What do you think of it so far? A survey of 20 Priory Court residents, *Mental Handicap*, 11(3): 97–9.

Pilgrim, D. (1993) Anthology: policy, in J. Bornat, C. Pereira, D. Pilgrim and F. Williams (eds) *Community Care: A Reader*. London: Macmillan.

Potts, M. and Fido, R. (1991) *'A Fit Person to be Removed': Personal Accounts of Life in a Mental Deficiency Institution*. Plymouth: Northcote House Publications.

Race, D. (1995a) Classification of people with learning disabilities, in N. Malin (ed.) *Services for People with Learning Difficulties*. London: Routledge.

Race, D. (1995b) Historical development of service provision, in N. Malin (ed.) *Services for People with Learning Difficulties*. London: Routledge.

Race, D.G. (1999) Hearts and minds: social role valorization, UK academia and services for people with a learning disability, *Disability and Society*, 14(4): 519–38.

Richards, S. (1985) A right to be heard, *Social Services Research*, 14(4): 49–56.

Rogers, C. (1951) *Client Centred Therapy*. London: Constable.

Rudgley, R. (2000) *Secrets of the Stone Age*. London: Century.

Ryan, J. and Thomas, F. (1980) *The Politics of Mental Handicap*. Harmondsworth: Penguin.

Ryan, J. and Thomas, F. (1991) *The Politics of Mental Handicap*, revised edn. London: Free Association Books.

Scull, A. (1979) *Museums of Madness: The Social Organisation of Insanity in Nineteenth Century England*. London: Penguin.

Stanworth, M. (1989) The new eugenics, in A. Brechin and J. Walmsley (eds) *Making Connections: Reflecting on the Lives and Experiences of People with Learning Difficulties*. London: Hodder and Stoughton.

Swain, J. (1989) Learned helplessness theory and people with learning difficulties: the psychological price of powerlessness, in A. Brechin and J. Walmsley (eds) *Making Connections: Reflecting on the Lives and Experiences of People with Learning Difficulties*. London: Hodder and Stoughton.

Symonds, A. and Kelly, A. (eds.) (1998) *The Social Construction of Community Care*. Basingstoke: Macmillan.

Thompson, E.P. (1968) *The Making of the English Working Class*. Harmondsworth: Penguin.

Tizard, J. (1964) *Community Services for the Mentally Handicapped*. Oxford: Oxford University Press.

Tizard, J. and O'Connor, N. (1952) The occupational adaptation of high grade defectives, *Lancet*, 2: 620–3.

Walton, J.K. (1980) Lunacy in the Industrial Revolution: a study of asylum admissions in Lancashire, 1848–50, *Journal of Social History*, 13: 1–22.

Whittlemore, R., Langness, L. and Coegel, P. (1986) The life history approach to mental retardation, in L. Langness and H. Levine (eds) *Culture and Retardation*. London: Reidel.

Williams, F. (1989) Mental handicap and oppression, in A. Brechin and J. Walmsley (eds) *Making Connections: Reflecting on the Lives and Experiences of People with Learning Difficulties*. London: Hodder and Stoughton.

Wolfensberger, W. (1972) *The Principle of Normalization in Human Services*. Toronto: National Institute on Mental Retardation.

Wolfensberger, W. (1983) Social role valorization: a proposed new term for the principle of normalization, *Mental Retardation*, 21(6): 234–9.

Wolfensberger, W. (1989) The killing thought in the eugenic era and today: a commentary on Hollander's essay, *Mental Retardation*, 27(2): 63–74.

3

The roots of biomedical diagnosis

Fiona Mackenzie and Heather McAlister

Introduction

There have been significant advances in the lives of people with learning disabilities since the White Paper *Better Services for the Mentally Handicapped* (Department of Health and Social Security 1971) legislated for the closure of large institutions and the development of community services (see Chapter 5). The end of the era of institutional living has been associated with what has been called a 'demedicalization' of learning disabilities and a recognition that needs are social and cannot be wholly catered for by doctors and nurses. Concern about the overuse of drugs to manage behavioural problems and the involvement of doctors in the eugenics movement has added impetus to the move away from a medical model. Learning disabilities have come to be understood as a socially constructed condition to which the most helpful response is social inclusion.

One important aspect of social inclusion, which has been neglected for people with learning disabilities, is health. Political changes set in motion by the human rights movement and now legislated for in the Disabilities Discrimination Act 2005 have given us a principle of equality of access to health services. People with learning disabilities have greater health needs than the general population (e.g. Moss and Patel 1993; McGrother *et al.* 2002; Kerr *et al.* 2003) but make less use of health services. Publications such as *Treat me Right!* (Mencap 2004) and *Death by Indifference* (Mencap 2007) have brought these inequalities in health care to the forefront. The government responded to Mencap's *Death by Indifference* with an Independent Inquiry, *Healthcare for All* (Department of Health 2008), which made ten essential recommendations for change. These recommendations are reviewed in *Valuing People Now* (Department of Health 2009), along with a delivery plan of how organizations should address them. One of these plans is to commission a scoping study for a Confidential Inquiry into the premature deaths of people with learning disabilities.

The high level of unmet physical and mental health needs recognized in people with learning disabilities (see Chapters 12, 26, 28 and 34) also occurs among other socially and economically disadvantaged groups such as the homeless, and the solution may, for the large part, be social. However, in addition to the health needs that they share with the general population, some people with learning disabilities, particularly those with severe disabilities that may be multiple, have special health needs associated with the biomedical cause of their disability. In this chapter I will discuss how the diagnosis of the biomedical cause of an individual's learning disabilities can facilitate identification and appropriate management of these health needs over their lifespan. This is likely to have a significant impact on an individual's quality of life.

The bio-psycho-social model

A simplistic view of the medical model is that it implies the presence of pathology in an individual, which the doctor has the skills to identify and cure. The patient's role, once he or she has provided the doctor with the information required to make a diagnosis, is that of a more or less passive and compliant recipient of treatment.

This model has been heavily and rightly critiqued and is now regarded as an outmoded way of understanding and responding to the health needs of the general population. It is clearly an unhelpful and potentially devaluing way of thinking about the health needs of people with learning disabilities at either the individual or population level. The medical profession has long been aware of the complex interaction of biological, psychological and social factors in the conditions they treat and this has now been made explicit in what is termed the 'bio-psycho-social' model. This model, which is now taught in medical schools, places patients (as unique individuals with biological, psychological and social needs) at the centre of their interaction with health services. It is within this framework that the process of diagnosis and assessment of the health needs of individuals with learning disabilities and the planning of health services to meet their needs should take place.

Terminology and definitions

There is a confusing proliferation of terms in everyday use to describe people with learning disabilities. In this section we will define the terms we use in this chapter and discuss the use of terminology in practice. In clinical situations, most doctors use the term which the patient prefers and uses to refer to their condition. In the UK this is frequently 'learning disabilities', the term adopted by the Department of Health in 1991 for use in government publications. We will use it in this chapter except where we are referring to a recognized classification of diagnosis. Such classification requires some understanding of how various categories are defined, and a summary is provided below.

The international *Classification of Mental and Behavioural Disorders,* currently in its tenth edition (*ICD-10*) (World Health Organization 1992) and the *Diagnostic and Statistical Manual of Mental Disorders,* currently in its fourth edition (*DSM-IV*) (American Psychiatric Association 1994), are the main classification systems currently in use. They assign numerical codes to the disorders they describe. The term 'mental retardation' is used in both *ICD-10* and *DSM-IV* and equates with learning disability. This term was associated with the eugenics movement (Williams 1995) and 'retard' has become a term of abuse. Hence the term mental retardation is unacceptable for use in clinical practice but because it is operationally defined in *DSM* and *ICD* it remains in use when precise communication between professionals is a priority – for example, in research publications and legal reports.

The World Health Organization (1980) defined the terms 'impairment', 'disability' and 'handicap'. Impairment is any loss or abnormality of physical or psychological function. A disability is defined as interference with activities of the whole person (often referred to in the field of learning disabilities as 'activities of daily living'). A handicap is the social disadvantage to an individual as a result of impairment or a disability. The term 'intellectual impairment' is used in the medical literature and does not necessarily equate with learning disability, as a learning disability does not necessarily result from mild degrees of intellectual impairment which do not interfere with the individual's capacity to carry out activities of daily living. Intellectual disability is sometimes preferred to learning disability because in disorders associated with intellectual impairment it is usual for other aspects of cognitive function such as attention and comprehension to be impaired as well as the ability to learn.

'Learning disabilities' sounds similar to 'learning difficulties', a term which can have different meanings in different contexts. Some people prefer the latter term, perhaps because it is inclusive (many people identify themselves as having difficulty learning in some area of their life). Learning difficulties is used in educational settings to describe children who are underachieving scholastically for a variety of reasons, which might include emotional or behavioural problems which are interfering with their ability to learn. Not all of these children have an intellectual impairment. The educational category of severe learning difficulties corresponds more closely with learning disabilities as used in health settings and many children who have been identified as having severe learning difficulties in school will need support from child and adult learning disabilities services. The term 'special needs' refers to children who have been given a Statement of Special Educational Needs (SEN) by their education authority. This is based on the assessment of all professionals involved in their care and outlines the education authority's responsibilities to provide an education appropriate for the individual's needs.

ICD-10 uses the term 'disorder' to describe conditions with symptoms or behaviour associated, in most cases, with distress or interference with personal functions. I use it in the same way in this chapter when referring to developmental disorders. It does not imply a specific causation although there is good quality scientific evidence that many developmental disorders are associated with physical pathology in the brain.

A syndrome is the medical term for a set of clinical

features which commonly occur together (e.g. in velo-cardio-facial syndrome, cleft palate, cardiac abnormalities and distinctive facial features occur together and are associated with learning disabilities). Some syndromes (e.g. Down's syndrome) are named after the researchers who first described them. Syndromes have also been named after characteristic features. Three children with learning disabilities were described in a paper entitled 'Puppet children' by Angelman (1965), who used this term to convey the children's jerky, string-puppet like movements. The term 'puppet children' is devaluing and has been replaced by 'Angelman syndrome'. Cri-du-chat syndrome is, however, still used to describe a syndrome in which, as a result of abnormal development of the larynx, the child has a high-pitched cat-like cry.

The term 'mental handicap' is now widely regarded as unhelpful because it implies that to be handicapped is the inevitable outcome of intellectual impairment. Nevertheless, some parents continue to refer to their learning disabled children as mentally handicapped because they feel that, for example, for a person with cerebral palsy who is incontinent and unable to walk or talk, the term 'learning disability' does not convey the extent of their care needs.

The psychoanalyst Valerie Sinason has described and critiqued the repeated change of terminology used to describe those with learning disabilities (Sinason 1992). She argues that while new terms, apparently more accurate or without unpleasant associations, are coined with good intentions, the process is driven by a defensive need to wish away the reality of actual damage and painful differences. There is a denial of the trauma which is intrinsic to having a condition in which development has gone awry. This primary trauma experienced by people with learning disabilities needs to be acknowledged and accepted.

Exercise 3.1

'I've got four handicaps. I've got Down's syndrome, special needs, learning disabilities and a mental handicap' (Young woman with Down's syndrome, quoted in Sinason 1992).

Discuss the use of terminology to refer to people with learning disabilities from the perspectives of a person with learning disabilities and their family.

Classification in learning disabilities

Learning disabilities are socially constructed (see Chapter 2). An individual comes to meet diagnostic criteria for learning disabilities and to be identified as learning disabled as the end point in a complex interplay of biological, psychological and social processes. As a result, who comes into the category varies over time and between societies. An individual may move in and out of the category of mild learning disabilities over their lifespan depending on the balance between their state of mental and physical health and the supports and demands of the environment. A mild degree of intellectual impairment may be less disabling in a developing economy where rates of literacy are low and there is a wider range of valued social roles available. Historically, deficits in the capacity to cope with the demands of the environment, now called 'adaptive behaviour', were used to define those who would now be regarded as learning disabled (Wright and Digby 1996). Intelligence as a unitary and potentially measurable entity began to be conceptualized at the end of the nineteenth century and was then incorporated into the definition of learning disabilities.

The *ICD* and *DSM* definitions of mental retardation are broadly similar (see Boxes 3.1 and 3.2). Each is based on the presence of impairments in adaptive

Box 3.1: *DSM-IV* definition of mental retardation

A. Significantly subaverage intellectual functioning: an IQ of approximately 70 or below on an individually administered IQ test (for infants, a clinical judgement of significantly subaverage intellectual functioning).
B. Concurrent deficits or impairments in present adaptive functioning (i.e. the person's effectiveness in meeting the standards expected for his or her age by his or her cultural group) in at least two of the following areas: communication, self-care, home living, social/interpersonal skills, use of community resources, self-direction, functional academic skills, work, leisure, health and safety.
C. The onset is before 18 years of age.

Box 3.2: *ICD-10* definition of mental retardation

Mental retardation is a condition of arrested or incomplete development of mind, which is characterized by impairment of skills manifested during the developmental period, which contribute to the overall level of intelligence, i.e. cognitive, language, motor and social abilities.

Box 3.3: *ICD* classification of developmental disorders

Mental retardation
Mild
Moderate
Severe
Profound

Pervasive developmental disorders
Autism
Atypical autism
Asperger syndrome
Disintegrative disorder
Rett's syndrome
Other and unspecified

Specific developmental disorders
Speech and language: articulation; expressive speech; mixed expressive and receptive speech
Literacy: reading; spelling
Numeracy
Motor co-ordination
Mixed specific developmental disorder

function in association with low IQ and both require the impairments to be present during the developmental period, which separates people with mental retardation from those who acquire intellectual impairment in adult life, for example as a result of brain injury.

ICD is the system used in the UK. It emphasizes the need to draw on wide sources of information when assessing an individual's adaptive function and to use standardized assessment schedules for which local cultural norms have been established. When comprehensive information is not available, a provisional diagnosis can be made. The limitations of IQ tests are recognized and the IQ levels specified for mild (50–69), moderate (35–49), severe (20–34) and profound (<20) mental retardation are intended only as a guide. Detailed clinical descriptions of each category of learning disability are provided.

ICD also emphasizes that while mental retardation can occur in the absence of any other disorder, the full range of mental disorders coded elsewhere in the manual can occur in people with mental retardation. The developmental disorders, including specific disorders of speech and language and pervasive disorders (autism) are of particular relevance (see Box 3.3). The manual recognizes the clinical difficulty in distinguishing, for example, a specific disorder of speech and language from delayed speech and language in the context of global developmental delay in mental retardation. It points out that it is common for there to be an uneven profile of skills in mental retardation. For example, there may be a relative strength in non-verbal skills in comparison to language skills but when this discrepancy is marked, a specific developmental disorder should be coded in addition. *ICD* states that if the medical cause of the learning disability is known it should be coded separately.

Classification in service settings

Decisions made every day in service settings to categorize service users as having a learning disability are not generally based on the rigorous application of the operational diagnostic criteria described above (Hatton 1998). There are users of learning disability services who clearly do not meet diagnostic criteria, particularly some who were institutionalized many years ago for social reasons (see Chapters 1, 2 and 5). If they are settled and fit in well with their peer group there may be no impetus to review their classification. There are also many people who receive support from health and social services whose learning disability is not recognized as such. There is some evidence that failure to identify a learning disability may adversely affect outcomes in mental health services (Lindsey 2000).

In practice, indicators that a learning disability may be an issue, such as a history of SEN, poor language skills as well as the individual's own identity and how their needs are understood by carers, influence referral to learning disability services. Local service configurations and professional attitudes also have an impact on the decision to refer (Hatton 1998). When a referral for assessment is accepted by a learning disability service the response to immediate difficulties may appropriately take priority over the time-consuming and potentially threatening detailed assessments of adaptive behaviour. The limitations of IQ testing have been widely acknowledged. Factors such as an individual's level of motivation and state of health as well as cultural and linguistic diversity reduce the validity and utility of formal assessment of IQ in clinical practice (Jacobson and Mulick 1996). It is usual for experienced practitioners to make clinical judgements concerning whether or not it is appropriate and helpful to describe a person as learning disabled and to provide them with a service. The decision is based on information from as many sources as possible including interviews with family members and carers, health and education records, and the opinions and assessments of members of the multidisciplinary team. Diagnostic criteria are only rigorously applied when there is disagreement, doubt or pressure to prioritize access to limited resources. Then, standardized IQ tests such as the 1981 Wechsler Adult Intelligence Scale may be used. Checklists of adaptive function are also available but these should be supplemented with direct observation (Widaman and McGrew 1996).

In medical practice little time is devoted to assigning individuals to the socially defined category of learning disabilities. The approach to diagnostic assessment of a person with an apparent intellectual impairment is similar whether or not their impairment results in their being defined as learning disabled. The priority is to identify the presence of additional mental and physical disorders, which may be contributing to the individual's impairment in adaptive function, particularly the specific developmental disorders and autism. Thought will also be given to the causes of the impairment and an attempt may be made to identify an underlying biomedical cause if this is likely to influence the individual's management plan.

Exercise 3.2

How useful are diagnostic criteria in informing decisions about who has priority of access to learning disability services? How would you go about developing eligibility criteria in a service with limited resources?

The causes of learning disabilities and their diagnosis

'Aetiology' is the word used in medical practice to refer to the cause or set of causes of a disease or condition. There is now evidence for a complex interaction of the social, the psychological and the biological in the aetiology of conditions such as heart disease, which have previously been thought of as having a physical cause. The process by which an individual comes to be defined as having a learning disability also depends on this interaction of the biological, psychological and social over their lifespan.

Intelligence as measured using standardized IQ tests is normally distributed in the population. If a graph is drawn to plot the results of IQ tests of a representative sample of the population it is a bell-shaped curve, which is almost symmetrical around a mean of 100. Statistical methods would predict that 2.27 per cent of the population would have an IQ of less than 70, which is two standard deviations below the mean. As the definition of learning disabilities also includes the presence of associated impairments in adaptive function, fewer than 2.27 per cent of the population would be expected to be defined as learning disabled. Some people with mild learning disabilities are likely to represent the lower end of the normal distribution of intelligence in the population. Mild learning disabilities tend to be associated with social disadvantage and to cluster in families. This may be the result of adverse environmental factors ranging from lead poisoning due to traffic fumes to child abuse and neglect in the developmental period interacting with genetic determinants of intelligence. In mild learning disabilities there is likely to be an identifiable cause in about 50 per cent of people. For the remainder, low intelligence may be a qualitative variation from normality.

In practice, the number of mildly learning disabled individuals in a given population is difficult to estimate. The administrative prevalence based on numbers known to learning disabilities services varies according to the availability of services and other factors such as the degree of stigma attached to being defined as having a learning disability. The number of people in a population with severe learning disabilities is likely to be estimated more accurately as most will be known to services. This number is greater than would be predicted, based on a normal distribution. The increased number of people with low IQ is seen as a bump in the curve, which has been referred to as the 'pathological tail'. This implies that this group includes people whose intellectual development is qualitatively different from normality as a result of a biological insult to their central nervous system, rather than just a quantitative variation on normality.

In 80 per cent of people with severe learning disabilities, a specific biomedical cause can be diagnosed. However, even in the presence of a disorder that has a significant impact on the development of the brain, the outcome in terms of the individual's eventual intellectual capacity and adaptive function will be significantly influenced by additional biomedical and environmental factors during the developmental period. The biomedical condition might be understood as defining the range of eventual outcomes – for example, people with Down's syndrome range from severely to mildly disabled. Factors which influence the eventual outcome include the presence of additional impairments, which might be intrinsic to the biomedical cause (e.g. motor impairment in cerebral palsy; hearing impairment following repeated respiratory infection in Down's syndrome). These additional impairments limit the developing child's capacity to interact with and learn from their social and physical environment and may cause frustration or damage to self-esteem, which adversely affects their emotional development.

Classifying the biomedical causes of learning disabilities

A useful way of classifying the biomedical causes of learning disabilities is by the timing of the earliest factor which affected the development of the central nervous system. Diagnosis can be divided into six main groups, which are listed in Table 3.1 with common examples (for more see Chapter 10).

Diagnosis over the lifespan

The significance of a search for a main biomedical cause of learning disabilities changes over the life cycle and relates to care of the individual by their family. In this section we will discuss the relevance and implications of biomedical diagnosis at different life stages.

Perinatal diagnosis

Screening for Down's syndrome and neural tube defects (associated with spina bifida) is offered routinely in pregnancy. When risk factors are present (e.g. a family history), additional tests may be offered. Parents may interpret normal results from these tests as meaning that such disorders have been ruled out, however their sensitivity is not 100 per cent. Infants born in the UK are routinely screened for congenital hypothyroidism and phenylketonuria. Some conditions are identifiable or suspected at birth such as Down's syndrome. Children who have suffered from birth asphyxia or prematurity are at higher risk of subsequent learning disability and paediatricians will follow up and arrange diagnostic investigations as required. The presence of a specific combination of malformations may suggest that the baby has a less common dysmorphic syndrome that requires investigation by clinical geneticists.

The impact on a family of the birth of a significantly impaired child has been likened to the grieving process (Bicknell 1983) in which what has been lost is a normative expectation that Bicknell describes as the 'fantasy' of having a 'perfect' child. There are phases of numbness, disbelief, guilt and anger followed by active adaptation. The validity of this comparison, which seems to devalue those with impairments, has since been questioned (see Chapter 11 in this volume) and an alternative model proposed. It is nevertheless a time in which families have to make considerable psychological and practical adjustments to the special needs of their child and the provision of a clear diagnosis is likely to be helpful.

Cause	Examples
1 Genetic	
Chromosomal disorders	Down's syndrome
Syndromes associated with microdeletions	Velo-cardio-facial, Prader-Willi syndrome
Single gene disorders	Tuberous sclerosis, fragile X syndrome, phenylketonuria
Multifactorial inheritance	Neural tube defects
2 Central nervous system malformations	
Unknown	Sotos syndrome
3 Factors in prenatal environment	
Toxic	Foetal alcohol syndrome, maternal rubella, HIV
Infectious	Prematurity, birth injury
4 Disorder acquired around the time of birth	
Various	
5 Disorder acquired postnatally	
Infections of the central nervous system	Measles, encephalitis
Accidents	Brain injury
Toxins	Lead poisoning
6 Unknown cause	
Learning disabilities associated with other symptoms and signs of brain damage	e.g. autism, cerebral palsy
Learning disabilities where low IQ is a quantitative variant of normality	

Table 3.1 Summary of biomedical classification of causes of learning disabilities

Source: adapted from Gelder *et al.* (2000)

Each individual is unique and it is not possible to predict exactly how a child will develop. If, however, the range of impairment associated with a syndrome is known it may be possible to provide parents with some information about prognosis, in reply to such questions as 'Will he ever talk?', 'Will she be able to live independently as an adult?'. Much has been written about how best to inform parents of the news that their child has a developmental disability (see Chapter 11 in this volume). When things go well the outcome will be the formation of a healthy partnership between the family and health professionals, which will enable them to work together to meet the needs of the child over its lifespan.

The family will be able to make contact with other families caring for children with similar disorders, to share information and support. There are well-established associations for the more common disorders such as Down's syndrome and cerebral palsy and the internet has allowed both parents and professionals involved in the care of those with rare disorders to link up and share information and support (see Box 3.4).

When an inheritable disorder is diagnosed, parents will be offered information about the probability of this reoccurring in future pregnancies and the implications for other family members. This can raise complex ethical dilemmas for families and professionals. Referral to genetic counselling services, which can provide accurate information and support, may be helpful.

In some conditions associated with learning

Box 3.4: Websites of support groups and associations

The Down's Syndrome Association	www.downs-syndrome.org.uk
The Fragile X Society	www.fragilex.org.uk
The Prader-Willi Syndrome Association	www.pwsa.co.uk
The Tuberous Sclerosis Association	www.tuberous-sclerosis.org
The National Autistic Society	www.nas.org.uk

disabilities, early diagnosis and treatment can significantly improve the outcome. An example is phenylketonuria in which, due to gene mutation, the presence of the protein phenylalanine produces toxic metabolites which damage the developing nervous system. A low phenylalanine diet can prevent subsequent learning disabilities. In most other conditions there are no effective preventative treatments currently available, although there are future prospects for gene therapy in some genetic disorders, for example Duchenne muscular dystrophy, which is associated with mild learning disabilities. The value of diagnosis for the child is the creation of the potential for early identification of additional physical and psychological impairments that are known to be associated with the condition. The optimal management of these can minimize their impact. It is well recognized that in some circumstances medical intervention can cause further problems (e.g. the treatment of epilepsy with sedating medication or the trauma of surgery to correct orthopaedic problems). A thoughtful approach based on a thorough understanding of the child's physical, psychological and social needs is needed to enable the child to develop optimally within the limits imposed by their condition.

Preschool diagnosis

For the majority of children with learning disabilities the presence of a developmental disorder becomes apparent as, over time, delays in achieving milestones or qualitative differences from the usual pattern of development are recognized by parents or professionals. There are protocols for the developmental screening of children by health visitors and guidelines for specialist referral. The incidence of severe developmental disorders is low in primary care. A working party of the British Paediatric Association

(Valman 2000) estimated that one child with a severe learning disability is born in ten years to a family on a GP's average list of about 2000 patients. It is therefore unrealistic to expect primary care teams to develop expertise in diagnosis and assessment, but the hope is that children with significant developmental delay, or whose development is qualitatively different, will be identified and referred to paediatric services for diagnostic assessment.

When a significant developmental delay is identified, whether or not a biomedical cause can be identified, the family is offered a multi-disciplinary assessment in a Child Development Centre. The aim of this is to get a detailed picture of the child's mental and physical function and family context. Particular attention is given to identifying sensory impairments and medical conditions such as epilepsy, which might need specific intervention. There is also assessment for the presence of specific developmental disorders of speech, language and motor function, and pervasive developmental disorders such as autism. The assessment informs a care plan, which aims to optimize the child's development and prevent as far as possible the emergence of secondary impairments. The care plan may include physiotherapy to develop gross motor co-ordination and occupational therapy to develop motor skills. The parents will be given advice about how to respond to their child to promote their physical and psychological development. They will also be advised as far as possible about what to expect from their child over their lifespan and given information about services, support groups and emotional support. The care plan will be regularly reviewed and adapted.

Diagnosis in the school-aged child

The presence of learning disabilities may not become apparent until the child starts to attend school and fails to progress for whatever reason. This group of children is diverse; they may have a generalized learning disability, specific learning disability or other neurodevelopmental disorder, e.g. attention deficit hyperactivity disorder (ADHD). Children may present with behavioural difficulties masking significant underlying diagnosable conditions. Levels of co-morbidity are high with greater functional impairment resulting from the combination of two or more disorders, e.g. autism, epilepsy and attention deficit hyperactivity disorder. Recognition of these co-morbid disorders is essential to guide interventions, particularly as some of these conditions may be alleviated by appropriate treatment. Some children have developmental disorders with a biomedical condition, which has not been recognized in the early years. An example is foetal alcohol syndrome, which is a result of drinking alcohol in pregnancy and ranges in severity according to the timing and degree of foetal exposure to alcohol. Other children may fall behind as a result of emotional and social deprivation.

It is generally accepted that people with learning disabilities have a higher risk of all mental health disorders (Emerson and Hatton 2007), often quoted at around three to five times greater than the general population (Kerker et al. 2004). The school years are a time when these additional difficulties may begin to manifest themselves.

The identification and referral for specialist assessment of children who present in school years is less systematic than the screening provided by health visitors for preschool children. It relies on teacher and parents/carers recognizing qualitative differences in the child which are likely to be associated with a developmental disorder. Referral from school health services to child and adolescent mental health or paediatric services should then be made, dependent on the nature of the difficulty.

Diagnosis in adulthood

At the time of transition from children's to adult services individuals with learning disabilities are, under present policy in England, to be offered a Health Action Plan which forms a basis for planning to meet their health needs in adult life. It will include assessments of any special health needs which are associated with the biomedical cause of their learning disability and associated conditions.

Although the majority of those with severe learning disabilities entering adult services will now have an identified biomedical cause, there are a significant number of adults already in services who do not, and for whom developments in scientific knowledge mean that a biomedical diagnosis is now possible. Children with developmental delay are seen at intervals by paediatricians and if a specific cause has not been identified the issue of diagnosis will be reviewed in the light of any emerging signs and developments in medical knowledge. Such specialist medical care is not routinely provided for adults with learning disabilities. Most adults will be known only to social and primary health care services, which may not be familiar with the less common biomedical causes of learning disabilities and associated specific developmental disorders.

In some learning disabilities services there has been a reluctance to use diagnosis of any sort as this is felt to label the individual in such a way as to create negative expectations of them and deny their individuality. A counter argument is that if we live in an inclusive society in which individual differences are recognized and valued, there may be something to be gained from understanding as much as possible about the nature of those differences through the assessment of the biological, psychological and social aspects of learning disabilities.

The diagnostic assessment of adults with learning disabilities raises clinical and ethical dilemmas. Family members or professionals involved with an adult with a learning disability may request diagnostic assessment because they think it may provide useful information about how to care for the individual or access services – for example, those for people with autism. A family member may request investigation for a genetic syndrome to inform an assessment of their risk of having a child with a developmental disorder. In each of these circumstances, the first issue to be considered is the person with a learning disability's capacity to consent to investigation. This will require assessment of their understanding of the nature and possible outcomes of such an investigation.

When an individual lacks the capacity to consent to investigation it is the responsibility of the clinician carrying out the investigation to proceed on the basis of the individual's best interests, involving them as far as possible and those family members and professionals that know them best in the decision (issues of capacity and consent are dealt with more fully in Chapter 4). A useful question to consider is how likely is there to be an identifiable biomedical cause for this individual's learning disability. For example, the presence of congenital malformations or a family history suggestive of an inheritable condition makes this more likely. Factors then to be considered are the likely benefit to the individual's health, for example through a better understanding of their condition. The discomfort and distress likely to be associated with an investigation (e.g. blood tests) also needs to be taken into account.

When an adult with learning disabilities is referred to specialist health services because they have developed a problem with their physical or mental health (see Chapter 28) the investigation of the aetiology of their intellectual impairment may in some situations help in the understanding of this and therefore inform its management. Another situation in which the diagnostic investigation of an adult with learning disabilities may be considered is when they have not had access to specialist health care in childhood – for example, immigrants or refugees from economically disadvantaged countries. Again, the individual's capacity to consent and the likely impact on them of a diagnostic assessment need to be considered. When a developmental disorder that is known to be associated with serious health problems, such as tuberous sclerosis, is suspected, diagnosis is likely to be of benefit so that the health issues can be identified and treated promptly. In other developmental disorders not known to be associated with serious health problems the benefit for the individual may be less clear.

A related area is that of behavioural phenotypes, a concept first used by William Nyhan (1972) in relation to Lesch-Nyhan syndrome, in which he described self-mutilating behaviour. He emphasized the role of biomedical factors in producing this behaviour and defined the behavioural phenotype as 'behaviours which are an integral part of certain genetic disorders'. Since then, behavioural pheno-

types have been described for a number of conditions and it can be argued that an understanding of the pattern of motor, cognitive, linguistic and social behaviour which is characteristic of a condition can help inform the planning of education and support. There is, however, debate about the quality of the evidence for behavioural phenotypes and concern about the risk of creating negative expectations in conditions in which there is much individual variation. A description of the behavioural phenotype and a case example of a young woman with Prader-Willi syndrome is given below. It is followed by a description of Down's syndrome which is a common biomedical cause of learning disabilities.

Prader-Willi syndrome

Prader-Willi syndrome is caused by a deletion in chromosome 15. There are two copies of chromosome 15, one inherited from each parent. The deletion usually affects the chromosome inherited from the father. A similar deletion in chromosome 15 inherited from the mother results in Angelman syndrome, which has very different characteristics. Prader-Willi syndrome does not usually (but can occasionally) reoccur in families. It is now normally diagnosed by genetic testing in infancy when it is associated with low muscle tone and poor feeding, with failure to gain weight at the expected rate. There is developmental delay in childhood and most but not all adults have mild to moderate learning disabilities. At around the age of 3, children begin to overeat and this tendency continues throughout the lifespan. Other features include delayed and incomplete puberty and behavioural problems, some of which may be linked to carers' attempts to restrict their eating. People with Prader-Willi syndrome have difficulty restricting their food intake, and there are no specific treatments that are effective in preventing resultant obesity. Unless carers restrict access to food, lifespan is limited by the complications of obesity including Type II diabetes and respiratory problems. There has been debate about the ethical basis for the control of access to food for adults with Prader-Willi syndrome (Holland and Wong 1999).

Case study 1

Julie is a 38-year-old woman with moderate learning disabilities who has lived in a staffed group home for two years since the death of her mother. Her GP referred her to the health support team GP because of concerns about her weight, which has increased from 16 to 21 stone over two years. Her carers have noticed her tendency to overeat and think that this is due to boredom. They have supported her to gain the confidence to go out into the local town unaccompanied but this has led to an increased food intake as she often buys sweets and chips. With her agreement her carers have encouraged her to follow a healthy eating plan but she has become angry whenever she has felt under pressure to cut back on food. Julie does not understand the health risks associated with obesity, but is aware that she is not able to walk uphill without becoming breathless and finds this distressing. She is not able to say very much about her weight and eating patterns before her move to the group home and there is limited information from records apart from the fact that she has been obese since starting at primary school. Her brother describes how her mother consistently limited Julie's access to food and even obtained a lock for the fridge. He believes that this was the only way of ensuring that his sister did not massively overeat.

Exercise 3.3

Should genetic investigation of Julie for Prader-Willi syndrome be considered and if so how should an assessment of her capacity to consent to this be approached? If Julie were found to lack the capacity to consent, would it be in her best interests to carry out the investigation? If Julie is found to have Prader-Willi syndrome, how would this influence the response to her obesity?

Down's syndrome

Approximately 4.6 in 10,000 people have Down's syndrome (Steele 1996). Down's syndrome results when an individual has extra genetic material in the form of an additional copy of chromosome 21 (Lejeune *et al.* 1959). It is usual for human cells to contain 23 pairs of chromosomes, one of each pair being inherited from each parent. The majority of people with Down's syndrome have an additional copy of chromosome 21 and the condition may be referred to as 'trisomy 21'. In 3 per cent of cases the extra genetic material is joined to another chromosome (this is referred to as a translocation) and in these cases the condition may be inherited, usually from the mother, who has a one in six chance of conceiving a child with Down's syndrome.

People with Down's syndrome have a variety of physical characteristics, which include short stature, skin folds at the inner corners of their eyes, broad hands and a large tongue. People with Down's syndrome are easily identified as learning disabled by the general public which may impact on the formation of their identity. About half of babies born with Down's syndrome have heart defects. The motor and intellectual development of infants with Down's syndrome is delayed in comparison with the general population, and people with the syndrome have reduced muscle tone, which contributes to delay in the average age of walking unsupported to between 19 and 29 months. The average IQ of a young adult with the syndrome is around 50 and the majority of people have severe learning disabilities. There is however a large range of IQ (from 17 to 75) and of ability in daily living skills in the population of people with Down's syndrome. The most severely disabled people with the syndrome require a high level of care, whereas the most able people with Down's syndrome acquire literacy and numeracy skills, are able to live and work without special support and do not necessarily have a learning disability as socially constructed.

Down's syndrome has historically been associated with a decreased life expectancy. This has changed dramatically in recent years from an average age of 12 years in 1947 (Penrose 1949) to at least 45 years at present (Carr 2000) as a result of health care interventions, particularly surgery to treat heart defects. One consequence of this is that parents of middle-aged people with Down's syndrome who may have

Box 3.5: Health problems associated with Down's syndrome

Congenital heart defects
Respiratory infections
Hearing and visual impairments
Hypothyroidism
Skin problems
Gum disease and tooth loss
Obesity
Depression
Alzheimer's disease

Conditions of particular note are Alzheimer's disease, which occurs at an earlier age in people with Down's syndrome, and hypothyroidism which occurs in 40 per cent of adults with Down's syndrome (Anneren and Pueschel 1996) and can mimic the early stages of Alzheimer's disease. The physical health and development of children with Down's syndrome is routinely monitored by community paediatric services. There is an argument for this monitoring to continue into adult life (Prasher 1994), although the majority of conditions should be identified in well-person clinics in primary care.

been led to expect that they would outlive their children now have to readjust their expectations.

Although the majority of people with Down's syndrome enjoy good physical and mental health for much of their lifespan they are at an increased risk of a number of conditions, the prompt detection, accurate diagnosis and appropriate treatment of which is likely to be of benefit (see Box 3.5).

Exercise 3.4

Using a bio-psycho-social model, discuss how you would approach the construction of a Health Action Plan for a 19-year-old man with Down's syndrome who is leaving school and moving into adult services.

Conclusion

By applying the bio-psycho-social model it is possible to attach a label or diagnosis to a person with a learning disability. This is not done with the intention of labelling a person as having less value than anyone else. It is, rather, a means of ensuring that access to appropriate health and medical interventions through the life course is achieved. The name or label is the most efficient way of knowing what to look out for in terms of health and medical needs. It may be a way of understanding behaviours and the ways in which people communicate. It can also be of huge value to professional staff seeking to ensure that major physical and health needs are understood and met (see Chapter 12). And if this is the case it can be argued that the role of biomedical diagnosis, used in the appropriate way, is central to improving the quality of life of people with learning disability and maximizing their developmental potential.

References

American Psychiatric Association (1994) *DSM-IV Diagnostic and Statistical Manual of Mental Disorders*. Washington, DC: The American Psychiatric Association.

Angelman, H. (1965) Puppet children: a report on three cases, *Developmental Medicine and Child Neurology*, 7: 681–3.

Anneren, G. and Pueschel, S. (1996) Preventive medical care, in B. Stratford and P. Gunn (eds) *New Approaches to Down Syndrome*. London: Cassell.

Bicknell, J. (1983) The psychopathology of handicap, *British Journal of Medical Psychology*, 56: 167–78.

Carr, J. (2000) Intellectual and daily living skills in 30 year olds with Down's syndrome: a continuation of a longitudinal study, *Journal of Applied Research in Intellectual Disabilities*, 13: 1–6.

Department of Health (2008) *Healthcare for All, Report of the Independent Inquiry into Access to Healthcare for People with Learning Disabilities, Sir Jonathan Michael*. London: Department of Health.

Department of Health (2009) *Valuing People Now: A New Three-year Strategy for People With Learning Disabilities*. London: Department of Health.

Department of Health and Social Security (1971) *Better Services for the Mentally Handicapped*. London: DHSS.

Emerson, E. and Hatton, C. (2007) Contribution of socioeconomic position to health inequalities of British children and adolescents with intellectual disabilities, *American Journal of Mental Retardation*, 112: 140–50.

Gelder, M.G., Loez-Ibor Jr., J.J. and Andreasen, N.G. (2000) *The New Oxford Textbook of Psychiatry*. Oxford: Oxford University Press.

Hatton, C. (1998) Intellectual disabilities – epidemiology and causes, in E. Emerson, C. Hatton, J. Bromley and A. Caine (eds) *Clinical Psychology and People with Intellectual Disabilities*. Chichester: Wiley.

Holland, A.J. and Wong, J. (1999) Genetically determined obesity in Prader-Willi syndrome: the ethics and legality of treatment, *Journal of Medical Ethics*, 25: 230–6.

Jacobson, J.W. and Mulick, J.A. (1996) Psychometrics, in J.W. Jacobson and J.A. Mulick (eds) *Manual of Diagnosis and Professional Practice in Mental Retardation*. Washington, DC: American Psychological Association.

Kerker, B.D., Owens, P.L., Zigler, E. and Horwitz, S.M. (2004) Mental health disorder among individuals with mental retardation: challenges to accurate prevalence estimates. *Public Health Reports*, 119: 409–17.

Kerr, A.M., McCulloch, D., Oliver, K., McLean, B., Coleman, E. and Law, T. (2003) Medical needs of people with intellectual disability require regular assessment, and the provision of client- and carer-held reports, *Journal of Intellectual Disability Research*, 47: 134–45.

Lejeune, J., Gautier, M. and Turpin, R. (1959) Les chromosomes humaine en culture de tissus, *Compte rendu de l'Academie Science*, 248: 602.

Lindsey, M. (2000) Services for people with learning disabilities and mental health problems, *Mental Health Review*, 5: 5–18.

McGrother, C., Bhaumik, S., Thorp, C., Watson, J. and Taub, N. (2002) Prevalence, morbidity and service need among South Asian and white adults with intellectual disability in Leicestershire, UK, *Journal of Intellectual Disability Research*, 46: 299–309.

Mencap (2004) *Treat me Right!* London: Mencap.

Mencap (2007) *Death by Indifference*. London: Mencap.

Moss, S. and Patel, P. (1993) The prevalence of mental illness in people with intellectual disability over 50 years of age, and the diagnostic importance of information from carers, *Irish Journal of Psychology*, 14(1): 110–29.

Nyhan, W. (1972) Behavioural phenotypes in organic genetic disease: presidential address to the Society for Paediatric Research, May 1, 1971, *Paediatric Research*, 6: 235–52.

Penrose, L.S. (1949) The incidence of mongolism in the general population, *Journal of Mental Science*, 95: 685–8.

Prasher, V.P. (1994) Screening of medical problems in adults with Down syndrome, *Research and Practice*, 2(2): 59–66.

Sinason, V. (1992) *Mental Handicap and the Human Condition*. London: Free Association Books.

Steele, J. (1996) Epidemiology: incidence, prevalence and the size of the Down's syndrome population, in B. Stratford and P. Gunn (eds) *New Approaches to Down's Syndrome*. London: Casseu.

Valman, H.B. (2000) *The ABC of One to Seven*. London: BMJ Books.

Widaman, K.F. and McGrew, K.S. (1996) The structure of adaptive behaviour, in J.W. Jacobson and J.A. Mulick (eds) *Manual of Diagnosis and Professional Practice in Mental Retardation*. Washington, DC: American Psychological Association.

Williams, C. (1995) *Invisible Victims*. London: Jessica Kingsley.

World Health Organization (1980) *International Classification of Impairments, Disabilities and Handicaps*. Geneva: WHO.

World Health Organization (1992) *The ICD-10 Classification of Mental and Behavioural Disorders*. Geneva: WHO.

Wright, D. and Digby, A. (eds) (1996) *From Idiocy to Mental Deficiency: Historical Perspectives on Learning Disabilities*. London: Routledge.

4

Learning disability and the law

Alison Brammer

Introduction

The focus of this chapter is how law relates to people with learning disabilities. 'Law' refers to both legislation (e.g. the Disability Discrimination Act 1995) and case law (e.g. *R (on the application of A)* v. *East Sussex CC (no. 2)* [2003] EWHC 167). Most of the time, people with learning disabilities (particularly where mild or moderate) are treated no differently in law than any other citizens. The law assumes that all individuals have the capacity to make their own decisions unless proven otherwise. The provisions of the Human Rights Act 1998 apply equally to all citizens regardless of disabilities or other characteristics.

There are exceptions, however, and in each area where the law differentiates it defines the characteristics of those individuals to whom it applies. For example, if a crime is committed, the criminal law will operate to identify and punish the perpetrator and protect the victim. If a person with a learning disability is involved then the law provides additional safeguards, recognizing that they might otherwise be disadvantaged in the legal system. If it is alleged that a learning disabled adult has committed a crime an 'appropriate adult' will be present during police questioning to advise, observe and facilitate communication (see Chapter 20). If a learning disabled person is a witness in criminal proceedings, as a victim or otherwise, 'special measures' may apply to enable them to give evidence more effectively.

In other circumstances the learning disabled adult may benefit from support services and such need is assessed under the National Health Service and Community Care Act 1990. People with learning disabilities are sometimes considered alongside people with physical disabilities in legal terms and definitions may extend to incorporate both, as for example in the Disability Discrimination Act 1995. Elsewhere, particularly if capacity is relevant, learning disability may be addressed separately, as under the Sexual Offences Act 2004.

In law, for the purpose of clarity, categories are drawn based on different individual characteristics (e.g. age, mental illness, physical or learning disability). Such clarity is not always reflected in reality. Importantly, some individuals will cut across categories and may for example be aged and have learning and physical disability. Generalized assumptions should be avoided and diversity fully recognized. A practice response to the limitations of legal definitions has been to utilize the term 'vulnerability'. This term is not without criticism and carries some negative connotations, but it is increasingly used to refer to an individual who may require support or protection due to a variety or combination of characteristics including age and disability.

In considering the role of law there is an apparent conflict. It may be empowering. There are provisions that may be employed to promote the four principles contained in *Valuing People* (Department of Health 2001), namely rights, independence, choice and inclusion. Further support is provided by the UN Convention on the Rights of Persons with Disabilities, 2006, to which the UK is a signatory.

Despite the existence of anti-discrimination legislation, the law itself may also be discriminatory in both its terminology and its application. The term 'subnormality' was used until 1983 in mental health legislation. Until the Sexual Offences Act 2003 replaced its 1956 counterpart, 'defective' was used to refer to a 'person suffering from a state of arrested or incomplete development of mind which includes severe impairment of intelligence and social functioning'. Moreover, perpetrators of offences against people with learning disabilities are less likely to be brought to justice, due to failure to initiate proceedings, failure to understand the nature of learning disability and its relevance to competence in giving evidence (see also Chapter 20).

The first section of this chapter will consider definitions in current use and their significance in terms of service provision and other measures, including protection. Closer examination of the legal status of individuals with learning disabilities where capacity is impaired follows, along with legal aspects of competence and informed consent contained in the provisions of the Mental Capacity Act 2005. The remainder of the chapter considers application of the law to three case studies.

Definitions

The status and needs of children and young people with learning disabilities are specifically addressed in the Children Act 1989, as children in need. Like the Special Education Needs and Disability Act 2001, it views children as children first, though there are some references to disabled children in the Act (e.g. Schedule 2, Part 1, Para. 6).

A child who is disabled is defined in the Children Act in the same terms as contained in the National Assistance Act 1948 in relation to adults, as one who is blind, deaf or dumb (or suffering from mental disorder of any description), substantially and permanently handicapped by illness, injury or congenital deformity or other such disabilities as may be prescribed. In effect, this provides a statutory definition of disability including both learning and physical disability. The terminology is that adopted in 1948.

In respect of adults, Section 21 of the National Assistance Act 1948 contains the duty of local authorities to provide residential accommodation for persons who by reason of age, illness, disability or any other circumstances are in need of care and attention not otherwise available to them. Local authorities are required to inform themselves of the number of people who fall within the definition contained in Section 29 of the National Assistance Act 1948 (above) and to make arrangements for them (see Section 1 of the Chronically Sick and Disabled Persons Act 1970). Under Section 2, local authorities are required to assess individual needs and provide services to meet the needs of disabled persons. The definition in Section 29 is also employed in the National Health Service and Community Care Act 1990, the legislation which provides for the assessment of eligibility for services established under a

range of other pieces of legislation. The whole area of adult social care law, including those provisions which enable support to be provided to disabled adults, is currently being reviewed by the Law Commission; at present the law is extensive, complex and has been developed in a piecemeal fashion. Some terms and elements of the law are therefore outdated and may conflict with human rights principles and require the Commission to provide a clearer, more coherent framework, possibly in the form of a new single statute.

The Disability Discrimination Act 1995 made it unlawful to discriminate against a person on the grounds of disability in relation to employment and the provision of goods and services. Disability in this context is defined as 'a physical or mental impairment which has a substantial and long-term adverse effect on ability to carry out normal day-to-day activities'. The updated Disability Discrimination Act 2005 introduces a disability equality duty on public authorities (i.e. those whose functions are of a public nature), including local authorities, to work towards elimination of discrimination and, more positively, to promote equality of opportunity. The Equality Act 2006 has established a single enforcement body, the Equality and Human Rights Commission, with responsibility for all forms of discrimination and human rights. It replaces and assumes the role of the Disability Rights Commission.

The Mental Health Act 2007 (MHA) (amending the 1983 Act) now defines mental disorder as 'any disorder or disability of the mind'. This replaces the previous definition of mental disorder as 'mental illness, arrested or incomplete development of mind, psychopathic disorder and any other disorder or disability of mind'. The four separate classifications of mental impairment, severe mental impairment, mental illness and psychopathic disorder are removed. Learning disability is defined as 'a state of arrested or incomplete development of mind which includes significant impairment of intelligence and social functioning' (S1(4). A person will not be considered to be suffering from a learning disability for some sections of the MHA (including long-term admission and guardianship) unless their learning disability is 'associated with abnormally aggressive or seriously irresponsible behaviour'. The new legislation also introduces a new community treatment order and deprivation of

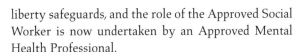

liberty safeguards, and the role of the Approved Social Worker is now undertaken by an Approved Mental Health Professional.

The last few years have therefore seen significant reforms of the law in relation to disability-specific legislation and mental health legislation which may apply to people with learning disabilities as well as human rights. For much of this legislation the notion of capacity is vital and it is therefore described further below.

> ### Exercise 4.1
>
> Which laws treat people with learning disabilities the same as other people?
>
> Are there exceptions?
>
> Split into groups and debate whether there should be exceptions.

Capacity

The question of capacity or legal competence is central to any consideration of the law and learning disability. It is a complex area of practice, involving significant ethical dilemmas. A legal framework is now provided by the Mental Capacity Act 2005 (MCA), together with a supporting Code of Practice, applying to those aged over 16. Until this legislation was introduced the law in this area was mainly based on common law principles from decided case law. Loopholes in the previous law have been addressed by the Law Commission particularly in relation to mental capacity and substitute decision-making. In stating the need for reform the Law Commission stated:

> It is widely recognised that, in this area, the law as it now stands is unsystematic and full of glaring gaps. It does not rest on clear or modern foundations of principle. It has failed to keep up with social and demographic changes. It has also failed to keep up with developments in our understanding of the rights and needs of those with mental disability.
>
> (Law Commission 1995)

Certain of the common law principles have been retained and incorporated into the new law, notably the presumption *in favour* of capacity; and the reasoning from early case law on, for example, best interests remains valid.

As law incorporates a presumption in favour of capacity, it is pertinent first to question what the law defines as 'capacity'. Elements of capacity were set out in *Re C (Adult: Refusal of Treatment)* [1994] 2 WLR 290. To be deemed 'competent', following this case, a patient must comprehend and retain treatment information; believe it to be true; and weigh it in the balance to arrive at a choice. It is a functional approach. This case also made it explicitly clear that mental incapacity and mental illness are separate issues in law. The adult concerned in *Re C* was detained for treatment in a mental hospital suffering from schizophrenia. He nevertheless had the capacity to refuse proposed treatment for a physical condition.

There are different standards of capacity in law – it is not a fixed concept. For example, the capacity required to enter into a sexual relationship is different to that required to manage property and financial affairs. The level of capacity required attempts to reflect the complexity of the issue at stake. In practice this means that no one should be considered incapable in a total sense as most people, including those with severe learning disabilities, will have the capacity to make some decisions for themselves. An individual's capacity to make a decision may fluctuate and it is therefore obviously good practice to take steps to enhance capacity and to enable decision-making during lucid periods. The MCA provides a definition of capacity and encourages first-hand decision-making wherever possible, through application of key principles.

The Act defines capacity as follows:

> A person lacks capacity if at the material time he or she is unable to make a decision for himself or herself in relation to the matter because of an impairment or a disturbance in the functioning of the mind or brain (s. 2(1)). It does not matter whether the impairment or disturbance is permanent or temporary (s. 2(2)).

There are two stages: establishing an impairment or disturbance, and a resulting inability to make the decision. Examples of impairment or disturbance in the functioning of the mind or brain could include a range of conditions such as: dementia; learning disabilities; effects of brain damage; physical or medical conditions that cause confusion, drowsiness or loss of consciousness; concussion following a head injury, and the symptoms of alcohol or drug use.

Being unable to make a decision means that the person is:

> unable to understand the information relevant to the decision; unable to retain the information; unable to use the information as part of the process of making the decision; or unable to communicate the decision (s. 3(1)).

An 'unwise' decision will not be treated as inability. 'Relevant information' includes the reasonably forseeable consequences of deciding or failing to make a decision.

The Act commences with a set of principles which are to apply across the whole of the Act and which endorse the focus of the Act as an empowering piece of legislation encouraging first-hand decision-making by the individual wherever possible. The principles are:

- A person must be assumed to have capacity unless it is established that he does not (s. 1(2)).
- A person is not to be treated as unable to make a decision unless all practicable steps to help him to do so have been taken without success (s. 1(3)).
- A person is not to be treated as unable to make a decision merely because he makes an unwise decision (s. 1(4)).
- An act done, or decision made for or on behalf of a person who lacks capacity must be in his best interests (s. 1(5)).
- Before the act is done, or the decision made, regard must be had to whether the purpose for which it is needed can be as effectively achieved in a way that is less restrictive of the person's rights and freedom of action (s. 1(6)).

Difficulties can arise where an individual does not have the capacity to make a particular decision. Under the old law, proxy decision-making was only recognized in respect of legal and financial matters and took effect through the operation of the Court of Protection, Enduring Powers of Attorney (documents which provide for an attorney to deal with the finances of a person if that person loses that capacity in the future), and use of a litigation friend (a person appointed to commence or defend legal proceedings on behalf of an individual who lacks capacity). There was an absence of formal machinery to delegate decision-making in other areas, including health and welfare matters.

Medical treatment without consent actually constitutes the tort of battery (i.e. a civil wrong which comprises infliction of physical force for which damages may be payable). A defence to this is provided by the principle of necessity which allows a doctor to give treatment when it is in the patient's best interests (F v. *West Berkshire HA* [1989] 2 All ER 545). A series of cases have dealt with the sterilization of mentally handicapped women, based on this principle. Critics have argued that this line of case law demonstrates a paternalistic application of law which gives great credence to medical evidence in the absence of a full consideration of social circumstances (Keywood 1995). For example, in *Re M (A Minor) (Wardship: Sterilization)* [1989] 1 FLR 182, the court accepted the view of doctors regarding sterilization as a form of contraceptive and was persuaded that sterilization was justified as there was a 50 per cent chance that the woman would conceive a mentally handicapped (the term used by the judge) child.

The case of *Re A (Mental Patient: Sterilization)* [2000] 1 FLR 549 CA, where an application to authorize sterilization of a learning disabled man was refused, implicitly supports this reasoning. In this case an application was made to the court for a 'declaration' that the proposed treatment was not unlawful, eliminating the risk of a legal action for battery afterwards. In recent years the use of 'declaratory relief' has extended beyond medical cases to some 'welfare' areas. This is discussed further in case study 1.

The Mental Capacity Act 2005 considerably extends the options and provides a clearer framework for substitute decision-making. These include a general power to act in a person's best interests, the use of a Lasting Power of Attorney (LPA) and orders of the newly constituted Court of Protection, including the appointment of a deputy, each of which are considered below. In any instance of substitute decision-making the best interests principle applies. The new legislation, replacing piecemeal case law, actually specifies certain matters which (as a minimum) provide some guidance and structure to the process. The factors are:

- the ascertainable past and present wishes and feelings of the person (including any relevant written statements);
- the beliefs and values that would be likely to influence the person's decision if they had capacity (including religious beliefs and cultural values);
- other factors the individual would be likely to consider if able to do so (this might include a sense of family obligation);
- the views of others it is considered appropriate to consult including anyone so named, carers and others interested in the person's welfare and any donees of an LPA or deputies appointed under the Act (s. 4).

In practice this list is not intended to be exhaustive and, while it can help to structure decision-making, the concept of 'best interests' is likely to remain a challenging one. As a matter of good practice, the Code of Practice stresses the need for both assessments of capacity and 'best interests' decisions to be recorded properly. For certain types of decisions, where individuals do not have close family or friends, they can consult an Independent Mental Capacity Advocate (IMCA) who may be appointed to assist in arriving at a best interests decision. This is a new role created by the Act and applies where either serious medical treatment or long-term changes of accommodation is contemplated. There is also a discretion to involve an IMCA in cases where adult abuse is suspected.

Substitute decision-making

Section 5 of the Act introduces a provision which gives some legal security to those people making a range of day-to-day decisions for a person who lacks capacity. The Mental Capacity Act refers to such acts in connection with care or treatment, stating that,

> where a person ('D') does an act in connection with the care or treatment of another person ('P'), he will not incur liability so long as he reasonably believes that P lacks capacity in relation to the matter, and that it will be in P's best interests for the act to be done (s. 5(1)).

It is intended to be a positive permission-giving provision. Examples of acts in connection with personal care are given in the Code of Practice, including: assistance with washing and dressing; help with eating and drinking; shopping; help with mobility; acts performed in relation to domiciliary services required for the person's care (such as home care or meals on wheels) or in relation to other community care services. It is important to note that the provision cannot be used to justify use of force, or restrict a person's liberty.

A further mechanism for substitute decision-making applies where an individual has capacity but anticipates possible loss of capacity in the future. The individual with capacity may execute an LPA. This replaces and extends beyond the currently used Enduring Power of Attorney and can apply to decisions relating to health and welfare as well as property and affairs. An LPA will have to be registered with the Public Guardian to take effect.

Inevitably there will be some situations which involve more complex decisions or where there are disputes about aspects of an individual's capacity to make a decision. The Act establishes a new Court of Protection with jurisdiction to determine such disputes. The court may make single orders about particular issues, such as contact or residence. Previously the High Court may have made a declaration covering such issues, but the Court of Protection is intended to be more accessible than the High Court and with a specialist jurisdiction relating to capacity. The Court may also appoint a 'deputy' to make welfare and financial decisions for a person who either has not made an LPA and subsequently loses capacity, or could not have made an LPA because of a long-term disability. This system will replace and extend the use of receivership currently operating from the Court of Protection. As with other substitute decision-making, the court will apply the 'best interests' principle.

A new criminal offence

Finally, the Act extends the scope for prosecutions of abuse of adults with learning disability with the introduction of a new offence. A person is guilty of an offence if she or he has the care of a person who lacks capacity or is reasonably believed to lack capacity, or is the donee of an LPA or a deputy, and she or he ill-treats or wilfully neglects the person. The offence carries a maximum sentence of five years' imprisonment. Early instances of prosecutions have included staff in care homes whose behaviour caused a resident to be scalded in a hot bath and another case where three men were left in a locked car for several hours.

Below, case studies are presented which examine more closely case law and the application of the law in practice.

> **Exercise 4.2**
>
> When is a person taken to have capacity?
>
> How is it decided that a test of capacity should be undertaken?
>
> In what does such a test consist?

Case study 1

This case study illustrates how the courts have innovated and extended the use of the High Court power to rule whether a proposed action is lawful, by making a declaration (also referred to as declaratory relief) to make decisions in respect of adults who lack mental capacity. This line of case law has its origins in medical treatment cases based on the doctrine of necessity. As an example, in *Airedale NHS Trust v. Bland* [1003] 1 All ER 821, a declaration was made that it was unlawful to discontinue life-sustaining treatment for a person who was in a persistent vegetative state. The law has developed in a piecemeal fashion with issues being determined on a case-by-case basis.

On more than one occasion the courts signalled the need for Parliament to introduce legislation and prior to the Mental Capacity Act 2005 declaratory relief was developed by the courts to fill the legal loophole that exists whereby it was not possible to formally delegate decision-making to another individual concerning social and welfare matters. As discussed above, since the introduction of the Act it has become possible for individuals with capacity to appoint a Lasting Power of Attorney to make social, health and welfare decisions for them on loss of capacity. Where there is no LPA the new Court of Protection can make such decisions. It will do so following the line of case law on declaratory relief decided before the Act, particularly drawing on the precedents relating to best interests.

Extension of declaratory relief beyond medical cases was first noted in *Re S (Hospital Patient: Court's Jurisdiction)* [1996] Fam 1. Here, the court indicated that declaratory relief might be available wherever a 'serious justiciable issue' arose and with flexibility in order that the court could respond to social needs as they are manifested on a case-by-case basis. A few years later in *Re D-R (Adult: Contact)* [1999] 1 FLR 1161 the court considered a claim by a father for access to his adult daughter who had a learning disability. The Court of Appeal confirmed that, for an adult with a disability, the question the Court must address was whether it was in her best interest to have contact, relying on *Re F (Sterilization: Mental Patient)* [1990] 2 AC 1. To determine best interests where there was family conflict, it was necessary to look at all the circumstances, which included the history and former relationship of the father and daughter, the current situation and the prospects for the future.

Susan

Susan is aged 33. She has a moderate to severe learning disability. She was cared for by her parents in the family home until 1995 when, following her mother's death, she was cared for by her father with support from care assistants. An allegation was received from the district nurse that Susan was punched in the face by her father (while drunk). Susan lacks capacity to choose where to live. Her father's love is not disputed but his health is deteriorating. He does not allow contact with her siblings. The local authority sought a declaration that it would be lawful for them to remove Susan from the family home, place her in specialist residential accommodation and restrict access between her and her father.

Exercise 4.3

How should Susan's needs be met?

The facts outlined are drawn from *Newham London Borough Council* v. *S* [2003] EWHC 1909 Fam. In cases where a declaration is sought the court describes the decision-making process in terms of 'four essential building blocks':

- Is mental incapacity established?
- Is there a serious justiciable issue relating to welfare?
- What is it?
- With welfare of the incapable adult as the court's paramount consideration, what are the balance sheet factors which must be drawn up to decide which course of action is in a person's best interests?

The factors that weighed against the authority's application in Susan's case were the father's love and sense of duty towards her, the fact that he had cared adequately for her since her mother's death and the fact that the allegations against him were not substantiated. Factors in favour of the application included the relevance of the father's age and health which meant his ability to care would diminish. Contact between Susan and her siblings had ceased due to a rift between the father and his other children and this contact could resume if Susan were accommodated by the council. Also, the proposed accommodation was purpose-built for Susan and would enable her to socialize with people of her own age. Finally, independent evidence of a consultant psychiatrist supported Newham's plans as the best way of meeting her needs.

The father's argument that a 'significant harm' threshold needed to be satisfied (analogous to that in the Children Act 1989) before Newham could intervene was rejected. The court stated that as long as the adult concerned lacked the capacity to make decisions about future care and there was a serious justiciable issue requiring resolution, the court's inherent jurisdiction was available to it.

Prior to this decision it had been assumed that declarations would only be sought by local authorities where they had concerns about possible abuse. That was precisely the case in *Re F (Adult: Court's Jurisdiction)* [2000] 3 WLR 1740 CA, where the local authority sought a declaration as to the place of residence and contact arrangements for a woman with a learning disability who was unable to care for herself. It was accepted that the woman lacked capacity to make decisions as to her future. She did not fall within the guardianship provisions of the Mental Health Act 1983, and as she was aged over 18, the wardship jurisdiction could not be utilized. The family circumstances were complex but evidence was provided of chronic neglect, a lack of minimum standards of hygiene and cleanliness in the home and possible sexual abuse.

The court confirmed that where there was a risk of possible harm in respect of an adult who lacked the capacity to make decisions as to their own future the court had power, in the best interests of that person, to hear the issue involved and to grant the necessary declarations. Subsequent decisions have dealt with a range of issues, including in the case of *M* v. *B* [2005] EWHC 1681 Fam, the proposed arranged marriage of a woman with a severe learning disability to which she lacked capacity to consent. The court noted the need to bar the marriage to protect her right to respect for her private life within the terms of the Human Rights Act 1998.

The Newham case (Susan) apparently opens the way for declarations to be sought to resolve any 'best interest' decision regarding an incapacitated adult. This pre-empted the role envisaged for the new Court of Protection under the Mental Capacity Act 2005.

Case study 2

It is well documented that residential accommodation, whether providing homes for children, adults with disabilities or very elderly people, has provided opportunities for abuse of individual residents and for abusive practices to develop (see Chapter 16). This case study illustrates the need for close regulation of residential accommodation.

Alan

Alan, who had a severe learning disability, lived in a home in Northamptonshire which was registered to accept 16 people with physical disability, or mental handicap (the term used in the conditions of registration) and mental disorder. Registration of the home was cancelled for reasons including failure to care for Alan and recognize his care needs. Alan had been kept in conditions of squalor and degradation, deprived of his liberty. His dignity was ignored, his right to property compromised, and he was in pain with a dental abscess and no action was taken to treat him. One of the inspection officers commented that she had never seen an animal kept in that way. He was effectively abandoned by Essex County Council 12 years before and kept in conditions reminiscent of those which led to the closure of many large mental institutions. He spent time sitting on a plastic chair dressed in only a ripped T-shirt, surrounded by urine in a cold room with no bed linen and a high handle on the door to prevent escape. Of the 15 residents, only four had a care plan. The human rights implications were noted in the judgement of the Registered Homes Tribunal:

> We had in mind that local authorities now have a duty under the Human Rights Act 1998 to safeguard the rights of those, like Alan, for whom they are responsible. We consider that both Essex and Northampton, as public authorities by virtue of section 6 of the Act, behaved in a way which was incompatible with Alan's convention rights. Inspection units and Registered Persons should consider that it may be appropriate to look at how convention rights are promoted and protected in Registered Homes when questions of registration and fitness arise. [Essex was the placing authority and Northamptonshire was the registration authority.]

The case is reported as *Freeman and Goodwin* v. *Northamptonshire CC* 2000, Decision 421 and it reached the Registered Homes Tribunal while the Registered Homes Act 1984 was in force. A similar scenario would now be dealt with by tribunal under the Care Standards Act 2000 supported by National Minimum Standards. Any concerns of possible abuse, of which the home is aware, should be notified to the registration authority, now a national body, the Care Quality Commission, which has replaced the Commission for Social Care Inspection (CSCI).

This case study presents an opportunity to discuss the application of the Human Rights Act 1998 in relation to people with learning disabilities. It has already been noted that the Act applies equally to all citizens, and people with learning disabilities may rely on its provisions to secure a guarantee of their basic human rights. The Act incorporates the *European Convention on Human Rights* 1951 (which contains various rights and prohibitions, in the form of articles, e.g. article 2 is the 'right to life') and enables individuals for the first time to enforce compliance with the articles in the UK courts. Previously cases could only be brought against the UK in the European Court of Human Rights in Strasbourg, a costly and time-consuming process. Under the Human Rights Act 1998 it is unlawful for a public authority to act in a way which is incompatible with a convention right (Section 6). The term 'public authority' includes the courts, central and local government, social services, police, health authorities, the Care Quality Commission and others carrying out functions of a public nature. The effect of this provision is that the placing and receiving authority in Alan's case as well as the inspection body would be obliged to ensure that Alan's rights under the *Convention* were not violated.

In Alan's case it could be argued that aspects of the regime could amount to inhuman or degrading treatment under Article 3 of the *Convention*. Application of this article hinges on definition of the terms used. In

Ireland v. *UK* 1978 five techniques, wall standing, hooding, subjection to noise, sleep, food and drink deprivation were found to be degrading treatment. 'Torture' was defined as deliberate inhuman treatment causing very serious and cruel suffering; 'inhuman treatment' as intense physical and mental suffering and acute psychiatric disturbances; and 'degrading' as behaviour which aroused in the victim feelings of anguish and inferiority capable of humiliating and debasing them and possibly breaking their physical or moral resistance. The case also said that ill treatment must attain a minimum level of severity. That is a relative issue and will depend on all the circumstances of the case, including duration of treatment, its physical and mental effects, and the age, sex and state of health of the victim. Alan's right to respect for private and family life, contained in Article 8, may also have been violated. Much of existing human rights case law has focused on application of Article 8, the right to respect for private and family life, which has been described as:

> a broad term not susceptible to exhaustive definition. It covers the physical and psychological integrity of the person. Elements such as gender identification, name and sexual orientation and sexual life fall within the personal sphere protected by Art. 8. Art. 8 also protects a right to personal development, and to establish and develop relationships with other human beings and the outside world.
>
> *(Pretty* v. *UK* [2002] 35 EHRR 1)

Article 8 is a qualified article. This means that there are some permitted exceptions to the rights protected by it. A breach or interference with the right may be permissible where it is in accordance with law, necessary in a democratic society and in the interests of named justifications including public safety, prevention of disorder or crime, or the protection of the rights and freedoms of others. In the latter circumstances this may involve a balancing exercise between the competing rights of two or more parties. For example, a resident in a home might argue that his right to freedom of expression permits him to make offensive comments about people with learning disabilities. A resident with a learning disability, however, might well argue that this behaviour infringes their right to respect for private and family life. It is also important that any interference under Article 8 is a 'proportionate' response, and that proper procedural safeguards are followed. As an example, closure of a home following a minor incident of poor record-keeping by the owners would not seem to be a proportionate response to the need to safeguard the residents.

The other important concept embraced by 'physical and psychological integrity', which are protected by Article 8, is the right of the disabled person to participate in the life of the community and to have 'access to essential economic and social activities and to an appropriate range of recreational and cultural activities'. This is matched by the positive obligation of the State to take appropriate measures designed to ensure to the greatest extent feasible that a disabled person is not 'so circumscribed and so isolated as to be deprived of the possibility of developing his personality'.

The Human Rights Act 1998 offers an opportunity to ensure best practice in respecting the human rights of people with learning disabilities and provides an effective route to challenge any violations by public authorities.

It is significant that Alan suffered mistreatment at the hands of a professional carer. One of the most effective ways of reducing abuse must be to ensure that unsuitable adults do not come into contact with vulnerable adults in a caring role. The Care Standards Act 2000 introduced the Protection of Vulnerable Adults (POVA) index, a list of individuals who are considered unsuitable to work with vulnerable adults (Section 81). As an example, in *Close* v. *Secretary of State for Health* [2008] EWCST 852, the Care Standards Tribunal found that a care home worker who slept on waking shifts and verbally abused residents was unsuitable to work with vulnerable adults. The Safeguarding Vulnerable Groups Act 2006 has established a new vetting and barring scheme which replaces POVA. An individual who intends to work with vulnerable adults or children must seek registration under the scheme before doing so. It will be illegal to engage anyone in a regulated activity, such as work in a care home, without checking the register.

Case study 3

Research suggests that people with learning disabilities may be particularly vulnerable to sexual abuse. The operation of the criminal law is the focus of this case study. It should also be remembered that such behaviour would be covered by adult protection guidelines and joint investigation by the police and social services would be appropriate at least in the initial stages. Multi-agency guidelines are in place nationally following publication of *No Secrets: Guidance on Developing and Implementing Multi-agency Policies and Procedures to Protect Vulnerable Adults from Abuse* (Department of Health 2000). *No Secrets* defines abuse as follows: 'Abuse is a violation of an individual's human and civil rights by any other person or persons.' The guidance describes abuse further:

> It may be physical, verbal, or psychological. It may be an act of neglect or an omission to act, or it may occur when a vulnerable person is persuaded into a financial or sexual transaction to which he or she has not consented or cannot consent. Abuse can occur in any relationship and may result in significant harm to, or exploitation of, the person subjected to it.
>
> (Department of Health 2000: para. 2.6)

The issue of consent is central to the determination of whether sexual behaviour is abusive. This approach is also taken in the criminal law. However, as this case study details, there has been a lack of legal clarity as to what constitutes consent in this context.

Jenkins

David Jenkins, aged 61, worked at a project providing supported housing for people with learning disabilities, as a support worker. He admitted a sexual relationship with a woman resident after she was found to be pregnant and a DNA test proved paternity. She was described as having a mental age of 2 years and 8 months and had no concept of sexual relationships nor of their consequences. He was charged with rape. An alternative charge would have been 'sexual intercourse with a defective' under the Sexual Offences Act 1956. This, however, carries a maximum sentence of only two years compared to rape which carries a life sentence. The key question before the court was whether she had given her consent. Expert evidence was provided to the court based on the Law Society and British Medical Association (BMA) guidelines on capacity. It was argued that in order to consent to sex a woman must be able to understand what is proposed and its implications and must be able to exercise choice. On this analysis the woman could not have given consent.

The court rejected this evidence, preferring to rely on a judgment from the 1800s which suggested that consent could be given by following 'animal instinct'. In the circumstances the prosecution was not able to offer any further evidence on the rape charge and Jenkins was acquitted.

Clearly in the above case the law failed to offer protection to an alleged victim of sexual abuse in circumstances involving abuse of trust. The law on sexual offences, including those where the victim is unable to consent, has been reformed and is now contained in the Sexual Offences Act 2003. The act includes a range of sexual offences relating to people with mental disorder, where the mental disorder impedes choice. For example, under Section 30 a person (A) commits an offence if he (or she) intentionally touches another person (B) in a sexual way, where B is unable to refuse because of or for a reason related to a mental disorder, and A knows or could reasonably be expected to know that B has a mental disorder and that because of it or for a reason related to it B is likely to be unable to refuse. A person is unable to refuse if he or she lacks the capacity to choose whether to agree to engaging in the activity because he or she lacks sufficient understanding of the nature or reasonably foreseeable consequences of the activity, or for any other reason, or he or she is unable to communicate such a choice to A.

There are further offences where a person uses inducement, threat or deception to procure sexual activity with a person with a mental disorder, or engages in sexual activity in the presence of a person with a mental disorder, or causes a person with a mental disorder to watch a sex act (including one on film).

The Act also introduces a new 'breach of a relationship to care' offence, where a 'care worker' who has face-to-face contact through employment (paid or unpaid) in a care home, National Health Service body or independent health setting engages in sexual activity with a person with a mental disorder. With the exception of rape, all offences contained in the Act are 'gender neutral'. Maximum sentences range from ten years to life imprisonment. The new legislation provides a range of offences that may be charged where some form of sexual behaviour takes place with a person with a learning disability to which they did not or could not consent.

It is important to remember that the aim of this legislation is to protect individuals from inappropriate and abusive sexual acts. It is not in any way intended to give the message that people with learning disabilities should be prohibited from enjoying an appropriate and consenting sex life. Guidance to the Act reminds us that 'It is important to appreciate that where a person with a mental disorder is able to consent freely to sexual activity, they have the same rights to engage in sexual activity as anyone else' (Home Office 2003).

It was encouraging in the Jenkins case that the Crown Prosecution Service was committed to pursuing the case and charging rape. It has been suggested that many sexual (and other) offences are not prosecuted for reasons associated with actual or perceived lack of credibility of the person with a learning disability when giving evidence (Mencap 1997, see Chapter 20). Provisions in the Youth Justice and Criminal Evidence Act 1999 recognize that giving evidence may be particularly stressful for some vulnerable witnesses and allow for special measures to be employed. A vulnerable adult witness is defined as a person suffering from mental disorder or otherwise having a significant impairment of intelligence and social functioning or a physical disability (Section 16 (2) (b)). Further, a witness may be entitled to special measures if the court is satisfied that the quality of their evidence is likely to be diminished by reason of fear or distress in connection with testifying (Section 17). Special measures available include screening the witness from the accused, giving evidence via a live link, removal of formal wigs and gowns during testimony, giving evidence in private (particularly in sexual cases), video-recording of evidence, cross-examination and re-examination, use of an intermediary and use of communication aids.

Conclusion

At all times, the law starts with the premise that an adult with a learning disability has the same rights to participate fully in society as any other adult. This is supported by legislation which prohibits discrimination. Exceptions to this principle have been incorporated into law. Where individuals with learning disabilities may benefit from support services, legislation contains powers to provide such services. Sadly, we know that adults with learning disabilities may be abused in different ways in different contexts and by a range of individuals, who may or may not have a professional relationship with the adult. The law provides certain avenues to secure protection of the individual. The criminal law may prosecute perpetrators, punish them and act as a deterrent to others. Some specific sexual offences recognize that learning disability may impede genuine choice to enter into sexual relations and prohibit others from taking advantage of invalid consent.

Case studies used in this chapter illustrate the application of law to different scenarios concerning adults with learning disabilities. In each area, actual and potential law reforms present more positive outcomes. A major development has been provided by the Mental Capacity Act 2005 which reinforces the positive presumption in favour of capacity and delivers a clear framework applying to cases where individuals lack capacity to make their own decisions. Supported by provisions of the Human Rights Act 1998, the law is developing positively to uphold the rights of individuals with a learning disability.

Exercise 4.4

Consider the potential violations of human rights an individual with learning disabilities might experience, living at home with family members or in a supported living environment.

When an individual lacks the capacity to make a particular decision, who can make the decision and on what basis?

What should be the role of law where a person with a learning disability suffers abuse by a carer?

Should the primary purpose of law be to uphold the human rights of adults with learning disabilities, provide support services, or offer protection from abuse?

Further reading

Bartlett, P. (2003) Adults, mental illness and incapacity: convergence and overlap in legal regulation, *Journal of Social Welfare and Family Law*, 341.

Brammer, A. (2000) Human Rights Act 1998: implications for adult protection, *Journal of Adult Protection*, 3(1): 43. The *Journal of Adult Protection* includes a range of practice, law and research articles concerned with vulnerable adults including adults with learning disabilities.

Brammer, A. (2009) *Social Work Law*, 3rd edn. Harlow: Pearson Education.

Brown, R. and Barker, P. (2008) *The Social Worker's Guide to the Mental Capacity Act 2005*. Exeter: Learning Matters.

Lord Chancellor's Department (1999) *Making Decisions: The Government's Proposals for Making Decisions on Behalf of Mentally Incapacitated Adults*. London: The Stationery Office.

Resources

www.carestandardstribunal.gov.uk/index.htm. This website provides details about decisions of the Care Standards Tribunal and archive decisions of the Registered Homes Tribunal.

www.cqc.gov.uk. The Care Quality Commission is the new inspectorate for all social care services in England.

www.doh.gov.uk/learningdisabilities. The section of the Department of Health website that addresses learning disability issues.

www.drc-gb.org/. The Disability Rights Commission (DRC) is an independent body established by an Act of Parliament to stop discrimination and promote equality of opportunity for disabled people.

www.equalityhumanrights.com. The website of the new enforcement body, the Equality and Human Rights Commission.

www.voiceuk.org.uk. Voice UK is an organization that supports people with learning disabilities, their families and carers, who have experienced crime or abuse. The organization campaigns for changes in law and practice.

References

Department of Health (1991) *The Children Act 1989 Guidance and Regulations*, vol. 6. London: HMSO.

Department of Health (2000) *No Secrets: Guidance on Developing and Implementing Multi-agency Policies and Procedures to Protect Vulnerable Adults from Abuse*. London: The Stationery Office.

Department of Health (2001) *Valuing People: A New Strategy for Disability in the 21st Century*. London: The Stationery Office.

Home Office (2003) *Guidance on Part 1 of the Sexual Offences Act 2003*, circular 021/2004. London: Home Office.

Keywood, K. (1995) Sterilising the woman with learning difficulties, in S. Bridgman and S. Mills (eds) *Law and Body Politics: Regulating the Female Body*. Aldershot: Dartmouth Publishing Co.

Law Commission (1995) *Mental Incapacity* (No. 231). London: HMSO.

Mencap (1997) *Barriers to Justice*. London: Mencap.

5

Models of service delivery

Eric Emerson and Paul Ramcharan

Introduction

The last 150 years, and in particular the last 30 years, have witnessed a revolution in the way in which public agencies have sought to provide 'care' or 'support' for people with learning disabilities. The period has seen a revolution in models of service delivery. These changes have been most noticeable in the way in which 'care' or 'support' has been provided for people with learning disabilities who do not live with their family.

A hundred and fifty years ago, England's first publicly funded 'asylum' for people with learning disabilities was opened. The number of such institutions and the number of people with learning disabilities who were placed in them rose steadily through the last quarter of the nineteenth century and the first half of the twentieth century (see also Chapter 2). Only 30 years ago over 50,000 people with learning disabilities were living in these large institutions (by then renamed 'hospitals'). These numbers dropped precipitously during the 1980s and 1990s. In 2001 the government announced in the White Paper *Valuing People* that all remaining learning disability hospitals would close (Department of Health 2001). This target should have been achieved by April 2006. Changes have taken place not just in living arrangements but also in education, criminal justice and employment (see Chapters 14, 20 and 27). This chapter will concentrate on examining supported accommodation so as to understand what has driven these changes and assess the impact of the changes on the lives of people with learning disabilities.

But what exactly do we mean by 'models' of service delivery? For example, while the term 'institution' is often associated with images of Dickensian deprivation, it is important to keep in mind that this term is used by different people at different times to refer to:

- the physical structure of services (e.g. large socially isolated accommodation arrangements);
- administrative categories of services (e.g. learning disability hospitals);
- practices and social arrangements (e.g. 'institutional' regimes);
- the ideological underpinnings of approaches to providing support.

As we will see, while these dimensions of what constitutes a 'model' may often overlap, the fit between them is often far from perfect. In what follows the history of such institutions and the development of alternatives since the commitment to their closure is traced using information extracted from a range of secondary sources including Wolfensberger (1975, 1981), Malin *et al.* (1980), Simmons (1982), Scheerenberger (1983), Scull (1984, 1993), Ryan and Thomas (1987), Alaszewski (1988), Race (1995) and Wright and Digby (1996).

Institutional living for many children and adults with learning disabilities in the developed world has been a 'short interlude' and the majority have historically always lived with their families or have lived independently (see Chapter 2). An important question for societies has been what type of accommodation should be provided to those people with learning disabilities for whom neither independent living nor family support is an option. The answer to this question has been shaped by (and itself served to shape) several factors including:

- public and professional conceptions of the nature of 'learning disability';
- public and professional expectations regarding notions of 'common decency';
- pre-existing mechanisms for the delivery of welfare support.

Changing patterns and practices in supported accommodation

The evolution of institutional provision

Wolfensberger (1975) describes four phases in the evolution of institutional models: making the deviant undeviant; protecting the deviant from society; protecting society from the deviant; and finally a 'loss of rationale'. Unfortunately, the early optimism of the power of education to 'solve' the problem of out-of-home support for people with learning disabilities proved unfounded.

First, such options were only available to a minority of people with learning disability. The 1908 Royal Commission estimated that most people with mild learning disabilities were paupers under no authority, or in generic institutions for the destitute. The Commission estimated that 18 per cent of the population in workhouses had learning disabilities, 10 per cent of those in prison and 2 per cent of those on outdoor relief. Second, it proved highly problematic to return people to their communities after several years in an isolated asylum. In the light of these difficulties, professional pronouncements of appropriate models of support began to gradually shift from those that emphasized education to those that emphasized long-term care and protection. Consider, for example, the following two quotes, both from past presidents of the American Association on Mental Retardation and both quite remarkable for their paternalistic/maternalistic tone:

> A well fed, well cared for idiot, is a happy creature. An idiot awakened to his condition is a miserable one.
>
> (Butler 1885)

> They must be kept quietly and safely away from the world, living like the angels in heaven, neither marrying nor given in marriage.
>
> (Johnson 1889)

The shift from short-term education to a more paternalistic/maternalistic ethos was accompanied by a rapid expansion in the number of institutions and the number of people living in them. For example, the Royal Albert Asylum was founded in Lancaster in 1870 as a charitable institution for young people with less severe learning disabilities. In 1873, 141 people lived there. By 1893, this number had grown to 600. It would eventually rise to over 1000.

This paternalistic/maternalistic ethos was, however, to prove to be another relatively short-lived phase (although again, we shall see the resurgence of such ideas a century later). The early twentieth century saw a fundamental shift in public discourse about people with learning disability. No longer to be seen as part of the 'worthy poor', instead they came to be seen as a significant threat to the current and future social order.

Three sets of beliefs were combined by eugenicists (see Chapter 2) to argue that people with learning disabilities (and in particular people with less severe learning disabilities) posed a significant threat to English society. First, it was believed that intelligence and ability were inherited (a belief supported by the growing 'science' of psychology). Second, it was believed that people with learning disability were 'breeding' faster than the rest of society. Third, it was believed that there were strong links between 'feeble-mindedness' and most of the major social problems of the day. On the basis of these three beliefs, eugenicists argued that without 'appropriate action' the gene pool would gradually but inevitably become corrupted and the extent of associated problems would increase (see Chapter 2).

These ideas were taken seriously. The findings of the 1908 Royal Commission on the Care of the Feeble Minded stressed the importance of hereditary factors and the association between feeble-mindedness and promiscuity, delinquency, alcoholism and illegitimacy. In 1898, Lord Hershel moved a resolution at a meeting of the National Association for the Care of the Feebleminded (NACFM) that: 'the existence of large classes of feeble minded persons is a danger to the physical and moral welfare of society and calls for immediate attention both on the part of public authorities and charitable enterprise'. What would constitute such 'immediate attention'? The 1908 Royal Commission recommended the segregation of people with learning disabilities, while rejecting the Eugenics Education Society's call for 'genetic purification'. In 1909, Tredgold argued that:

> I have come to the conclusion that, in the case of the majority of the feebleminded, there is

one measure, and one measure only . . . which is practically possible, namely the establishment of suitable farm and industrial colonies . . . Society would thus be saved a portion, at least, of the cost of their maintenance, and more important, it would be secure from their depredation and danger of their propagation.

In 1910, the NACFM met with Prime Minister Asquith and Home Secretary Winston Churchill. Following this, Churchill stated that people with learning disabilities should 'be segregated under proper conditions [of sexual quarantine] so that their curse dies with them'. In the 1910 general election the NACFM petitioned all candidates to support measures that would 'tend to discourage parenthood on the part of the feebleminded and other degenerate types'. In 1912, a Mental Deficiency Bill was introduced into Parliament with a clause prohibiting marriage among people with learning disabilities. This Bill was later withdrawn.

These ideas were taken to their logical conclusion in Germany. In October 1939, Hitler authorized a euthanasia programme targeted at people with disabilities. It is estimated that approximately 100,000 people with learning disabilities and 200,000 people with other disabilities were killed in this programme, primarily administered in medical institutions. For example, of the 16,300 inmates of psychiatric institutions in Berlin, only 2400 (15 per cent) survived the euthanasia programme.

While no parallel to these atrocities actually occurred in England, support for the 'mercy killing' of people with learning disabilities was (and continues to be) voiced. Consider the following quote taken from the eighth edition of Tredgold's *Textbook on Mental Deficiency* that was published in 1952:

The 80,000 or more idiots and imbeciles in the country . . . are not only incapable of being employed to any economic advantage, but their care and support, whether in their own homes or in institutions, absorbs a large amount of time, energy and money of the normal population which could be utilised to better purpose. Moreover, many of these defectives are utterly helpless, repulsive in appearance, and revolting in manners. Their existence is a perpetual source of sorrow and unhappiness to their parents, and those who live at home have a most disturbing influence upon other children and family life . . . In my opinion it would be an economical and humane procedure were their existence to be painlessly terminated.

These ideas did, however, help to support a system of 'care' or 'support' that was based on the establishment of large physically segregated institutions in which men and women with learning disabilities led regimented and separate lives. Gray (1997), for example, assisted Herbert (Bertie) Lawford to tell his story of life in Church Hill House Hospital. Bertie was admitted to Church Hill House in August 1934 when he was 9 (he was told he was going for a day at the seaside). He lived there for the next 60 years. His memories include hard physical work on the farm or scrubbing and polishing the wards, and the 'boys' (who were grown men by then) always having to walk two by two whenever out of the institution's grounds, a practice which persisted until the 1960s.

> **Exercise 5.1**
>
> Make a case for keeping people with learning disabilities in closed institutions, separated by gender and engaged in the work of the institution. Write down the struggles you have with this vision. What values does it challenge? What service alternatives are there?

Deinstitutionalization

In 1976, there were just over 50,000 people with learning disabilities living in large-scale segregated institutions (by now renamed 'mental handicap hospitals') in England. Over the next 25 years this number dropped to around 4000 (Emerson 2004a). In 2001 the White Paper *Valuing People* announced that all remaining 'learning disability hospitals' would be closed by April 2006. Within 30 years the approach which had completely dominated the way we have sought to provide 'supported accommodation' for 100 years will have been dismantled. What drove these remarkable changes and what has replaced these institutions?

At least three factors were important in bringing about these changes. First, the 1960s was a period of significant economic growth, increasing living standards and a more liberal approach to social policy. The atrocities of the Second World War had contributed to an increasing international focus on defining and defending people's 'human rights' (e.g. the *Universal Declaration of Human Rights* of 1948, the *European Convention on Human Rights* of 1951), and this focus extended to marginalized groups including people with disabilities in the late 1960s, culminating in 1971 with the United Nations General Assembly adopting the *Declaration on the Rights of Mentally Retarded Persons*. Four years later in 1975 the UN adopted the wider *Declaration of the Rights of Disabled People*.

Second, increasing living standards for the majority, and human rights, threw into stark contrast the regimes operating in large-scale state-operated institutions in the UK and North America. In the UK, a series of public scandals and inquiries highlighted the degrading conditions under which people with learning disabilities (and people with mental health problems and elderly people) were being 'cared for' or 'supported' by the state (Martin 1984). Similar scandals were occurring across North America (e.g. Blatt and Kaplan 1966); scandals that prompted John F. Kennedy in 1963 to call upon Congress for action 'to bestow the full benefits of our society on those who suffer from mental disabilities [and] to retain in and return to the community the mentally ill and mentally retarded, and there to restore and revitalize their lives'.

Third, there was a re-emergence of the interest by professionals in the possibilities of education for people with learning disabilities. Jack Tizard, for example, suggested in 1952 that: 'Young feebleminded adults are the greatest single group in mental deficiency hospitals. There seems no reason why most of them cannot be restored to the community after a period of education and training' (Tizard 1954: 164). In the 1960s and 1970s, behavioural psychologists demonstrated time after time the ability of people with learning disabilities (including people with severe learning disabilities) to acquire new skills and competencies (Remington 1991). Furthermore, Scandinavian services had during the 1950s and 1960s begun to develop a range of much smaller living arrangements whose aim, in the terms used in a 1959 Danish Act, was to 'create an existence for the mentally retarded as close to normal living conditions as possible' (Bank-Mikkelsen 1980).

The policy response in the UK was contained in the White Paper *Better Services for the Mentally Handicapped* (Department of Health and Social Security 1971). While not calling for the abandonment of institutional provision, *Better Services* did place considerable emphasis on developing alternative, smaller scale, community-based residential services for people with learning disabilities. By 1980, however, a policy commitment had been made to ensure that children with learning disabilities would not be placed in 'mental handicap hospitals'. It was not until 2001, however, that the Department of Health explicitly stated that all 'learning disability hospitals' should close.

So what has replaced 'learning disability hospitals'? The answer to this question is complex since de-institutionalization has not been a unified policy in England. With very little central guidance, responsibility for developing alternative forms of supported accommodation fell to two main agencies, the social services departments of local authorities, and health authorities (and more recently Trusts) operating under the auspices of the National Health Service (NHS). As a result, there was (and continues to be) extensive variation across England with regard to how the policies of deinstitutionalization were transacted. There were, however, some common themes.

In the 1970s, deinstitutionalization primarily involved the movement of people with mild learning disabilities (the old 'feeble-minded') into a range of often pre-existing services including hostels, semi-supported group homes, family placement (adult 'fostering') schemes, bed and breakfast arrangements and independent living. Attention also began to turn to developing community-based support for people with more severe disabilities involving the development of medium-sized locally based hospital (or community) units. These were developed and operated by health authorities (who also operated the mental handicap hospitals). Simon, a highly influential psychiatrist, described them thus:

Community units that already exist vary in size from 12 to 30 beds. The most convenient and economic size has been found to be 24 beds, 8 catering for long-term residents, 8 providing residential care with training for up to a two-year period and 8 being retained to meet the need for short-term, on demand services. Community units of this size should serve a population of about 80,000.

(Simon 1981: 24)

Interestingly, Simon also suggested that the learning disability 'hospital of the future will be a great deal smaller, 200 beds or less' (1981: 26).

During the 1980s, however, the development of these medium-sized medicalized facilities was subject to increasing challenges. The Danish aim to 'create an existence for the mentally retarded as close to normal living conditions as possible' (Bank-Mikkelsen 1980) led to the notion, or more accurately notions (see Emerson 1992) of normalization. The most influential definition of normalization was provided by a North American psychologist, Wolf Wolfensberger. Subsequently renaming it social role valorization (Wolfensberger 1983), he defined normalization as the 'utilization of means which are as culturally normative as possible, in order to establish and/or maintain personal behaviours and characteristics which are as culturally normative as possible' (Wolfensberger 1972: 28). In the UK, notions of normalization found their voice in an influential series of publications from the King's Fund (King's Fund Centre 1980, 1984). Grouped under a banner proclaiming 'An Ordinary Life', these papers argued that services should aim to provide the level of support necessary to enable *all* people with learning disabilities to live in ordinary domestic housing and to be employed in ordinary jobs. These ideas now underpin official health and social care policy for people with learning disabilities in England (Department of Health 2001).

During the 1980s a number of pilot schemes involving small group living arrangements for people with severe learning disabilities in 'ordinary' domestic housing (group homes or staffed houses) had been developed and evaluated (e.g. Felce 1989; Lowe and de Paiva 1991), including pilot schemes for people with extremely disturbed or 'challenging' behaviour (Mansell *et al.* 2001). By the end of the 1980s, use of staffed domestic housing for people with

learning disabilities had become the dominant approach in many localities. For example, in Wales the innovative *All Wales Strategy* (Welsh Office 1983) marked a sea change in policy towards the development of ordinary housing and individualized planning and support for people with learning disabilities. However, in other localities deinstitutionalization was accomplished (at least in part) by the development of cluster housing or large campus-style facilities, or by the development of relatively large 'residential care homes'.

Current provision

Figure 5.1 illustrates the patterning of provision across different sectors in England in 2001.

NHS provision

The NHS provides both long-stay 'beds' and residential 'places' for people with intellectual disability, accounting for 12 per cent of total recorded provision in 2001. Long-stay 'beds' represent provision in which the person has the legal status of being a patient within the NHS. There has been a marked and continuing reduction in the number of NHS long-stay beds since 1976. In 2001 there were just over 3500 NHS long-stay beds for people with intellectual disability in England (representing 50 per cent of NHS residential provision for people with intellectual disability). Of these, approximately 1000 were spread across the 22 remaining NHS long-stay hospitals for people with intellectual disability. The nature of the remaining 2500 long-stay beds is unclear. It is likely, however, that they are primarily composed of either 'campus-style' or 'cluster housing' arrangements or long-term 'treatment' facilities. Recent research has seriously questioned the cost-effectiveness of such services (Emerson *et al.* 2000a, 2000b; Emerson 2004b). As a result, the Department of Health has finally made a commitment to close all 'campus-style' arrangements (Department of Health 2001, 2009a: 79).

The NHS also provides residential 'places' for people with intellectual disability. This includes all forms of residential provision operated by the NHS in which residents have been legally 'discharged' from hospital care. Again, the nature of this type of provision is unclear. It is likely, however, that they are

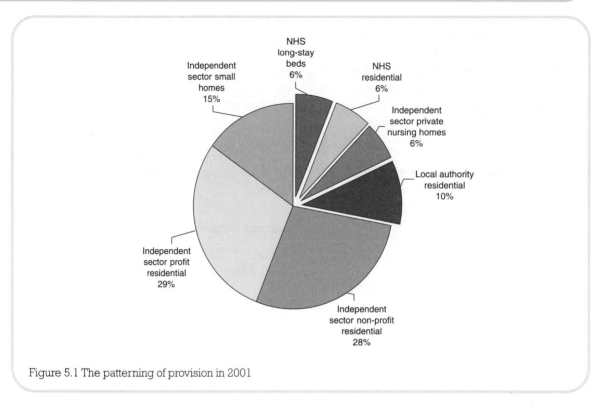

Figure 5.1 The patterning of provision in 2001

composed of either 'campus-style' or 'cluster housing' arrangements, dispersed group homes or staffed housing schemes.

Local authority provision

In England, local authorities are responsible for arranging social care (but not health care). The initial phases of deinstitutionalization saw the amount of residential services that were directly managed by the local authorities rise from just under 7000 in 1976 to over 12,500 in 1988/89. The introduction of 'internal markets' in social care in 1990 resulted in falls down to under 6000 with continuing falls expected. Local authority provision currently accounts for 10 per cent of all provision. Thus, provision directly managed by statutory sector organizations accounted for 22 per cent of all residential provision for people with learning disabilities in England in 2001 with the average falling between 1994 and 2001 from 15.4 to 13.0 places per home.

Independent sector provision

Deinstitutionalization (and the more recent pressure to reduce residential services directly managed by

local authorities) has been associated with a significant increase in provision managed by independent sector organizations.

Total provision by the independent sector has risen nearly 15-fold from just over 3000 in 1976 to over 50,000 in 2001, about 57 per cent of all provision. The majority of this provision is in group homes for four or more people and is equally split between 'voluntary' non-profit and 'private' profit-making organizations. Information on group homes for fewer than four people has only been collected since 1993/94. Since that time, provision in small homes has risen by over 200 per cent (compared with 63 per cent for independent sector 'residential' provision over the same period).

The average size of independent sector non-profit provision (excluding all 'small homes' for three or fewer people) fell between 1994 and 2001 from 9.3 to 8.4 places per home. The average size of independent sector for-profit provision (excluding all 'small homes' for three or fewer people) fell between 1994 and 2001 from 10.7 to 9.5 places per home.

Community-based residential support is not, however, the only alternative to traditional forms of institutional care. Other options include intentional or village communities (Cox and Pearson 1995) upon which little reliable information exists. However, it appears that: (1) all such services are operated by independent sector non-profit organizations; (2) they account for approximately 2 per cent of supported accommodation services for people with intellectual disabilities in England (Department of Health 1999); (3) the majority of people who live in such communities are relatively able and moved there from their family home or from residential schools. As such, the village community movement has developed independent of deinstitutionalization.

Overall levels of provision

The currently recorded overall level of provision is equivalent to 129 places per 100,000 of the general population. This level of provision is markedly lower than that reported in the US (155) and markedly higher than that reported in Australia (100) (Braddock et al. 2001). Our best estimate is that there has been no change in the overall level of provision over the last 25 years, which is widely recognized (Department of Health and Social Security 1971).

The impact of changing patterns and practices in supported accommodation

Deinstitutionalization was perceived as a contentious and risky policy. While there was general agreement that existing institutional provision was often of an unacceptable quality, there was no consensus on what the most appropriate alternatives would be. As a result, deinstitutionalization came under close scrutiny and generated a significant volume of applied research (Walsh et al. 2008; Kozma et al. 2009). Initially, most of this research tried to answer the question: are people with learning disabilities better off in community-based services than they were in institutions? But what was and is meant by 'better off' and who decides what 'better off' means? In terms of the latter question and, with very few exceptions indeed, researchers and the policy-makers who commission research have decided what 'better off' means, with people with learning disabilities and their relatives having virtually no say in deciding what outcomes research should focus on. As a result, the definition and measurement of being 'better off'

tended to reflect the biases and preoccupations of academics (like myself) and senior policy-makers. Fortunately, these interests were sufficiently wide and varied for some generally robust conclusions to be drawn (Walsh et al. 2008; Kozma et al. 2009). Table 5.1 summarizes the conclusions and draws largely on Kozma et al.'s (2009) comprehensive review of 68 studies published since 1997.

Several years ago the Office of the Deputy Prime Minister and the Department of Health began developing new guidance for housing and support services (guidance that was never released). However, the consultation document (released in 2003) summarized the existing evidence base in three brief statements:

- Smaller community-based housing and support services provide higher quality support and better outcomes for people with learning disabilities than larger more 'institutional' forms of provision.
- The quality of support and outcomes provided by community-based housing and support services is often unacceptable when judged against the aspirations of *Valuing People*.
- There are few robust relationships between measures of resource input and either the quality of support or outcomes for people with learning disabilities. Quality is determined by how resources are used.

The evidence, therefore, suggests that deinstitutionalization has been a qualified success. It is clear that while smaller community-based supports are associated with better outcomes, there still exists a marked gap between what is being delivered and the aspirations of social inclusion and empowerment that underlie current policy.

This gap has led to increasing criticism of the reliance of public agencies on staffed housing or group homes as the dominant model of provision. Some commentators have argued that this model did not go far enough and promote more 'supported living' options (e.g. Kinsella 1993; O'Brien 1994; Simons 1997), while others claim it has gone too far and have promoted 'village communities' (Cox and Pearson 1995; Grover 1995).

Proponents of 'supported living' argue services should be provided to enable people with learning disabilities to live in their own homes, rather than in a

Outcome area	Findings	Mediating factors or explanation for variation in results
Community presence and participation	Limited across all settings but generally better in smaller scale settings	Adaptive behaviour: complexity of needs; social competence; service factors and quality support
Social network and community presence	More friends in smaller setting with low staff turnover; those in supported accommodation had more friends, contact with neighbours and visitors Loneliness is a product of incompatibility of clients and feelings of safety in smaller settings Friendships with other people with learning disabilities were stable, reciprocal and valued	Active support; adaptive skills and level of challenging behaviour
Family contact	No difference found between settings	Distance from family; family and resident age
Self-determination and choice	Most people have relatively limited choice in minor everyday decisions Smaller and less congregate settings offer more choice and opportunities but did not guarantee better outcomes	Staff practices, active support, home-like environment, adaptive skills and level of disability
Quality of life	Community living options including cluster, small groups homes, semi-independent and independent living produced better quality of life	Individual characteristics, staff practices and service procedures
Adaptive behaviour	Conflicting data: studies have shown no change, static skills and improvements in only some domains People with severe and profound disabilities show most gains once they move to the community	Environmental and service factors; attractiveness of setting; stimulation in the environment and choice-making; active support; skills teaching
Challenging behaviour	No significant changes on the move to different community residences; some evidence the nature of challenging behaviour changes	More restrictive practices
Medication	More medication used in community settings though not in all studies; smaller use of polypharmacy in the community	Environment and conditions

Outcome area	Findings	Mediating factors or explanation for variation in results
Health, risk and mortality	No evidence of transfer trauma in moves. Less restrictive environments in the community give rise to increased smoking and obesity but overall there is reduced inactivity. The smaller settings, semi-independent and independent living give rise to greater exposure to crime and verbal abuse	Gender has effect on health outcomes Inadequate access to health care determines rates of morbidity
User and family views and satisfaction	High satisfaction from families and users for community living arrangements; more critical of institutions and did not want to return But parents report high satisfaction with institutional living for relatives	Retrospective measures favour current living arrangements making these measures unreliable

Table 5.1 Summary of outcomes of community living options, mediating factors and factors explaining variation in results

residential facility (whether large or small) that is owned and operated by a welfare agency, providing for them a secure sense of place over which the person exerts considerable control (O'Brien 1994). As a result, approaches to supported living have sought to provide people with legal security regarding their accommodation (e.g. by ensuring that people hold legal tenancies) and to maximize the degree of control they have over where and with whom they live. The little evidence that is available suggests that the gains associated with supported living are relatively modest when compared against group homes of similar size (Emerson *et al.* 2001).

The guiding ethos behind village communities is that, by paralleling the operation of rural villages, they can provide a relatively self-contained, rich and varied life for people with learning disabilities in a setting that is to a certain extent physically separate from mainstream society. As such, village communities demonstrate continuity in ideas with romantic notions of village life and the rationale for institutions for people with intellectual disabilities that emerged at the end of the nineteenth century.

A number of village communities have a clear religious or philosophical foundation. The latter include Camphill communities that are based on life-sharing arrangements between people who do and who do not have disabilities (see www.camphill.org.uk). As Fulgosi (1990: 43) describes:

> As the word 'village' implies, each Camphill village centre endeavours to create and maintain an environment where the economic, social and spiritual life of the community complement each other. Villagers [people with intellectual disabilities] and co-workers live and work side-by-side, running their homes, and sharing what needs to be done. Some villages have a village store, a gift shop, café, and even a post office ... The rhythm of the farming year, the seasons and the celebration of the Christian festivals play an important part in the life of each community.

The little evidence that is available suggests that such communities offer a different, though not necessarily inferior, quality of life to community-based approaches (Emerson *et al.* 2000a).

Moves towards personalization

Arguably, for the best part of 50 years it has been possible to trace gradual steps towards what can now be described as personalization in the evolution of service models. Perhaps the earliest significant step in this direction was the 'Brooklands Experiment' that involved evaluating the effects of regime change on the behaviour and attainments of children previously living in institutions. Following a matched pairs study design, half the children were divided into small family groups, each with its own housemother; here they were encouraged to engage in natural play; there was an emphasis on language development, not through over-formalized lessons; and the overarching culture was child-centred, emphasizing the development needs of each child. The hugely successful outcomes of the Brooklands Experiment have been amply described in the seminal work of Lyle (1960a, b) and Tizard (1964). This step change towards a much more humanistic, person-centred environment stood in stark contrast to the prevailing institutional cultures well characterized by King et al. (1971) in terms of rigidity of routine, block treatment, de-personalization and social distance.

Subsequently, with the push towards deinstitutionalization, community care and development of supported accommodation, successive governments have continued to push the pendulum from a concern with 'fitting the person to services' to the 'creation of supports designed to address the needs and aspirations of individuals', an altogether more ambitious goal. This can be seen in the arrangements for engaging service users and families in decisions about their own care and support. In setting out the Green Paper for a new agenda for community care in 2009, the government specifies that 'it must be underpinned by national rights and entitlements, but personalised to people's individual needs' (Department of Health 2009b: 25). Stakeholders already familiar with learning disability services can be forgiven for thinking that they have 'heard about this before' over recent decades given, in some cases, dalliances, in other serious national commitments, respectively to: goal planning, individual service plans, individual programme plans, lifestyle planning, case management and care management (Houts and Scott 1975; Blunden 1980; Welsh Office 1983; Challis and Davies 1986; Cummins et al. 1996; Rudkin and Rowe 1999) – all of these being a family of approaches concerned with organizing assistance to individuals and their families.

Within the UK the Welsh Office (1983) can claim a first in making individual plans (IPs) both a requirement and a cornerstone of its national strategy for people with learning disabilities (see Chapters 22 and 25) but with limited success (Felce et al. 1998).

Valuing People (Department of Health 2001a) sought to extend choice and control to people by developing advocacy, Direct Payments and a national framework for person-centred planning (PCP). Official guidance issued about PCP described PCP as 'a process for continual listening and learning, focusing on what is important to someone now and in the future, and acting on this in alliance with their family and friends' (Department of Health 2001b: 12). Mansell and Beadle-Brown (2004) suggest that though PCP shares characteristics with the individualized planning approaches, it transcends them in a number of ways:

- it seeks to take account of aspirations and capacities expressed by the service user, rather than needs and deficiencies, thereby strengthening the user's voice and the idea of their contributions;
- it attempts to mobilize the individual's family and social network as well as services and community resources; in so doing it therefore recognizes familial and relational commitment and expertise;
- it aims to provide the support required to achieve goals rather than to limit goals to what services can typically manage, thereby seeking to address raised expectations.

With PCP, therefore, the stakes are high since it is central to the core ambitions of Valuing People (Department of Health 2001a) for achieving rights, choice, independence and inclusion for people with learning disabilities. In this it has to embrace people's ambitions as well as their needs, their future as well as present requirements, the resources and knowledge of their familial and social networks, and the support that can be provided by civil society as well as services.

Not surprisingly, considerable implementation challenges for PCP have presented themselves, including the availability of trained facilitators, service availability, lack of time for what can be a labour-intensive process, and reluctance of people other than support staff to engage in the process (Robertson *et al.* 2007). Other commentators have provided evidence that questions whether having a higher quality plan necessarily leads to better outcomes. Chapters 22 and 25 address these details much more fully, especially in relation to the question of outcomes, drawing on evidence from the UK's largest and most robust outcome study of PCP.

Three of the approaches identified earlier – case management, care management and Direct Payments – are examples of micro-budgeting. By this is meant an arrangement that explicitly links assessment (of needs, circumstances and aspirations) to funding and resources for individual packages of tailored support.

With case management and care management, control of budgets were left in the hands of front-line staff or their line managers whereas, with Direct Payments, funding and control of contracts lies with the individual service user. As such Direct Payments are designed to enable people to buy a service that meets their needs or allows them to realize ambitions expressed in their PCP. (Chapter 22 reports research findings from evaluations of Direct Payments and its derivative, Individualized Budgets). For the moment it is worth recording that PCP, Direct Payments and Individualized Budgets are the latest manifestations of arrangements that seek to place service users in fuller charge of their destinies – a far cry from the institutional environments where they were dehumanized and largely forgotten.

Conclusion

As we have seen, the last 150 years, and in particular the last 30 years, have witnessed a revolution in the way in which public agencies have sought to provide 'care' or 'support' for people with learning disabilities who live outside the family home. Overall, the changes of the last 30 years appear to have been to the benefit of people with learning disabilities. Different 'models' have been associated with different outcomes, although the magnitude of these differences is often quite modest. As the Office of the Deputy Prime Minister and Department of Health suggested in 2003, the quality of support and outcomes provided by community-based housing and support services is often unacceptable when judged against the aspirations of *Valuing People*.

What are we to make of this? First, it suggests that there is often a significant gap between policy rhetoric and people's lived reality. All too often, the aims and aspirations of different models prove remarkably difficult to realize in practice. Perhaps part of the problem here has been our tendency to think about different 'models' of support as radical departures from the status quo (e.g. King's Fund Centre 1980; Kinsella 1993). Maybe we need to turn our attention to understanding the basis for continuity in supported accommodation rather than discontinuity and change and use this knowledge to attempt to close the gap between policy aspirations and reality.

Recently, a number of research studies have adopted this focus. That is, instead of asking whether people are 'better off' in model A or B, they have attempted to identify what it is that leads to better outcomes in some circumstances than in others (see Felce 2000; Stancliffe and Keane 2000; Hatton 2001; Felce *et al.* 2002; Robertson *et al.* 2004; Emerson *et al.* 2005; Young 2006; Walsh *et al.* 2008; Kozma *et al.* 2009). The results of these studies have indicated that:

- Considered on their own, resources (e.g. costs, staffing levels, staff values, skills or qualifications) are, at best, only weakly associated with the quality of support or outcomes.
- Strong evidence for all 'models' indicates that people with less severe learning disabilities are likely to enjoy a better quality of life than people with more severe learning disabilities.
- The internal organization and management of support are key to assuring quality outcomes. Institutional working practices have been consistently associated with a wide range of poor outcomes. The use of systematic individualized working practices has been associated with the provision of increased

and more effective support, increased participation, increased social inclusion and increased user satisfaction.

These findings suggest that attention needs to be paid to aspects of the day-to-day operation of services, rather than broad aspects of the 'model' of provision.

Then again, perhaps we should not be surprised about the often modest progress made towards promoting full inclusion and an equitable quality of life for people with learning disabilities. To be surprised, in effect, subscribes to a simple 'idealist' view of history which sees gradual progress as a result of benevolent implementation of changes resulting from new ideals, theories, visions and advances in knowledge. In this view, the development of services is seen as a victory of humanitarianism/science over irrational prejudice. Failure is seen in terms of remaining irrationality, poor communication, public prejudice and lack of resources.

There are, however, alternative (and some would say more pessimistic) views. In some, intentions are seen as solutions to conflicts arising from social change, and change is considered to result from the complex interdependence of 'conscience and convenience'. In this model, unholy alliances between benevolent rhetoric and operational needs lead to the symbolic rather than actual implementation of 'advances' in knowledge (e.g. Rothman 1980). Still others argue that all we are seeing are changing patterns of social control in response to changes in the social order. In this approach, ideals and intentions are seen as mystifying rhetoric concealing the true nature of the control process (e.g. Scull 1984). Understanding the nature and impact of 'models of service delivery' requires us to address these broader issues concerning the nature of change in social responses to people with disabilities.

Exercise 5.2

Consider what makes a home for you.

From the evidence (Table 5.1) about types of supported accommodation, and from your wider reading, compare what you consider to be the most desirable features of community-based types of accommodation for people with learning disabilities.

Given the weak association between staffing levels and user/resident outcomes across types of supported accommodation, consider what staff-related and organization-related factors are most likely to make a difference to the quality of a person's everyday life in those settings. Discuss your views and evidence with one of your peers and a person with learning disabilities.

References

Alaszewski, A. (1988) From villains to victims, in A. Leighton (ed.) *Mental Handicap in the Community*. Cambridge: Woodhead-Faulkener.

Bank-Mikkelsen, N.E. (1980) Denmark, in R.J. Flynn and K.E. Nitsch (eds) *Normalization, Social Integration and Community Services*. Austin, TX: Pro-Ed.

Blatt, B. and Kaplan, H. (1966) *Christmas in Purgatory: A Photographic Essay on Mental Retardation*. New York: Allyn and Bacon.

Blunden, R. (1980) *Individual Plans for Mentally Handicapped People: A Draft Procedural Guide*. Cardiff: Mental Handicap in Wales Applied Research Unit, University of Wales College of Medicine.

Braddock, D., Emerson, E., Felce, D. and Stancliffe, R. (2001) The living circumstances of children and adults with mental retardation or developmental disabilities in the United States, Canada, England and Wales, and Australia, *Mental Retardation and Developmental Disabilities Research Reviews*, 7: 115–21.

Cambridge, P. and Carnaby, S. (2005) *Person-centred Planning and Care Management for People with Learning Disabilities*. London: Jessica Kingsley.

Challis, D. and Davies, B. (1986) *Case Management in Community Care*. Aldershot: Ashgate.

Cox, C. and Pearson, M. (1995) *Made to Care: The Case for Residential and Village Communities for People with a Mental Handicap*. London: The Rannoch Trust.

Cummins, R.A., Baxter, C., Hudson, A. and Jauernig, R. (1996)

A model system for the evaluation of individual program plans, *Journal of Intellectual and Development Disability*, 21: 59–70.

Department of Health (1999) *Facing the Facts: Services for People with Learning Disabilities – A Policy Impact Study of Social Care and Health Services*. London: Department of Health.

Department of Health (2001a) *Valuing People: A New Strategy for Learning Disability for the 21st Century*. Cm 5086. London: The Stationery Office.

Department of Health (2001b) *Valuing People: A New Strategy for Learning Disability for the Twenty-first Century. Towards Person Centred Approaches. Planning with People: Guidance for Partnership Boards*. London: Department of Health.

Department of Health (2009a) *Valuing People Now: a new three-year strategy for people with learning disabilities. Making it happen for everyone*. Wellington House: London.

Department of Health (2009b) *Shaping the Future of Care Together*. London: Department of Health.

Department of Health and Social Security (1971) *Better Services for the Mentally Handicapped*. London: Department of Health.

Emerson, E. (1992) What is normalisation? in H. Smith and H. Brown (eds) *Normalisation: A Reader for the 1990s*. London: Routledge.

Emerson, E. (2004a) Deinstitutionalisation in England, *Journal of Intellectual and Developmental Disability*, 29: 17–22.

Emerson, E. (2004b) Cluster housing for adults with intellectual disabilities, *Journal of Intellectual and Developmental Disability*, 29: 187–97.

Emerson, E. and Hatton, C. (1994) *Moving Out: The Impact of Relocation from Hospital to Community on the Quality of Life of People with Learning Disabilities*. London: HMSO.

Emerson, E., Robertson, J., Gregory, N., Kessissoglou, S., Hatton, C., Hallam, A. *et al.* (2000a) The quality and costs of village communities, residential campuses and community-based residential supports in the UK, *American Journal of Mental Retardation*, 105: 81–102.

Emerson, E., Robertson, J., Gregory, N., Kessissoglou, S., Hatton, C., Hallam, A. *et al.* (2000b) The quality and costs of community-based residential supports and residential campuses for people with severe and complex disabilities, *Journal of Intellectual and Developmental Disability*, 25: 263–79.

Emerson, E., Robertson, J., Gregory, N., Hatton, C., Kessissoglou, S., Hallam, A. *et al.* (2001) The quality and costs of supported living residences and group homes in the United Kingdom, *American Journal of Mental Retardation*, 106: 401–15.

Emerson, E., Robertson, J., Hatton, C., Knapp, M., Walsh, P. N., and Hallam, A. (2005) Costs and outcomes of community residential supports in England, in R.J. Stancliffe and K.C. Lakin (eds) *Costs and Outcomes of Community Services for People with Intellectual Disabilities*. Baltimore, MD: Paul H. Brookes Publishing.

Felce, D. (1989) *The Andover Project: Staffed Housing for Adults with Severe or Profound Mental Handicaps*. Kidderminster: British Institute for Mental Handicap.

Felce, D. (2000) *Quality of Life for People with Learning Disabilities in Supported Housing in the Community: A Review of Research*. Exeter: Centre for Evidence based Social Services (www.ex.ac.uk/cebss).

Felce, D., Kushlick, A. and Mansell, J. (1980) Evaluation of alternative residential facilities for the severely mentally handicapped in Wessex: client engagement, *Advances in Behaviour Research and Therapy*, 3: 13–18.

Felce, D., Grant, G., Todd, S., Ramcharan, P., Beyer, S., McGrath, M. *et al.* (1998) *Towards a Full Life: Researching Policy Innovation for People with Learning Disabilities*. Oxford: Butterworth Heinemann.

Felce, D., Lowe, K. and Jones, E. (2002) Association between the provision characteristics and operation of supported housing services and resident outcomes, *Journal of Applied Research in Intellectual Disabilities*, 15(4), 404–18.

Fulgosi, L. (1990) Camphill communities, in S. Segal (ed.) *The Place of Special Villages and Residential Communities: The Provision of Care for People with Severe, Profound and Multiple Disabilities*. Bicester: AB Academic Publishers.

Gray, G. (1997) *A Long Day at the Seaside*. Windsor: Reedprint.

Grover, R. (1995) *Communities that Care: Intentional Communities of Attachment as a Third Path in Community Care*. Brighton: Pavilion.

Hatton, C. (2001) *Developing Housing and Support Options: Lessons From Research*. Lancaster: Institute for Health Research, Lancaster University (www.lancaster.ac.uk/depts/ihr/ld/download/housing_support.pdf).

Hatton, C. and Emerson, E. (1996) *Residential Provision for People with Learning Disabilities: A Research Review*. Manchester: Hester Adrian Research Centre, University of Manchester (www.lancaster.ac.uk/depts/ihr/ld/download/res_review.pdf).

Houts, P.S. and Scott, R.A. (1975) *Goal Planning with Developmentally Disabled Persons: Procedures for Developing an Individualised Client Plan*. Hershey, P.A.: Milton S. Hershey Medical Center.

King, R.D., Raynes, H.V. and Tizard, J. (1971) *Patterns of Residential Care: Sociological Studies in Institutions for Handicapped Children*. London: Routledge and Kegan Paul.

King's Fund Centre (1980) *An Ordinary Life: Comprehensive Locally-based Residential Services for Mentally Handicapped People*. London: King's Fund Centre.

King's Fund Centre (1984) *An Ordinary Working Life: Vocational Services for People with Mental Handicap*. London: King's Fund Centre.

Kinsella, P. (1993) *Supported Living: A New Paradigm*. Manchester: National Development Team.

Kozma, A., Mansell, J. and Beadle-Brown, J. (2009) Outcomes in different residential settings for people with intellectual disability: a systematic review, *American Journal on Intellectual and Developmental Disabilities*, 114: 193–222.

Lowe, K. and de Paiva, S. (1991) *NIMROD – An Overview*. London: HMSO.

Lyle, J.G. (1960a) The effects of an institutional environment upon the verbal development of imbecile children. II Speech and Language, *Journal Mental Deficiency Research*, 4(1): 1–13.

Lyle, J.G. (1960b) The effects of an institutional environment upon the verbal development of imbecile children. III The Brooklands Residential Family Unit, *Journal of Mental Deficiency Research*, 4(1): 14–23.

Malin, N., Race, D. and Jones, G. (1980) *Services for the Mentally Handicapped in Britain*. London: Croom Helm.

Mansell, J. and Beadle-Brown, J. (2004) Person-centred planning or person-centred action: policy and practice in intellectual disability services, *Journal of Applied Research in Intellectual Disabilities*, 17: 1–9.

Mansell, J., McGill, P. and Emerson, E. (2001) Development and evaluation of innovative residential services for people with severe intellectual disability and serious challenging behaviour, in L.M. Glidden (ed.) *International Review of Research in Mental Retardation*. New York: Academic Press.

Martin, J.P. (1984) *Hospital in Trouble*. Oxford: Blackwell.

O'Brien, J. (1994) Down stairs that are never your own: supporting people with developmental disabilities in their own homes, *Mental Retardation*, 32: 1–6.

Office of the Deputy Prime Minister/Department of Health (2003) *Housing and Support Options for People with Learning Disabilities* (draft released for consultation). London: DoH.

Race, D. (1995) Historical development of service provision, in N. Malin (ed.) *Services for People with Learning Disabilities*. London: Routledge.

Remington, B. (1991) *The Challenge of Severe Mental Handicap: A Behaviour Analytic Approach*. Chichester: Wiley.

Robertson, J., Emerson, E., Pinkney, L., Caesar, E., Felce, D., Meek, A. *et al*. (2004) Quality and costs of community-based residential supports for people with mental retardation and challenging behavior, *American Journal on Mental Retardation*, 109(4): 332–44.

Robertson, J., Emerson, E., Hatton, C., Elliot, J., McIntosh, B., Swift, P. *et al*. (2007) Person-centred planning: factors associated with successful outcomes for people with intellectual disabilities, *Journal of Intellectual Disability Research*, 51(3): 232–43.

Rothman, D.J. (1980) *Conscience and Convenience: The Asylum and its Alternatives in Progressive America*. Boston, MA: Little, Brown.

Rudkin, A. and Rowe, D. (1999) A systematic review of the evidence base for lifestyle planning in adults with learning disabilities: implications for other disabled populations, *Clinical Rehabilitation*, 13: 363–72.

Ryan, J. and Thomas, F. (1987) *The Politics of Mental Handicap*, revised edn. London: Free Association Books.

Scheerenberger, R.C. (1983) *A History of Mental Retardation*. Baltimore, MD: Brookes.

Scull, A. (1984) *Decarceration: Community Treatment and the Deviant – A Radical View*, 2nd edn. Cambridge: Polity Press.

Scull, A. (1993) *The Most Solitary of Afflictions: Madness and Society in Britain, 1700–1900*. New Haven, CT: Yale University Press.

Simmons, H.G. (1982) *From Asylum to Welfare*. Downsview, Ontario: National Institute on Mental Retardation.

Simon, G.B. (1981) *Local Services for Mentally Handicapped People*. Kidderminster: British Institute of Mental Handicap.

Simons, K. (1997) *A Foot in the Door: The Early Years of Supported Living for People with Learning Difficulties in the UK*. Manchester: National Development Team.

Stancliffe, R. and Keane, S. (2000) Outcomes and costs of community living: a matched comparison of group homes and semi-independent living, *Journal of Intellectual and Developmental Disability*, 25(4): 281–305.

Tizard, J. (1954) Institutional defectives, *American Journal on Mental Deficiency*, 59: 158–65.

Tizard, J. (1964) *Community Services for the Mentally Handicapped*. Oxford: Oxford University Press.

Walsh, P., Emerson, E., Lobb., C., Hatton, C., Bradley, V., Schalock, B. *et al*. (2008) *Supported Accommodation Services for People with Intellectual Disabilities: A Review of Models and Instruments Used to Measure Quality of Life*. Dublin: National Disability Authority.

Welsh Office (1983) *All Wales Strategy for the Development of Services to Mentally Handicapped People*. Cardiff: Welsh Office.

Wolfensberger, W. (1972) *The Principle of Normalization in Human Services*. Toronto: National Institute on Mental Retardation.

Wolfensberger, W. (1975) *The Origin and Nature of Our Institutional Models*. Syracuse: Human Policy Press.

Wolfensberger, W. (1981) The extermination of handicapped people in World War II Germany, *Mental Retardation*, 19(1): 1–7.

Wolfensberger, W. (1983) Social role valorization: a proposed new term for the principle of normalization, *Mental Retardation*, 21: 234–9.

Wright, D. and Digby, A. (1996) *From Idiocy to Mental Deficiency: Historical Perspectives on People with Learning Disabilities*. London: Routledge.

Young, L. (2006) Community and cluster centre residential services for adults with intellectual disability: long-term results from an Australian-matched sample, *Journal of Intellectual Disability Research*, 50(6): 419–31.

Maintaining a commitment to quality

Lesley Montisci and Gordon Grant

6

Introduction

Maintaining a commitment to quality in the planning, design, delivery and review of services for people with learning disabilities is an important requirement in ensuring that public money is wisely spent. Equally important is the task of enabling people with learning disabilities to achieve a quality of life (QoL) comparable to that of other citizens. In this chapter the reader is therefore introduced to some of the contemporary thinking about QoL, and how this can be used to inform quality in services. The first part of the chapter reviews QoL concepts and their applications. Drawing from research evidence an attempt is then made (1) to highlight the wide array of factors informing judgements about quality, leading to a consideration of (2) how these can be integrated in order to understand variations in life experience and (3) to remain conscious of possible linkages between service quality and QoL.

Quality of life

'Quality of life' is a term used in everyday talk but its meaning is very much dependent on context. In their review of conceptual and measurement issues about QoL, Schalock and Felce (2004) suggest that it is a multi-dimensional construct, used in different ways throughout the world, for example as:

- *A sensitizing notion* that provides a frame of reference from the individual's perspective, about the person and his or her environment. In this sense, 'quality' makes us think about individual characteristics such as happiness, success, wealth, health and satisfaction, whereas 'of life' suggests a concern with the essential aspects of human existence for the individual.
- *A social construct* that can be used as the basis for evaluating person-referenced outcomes and to enhance a person's perceived QoL. This ties in with ideas about service designs and how these might inform valued outcomes for individuals.
- *A unifying theme* that provides a systematic framework for understanding and applying the concept of QoL. This typically involves knowing about the linkages between the 'microsystem' (the person, family, friends, advocates and wider social network), the 'mesosystem' (neighbourhood, community or organization providing services or support) and the 'macrosystem' (overarching patterns of culture, society and sociopolitical influences).
- *A motivational construct*, meaning that sensitivity to important and desirable outcomes in one's personal life reinforces a heightened awareness of, and commitment to, the means to achieve them.

There is a huge literature on QoL, much of it focusing on conceptualization and measurement, heralding many scales and instruments that claim to assess QoL. Different models of QoL have therefore emerged.

QoL models

There are now many QoL models that have been developed and applied to varying extents to the lives of people with learning disabilities. Three of the more distinctive QoL models are summarized in Table 6.1 so a few words of explanation about them are in order here.

In the Felce and Perry (1996) model, QoL is seen as the product of three interacting elements: personal values, life conditions and personal satisfaction. Briefly stated, QoL is defined as overall well-being comprised of objective and subjective evaluations of the domains of physical, material, social and emotional well-being, together with the extent of personal development and purposeful activity. All these evaluations are then weighted by personal

Felce and Perry (1996): a model for people with and without disabilities	Bach and Rioux (1996): a social well-being framework	Renwick and Brown (1996): centre for health promotion model
QoL constructs: *Physical well-being* *Material well-being* *Social well-being* *Development and activity* *Emotional well-being* **Measurements:** Objective assessment of life conditions, and subjective assessment of personal satisfaction **Mediating influences:** Personal values	**Social well-being constructs:** *Self-determination:* making decisions and choices without coercion; exercising control *Equality:* equal access to the means of self-development, coupled with freedom from political control, social pressure, economic deprivation and insecurity in order to engage in valued pursuits *Democratization:* participation in decision-making that directly affects well-being	**QoL constructs:** *Being:* who the person is as an individual *Belonging:* how environments and others fit with the person *Becoming:* what the person does to achieve hopes, goals and aspirations **Mediating influences:** Opportunities and constraints presented both by chance and by choice

Table 6.1 QoL models compared

values – i.e. by what is important to individuals. Objective evaluation concerns those everyday conditions in which people live their lives, such as health, income, housing quality, friendships, activities and social roles. Subjective evaluation refers to satisfaction with these life conditions. However, the key to these lies in the value or importance the individual attaches to each domain.

In this model, physical well-being is comprised of health, personal safety, fitness and mobility. Material well-being comprises finance, income, transport, security and tenure, as well as other aspects of the living environment. Social well-being includes the quality and breadth of interpersonal relationships, and community involvement. Emotional well-being is characterized by affect, fulfilment, mental state, self-esteem, status and respect, faith and sexuality. Finally, development and activity concerns the acquisition and use of skills in different arenas – at home, work, education and leisure for example.

The social well-being framework described by Bach and Rioux (1996) takes a different direction. At its core are three elements: self-determination, democra-

tization and equality. These elements are founded on the empirical literature on well-being, philosophical literature and human rights declarations and conventions (Roeher Institute 1993).

It is claimed that self-determination can be exercised when people, communities and governments can make known their hopes and aspirations, and make plans and decisions to achieve them. Self-determination is expressed both as freedom from resistance and as freedom to do things that are worth doing. Hence the model emphasizes the interdependent relations between people, communities and governments in nurturing the resources and conditions for aspirations to be realized. Put another way, it highlights the help and support people require for exercising self-determination, rather than assuming that self-determination is an inherent or voluntary capacity of individuals. The second element in the model, democratization, is closely linked to the idea of self-determination. The reason for this is that it is concerned with enabling the participation of individuals and diverse groups in decisions that directly affect their own lives and well-being. Social well-being is more likely, it is claimed, where democratization becomes an integrating force. The third element, equality, is defined as the absence of barriers to mutual respect and recognition between people. It implies freedom from political control, social pressure, economic deprivation and insecurity (Lukes 1980).

The model proposed by Renwick and Brown (1996) is based on the humanist–existential tradition that acknowledges a person's needs to belong, in both physical and social terms, and to develop and pursue personal goals, making decisions and choices along the way. Renwick and Brown stress the importance of how individuals view their own QoL and identify three core components: being, belonging and becoming. Being refers to an individual's physical, psychological and spiritual identities. Belonging is about the links individuals have with their physical, social and communal environments, and whether they feel 'at home' in these environments. Finally, becoming relates to personal aspirations in terms of purposeful activity, leisure and personal growth. Importance and enjoyment are considered to be factors determining QoL, moderated by how much control individuals can exert over the perceived opportunities they have to exploit change to enhance each area of life.

These models continue to be tested and to evolve. Though each has rather different philosophical roots there are nevertheless some unifying themes. Brown and Brown (2003: 30–1) suggest that five ideas about QoL need to be kept constantly in mind:

1 QoL addresses similar aspects, attributes and processes of life for all of us, disabled and non-disabled. It concerns things that are important to all, such as nutrition, health, social connections, housing and leisure, irrespective of country or region, or of historical period.
2 QoL is personal. In this view, QoL is largely dependent therefore on the unique interactions between a person, services and their environment – i.e the microsystem, mesosystem and macrosystem identified by Schalock and Felce (2004). Understanding these interactions therefore becomes a key in designing interventions and support to help people improve QoL. Typically, this is best understood from the individual's own perspective.

3 We can judge specific aspects of our own lives even if these views diverge from those of practitioners.
4 All parts of our lives are interconnected. This can make QoL quite complicated, but then it can help practitioners and others to look at individuals more holistically and judge how well-intentioned interventions might improve QoL in one domain but perhaps undermine it in another.
5 QoL is ever-changing. As has been stressed elsewhere, people's lives are rarely if ever static given the demands, unplanned events and changing circumstances that occur over the life cycle. Accordingly, QoL may change from day to day and year to year, and things that contribute to QoL at one life stage may be quite different to those that contribute to it later on.

We might also add that:

6 QoL is one way of conceptualizing what might constitute valued outcomes for individuals. Hence it may be feasible to incorporate elements of QoL into the evaluation of person-centred or family-centred interventions (Kober and Eggleton 2009), concentrating attention on the things individuals value in life. Used wisely, it can therefore act as a counterpoint to dominant professional, academic and political agendas.
7 QoL literature sometimes appears to imply that the person's life is purely a product of services. Evaluation should therefore start with biographical, social and environmental factors prior to evaluating the contribution of services in shaping the quality of everyday life. More is said of this later.
8 Robust measures of QoL need to be applicable across people with all conditions, including those with limited articulacy. Plimley (2007), for example, has shown how, for people with autistic spectrum disorders (ASD), established QoL measures can be adapted to take account of features of the Triad of Impairments (social interaction, communication and flexibility of thought) that can shape the behaviours and responses of individuals with ASD.

Although QoL measures have typically been applied to individuals, they have also been developed

Case study: *Ernie*

Ernie is 54 years old. He lives by himself in a bungalow that he used to share with his mother until she died five years ago. He is supported by a home help, Sue, four to five mornings a week though he rarely sees her as he is typically at work. Ernie has a family aide, Jemma, who takes him out for three to four hours at weekends, though he says that they often go to places that Jemma decides, including her own home where he sometimes has a meal with Jemma and her husband. Ernie has eyesight problems with cataracts and is awaiting surgery. He has a heart condition and is checked every six months by his GP. Ernie attends the local social activity centre but he also has some work experience where he assists with the running of a community centre. When interviewed about his everyday life, Ernie revealed that his support network and the wider environment influenced the quality of his everyday experiences: his support worker took him shopping but insisted on making decisions for him; he spent a lot of time watching TV but because of news stories became afraid of venturing out into the community; and he confessed to feeling lonely after the death of his mother.

Exercise 6.1

From these brief extracts about Ernie taken from a longer interview:

List which 'objective' features of Ernie's environment you consider to affect the quality of his everyday experiences.

Which 'objective' features would you identify with the microsystem, mesosystem and macrosystem in turn?

Taking any one of the three QoL models shown in Table 6.1, write down what you think are the best 'indicators' that capture Ernie's main sentiments in the above interview extracts. What do the indicators you have identified tell you about Ernie's social environment?

In collaboration with Ernie, how might you address the environmental factors that influence his QoL?

---

in work with families (Park *et al.* 2003; Wang *et al.* 2006; Schippers and Van Boheemen 2009 for example), especially in early intervention studies of families with young children. However, there continues to be a methodological challenge about how best to make sense of family perceptions based on data from multiple family members where the unit of analysis is the whole family.

QoL: critiques and challenges

QoL has a strong allure, yet there remains a deal of healthy scepticism about it. Several points are worth bearing in mind in this respect:

- Most of the research on QoL among people with learning disabilities has been conducted with people who have speech. The validity of underlying QoL constructs in people without speech is not yet clear.

- There is a high dependency on using proxies (third parties like advocates, allies or support workers) to speak for people who cannot speak for themselves. According to Schalock and Felce (2004), little is known about concordance between self-reports and proxy accounts and discrepancies are most likely in questions requiring people to make subjective appraisals.

- Most of the QoL models in use with people with learning disabilities, including the three highlighted in this chapter, were developed before substantive advances in oral history, life history and narrative research within this field, and before the emergence of the user movement with its increasingly powerful articulations. The models have primarily been academic-led instead of being designed and controlled by people with learning disabilities themselves (see Chapter 35).

- Improving the quality of services may not

necessarily lead directly to improvements in QoL. This is because services reflect shifting policy priorities that may not be fixed around QoL dimensions; most people spend only part of their lives using services so it is easy to exaggerate the influence of services on QoL; and evidence suggests that satisfaction, as one way of measuring subjective well-being, is unresponsive to important changes in people's lives. This has left some commentators to question the relevance of QoL (Hatton 1998; Hensel 2001). In addition, the relationships between judgements of importance and people's aspirations, preferences and opportunities for choice need closer attention, and may give a better sense of what is more important than QoL constructs (Hensel *et al.* 2002). But then again, to be valid, QoL constructs need to be rooted in people's core values about what matters to them.

- In regard to Family Quality of Life (FQoL) there appear to be unresolved tensions between looking upon the family as the unit of analysis in contrast to individual differences in the views held by each family member (Wang *et al.* 2006), though recent research (Schippers and Van Boheemen 2009) does argue that an emphasis on FQoL demonstrates the key role of partnerships and agreements between people with learning disabilities, their families and service providers.

The next section of the chapter takes a closer look at connecting service quality with QoL.

Is there a link between quality of support and quality of life?

While knowledge of service quality has developed considerably in recent years, there is much more to do to link that experience to how people with learning disabilities and their families evaluate the quality of their own lives.

In efforts to condense a burgeoning but still rather unco-ordinated body of knowledge, the first and second parts of this section will relate common findings of two programmes of applied research that have grappled with evaluations of national strategies for people with learning disabilities. Both provide some insights into issues relating to service quality and quality of life. The first concerns an attempt to synthesize the findings of two research teams commissioned to evaluate the innovative All Wales Strategy, AWS (Welsh Office 1983) over a period of ten years (Felce *et al.* 1998). The AWS was widely acclaimed for its commitment to principles of rights, inclusion, consultation and independence and was, in many ways, an early marker for what *Valuing People* (Department of Health 2001) set out to accomplish. The second concerns the outcomes of the Department of Health Learning Disability Research Initiative (Grant and Ramcharan 2007), established to evaluate the implementation and early experiences of *Valuing People*.

Quality of the service experience

At the level of interactions between service users, families and professionals, or what might be termed the *service microsystem*, some recurrent findings confirmed what users and families rated most highly. First, having access to an individual plan (IP) or person-centred plan (PCP) was crucial to the quality of the service experience, but so too was ensuring that it was implemented, and then followed up for review. This did not happen enough. Having access to a known and trusted named worker was integral to success in this particular respect. This worked even better when professionals were perceived as being able to empathize with service users and families and to be proactive rather than crisis-driven.

Service users and families were acutely aware of whether or not they were being listened to and they were quick to highlight shortcomings in the communication competence of professionals they met. Finally, feeling that control could be exercised over what was happening over personal planning arrangements was highly important to service users and families. Identifiable features of the service system, the mesosystem at the local level, facilitated this level of personalization that service users and families valued so much.

It now seems well accepted that expectations for meeting the core ambitions of *Valuing People Now* cannot be singularly dependent on *service microsystem* factors. Person-centred planning or Direct Payments, alone, simply do not work. A primary requirement of the *service mesosystem* is therefore comprehensive local services for, without them, huge constraints are placed on choice-making and the capacity to match resources to individual needs and aspirations. For example, Mansell (2007) shows that, for people with challenging behaviour or mental health needs, higher dependency, expensive and potentially dysfunctional out-of-area placements can ensue. But local services also needed to be well marshalled and co-ordinated, placing a high value on interdisciplinary teamwork and interagency work.

Person-centred planning and care management functions and responsibilities need to be closely aligned to provide people with seamless support, as previously suggested by other commentators (Cambridge and Carnaby 2005), rather than to be running as disconnected parallel systems. Investment in leadership and supervision, with the vision and managerial competence to align local strategies with population needs and resources and to stimulate innovation in front-line practice, was found to be vital. A commitment to continuing professional development was crucial to the maintenance of high professional standards, though there is now evidence that service users, families and professionals may not necessarily share the same views about what constitute 'core skills' required of staff (Hatton et al. 2009).

Finally, monitoring, inspection and regulatory systems have for too long been measuring the wrong things – service processes and service inputs mostly – rather than service outputs and QoL outcomes for service users and families, undermining the capacity for local services to consolidate learning about what works best for whom and in what circumstances. It is not clear whether Valuing People Now has gone far enough in emphasizing this last point or in making provision for it.

Civil society

Important though services are, service users and families only spend part of their lives using them. The quality of people's lives to a large extent depends, therefore, on the capacity of services to harness the resources, interests and expertise of civil society, and to work in close partnership with the many institutions involved.

At the level of community, it was found that the lives of many people with learning disabilities were blighted by unwelcoming neighbourhood attitudes and outright rejection (from social clubs for example) or, worse, forms of abuse and crime. Two factors emerge from this. First, trust was the key component in relationships with local people and civic agencies, making the difference as to how people with learning disabilities felt about being part of wider social networks and local communities. But trust is not an objective condition; it was something to be worked upon, and could take much time to develop, involving a lot of trial and error, and careful judgement about the balance between independence and personal safety. Too often fears and anxieties overcame people, the inevitable result being decisions to limit associations and community involvement. Second, people with learning disabilities needed to have opportunities to make contributions to the community, and to receive contributions from the community – in both paid and non-paid roles – like other citizens. This is part and parcel of being affirmed as a citizen. Too often this did not happen.

What emerges from this is the importance of ties and connections people have with their local communities and communities of interest to the quality of their everyday lives. Few individuals were able to manufacture those ties and connections themselves, and were dependent on others to broker them (see Chapter 30). This would seem to lend support to the notion central to the Renwick and Brown (1996) QoL model that fulfilment of QoL is mediated by opportunities and constraints presented both by chance and by choice. Individual agency alone was insufficient. The fostering and maintenance of meaningful relationships appears to lie at the very core of understanding what QoL or life satisfaction means for people with learning disabilities (Miller and Chan 2008).

Individuals for the most part were able to rely on the unconditional support, love and companionship of their own families, though families were too often left with inadequate information, support and respite from services. When acknowledged and reinforced by services, the expertise and strengths of families was a tremendously powerful resource that could make a huge impact on the lives of people with learning disabilities (see Chapter 13). It was also a context in which mutual exchange, confidences and intimate relations could be maintained, providing a sense of security and integrity.

Individuals' social position

As many other chapters in this book demonstrate, what individuals experience in their lives and how they evaluate that experience is affected by individual factors also. We are all born with genetic dispositions and have personal characteristics that by and large cannot be changed. Thus far, little attention has been focused on how these individual-level factors might shape service experiences and, at a higher level, quality of life.

Findings from the first national sample survey of 2898 adults with learning disabilities in England in 2003/04 (Emerson *et al.* 2005) are helpful here. A few headline findings provide some indications of dimensions of QoL relevant to all three of the models outlined earlier (Table 6.1):

Inclusion in civil society: 92 per cent never married, 17 per cent had a paid job, 31 per cent voted in the 2001 general election;
Personal relationships: 31 per cent had no contact with friends, 25 per cent had friends without learning disabilities, only 7 per cent had children (in several cases looked after by someone else);
Personal safety: 43 per cent had been bullied at school, 32 per cent did not feel safe in their own homes, their local area or when using public transport;
Control: 64 per cent had no control about who they lived with or where they lived, 39 per cent did not have enough privacy, 54 per cent said someone else decided how much money they could spend each week.

Disadvantages in regard to the above criteria were worse for people who were poor or who lived in poor areas, people from black and minority ethnic (BME) communities, people with higher support needs and people with poor health. Services need to be reminded that, in relation to achieving citizenship and full inclusion in society, people with learning disabilities start from a very low base. We also know from the Learning Disability Research Initiative (LDRI) programme (Grant and Ramcharan 2007) that women's health issues were dealt with very poorly by GPs, some being put at risk, so gender is self-evidently important. Plenty of research also demonstrates problems with clinical diagnosis and diagnostic overshadowing where people have multiple dis-

abilities and conditions (see Chapter 3). As a result some individuals are not receiving the best available care and support because they have as yet undiagnosed conditions, so their health status is put at risk. People with profound and complex disabilities also continue to receive very poor care, as *Valuing People Now* attests. Only a minority of people with learning disabilities are economically active, and a disproportionate number live in poor areas, so relative poverty is an issue for many. Very few are married/living with a partner and so do not enjoy a level of enduring intimacy typical of other adults. It is also recognized that to date little has been done to map service experience or quality of life by life stage, despite the availability of theoretical frameworks that may help us to understand successful ageing (see Chapter 34).

These individual-level factors are important markers of difference. There are undoubtedly others of relevance to quality issues, but they are a reminder about *respect for* difference and about a service system and society that *respects all*.

Social structure

The social model of disability forces us to ask critical questions about the possible influences of macro-level factors on people's lived experiences. Legal instruments (see Chapter 4) such as the Human Rights Act 1998 and Disability Discrimination Act 2005 give individuals certain basic rights and freedoms as well as responsibilities although at least to date these have not been widely enforced. The labour market, especially during a period of world recession (at the time of writing), is highly competitive and weighted against people who have suffered long exclusion from the labour force, contributing to their continued marginalization and relative poverty compared to other citizens. The built environment can present physical access obstacles and leave people feeling unsafe, though this need not be so. Neighbourhoods too can exclude people, not only for the reasons mentioned earlier, but also because of where they are, what they are and whether there are adequate public transport links that people can use safely. How people fare in adolescence and adulthood can, quite plainly, be dependent on what they have gained from the education system at an earlier stage in their lives.

These might seem like rather indistinct factors that have little to do with the quality of personal experience in everyday life but such macro-level factors have all too enduring influences.

Integration

In Table 6.2 an attempt has been made to bring together all the factors discussed above within a common framework. It suggests that the social structure is likely to have an overarching, as well as enduring influence on an individual's social position. And this effect is more likely to be negative where service experiences as structural factors are beyond the individual's control. The framework suggests what individual factors need to be accounted for in exploring service quality and QoL in order to account

for individual differences. Importantly, it is suggested that the combinations of, and interactions between, civil society (family and community) variables and services (microsystem and mesosystem) variables are therefore crucial to a contemporary understanding of QoL and FQoL appropriate for people with learning disabilities and their families. This framework is not definitive, however. It should be looked upon as an heuristic, an aid to reflection and learning. Growing evidence will allow for the expansion of factors that inform what is conducive to service quality and also QoL and FQoL. Hopefully, the framework will attest to the fact that QoL and FQoL are far from being the product of services alone, however good these may be. However, professional workers have responsibilities to ensure that high standards are being met.

Social structure	Social position	Mediating factors	Outcomes

legal entitlements
labour market
neighbourhood type
built environment
transport
education system
	gender
	civil status
	ethnicity
	economic activity
	  status
	relative poverty
	life stage
	health status
	disability:
	  severity
	  syndrome
		Community
		  trust
		  safe public spaces
		  contributions to
		  contributions from
		
		Family
		  supportive care network
		  confidant(e)
		  reciprocities and exchanges
		
		Services – micro
		  IP or PCP availability
		  named worker
		  user/family control
		  communicative competence
		  empathic relationship
		
		Services – meso
		  local, comprehensive
		  integrated
		  professional standards
		  'system architecture'
		  outcome-based IT systems
			QoL or FQoL
			domains

Table 6.2 Quality of life and its antecedents

How can professionals add value to service quality and quality of life?

At this point it is important to say something about the stake of front-line health and social care staff in driving up quality standards.

The reforming health agenda of New Labour (Department of Health 1997), of which *Valuing People* was a part, emphasized three key aspirations: improve the overall standards of clinical practice; reduce unacceptable variations in clinical practice; ensure best use of resources – so that care is appropriate, effective, efficient and economic.

In its determination to set and monitor standards the government proposed a new framework (see Figure 6.1). Central to the framework was clinical governance, essentially an umbrella term for structures such as clinical audit, clinical effectiveness, evidence-based practice, risk assessment and performance management. While clinical governance is still relatively new, these individual structures have been around in the National Health Service for a number of years.

What the framework seeks to do is integrate the different elements and drive up standards. This aspiration is applicable to social care as well as health staff, with the government seeking to create a situation where standards rather than national targets are the driving force for continuous quality improvements (Department of Health 2004). While the onus is on all staff to be accountable for their practice, the government has made its commitment to improve standards at local and national level through the National Institute for Clinical Excellence (now National Institute for Health and Clinical Excellence), National Service Frameworks, the Commission for Health Improvement (subsequently Healthcare Commission), the Commission for Social Care Inspection, the Care Quality Commission (replacing the Healthcare Commission, Commission for Social Care Inspection and Mental Health Commission from 2009), the Equality and Human Rights Commission and World Class Commissioning (see website references and notes at the end of the chapter).

This quality assurance (QA) infrastructure is designed to ensure that care and support are appropriate,

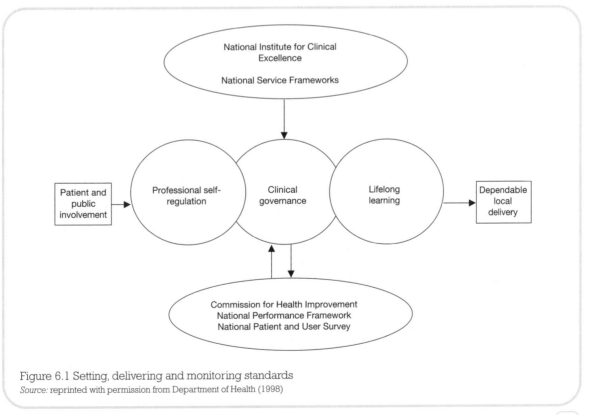

Figure 6.1 Setting, delivering and monitoring standards
Source: reprinted with permission from Department of Health (1998)

timely, of the highest quality and based on the best available evidence at the time. Professional activity is now more open to public scrutiny than it has ever been, with the introduction of open forums and published service performance indicators following inspections and Annual Quality Assurance Assessments.

This is a challenging agenda for professionals. While the emphasis in the health service has been on improving quality and maintaining safe systems of care (Walshe 2001), it has been argued that fear of litigation and increasing costs of compensation can undermine this aspiration. Symon (2003) suggests that this may have a critical effect on how health care practitioners act or react in respect of client care because they may be unduly cautious so as to prevent anything untoward from happening. Risk management then presents a challenge in terms of working with people with learning disabilities because in trying to promote independence and choice there is always an element of risk. The spate of serious case reviews, like that following the torture and murder of Stephen Hoskin (Flynn 2007), remind us that personal safety issues are far from being met and that there is a premium on close, transparent interagency working across health, social care and the criminal justice services.

A complicating concern for professionals concerned about driving up standards is the application of fair access to care services criteria (Department of Health 2003). There are four criteria within the framework and people are judged to have either 'critical', 'substantive', 'moderate' or 'low' needs. Local authorities have been expected to prioritize individuals whose level of risk is deemed to be critical and although the framework is intended to widen the entry gate to care services, this is not in practice the case. Local authorities that feel they only have sufficient resources to meet the needs of people falling into high-risk categories can set their criteria to critical and substantive bands only. Tanner (2003) argues that although the language of assessment is 'need', it is 'risk' that takes precedence when it comes to service provision. This has major implications for people with mild learning disabilities who often have difficulty accessing appropriate services, as *Valuing People Now* attests.

In relation to achieving citizenship and full inclusion in society, people with learning disabilities start from a very low base (Emerson *et al.* 2005). This raises two key considerations about equality: first, service standards for individuals should be measured against norms and standards enjoyed by the rest of the general population (external criterion) in the interests of fairness and equality; second, the same standards need to apply to all people with learning disabilities regardless of their gender, ethnicity or socio-economic position (internal criterion).

Finally, there are concerns that national minimum standards in some settings do not match important user outcomes (Beadle-Brown *et al.* 2008), suggesting that the inspection industry may sometimes be measuring largely irrelevant things.

Implications for service providers

Even from this all too brief description of regulatory and QA mechanisms it is easy to lose sight of what is implied by quality standards criteria. From the foregoing discussion the following appear to be relevant:

- *Access*: are services available to people with respect to information (are services known), location (are they conveniently placed), means of access (physical barriers like steps) and eligibility criteria (some services still exclude people because of the way their needs are defined)?
- *Acceptability*: do services reflect the cultural and moral norms of a diverse multi-ethnic society? Do they meet the same standards expected by service users and families?
- *Reliability*: are services available at the right time? Do they fit personal and family schedules? Are services dependable?
- *Co-ordination*: are health and social care services sufficiently well integrated so as to meet the unique needs of individuals and families? Is there a single point of access to services? Are care management and person-centred planning co-ordinated by a named person?
- *Efficiency*: can service users be assured of best value? Is service duplication and waste avoided or minimized?
- *Effectiveness*: is support provided on the basis of best evidence, and in ways that maximize a person's QoL or other valued personal outcomes?

- *Equality*: are all citizens with learning disabilities experiencing the same care and support standards or is this limited to certain groups? Do all people with learning disabilities enjoy the same citizenship rights as everybody else, and are they able to express them?
- *Rights and redress*: do services respect people's individual civil rights? Do people know what recourse they have to complain and seek redress should they wish to?
- *Personal safety and protection*: is each person's health, well-being and safety assured under all conditions?

Exercise 6.2

Think of a local service well known to you, then ask yourself how well it would evaluate in terms of the criteria suggested above.

If services were improved in regard to some or all of the above criteria:

> in what ways might the QoL of service users change?
> why might QoL not change?

Put together, these benchmarks of quality in services represent a challenging agenda. It has already been demonstrated that services often fail at the first hurdle of *access*, and it will be seen later (Chapter 26) that users' cultural norms are not always accommodated, meaning that the *acceptability* of services can be left wanting. Hospital waiting times are apparently coming down but delays and interruptions still perpetuate difficulties with service *reliability*. *Co-ordination*, as illustrated earlier, remains an ever-present challenge for all health and social care services, yet is vital in helping people to secure seamless support. *Efficiency* improvements in an organization as large and complex as the NHS can always be made.

In learning disability services values and visions often precede good evidence about what works, so *effectiveness* too is an issue to be constantly checked since there is still rather sparse evidence about supports and interventions that work well for people with learning disabilities. Service achievements need to be measured against all people with learning disabilities to demonstrate that gains for some are not at a cost to, or to the neglect of, others. Better still, the achievement of civil rights and inclusion needs to be measured against what is typical for the rest of the general population. *Equality* is key. Then finally, even when systems of *redress* are in place, people may still regard some of their rights as strictly 'non-negotiable' – there is no point trying to satisfy a vegetarian with even a Harry Ramsden serving of fish and chips! One of the 'non-negotiables' must be *personal safety*, and hopefully the eradication of abuse, neglect and bullying in all their forms.

Even were all of these criteria to be met there remain prospects of discontinuities between service quality and QoL. The reason for this is that these criteria represent service outcomes reflecting service priorities *of the day*. Moreover, they are typically pursued singly rather than as a package. It takes a leap of faith to assume that QoL improvements will come about as a result of, say, improving service access or boosting service reliability. Promoting service improvements according to these criteria is one thing; ensuring that they connect to valued QoL outcomes in service users and families is another.

A cautious conclusion

As will now be evident, there is an almost bewildering array of government policies emphasizing the quality agenda through a variety of QA mechanisms, regulatory and inspection systems. Readers may be forgiven for feeling a trifle confused about what this adds up to. Those taking a cynical view like Watson (2002) would suggest that this 'quality speak' merely reinforces the power and position of managers rather than fundamentally challenging existing power structures within services that so easily disable service users. It has been suggested that benchmarking and performance measurement are less straightforward than claimed, and that front-line workers obligated into taking part in these activities frequently find therapeutic work with service users being displaced or passed on to those with lesser qualifications.

Further, it is sometimes claimed that the industry of quality measurement tends to focus on those aspects of services that are more tangible – these being rather more concerned with efficiency and economy rather than effectiveness or personal safety. Qureshi (1999: 264), describing a project about collecting outcome information as a part of routine practice in social care, sums up the position well:

> If the collection of outcome information is to form part of routine practice it must fit with what is already done, or staff must be convinced of its ultimate benefits to them or to service users, otherwise the information will either not be collected, or it will be subject to 'gaming' as people try to fit with the letter of requirements instead of the spirit.

In their exploration of performance measurement in sheltered housing, Foord *et al.* (2004) made similar observations, suggesting that the 'expert' knowledge required by regulatory bodies remains privileged over service user knowledge. They found, like other observers, that the voice of users should be central to measuring satisfaction or outcomes, but that in practice the methods and systems in use failed to capture issues of importance to users. For Watson (2002: 885), the solution is seen to lie in reasserting the agenda of empowerment which 'should open up all the decision-making processes to provider and user involvement, including those at a day-to-day level, which impact directly on individual lives and make up the fine texture of the organization'.

Quality, in this sense, is therefore inextricably tied up with the democratization of services at a national and local level – that is, with opening up services to scrutiny in order to ensure that they are not only moulded but driven by the interests and aspirations of service users, a core ambition for *Valuing People Now* (Department of Health 2009). Professionals are in a unique position to influence what happens in this regard, and to ensure that high-quality services and supports remain dedicated to people with learning disabilities and their families, as Kober and Eggleton (2009) have tried to demonstrate.

Finally, achieving sustained change of this kind is likely to test the capacity for 'whole-system leadership' (Towell 2009), something requiring the active partnership of three main sets of stakeholders – civil society, government and services. According to Towell the UN Convention on the Rights of Persons with Disabilities (United Nations 2008), ratified by the UK recently, will have the force of law. If adopted it may yet be the best instrument for enabling people with learning disabilities to attain full citizenship and to be liberated to live life to the full.

Resources

www.cqc.org.uk. The Care Quality Commission is the independent regulator of health and social care in England. Its aim is to make sure better care is provided for everyone, whether that is in hospital, in care homes, in people's own homes, or elsewhere. The CQC regulates health and adult social care services, whether provided by the NHS, local authorities, private companies or voluntary organizations. The organization also protects the rights of people detained under the Mental Health Act.

www.nice.org.uk. The National Institute of Health and Clinical Excellence (NICE) is an independent organization responsible for providing national guidance on promoting good health and preventing and treating ill health. NICE produces guidance in three areas of health:

- public health – guidance on the promotion of good health and the prevention of ill health for those working in the NHS, local authorities and the wider public and voluntary sector;
- health technologies – guidance on the use of new and existing medicines, treatments and procedures within the NHS;
- clinical practice – guidance on the appropriate treatment and care of people with specific diseases and conditions within the NHS.

www.equalityhumanrights.com. The Equality and Human Rights Commission aims to promote equality and human rights and to create a fairer society. It does so by publishing advice and guidance, and by working to implement an effective legislative framework, and raising awareness of rights. Its guidance concerns core health and social care issues relating to access, equality, inclusion, protection and redress.

References

Bach, M. and Rioux, M.H. (1996) Social well-being: a framework for quality of life research, in R. Renwick, I. Brown and M. Nagler (eds) *Quality of Life in Health Promotion and Rehabilitation*. Thousand Oaks, CA: Sage.

Beadle-Brown, J., Hutchison, A. and Mansell, J. (2008) Care standards in homes for people with learning disabilities, *Journal of Applied Research in Intellectual Disabilities*, 21: 210–18.

Brown, I. and Brown, R.I. (2003) *Quality of Life and Disability: An Approach for Community Practitioners*. London: Jessica Kingsley.

Cambridge, P. and Carnaby, S. (2005) Introduction and Overview, in P. Cambridge (ed.) *PCP and Care Management with People with Learning Difficulties*. London: Jessica Kingsley.

Department of Health (1997) *The New NHS: Modern, Dependable*. London: The Stationery Office.

Department of Health (1998) *A First Class Service: Quality in the New NHS*. Leeds: DoH.

Department of Health (2001) *Valuing People: A New Strategy for Learning Disability for the 21st Century*. London: The Stationery Office.

Department of Health (2003) *Fair Access to Care Services. Guidance on Eligibility Criteria for Adult Social Care*. London: The Stationery Office.

Department of Health (2004) *National Standards, Local Action: Health and Social Care Standards and Planning Framework 2005/06–2007/08*. London: The Stationery Office.

Department of Health (2009) *Valuing People Now: A New Three Year Strategy for People with Learning Disabilities*. London: HM Government.

Emerson, E., Malam, S., Davies, I. and Spencer, K. (2005) *Adults with Learning Difficulties in England 2003/4*. Leeds: Health and Social Care Information Centre.

Felce, D. and Perry, J. (1996) Exploring current conceptions of quality of life: a model for people with and without disabilities, in R. Renwick, I. Brown and M. Nagler (eds) *Quality of Life in Health Promotion and Rehabilitation*. Thousand Oaks, CA: Sage.

Felce, D., Grant, G., Todd, S., Ramcharan, P., Beyer, S., McGrath, M. *et al.* (1998) *Towards a Full Life: Researching Policy Innovation for People with Learning Disabilities*. Oxford: Butterworth Heinemann.

Flynn, M. (2007) *The Murder of Stephen Hoskin – A Serious Case Review*. Cornwall Adult Protection Committee.

Foord, M., Savory, J. and Sodhi, D. (2004) Not everything that can be counted counts and not everything that counts can be counted – towards a critical exploration of modes of satisfaction measurement in sheltered housing, *Health and Social Care in the Community*, 12(2): 126–33.

Grant, G. and Ramcharan, P. (2007) *Valuing People and Research: The Learning Disability Research Initiative. Overview Report*. London: Department of Health.

Hatton, C. (1998) Whose quality of life is it anyway? Some problems with the emerging quality of life consensus, *Mental Retardation*, 36: 104–15.

Hatton, C., Wigham, S. and Craig, J. (2009) Developing measures of job performance for support staff in housing services for people with learning disabilities, *Journal of Applied Research in Intellectual Disabilities*, 22(1): 54–64.

Hensel, E. (2001) Is satisfaction a valid concept in the assessment of quality of life of people with intellectual disabilities? A review of the literature, *Journal of Applied Research in Intellectual Disabilities*, 14: 311–26.

Hensel, E., Rose, J., Stenfert Kroese, B. and Banks-Smith, J. (2002) Subjective judgements of quality of life: a comparison study between people with learning disability and those without disability, *Journal of Intellectual Disability Research*, 46(2): 95–107.

Kober, R. and Eggleton, I.R.C. (2009) Using Quality of Life to evaluate outcomes and measure effectiveness, *Journal of Policy and Practice in Intellectual Disabilities*, 6(1): 40–51.

Lukes, S. (1980) Socialism and equality, in J. Sterba (ed.) *Justice: Alternative Political Perspectives*. Belmont, CA: Wadsworth.

Mansell, J. (2007) *Services for People with Learning Disabilities and Challenging Behaviour or Mental Health Needs*. London: HMSO.

Miller, S.M. and Chan, F. (2008) Predictors of life satisfaction in individuals with intellectual disabilities, *Journal of Intellectual Disability Research*, 52(12): 1039–47.

Park, J., Hoffman, L., Marquis, J., Turnbull, A.P., Poston, D., Mannan, H. *et al.* (2003) Toward assessing family outcomes of service delivery: validation of a family quality of life survey, *Journal of Intellectual Disability Research*, 47(4/5): 367–84.

Plimley, L. (2007) A review of quality of life issues and people with autism spectrum disorders, *British Journal of Learning Disabilities*, 35(4): 205–13.

Qureshi, H. (1999) Outcomes of social care for adults: attitudes towards collecting outcome information in practice, *Health and Social Care in the Community*, 7(4): 257–65.

Renwick, R. and Brown, I. (1996) The Centre for Health Promotion's conceptual approach to quality of life: being, belonging and becoming, in R. Renwick, I. Brown and M. Nagler (eds) *Quality of Life in Health Promotion and Rehabilitation*. Thousand Oaks, CA: Sage.

Roeher Institute (1993) *Social Well-Being: A Paradigm for Reform*. North York, Ontario: Roeher Institute.

Schalock, R. and Felce, D. (2004) Quality of life and subjective well-being: conceptual and measurement issues, in E. Emerson, C. Hatton, T. Thompson and T. Parmenter (eds) *The International Handbook of Applied Research in Intellectual Disabilities*. Chichester: Wiley.

Schippers, A. and Van Boheemen, M. (2009) Family Quality of Life empowered by family-oriented support, *Journal of Policy and Practice in Intellectual Disabilities*, 6(1): 19–24.

Symon, A.G. (2003) Reactions to perceived risk defensiveness in clinical practice, *Clinical Risk*, 9: 182–5.

Tanner, D. (2003) Older people and access to care, *British Journal of Social Work*, 33(4): 449–515.

Towell, D. (2009) Achieving equal citizenship: meeting the challenges of the UN Convention on the Rights of Persons with Disabilities, *Tizard Learning Disability Review*, 14(2): 4–9.

United Nations (2008) Convention on the Rights of Persons with Disabilities. (See www.un.org/disability.)

Walshe, K. (2001) The development of clinical risk management, in C. Vincent (ed.) *Clinical Risk Management: Enhancing Patient Safety*. London: BMJ Books.

Wang, M., Summers, J.A., Little, T., Turnbull, A., Poston, D. and Mannan, H. (2006) Perspectives of fathers and mothers of children in early intervention programmes in assessing family quality of life, *Journal of Intellectual Disability Research*, 50(12): 977–88.

Watson, D. (2002) A critical perspective on quality within the personal social services: prospects and concerns, *British Journal of Social Work*, 32: 877–91.

Welsh Office (1983) *All Wales Strategy for the Development of Services to Mentally Handicapped People*. Cardiff: Welsh Office.

7

Advocacy, campaigning and people with learning difficulties

Dan Goodley and Paul Ramcharan

Introduction

After a substantial history of silence people labelled as having learning difficulties have in the last 30 years made substantial moves to have their voices heard, to reclaim their lives and to take charge of their own destiny and identity. Public records of their work (see Ramcharan and Grant 2001), campaigns for their rights, largely through the self-advocacy movement and more personalized forms of advocacy and through everyday resistance and protest, have emerged that challenge their exclusion.

In this chapter we begin by outlining various types of advocacy and then ask questions about the place of professionals under the 'advocacy umbrella'. Having established some of the limitations for professional service workers within the wider advocacy movement, we focus on the history, emergence and practicalities of self-advocacy before examining a growing arm of campaigning by people labelled with learning difficulties.

Forms of advocacy

Perhaps one of the first ideas that emerges when we are presented with the words 'advocacy' and 'campaigning' is the notion of making our own views and ambitions heard through a variety of individual and collective means. We are all aware when we are not being listened to, sometimes at home, with partners, family and friends or at work with colleagues. It is, to say the least, a particularly frustrating experience, making us feel worthless and devalued. For many people with learning difficulties this is a common, daily experience.

People with mental health problems, individuals with physical and sensory impairments, those labelled with 'learning difficulties' and older adults are among the social groups that have historically been mar-ginalized. Their experiences and ambitions have been ignored or simply not acknowledged. Often there is a pervasive idea, a common-sensical notion, that individuals within such groups have little of importance to say. They are ignored because they are considered to be somehow 'lacking' the skills, abilities or self-awareness to say anything of worth. Furthermore, they are often viewed as being 'at risk' (to themselves and others). Here professionals are positioned in ways that permit them to talk on behalf of these labelled groups: to speak for those who cannot or are taken not to be able to do so either 'rationally' or 'responsibly'.

> ### Exercise 7.1
>
> Think about a time when you felt your voice was not being heard, for example in your family or at work. What did you do about the situation?
>
> Now think of a person with a learning difficulty whose voice, views or feelings were being ignored. How could this person make his/her voice heard?

You may find similarities between the two situations in Exercise 7.1. For example, it is difficult to speak up in situations where there is a power difference between yourself and others. So, while it may be difficult to question your charge nurse or manager it might similarly be as difficult for people with learning difficulties to challenge service workers or parents. In certain circumstances a person may not have a legitimate voice. They may, for example, be an asylum-seeker who does not speak the dominant language or a person in a court of law who cannot speak for himself or herself because of the specialist language involved or, indeed, a person who communicates in ways that others find difficult to understand (see Chapter 9). We all need someone to speak on our behalf at some times in our life. But for people whose predominant experience is of having their voice appropriated by others this has been problematic. The central idea of advocacy is that the person speaks for themselves or that an advocate speaks for that person as if that person's voice was his or her own.

Advocacy models

What has been termed 'advocacy' has taken many forms. It has been associated with a formal and paid role (professionals, paid advocates or lawyers) and with an informal volunteer role (e.g. friends or other self-advocates). Advocacy has also been categorized as being 'instrumentally' orientated to the resolution of an issue/problem or 'affective' in terms of long-term friendship (see Butler *et al.* 1988).

In describing advocacy as it relates to people with learning difficulties, Atkinson (1999: 5) relates that:

> Advocacy takes many forms but is essentially about speaking up – wherever possible for oneself (self-advocacy), but sometimes with others (group or collective advocacy) and, where necessary, through others. Speaking up through others can involve another 'insider' (a peer advocate), an 'ordinary'

person or volunteer (a citizen advocate), or a person paid and trained as an advocate (a paid advocate).

Simons (1992) adds to this list 'professional advocacy', where a professional seeks to support a client. Indeed, *Valuing People Now* (Department of Health 2009) identifies self-advocacy, citizen advocacy, professional/representational advocacy and peer advocacy as key advocacy areas for the future. In extending the original monetary commitment to self- and citizen advocacy in *Valuing People*, the new document states that

> people with learning disabilities say that being part of a self-advocacy group or getting support from an advocate is a really important part of being able to take control of their lives.
> (Department of Health 2009: 100)

There are, then, a multitude of potential advocacy forms and these are summarized along with their strengths and weaknesses in Table 7.1.

Advocacy and 'best interest'

One of the key themes in the early advocacy literature was the importance of 'advocate independence'. In the column marked 'weaknesses' in Table 7.1 this issue of 'independence', a major principle of advocacy

Type of advocacy	Strengths	Weaknesses
Citizen advocacy (see e.g. Wolfensberger 1983; Butler *et al.* 1988; Simons 1993; Williams 1998; Brooke 2002)	Unpaid volunteers offer wide-ranging one-to-one support, both instrumental and affective If the advocate partner relationship lasts it can be a highly significant one Independence from services gives them a strong voice	Maintains a distinction between 'advocate' and 'partner/protegé' Difficult to recruit volunteers who have the time and motivation to commit to a long-term relationship There can be a skills gap in terms of the instrumental side of advocacy There remains a patchwork of projects because it is not cheap to run citizen advocacy programmes Advocates impart idealistic and overly ambitious views

Type of advocacy	Strengths	Weaknesses
Peer advocacy (see e.g. Brandon 1994, 1995)	Advocates share experiences with similar others, not least of service experiences Advocacy is independent of the service sector Friendships can blossom and similar groups be brought together	Advocates' experiences may not be in line with those for whom they are working Advocates might impart idealistic and overly ambitious views
Parent/carer advocacy (see e.g. FEU 1989)	Care and love define the relationship over a lifetime Advocacy located in dynamics of family Advocacy skills translated into family	Parents/carer needs may dominate at the expense of individual choices Potential for over-protection and conflict of interest over key issues Emotional involvement *may* negatively affect both relationships with professionals and decisions being taken
Professional advocacy (see e.g. Crawley 1990; Simons 1992; Atkinson's 1999 argument in relation to advocacy as social work)	Close one-to-one relationships can blossom Sophisticated and trained approach to advocacy	Professionals tied to demands of services rather than the ambitions of the individuals they are supporting Reaffirms professional expertise Professionals move on and leave a vacuum in people's lives
Individual and collective self-advocacy (see e.g. Dybwad and Bersani 1996; Shoultz 1997; Ward 1998; Goodley 2000)	Promotes positive self-identity and capacity for advocating for oneself Challenges professional expertise and contributes to development of the self-advocacy social movement	Some individuals may be unable to advocate for themselves May require substantial support from others and is not cheap Suffers from lack of professional and service resources

Table 7.1 Types of advocacy and their strengths and weaknesses

since its earliest days, appears against a number of forms of advocacy. For example, a citizen advocate should neither be service worker nor be funded by services (Butler *et al.* 1988) but an ordinary citizen willing to partner a person 'for life', offering both instrumental help to change their lives and expressive help (i.e. friendship). Dowson (1991) argued similarly strongly for the need for independence within self-advocacy, though many self-advocacy groups are both funded by statutory authorities and facilitated by service workers. There are some fundamental issues here to be considered in terms of an argument concerning 'conflicts of interest'.

It is easy to see how funding from the statutory sector might be easily curtailed were an advocacy organization to become too critical of that statutory service. Other conflicts of interest identified with the service sector are: conflicting demands between users; managing limited resources; professional socialization means relying on clinical judgements or professional cultures at the expense of what the user wants; professional hierarchies operate; and professionals are apt to settle for the 'quiet life' (Simons 1993). Some argue that such conflicts mean professionals cannot advocate at all (Allmark and Klarzynski 1992) but should instead always act in the person's best interests.

Table 7.1 also points out potential conflicts in respect of family carers advocating for their relative where it is often difficult to disentangle the family's interest and values from those of the person with a learning difficulty (Mitchell 1997). For example, it may be that parents feel their son or daughter will never be able to live in supported accommodation or become employed or have relationships. The intricacies of family life may cloud judgement and make decision-making that incorporates the person's voice very difficult and less than independent.

Exercise 7.2

Brad has recently flown into a rage in his home, which he shares with five other people with learning difficulties. When he does not get his choice of television channel to watch and when he is not allowed to take his own snacks out of a locked fridge when he chooses Brad has become so threatening that it has upset some of the other

residents. A behavioural assessment has taken place and staff have a plan which involves sending Brad to his room when de-escalation strategies have failed. Staff know they cannot open the fridge as one of the residents has Prader-Willi syndrome and will raid the fridge if allowed open access.

What could you do to advocate for Brad? What would stop you from advocating on his behalf if you were:

- a member of staff?
- an independent advocate?
- a parent?

For both professionals, families and other advocates, though, what seems to be vital is that where conflicts of interest arise the advocate recognizes the limits to their advocacy role and finds another able to advocate with continued independence at that point.

Advocacy developments and people with learning difficulties

In what follows we place emphasis on the historical development of self-advocacy and campaigning, reflecting their continued UK growth in recent years as well as the authors' own interests.

The rise of self-advocacy

It is fitting to start this section by pointing out that in this chapter we have adopted the term 'learning difficulties' (rather than 'mental handicap', 'mental impairment' or 'learning disabilities'), because it is the term preferred by many in the British self-advocacy movement. As one member of the movement puts it, 'If you put "people with learning difficulties" then they know that people want to learn and to be taught how to do things' (quoted in Sutcliffe and Simons 1993: 23). As one of the best known aphorisms of the People First self-advocacy movement puts it, 'Label jars, not people.' The adoption of their preferred term challenges administrative definitions that appear to locate disability within the impaired individual, a pathological focus. By viewing disability as causally related to some form of individualized impairment these definitions say something very simple – that impairment, whether it be physical or 'of mind' results in and creates disability. Hence, in that view, impairment and disability are synonymous, inseparable concepts (Goodley 1997).

Following this, 'impaired thought' leads *to* a myriad of disabilities – disabled thinking, disabled educational potential, disabled relationships with others, disabled sex lives and disabled parenting. Noteworthy too is that professional and service interventions are geared towards providing inputs that are based on these assumptions. The emerging image of the person with learning difficulties, then, is not one of autonomy but of a loss of wholeness and a personal tragedy that renders the individual the focus of a specialist professional intervention. Barnes (1990) argues that this results in disabled people being assigned a position in a culture of dependence, as burdens to their families and to society at large, i.e. as a problem or challenging category, rather than as people.

In contrast, campaigns by people with learning difficulties have emphasized their views of themselves as 'people first'. This posits a key tenet of new social movements to re-present another vision of humanity that may have been ignored by dominant discourses of the health and social welfare professions. Hence, self-advocacy, as we shall see, taps into a more critical view of disability and impairment (see also Goodley 1997) as exemplified through the following argument:

> Mental retardation is, in fact, a sociopolitical not a psychological construction. The myth, perpetuated by a society which refuses to recognise the true nature of its needed social reforms, has successfully camouflaged the politics of diagnosis and incarceration.
>
> (Bogdan and Taylor 1982: 15)

Self-advocacy has the potential to publicly revisit and challenge the very political processes that position people with the label of learning difficulties as a different, 'othered' social group. In this sense, then, self-advocacy and campaigning are crucially involved in challenging the very processes of diagnosis, incarceration and treatment, on a variety of private and public, individual and group, short- and long-term levels.

Exercise 7.3

Explain to a friend or colleague why the term 'people with learning difficulties' has been adopted. Can you do this without mentioning a previous collective description? What response did you get?

The beginnings of the self-advocacy movement

The self-advocacy movement is a living testament to the group activity of people with learning difficulties in challenging institutionalized prejudice within society (Williams and Shoultz 1982), claiming power over their own destiny (Worrell 1988) and re-historicizing their personal and collective histories (Potts and Fido 1991: Chapter 1 this volume).

The origins of the self-advocacy movement can be traced back to the late 1960s and have, not surprisingly, moved from a professional/practice-based approach initially to one that is now led by people with learning difficulties themselves. Following the historical overview provided in Goodley (2000), a small group of people with learning difficulties in Sweden developed a list of requests about how their services should be provided. They gave this list to the parent organization that supported them. Whether or not the requests were acted upon remains unknown, but something unprecedented and previously undocumented had occurred. Perske (1996: 20–1) describes another similar episode:

> STOCKHOLM, SWEDEN, November 8, 1969. Ten persons with mental retardation and six university students – all good friends – came together for a special adventure . . . [They met in a club and intended to go to the theatre] . . . The sixteen went to a coffee shop and discussed all that they had experienced. Everyone decided that they wanted to see the play at a later date. So, they began making a checklist of preparations. As they left, the group decided not to return to the club. They agreed to break up at this new and strange location and each find his or her own way home.

The work of Nirje in Northern Europe and later Wolf Wolfensberger and John O'Brien in the US sought to formulate processes through which empowerment could be accomplished by supporting people to live 'normal' and 'socially valued' lives. The normalization movement used the Program Analysis of Services Systems (PASS) tool (Wolfensberger and Glenn 1975) to compare services to a 'culturally valued analogue' (i.e. to the life one would expect for any person within mainstream society). Later, O'Brien's 'five accomplishments' aimed to provide a starting point for putting normalization into practice (O'Brien 1987). O'Brien's philosophy was that if services were to 'empower' they must have ensured that their users were:

- present in the community;
- supported to make choices;
- participants in community environments;
- respected;
- participating in the community.

Exercise 7.4

The early 1970s saw a number of attempts to make available to people with learning difficulties patterns of life and conditions of everyday living that were as close as possible to the regular circumstances of life in society. Can you think of ways of making available such patterns of life for people with learning difficulties through your professional work?

The beginnings of self-advocacy can be traced back to the first and second Swedish National Conferences of Retarded Adults in 1968 and 1970, which coincided with the emergence of normalization and the first experiences of autonomy, choice and independence as described earlier. The staging of these conferences contributed substantially to public visibility of adults with learning difficulties (Dybwad 1996) and their interests, and were followed closely by many more such conferences, for example the National Youth Conference on Mental Retardation in Miami, 1969, and what were then called 'participation events' such as Our Life, organized by the Campaign for the Mentally Handicapped in London 1972, which were subsequently repeated for a further three years.

This kind of overt participation represented a radical departure and covered topics such as where to move after leaving hospital, employment and relationships with peers and professionals. The delegates demonstrated their desire to talk about themselves as people first and to challenge others' preoccupation with impairment. Hersov (1996) states that these events had an immeasurable impact upon the UK self-advocacy movement. Furthermore, many delegates felt that the one-off nature of the CMH conferences was inadequate: 'We should have a meeting once a month.' On writing up the 'Listen' conference report, Shearer's (1973: 34) concerns and ambitions typify many feelings prominent in the early days:

> 'Listen' and 'Our Life' have shown the potential for development and have indicated the waste if this potential is neglected. It is now up to others to ensure that the future is one of development and not neglect. It is up to everyone ... to do them justice and show that something lasting was achieved at the conference.

CMH's American links culminated in Paul Williams and Bonnie Shoultz co-writing *We Can Speak for Ourselves* (1982), reviewing international developments. This highlighted the variety of groups that were taking off in the UK and the US, reflecting the United Nations *Declaration of the Rights of Disabled Persons* (1975, cited in Campbell and Oliver 1996: 19), which asserted that 'organisations of disabled persons may be usefully consulted in all matters regarding the rights of disabled persons' (Section 3447.12).

The early days of the self-advocacy movement therefore gave way to a fast and earnest growth in the following years!

Self-advocacy and people first

> Until I started going to a self-advocacy group, which set me free, I couldn't put my views across, tell people what I thought of them, tell the DHSS, tell anyone. I couldn't tell the staff where they were going wrong.
> (Patrick Burke, self-advocate, quoted in Goodley 2000: xii)

Self-advocacy groups continued to grow in dance companies, sport and recreational clubs, through to adult training centres and hospitals. According to Hersov (1996), in the UK, two of these, the Mencap London Division's Participation Forum and City Lit, grew in stature in the early 1980s (reflecting strong financial support gained through charity funds). In 1984, they sent representatives to the First International Self-Advocacy Leadership Conference in Tacoma, North America. By this time the movement had grown markedly in the US, with the People First organization holding its first convention for North American members as early as 1974 (Dybwad 1996). By 1975 there were 16 People First chapters formed in 12 cities (Crawley 1988). According to O'Brien and Sang (1984), the links between English and American self-advocates continued to be productive. Things were starting to take off.

At the First International People First Conference in 1984, a number of English delegates were inspired to set up People First of London and Thames. This self-advocacy group was independent of a service base, with members attending voluntarily, and by 1997 had a number of paid independent supporters. It has continued to be one of the most influential collectives within the movement. In 1988 the Second International People First Conference was held in Twickenham, entitled 'A Voice of Our Own – Now and In the Future', followed in 1993 by the Third International Conference which took place in Toronto, Canada, with many UK People First groups attending. The fourth was held in Alaska in 1998.

While the UK movement has grown in strength internationally, it has also made some links with the larger disability movement in the UK. Hersov (1996) records how the well-known self-advocate, Gary Bourlet, represented London People First on the 1992 national council of the British Council of Organizations of Disabled People as it was then known (now the British Council of Disabled People, BCODP). More recently, Simone Aspis, previously Campaigns Officer at People First London, has maintained links with the BCODP, and was the self-advocacy movement's only representative in Campbell and Oliver's (1996) account of the British disability movement.

Moreover, self-advocates have become involved in formal studies of services (see e.g. Gramlich *et al.* 2002), published widely, produced video materials and other learning packages (see Ramcharan and Grant 2001), appeared on TV and in the broadsheets, and taken part in civil rights demonstrations:

> In the last decade, there have been important landmarks in the growth of self-advocacy throughout the country ... There is every reason to believe that the [movement] ... will continue to gain new members and widespread support, and that it will reach even greater heights in the future.
>
> (Hersov 1996: 139)

In introducing this chapter we highlighted the ways in which the public voices of people with learning difficulties were left unheard. As this history shows, the self-advocacy movement has, over time, fought hard to unshackle itself from ownership by professionals and service workers and to gain independence. Herein lies an interesting issue. We will shortly talk more about the success of campaigning and the independent self-advocacy lobby. However, there has been an unparalleled growth in self-advocacy in recent years and, despite wider understanding of the ideal of independence, a closer relationship to government has emerged.

It is vital to note that in recent years self-advocacy has become not simply accepted, but both expected and indeed funded by government. For example, alongside the White Paper *Valuing People* (Department of Health 2001a), a document termed *Nothing About Us Without Us* (Department of Health 2001b) was produced by self-advocates after consultation with members of the self-advocacy movement. *Valuing People* committed £3m per annum over three years to the development of both self- and citizen advocacy; the learning disability research initiative (Grant and Ramcharan 2007: 2009) involved people with learning difficulties as reviewers of research proposals and as managers of research and it promoted the involvement of people in all areas of research. Of two co-directors of the Valuing People Support Team, the team with overall responsibility for the implementation of *Valuing People*, one is a person with a learning difficulty who is paid the going rate for their role. In short, the slogan 'nothing about us without us' has built increasingly strong levels and mechanisms for participation since the publication of *Valuing People*.

Local citizen and self-advocacy groups were reported to have increased substantially four years after, and as a result of, *Valuing People* (Valuing People Support Team 2005). Moreover, it was reported in this document that over 1000 self-advocates were involved in regional forums in the nine administrative areas covered by *Valuing People*, each in turn having representatives on a national forum of self-advocates. Representatives from the national forum also sat on the Task Force, a group directly advising the government minister on *Valuing People* implementation and emergent issues.

Taking one example of one such emergent issue, minutes from the National Forum and Task Force indicate that their consideration of hate crimes emerged from worries expressed by local self-advocates in relation to safety in public. While self-advocacy groups were free to meet police and police authorities at local and regional levels, the meeting minutes at national level indicate the issue as having been brought to the attention of the Home Office, indicating a creative way of establishing joined-up government around the issues people with learning disabilities face in their everyday lives. The Learning Disability Taskforce (2007) also notes the contribution of self-advocates to *Our Health, Our Care, Our Say* (Department of Health 2007), to *Improving the Life Chances of Disabled People* (Office for Disability Issues 2006) and to the consultation on primary health care undertaken by the Disability Rights Commission.

Some commentators have voiced concern at the extent to which the agenda has been set for self-advocacy by government since *Valuing People* was first published, leading to new forms of colonization which have the potential to undermine an independence of voice. The proposal that a new advocacy programme lead appointed by the government to develop advocacy, write a tool kit and work to involve people from BME communities and those with complex needs can be seen as government setting the self-advocacy agenda itself.

Similar debate surrounds the emergence of learning difficulty Parliaments. In these Parliaments, of which there are a growing number in the UK, representatives with learning difficulties are generally elected by other people with learning difficulties in their area. The Parliamentarians meet, usually in

council chambers, to discuss key issues and invite people to report to, and answer questions from, the group. Perhaps the best known of these Parliaments is in Cambridge. It has 35 Members of Parliament and they meet every two months. Their website tells us how they invite people with the power to make a real difference (Cambridge Parliament, http://www.speakingup.org/innovative-projects/index.php?action=40) – the Mayor, Parliamentary MPs, Partnership Board members, Bank CEOs and so forth. Where their response to issues raised is not considered sufficient the group launch campaigns in the media and elsewhere. The Parliaments are therefore designed to invert power, to make those with power answerable and to harness support for lobbying where their voice is not being heard.

Andrew Holman, a long-time supporter of self-advocacy in England, proposed in a social care experts' blog run by Community Care in November 2008 (http://www.communitycare.co.uk/blogs/social-care-experts-blog/2008/11/learning-disability-parliament.html) that such Parliaments were people 'playing at being Parliamentarians' with no power, ignoring the Partnership Board mechanisms set up under *Valuing People* and those for regional and national forums of self-advocates. Such Parliaments were also taking money that might have been spent on the established self-advocacy movement. The swift response signed by a number of the Cambridge Parliamentarians notes (among other things) that:

> Our Parliament is not about having nice lunches, it is about making change and we have been successful in making real change happen. It also gives us the opportunity to have our voices heard and we can't understand how that could be a bad thing. You mention the importance of Partnership Boards, and are obviously unaware that our Parliament works closely with our local Partnership Board, sitting on it, chairing it and reporting to it. In fact our Partnership Board lead Jean Clark believes the Parliament 'legitimises the voice of the service users on the board and ensures the user voice influences developments in Cambridgeshire', as MP's are not just speaking from their own experience but also representing others.

Once again there are real issues in this debate around the independence of groups, the extent to which they hold the agenda and how much power they can wield for change. How far has self-advocacy come in these respects? Has it broken the links with services and, if so, how successful has independent lobbying and campaigning been in affecting change?

Self-advocacy and services

Self-advocacy groups have inevitably required support workers or advisers. However, as one self-advocate puts it,

> I think there's a problem with advisers who are staff because you see them every day . . . She was always watching you.
>
> (Joyce Kershaw, self-advocate, quoted in Goodley 2000: 127)

For some, the People First movement *is* the self-advocacy movement. However, the foundations of the British movement are not found solely in independent People First (nor the London groups focused on by commentators like Hersov). The movement's origins can be also be traced back over the last three decades of trainee committees in adult training centres, social education centres, hospitals, long-stay institutions and group homes. Crawley (1988) has documented the rush of self-advocacy issues into adult training centre curricula, while Whittell and Ramcharan (1998) report similar groups in Wales not operating as part of the independent self-advocacy and People First movements. Similarly, Paul Williams's paper on participation and self-advocacy reflects some small-scale translation of self-advocacy issues into service decision-making (participation). He argued that:

> Participation seeks to provide handicapped (*sic*) people and others with experiences of equality and sharing. Self-advocacy enables handicapped people to take their own decisions and exercise control over their own affairs.
>
> (Williams 1982: 3)

In terms of recognizing diversity, it is clear that the doing of self-advocacy in service bases fits the user participation and community care discourses in government policy that have proliferated since the mid-1980s in Britain. As learning difficulties services experience a transition from public sector organizations to private sector management, and a shift from residential to community bases, self-advocacy appealed to those promoting service innovation in a market economy. Service personnel may therefore have a role in supporting the development of a 'consumer voice'.

Viewed in this light, the critics of self-advocacy under *Valuing People* might assert that, while the number of groups has increased, the agenda simply represents the latest iteration of that consumer voice speaking about a service agenda set by government. At the very least it speaks of the central importance of the support worker or adviser working in ways that promote independence of voice.

Dowson and Whittaker (1993) conceptualize 'good support' by introducing the notion of intervention. They argue that at particular times different types of intervention are required on the part of the supporter, including ones that are:

- *prescriptive* (i.e. aim to give advice, recommend a behaviour or course of action);
- *informative* (i.e. aim to give knowledge or information);
- *confronting* (i.e. challenge attitudes, beliefs or behaviours);
- *cathartic* (i.e. provoke a release of tension);
- *catalytic* (i.e. elicit information or opinion from the group);
- *supportive* (i.e. affirm the value or worth of the group).

Any intervention that (re)creates dependency is an intervention that is at odds with the aims of self-advocacy and campaigning (Goodley 1997). Service workers in support roles may therefore be contentious, especially where such support is not seen by managers as a priority or as a moveable feast dependent on their other roles. Because of this, some support workers have chosen to operate in a voluntary capacity and in 'their own time'. Moreover, the conflicts of interest outlined earlier are always likely to cause additional troubles.

Exercise 7.5

What constitutes 'good support' in relation to facilitating self-advocacy groups?

Are the people with learning difficulties with whom you work involved in a self-advocacy group? If so, what sort of group is it? What sort of things are they advocating for?

If they are not involved in such a group consider whether they should be, and what role you might play in supporting them.

Self-advocacy, politicization and campaigning: the new politics of the twenty-first century

Over the last 30 years, a rise in the amount of advocacy and campaigning by a variety of labelled groups has demonstrated the potential of such approaches in challenging societal ignorance. A popular point of analysis in contemporary sociology and social policy at the start of this century was the argument that the old grand narrative political identities of class, 'race' and gender have given way to more diverse and varied political identities and aspirations.

The move towards diversity in the latter part of the twentieth century was characterized by a struggle for access to the production of knowledge. Here individuals and groups, with particular political interests, were increasingly engaged actively with the 'knowledge society's' production of information about them and others. Knowledge is power, and who owns or utilizes knowledge has important consequences. A variety of political concerns have increasingly been represented through the emergence of a diverse collective of campaigning groups.

A number of examples can be cited where disabled people around the globe organize themselves under the banner organization of Disabled People's International. All of these collectives can be seen as contributing to the emergence of new social movements. Such movements encompass a whole host of groups impacting upon various private, public, statutory and voluntary institutions and contexts.

Bersani (1996: 265–6) and Shakespeare (1993) characterize the self-advocacy and disability rights movements, respectively, as new social movements with a number of common features:

- *Members go beyond typical roles*: here people transcend typical positions that have been assigned to them (in this case by health and social welfare professionals). So, for example, people labelled with a learning difficulty have chosen on the basis of sharing an interest to collaborate with the British Council of Organizations of Disabled People.
- *Representation of a strong ideological change*: new social movements re-address traditional ideologies that have shaped the life worlds of members. The control of the production of information by people with learning difficulties for people with learning difficulties represents a major attempt to represent their interests independently of those voices that have traditionally spoken on their behalf.
- *Emergence of a new identity*: here, people choose their own identity and are not forced into identities others choose for them. Thus the People First movement, as its name implies, insists that each person labelled with a learning difficulty is seen as a person first and not a member of a labelled group.
- *Relationship between the individual and movement is blurred*: one of the key points of a new social movement is its emphasis on collective as well as individual action. People with learning difficulties have chosen the name they prefer for themselves as a collective and, through the People First movement, they have been represented in pushing for disabled people's rights.

It is possible to view the disability movement as a new social movement in four ways. First, disabled people have become recognized as 'disabled activists' lobbying governments for adequate anti-discriminatory legislation, pushing for independent living. Second, the disabled people's movement has recast 'disability' as a social and political issue – the exclusion of people with impairments – rather than simply viewing it as the product of an individual impairment. Third, disabled people have embraced this new politicization of disability and have provided alternative views of disability and impairment through, for example, disability arts where theatre companies such as 'The Lawnmowers' present people with the label of learning difficulties as skilled, competent performers rather than 'tragic' victims of 'mental impairment'. Finally, the concerns of disabled individuals and the wider disability movement overlap, for example in demands for supported living in the community and for extending access to direct payments.

Take the following example relating to campaigning for the implementation of 'direct payments', now a major element of government policy (Department of Health 2007). Barnes and Mercer (2006) suggest that the introduction of such payments has been significantly influenced by lobbying and pressure of 'disabled people'. Initially achieved through lobbying by disabled people for a cash payment in lieu of a shortfall in benefits payments, the Independent Living Fund introduced in 1988 was found to break away from off-the-shelf care packages, giving each person freedom to employ the support they felt met their own needs, wishes and aspirations. The substantial success in achieving independence through this mechanism saw the emergence of the first Independent Living Centres (ILCs), which assisted numerous local authorities to set up direct payment schemes. Research has found that the take-up in 150 such authorities is directly related to the level to which ILCs were engaged in local decision-making and negotiations with local authorities (Glasby and Littlechild 2002).

However, the initial implementation of direct payments (Department of Health 1996: 2000) only allowed access to those able to 'manage' their own direct payment, with the result that people labelled with physical disability had greater access to direct payments than people with learning difficulties (Fruin 2000). It took a substantial amount of lobbying by People First, the national independent self-advocacy movement for people with learning difficulties, together with the National Centre for

Independent Living (NCIL), to change the government's mind, along with research by people with learning difficulties (Gramlich et al. 2002). The result was that the 2003 guidance redefined 'ability to manage' as 'capacity (with or without support) to arrange a direct payment service to meet an assessed need. The ability to "direct" is more important [than] the ability to manage' (Department of Health 2003: Glossary). It further proposed that:

> When discussing DPs with people, local councils will wish, wherever possible, to offer the option for them to be put in touch with [a] support group or local centre for independent living, or a peer support group of people who already manage direct payments.
>
> (Department of Health 2003: 9)

and,

> Councils might decide that they can provide a support service directly in partnership with the local voluntary organisations, or by some other means. Support provided through voluntary/recipient run organisations has been shown to be particularly effective and valued by participants.
>
> (Department of Health 2003: 9)

The advice about development in the implementation of direct payments has continued to adapt to the voices of disabled people and people with learning difficulties. What can be readily said is that such change was a triumph for the independent voice of people with learning difficulties in pressing for mechanisms and practices that best reflected their goals. It sometimes placed them in paid roles and, through acting collectively, they have taken on leadership and supporting roles to the sector, hence inverting the relations of power and dependence that have historically seen people with learning difficulties in powerless roles.

Conclusion

From what has been argued above it is fair to say that advocacy and campaigning are overlapping approaches. Both require some form of speaking for oneself and/or others in ways that put certain ambitions and aims in a public arena. Both appear to be associated with individuals and groups challenging authorities and institutions to take on board concerns otherwise marginalized by other individuals or wider society. Furthermore, both are terms and actions bound up with the notion of power. Advocacy and campaigning can both engage with powerful institutions and individuals and attempt to challenge or disrupt the distribution of power. We have also shown that advocacy itself has evolved and that in its original incarnation it was still, perhaps unavoidably, a professional and service-orientated approach. Establishing power has therefore involved a struggle over time towards reclaiming voice, power and identity.

In this chapter we have argued that the development of advocacy has moved from being led by professionals to being supported by professionals, and further to being forged under the rubric of 'people first'. We might also argue, using a consumerist framework, that the development has been from a position in which people with learning difficulties were *given* a say, through one in which they were involved and in which they participated in services, to a contemporary position in which they have claimed their own voice and campaigned for their own interests. In terms of voice we might also assert that the movement started with the voice of people with learning difficulties being heard for the first time through professional support, prior to becoming an independent voice, and finally a voice heard in unison with others with whom interests are shared. In other words, advocacy and campaigning seem to have a natural history which, over time, relocates power to, with and for people themselves.

Such a progression is not one that is pursued by all people with learning difficulties today. There remain some questions about whose voice is being heard, at the expense of whom and representing which interests. However, if the key elements of this progression are towards 'empowerment', if they are about reclaiming equal rights to each person within society, then they are fundamental to each of us in demonstrating 'civility' in all our interactions and, in wider terms, accomplishing a 'civil society' and a civilization of 'people first'.

Acknowledgements

The following sections of this chapter draw on the Open University Press text *Self-Advocacy in the Lives of People with Learning Difficulties* (Goodley 2000: Ch. 2): the rise of self-advocacy; the beginnings of the movement; self-advocacy and civil rights; services and People First; and setting up. We would like to thank Open University Press for granting us permission to draw upon this text in the writing of this chapter.

References

Allmark, P. and Klarzynski, R. (1992) The case against nurse advocacy, *British Journal of Nursing*, 2(1): 33–6.

Atkinson, D. (1999) *Advocacy: A Review*. Brighton: Pavilion Publishing.

Barnes, C. (1990) *The Cabbage Syndrome: The Social Construction of Dependence*. London: Falmer Press.

Barnes, C. and Mercer, G. (2006) *Independent Futures: Creating User-led Disability Services in a Disabling Society*. Bristol: The Policy Press.

Bersani, H. (1996) Leadership in developmental disabilities: where we've been, where we are, and where we're going, in G. Dybwad and H. Bersani (eds) *New Voices: Self-advocacy by People with Disabilities*. Cambridge, MA: Brookline Books.

Bogdan, R. and Taylor, S. (1982) *Inside Out: The Social Meaning of Mental Retardation*. Toronto: University of Toronto Press.

Brandon, D. (1994) Peer advocacy: care in place, *The International Journal of Networks and Community*, 1(3): 218–24.

Brandon, D. (1995) Peer support and advocacy – international comparisons and developments, in R. Jack (ed.) *Empowerment in Community Care*. London: Chapman and Hall.

Brooke, J. (2002) *Good Practice in Citizen Advocacy*. Kidderminster: BILD Publications.

Butler, K., Carr, S. and Sullivan, F. (1988) *Citizen Advocacy: A Powerful Partnership*. London: National Citizen Advocacy.

Campbell, J. and Oliver, M. (1996) *Disability Politics: Understanding our Past, Changing our Future*. London: Routledge.

Crawley, B. (1988) *The feasibility of trainee committees as a means of sef-advocacy in adult training centres in England and Wales*. Unpublished PhD Thesis. University of Manchester.

Crawley, B. (1990) Advocacy as a threat or ally to professional practice? in G. Brown and G. Wistow (eds) *The Roles and Tasks of CMHTs*. Aldershot: Avebury.

Department of Health (1996) *Community Care (Direct Payments) Act*. London: HMSO.

Department of Health (2000) *Community Care (Direct Payments) Act: Policy Guidance*. London: Department of Health.

Department of Health (2001a) *Valuing People: A New Strategy for Learning Disability for the 21st Century*. London: Department of Health.

Department of Health (2001b) *Nothing About Us Without Us: The Service Users Advisory Group Report*. London: Department of Health.

Department of Health (2003) *Direct Payments Guidance: Community Care, Services for Carers and Children's Services (Direct Payments) Guidance, England 2003*. London: Department of Health.

Department of Health (2007) *Our Health, Our Care, Our Say: A New Direction for Community Services*. Cm 6737. London: Department of Health.

Department of Health (2009) *Valuing People Now: A New Three-year Strategy for People with Learning Disabilities. Making it Happen for Everyone*. London: Wellington House.

Dowson, S. (1991) *Keeping It Safe: Self-advocacy by People with Learning Difficulties and the Professional Response*. London: Values into Action.

Dowson, S. and Whittaker, A. (1993) *On One Side: The Role of the Advisor in Supporting People with Learning Difficulties in Self-Advocacy Groups*. London: Values into Action in association with the King's Fund Centre.

Dybwad, G. (1996) Setting the stage historically, in G. Dybwad and H. Bersani (eds) *New Voices: Self-advocacy by People with Disabilities*. Cambridge, MA: Brookline Books.

Dybwad, G. and Bersani, H. (eds) (1996) *New Voices: Self-advocacy by People with Disabilities*. Cambridge, MA: Brookline Books.

FEU (Further Education Unit) (1989) *Working Together? Self-advocacy and Parents: The Impact of Self-advocacy on Parents of Young People with Disabilities*. London: FEU.

Fruin, D. (2000) *Moving into the Mainstream: The Report of a National Inspection of Services for Adults with Learning Difficulties*. London: Department of Health.

Glasby, J. and Littlechild, R. (2002) *Social Work and Direct Payments*. Bristol: The Policy Press.

Goodley, D. (1997) Locating self-advocacy in models of disability: understanding disability in the support of self-advocates with learning difficulties, *Disability and Society*, 12(3): 367–79.

Goodley, D. (2000) *Self-advocacy in the Lives of People with Learning Difficulties: The Politics of Resilience*. Buckingham: Open University Press.

Gramlich, S., McBride, G., Sneham, N., Myers, B. with Williams, V. and Simons, K. (2002) *Journey to Independence: What Self-advocates Tell Us About Direct Payments*. Kidderminster: BILD.

Grant, G. and Ramcharan, P. (2007) *Valuing People and Research: The Learning Disability Research Initiative: Overview Report*. London: Department of Health.

Grant, G. and Ramcharan, P. (2009) Researching *Valuing People and Research*: outcomes of the Learning Disability Research Initiative, *Tizard Learning Disability Review*, 14(2): 25–34.

Hersov, J. (1996) The rise of self-advocacy in Great Britain, in G. Dybwad and H. Bersani (eds) *New Voices: Self-advocacy by People with Disabilities*. Cambridge, MA: Brookline Books.

HMSO (1995) *Disability Discrimination Act*. London: HMSO.

Learning Disability Task Force (2007) *Could Do Better: Annual Report*, 2006/07.

Mitchell, P. (1997) The impact of self-advocacy on families, *Disability and Society*, 12(1): 43–56.

O'Brien, J. (1987) A guide to life style planning: using the activities catalogue to integrate services and natural support systems, in B.W. Wilson and G.T. Bellamy (eds) *The Activities Catalogue: An Alternative Curriculum for Youth and Adults with Severe Disabilities*. Baltimore, MD: Brookes.

O'Brien, J. and Sang, B. (1984) *Advocacy – The UK and American Experiences*. London: King Edward's Hospital Fund.

Office for Disability Issues (2006) *Improving the Life Chances of Disabled People*. London: Office for Disability Issues.

Perske, R. (1996) Self-advocates on the move, in G. Dybwad and H. Bersani (eds) *New Voices: Self-advocacy by People with Disabilities*. Cambridge, MA: Brookline Books.

Potts, M. and Fido, R. (1991) *'A Fit Person to be Removed': Personal Accounts of Life in a Mental Deficiency Institution*. Plymouth: Northcote House.

Ramcharan, P. and Grant, G. (2001) Views and experiences of people with intellectual disabilities and their families: (1) The user perspective, *Journal of Applied Research in Intellectual Disabilities*, 14: 348–63.

Shakespeare, T. (1993) Disabled people's self-organisation: a new social movement? *Disability, Handicap and Society*, 8(3): 249–64.

Shearer, A. (1973) *Listen*. London: CMH/VIA.

Shoultz, B. (1997) *More Thoughts on Self-advocacy: The Movement, the Group, and the Individual*. Center on Human Policy, Syracuse University, New York, http://soeweb.syr.edu/.

Simons, K. (1992) *'Sticking Up For Yourself': Self Advocacy and People with Learning Difficulties*. London: Joseph Rowntree Association.

Simons, K. (1993) *Citizen Advocacy: The Inside View*. Bristol: Norah Fry Research Centre.

Sutcliffe, J. and Simons, K. (1993) *Self-advocacy and Adults with Learning Difficulties: Contexts and Debates*. Leicester: The National Institute of Adult Continuing Education in Association with the Open University.

Valuing People Support Team (2005) *The Story So Far . . . Valuing People: A New Strategy for Learning Disability for the 21st Century*. London: Valuing People Support Team.

Ward, L. (ed.) (1998) *Innovations in Advocacy and Empowerment for People with Intellectual Disabilities*. Whittle-le-Woods: Lisieux-Hall.

Whittell, B. and Ramcharan, P. (1998) The All Wales Strategy: self advocacy and participation, *British Journal of Learning Disabilities*, 20(1): 23–6.

Williams, P. (1982) Participation and self-advocacy, *CMH Newsletter*, 20 (spring): 3–4.

Williams, P. (1998) *Standing by Me: Stories of Citizen Advocacy*. London: CAIT.

Williams, P. and Shoultz, B. (1982) *We Can Speak for Ourselves*. London: Souvenir Press.

Wolfensberger, W. (1983) *Reflections on the Status of Citizen Advocacy*. Ontario: National Institute of Mental Retardation.

Wolfensberger, W. and Glenn, S. (1975) *PASS 3: Program Analysis of Service Systems. Handbook and Manual*. Toronto: National Institute on Mental Retardation.

Worrell, B. (1988) *People First: Advice for Advisors*. Ontario: National People First Project.

Part Two
Childhood and early parenting

In Part One of this book, attention was given to different constructions of learning disability and the implications for service design and development. We now turn to the first of the life cycle sections. It is important to provide a space for the voice of children with disabilities themselves, and family members, parents in particular, so as to hear what they say about their own identities, social relationships and support needs. We hope that the narratives and case material will provide readers with important points of reference for weighing and evaluating professional, policy and academic perspectives about the lives of children and young people with learning disabilities and their families.

Two of the new chapters in this edition consider the birth of a child with a suspected disability, disclosure and early support to families (Chapter 11), and the aetiological and ethical challenges that arise for professionals and families (Chapter 10). Chapters also give attention to ways of communicating with young children who face different kinds of challenges expressing themselves orally, and one chapter focuses entirely on supporting children with high support needs, especially those with profound and multiple learning disabilities. Both these chapters provide clear indications of the kinds of expertise and skills required of front-line staff to support individuals with these challenging needs.

This section of the book begins to elaborate some of the grander themes that permeate work with categories of vulnerable people described here and elsewhere in the book, especially in relation to the balancing of rights and risks, independence and inclusion, personal development and familial obligations, together with an appreciation of professional responsibilities.

Chapter 8 by Kirsten Stalker and Clare Connors demonstrates that children with learning disabilities, given the opportunity and necessary support, can give interesting and insightful narrative accounts about

their everyday lives. Children's talk reveals that they do not necessarily look upon themselves in terms of a disability identity. For the most part they talk about and do the things that most young children do and talk about. However, the narratives illustrate that relationships with siblings can be very mixed, and that bullying can occur at home, from siblings, and also at school. Circumstances can limit friendships with other children and boredom can be common, especially at weekends and during holidays. The chapter will help the reader to gain an appreciation of:

- the value of listening to children with disabilities talking;
- important people in children's lives;
- children's experiences of school and other services;
- theoretical frameworks from the sociology of childhood and the social relational model of disability, and how these can inform an understanding of children's narratives;
- the practice implications of working with young disabled children.

Chapter 9 by Lesley Cogher is themed entirely on communication since this is something that challenges many children and young people with learning disabilities and also those that support them – families, friends, allies and professionals – from the early years. Since most language development takes place in the early years much attention is given to this life stage, though case examples also include adolescents and adults. By means of a language skills model the reader is presented with a way of taking stock of the different communication challenges that people with learning disabilities often face. Strategies for supporting people with communication difficulties are outlined, including the use of augmentative and alternative communication systems. The reader is guided towards an understanding of:

- critical features of interpersonal communication, illustrated by use of a language skills model;
- development of communication in the infant and young child, the school-aged child, and young people and adults;
- tasks of the communicator and communication partner;
- what can go wrong with communication;
- augmentative and alternative communication systems.

Chapter 10 by Chris Oliver, Kate Woodcock and Dawn Adams is entirely new. Genetic disorders that result in specific syndromes are evident in a substantial proportion of people who have an intellectual disability. The majority of syndromes are associated with different physical, cognitive, motivational, emotional, sensory and behavioural profiles. Understanding and describing these profiles has implications for people's psychological and physical well-being and, ultimately, their quality of life. The following are the main learning points:

- there are over 1700 genetic disorders associated with intellectual disability and many are associated with specific physical, cognitive and behavioural phenotypes;
- physical health conditions and cognitive differences over and above a general intellectual disability are associated with some syndromes and can be directly related to some forms of challenging behaviour;
- strong preferences or aversion for some sensory and social experiences are evident in some syndromes;
- knowing and understanding the nature of these differences enables those supporting people with genetic disorders to seek help for physical, emotional, cognitive and behavioural problems, plan for the future and create supportive environments;
- the consequences of genetic causes of intellectual disability must be considered within the social context to gain a full understanding of people's experience.

Breaking news about disability, especially when it is unexpected, is one of the most difficult tasks professionals face, and at this critical moment it is important to put in place sound arrangements for early support. This is the theme of Chapter 11 by Bronach Crawley,

which is entirely new. The author provides a first-hand account of this experience, initially as a parent herself, but also as a clinical psychologist. The reader is led through evidence about what seems to support good disclosure practice, and what support professionals may themselves need in order to feel protected and empowered in carrying out this difficult practice. The chapter provides the reader with an understanding of:

- theories and frameworks for locating good practice about the disclosure of disability;
- disclosure as a process rather than an event;
- guidelines for disclosure, their advantages and disadvantages;
- early support required by parents.

Promoting healthy lifestyles in people with learning disabilities who have additional physical and sensory impairments is the subject of Chapter 12 by Bronwyn Roberts. This chapter addresses issues about children and young people with profound and multiple learning disabilities or high support needs, concentrating in particular on youngsters with cerebral palsy, visual impairments or hearing loss. People with high support needs are enjoying longer lives than before, so it is important for professionals to acquire the skills that can help them to contribute to and enrich the lives of the growing number of people in these circumstances. This chapter will acquaint the reader with:

- conceptual and definitional issues about the identification of people with profound and multiple learning disabilities;
- ways of enriching the environments of people with profound and multiple learning disabilities;
- a detailed account of cerebral palsy, visual impairments and hearing loss;
- ways of being sensitive to the personal communication repertoires of individuals;
- evidence-based helping strategies.

Chapter 13 by Gordon Grant considers how families experience care and what support they want from services. It begins with a critique of stereotypes about families with caregiving responsibilities, and then moves to a discussion about stress, coping and resilience in families across the life cycle. The practice implications of supporting families are reviewed in light of a discussion about 'family-centred' or family systems thinking. The chapter is intended to provide the reader with an appreciation of:

- who and what the family is in twenty-first century postmodern societies;
- how families manage caregiving;
- the experience of stress, coping and resilience across the life cycle;

- practice requirements of family-centred thinking.

At the end of Part Two you may want to ask yourself what you think you have gleaned about the capacities and identities of children and young people with learning disabilities, how they communicate, and how you can most effectively engage with them. You may want to reflect on your role relationship with families given the many demands they face but also their emergent expertise, and how you can play your part in ensuring that young people enjoy a smooth pathway to adult services.

There is always one moment in childhood when the door opens and lets the future in.
(Graham Greene, *The Power and the Glory*, 1940)

Children with learning disabilities talking about their everyday lives

Kirsten Stalker and Clare Connors

Introduction

Over recent years, many studies have examined children's lives from their own perspective. A smaller literature reports the views of disabled children, most of which focuses on young people's experiences of school or support services. Few studies have sought disabled children's accounts of their everyday lives, although Hirst and Baldwin (1994), Watson *et al.* (2000), Lewis *et al.* (2006) and Singh and Ghai (2009) are among the exceptions. The views of children with learning disabilities are particularly poorly represented in the literature. In this chapter, we report what children with learning disabilities involved in one study had to say about their everyday lives.

The chapter begins by identifying some theoretical frameworks which can help us understand the children's accounts and place them in a wider context. These are drawn from the social studies of childhood and the social relational model of disability. The reader is encouraged to find out more about these ideas by following up the references given. Next, we describe the aims and methods of our study: 26 disabled children took part but this chapter presents an analysis of the interviews with those who had learning disabilities – 13 in all. The bulk of the chapter reports their accounts of their lives, looking in turn at home, school, services and 'views of self', followed by pen profiles of two children. The final section draws out conclusions and implications for policy and practice. All real names have been changed. Fuller accounts of the study can be found in Connors and Stalker (2003, 2007).

Theoretical frameworks

Where childhood is seen as a period of predictable development leading to independence and autonomy, then, Priestley (2003) argues, disabled children are bound to 'fail'. Traditionally, research about children has focused on their biological or psychological development: viewed through adult eyes, children were seen as playing a relatively passive role, reacting in a fairly predictable way to 'natural' processes going on within them and social processes going on around them. The social studies of childhood, however, view childhood as socially constructed (James *et al.* 1998; Mayall 2002). Being a child has carried a wide variety of meanings across different cultures and times. For example, young working-class people in early Victorian Britain enjoyed precious little 'childhood' before being sent to work down mines or up chimneys, and many in the 'majority world' have similar experiences today. For much of the twentieth century, children with learning disabilities were excluded from mainstream childcare legislation and treated as 'small' or 'pre-' adults with learning disabilities. The social studies of childhood recognize the cultural and historical diversity of children's lives, which are further differentiated by class, gender, race and disability. Children have a unique perspective which differs from that of adults and are active in shaping their own lives: thus we need to recognize the contribution which their accounts can make to a broader analysis of childhood itself.

Another set of ideas which can usefully inform our thinking about disabled children can be found in the social model of disability. This was developed by disabled people to explain, and help overcome, oppression and discrimination (Oliver 1990; Barnes 1991). The social model draws an important distinction between 'impairment', meaning the loss or limitation of functional ability (such as the inability to see, hear or walk) and 'disability', which refers to social, material and cultural barriers (such as inaccessible buildings or information) that exclude people from mainstream life. This way of looking at disability, widely promoted by the disabled people's movement, has won considerable political success, for example in campaigns for anti-discrimination legislation (see also Chapter 35).

At the same time, some disabled people have pointed out limitations within the social model. These include its lack of attention to the implications of living with impairment on a daily basis and its neglect of the importance of personal experience (Shakespeare and Watson 2002; Shakespeare 2006). Thomas (1999, 2004) has developed what she calls a *social relational model of disability* which addresses these issues. She suggests that disabled people face two types of barrier. First, there are 'barriers to doing' which restrict what people can do: these are the buildings with steps which prevent wheelchair users from entering, or written information leaflets which cannot be read by people with visual impairment. Second, Thomas identifies 'barriers to being', caused by the hurtful or hostile attitudes and behaviour of other people or by exclusionary policies and practices within institutions. Over time, these can undermine a person's psycho-emotional well-being, restricting who they can 'be' or become by damaging their self-esteem and confidence. Thomas also talks about 'impairment effects': these are restrictions of activity which result directly from impairment, as opposed to physical barriers or other people's attitudes. For a child with learning disabilities, for example, difficulty with reading may well be related to intellectual impairment. However, there could be other contributing factors: people may have undermined the child's confidence, and thus willingness to persevere with reading, by making thoughtless remarks about their ability or achievement.

Study aims and methods

This was a two-year study funded by the Scottish Executive. Its aims were to explore:

- disabled children's understandings of disability;
- how they negotiate the experience of disability in their everyday lives;
- their experiences of using services;
- siblings' views about having a disabled brother or sister.

We did not set out to recruit children who would be representative of the wider population of disabled children; rather, we aimed to include youngsters with a range of ages and impairments, attending a variety of schools. Families were recruited to the study through schools and voluntary organizations. These agencies were asked to send information and consent forms to parents on our behalf. Once a positive response was received, we sent information and consent forms to the disabled children and their siblings. Three or four visits were made to each family, the first meeting being an opportunity to discuss their participation in the study. Semi-structured interviews were carried out with the disabled children, spread over two or three interviews. In most cases we talked to the children alone but mothers of young people with learning disabilities 'sat in' on two occasions.

Two different versions of the interview schedule were used in the study, one with children aged 11–15, the other with those aged 7–10. The latter schedule, which included various activities and visual aids to engage the children's interest and facilitate communication, was used for all those with learning disabilities. While it is important to use age-appropriate material with children, piloting showed that the more structured schedule worked better with this group. We offered the younger children and those with learning disabilities various activities (such as drawing or writing a story), as well as certain games and exercises, so that those who were not verbally skilled, or not very forthcoming, had alternative means of expressing themselves. Two children used British Sign Language and two used Makaton, a signing system which accompanies speech: they were interviewed by one of the authors who has these communication skills. Another child used facilitated communication: his mother went through some of the questions with him and passed on his responses to us. The following chapter goes into more detail about communication in childhood.

Booth and Booth (1994: 36) report that their respondents – parents with learning disabilities – tended to answer questions with 'a single word, a short phrase or the odd sentence'. This sometimes happened in our study, presenting challenges in terms of analysis and writing up. Some of the data are quite 'thin'; the key points are sometimes expressed only briefly and intermittently – or they may be repeated many times over. Booth (1996) discusses possible ways of editing such material. Is it acceptable, for example, to rewrite someone's words if they will otherwise be unclear or even incoherent to the reader, if the researcher 'knows' what the respondent meant? We think not. Booth also talks about 'cutting and pasting' data from different parts of the same interview to form a coherent narrative or develop a theme. As this involves neither adding to nor changing the respondent's words, at times we have used this method in presenting the data below. Where we have run together data from different parts of the interview, we indicate this with '. . .' to show that some material has been omitted. Elsewhere we reproduce chunks of data including the interviewer's questions or responses, which allows the reader to follow the meaning and flow of the conversation.

Exercise 8.1

Find out what legislative rights children with learning disabilities have to be consulted about their views, and to be protected from discrimination.

The sample

Of the 26 disabled children in the study, 15 had learning disabilities. Two had profound multiple impairments and here we interviewed their parents. Thus, the following sections focus on the accounts of 13 children – nine boys and four girls. Some had additional diagnoses, including attention deficit hyperactivity disorder, hearing impairment, autism and, in one case, a combination of cerebral palsy, epilepsy and 'challenging behaviour'. Six attended special (segregated) schools, including one residential establishment, four were in integrated units (special units within mainstream schools) and three were in mainstream schools. Only five lived with both birth parents: four were in single parent families and four had step-parents. All lived in central or southern Scotland – three in a city, eight in towns and two in rural settings.

Findings

Important people in the children's lives

We asked the children to tell us about important people in their lives. Their comments showed that most had close, loving relationships with their parents, especially mothers. One boy gave his mum 'ten out of ten' for helping him. Asked what was his most valuable possession, he said: 'My mum and dad, my family . . . 'cos they're kind.' One girl said of her mother, 'She's the best.' Most children described their brothers and sisters as important and several mentioned members of their extended family – grandparents, aunts, uncles and cousins – who played significant roles in their lives. Several told us they were worried about a close relative who was ill, or had been upset by the death of a family member (usually a grandparent). Some named particular friends, and a couple included a teacher, as important people in their lives.

Three children seemed to have an ambivalent relationship with their parents, not including them as 'important people'. A 9-year-old girl, prompted to say something about her mother, replied, 'I'm not quite sure about my mum . . . there's not much about her.' A boy, also aged 9, who declined to take part in a second interview, said little about his father and nothing about his mother during the first interview. Asked who helped him at home, he replied, 'Nobody. My dad gives me my medicine and my dad makes the breakfast all the time.' This child's mother had experienced mental health difficulties leading to several hospital admissions: data collected from his siblings suggest the boy was very close to his mother and upset when separated from her. Perhaps it was too painful a subject to talk about.

Among the wider sample of 26 children, relationships with siblings were mostly positive: the children talked about the fun they had playing together and their appreciation of support offered. There was some conflict too, as would be expected among any brothers and sisters, with arguments about ownership of toys, uninvited incursions onto each other's territory or which television channel to watch. Looking just at the group of children with learning disabilities, it is evident that their relationships with siblings were generally more fraught. A couple of youngsters seemed to get on well with their brothers or sisters most of the time while some got on better with one sibling than another. However, the three children in the study who reported being bullied by their siblings all had learning disabilities, while two others only referred to their siblings in negative terms. One 9-year-old boy had this exchange with the interviewer about his older brother, Paul:

Child:	Bully.
Interviewer:	Oh, is he a bully?
Child:	Yes.
Interviewer:	When is he?
Child:	What?
Interviewer:	When?
Child:	Just now he's a bully.
Interviewer:	Is he? Does he bully you?
Child:	He bullies every single one, even Jane and Elspeth [older sisters] . . .
Interviewer:	And what does Paul do?
Child:	I don't know. Punch, kick, whack.
Interviewer:	Why does Paul punch you?
Child:	Because he's a bully and he likes it.

Another child described being hit by her older brother. In these cases, the siblings interviewed also described physical aggression on the part of the disabled child, and the problematic sibling relationships were confirmed by parents' accounts. However, when talking to us, the disabled children all strongly denied ever provoking their brothers or sisters!

Friends and foes

Friendships were very important to the children. Seven said they had friends locally with whom they played. Shared activities included riding bikes, building dens, shopping and going to the park. However, in four cases comments about friendships were qualified by later remarks. For example, one boy began by saying he had friends round about, but later stated he did not have many 'pals' locally. An older boy named a couple of his neighbours as friends with whom he played, but it then transpired that for some time they had refused to talk to him. In the separate interviews with siblings and parents, we learnt more about the children's experiences with other youngsters in the area. They described incidents where children had been called nasty

names, taken advantage of and, in one case, returned home with torn clothes, apparently as a result of physical aggression from other children. One girl had been the subject of particularly cruel harassment, not just by children but also by adults: this is described in more detail in a pen profile below. The children's friendships at school are also discussed later.

Activities

Between them, the children were involved in a wide range of activities, most of which were very typical pastimes for children of their age. The boys tended to like football, basketball, computers, riding bikes and swimming while the girls enjoyed drawing, dancing, drama, music and swimming. Other pastimes included going to the park, shopping, visiting relatives, and watching TV and videos. Some children attended organized activities, such as youth clubs, Brownies or Sunday School. A few proudly described holding positions of responsibility, such as being an altar server in church. One boy said he was a member of a gang which had several secret dens locally. His exploits included the following:

Child:	The best thing that happened to me during the weekend would have to be being able to climb a tree that nobody else could climb.
Interviewer:	Right, and you didn't fall out?
Child:	Yes, I fell down.
Interviewer:	At the weekend you fell out the tree?
Child:	Yes.
Interviewer:	So that was the best thing and the worst thing is it?
Child:	Yes.
Interviewer:	Oh, did you hurt yourself?
Child:	Yes.
Interviewer:	Did you?
Child:	See when I fell down it right, I was holding onto a branch then suddenly I kinda caught between bits of my arm so I fell and I didn'ae stop till I hit the bottom so it would be very painful.
Interviewer:	I'm sure it would have been.
Child:	So what do you think of that?

Interviewer: Did you tell your mum you'd hurt yourself?

Child: No. I just crawled down underneath the hedge and I went to bed.

However, a few children felt bored at times, lacking interesting occupation. One 12-year-old girl said that weekends were *not* better than school, while a 9-year-old boy, asked what he did at weekends, commented, 'We do nothing on thae days', adding that he never went out to play.

Overall, the children's accounts of the time they spent in and around home suggest lives that have much in common with any other youngsters. While there is relatively little evidence of impairment effects, there are reports of other children's hurtful and hostile behaviour upsetting these children, which may lead to what Thomas (1999) calls 'barriers to being'.

At school

Ten of the 13 children said they liked school – some were very enthusiastic about it. One boy described school as 'brilliant'; one girl, asked 'What was the worst thing about school yesterday?' replied 'Nothing'. One boy (who was not always happy at home) reported always being happy at school. Similarly, another child, who sometimes felt bored at home, commented 'There are a lot of things we can do. But when the weekend comes I think oh, no school, no school, I want to go back to school.'

All the children but one named at least one teacher whom they liked – often this was a class teacher who took the children for most of their lessons. They described teachers as kind and helpful: 'She helps me count ... help me do my maths and tell me what to do'; 'Mr Murray is ... helps me and Ross and John ... He's very important. Because he helps the school. He helps the people, helps people that's stuck on work'; 'Sometimes nice, sometimes angry at people.'

However, as discussed shortly, although these children's overall view of school was very positive, the majority reported falling out with friends or being bullied at times.

Three children were unhappy at school. Two had moved from a mainstream school, which they had liked, to a special school (in one case, a residential establishment) which they did not enjoy. One boy compared his new school unfavourably with the last one: 'I dinnae like getting transport to school ... I'd rather walk it or cycle or something ... I hate that school ... Up at [previous school] you dinnae get detention ... I dinnae like the school uniform and all ... at [previous school] we dinnae wear a school uniform.' This boy had a twin who remained at the local mainstream school: being separated from his brother, perhaps coupled with the implication that he was managing less well at school, may have added to his unhappiness – although he did not say so himself. In contrast to most of the other children, when asked to name the best thing about school, he replied 'nothing' while the worst thing was 'everything'.

The child at residential school had autism and was not very vocal. Here is an extract from the interview:

Mum: What do you do at [new school]? What's that? Happy or sad?

Child: Sad.

Mum: Does Jo like that one? What's that one?

Child: [Previous school].

Mum: [Previous school]. Is that happy or sad?

Child: Happy.

In two cases, the child's parents were also unhappy with the current school placement and were seeking an alternative.

Nine of the 13 children reported difficulties with other children at school. It was not always easy to gauge the extent of the problem, but in some cases it appeared the child had experienced a serious 'falling out' with friends. One girl, for example, reported she was sad at school: 'When my friends leave me ... my friends normally leave me.' Four children reported what appeared to be isolated incidents of bullying; they had been 'picked on', called names or 'punched'. Others had been bullied on a more continuing basis. The transcript from an interview with a 12-year-old boy suggests he did not want to discuss this topic:

Interviewer: When it's playtime, who do you play with?

Child: I kicked the football right over the fence.

Interviewer: Was that at school or at home?

Child: At home.

Interviewer:	So what about in school, who do you play with in school?
Child:	I kicked the yellow one up over the house and [the cat] went climbing up there and ran away.
Interviewer:	So that was at home too. What about in school? Who do you play with in school?
Child:	I stay in the classroom. I don't play in school.
Interviewer:	You don't go outside at playtime?
Child:	Uhu.
Interviewer:	Who stays with you in the classroom?
Child:	Miss Bryson.

Later, he reported sometimes feeling sad at school:

Interviewer:	What happens in school to make you sad?
Child:	Bully me.
Interviewer:	Who bullies you?

At this point, he changed the subject again.

Thus there is evidence of what Thomas (1999) calls psycho-emotional disablism which, in the example given above, stopped the child from playing outside during breaks (a barrier to doing) but also made him sad (possibly resulting in a barrier to being). However, the children were by no means passive victims of bullying. Although these incidents were clearly distressing, the children described how they took steps to deal with them. Some reported the matter to teachers, others to their parents who passed on the information to the school. One child, who said he had not been bullied, commented: 'No, I just bully them back ... Or if they started kicking us, I'd kick them back.' This boy had received a number of detentions for fighting. Two of the children who had been 'sent to Coventry' by their 'friends' had not told their parents about these incidents; a third had not told her mother about a recent name-calling incident. On the whole, however, the children's prompt action in dealing with bullying is worth noting, since this flies in the face of the more common perception of children with learning disabilities as helpless and lacking in agency.

Children's experiences of using services

The children were asked about any services they had used. They were shown picture cards depicting various professionals (doctor, nurse, social worker – although that was more difficult to convey pictorially) and services (hospital, short breaks unit, play scheme) and asked, for example, if they had ever been to 'a place like that' and, if so, what happened and what it was like. Apart from the comments about school and teachers reported above, the children had relatively little to say about services. This could be seen as a finding in itself, showing that the children did not frame their lives in terms of using services and/or it may be that children saw this as their parents' concern, since they themselves were not directly involved in accessing and negotiating with services. This may explain why the only service which several children talked about was their experience of being in hospital, which had a direct, immediate impact on them.

Nine children spoke – or expressed feelings – about being in hospital, including six who had unpleasant memories. Here is a 10-year-old boy talking:

Child:	Um, I must have been about 5 or 6 when I got an operation on my eye ...
Interviewer:	What was it like?
Child:	Scary at the time.
Interviewer:	Scary? What ways was it scary? Can you still remember it?
Child:	Yes.
Interviewer:	What happened? Did you go into hospital on your own?
Child:	My mum wasn't allowed to come in with me.

Interviewer:	Was she not?
Child:	Into the theatre.
Interviewer:	Into the theatre. Was she allowed to be with you in the ward?
Child:	Yes. Uh-huh.
Interviewer:	Good.
Child:	What made me scared most was, there were these tongs, they were like that with big bridges with lights on them, you know, and 'oh, oh, what are they for? What are they for?'
Interviewer:	Hmm. Hmm.
Child:	And there were things all in my mouth.
Interviewer:	Hmm hmm.
Child:	Then everybody was there.
Interviewer:	Ah ha.
Child:	Then I went 'Mum!'
Interviewer:	Hmm. So it's quite scary. Did it help?
Child:	Yeah.

None of the other children went into details about why they didn't like hospital, although one referred to being in pain and bleeding. A particularly concerning report came from a girl who said that while in hospital, a man 'had done a bad thing to her'. She went on to say that although her mother believed her, the police had not. She did not elaborate on the incident, and we did not ask her to. Three children had more cheerful accounts of being in hospital. One awarded a doctor '20 out of 10' points for helping her, while another said his hospital consultant was 'brilliant'. He enjoyed going back to the hospital because he 'was the first tiny baby born there' and all the nurses knew him.

Overall, the families in the study had little contact with social work departments and only four had an allocated social worker. Two of the children with learning disabilities commented on a social worker. One girl, asked if a social worker had ever helped her, responded, 'No, she just makes it worse.' However, further details were not forthcoming. The other described the social worker as unhelpful (see pen profile below).

Only one child had a befriender and none had an independent advocate. A few attended regular youth clubs or groups run by voluntary agencies, which they seemed to enjoy.

Exercise 8.3

Imagine you are working with a child with learning disabilities, high support needs and no speech. One weekend a month, she goes to a short breaks residential unit. How would you find out what she feels about going there?

What could be done to make things easier for children with learning disabilities going into hospital for medical treatment?

Views of self

In this section, we bring together data which throw light on how the children saw themselves and in what ways they tried to make sense of their experiences of impairment and disability.

The children were asked to complete a 'word choice' exercise which involved picking out words, from a given list, which matched 'what they were like' at school. There were 12 words in all, representing a mix of positive, negative and neutral words. The findings suggest that children generally saw themselves as good friends, helpful pupils and active participants in school life. Sometimes their responses were backed up with examples: several named their best friends while one boy, who was a 'class helper', commented, 'I do letters, helping the little ones because we have new ones in the classroom because they're only little and I'm helping them.' While most denied ever being 'naughty', several did admit to being 'dreamy' at times.

Most of the children, when asked, could name some activities they were 'good at': this ranged from achievements which had received formal recognition – one child was a member of a Junior Olympics sports team, others had trophies, medals or certificates to show off – to children describing themselves as 'good at playing' or 'good at pretending'.

However, the children could also be self-deprecating at times. When asked if there was anything they found hard, several referred to particular school subjects: 'The only thing I don't like, naw, the only thing I'm not good at is money problems and that.' Another said, 'Sometimes reading big words but I try to do them myself.' Some children had been told they were not good at something: 'They tell me my spelling and reading's no good.' Conversely, one girl did not believe the praise she had been given: 'The teacher says I am really good at maths but I don't think I am.'

Some of the most interesting findings from this study relate to how the children with physical and sensory impairments saw and understood disability. Those children were all aware of their impairments, but most took a practical and pragmatic approach, encapsulated in one boy's comment: 'That's it. I'm in a wheelchair so just get on with it. Just get on with what you're doing.' These children also identified a number of disabling barriers, such as inaccessible buildings and transport and ineffective inclusion policies. They were sometimes made to feel aware of their difference in a negative way by other people's insensitive, hurtful or hostile comments or behaviour. When such incidents occurred, they knew that they were connected to other people's response to them as a person with an impairment.

Matters were rather different for the children with learning disabilities. They made fewer references to their impairment. Only one child referred to her diagnosis. She had written a piece about herself for the researcher, with whom she had this exchange as they read it together:

Interviewer: What's that? My name is . . .
Child: Jenny Hoskin. I have X syndrome.
Interviewer: Right. Tell me what X syndrome is.
Child: Em . . . eh . . . what is it again?
Interviewer: How does it make you feel?
Child: Different.

It is not clear how far the other children were aware of having a learning disability. Certainly there was evidence that some were aware of being treated differently by those around them, and subject to different interventions or policies from, say, their siblings. One boy, talking about his friend, said:

Child: He's the last to get dropped off the bus because he's in a . . . he's like me too.
Interviewer: Like you?
Child: In the special class.

This child's mother reported that he had once asked her what he had 'done wrong' to be placed in a special class. This question points to a lack of clear information and explanation given to the child, but also suggests that he had come to associate difference with badness. This in turn indicates that he had not been given positive messages about diversity.

The children were asked what they would be doing when they were the same age as their parents. Overall, they had very similar aspirations to any other children of their age. One boy wanted to be in the army, another wanted to be a builder and a third, a fireman ('go to fires and save people'). One girl wanted to be a singer and dancer, another a vet or nurse. Two said they would not need any help to achieve their ambitions.

The children's hopeful yet 'ordinary' aspirations might be seen as a good thing except for the fact that, whether through impairment effects, disabling barriers or a mixture of the two, we may not be optimistic about how many will go on to achieve their ambitions. There were indications that a couple of children with physical/sensory impairment believed they would outgrow their impairment. The mother of a deaf child, for example, told us she had recently discovered that her son thought that he would be able to hear when he grew up. We do not know if any of those with learning disabilities thought they would outgrow their impairment. Alternatively, research with adults with learning disabilities suggests that while some individuals are aware of those around them having a learning disability label, they may choose to distance themselves from that label, being aware of the perceived stigma (Finlay and Lyons 1998). We do not know how common this is, nor at what age the distancing process begins. Alternatively, the children's views of the future may have been shaped by the combination of (in most cases) their relatively young age and a lack of awareness of impairment effects.

The following section presents pen profiles of two children. They are not intended to be 'representative' of the wider sample but to illustrate the richness of children's lives. This girl was very articulate; thus, there is more 'meat' in her story than in some others.

Pen profile: *Jenny Hoskin*

Jenny, aged 13, lived with her single mother in a Scottish city. She had no contact with her father. Jenny attended a special school.

Jenny had experienced a high level of change and disruption in her life. She had previously lived in England, where she had been subjected to some cruel treatment by other children: 'When I lived in London, nine children between the ages of 7 and 13 stood me by the garage wall and stoned me.' Jenny had drawn a picture of this incident for the researcher. She went on: 'We moved to Scotland when I was 5. First, I went to Highfield, and I got spat on and urine and, is it shit, and called a 'spazzy' . . . and my swing set got slashed and then we went to Monument Street . . . then it got worse when I lived there. Then I went to my uncle's . . . then my gran's, then my uncle's again . . .'

Jenny recounted how she and her mother eventually ended up in homeless accommodation, as well as being placed in a succession of local authority housing. This included one house where: 'We were not there three months when the man next door came to our door and rattled the letter-box and shouted "come out you cows or I will get you". So we called the police and then they did not believe us because I was a special needs.' She had drawn a picture of this frightening incident as well.

Jenny had a number of important people in her life. Her mum came first – 'Who else?' – followed by a friend and various members of her extended family who lived locally. It was sometimes Jenny and sometimes her mother who made decisions about different day-to-day aspects of Jenny's life. Sometimes they disagreed, for example about what Jenny should wear to school. She had a wide range of interests: apart from her sporting achievements, which were clearly exceptional, Jenny enjoyed going shopping, watching videos and listening to music.

Jenny said that school was 'okay': there were six children in her class. She had various friends there and enjoyed playtime most. Jenny had had a boyfriend at school – she was the only young person to mention having a boy- or girlfriend – but was no longer talking to him because he had started going out with someone else. Although she had friends at school, Jenny reported having no friends to play with locally. She did have a befriender, who was clearly an important figure, and had taken Jenny to see her favourite pop group. Jenny was also aware of a social worker coming to the house but this person had made little impact on her:

Interviewer:	Do you know why you saw the social worker?
Jenny:	No.
Interviewer:	No? When she came, what did she talk to you about?
Jenny:	She spoke to my mum usually.
Interviewer:	So she didn't come to see you. If you were going to give the social worker a mark out of ten for how helpful she was, what mark would you give her?
Jenny:	One.
Interviewer:	One? Why was that?
Jenny:	Because she doesn't – she is always on sick leave and that.

Jenny's ambitions for the future were to tour the world with her favourite pop group and be a swimming teacher.

Pen profile: *Colin Baxter*

Colin was an 11-year-old boy who lived in a Scottish town with his parents, brother and sister. He attended an integrated unit. Colin referred several times to his extended family – grandparents, aunts and uncles – but did not choose to include his parents as 'important people'. He did, however, describe good relationships with his siblings. He said he got on with his younger brother 'when we help each other . . . sometimes in the mornings getting ready', and with his sister, 'when we play and sometimes we have wee chats about what it's like to get a bit bigger.'

Colin had several friends living locally. He had a particular friend of whom he said, 'He's so kind, helps people and, eh, we play games.' Colin had been befriended by a teenage boy who, his mother explained, was helping Colin become accepted within the community because 'a lot of people were picking on him'.

Colin identified a number of things he was good at. He said he was 'too good' at drawing and was also proficient at swimming, typing and woodwork: 'I'm good at craft things like putting two nails into a piece of wood to put it together.' He also proudly told us that he was responsible for helping look after the family dogs, taking them for walks with his mother: 'I make sure they're fed and I check their legs and make sure they're alright.'

There were some things that Colin found less easy. He described French as 'hard and strange' and said that it was difficult 'trying to understand about things that you've no' seen and you've no' heard'. Colin had an awareness but, it seems, limited understanding of being 'different' from other children. He was the child, mentioned above, who asked his mother if he was attending an integrated unit because he had done something wrong.

At the same time, however, Colin was very enthusiastic about school. He gave an engaging account of a typical school day. He began by describing who was on the school bus:

> A lot of big people, a lot of big people, and there's a driver and it's got seatbelts on the bus. There's an escort and she opens the door and she lets us in. And then we're going to pick everyone up and we go to the school and when the bell goes we go in, then the bus goes away, then we're just sitting in the desk . . . then we do our work, like hard work, hard work . . . counting all the sums up and it's hard work . . . Then, we come home and the escort says 'Have a good afternoon' and I come home and the dog jumps on me and I say, 'I see, I see you.' Then I get my jammies on and we watch telly and we go to our beds.

Colin had some intense friendships with other boys and took relationships with his peers very seriously. He was willing to go far to help one boy stay on track: 'He's a wee troublemaker. I watch what he's doing because he gets into big bother and I get him out of it. When we're speaking I'll say "Martin, if you're going to be like that, I want you to go out and have a wee walk and take two deep breaths and you'll be alright".'

Colin had been 'picked on' at school by one particular boy. Although he had reported this to his teacher, who had apparently reprimanded the culprit, Colin described it as an ongoing problem. However, he was not averse to taking the law into his own hands: 'One person bullied me once . . . in school and my old school and that was Tracey but I got her back. In the girls' toilets I got her back.'

Colin had great ambitions for the future: 'I'd like to be a film expert and art too because I'm into art and film.'

Exercise 8.4

Note down your responses to these two pen profiles – does anything in them surprise you? Compare notes with a fellow student or in a small group. Discuss how far and in what ways children with learning disabilities are like any other children, and in what ways they might be seen as different.

Conclusion

This study demonstrates that many children with learning disabilities are able to give narrative accounts of their everyday lives which are interesting and useful, often engaging, sometimes insightful. Some young people are very articulate and will happily talk at length; others need prompting and encouragement; some will benefit from, or require, alternative forms of communication. Practitioners should assume that every child can communicate and, at the least, can express likes, dislikes and preferences. It is no longer acceptable to avoid seeking a child's views on the grounds that she or he does not have an opinion or cannot communicate it. Indeed, there is a raft of legislative and policy initiatives across the UK which requires authorities to promote children's participation.

The findings show that in many ways these children had ordinary lives and much in common with their non-disabled peers. In most respects, they were similar to any other youngsters, underlining the importance of practitioners approaching all children as children first and foremost.

At the same time, it is important to be aware of areas where difficulties may arise. The findings suggest that relationships with brothers and sisters were mixed. As well as giving children with learning disabilities a chance to talk about their feelings towards siblings, practitioners can offer support to brothers and sisters, which may help reduce conflict. Tozer (1996) argues that attention to siblings' needs should begin at the point of birth or diagnosis: they should be given clear age-appropriate information about the disabled child's impairment, with ongoing opportunities to ask questions and discuss any concerns. They can be offered support through one-to-one counselling if required, or simply space and time to enjoy themselves through siblings' groups or other activities.

Some of the children said they were bored at weekends and in school holidays. Other research has shown a paucity of social and leisure activities for disabled children (Murray 2002). Practitioners can help by encouraging local play groups and youth clubs to become more inclusive, by recruiting befrienders and by encouraging families to apply for direct payments from the local authority, whereby they may be able to purchase one-to-one support for their child to access leisure activities.

Most children made no direct reference to their impairment. Nevertheless, their accounts include some experiences which may reflect impairment effects, notably difficulty with schoolwork. The children in the study who had physical or sensory impairment were brought up against difference through – among other things – inaccessible buildings or transport. These 'barriers to doing' were less evident to those with learning disabilities in this study, with most having positive aspirations for their future. It was the hurtful or hostile reactions of other people which upset them most.

Some of the disabled children had been ignored or taunted by 'friends' or experienced difficulties with other children at school, ranging from 'being sent to Coventry' to fairly relentless bullying. Although all schools nowadays have anti-bullying strategies, the children's accounts, supported by findings from other studies (Watson et al. 2000; Mencap 2007), show that these policies need to be regularly monitored and reviewed. The problem has been recognized at national level, with the Department for Children, Schools and Families (2009) writing to head teachers and school governing bodies urging them to take practical steps to tackle the bullying and exclusion of children with 'special educational needs'. Practitioners in all agencies working with children need to be alert to signs of bullying and act quickly to stop it.

One young girl reported having been abused but said the police had not believed her. Large-scale research in the US has shown that disabled children are 3.4 times more likely than non-disabled young people to be abused (Sullivan and Knutson 2000), yet there is evidence that adults do not always take disabled children's reports of abuse seriously (Hershkowitz et al. 2007). Therefore it is of paramount importance that practitioners are aware of the risks and how to deal with them (see information about Triangle in 'Resources' section below). Worryingly, Cooke and Standen (2002) found that, in the UK, child protection cases involving disabled children are less likely to receive care plans or be placed on child protection registers.

The children had relatively little to say about formal services other than hospitals. The findings underline the need for medical staff to be aware that children with learning disabilities experience the same range of feelings as any others and are likely to feel anxious, and perhaps frightened, when admitted to hospital, especially if this involves separation from parents. Children should be given information and explanations about medical procedures in a format appropriate to their age, ability and, perhaps, desire to hear (see Coad 2007 for good practice suggestions regarding disabled children in hospital).

As only a couple of the children commented on their social workers, it would be wrong to draw conclusions from what they said. Research elsewhere has shown the beneficial effects of having a dedicated key worker, with an advocacy and co-ordinating role, who spends time building up a relationship with all family members (Stalker *et al.* 2008).

Other research has found that young disabled people value exchanging information and support with young people of similar age who have the same condition, in informal social settings (Beresford and Sloper 2000). If this were to work for those with learning disabilities, they would need good support from a skilled facilitator: voluntary organizations could play an important role here. Organizations of people with learning disabilities also have huge potential, albeit limited resources, to offer positive adult role models to children with learning disabilities. Along with schools and local authorities, they could support children to participate in self-advocacy groups and learn about their right to speak up for themselves. Young disabled people's peer mentoring projects are already having some success in this area (Bethel and Harrison 2003). Given adequate funding, such organizations would be ideally placed to deliver disability awareness and inclusion training to staff at all levels in schools, public authorities and voluntary agencies.

Further reading

Abbott, D. and Carpenter, J. (forthcoming) *Transition to Adulthood for Young Men with Duchenne Muscular Dystrophy and their Families*. London: Muscular Dystrophy Society.

Ali, Z., Qulsom, F., Bywaters, P., Wallace, L. and Singh, G. (2001) Disability, ethnicity and childhood: a critical review of research, *Disability & Society*, 16(7): 949–68.

Department of Health (2009) *Valuing People Now: A New 3-year Strategy for People with Learning Disabilities*. This identifies three key areas for work with children – access and empowerment, responsive services and timely support, and improving quality and capacity.

Morris, J. (1998) *Don't Leave Us Out: Involving Disabled Children and Young People with Communication Impairments*. York: Joseph Rowntree Foundation.

Scottish Executive: The same as you? National Implementation Group (2006) *Changing Childhoods: Report of the Children's Sub-Group*. Edinburgh: Scottish Executive. Also available on www.scotland.gov.uk. This sets out ways of improving services and support to children and young people.

Resources

www.bris.ac.uk/Depts/NorahFry. The Norah Fry Research Centre, University of Bristol: for summaries of research projects and information about current research on disabled children and their families.

www.cafamily.org.uk. Contact-a-Family: for information on support networks, a database of specific conditions and rare disorders, publications and a helpline.

www.familyfund.org.uk. The Family Fund: for information, publications and research. The Fund gives grants to families with 'severely disabled' children.

www.jrf.org.uk. The Joseph Rowntree Foundation: for summaries of research projects, and information on current research about disabled children and their families.

www.ncb.org.uk. Council for Disabled Children: for details of projects, a parent partnership network, early support pilot programmes, events and publications.

www.triangle-services.co.uk. Triangle: an independent organization promoting good practice in communication, inclusion and child protection for disabled children and young people. The website outlines training and consultancy available to professionals throughout the UK, and some outreach work with families; also provides details of publications and other relevant organizations.

References

Barnes, C. (1991) *Disabled People in Britain and Discrimination: A Case for Anti-Discrimination Legislation*. London: Hurst/BCODP.

Beresford, B. and Sloper, P. (2000) *The Information Needs of Chronically Ill or Physically Disabled Children and Adolescents*. York: Social Policy Research Unit, University of York.

Bethel, J. and Harrison, M. (2003) *'Our life! Our say!' A Good Practice Guide to Young Disabled People's Peer Mentoring/ Support*. Brighton: Pavilion Publishing.

Booth, T. (1996) Sounds of still voices: issues in the use of narrative methods with people who have learning difficulties, in L. Barton (ed.) *Disability and Society: Emerging Issues and Insights*. Harlow: Longman.

Booth, T. and Booth, W. (1994) *Parenting Under Pressure: Mothers and Fathers with Learning Difficulties*. Buckingham: Open University Press.

Coad, J. (2007) *Voices of Children and Young People*. Action for Sick Children.

Connors, C. and Stalker, K. (2003) *The Views and Experiences of Disabled Children: A Positive Outlook*. London: Jessica Kingsley.

Connors, C. and Stalker, K. (2007) Children's experiences of disability: pointers to a social model of childhood disability, *Disability & Society*, 22(1): 19–33.

Cooke, P. and Standen, P.J. (2002) Abuse and disabled children: hidden needs? *Child Abuse Review*, 11(1): 1–18.

Department for Children, Schools and Families (2009) *Letter to all Head Teachers and Chairs of Governing Boards at Schools in England*, 22 January, http://www.teachernet. gov.uk/_doc/13246/Letter%20to%20schools.pdf (accessed 16 June 2009).

Finlay, M. and Lyons, E. (1998) Social identity and people with learning difficulties: implications for self-advocacy groups, *Disability & Society*, 13(1): 37–52.

Hershkowitz, I., Lamb, M.E. and Horowitz, D. (2007) Victimization of children with disabilities, *American Journal of Orthopsychiatry*, 77(4): 629–35.

Hirst, M. and Baldwin, S. (1994) *Unequal Opportunities: Growing Up Disabled*. London: HMSO.

James, A., Jenks, C. and Prout, A. (1998) *Theorising Childhood*. Cambridge: Polity Press.

Lewis, A., Parson, S. and Robertson, C. (2006) *My School, My Family, My Life: Telling It Like It Is*. Disability Rights Commission, http://83.137.212.42/sitearchive/DRC/ about_us/drc_wales/newsroom/events/my_school__my_ family__my_life.html (accessed 16 June 2009).

Mayall, B. (2002) *Towards a Sociology for Childhood: Thinking from Children's Lives*. Buckingham: Open University Press.

Mencap (2007) *Bullying Wrecks Lives: The Experiences of Children and Young People with a Learning Disability*, www.mencap.org.uk (accessed 16 June 2009).

Murray, P. (2002) *Disabled Teenagers' Experiences of Access to Inclusive Leisure, Findings 712*. York: Joseph Rowntree Foundation.

Oliver, M. (1990) *The Politics of Disablement*. London: Macmillan.

Priestley, M. (2003) *Disability: A Life Course Approach*. Cambridge: Polity Press.

Shakespeare, T. (2006) *Disability Rights and Wrongs*. London: Routledge.

Shakespeare, T. and Watson, N. (2002) The social model of disability: an outdated ideology? in S. Barnarrt and B.M. Altman (eds) *Exploring Theories and Expanding Methodologies: Where Are We and Where Do We Need to Go?* Research in Social Sciences and Disability, Vol. 2. Amsterdam: JAI.

Singh, V. and Ghai, A. (2009) Notions of self: lived realities of children with disabilities, *Disability & Society*, 24(2): 129–45.

Stalker, K., Malloch, M., Barry, M. and Watson, J. (2008) Local area co-ordination: strengthening support to people with learning disabilities in Scotland, *British Journal of Learning Disabilities*, 36(4): 215–19.

Sullivan, P.M. and Knutson, J.F. (2000) 'Maltreatment and disabilities: a population-based epidemiological study', *Child Abuse & Neglect*, 24(10): 1257–73.

Tozer, R. (1996) My brother's keeper? Sustaining sibling support, *Health and Social Care in the Community*, 4(3): 177–81.

Thomas, C. (1999) *Female Forms: Experiencing and Understanding Disability*. Buckingham: Open University Press.

Thomas, C. (2004) 'Disability and impairment', in J. Swain, S. French, C. Barnes and C. Thomas (eds) *Disabling Barriers, Enabling Environments*, 2nd edn. London: Sage.

Watson, N., Shakespeare, T., Cunningham-Burley, S., Barnes, C., Corker, M., Davis, J. et al. (2000) *Life as a Disabled Child: A Qualitative Study of Young People's Experiences and Perspectives*. Final report to the ESRC Research Programme '5–16: growing into the twenty-first century', http:// www.leeds.ac.uk/disability-studies/projects/children.htm (accessed 16 June 2009).

Communication with children and young people

Lesley Cogher

9

Introduction

In trying to understand how people with a range of learning disabilities experience communication, it is useful to define the characteristics of communication. The following working definition is suggested: 'Communication occurs when two or more people correctly interpret each other's language and/or behaviour.'

There are many possible definitions of communication but the following characterization has been developed from a number of writers on language and communication such as Grice (1975), Chomsky (1976) and Miller (1981). Critical features of communication are that:

- *it is at least two-way* (two or more people are always involved in a communicative act, sometimes directly, sometimes indirectly, over the telephone or through the written word);
- *it may be verbal or non-verbal* (behaviour that may have a meaning for someone is common; for example, yawning may indicate that someone is bored; however, to be communicative, a behaviour has to be intentional);
- *it may not always be successful* (either party to the communication might need to work hard to repair misunderstandings or misinterpretations);
- *interpretation is needed* (successful communication involves a shared code or culture; the code need not be spoken language, it can be mimes, signs or gestures, pictures or writing).

The above list highlights the social and cultural context in which communication occurs. Each of us brings knowledge of our world and our experience in social situations to bear on our understanding of other people and what they might mean by what they say. Our knowledge of the world may be similar to a degree if we have been raised in a similar way, for example attended the same school, lived in the same

area or watched the same programmes on television. It will never be *exactly* the same because of our own unique experiences in our family groups. So, if a person with learning disabilities went to a special school and lived in sheltered housing, their knowledge of the world would differ from that of their communication partners who may have gone to mainstream schools or even university, and each of these would differ from those who had travelled on a gap year. How would these differences affect the content and quality of the communication interactions that might occur between these groups of people?

In this chapter I will describe the underlying skills required for communication to develop, the overall sequence of communication development, what can go wrong with communication, the effect that communication breakdown can have on potential interactions and the role of communication partners.

Communication skills

By the time we reach adulthood, our communication skills have largely been acquired. Infancy and childhood are therefore critical periods in which to acquire, practise and develop the skills of communicating.

The skills required for communication to develop, for the purposes of explanation, can be split into individual skills, although all skills work in interaction with each other during communication. This can be seen in the language skills model (see Figure 9.1). The left-hand side of the figure shows the skills and opportunities that are required for communication to develop.

Input

Opportunity to hear language

It is possible to gain much language experience from listening to the conversations of others, if meanings are made clear by the context (e.g. at the dinner table

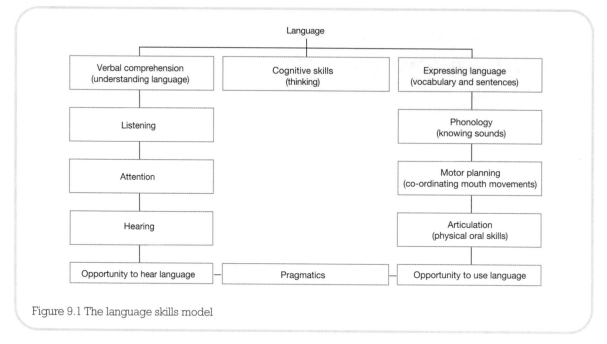

Figure 9.1 The language skills model

or when dressing). Background language forms a large part of a young child's experience and is as important to them as direct conversation.

However, some language learners may not have the opportunity to hear good-quality language from which they can learn. If students have limited mobility and cannot move towards the source of their interest or if their fellow students or those with whom they have most interaction do not use language, their opportunities may be severely reduced.

Hearing

Clearly the language learner also needs the ability to hear and it is quite clear what limitations hearing impairment puts on the development of speech and language (see Chapter 12).

Attention and listening

It is not enough just to hear sounds and language. There has to be an intention to interpret what is said, and we call this listening. Listening can be defined as hearing with the purpose of understanding. Language development can be vulnerable where the person has difficulty in giving attention to the language in their environment, such as people with concentration problems as part of their learning difficulties.

Language processing

The next stages of language ability include both input (understanding of language) and output (expression of language) as well as a central processing component. In order to understand what is being said it is necessary to:

- extract the meaning from words and the sentences used (language comprehension);
- process what is understood by comparing with experience and developing a response (thinking);
- generate the appropriate vocabulary and sentence structures to convey this meaning back to the communication partner (expressive language).

Language output

There are several stages to language output. Having decided which words and sentence structures will best represent what the speaker wants to say, further planning is required, involving:

- linguistic rules which refer to style of pronunciation, intonation and stress patterns;
- motor planning, the organization and sequencing of appropriate mouth movements;
- the ability to move the mouth in a co-ordinated way in order to produce speech sounds;

- the opportunity to use the speech and language in an interactive way.

It should be noted that output can be via oral speech, signs, pointing to pictures, use of objects of reference, writing, the use of a talking book, or even a high-tech communication aid, but all of these require some sort of motor planning and output ability, from the complex physical act of writing to pressing a switch to activate a synthesized or digitized speech machine.

Exercise 9.1

Imagine a person was unable to speak. In what ways might they make themselves understood?

Pragmatic competence

The final central box in Figure 9.1 is labelled 'pragmatics', which refers to the use of language in social situations. In order to do this successfully the communicator needs to understand which of a range of social styles to use in a given situation. For example, it would not be appropriate for a child to refer to his teacher as 'mate' or for a football supporter to be formal in interaction with others on the terraces. Most adults know when swearing is inappropriate and in which circumstances it can be tolerated, but this is learned behaviour and relies on subtle interpretation of social clues and rules, memory and awareness of social timing.

Pragmatics, then, is knowledge about linguistic communication and includes recognition of the social uses of language and the importance of context in making speaking and listening choices. As children become skilled language users they interact with a variety of speakers and gain access to differing patterns of input. They engage in disputes with their peers, report on their activities, ask questions and generally experiment with language acquisition.

For a person with learning difficulties, the complex interaction of all the above communication skills may make effective communication one of the more vulnerable areas of their lives.

Development of communication

The detailed developmental sequence of speech and language in babies and children is well documented (e.g. Sheridan 1973). In typically developing people, the bulk of language competence is learned by age 6, with further refinement of vocabulary and sophistication of sentence structure continuing to develop throughout their lives. For people with learning difficulties, the pace of language and communication development may sometimes be significantly slower, such that there appears to be very little intentional communication. It will be useful therefore to outline some of the key developmental stages of communication.

Infants usually start to say their first words around 1 year old and put two words together at 18 months old. If a child has not started to talk by the time he or she is 2 there is usually concern on the part of parents and health visitors. However, other stages of language development may be less well understood. When, for example, do children understand the prepositions 'in', 'on' and 'under'? When can they use pronouns like 'he' and 'she' correctly? When do they learn the difference between 'ask' and 'tell'?

In a sense, these milestones are quite unimportant. When we meet a new person, particularly a person who may have learning difficulties, we are not assessing whether or not they understand pronouns, we are engaged in the business of communication with them and the most important question that we ask is, 'What is the person intending to communicate?', and when we interpret their intention this gives us clues towards their meaning. So it is important to look at the development of language, speech and communication skills in the context of the main task of the communicator, which is to 'learn how to mean'.

The infant and young child – learning to talk

Early meaning

Children must develop basic communication skills before they can be expected to use language for the purpose of communicating. This prelinguistic development starts at birth.

Early experience of the human voice in pleasurable situations helps the baby to attune to language. Baby games and songs help the infant to learn rhythm and anticipation of events that become associated with language. Understanding develops in close reciprocity with expression.

Joint attention

For communication to take place, the participants must be able to share a 'frame of reference'. In the early stages of language development babies and children establish reference by looking and/or pointing and/or sound-making. In babies and very young children the communication partner tends to follow the child's attentional lead and interpret meaning in their behaviour accordingly. This ability of people to share attention on an object or activity is central to successful communication and is known as 'joint attention'. As the baby becomes older, the communication partner can increasingly draw the child's attention to something instead of just following the child's attentional lead, and the balance gradually shifts so that subsequently attention can be shared on more equal terms. At around 9 months, the baby can look at an object, towards his or her mother and back to the object to indicate interest.

Children of around 4 to 5 years of age can co-operate for short periods of time in attending entirely to an adult-directed task.

Evidence that the communicator is trying to get a specific message across is gained from eye contact, eye direction and body language, as well as speech. For a person with learning disabilities it may be necessary to increase the parent's or carer's awareness of where the communicator's interest is directed. They also develop the ability to recognize reference by watching eye direction or by pointing.

Participation

Early language is learnt through verbal routines in familiar situations. The baby comes to anticipate and expect events to follow the build-up (e.g. dinner arrives after clattering of plates, cooking smells and preparation of the table).

In contexts such as these, a person with learning difficulties begins to expect certain language strings (e.g. 'dinner's ready', 'wash your hands' or 'sit down'). Having learnt this framework he or she can begin to recognize word boundaries when other situations arise (e.g. 'it's bedtime', 'wash your face'

and 'lie down') (Bruner 1975). This sort of social and environmental scaffolding for language development is vital but should not preclude choice-making on the communicator's part.

Intention

Perhaps the most powerful factor in the development of communication is the interpretation of intent even if, as in the very young baby, the intent does not exist. Interpretation allows the interaction to be spontaneous and child-led and teaches turn-taking, contingency (i.e. the consequences of behaviour – children learning communication skills learn that their vocalizations have an effect on their environment, e.g. the child says 'more' and gets more food), timing and joint attention, as well as specific verbal and non-verbal representations of the world. Understanding and expressive language can develop in a social context as the baby learns that certain behaviours lead to a predictable outcome. This helps to bring the behaviour under voluntary control.

Interaction with a baby often involves exaggerated facial expression and seemingly bizarre vocal pitch changes which hold the baby's attention and maximize learning. Stern (1977) called these adult behaviours 'infant-elicited social behaviours'. With the development of the smile and its potent effect on adult behaviour, opportunities arise for the baby to learn such communicative prerequisites as turn-taking and cause and effect. The baby also learns about initiating, responding to and maintaining social interaction in that, with the smile, he or she signals a readiness to interact, then that the interaction is going well and, in the event of a breakdown, a desire to re-engage in the interaction.

Early characteristics contributing to communication

Most babies are predisposed to look at faces (Fantz 1966), their principal interest being in the eyes and mouth. This predisposition helps the baby to learn that important messages are sent by the face and not just by using eye contact. Also, the infant can attract and hold the attention of adults. Joint attention and reference have their roots in the early months when parents watch the direction of the baby's eyes and reinforce the interest by moving the object closer and/or talking about it. Eye contact and eye pointing become meaningful and communicative.

Language learning

The young infant does not co-operate with any of his or her carers' requests or demands at this stage. However, from 3 months up to 4–5 years, there is a gradual shift towards a more equal balance of turn-taking and co-operation, listening and talking. Many parents intuitively provide the child, during daily activities, with language he or she can for the most part understand, with new elements introduced gradually, basing their language on knowledge of the child's current vocabulary. The child therefore receives understandable language input in an environment where he or she is able to make more sense of new vocabulary.

Much of the child's language is learnt actively through play and daily activities. The child learns not only the names of objects but also actions (e.g. run, clap, eat); positions (e.g. in, on, under); and qualities (e.g. big, red, long). In facilitating language it is important to include all types of words and resist the temptation to restrict language to labels. The child's language acquisition will be helped if he or she has experience of as many activities as possible and these activities are discussed in terms of past, present and future, positive and negative. Understanding is an active process usually learnt in the context of expressive physical interaction with the environment – talking, showing, looking and so on. A person with learning disabilities may have limited opportunities in this regard.

Communication in the school-age child

The school-age child is expected to be able to communicate fully and to use language to interact with family, peers, teachers and others. As well as verbal development, the school-age child should have grasped many of the rules of social interaction, for example acceptable strategies for initiating, maintaining and terminating conversations. Language and communication skills are also used in a child's social life outside school, in play sessions with other children and in organized activities such as Cubs or Brownies.

A child with learning disabilities may have a limited range of social opportunities and may also have to rely on alternative methods of communication such as Makaton signing or a symbol system to augment their communication. They may only participate to a small extent in the rough and tumble of primary-age children communicating. This is exacerbated in situations of segregation where, for example, the child attends a special school.

Communication in young people and adults

Raffaelli and Duckett (1989) suggest that, in adolescence, conversation becomes the major medium of social interaction rather than the shared activities typical of the younger child. Moreover, in adolescence and adulthood friendship is often negotiated by just talking. Adolescents are able to think more abstractly and this is reflected in the language that they use.

In young people there is continuing development of vocabulary and language structure skills towards those of an adult, but there will be a significant use of slang and the dialect of the adolescent. This is also the time when the younger person tends to move away from the intensity of family relationships and seek out an identity within his or her peer group. Attendance at a special school can be isolating because school friends are unlikely to live nearby. However, this broadening of relationships does not necessarily mean that relationships are benign or fulfilling. Bullying and abuse can of course occur (see Chapter 16).

By adolescence, children have mastered the basic skills of language learning and have started to achieve goals in producing and understanding narratives and complex sentences. They are able to make inferences and do some critical thinking. Their sentences are longer, with more subordinate clauses, and show an increase in technical terms. They learn to manipulate meanings through understanding the multiple meanings of words, and they start to understand language that has a figurative rather than literal function. They are much more able to make coherent jokes and use metaphors, proverbs and idioms correctly. They pick up and use slang as part of their social group, and this is important for peer acceptance.

As an adult the development of language and communication skills seems to be inextricably bound up with achieving personal autonomy and independence.

From 18 years we expect people to vote, be able to drink in pubs and make most major life decisions. However, young people with learning disabilities have often not been able to achieve such independence, and it may therefore be hard for them to establish an adult role in the community and access adult decision-making. Work opportunities often depend on an ability to communicate effectively in a number of settings, from requesting more work materials to commenting on the food in the cafeteria, and an environmental analysis may be necessary to develop a comprehensive list of possible communication situations and partners. By environmental analysis I mean a review of all the possible communication partners in a person's life and a breakdown of their opportunities for communication. The importance of this point is illustrated by findings from a study of supported employment that shows that people with learning disabilities can often find themselves working by themselves, and that social inclusion in the workplace is yet to be claimed (Wistow and Schneider 2003).

In order to consider this further the next section will focus on the tasks of the communicator and the tasks of the communication partners in communication.

> ### Exercise 9.2
>
> Think of a person with learning disabilities that you know. How would he or she communicate: in a work setting; in a social situation with friends; at home?
>
> What are the issues for this person?

Communication tasks

In any communication there are parties whose roles vary throughout the interaction.

The tasks of the communicator

In order to be effective the communicator must show intention to communicate. So what are the indicators of intentional communication? Evidence that:

- the communicator is trying to get a partner's attention;

- the communicator is trying to get a specific message across;
- the communicator is clearly waiting for a response; and
- if no response is forthcoming, further attempts will be made through repetition or showing displeasure.

The communicator must also intend to make sense of the communication attempts of their communication partners.

The tasks of the communication partner

The range of a person's potential communication partners will vary during the course of their life, and the main task of the communication partner is to intend to make sense of the interaction.

Communication partners need not be just one person. Communicators could be having a conversation with one other person, taking regular turns, interrupting or being interrupted, or could be having a night out in a small group with people chatting freely and simultaneously with someone occasionally holding the floor. Alternatively, the communicator could be at a lecture or gathering of a larger group, either as part of the audience or indeed the speaker. These, and many more possible scenarios, need to be taken into consideration when evaluating what a person's communication needs might be in any given situation. Consideration of the type and number of communication partners will determine the type of communication that needs to take place if it is to be successful. What does the communication partner need to do which helps the communication?

- expect the communicator to want to communicate and look for active signals;
- apply active understanding (i.e. rich interpretation of what the communicator may be trying to convey);
- reframe the communication in his or her own words to show understanding, requesting clarification or physical clues such as pointing if the message is not understood;
- be aware that the communicator may need time to get their message across, and be receptive to potential communication;
- respond in a timely and appropriate manner;

- be consistent in responding to the same behaviour or sound in the same way.

Activities that do not help the success of interactions include the following:

- distracting the communicator to a new activity or issue;
- ignoring;
- making an unrelated response;
- interrupting;
- not giving time to complete the utterance;
- breaking off to talk to another;
- being too helpful in talking for the communicator.

What can go wrong with communication?

Age-related difficulties

In this section I consider developmental stages once again, drawing attention to some of the more specific communication challenges facing people with learning disabilities.

Across the age range many difficulties can occur, and it is also important to note that early experience of communication failure can influence future development into adulthood.

Babyhood

The baby's sounds and gestures encourage interaction from adults, and evidence that the baby can understand, such as waving 'bye bye' or clapping along to a song, leads adults to expect and try to elicit yet more. The baby with learning difficulties may be slow to respond to these initiatives and this may result in extinction of the adults' positive communication behaviour.

Speech output skills can be affected as babies with learning difficulties may have low muscle tone (see Chapter 12). This can result in a difficulty in producing babble sounds which contain consonants, and they may lack experience in producing sounds, thus affecting their acquisition of a phonological system. Disordered oral sensation may also occur and be compounded by the lack of experience of mouthing toys if the baby has been late to do so. Using speech in a communicative act requires accuracy and timing, skills usually learnt in the baby stage through babble, imitation and interactive games.

Babies also use body posture, gaze and facial expression to augment their speech attempts. A baby with learning disabilities whose intention to communicate is hampered by physical or cognitive impairment may experience frustration.

Illness in the early months can disrupt the balance of early interactions with parents, as described in the section on communication development in young children. The sick baby may not be available for social interaction; the anxiety of the parents may jeopardize the interaction; and the disclosure of a diagnosis which suggests learning disabilities in the future may also throw the development of interaction off-balance.

Preschool

It is central for the preschool experience of all children to learn to interact with a variety of other children. Communication skills provide the primary means of controlling the social environment – friends, siblings, classmates, parents, caregivers, relatives and teachers – but simply placing children with disabilities in the same educational environment as preschool children without disabilities does not automatically facilitate high-quality social interactions.

Children need early socialization experiences in order to build up a variety of language functions. Breakdowns occur when one participant in the communicative interaction fails to respond to a partner's utterance requiring a response. For example, if a child says, 'Do you want to play ball?' to a friend and the friend fails to say anything, a breakdown has occurred. Communicative breakdowns may be attributable to sensory impairment, memory deficit, or delayed or disordered aspects of language. Repairs of communicative behaviour tend to rest with the more sophisticated communication partner but research has shown that children with specific difficulties with language tend not to request clarification if they do not understand (Donahue *et al.* 1982).

Children with expressive speech problems who find it difficult to be understood may become aware of their failure to communicate and may become reticent to speak or may rely on simple predictable context-based language structures.

Primary school

Research suggests that children between the ages of 2 and 7 engage in verbal interaction between one-third and two-thirds of the time spent in free play (Goldstein and Kaczmarek 1992). Mueller (1972) reported an average of 3.3 utterances per minute per child, with a suggestion that children adapt the frequency of their contribution to that of their partners (Kohn 1966). However, Beckman (1983) found that children without disabilities interact more frequently with other children without disabilities than they do with children with disabilities in integrated settings.

Guralnick and Paul-Brown (1986) have shown that children without disabilities reduce the level of their language in accordance with the developmental sophistication of their playmates with disabilities. This works to the advantage of children with disabilities but may overall give them fewer communicative experiences (Goldstein and Kaczmarek 1992). Nuccio and Abbeduto (1993) found that school-age children with mild-to-moderate learning difficulties tended to use what would be regarded as impolite non-interrogative (demanding) forms when requesting an object, whereas their learning-age peers without disabilities tended to use polite forms (e.g. 'Can I have another toy?').

Secondary school

Bliss (1985) found that adolescents with learning disabilities were less good at selecting socially acceptable forms for their request than would be expected from the evidence of their cognitive functioning. There is also evidence that understanding social motivation during interactions can pose a problem to people with learning difficulties, particularly if the speaker is not familiar to them, or if the interaction is not embedded in their highly familiar routine.

Exercise 9.3

Discuss how you might support Pauline to express her views in work, social or familial situations.

Adulthood

Research has shown that people with learning difficulties reveal delays in all aspects of their speech, language and communication performance (Abudarham and Hurd 2002). As well as limited language use and problems with speech intelligibility, they also show delays in their use of social information to make decisions about the appropriate social style to adopt, and may be delayed in understanding social motivations. However, in adulthood they do tend to show some ability in understanding language when it is embedded in highly familiar interaction routines (Abbeduto and Rosenberg 1992).

It is not uncommon for people with learning disabilities to appear socially gauche or inappropriate in interactions. Abbeduto and Rosenberg (1992: 347) attempt to account for this in terms of difficulty with skills at a pragmatic level:

> When making a request such a speaker may select a linguistic form at random because they are unable to retrieve information about their addressee, e.g. his or her status because, as part of their cognitive problems, they have poor organisation of retrieval from long-term memory, poorly developed interpersonal goals and motive, a lack of knowledge about other people's intentions and beliefs, and other limitations in social competence or knowledge of and reasoning about the social world which

Case study: *Pauline*

Pauline is a very articulate person with Asperger syndrome. She has good spoken language and is very interested in No Smoking signs. However, she doesn't understand other people's language well. People overestimate her skills because she can talk well and, when she does not understand or respond to what they say directly, they think she is being difficult or ignorant. As she has Asperger syndrome, Pauline finds it difficult to make reciprocal relationships on equal terms with other people, but her good expressive language skills in the context of poor understanding make her seem aggressive and uncaring and make it even harder for her to develop relationships.

can limit the effectiveness of linguistic communication. For example, people may have difficulty making polite requests because their poor perspective-taking skills prevent them from anticipating the reaction of their addressee to an impolite request.

It may be that the person with learning difficulty lives in a supported environment where there is a high turnover of care staff, and the concomitant difficulties in establishing rapport and relationships can result in communication breakdown. Where there are a number of carers on shifts it may be that nobody fully understands the extent of the person's understanding and may pitch the language too high or too low for the language learner. It has also been shown that staff can sometimes overestimate a person's understanding of verbal language, or fail to identify non-verbal behaviour as a means of communication (Purcell *et al.* 1999).

Exercise 9.4

Think of one person with learning disabilities with whom you have worked. Can you think of ways you might facilitate his or her ability to communicate?

A person with learning disability has to communicate with a range of people on a personal level and, indeed, on a service level, and here further risks can arise. Depending on the degree of support required, a person with learning disability will have to react to life events with appropriate actions (e.g. illness should lead them to consult a doctor, but they may be required to communicate their symptoms to a precise degree, which might lead to misunderstanding or misdiagnosis in a busy consultation.

The National Patient Safety Agency (NPSA) (2004) highlights the communication difficulties of patients with learning disabilities and the fact that they may not be listened to as carefully in matters of health, which can result in severe risk for them.

Similarly, housing issues or respite arrangements may need to be negotiated and the person with a learning disability will need support with this – as long as, of course, the support person takes the time to listen accurately and check that they have correctly interpreted the wishes of the communicator.

Above all, on the issue of communication, services must, while respecting confidentiality and dignity, communicate with each other in the best interests of the person with a learning difficulty. Vulnerable people need services to work sensitively in tandem with each other, with the person with a learning

Case study: *Nigel*

Nigel has autism and lives in a very caring home with quite a strict routine because of shift patterns and care routines. Meals are always provided on time. Staff are concerned that Nigel sometimes becomes angry around supper time and when he does it tends to be on a Saturday. Supper is always at 5.00 p.m. on a Saturday, when Nigel enjoys watching the football results. Because of the rather strict routine he does not have the opportunity to watch the football results and then eat his supper or say that he wants to eat earlier. Nigel does not have the skills to refuse his supper or negotiate postponing it. Living in a routine has meant that Nigel does not need to ask for food, nor does he have the opportunity to reject it. He does not have the opportunity to hear anyone else negotiating or making choices about food. As well as his primary difficulty of autism, therefore, Nigel lacks experience in managing choices and negotiating. He does not know that he can ask for change and therefore doesn't or hasn't the motivation to learn the language he needs to do so. When there is a conflict between his routine meal times and his focused interest, Nigel finds it difficult to cope and tends to have a tantrum, which requires help to calm him down.

In spite of and perhaps as a result of the staff in Nigel's home making every effort to make residents comfortable, Nigel has lacked the opportunity and experience for developing skills of negotiation and he has only aggression to resort to when he is frustrated.

disability at the centre. To this end person-centred planning (see Chapter 25) using MAP and PATH (Pearpoint *et al.* 1993) techniques can be a major communication resource. These are techniques involving drawing or other visual representation that actively involve the person with a learning disability in planning their environment, activity and life aims.

Looking back to the input/output communication model (Figure 9.1), difficulties or vulnerabilities in any of these areas can cause speech, language or communication problems. Communication break-down can occur if communication partners have expectations that cannot be met.

Fostering communication

Communication occurs all day and every day, and the fostering of communication in children and adults with learning disabilities should reflect this by recognizing that the families, teachers and other communication partners are the best resource. Written programmes may cause stress as they have to be read and assimilated into child rearing and interactional practices. Also, the programme writer's style of interaction with children may not correspond with that of the parents, and their interaction may become stilted and unnatural. If, as a result, they then abandon the programme, they may feel guilt and their relationship with the child and therapist may suffer as a result. As experts on their child (see Chapter 11), parents and carers can be equal partners in the facilitation process with the therapist, and it is important to develop the team for the person with learning difficulties, who can make joint decisions about appropriate strategies for improving communication.

All potential communication partners of the person with learning disabilities can be responsible for enhancing and facilitating the communication partnership. MacDonald (1985) outlines some natural teaching principles, the understanding of which can contribute to a positive communicative environment, for example:

1 *The ubiquity principle* – all behaviours communicate. Every behaviour potentially carries a communicative message and the communication partner can richly interpret behaviours to facilitate the communication, except possibly in the case of self-stimulatory stereotypical behaviours where it might be best to distract the communicator.

2 *The systems principle* – this is the principle that there are multiple members of the team or system for any one person and each needs to be a target for training. The child or person with learning difficulties is not the only receiver of therapy or training. Communication partners should also receive training.

3 *The joint attention principle* – communication is more likely to occur if the communication partners can focus on the interest and activity of the communicator.

4 *The expectancy principle* – communication partners need to behave as if they expect the child or person with learning difficulties to communicate; they need to wait and listen.

5 *The trade-off principle* – if the person has an effective but non-desirable method of communication there must be a significant and immediate result if they are to be encouraged to replace this effective behaviour with a new one that has no proven benefit, as in the following case study.

Case study: *Robert*

Robert is a young man with severe learning difficulties and visual impairment. As a young child he regularly put his hand down his nappy and smeared faeces. When he did this he would be attended by a carer who would change and clean him. In time Robert became aware that smearing could be an alerting tool. He began to reach for his nappy to get attention or to avoid an activity. If Robert were successfully to use a single-message communication aid or an object of reference the 'payoff' for him would have to be immediate, clear and effective enough to prevent the undesirable behaviour.

There are a number of facilitation strategies which aim to enhance the communication skills of a person with learning disabilities, for example intensive interaction (Nind and Hewett 2001), in which the communication partner pays close attention to and responds adaptively to behaviours which may be communicative. Speech and language therapists may develop, in conjunction with users and carers, strategies that are designed to build vocabulary, grammatical or speech or social skills. However, in an interaction it is most important that the intention behind the communication is recognized and acknowledged so that it can be 'functional' even if not age-appropriate in terms of language or clear in speech production.

Roland and Schweigert (1993) suggest that functional communication:

- occurs in everyday real life and natural situations;
- results in real consequences, the act affecting the environment, with changes in accordance with the intent of the communication;
- includes but is not limited to spontaneous communication – communication skills are not fully functional if the communicator is incapable of using them except when prompted to do so.

Some people may not be able to use speech at all as their main method of communication and may need to use alternatives. As recognizing and responding to alternatives to oral communication is not currently a common experience for most people, it may be necessary for supporting organizations to arrange regular training for groups of carers and people working within the learning disability community.

Alternative methods of communication

People with learning and physical disability, particularly those with the more severe types, may have significant difficulty in producing mouth movements which can be co-ordinated to make intelligible speech (Cogher et al. 1992). Some people with learning and physical disability rely on alternative methods of communication, such as communication books or digitized speech aids.

Franklin and Beukelman (1991) found that augmentative communicators primarily respond to rather than initiate communication interactions. They tend to produce a limited number of turns and a limited number of communicative functions, and often fail to repair, i.e. they often fail to bring the communication back on track if there has been a breakdown. Franklin and Beukelman found that the speaking partners tended to dominate conversations and structure interactions to require minimal responses from users of augmentative communication systems. People who use augmentative and alternative communication (AAC) systems act on as few as 50 per cent of the available conversational opportunities during the course of an interaction (Light et al. 1985). AAC supports oral speech. For example, we all tend to use natural gestures when speaking and this 'augments' our meaning by giving extra clues.

AAC is required when a person is unable to use speech at all and needs to communicate in other ways. AAC systems can involve signing and/or visual systems (e.g. pictures, symbols, letters) or voice output communication aids (VOCA).

Signing

There are a number of signing methods mainly developed by the hearing impaired community: e.g. British Sign Language, the Paget Gorman sign system. These languages vary in how the signs are made with hand shape and position and also in terms of how many grammatical markers such as tense and plurality that they convey.

The Makaton Vocabulary Development Project used signs from British Sign Language to develop a vocabulary of signs presented in stages which are relevant to the experiences and needs of people with learning disability. 'Signalong' works on similar principles.

Signing should be considered as a positive alternative or augmentative method of communication. Makaton signing, British Sign Language and Signalong are signing systems that have been used positively with populations of children and adults with learning disabilities as they provide a multisensory approach to communication (Paul 1995) and can help with understanding as well as expression.

Integrating signing into a setting may not always run smoothly. A pilot investigation into the efficacy of a signing training strategy for staff working with adults with learning disabilities found that although staff were positive about receiving the training, few used the signs when communicating in everyday situations (Chadwick and Joliffe 2008). This highlights the need to make signing part of the environment and increase expectations that it will be used consistently.

Visual systems

Depending on the person's cognitive ability to process visual information, objects, photos, drawings, symbols or letters can be used within AAC. It is possible to use photos, pictures or symbols to point to by hand, fist, head or eye, to indicate meaning. These can be on a board, tray or in the form of a 'talking book' or 'talking mat' (for example Cameron and Murphy 2007). The child can also hand over these pictures to convey meaning as in PECS (Picture Exchange Communication System) (Bondy and Frost 1992). Symbols systems such as Rebus and Mayer-Johnson can be generated using computer programs such as Widgit and allow more condensed meaning, giving more options for communication providing the person has cognitive skills to that level.

Use of visual systems

Objects of reference are miniature objects or parts of objects which represent very closely an activity or an idea. For example, a key may be used to indicate going out as it refers to the key of the door, car keys etc., or a piece of coat fabric or shoelace may indicate going out. A cup, or a bottle, or a straw, whatever is relevant to the person, may indicate drink. When the planned activity is about to take place, the person is given the object of reference to hold and then the activity continues. They come to associate the object with the activity and are passed the object every time the activity is imminent. In time, some people learn to select an object and hold it or hand it to someone to indicate that they want the activity to take place. Each person has their own customized vocabulary and set of objects that are easily understood by them.

Some people with learning difficulties will benefit from using *pictures* as an aid to communication. There are a number of different types of pictures from photographs which represent as close to real objects as possible, through to line drawings which represent the idea in some detail, to symbols which are abstract representations of the idea. The pictures can be used in a number of ways: the person can be encouraged to pick a picture and hand it to their communication partner to get an idea across. A structured programme to enable this is called the Picture Exchange Communication System (Bondy and Frost 1992); alternatively, the pictures can be assembled into a sequence to give the users information and allow them to continue to look at the sequence over time to remind themselves of the information. Picture sequences may be used in, for example, dressing or work tasks. Pictures and symbols can be used successfully to augment written statements, for example in standardized assessment procedures like the CORE-OM (Marshall and Willoughby-Booth 2007), in order to improve wider application and use.

Communication passports contain key customized information about a person and can be presented as a booklet or other form of display relevant to the user; this is especially helpful in transitions or where there is rapid staff turnover.

Case study: *George*

George is a young man with cerebral palsy. He has preserved intelligence and understands the language of others very well, but has no intelligible speech. Through support workers and the internet, he is working for a degree in computer science and he has several 'buddies' who help him take part in a number of social activities. However, George uses a wheelchair and has to use a communication aid as he does not have adequate oral movement for speech. Programming what he wants to say into his communication aid takes slightly longer than spontaneous speech, and he therefore finds it hard to interact in group conversation in the pub. He is always two or three sentences behind, and the group dynamic means that it is hard for people to wait for him to speak. People who don't know George imagine that, because he can't speak, he has difficulty in understanding. When they talk to George, they may talk to his carers rather than directly to him.

Exercise 9.5

How do you think George feels when people don't hear what he has to say?

What would make it easier for George to communicate in this environment?

Use of communication aids

Another form of AAC used in combination with visual systems is battery-operated or electronic communication aids (VOCA) which the child activates to produce spoken words, phrases or sentences. These aids vary in complexity from one-hit, single message aids (e.g. Big Mack made by Prentke Romich) through to 4, 8 or 32 message aids

and more. The more complex the aid, the greater is the intellectual ability required to use it.

A Big Mack, a single message switch, can help a person with very limited communication skills to signal that they need attention or request that an activity is repeated. Clearly just one message significantly limits communication options but there are communication aids which can convey longer and more complex messages, the level of aid being influenced by the person's general learning capacity. Because communication and language play a central role in human development and behaviour throughout a person's life, the facilitation of communication and any therapeutic intervention that needs to take place must work across disciplines. It should not be exclusively the province of the speech and language therapist to manage communication.

Conclusion

Good communication lies at the heart of enabling people with learning disabilities to be heard, understood and respected. It requires that we pay attention both to the foundations of how people with limited verbal articulacy seek to communicate and to the skills and communicative competencies of families and health and social care practitioners.

People with learning disabilities may not understand as much language as you would expect of a person of their age, so:

- use short sentences;
- use gestures/pointing to support what you say;
- don't talk too fast, but there is no need to talk loudly.

People with learning disabilities may take longer to process language, so:

- give them a little more time to make a response;
- wait and listen.

People with learning disabilities may find it hard to express themselves, so:

- give them time and listen;
- try hard to understand what they are trying to express;
- help out if you can, but don't put words in their mouth or rush them;
- if you don't understand, say so and see if the person can tell you another way.

People with learning disabilities may have been limited in their life experiences, so:

- offer communication opportunities (i.e. give choices, try not to assume).

You might use a number of augmentative or alternative communication approaches to enable the systems of input, processing and output to be successfully achieved.

A sensitivity to features of the language skills model described in this chapter may be helpful in reminding us of how to take account of these matters in an integrated way. Rolling out arrangements for advocacy, person-centred planning and the inclusion of people with learning disabilities in decision-making forums will heighten the importance of the contributions they can make in shaping their own lives and influencing others. Allied to these important changes, helping staff to communicate more effectively will have a centrally important part to play in promoting the well-being and social inclusion of people who are too easily marginalized because of a 'poverty of speech and language'.

Resources

www.blissymbols.co.uk. BLISS.
www.bda.org.uk/bsl/. British sign language.
www.makaton.org. Makaton.
www.mayer-johnson.com. Mayer Johnson Symbols.
www.pecs.org.uk. PECS.
www.pgss.org. Paget Gorman.
www.prentrom.com. Big Mack.
www.psychology.stir.ac.uk/AAC/infosheet.htm.
    Talking Mats.
www.signalong.org.uk. Signalong.
www.widgit.com. Rebus.

References

Abbeduto, L. and Rosenberg, S. (1992) Linguistic communication in persons with mental retardation, in S.F. Warren and J. Reichle (eds) *Causes and Effects in Communication and Language*. Baltimore, MD: Paul H. Brookes.

Abudarham, S. and Hurd, A. (2002) *Management of Communication Needs in People with Learning Disability*. London: Whurr.

Beckman, P.J. (1983) The relationship between behavioural characteristics of children and social interaction in an integrated setting, *Journal of Early Intervention*, 7: 69–77.

Bliss, L.S. (1985) The development of persuasive strategies by mentally retarded children, *Applied Research in Mental Retardation*, 6(4): 437–47.

Bondy, A.S. and Frost, L.A. (1992) *The Picture Exchange Communication System (PECS)*. Newark, DE: Pyramid Educational Consultants, Inc.

Bruner, J.S. (1975) The ontogenesis of speech acts, *Journal of Child Language*, 2: 1–40.

Cameron, L. and Murphy, J. (2007) Obtaining consent to participate in research: the issues involved in including people with a range of learning and communication disabilities, *British Journal of Learning Disabilities*, 35: 113–20.

Chadwick, D. and Joliffe, J. (2008) Pilot investigation into the efficacy of a signing training strategy for staff working with adults with intellectual disabilities, *British Journal of Learning Disabilities*, 37(1): 34–42.

Chapman, R.S. and Hesketh, L.J. (2000) Behavioral phenotype of individuals with Down syndrome, *Mental Retardation and Developmental Disabilities Research Reviews*, 6: 84–95.

Chomsky, N. (1976) *Reflections on Language*. Glasgow: Fontana.

Cogher, L., Savage, E. and Smith, M.F. (1992) *Cerebral Palsy: The Child and Young Person (Management of Disability)*. London: Chapman & Hall.

Donahue, M., Pearl, R. and Bryan, T. (1982) Learning disabled children's syntactic: proficiency on a communicative task, *Journal of Speech and Hearing Disorders*, 47: 397–403.

Fantz, R.L. (1966) Pattern discrimination and selective attention as determinants of perceptual development from birth in A.H. Kidd and J.L. Rivoire (eds) *Perceptual Development in Children*. New York: International University Press.

Franklin, K. and Beukelman, D. (1991) Augmentative communication: directions for future research, in J. Miller (ed.) *Research on Child Language Disorders*. Austin, TX: Pro-Ed Inc.

Goldstein, H. and Kaczmarek, L. (1992) Promoting communicative interaction among children in integrated intervention settings, in S.F. Warren and J. Reichle (eds) *Causes and Effects in Communication and Language*. Baltimore, MD: Paul H. Brookes.

Grice, H.P. (1975) Logic and conversation, in P. Cole and J. Morgan (eds) *Syntax and Semantics, Volume 3: Speech Acts*. New York: Academic Press.

Guralnick, M.J. and Paul-Brown, D. (1986) Communicative interactions of mildly delayed and normally developing preschool children: effects of listener's developmental level, *Journal of Speech and Hearing Research*, 29(1): 2–10.

Kohn, M. (1966) The child as determinant of his peers' approach to him, *Journal of Genetic Psychology*, 109: 91–100.

Light, J., Collier, B.K. and Parnes, P. (1985) Communicative interaction between nonspeaking physically disabled children and their primary caregivers: Part II – communicative function, *Augmentative & Alternative Communication*, 1(3): 98–107.

MacDonald, J. (1985) Language through conversation: a model for intervention with language-delayed persons, in S. Warren and A. Rogers-Warren (eds) *Teaching Functional Language: Generalization and Maintenance of Language Skills*. Baltimore, MD: University Park Press.

Marshall, K. and Willoughby-Booth, S. (2007) Modifying the clinical outcomes in routine evaluation measure for use with people who have a learning disability, *British Journal of Learning Disabilities*, 35: 107–12.

Miller, G.A. (1981) *Language and Speech*. San Francisco, CA: W.H. Freeman.

Mueller, E. (1972) The maintenance of verbal exchanges between young children, *Child Development*, 43: 930–8.

National Patient Safety Agency (2004) *Understanding the Patient Safety Issues for People with Learning Disabilities.* London: NPSA.

Nind, M. and Hewett, D. (2001) *A Practical Guide to Intensive Interaction.* Kidderminster: BILD Publications.

Nuccio, J.B. and Abbeduto, L. (1993) Dynamic contextual variables and the directives of persons with mental retardation, *American Journal of Mental Retardation*, 5: 547–55.

Paul, R. (1995) *Language Disorders from Infancy through Adolescence: Assessment and Intervention.* St Louis, MI: Mosby.

Pearpoint, J., O'Brien, J. and Forest, M. (1993) *PATH: A Workbook for Planning Positive Possible Futures*, 2nd edn. Toronto: Inclusion Press.

Purcell, M., Morris, I. and McConkey, R. (1999) Staff perceptions of the communicative competence of adult persons with intellectual disabilities, *British Journal of Developmental Disabilities*, 45(1): 16–25.

Raffaelli, M. and Duckett, E. (1989) 'We were just talking . . .': conversations in early adolescence, *Journal of Youth and Adolescence*, 18: 567–81.

Roland, C. and Schweigert, P. (1993) Analyzing the communication environment to increase functional communication, *Journal of the Association for Persons with Severe Handicaps*, 18: 161–76.

Sheridan, M.D. (1973) *Children's Developmental Progress: From Birth to Five Years.* Windsor: NFER.

Stern, D.N. (1977) *The First Relationship: Infant and Mother.* Cambridge, MA: Harvard University Press.

Tager-Flusberg, H. (ed.) (1999) *Neurodevelopmental Disorders.* Cambridge, MA: MIT Press.

Wistow, R. and Schneider, J. (2003) Users' views on supported employment and social inclusion: a qualitative study of 30 people in work, *British Journal of Learning Disabilities*, 31(4): 166–74.

10

The importance of aetiology of intellectual disability

Chris Oliver, Kate Woodcock and Dawn Adams

Introduction

In this chapter we will describe how different causes of intellectual disability can be related to important differences in physical, cognitive, behavioural and emotional domains. We will develop the argument that these differences can significantly influence an individual's well-being and consequently such differences and their causes warrant identification to indicate points of possible change. We do not intend to detail all causes of intellectual disability or all known associations between causes of intellectual disability and their outcomes. Rather, via exploration of a number of specific genetic disorders we will demonstrate that knowing something about a cause of intellectual disability can help us to understand the experience of people who have an intellectual disability due to that cause.

The position we adopt, that genetics is relevant and important to the well-being of people with intellectual disability, can be construed as contentious. Genetics and psychology have at times combined to oppress people with intellectual disability and segregate them from others within a society. The eugenics movement, evident in the UK at the start of the last century, had at its heart the assumption that intellectual disability, defined by performance on psychological assessments, was inextricably linked with genetics and that social engineering was a justifiable policy that would change the nature of a society beneficially (see Kelves 1995 and Chapter 2 of this volume). This discredited and morally bankrupt view has left a legacy that any association between genetics, psychology and intellectual disability is unlikely to be in the interests of those who have an intellectual disability. In this chapter we will argue that this assumption is unwarranted and that inclusion in society can be enhanced by understanding individual difference

that, in the examples we cite, can be traced to a specific genetic disorder.

There is little doubt that having a genetic disorder associated with an intellectual disability can still lead to discrimination at a number of levels. In the late 1980s there was extensive media coverage of the decision to withhold heart surgery for some children with Down's syndrome. One justification given for this was related to economic costs and benefits, an argument not dissimilar to that proposed at the height of the eugenics movement (see Walter 1922). Additionally, it has been argued that laissez-faire eugenics is evident within contemporary society, for example inherent in the antenatal screening programme for Down's syndrome (see Ridley 1999). Furthermore, an argument has been made that behaviour associated with a particular syndrome might be an important consideration for such screening programmes (Kitcher 1996).

It is clear from these examples that an association between genetics, psychology and intellectual disability allied to a specious argument of societal benefit persists, at least to some extent. This association has played a role in the rejection of the use of diagnostic labels, such as syndrome names. Additionally, it is argued that the use of syndrome names emphasizes difference and a medical model of disability. This is counter to the trend toward a social construction of disability that identifies a significant role for societal attitudes and values in determining, for example, the level of inclusion that people with intellectual disability experience. In combination these perspectives and trends have cultivated a view that there is little merit in knowing that someone has a particular genetic disorder. However, this argument must be balanced by the evidence for the possibility that the cause of intellectual disability can be of equal or greater importance than the immediate and broader environment as a determinant of well-being.

When faced with this debate it is necessary to examine whether differences that arise as a result of a genetic disorder are important: the most obvious example in the history of intellectual disability is that of the genetic disorder giving rise to phenylketonuria (PKU) in which a diet free from phenylalanine will result in less cognitive impairment. Consequently, knowing that a genetic disorder is present can, on balance, promote a beneficial outcome. Understanding a genetic disorder may also improve our understanding of whether and how people view and experience a shared environment, which may impact on how these people behave. It will also help us to track the pathway from the nature of an impairment, to disability and ultimately to handicap. This will allow a response that is more likely to facilitate social integration by being able to adapt the environment in a way that is helpful specifically to a person's impairment. The most visible examples of adaptations are the provision of ramps to enable access for wheelchair users and audio induction loops for those with hearing impairments. In each case the disability is minimized when there is a relevant and specific response to the impairment. Knowing more about specific cognitive, emotional and behavioural differences that are associated with a particular genetic cause can allow us to create and adapt environments in similar ways.

The preceding arguments raise the possibility that perspectives that traditionally differ on the importance of knowing something about the cause of intellectual disability are compatible. We would argue that it is the assumptions that underpin the importance of difference that are the real issue as opposed to the cause of difference in itself. In this chapter we will develop the argument that knowing the cause of intellectual disability can be important and beneficial and that this is clearly demonstrated from the study of the physical, behavioural, cognitive and emotional profiles associated with specific genetic disorders.

Genetic causes of intellectual disability

With regard to genetic causes, generally speaking an intellectual disability can arise as a result of dif-ferences in the number of chromosomes or structural differences on chromosomes. An example of a specific syndrome normally associated with intellectual disability that arises from a difference in the number of chromosomes is Down's syndrome (usually caused by trisomy of chromosome 21). Syndromes associated with structural differences on specific chromosomes are Cornelia de Lange syndrome (deletion on either chromosome 5, 10 or X in approximately 50 per cent of people with the syndrome), Fragile X syndrome (an excessive number of repeats of the CGG repeats on the X chromosome) and Prader-Willi and Angelman syndromes (both caused by the loss of genetic information from the q11–13 region of chromosome 15). It is important to note that within each syndrome there can be variability in terms of the nature and degree of the genetic change, which can be associated with 'within syndrome variability' in individual developmental outcomes.

All of the genetic disorders that are associated with an intellectual disability are rare. Incidence at birth can range from 1:800 to 1:1000 for Down's syndrome to 1:380,000 for Lesch-Nyhan syndrome. This does not mean, however, that the number of people with an intellectual disability who have a genetic disorder is small. There are approximately 1700 genetic disorders associated with intellectual disability and for those with severe intellectual disability approximately 50 per cent have a genetic disorder, while for those with a mild intellectual disability approximately 20 per cent have a genetic disorder. Across the UK, therefore, the estimate of the total number of people with a genetic disorder associated with intellectual disability ranges from approximately 350,000 to 750,000 (Oliver and Woodcock 2008). The number of people identified as having an intellectual disability caused by a genetic disorder is rising steadily as the technology for the identification of genetic disorders becomes more widely available.

Knowing the cause of intellectual disability appears to be of great importance to some parents. These parents describe enormous relief when they learned of a genetic disorder and often experience a release from guilt. It could be argued that an individual's ability to find out if they have a genetic disorder (if this information is available) is a fundamental human right. However, particularly with individuals with an intellectual disability, this raises complex issues related to confidentiality, capacity for informed consent and privacy. Finally, it is important to note when someone receives the diagnosis of a genetic disorder that this diagnosis does not define the person. Identity is multi-dimensional and a genetic disorder is simply one dimension that has greater or lesser importance in different contexts and at different times.

The historical link between genetics, intellectual disability and psychology should not lead to the assumption that this association will always be detrimental to people with an intellectual disability. There are important issues to consider with regard to labelling, assumptions about the value of people who are different and the merits of identifying the presence of a genetic disorder. It is this latter point that we believe is critical. The first step in evaluating the merit of identifying the presence of a genetic disorder is to ask whether there is any difference between people who have a genetic disorder and people who do not have that disorder when careful comparisons are made. The second step is to ask whether knowing something about a difference can lead to benefits for the person who has that genetic disorder.

Defining and identifying behavioural, cognitive and emotional phenotypes

A phenotype can be defined as the observable characteristics or traits of an organism. While some definitions of a phenotype emphasize only the genetic basis, others recognize that observable characteristics occur as a result of an ongoing interaction between genes and the environment. In humans, while it is easy to picture physical phenotypic characteristics such as hair colour, it is perhaps more difficult to imagine how thought processes, emotional profile and behaviour can be considered as an aspect of phenotype. Genetic syndromes, caused by specific genotypes, allow us to grasp more easily how a person's genetic make-up and developmental environment can affect thought processes, emotional and motivational profile and behaviour.

In this context, a behavioural phenotype can be defined as behaviours that are shown more frequently in individuals with a particular genetic syndrome than in individuals without the syndrome (Dykens *et al.* 2000). By defining a behavioural phenotype in this way we adopt a stance on the degree of specificity

involved in the relationship between genotype and behavioural phenotype (Hodapp 1997). It is, in theory, possible for a behaviour to occur as a direct result of only one specific genotype ('a total specificity approach'). In this case we would expect that all individuals with only that genotype would show the behaviour. There are examples of behavioural phenotypic characteristics that appear close to this definition, for example hyperphagia (overeating) in Prader-Willi syndrome, a high pitch, 'cat-like' cry during infancy in Cri du Chat syndrome and excessive laughing and smiling in Angelman syndrome. However, the majority of behavioural phenotypic characteristics are not shown by all individuals with a particular syndrome and they also form part of the behavioural phenotype associated with other genetic syndromes (partial specificity). An example of this is a preference for routine, which is shown by individuals with, for example, Prader-Willi and Fragile X syndromes and also typically developing children. The definition of a behavioural phenotype above allows us to work within a 'partial specificity approach'.

The definition of an endophenotype follows logically from that for a behavioural phenotype and refers to unobservable characteristics that are shown more frequently by individuals with a particular genotype than by individuals without that genotype. These can include cognitive characteristics (cognitive phenotype), emotional and motivational characteristics (motivational phenotype).

The contemporary position within phenotypic research of individuals with genetic syndromes considers pathways from genes to behaviour that pass through a number of levels with potential interaction with the environment at any stage. In this framework genetic expression gives rise to molecular pathways which can affect physical, physiological and neuronal development. Resultant neuronal characteristics can affect patterns of cognitive and emotional/motivational processing (which share a bidirectional relationship). The framework therefore describes how genotype can give rise to physical, neuronal, cognitive, emotional/motivational and behavioural difference (including both impairment or strength). Importantly, any of these levels of difference can interact with each other and also with the environment. Although behaviour can result from a pathway which passes through each of these levels of difference, it can also result from shorter pathways passing through just a few levels. This framework fits easily into a bio-psycho-social perspective for understanding the factors that, ultimately, influence the well-being of individuals with intellectual disabilities (see Chapter 3 this volume).

The framework highlights the potential for multiple levels of intervention aimed at helping individuals with genetic syndromes to overcome problems that they face. Behavioural interventions (acting at the level of behavioural difference and its interaction with the environment) are perhaps most common and employ the principles of operant learning to increase individuals' adaptive behaviours and/or decrease problematic behaviours. Cognitive interventions (acting at the level of cognitive difference) have been used less frequently in individuals with intellectual disabilities, but have been shown to be effective within other populations. These interventions employ training techniques aimed at increasing individuals' cognitive ability in a particular area of difficulty (e.g. training working memory in individuals with Attention Deficit Hyperactivity Disorder; Klingberg *et al.* 2002). Educational approaches can also act at the level of cognitive difference by tailoring an individual's educational environment to their cognitive strengths. Medical interventions can act at the level of physical difference and can treat a physical disorder which has implications for health.

The remainder of this chapter is structured according to the multiple levels of potential difference in individuals with genetic syndromes that are associated with intellectual disability and how these levels of difference can interact to influence the resultant phenotype. However, it is important to note that within the general population of individuals with intellectual disabilities, including those without genetic syndromes, these multiple levels of potential difference can play an important role in behavioural outcome and well-being, and thus a bio-psycho-social perspective is equally justifiable.

Exercise 10.1

Describe what is meant by the terms 'total specificity approach' and 'partial specificity approach'. Why are these terms helpful?

Behavioural phenotypes

Behavioural characteristics can be associated with difficulty for individuals and it is unsurprising that emphasis has been placed on describing and understanding these behaviours. In order to describe bio-psycho-social pathways to behaviour it is essential to have a clear description of the behaviour. In this section we describe examples of the behavioural phenotypes associated with certain genetic syndromes (although we must bear in mind that the same levels of difference and interactions can exist in pathways to behaviour for anyone). We have selected our examples in order to (1) illustrate the different levels of specificity that can exist in the behaviours comprising behavioural phenotypes and (2) set the scene for subsequent sections of this chapter when further levels of difference will be linked to behavioural phenotypes and bio-psycho-social pathways to behaviour will be discussed.

As noted above, certain components of some behavioural phenotypes appear to fit a total specificity approach, in that the behaviour is shown by all individuals with the syndrome and not by any individuals without the syndrome. One of the clinical diagnostic features of Angelman syndrome is 'excessive laughing and smiling'. To date this has not been shown to be characteristic of other syndromes. Prader-Willi syndrome is associated with hyperphagia, which is not generally reported in individuals without Prader-Willi syndrome (although there have been reports of a 'Prader-Willi like' phenotype of Fragile X and monosomy 1p36 deletion syndromes).

Another component of the Prader-Willi syndrome behavioural phenotype is temper outbursts (Einfeld *et al.* 1999). Although temper outbursts are reported more frequently in Prader-Willi syndrome than in a number of other groups of people without the syndrome, they cannot be described as totally specific to the syndrome. Temper outbursts are often seen in typically developing children and have been reported in individuals with, for example, Fragile X and Smith-Magenis syndromes. However, because a behaviour has been described at a crude level (e.g. temper outbursts) within different groups, this does not necessarily mean that a particular type of the behaviour (described at a more detailed level) will not be specific to one group. In fact the high level of uncontrollability and apparent physiological arousal associated with the temper outbursts in Prader-Willi syndrome may be more specific to the syndrome.

The fact that specificity of components of a behavioural phenotype for a particular syndrome appears to increase as behaviours are further refined is illustrated well by self-injurious behaviour within different behavioural phenotypes. Self-injurious behaviour is frequently reported in Cornelia de Lange syndrome and is also common in Lesch-Nyhan, Fragile X and Smith-Magenis syndromes and Autism Spectrum Disorder. However, a specific type of the behaviour (mild and directed towards the hands) is more common in Cornelia de Lange syndrome (Oliver *et al.* 2009). Similarly, self-injurious behaviour in Smith-Magenis syndrome (predominantly caused by a deletion on chromosome 17) includes the insertion of objects into body orifices, a behaviour which appears to be specific to this syndrome.

Repetitive behaviour is a component of the behavioural phenotype of many different syndromes (Moss *et al.* 2009). However, different syndromes are associated with different profiles of repetitive behaviour. For example, Fragile X and Prader-Willi syndromes are both associated with high levels of insistence on routine and repetitive questioning, but Fragile X syndrome is associated with more stereotypical movement (particularly hand stereotypy), tidying and repetitive speech (other than questioning). Individuals with Cornelia de Lange syndrome also show high levels of stereotypical movement and tidying, but not as much repetitive questioning or insistence on routine.

A diagnosis of autism is more common in individuals with Fragile X syndrome than in the general population of individuals with an intellectual disability and the prevalence of Fragile X syndrome is higher in individuals with autism than in the general population. Even within individuals with Fragile X syndrome without autism, there is substantial overlap in the Fragile X behavioural phenotype and the broad classes of behaviour that comprise autism spectrum behaviour (repetitive behaviour/restricted interests, deficits in communication and social behaviour). However, when we examine the Fragile X (without autism) behavioural phenotype, there are fundamental differences between the components and autistic spectrum behaviours. For example, individuals

with Fragile X syndrome show social anxiety and gaze avoidance (both frequently noted as autism spectrum behaviours), but do not appear to show lack of motivation for social contact, as is commonly reported in individuals with autism. This point is illustrated in other genetic syndromes whose behavioural phenotypes show overlap with broadly defined autistic spectrum domains, but that on closer examination can be distinguished from idiopathic autism (e.g. in Cornelia de Lange syndrome in which the social profile, as in Fragile X syndrome, appears to be characterized by social anxiety; Moss *et al.* 2008).

In stark contrast to the social anxiety evident in Fragile X and Cornelia de Lange syndromes, the behavioural phenotype of Williams syndrome (caused by a deletion on chromosome 7) is characterized by a profile of hypersociability, which may include lack of fear for strangers (Bellugi *et al.* 2007). Interestingly, while individuals with Williams syndrome clearly do not show social anxiety, specific (non-social) phobias do appear to be a component of the behavioural phenotype (Martens *et al.* 2008). Thus, a double dissociation appears to exist between individuals with Fragile X/Cornelia de Lange syndrome on the one hand and those with Williams syndrome on the other, between social behaviour and specific anxieties. This demonstrates how comparing behaviours across individuals with different genetic syndromes can provide an important starting point in attempting to understand the bio-psycho-social pathways to behaviour.

The discussion so far has focused on describing the similarities across groups of individuals with the same genetic syndrome. However, within-syndrome variability is clearly evident. Most of the research on which the above discussion is based uses group comparison designs. So, when describing a phenotypic behaviour we may only conclude that more people with the syndrome show a behaviour than people in a comparison group. Understanding which factors contribute to within-syndrome variability has important implications for understanding pathways to behaviour because to explain why a behaviour occurs in some individuals/at certain times, one must also be able to explain why that behaviour does not occur in others. The factors that contribute to within-syndrome variability are also important to consider when thinking about potential intervention strategies.

Exercise 10.2

Choose from Prader-Willi, Cornelia de Lange, Lesch-Nyhan, Fragile X, Rubinstein Taybi, Smith-Magenis or another syndrome of which you are aware. Find out the known components of the behavioural phenotype for this syndrome. Why is this information useful and important?

Sensory impairments and difference

Knowing that individuals with specific syndromes are susceptible to sensory impairments or differences can contribute to understanding an individual's behavioural presentation. Hearing impairments are frequently noted in individuals with Cornelia de Lange and Smith-Magenis syndromes (these are associated with chronic middle ear infections in children with Smith-Magenis syndrome) (Finucane et al. 2001). The acceptance of hearing aids by individuals with these syndromes is variable (see Sakai et al. 2002). This can lead to a situation where the development of verbal communication skills (as in Cornelia de Lange syndrome) is compromised by impaired hearing, highlighting the value of early intervention for hearing difficulties (Hawley et al. 1985). Importantly, this illustrates how understanding the causal pathway to an individual difference can have a positive influence on well-being.

Individuals with Lowe syndrome are very likely to experience childhood (and adult) cataracts, glaucoma and corneal keloids, which, if left untreated, can lead to blindness by the age of 6 months (see Tripathi et al. 1986). Such difficulties with vision may lead to specific behaviours, including moving the hands quickly in front of their eyes (strobing) in order to generate visual input (Lavin and McKeown 1993), demonstrating how sensory difficulties experienced by a particular group of individuals can inform on likely functions for some of their characteristic behaviours.

Sensory differences are as important as deficits. Almost all individuals (95 per cent) with Williams syndrome experience significant hyperacusis (oversensitivity to some noise frequencies) (Klein et al. 1990). Hyperacusis can be severe enough to disrupt everyday life and causes challenging behaviours in some individuals in noisy environments. However,

these difficulties can be minimized in a tailored environment.

Finally, a higher pain threshold is noted in many syndromes (e.g. Prader-Willi syndrome: Einfeld et al. 1999; Cornelia de Lange syndrome: Berney et al. 1999; Angelman syndrome: discussed in Cassidy and Schwartz 1998). This is not to suggest insensitivity or indifference to pain (see Foley and McCutcheon 2004 for a review) but highlights the need for sensitive assessment methods and tools within this area (see Davies and Evans 2001 for a review), carrying implications for a heightened pain threshold when identifying physical disorders.

Physical disorders and health

Levels of preventative care are lower for people with intellectual disability than for the general population, as is the frequency of contact with general practitioners and recognition and diagnosis of health problems (Ouellette-Kuntz 2005). Individuals with intellectual disabilities fit poorly into a health care system where no care is received unless requested, indicating the need for routine health screening (Beange et al. 1995), caregiver vigilance and eliciting reliable self-reports of health problems from individuals with mild to moderate intellectual disabilities. This is particularly pertinent for syndrome-specific health problems because knowing which health conditions can be associated with a syndrome can help to minimize the detrimental impact.

For example, people who have Down's syndrome are more likely to have congenital heart defects (e.g. Freeman et al. 1998), hypothyroidism (at least 30 per cent; Rubello et al. 1995), early menopause (Cosgrave et al. 1999) and Alzheimer-type dementia (discussed below). Individuals with Fragile X experience high rates of recurrent otitis media (Hagerman et al. 1987), heart disorders (Sreeram et al. 1989) and epilepsy (Musumeci et al. 1999) and adults with Williams syndrome are at a high risk for heart and kidney problems. Diabetes mellitus is common in Prader-Willi syndrome (Butler et al. 2002) and premature arteriosclerosis has been reported in Turner's and Klinefelter syndromes (see Wallace 2004 for a review). Seizures are noted in over 80 per cent of individuals with Angelman syndrome (see Clayton-Smith and Laan 2003), the presentation of which may be unusual and may be associated with the individual's specific genotype (see Minassian *et al.* 1998). In Cornelia de Lange syndrome gastro-intestinal disorders are common, resulting in painful reflux which is associated with self-injurious behaviour (Luzzani *et al.* 2003). Only by recognizing that painful chronic and acute health conditions are more likely within syndromes at given ages than we would expect by chance can we be proactive in identifying these conditions and assessing and treating them.

Emotional/motivational phenotypes

Thus far we have discussed the levels of potential difference between individuals (and between different groups of individuals) that are directly observable. Individual preferences are another level of potential difference that result from people's emotional/motivational phenotypes and play an important role in pathways to behaviour.

Excessive laughing and smiling seen in Angelman syndrome provides an example of a behaviour for which the pattern of expression across different situations allows us to appreciate aspects of a motivational phenotype. Although the laughing and smiling is described as excessive in Angelman syndrome, it shows a differential pattern of expression across social environments and is most likely to occur during social interaction (Horsler and Oliver 2006), indicating that interactions are experienced as extremely pleasurable. Aggressive behaviour and hair pulling in particular (also a component of the Angelman syndrome behavioural phenotype) also shows a differential pattern of expression across social environments and tends to function to obtain or maintain social interaction (Strachan *et al.* 2009). Thus, individuals with Angelman syndrome appear to show an emotional phenotype which results from a heightened motivation to obtain social contact. The special case of the genetics underpinning Angelman syndrome that involves absence of maternally but not paternally derived genetic material has led researchers to focus on the genetic underpinning of a pathway to behaviour via a difference in preference (Oliver *et al.* 2007).

The hypersociability in Williams syndrome also appears to be linked to a heightened motivation for social contact. However, whereas in Angelman syndrome the level of genetic difference has been emphasized in the pathway via the motivational phenotype to behaviour, in Williams syndrome researchers have focused at the level of neurological difference. In Williams syndrome a part of the brain that is responsive to emotional stimuli (the amygdala) shows accentuated response to happy faces but reduced response to sad faces. This fits well with the clinical picture of heightened motivation for positive social interactions (Porter *et al.* 2007). Another pathway to behaviour which has been described mostly at the levels of neurological and motivational difference involves the hyperphagia seen in Prader-Willi syndrome where the satiety centre in the brain does not respond in the normal manner to food intake (Hinton *et al.* 2006). Impaired satiety therefore comprises one aspect of the motivational phenotype in the syndrome and is linked with excessive food-seeking behaviour and overeating.

An additional aspect of the motivational phenotype of Prader-Willi syndrome that also comprises part of the phenotypes of Cornelia de Lange and Fragile X syndromes is a preference for sameness. This preference forms part of the pathway to behaviours that occur following change (in a specific environmental context), such as temper outbursts (Prader-Willi syndrome) and overt anxious reactions including stereotypical movement and self-injurious behaviour (males with Fragile X syndrome), likely to occur following the same environmental stressors (Woodcock *et al.* 2009a). In Cornelia de Lange syndrome transitions occurring around adolescence have been associated with increased avoidance of social interaction. This demonstrates how a bidirectional interaction can exist between aspects of the behavioural and motivational phenotypes and the environment. A preference for sameness can cause anxiety when changes occur in the environment, but because individuals already show a tendency towards social anxiety, avoidance of social interaction may be particularly heightened. The social anxiety may also be directly linked to a motivation to avoid the unpredictability inherent in social contact.

Cognitive phenotypes

Directly relevant to the preference for sameness seen in both Prader-Willi and Fragile X syndromes are difficulties with the cognitive capacity of attention switching (Woodcock *et al.* 2009b). Attention switching can be described as one of the executive functions (high-level cognitive processes that allow individuals to control and regulate lower level cognitive processes and behaviours). In individuals with Prader-Willi syndrome, the difficulty in attention switching can give rise to phenotypic behaviours (e.g. temper outbursts, repetitive questioning) when an unexpected change in the environment places a demand on this capacity. Additionally, the difficulty in attention switching is linked to neurofunctional difference. This forms an example of a pathway to behaviour that considers genetic difference (loss of paternal information on chromosome 15), neurological difference (differences in frontal brain activity associated with attention switching), motivational difference (preference for sameness), behavioural difference (temper outbursts) and environmental variability (unexpected changes; Woodcock *et al.* 2009c). Rubinstein Taybi syndrome is also associated with high levels of repetitive questioning. Cognitive differences in working memory and inhibition (also executive functions) have been linked to the repetitive questioning shown by individuals with the syndrome (Powis *et al.* 2009).

In addition to these associations between levels of cognitive and behavioural difference, cognitive difference has also been studied in its own right. As for our description of potential behavioural difference, cognitive difference may be more specific to particular groups of individuals as a specific cognitive capacity is further refined. For example, while individuals with Williams and Down's syndromes both show deficits in working memory, these appear to be specific to phonological working memory in Down's syndrome but to spatial working memory in Williams syndrome (Jarrold *et al.* 1999). These differences at a cognitive level have important implications for potential intervention and education strategies.

Exercise 10.3

Take the work you have already done in the previous exercise and find out any more you can about associated sensory impairments, health disorders and emotional/motivational and cognitive phenotypes. What implications would this knowledge have for you as a disability support worker?

Developmental change

The interaction between the gene and environment is made more complex given developmental change across the lifespan. We may be able to begin to understand an individual's physical differences or deficits, their preferences (motivational/emotional profiles) and cognitive style at one moment in time, but this, as with any individual, is subject to change with age.

A well-documented example of this is the development of dementia in individuals with Down's syndrome. The majority of adults with Down's syndrome over the age of 40 show the neuropathological signs of Alzheimer's disease at autopsy (Wisniewski *et al.* 1985). Age-specific prevalence rates for the clinical presentation of dementia in adults with Down's syndrome range from 0–2 per cent of 30- to 39-year-olds, to 33.3–54.5 per cent of 60- to 69-year-olds (Holland *et al.* 1998). The development of Alzheimer's disease has a significant impact upon the cognitive and behavioural phenotype in Down's syndrome, with changes in personality (akin to those noted in frontal dementia; Holland *et al.* 1998) appearing alongside decline in working memory, executive function and language (e.g. Oliver *et al.* 1998; Ball *et al.* 2006).

Age-related changes in behaviour have also been noted in other syndromes. The high levels of smiling and laughing behaviour noted in response to social contact in Angelman syndrome may decline over time (Horsler and Oliver 2006). Richards *et al.* (2009) report high levels of behaviours indicative of social anxiety (e.g. fidgeting or wringing hands, avoiding eye contact) in individuals with Cornelia de Lange syndrome, which may become more prominent as individuals enter adolescence and young adulthood (e.g. Collis *et al.* 2006). Being aware of syndrome-specific age-related changes to an individual's cognitive, behavioural and physical phenotype allows for proactive screening and planning.

Interactions with the environment

Throughout this chapter we have highlighted the importance of interactions with the environment in determining behavioural, sensory, motivational and cognitive difference and the pathways between them.

For example, anxiety appears to be linked to non-social phobic stimuli in Williams syndrome but to social stimuli in Cornelia de Lange syndrome. Hyperacusis in Williams syndrome can cause aversion to and avoidance of loud noises. The heightened motivation for social contact in individuals with Angelman syndrome is evidenced by increased laughing and smiling during social interaction and the display of aggressive behaviour that may maintain social contact. The cognitive difference in attention switching shown by individuals with Prader-Willi syndrome becomes apparent following unexpected changes in the environment which place a demand on this cognitive capacity.

Within all of these examples the interaction between the environment and genetic, neurological, cognitive, motivational and behavioural difference can be reciprocal. It is possible for a person to change the environment and for the resultant environment to change a person. This can be clearly illustrated for the laughing and smiling in Angelman syndrome. Individuals with Angelman syndrome show high levels of laughing and smiling during social inter-action. However, people in the environment are also more likely to smile after individuals with Angelman syndrome smile (Oliver *et al.* 2007). Presumably (as occurs in the general population) increased smiling by caregivers increases the positive emotional response to social interaction experienced by individuals with Angelman syndrome, which would in turn increase the motivation to obtain and maintain social contact.

Also important to note is that in the context of genetic differences associated with behavioural, motivational and cognitive phenotypic characteristics, it is easy to illustrate the concept of genetic predispositions to behaviour. A genetic predisposition is a genetic risk factor that increases the chance of a certain phenotypic outcome. For example, in Angelman syndrome the genetic abnormality appears to predispose to hair pulling, but hair pulling only occurs in environments in which it could function to obtain or maintain social interaction. Of course, environmental factors can affect genetic predispositions at any level and these may even include other genetic risk factors (the genetic environment).

Conclusions

We have argued that when trying to understand why people might think, feel and behave as they do, a bio-psycho-social perspective is useful. We believe this perspective is important given the documented evidence that biological, psychological and social factors can each influence how some people with genetic syndromes think, feel and behave. This empirical evidence cannot be easily dismissed. The importance of this perspective is that if a person wanted to change how they think, feel and behave, or they cannot express a desire to change but it is in their best interests to effect change (for example severe self-injury in someone with profound intellectual disability), then knowing the relative influence of biological, psychological and social factors will inform the most effective strategy for change. Within the broader psychological literature it is clear that for typically developing people comprehensive models of thinking, feeling and behaving draw on each of the three levels of explanation. There is no reason for models of thinking, feeling and behaving of people with intellectual disability to be markedly different or any less complex.

We have demonstrated that the biological level, and genetic aetiology specifically, is important for a number of reasons. First, knowing that a genetic disorder is evident means that the probability of painful chronic and acute health conditions can be known at given ages. Hence, we can be proactive in identifying these conditions, assessing and treating them. Second, we may know that sensory impairments of varying levels of specificity might be present but unrecognized and thus amenable to correction. It is important to note here that it is possible to intervene proactively because the genetic disorder is known. It is therefore possible to contribute to somebody's well-being by avoiding problems that immediately impact on quality of life even where people are unable to report health problems or sensory impairments directly.

Other implications are more subtle. For example, knowing that sensory or other stimuli may be experienced differently by some people allows us to understand why people might seek or avoid different experiences and environments. Also, knowing that specific genetic disorders might be associated with specific cognitive differences allows us to better understand the perspective of someone with that genetic disorder. Consequently we may understand that, for example, a task or situation that draws on specific cognitive processes might be experienced as carrying a higher load for some people than others. This suggests that cognitive training interventions may be possible and we may also understand why people might avoid such tasks or respond in a challenging way when they are presented. In each case, knowing something about a person's experience could help us tailor an environment in a way that promotes inclusion. Additionally, from a pragmatic point of view we may plan for the future if we know that cognitive difference will emerge at a given life stage. Finally, when specific health conditions have a high prevalence in a syndrome and are associated with challenging behaviour then effective intervention for that behaviour that is immediately appropriate can be implemented.

When we know that behaviours that are problematic in people who have genetic disorders can result from physical and psychological difference there are a number of beneficial outcomes. First, the attributions of those involved with the person may shift away from blame with a resultant increase in optimism to change and an increased willingness to help. There is also anecdotal evidence that parents and carers experience much less guilt regarding the attempts they may have made to change behaviour and their potential role in its cause. The models that we can build of the relationship between physical and psychological difference and behaviours that are problematic allow us to develop better interventions that incorporate medical procedures and cognitive strategies as well as more traditional behavioural methods. Knowing something about the presence of a genetic disorder can also help us to prioritize assessment and intervention strategies and to target interventions more specifically at underlying cause in a way that is likely to yield greater generalization. Finally, there is a possibility that the immediate social and physical environment can be tailored to cater for psychological difference in a way that might avoid a problematic behavioural outcome. This is immediately pertinent to quality of life and individual well-being.

While we have focused on genetic disorders and their relationship with physical, cognitive, emotional and behavioural outcomes it is likely that other causes of intellectual disability are associated with specific non-genetic causes. For example, the behavioural phenotype of foetal alcohol syndrome is becoming evident and the implications that are outlined above of knowing an association between this syndrome and given outcomes are therefore relevant. Throughout this chapter, in part because of the nature of the literature, we have focused on what might be considered impairments and behaviours that are problematic. However, it is important to emphasize that identifying cognitive emotional and behavioural difference does not, necessarily, carry a value judgement. It simply identifies a difference. Given the evidence it is clear that biological difference of demonstrable importance (as opposed to that which is irrelevant) should have equal recognition to, for example, cultural heritage or socio-economic position as it exerts a similar level of influence on a person's past and present experience. To do otherwise runs the risk of ignoring important information that might be of benefit to people with a genetic disorder.

Equally, it is clear that simplistic interpretations of gene behaviour associations are of significant concern and must be challenged, particularly given their potential connotations. A similar argument can be made for raising the profile of the importance of the physical, cognitive, emotional and behavioural outcomes of a genetic disorder at the level of practitioner training and policy. In this context the role of syndrome support groups (e.g. the Down's Syndrome Association, the Cornelia de Lange Syndrome Foundation) should be extended. There are numerous groups that collate and disseminate information more effectively than the traditional routes and so deserve both recognition and support.

Finally, there are two issues that we would make explicit. The first is that promoting the importance of knowing about genetic disorders and behavioural phenotypes is not inconsistent with embracing, rather than rejecting, diversity and difference. It does not follow that identifying difference leads to marginalizing or devaluing people who are in some ways different. There is an interim step that is unrelated to the knowledge. The second is that in order to promote the well-being of people who experience atypical neurological development it is important to recognize the complementary and supportive roles for advocacy, altruism and science while knowing when each is best deployed.

Acknowledgement

Preparation of this chapter was supported by funds from Cerebra.

References

Ball, S.L., Holland, A.J., Hon, J., Huppert, F.A., Treppner, P., and Watson, P.C. (2006) Personality and behaviour changes mark the early stages of Alzheimer's disease in adults with Down's syndrome: findings from a prospective population-based study, *International Journal of Geriatric Psychiatry*, 21: 661–73.

Beange, H., McElduff, A. and Baker, W. (1995) Medical disorders of adults with mental retardation: a population study, *American Journal on Mental Retardation*, 99: 595–604.

Bellugi, U., Jarvinen-Pasley, A., Doyle, T.F., Reilly, J., Reiss, A.L. and Korenberg, J.R. (2007) Affect, social behavior, and the brain in Williams syndrome, *Current Directions in Psychological Science*, 16: 99–104.

Berney, T.P., Ireland, M. and Burn, J. (1999) Behavioural phenotype of Cornelia de Lange syndrome, *Archive of Disease in Children*, 81: 333–6.

Butler, J., Whittington, J., Holland, A.J., Boer, H., Clarke, D. and Webb, T. (2002) Prevalence of, and risk factors for, physical ill-health in people with Prader Willi syndrome: a population-based study, *Developmental Medicine and Child Neurology*, 44: 248–55.

Cassidy, S.B. and Schwartz, S. (1998) Prader-Willi and Angelman syndromes. Disorders of genomic imprinting, *Medicine (Baltimore)*, 77: 140–51.

Clayton-Smith, J. and Laan, L. (2003) Angelman syndrome: a review of the clinical and genetic aspects, *Journal of Medical Genetics*, 40: 87–95.

Collis, L., Oliver, C. and Moss, J. (2006) Low mood and social anxiety in Cornelia de Lange Syndrome, *Journal of Intellectual Disability Research*, 50: 792.

Cosgrave, M.P., Tyrrell, J., McCarron, M., Gill, M. and Lawlor, B.A. (1999) Age at onset of dementia and age of menopause in women with Down's syndrome, *Journal of Intellectual Disability Research*, 43: 461–5.

Davies, D. and Evans, L. (2001) Assessing pain in people with profound learning disabilities, *British Journal of Nursing*, 10: 513–16.

Dykens, E.M., Hodapp, R.M. and Finucane, B.M. (2000) *Genetics and Mental Retardation Syndromes: A New Look at Behaviour and Interventions*. London: Paul Brookes Publishing Co.

Einfeld, S., Smith, A., Durvasula, S., Florio, T. and Tonge, B.J. (1999) Behavior and emotional disturbance in Prader-Willi syndrome, *American Journal of Medical Genetics*, 82: 123–7.

Finucane, B., Dirrigl, K. and Simon, E. (2001) Characterization of self-injurious behaviors in children and adults with Smith-Magenis syndrome, *American Journal on Mental Retardation*, 106: 52–8.

Foley, D.C. and McCutcheon, H. (2004) Detecting pain in people with an intellectual disability, *Accident and Emergency Nursing*, 12: 196–200.

Freeman, S.B., Taft, L.F., Dooley, K.J., Allran, K., Sherman, S.L., Hassold, T.J. et al. (1998) Population-based study of congenital heart defects in Down syndrome, *American Journal of Medical Genetics*, 80: 213–17.

Hagerman, R.J., Altshul-Stark, D. and McBogg, P. (1987) Recurrent otitis media in the fragile X syndrome, *American Journal of Diseases in Children*, 141: 184–7.

Hawley, P.P., Jackson, L.G. and Kurnit, D.M. (1985) Sixty-four patients with Brachmann-de Lange syndrome: a survey, *American Journal of Medical Genetics*, 20: 453–9.

Hinton, E.C., Holland, A.J., Gellatly, M.S.N., Soni, S., Patterson, M., Ghatei, M.A. et al. (2006) Neural representations of hunger and satiety in Prader-Willi syndrome, *International Journal of Obesity*, 30: 313–21.

Hodapp, R. (1997) Direct and indirect behavioral effects of different genetic disorders of mental retardation, *American Journal on Mental Retardation*, 102: 67–79.

Holland, A.J., Hon, J., Huppert, F.A., Stevens, F. and Watson, P. (1998) Population-based study of the prevalence and presentation of dementia in adults with Down's syndrome, *British Journal of Psychiatry*, 172: 493–8.

Horsler, K. and Oliver, C. (2006) Environmental influences on the behavioral phenotype of Angelman syndrome, *American Journal on Mental Retardation*, 111: 311–21.

Jarrold, C., Baddeley, A.D. and Hewes, A.K. (1999) Genetically dissociated components of working memory: evidence from Downs and Williams syndrome, *Neuropsychologia*, 37: 637–51.

Kelves, D.J. (1995) *In the Name of Eugenics*. London: Harvard University Press.

Kitcher, P. (1996) *The Lives to Come: The Genetic Revolution and Human Possibilities*. New York: Touchstone.

Klein, A.J., Armstrong, B.L., Greer, M.K. and Brown, F.R. III (1990) Hyperacusis and otitis media in individuals with Williams syndrome, *Journal of Speech and Hearing Disorders*, 55: 339–44.

Klingberg, T., Forssberg, H. and Westerberg, H. (2002) Training of working memory in children with ADHD, *Journal of Clinical and Experimental Neuropsychology*, 24: 781–91.

Lavin, C.W. and McKeown, C.A. (1993) The oculocerebrorenal syndrome of Lowe, *International Ophthalmology Clinics*, 33: 179–91.

Luzzani, S., Macchini, F., Valade, A., Milani, D. and Selicorni, A. (2003) Gastroesophageal reflux and Cornelia de Lange syndrome: typical and atypical symptoms, *American Journal of Medical Genetics Part A*, 119: 283–7.

Martens, M.A., Wilson, S.J. and Reutens, D.C. (2008) Research review: Williams syndrome: a critical review of the cognitive, behavioral, and neuroanatomical phenotype, *Journal of Child Psychology and Psychiatry*, 49: 576–608.

Minassian, B., Delorey, T., Olsen, R., Philippart, M., Bronstein, Y., Zhang, Q. *et al.* (1998) Angelman syndrome: correlations between epilepsy phenotypes and genotypes, *Annals of Neurology*, 43: 485–93.

Moss, J.F., Oliver, C., Berg, K., Kaur, G. and Jephcott, L. (2008) Prevalence of Autism Spectrum Phenomenology in Cornelia de Lange and Cri du Chat Syndromes, *American Journal on Mental Retardation*, 113: 278–91.

Moss, J., Oliver, C., Arron, K., Burbidge, C. and Berg, K. (2009) The prevalence and phenomenology of repetitive behaviour in genetic syndromes, *Journal of Autism and Developmental Disorders*, 39: 572–88.

Musumeci, S.A., Hagerman, R.J., Ferri, R., Bosco, P., Dalla, B.B., Tassinari, C.A. *et al.* (1999) Epilepsy and EEG findings in males with fragile X syndrome, *Epilepsia*, 40: 1092–9.

Oliver, C. and Woodcock, K.A. (2008) Integrating levels of explanation in behavioural phenotype research, *Journal of Intellectual Disability Research*, 52: 807–9.

Oliver, C., Crayton, L., Holland, A., Hall, S. and Bradbury, J. (1998) A four year prospective study of age-related cognitive change in adults with Down's syndrome, *Psychological Medicine*, 28: 1365–77.

Oliver, C., Horsler, K., Berg, K., Bellamy, G., Dick, K. and Griffiths, E. (2007) Genomic imprinting and the expression of affect in Angelman syndrome: what's in the smile? *Journal of Child Psychology and Psychiatry*, 48: 571–9.

Oliver, C., Sloneem, J., Hall, S. and Arron, K. (2009) Self-injurious behaviour in Cornelia de Lange syndrome: 1. Prevalence and phenomenology, *Journal of Intellectual Disability Research*, 53: 575–89.

Ouellette-Kuntz, H. (2005) Understanding health disparities and inequities faced by individuals with intellectual disabilities, *Journal of Applied Research in Intellectual Disability*, 18: 113–21.

Porter, M.A., Coltheart, M. and Langdon, R. (2007) The neuropsychological basis of hypersociability in Williams and Down syndrome, *Neuropsychologia*, 45: 2839–49.

Powis, L.A., Waite, J.E., Apperly, I., Beck, S. and Oliver, C. (2009) Linking social cognition and executive functioning to phenotypic behaviours in Rubinstein Taybi syndrome, *Journal of Intellectual Disability Research*, 53: 835.

Richards, C., Moss, J., O'Farrell, L., Kaur, G. and Oliver, C. (2009) Social anxiety in Cornelia de Lange syndrome, *Journal of Autism and Developmental Disorders*, 39: 1155–62.

Ridley, M. (1999) *Genome: The Autobiography of a Species in 23 Chapters*. London: Fourth Estate Ltd.

Rubello, D., Pozzan, G.B., Casara, D., Girelli, M.E., Boccato, S., Rigon, F. *et al.* (1995) Natural course of subclinical hypothyroidism in Down's syndrome: prospective study results and therapeutic considerations, *Journal of Endocrinological Investigation*, 18: 35–40.

Sakai, Y., Watanabe, T. and Kaga, K. (2002) Auditory brainstem responses and usefulness of hearing aids in hearing impaired children with Cornelia de Lange syndrome, *International Journal of Pediatric Otorhinolaryngology*, 66: 63–9.

Spencer, J., O'Brien, J., Braddick, J., Atkinson, O., Wattam-Bell, J. and Riggs, K. (2000) Form and motion processing in autism, *Perception*, 29: 98–9.

Sreeram, N., Wren, C., Bhate, M., Robertson, P. and Hunter, S. (1989) Cardiac abnormalities in the fragile X syndrome, *British Heart Journal*, 61: 289–91.

Strachan, R., Shaw, R., Burrow, C., Horsler, K., Allen, D. and Oliver, C. (2009) Experimental functional analysis of aggression in children with Angelman Syndrome, *Research in Developmental Disabilities*, 30: 1095–106.

Tripathi, R.C., Cibis, G.W. and Tripathi, B.J. (1986) Pathogenesis of cataracts in patients with Lowe's syndrome, *Ophthalmology*, 93: 1046–51.

Wallace, R.A. (2004) Risk factors for coronary artery disease among individuals with rare syndrome intellectual disabilities, *Journal of Policy and Practice in Intellectual Disabilities*, 1: 42–51.

Walter, E.G. (1922) *Genetics: An Introduction to the Study of Heredity*. New York: The Macmillan Company.

Wisniewski, K.E., Wisniewski, H.M. and Wen, G.Y. (1985) Occurrence of neuropathological changes and dementia of Alzheimer's disease in Down's syndrome, *Annals of Neurology*, 17: 278–82.

Woodcock, K.A., Oliver, C. and Humphreys, G.W. (2009a) Associations between repetitive questioning, resistance to change, temper outbursts and anxiety in Prader-Willi and Fragile-X syndromes, *Journal of Intellectual Disability Research*, 53: 265–78.

Woodcock, K.A., Oliver, C. and Humphreys, G.W. (2009b) Task switching deficits and repetitive behaviour in genetic neurodevelopmental disorders: data from children with Prader-Willi syndrome chromosome 15 q11–q13 deletion and boys with Fragile-X syndrome, *Cognitive Neuropsychology*, 26: 172–94.

Woodcock, K.A., Oliver, C. and Humphreys, G.W. (2009c) Hypothesis: a specific pathway can be identified between genetic characteristics and behaviour profiles in Prader-Willi syndrome via cognitive, environmental and physiological mechanisms, *Journal of Intellectual Disability Research*, 53: 493–500.

11

Breaking the news and early intervention

Bronach Crawley

Introduction

There are moments in any life when a familiar, well trodden pathway shifts course. Sometimes these moments arrive slowly, each step forward signalling the junction to come, such as the day of birth after nine long months of waiting, or the moment a loved one dies after a prolonged illness. But whether arriving slowly or abruptly, these moments create the 'before' and 'after' occasions through which a life is defined, as on the day a child achieves exceptional grades and is plucked out from the rest as having special potential; or the day a man hears out of the blue that he is to be made redundant from the job that he has loved and in which his identity is rooted; or the day on which parents hear that their beautiful child has a problem, a problem that will never go away.

For the practitioner, breaking the news of a diagnosis that has lifelong implications for a child and its family and carrying out interventions in the early years that follow is never easy. Being faced with a wide range of emotions, sometimes searing in their intensity, sometimes unrealistically demanding in their expectation of help, challenges not only one's skill and humanity but also one's confidence. For the child and the members of his or her family, how these moments unfold and are subsequently managed can have a profound impact and create repercussions reaching far into the years ahead.

As a clinical psychologist who has worked with children and adults with special needs, and as a parent of a child with Down's syndrome and autism, I have experience of both sides of this situation. I have spent time with families in the early weeks of a diagnosis, witnessing their confusion and their pain as the unexpected enters their lives, and I have cradled my own baby in a maternity ward wondering 'why me?' From this experience, I am keenly aware that there are actions that support parents, there are actions that make little difference despite effort and intention, and

there are some actions that make a difficult situation worse. The aim of this chapter is to provide guidance to help make professional support in the early days and years of diagnosis as effective as possible. The chapter focuses first on initial support with family members, the point at which they learn that their child has a disability. It then considers how the subsequent input to a family can add the greatest value. Families with whom I have been associated have given their permissions to be quoted.

When news is given

A diagnosis of disability can be made at any stage of a life and the timing of this news can have significant implications for who breaks the news, the way it is handled and reactions to it.

Antenatal screening

Advances in screening technology through amniocentesis, chorionic villus sampling and high-definition scanning have meant that in recent years the detection of disability has moved from using measures of probability to measures of near certainty. To add to this battery, a number of research centres are currently working on a simple, non-invasive blood test in which foetal markers are extracted from maternal blood (Fan *et al.* 2008). Screening of this nature opens up the possibility of genetic analysis during the very early part of pregnancy for those at high risk but also for those who previously would not have thought this necessary. Separate from the ethical considerations that medical advances of this nature provoke, mass screening will have considerable practical ramifications for which services must be prepared. Couples may not be fully aware of what they have undertaken when agreeing to screening and the decisions they will face if the result is not as they had wished. What support services will be available to them to help them come to terms with this news and with their decision regarding continuing or terminating the pregnancy? Little research has yet been done in understanding how information at this stage affects pregnant women, their partners or their children (Lalor *et al.* 2007). The load placed on the antenatal team in terms of breaking the news of test results will increase significantly. Will they be prepared for this task?

Experts in screening, who often have first contact with a parent at the time of, or soon after, a test may not be the best people to offer support or information beyond the test result. For example, a mother of a child with Down's syndrome who had chorionic villus sampling for a subsequent pregnancy was amazed that the highly regarded consultant carrying it out knew very little about the syndrome.

> Although he knew exactly how to detect the disorder in the womb, he had no concept of what it meant in real life. He hadn't met anyone with Down's syndrome. He presumed the downside but knew nothing of the upside, of the fulfilling and valuable lives that most people with Down's syndrome now live.

While those involved in screening may be in the front line of breaking news, helping a woman and her partner come to terms with this knowledge and make a decision about whether to continue with the pregnancy requires a different set of skills. Knowledgeable staff who can provide accurate information and sensitive, empathic help need to be on hand or readily accessible. Support groups composed of those who have been in this position, and others who have balanced knowledge of the disability, can be of tremendous value in enabling a couple deal with their situation.

At birth or soon after

We are familiar with the image of breaking news at birth or in the first few days of life when a child is born with tell tale signs that something is amiss. As most babies are still born in hospital, the doctors on call are most frequently charged with managing this situation. Texts on disability are littered with examples of how this has been mishandled. When it is, the adverse impact on parents can be significant. In

their study of families with children with Down's syndrome, Byrne *et al.* (1988) concluded:

> Throughout our contact with the cohort of families, a consistent theme has emerged of the importance of the way in which the diagnosis was told to parents and the support they were offered in the first few months . . . The way they were treated at this early, sensitive stage can influence how they feel about the child, about themselves and about professionals both in the short and long term.
>
> (Byrne *et al.* 1988: 138)

Fortunately, this study also found that training those involved produced a significant improvement in parental satisfaction with the way news was broken, a finding that has been replicated with those working in oncology (Abel *et al.* 2001) and elsewhere.

I recall my own experience of receiving the diagnosis of my son's Down's syndrome with total clarity. He was my first child. As I write this, I can almost feel the excitement that enveloped me on the journey to the hospital. I can see myself through every stage of labour and at the moment my baby arrived. My husband held him first then handed him to me and as I gazed at my son, unable to think of anything other than that the hardest part was over, he said quietly, 'I think our little boy has Down's syndrome.' My husband knew instantly but I chose not to see. 'All new babies look ugly', I said. The midwife was non-committal, suggesting that she would call the paediatrician because the baby was rather floppy. She also knew but felt she could not say. Then the mood around us began to change. Another midwife appeared and I was aware of quiet chattering in the background. When I looked again, I saw too but I still chose to deny it. 'Perhaps we are wrong', I said, hanging on to a thinning thread of hope. Then, a few minutes later, as I was being stitched up, with my legs in stirrups, the paediatrician arrived and proceeded to examine my tiny scrap of a son on the trolley next to me, talking to us as the midwife worked away with her needle. The paediatrician was softly spoken but direct. He asked us what we thought and then he simply confirmed our fears. We had done his job for him. He was sure that our son had Down's syndrome and at that moment everything in our lives spun. Our pathway pivoted violently.

Now I often laugh about the fact that this life-changing information was given when I was in such an undignified position but at the time that didn't matter to me one jot. The doctor did what he had to do. He spoke to us together. He recognized that our immediate need was to know but he checked first if we wanted him to come back later. He gave us the information we needed and told us what was to happen next. He was sensitive and empathic in his manner but he was not there to provide a shoulder to cry on. He did all he could, for he could not change the news he had to give.

At a later stage

Many disorders, such as autism, are not obvious at birth and only evidence themselves weeks, months or years later as concerns grow and professionals are alerted to the problem. If it comes as a surprise, the eventual diagnosis can be as painful as news given at birth, as in the instance of a couple who were informed that the delightful child they had taken home as a 'normal healthy baby' only six months earlier had a genetic condition that was likely to end her life within the following 12 months; or the parents who put their 3-year-old's difficult and uncommunicative behaviour down to him being a 'character' rather than the autism that the paediatrician confirms. For others, a formal diagnosis evolves over time and may eventually come as a relief as it provides not only some explanation about the difficulties their child has encountered but also access to services that may help:

> Our son has Down's syndrome and was diagnosed with autism at age 7. We knew from about 3 that he was different from other children with Down's syndrome and had to fight to get the second diagnosis. When it was finally confirmed, it came as a relief because we could now seek the help that he needed.

For some, particularly those with Aspergers syndrome, diagnosis may come very late indeed. Then, a system that is designed around diagnosis in childhood can be poor at responding:

> I had a late non-standard diagnosis of AS at the age of 25. I am very high functioning. I have very mild AS. I have a degree and a post-graduate qualification. I am taking professional exams having taken the second stage at the age of 29. I can get temporary work but not secure relevant employment. I received almost no post diagnostic support after my sloppy diagnosis . . . If I did not help myself, I would have little prospect in life.

It would seem that although our ability to detect some disorders accurately has improved at prenatal and the early stages of life, we have still some way to go to detect the more subtle disabilities that can still have a dramatic impact on the quality of an individual's life and those around him or or her.

Reactions to bad news

When given news of a diagnosis, whether confirming existing suspicions or as fresh information, individual families react in their own way. However, one model suggesting a common pathway through which negative experiences are processed has come to dominate thinking about loss. In a book first published in 1969 and still selling 40 years later, Elisabeth Kubler-Ross identified an emotional journey that she frequently observed in her work with those who were dying or had lost loved ones. She applied her model to any major negative event and called it 'The five stages of dealing with catastrophic loss'.

The stages she identified are:

- *Denial*: It's a mistake. It can't be happening.
- *Anger*: It's not fair! How can this happen to me? Who is to blame?
- *Bargaining*: Please God, let the results be wrong and then I'll . . .
- *Depression*: What's the point? I'm so sad, why bother with anything?
- *Acceptance*: It's not good but we can handle it. We'll make the best of it.

Kubler-Ross was an extraordinary campaigner who raised awareness of how those who experience loss can be supported. However, she built her model on her experiences and her intuition rather than detailed research. Indeed, there has been little research to substantiate her findings despite its almost universal application in the field of loss, although a recent study at Yale University (Maciejewski *et al.* 2007) did support some aspects but not others. Some critics have even suggested that the model has been more harmful than of value (Friedman and James 2008). Yet, for those who have worked with people experiencing significant loss, the model does have an intuitive integrity provided it is not applied in a prescriptive manner. Kubler-Ross did not intend that her model should be used as a rigid guide. She acknowledged that the stages do not always come in the order given and that people can move back and forth between the different emotions involved. The real lesson of her model was that emotions change with time.

When professionals over-rely on a particular model, they risk assuming that everyone experiencing the same event requires the same intervention. Immediately after the paediatrician confirmed that our son had Down's syndrome, we were moved into a room which we named the 'tragedy suite'. It was at the end of the corridor, away from all the other new mothers. Effort had been made to make the surroundings comfortable and homely. It had a pine double bed so that partners could stay, flowery curtains, comfy chairs and its own bathroom but the feature I remember most is the small hatch, in the otherwise solid door, that was raised at regular intervals so that the nurses could check on us. I ventured out of this room only to fill my plate from the food trolley, feeling like a prisoner in a cell, completely out of control, trapped and powerless. Being watched. Being expected to break.

The maternity staff had produced a packet of information on Down's syndrome which they were very keen to give us. As someone who had worked in the field and knew a fair amount about it, the last thing I wanted at that point was information. I had plenty of positive role models of people I had known with Down's syndrome to help me through. My mother-in-law had spent her entire career as a teacher and headmistress in special education so my husband was also already well informed. But each day, the nursing staff tried again to hand over their carefully constructed pack of papers. Even the consultant had a go. Clearly, we were not playing the game. I have no doubt that the staff believed they were acting in our best interests and were following good practice in providing information but what they didn't do was find out what *we* wanted. They didn't hear our desperate need to go home with our baby, to be as ordinary as we could and come to terms with the fact that our baby was different in our own surroundings.

Instead, we were kept in the hospital for a week, becoming more desperate to escape each day. Then, with only two hours' notice, I was told that I was to be discharged because they needed the room. Another tragedy had occurred.

Exercise 11.1

Think of a time when you've been told something that you did not want to hear, some news that you had not expected or hoped would be different.

How did you react at the moment of hearing the news?

How did your reaction change with time?

How do you feel about it now?

Guidance for telling parents difficult news

Guidelines for the process of giving difficult news abound so there is no excuse for entering this territory unprepared. For the prenatal period, Contact a Family (2006) have produced a short and straightforward checklist. For highly detailed guidance covering diagnosis at any stage, the material produced by the Irish National Federation of Voluntary Bodies Providing Services to People with Intellectual Disabilities (Harnett 2007), drawn from their Informing Families research project, provides a valuable resource. And for those who like acronyms to jog the memory, the SPIKES model (Baile *et al.* 2000) is a simple prompt for handling the initial meeting. The striking thing about these guidelines, and others, is the absence of anything technical or specialist. They are very straightforward, the kind of advice a wise grandparent would give, and they centre on one word – respect. Respect for parents, respect for their child, and respect for the professionals involved. The core themes they present are summarized below.

Respect for parents

Respect the parents' right to know

Parents have a right to know about their child's condition as soon as it is confirmed, or in some cases when it is first suspected. When parental suspicion is aroused by quiet comments, indirect references, nudges or stonewalling, anxiety and anger rise. Parents know when something is amiss. In the absence of words, they read the atmosphere. Try to avoid jargon and get to the point quickly but give families some control over the pace at which information is presented. Check out whether the pace is too fast or too slow. Ask what they already know or are concerned about. Ask what they want to know. Being excluded from information belittles parents. As one mother recalled:

> I knew as soon as he was born that he had Down's syndrome. I knew the midwife knew too but she clearly wasn't allowed to say. We had to wait right the way through the night before they could find a doctor to come out and confirm it. It was dreadful.

Parents who have little knowledge of a disability often crave information in the first few hours and days of their baby's life. Those likely to be in contact with such families should have a working knowledge of common conditions and easy access to information on less common disorders.

Respect the parents' right to be heard

Listen to what parents have to say, their questions, their concerns, their pure emotion. Listen not just to the words but to the feeling that goes with them, to the body language that may express what words cannot. Sit near enough so you can see this. Respond to the parents' questions and add additional information you believe to be relevant. And that means relevant, not everything you know.

Respect the parents' right to be treated with dignity

Breaking bad news in a hospital corridor, in view of others, when a mobile phone or bleeper keeps going off, with a student sitting in, or in a hurry because you've really got to be somewhere more important, all smack of disrespect. When told difficult news, parents are not at their best. Allow them privacy, time and dedication. Show them that they matter to you and that you appreciate the gravity of the situation.

Respect the parents' right to react in the way they want to react

Don't assume that parents will break down and sob in front of you but if they do, don't hurry it along or try to make anyone feel better. Just be there, showing that you care. Don't interpret lack of response as denial. Ask how people feel and respect the response given even if you think it does not accurately reflect what you can see and hear. It is not your job to provoke a response but simply to let parents know that you are there to provide what they need.

Respect for the child

Give full recognition that the child is first and foremost a child

However disabled, however unwell, a child brings positive value to the world even if that value may not be apparent to some parents in the early days of a diagnosis. To empathize with the mourning of the longed-for 'perfect' child is indeed appropriate but to ignore the value of the child that has arrived is unforgivable. I recall once going to see a psychologist about the behaviour of my son. She spoke only to me and took no interest in the beautiful little boy who played in her room. She wanted to know *about* him, not to know *him*. Needless to say, I did not go back.

Retain a balance

In response to initial parental despair, it is easy either to be drawn into agreement and thereby become overly pessimistic, or to try to counter grief by being overly optimistic. It is possible, however, to remain balanced by empathizing with the parents' concerns while still retaining a realistic view on the child's future in so far as it can be predicted. To do this, it is essential to be comfortable with emotional situations, to be able to sit with someone in the moment of their pain. In my experience, however distressed parents may feel when a diagnosis is given, it helps to remember that eventually few would choose to be without their child. Loving a child, and being loved in return, is not contingent on perfection as explained by this mother:

> My journey with my son has brought me to a place of acceptance I could never have imagined. For all his complex challenges I only

have to see his enormous smile each morning to be reminded to live in the moment as he does. When he does learn something new, such as pulling on his socks, as he did this year, I am moved to tears. My son has given me the opportunity to discover what it really means to love unconditionally.

Respect for the professional

Be more than a professional. Be human

However sophisticated our training, however experienced we may be, events with a strong emotional component do not, and should not, leave us untouched. We bring ourselves to these situations first and foremost as human beings, not just as people with qualifications but as people with hearts that are affected by others' sadness, with our own fears about what may lie ahead in our lives, with our own memories of grief that may be sparked by others' emotions. In their grief, parents do not want to be faced with a professional carrying out a task. They want people. In a review of medical literature on breaking neurological bad news to parents, Jan and Girvin (2002) conclude:

> Parents prefer professionals who show a genuine caring attitude, who encourage and allow them to talk and who show understanding of their emotional responses. Sensitivity to both informational content and parents' reactions is critical . . . In twenty first century medicine this part of the 'art' of medicine is too often sacrificed in deference to the science of medicine.
>
> (Jan and Girvin 2002: 81)

Recognize your own needs

Being with families who are in pain is no easy task as the pain impacts on everyone involved. As Auger (2006) notes, 'Physicians report that the stress associated with the delivery of difficult news persists hours or days after the interaction.' Unless we recognize our own need for support, we are unlikely to be effective in our professional life. Formal supervision or the friendly ear of a colleague can be enough to help make us more competent professionals and to grow as human beings.

Prepare

Practitioners can and should be prepared for their role in imparting life-changing news and supporting parents thereafter. However, we should not assume that because guidelines and training are available we are getting it right. In a large-scale Irish survey of parents of children with intellectual disabilities and practitioners, the practitioners rated their satisfaction with the way news was given much higher than parents (62 per cent compared with 36 per cent). The practitioners thought they were doing a good job but those on the receiving end often felt differently. In our preparation, therefore, we should hone our listening skills and our ability to show empathy. We should ensure that we have adequate knowledge about conditions that might arise and ready access to information to give to parents. We should test our own emotions about disability and practise the process of giving difficult-to-hear news. Such preparation improves the confidence of those involved and their ability to ask for support from senior colleagues (Horwitz and Ellis 2005) and improves competence (Byrne *et al.* 1988). However, we should not expect that brief training on its own is enough. Ongoing supervision should be given to ensure that professionals are undertaking their role effectively and that their own emotional needs are recognized.

Have a clear brief on what happens next

The giving of news is only the beginning. Parents want to know what will happen next, particularly if there are further tests needed to confirm the diagnosis or complications arising from it. A named person co-ordinating the next steps, and those leading into early intervention, enable parents to have a point of contact and to build a relationship during an extremely difficult time.

Be clear about your role

Who is doing what? Liaise with different professionals to present a common front to parents, particularly when a variety of health professionals are involved. In their work with children with cerebral palsy, Baird *et al.* (2000) found this co-ordination was often not in place and stress the particular importance of liaison between neonatal and community paediatric services. Families cannot afford us to be territorial.

Beyond diagnosis into early intervention

Ask any new parent how they feel about taking their newborn home and they'll probably say that they wished it had come with a manual. While advice and information are freely available to expectant mothers, after delivery, it is over to mum and dad to find their way. In most societies, however, informal support networks often come to the rescue. Grannies, in-laws, siblings and friends who have had children of their own are usually only too willing to give advice and, if you're lucky, to pitch in with some hands-on help. In the same way, the family of a child with a disability will have informal networks offering support although they may not always work as effectively. Family and friends can be wary of approaching parents, uncertain what to say or do. This distance can deny the family of much needed practical help:

> No one felt able to hold him, thinking they needed to do something special. As if he wasn't an ordinary baby.

Or with an older child, they may simply feel out of their depth:

> He was too much of a handful for my mum to help out. She wanted to but she just couldn't. We can't leave him with anyone now. They're very wary of being alone with him because he can be so unpredictable which means we have no cover for emergencies or any break except when he's at school.

Of course, it isn't always like this and many parents receive great comfort and help from their extended families and friends. When it does work, informal support feels natural because it is part of everyday life.

Appointments, visits, therapies and generally any intervention that comes from an organized body are recognized as formal interventions. Where things start to differ is when the other interventions fill up the calendar. Paediatricians, neurologists, physiotherapists, speech therapists, dieticians, social workers and many more create a growing list of practitioners with whom the child and its family may come into contact. Intervention may be preventative in nature, as in the case of physiotherapy for children with cerebral palsy to help stop their joints and muscles becoming stiff or 'contracted' (see Chapter 12). It can be remedial where a problem has developed and the intervention is designed to remove or manage it, such as dealing with behaviour problems or medical complications (see Chapters 10 and 17). Often, however, interventions are aimed at developing the child's potential where learning would otherwise be slow or unlikely to occur at all.

Why intervene early?

After the initial disorientation period following a diagnosis, parents often clamour for support. They want to know what can be done to help their child. There is a shared belief among both families and parents that getting in early is critical. For some, this intervention starts almost immediately, as at one centre in the US (The Bell Centre) where disabled children are enrolled onto programmes from as young as 2 days old. Indeed, when talking of early intervention, we mean mostly interventions started within the first three years of life. In their review of the literature on early intervention, Newman *et al.* (2009) found very few papers relating to children from age 4 onwards. Yet, we do not have evidence to show that the timing of intervention in the early years, as opposed to later, is as critical as it may feel to those involved. Michael Rutter (2002) writes that research on brain development in early childhood has been misleadingly extrapolated to suggest that higher quality experiences in the first two or three years of life will have a much greater effect than similar experiences later on, pointing out that 'brain development is far from over by age 3 years. On the contrary, important changes continue to occur through adolescence. Also, it is not the case that neuronal growth stops in early life or that plasticity is lost after infant years' (Rutter 2002: 13).

So why the rush to intervene? At a basic level, when something occurs that is unexpected, and we cannot change or remedy the event, we experience a significant blow to our fundamental need for security. We feel powerless and there is a hunger to regain control, to show that even if we cannot remove the fundamental problem, we can at least improve it. In addition, the early years of a child's life tend to be recorded in milestones – the first smile, the first word and so on. All are used as measures of progress and any parent of a disabled child is well aware of how their child's developmental path digresses from these norms. Support that aims to keep the developmental track as close as possible to the norm, or at least slowing the rate of divergence from it, is one way of retaining hope that the child's condition is not as disabling as at first feared, which may or may not be the case.

Is early intervention a 'good thing'?

At a strategic level, it has been suggested that intervention at an early age could make best use of limited resources. In a startling report, Knapp *et al.* (2007) estimate that the lifetime cost for someone with high-functioning autism is £3.1 million and £4.6 million for a less able individual. That's an aggregate national cost of £2.7 billion each year for supporting children with ASD and an eye-watering £25 billion for adults (including the cost of services, lost employment and family expenses). They suggest two reasons why these estimates are important:

> Firstly, there are early interventions available that help alter behaviour patterns. Would increased investment in these reduce high support costs in adulthood? Secondly, a greater availability of effective early interventions may reduce the impact of ASD on the UK economy as well as improve the quality of life for people with ASD and their families.
>
> (Knapp *et al.* 2007: 3)

But do we have the evidence that early intervention has the pay-off that Knapp *et al.* suggest? At

an individual level for the child, we probably do. There are many studies showing the improvements made in particular dimensions in a whole range of therapeutic interventions, autism included. Whether these improvements would have occurred anyway in the longer term, whether they would have been learned more speedily when the child was older, or whether the improvements lasted in the long term to make the kind of difference Knapp *et al.* hope for, is less certain. A recent review by Newman *et al.* (2009) concludes:

> Overall, the research literature on early years' interventions for disabled children is relatively rich in well-constructed outcome studies. These are, however, mostly of US origin, largely reflecting the strong introduction of the Headstart programme. They are also primarily short term, examining outcomes achieved following the completion of the programme or after a short, usually less than 12 months, follow up.
>
> (Newman *et al.* 2009: 12)

They continue:

> Whilst early years interventions may have an overall positive effect, not all children will benefit equally. A one size fits all approach in terms of achieving equivalent outcomes is not indicated by the research base. Effectiveness studies need to examine which kinds of programme produce developmental progress for specific children and/or families.
>
> (Newman *et al.* 2009: 13)

Models of intervention

Perhaps one reason why the efficacy of early intervention programmes is so difficult to track is that models of intervention have changed over the years. Not so long ago, it was typical for the expert to give direct, hands-on therapy to the child. In this 'professional as expert' model, the child was the focus of attention and the practitioner was the source of all knowledge. The parent was merely the escort, a bystander, a source of transport but little more. Out of necessity, approaches expanded to tap a willing and rich resource – parents. Family members thus became the agents of change, ready to implement expert-led programmes. A natural extension of this model was then to include family members as equal partners in the intervention process. In an excellent review of early intervention by Moore and Larkin (2005), this 'family-centred' model is described as an approach in which families are viewed as fully capable of making informed choices and acting on their choices. Professionals view themselves as agents of families who strengthen existing skills and promote the acquisition of new skills. Interventions emphasize capacity-building, resources and support. Family members are thus the experts on their child and become the designers of early intervention, flexing, developing and reviewing these interventions as appropriate. In this approach, the whole family is empowered and supported in the way family members believe will help them and their child most effectively.

Not only is the role of the family key in decision-making and design in the family-centred approach but the focus for intervention is the family as a whole. Intervening to improve the welfare of siblings, to strengthen the relationship between parents, to help lessen sources of stress in a family, to deal with practical day-to-day difficulties, and so on, all become valid goals, for whatever lifts the well-being of the family will impact on the well-being of the child. This type of systemic thinking in which the child is seen as part of a complex web of people and organizations is not easy. Family or social systems thinking tells us that an intervention at any point in a system can have an impact on other parts of the same system and that the other parts can influence the success or failure of an intervention elsewhere. If we really want to understand the value of an intervention, we have to think in a family-centred way which is why, as Moore and Larkin (2005) conclude, it is now the model of choice. For example, the UK Government's 'Children's Plan' (2007), which followed the 'Every Child Matters' agenda, is based on this philosophy. While its aim is stated as 'to improve the well-being of children and young people from birth to 19', it does so by the drive to 'place families at the heart of everything we do'.

Do families receive the best support?

The theory of best practice is one thing but reality is often a very different other. In a study of 6000 family service plans in the US, Perry et al. (2001) found that,

on average, only half of the service hours agreed on plans were actually delivered to children and families. In another study, when practitioners were observed on family visits, their actions were still primarily focused on hands-on intervention with the child rather than on broader actions concerning the whole family (McBride and Peterson 1997). Accordingly, it is not uncommon to hear families talk of the never-ending battle to obtain services.

Characteristics of positive support

Two recent literature reviews on early intervention (Moore and Larkin 2005; Newman et al. 2009) provide consistent indicators on what is required to make support a positive experience. They conclude that parents are most satisfied with support services that are:

- *Focused on the needs of the child and all those affected by the presence of a disabled family member.* The question at the beginning of early intervention must be 'what support needs to be given to the family to enable the disabled child to flourish in terms of health, development and fulfilment?' Only then can we help create the environment in which the child can progress in a sustainable way.

- *Accessible.* Designing the best intervention programmes, and informing families about them, has little merit if families do not have access to them. A finding in both UK and US studies is that eligibility criteria vary between funding bodies and lack transparency, which leads to unfairness and confusion for families (Scarborough et al. 2006; Council for Disabled Children 2009).

- *Based on clear goals developed in partnership with families.* Families are the experts on their children, on the needs of all family members and on their priorities for support. When my son was 3 weeks old, we received a visit from a speech therapist who described in detail the importance of getting children with Down's syndrome to drink as it was thought to improve the clarity of their speech. Strangely enough, speech was not on my agenda at that point! Putting the family in the driving seat does not make the professional redundant, for parents cannot make informed choices about intervention unless they are made aware of what is possible. Remember that parents are inexperienced in these matters at first. It will take time for them to become confident and competent at directing goals. One of the most valuable components of intervention is to help a family grow in this way.

- *Concerned with practical problems as well as more traditional therapies.* Families with a disabled child have higher levels of stress and are disadvantaged generally in a range of other areas. We know that poverty has the greatest influence on children's outcomes in the early years (Coghlan *et al.* 2009). Assisting with housing issues, the provision of physical aids, access to childcare, returning to work and so on can be of far greater value to the quality of life of the family and the child than intensive one-to-one development programmes.

- *Designed around the unique nature of each family.* Each child is unique and each family is different from any other. Both should be approached without assumptions about their difficulties or their requirements.

- *Flexible in terms of where, when, and changing priorities.* Services that are flexible to fit around the lifestyle and commitments of the family are far more likely to succeed than those that provide an extra burden on them. For example, interventions that are delivered in the child's natural surroundings have a greater chance of being generalized into the child's everyday life than those carried out in a therapist's office. Similarly, making appointments available outside working hours or when other small children have to be entertained, and recognizing that support needs do not go away at weekends or in school holidays, can significantly reduce the stress caused by interventions. Family circumstances are rarely static so practitioners need to be alive to this.

- *Wide-ranging and creative in their use of resources.* Support can come from anywhere. The more open we are to this notion, the more likely that we will provide the service that best meets the needs of the family. What a particular family requires may not yet exist and may require creative thought, and sometimes courage, to provide. If we are to make the best use of resources

and maximize the return on our efforts in early intervention, we need to see beyond existing menus of services.

- *Realistic in expectation.* While parental involvement in decision-making is key, parents cannot be responsible for providing the resources for all interventions. Much is asked of family members in implementing programmes in the home environment and elsewhere. Yet, these same family members are already responsible for the day-to-day care of their disabled child. What starts as a positive step can, at times, create an overwhelming burden of action, and a greater burden of guilt if it is not performed. One parent noted:

  > Reading and implementing things constantly is too depressing to contemplate. I believe I am not the only one craving some semblance of normality rather than spending every waking moment trying to be a behaviour specialist, nurse, physio, speech and language teacher, etc. etc. I just want to be a parent and have some fun in my family life.

  It is essential therefore for all to step back and reconsider the goal of intervention to ensure whether what is expected is realistic and sustainable, and whether it enables the family to experience enjoyment as well as a sense of achievement.

- *Supportive of the least advantaged.* Newman *et al.* (2009) conclude that while parents report significant long-term benefits from family-centred early interventions, the fewest benefits were reported by the most disadvantaged. Those with least 'social capital by virtue of illness, poor functioning, family structure, oppressive environments or poverty' are less equipped to take advantage of support services. They may also have more limited access to informal support and have a lower level of uptake of formal services, particularly when they speak a different first language (Hatton *et al.* 2002). These are the families who often suffer high levels of distress.

- *Co-ordinated, integrated and consistent.* Families ask for services where practitioners produce co-ordinated intervention plans, communicate freely with each other, and retain the family at the centre of their attention. Where possible, keeping the same core individuals involved with a family over time is of immense benefit in terms of building strong, supportive relationships. The key worker system has been found to be particularly valuable in this respect.

- *Staffed by professionals with both technical expertise and well-developed interpersonal skills.* Practitioners coming into contact with a family must have technical skill but, on its own, this is not enough. They also need the emotional maturity and sensitivity to share their expertise effectively. Being solely an expert or a counsellor does not work.
- *Positive in outlook.* While it is not appropriate to have unrealistic expectations, it is essential to hold out hope for a family, however small the steps concerned might be. Empathize with problems, but also ensure that the focus is on a solution to move the situation forward. This involves working with the strengths of the family rather than emphasizing what it lacks.

Exercise 11.3

Consider a formal or informal intervention in which you have been involved.

How well would it rate against the characteristics given above?

In retrospect, what would you have changed if you were to do it again?

Consider someone you know who receives support. How do their experiences compare with an ideal family-centred approach?

Conclusion

In the field of early intervention, as in many others, resources are scarce and demands are high. How effectively these scarce resources are used affects not only a financial balance sheet but the well-being of children, families and whole communities. Research findings now available provide us with sufficient guidance to ensure that the first major intervention with a family, the breaking of news of disability, is managed well. Research has also given us enough pointers to guide the policies on which subsequent early intervention services should be based. However, delivering the holistic service required is no small task. To do so, practitioners are required to be more than technical experts, more than banks of knowledge. They are called upon to befriend, to teach and to empower, to open doors and act as brokers for resources, to advocate and champion causes, to be agents of social change, to research and to inform, to be creative and systemic in approach and, perhaps hardest of all, to lay aside professional boundaries and work together. This is a tall order for those who design services and for the individuals who implement them but the potential rewards for children, families and ultimately society are great. As a parent of a disabled child, I feel we still have a long way to go before we achieve the ideal family-centred service that would have helped my family in the early years and would still help us now. As a practitioner, I feel we have no excuse not to keep striving to achieve it.

My family is ordinary. Having a child who has two disabilities is just normal to us. We live our lives as people, looking for fulfilment and joy. Although we face challenges at times, we know that many others do too for a wide variety of reasons. Everybody needs support at some time in their life. When someone walks through my door and offers that support, I want them to see us, not a family living with a disability. I want them to see the terrific young boy with whom we are lucky enough to share our lives.

References

Abel, J., Dennison, S., Senior-Smith, G., Dolley, T., Lovett, J. and Cassidy, S. (2001) Breaking bad news – development of a hospital-based training workshop, *The Lancet Oncology*, 2(6): 380–4.

Auger, R. (2006) Delivering difficult news to parents: guidelines for school counselors, *Professional School Counseling*, 10(2): 139.

Baile, W., Buckman, R., Lenzi, R., Glober, G., Beale, E. and Kudelka, A. (2000) SPIKES – a six-step protocol for delivering bad news: application to the patient with cancer, *The Oncologist*, 5(4): 302–11.

Baird, G., McConachie, H. and Scrutton, D. (2000) Parents'

perceptions of disclosure of the diagnosis of cerebral palsy, *Archives of Disease in Childhood*, 83: 475–80.

Byrne, E., Cunningham, C. and Sloper, P. (1988) *Families and their Children with Down's Syndrome: One Feature in Common*. London: Routledge.

Coghlan, M., Bergeron, C., White, K., Sharp, C., Morris, M. and Rutt, S. (2009) *Narrowing the Gap in Outcomes for Young Children through Effective Practices in the Early Years*. London: Centre for Excellence and Outcomes in Children and Young People's Services (C4EO).

Contact a Family (2006) *Working with Families Affected by a Disability or Health Condition, from Birth to Preschool. A Support Pack for Health Professionals*. London: Contact a Family.

Council for Disabled Children (2009) Statement issued on 24 August. London: CDC.

Fan, H.C., Blumenfeld, Y., Chitkara, U., Hudgins, L. and Quake, S. (2008) Noninvasive diagnosis of fetal aneuploidy by shotgun sequencing DNA from maternal blood. *Proceedings of the National Academy of Sciences*, published online 6 October. www.pnas.org/content/105/42/16266.full.

Friedman, R. and James, J. (2008) The myth of the stages of dying, death and grief, *Skeptic Magazine*, 14(2): 37–41.

Harnett, A. (2007) *Informing Families, National Best Practice Guidelines*. Galway: National Federation of Voluntary Bodies Providing Services to People with Intellectual Disabilities.

Hatton, C., Akram, Y., Shah, R., Robertson, J. and Emerson, E. (2002) *Supporting South Asian Families with a Child with Severe Disabilities: A Report to the Department of Health*. Lancaster: Institute for Health Research, Lancaster University.

Horwitz, N. and Ellis, J. (2005) Doctors' responses to the disclosure of a diagnosis of Down syndrome: what is the level of support and training available to specialist registrars for breaking bad news? *Archives of Disease in Childhood*, 90 (Supplement 11: A26).

Jan, M. and Girvin, J. (2002) The communication of neurological bad news to parents. *Canadian Journal of Neurological Sciences*, 29: 78–82.

Knapp, M., Romeo, R. and Beecham, J. (2007) *The Economic Consequence of Autism in the UK*. London: Foundation for People with Learning Disabilities.

Kubler-Ross, E. (1969) *On Death and Dying*. London: Macmillan.

Laler, J.G., Devane, D. and Begley, C.H. (2007) *Birth*, 34(1): 80–8.

McBride, S. and Peterson, C. (1997) Home-based early education with families of children with disabilities: who is doing what, *Topics in Early Childhood Special Education*, 17(2): 209–33.

Maciejewski, P., Zhang, B., Block, S. and Prigerson, H. (2007) An empirical examination of the stage theory of grief, *The Journal of the American Medical Association*, 297(7): 716–23.

Moore, T. and Larkin, H. (2005) *More Than My Child's Disability: A Comprehensive Review of Family-centred Practices and Family Experiences of Early Childhood Intervention Services*. Glenroy, Victoria: SCOPE.

Newman, A., McEwen, J., Mackin, H. and Slowley, M. (2009) *Improving the Wellbeing of Disabled Children (Up to Age 8) and their Families through Increasing the Quality and Range of Early Years Intervention*. London: Centre for Excellence and Outcomes (C4EO).

Perry, D., Greer, M., Goldhammer, K. and Mackey-Andrews, S. (2001) Fulfilling the promise of early intervention, *Journal of Early Intervention*, 24(2): 90–102.

Rutter, M. (2002) Nature, nurture, and development: from evangelism through science toward policy and practice, *Child Development*, 73(1): 1–21.

Scarborough, A., Hebbeler, K. and Spiker, D. (2006) Eligibility characteristics of infants and toddlers entering early intervention services in the United States, *Journal of Policy and Practice in Intellectual Disabilities*, 3(1): 57–64.

12

Addressing the physical and sensory needs of children with profound and multiple learning disabilities

Bronwyn Roberts

Introduction

As will be seen in this chapter, people with profound and multiple learning disabilities (PMLD) face enormous challenges in maintaining good physical health and well-being. Drawing upon both medical and social constructions of disability, this chapter examines conditions that affect many people with PMLD – cerebral palsy, visual impairment, hearing impairment – and the communication challenges they pose for practitioners. Based on the evidence, suggestions are made about how these challenges can be addressed.

Background

There is no universally accepted definition of PMLD. However, it is commonly associated with pronounced developmental delay with significant physical and sensory impairments and/or epilepsy (Ware 2003). Difficulties with effective communications are also common (Kelly 2000; Cavet and Grove 2005; Pawlyn and Carnaby 2008) and some 80 per cent of these individuals will have physical impairments that affect mobility. Some definitions have looked at functional skills to help classify individuals' abilities, while Ware (2003) recognizes that people with PMLD need maximum assistance and 24-hour support, in all aspects of daily living. For this chapter the definition of PMLD will include people with a profound learning disability, people with sensory impairments and people with a physical impairment. Co-ordination of muscles, cerebral palsy and asymmetrical body shapes will also be considered as many people with PMLD experience some or all these conditions. The Depart-

ment for Children, Schools and Families (2009) have a comprehensive definition stating:

> Children with profound and multiple learning difficulties have complex learning needs. In addition to very severe learning difficulties, the children will have other significant difficulties, such as physical disabilities, sensory impairment or a severe medical condition. They require a high level of adult support, for their personal care as well as for their learning needs. They are likely to need sensory stimulation and a curriculum that is broken down into very small steps. Some children with profound and multiple learning difficulties communicate by gesture, eye pointing or symbols; others communicate by using very simple language.
>
> (Department for Children,
> Schools and Families 2009)

It is essential that we recognize that people with profound and multiple learning disabilities are unique individuals with complex health care needs who require increased social support and often need help to meet their emotional needs (Foundation for People with Learning Disabilities 2005).

It has been estimated that there are about 210,000 people with PMLD and that around 65,000 of this number are children and young people (Department of Health 2001). The Department of Health also suggest that the number of people with severe learning disabilities may increase by around 1 per cent per annum for the next 15 years as a result of the growing numbers of children and young people with complex and multiple disabilities who are now surviving into adulthood (Department of Health

2001). Emerson and Hatton (2004) have also estimated that the total number of adults with a learning disability will increase by 8 per cent to become 868,000 in 2011 and by 14 per cent to become 908,000 by 2021. This upward rise in numbers is further emphasized by Emerson (2009) who recognizes a 4.8 per cent rise year upon year in children and adults with PMLD.

These figures highlight the increasing need for essential and personalized services to be developed for people with high support needs. The report *A Life Like Any Other?* (Joint Committee on Human Rights 2008) identifies the extensive failure of services to provide people with a learning disability with means to claim their basic rights. If services are unable to meet basic rights and needs, there is a real issue regarding their ability to develop the flexible and creative services needed for individuals with complex health and social needs (Social Care Institute for Excellence 2008).

The care and nurturing of a child is a complex and multi-dimensional process, involving emotional, cognitive, physical and psychological aspects. The complexity of care increases when the child concerned has profound learning and physical impairments. Care can often appear to revolve around the daily living activities of eating, drinking, intimate personal care and getting dressed and undressed, which are essential activities if fundamental needs are to be met. Roberts and Lawton (2001) showed that the majority of children with PMLD in their study required extra assistance or supervision with multiple areas of daily life. They looked at five activities (washing, dressing, meal times, during the night and keeping occupied) and found that more than 70 per cent of the children needed extra help to complete these activities. These findings further highlight the fact that children with severe disabilities have considerable extra care needs in many areas of daily life.

It is easy to think of people with PMLD as having a multitude of needs by concentrating on the impairments and the care needed, often utilizing a medical model of care – i.e. a predominant focus on medical conditions as defining the person. However, it is well documented (Department of Health 1995, 1998, 1999a, 1999b, 2001; Barr 1999; Mencap 2007; Michael 2008) that the health care experience of people with a learning disability is far from adequate. The recent report *Death by Indifference* (Mencap 2007) highlighted the 'widespread ignorance and indifference' towards people with a learning disability. The independent review which followed this, *Health Care for All* (Michael 2008) found 'appalling examples of discrimination, abuse and neglect across the range of health services'. People with PMLD are one of the most vulnerable groups in society; and if society is to be judged by how it cares for its more vulnerable members, there is clearly much yet to be accomplished.

The labels of 'profound', 'complex needs', 'multiple needs' and 'severe learning disability' also highlight obvious needs and impairments, often reflected in lists of what someone *cannot*, rather than *can* do. In developing services to promote a positive and healthy lifestyle it is essential that we recognize the individual: a person unique in what they can achieve with their skill base enhanced by appropriate support services. The medical model of care highlights the deficiencies the person has, while other models highlight social barriers (Richardson 1997; Race 2002). Barriers to good health care cited by the Scottish Executive (2002) include:

- *physical barriers*: poor wheelchair access to health care facilities;
- *administrative barriers*: appointment times too short for people who are non-verbal; waiting times to see GPs and consultants too long for people with poor concentration and for people who are hyperactive;
- *communication barriers*: inability of doctors to understand different communication styles, the difficulties of a person with PMLD to describe symptoms;
- *attitudinal barriers*: negative assumptions and attitudes about people with learning disabilities, for example not offering pain relief to people with a learning disability;
- *knowledge barriers*: limited theory and practice experience of the health needs of people with learning disabilities.

These barriers are recognized and supported by *Health Care for All* (Michael 2008), which

> found convincing evidence that people with learning disabilities have higher levels of

unmet need and receive less effective treatment, despite the fact that the Disability Discrimination Act and Mental Capacity Act set out a clear legal framework for the delivery of equal treatment.

(Michael 2008: 7)

For children with cerebral palsy and associated difficulties the task of undertaking basic physical activities of life can appear to be very simplistic. However, achieving a positive and healthy lifestyle and seeing the child from a positive perspective can be an enormous challenge.

The neophyte practitioner can feel daunted by early exposure to people with PMLD. Clare, a first year student nurse, had her first placement with people who have complex care needs. She felt hopeless, useless and completely overwhelmed by the people she met:

> I felt really nervous. I didn't realize really what complex needs had meant; I didn't realize what people would look like. I didn't want to hurt anyone and I certainly didn't know how to approach someone. I didn't know what to say. Lunchtime was a nightmare. It sounds a simple task helping someone with a meal but it was really difficult.

Addressing such challenges requires practitioner competencies in enhancing life opportunities, building choices into everyday living (Ware 2003) and learning to communicate rather than teaching communication (Nind and Hewett 2001). We need to recognize that the health of any group is about positive lifestyles based on abilities and strengths that guide and enable interventions. Due to the nature of having PMLD, some children miss out on essential learning opportunities which impact on how they know themselves and their environment. These missed opportunities are made worse if their environment is not manipulated to enhance their abilities. A visually stimulating room will not reward the child who has vision impairment, just as a room that utilizes sounds well will not reward a person with a hearing impairment. There are many different views regarding quality of life and how we perceive and measure it (see Chapter 6). However, in assessing quality, we must take into account all facets of the

person including their physical, social, emotional and spiritual abilities and interests (Robbins 2001). 'Hearing from the seldom heard' (British Institute of Learning Disabilities 2009), a special project to raise awareness and to enable people with complex needs to speak out about their services, identified six areas of need. Three of these needs, getting to know people really well, better communications and raising awareness of human rights, are considered within this chapter. Quality services must also pay attention to everyday environments that people experience, so that they stimulate and reward the person with PMLD. This chapter aims to identify practical strategies to help meet these challenges.

It has already been highlighted that people with PMLD will have a variety of health care needs. It is essential that these needs are met as fully as possible; in doing so it is possible to maximize their chance of having an active and fulfilling life. For example, a person with untreated chronic constipation will not be in the best state of health and will probably be lethargic and in pain. Understanding some of the main impairments faced by people with PMLD, and the barriers experienced in everyday life, helps to highlight what can be done to improve health, personal well-being and social inclusion. Once this is achieved we have an excellent starting point to develop empowerment, choice and control for the person with profound and multiple learning disabilities.

Cerebral palsy

Cerebral palsy (CP) is a condition that affects both movement and sensation. It is caused by damage to different parts of the brain. The damage may occur before birth, at birth or in early childhood. As a result of this damage the child might have poor co-ordination, difficulties in balancing and unusual patterns of movement. Some children's movement may only be slightly affected and they can learn strategies to manage their condition, while others may be more severely affected, requiring long-term support. At birth it is not always possible to identify which type of CP the child will have. Movement and co-ordination difficulties will be easier to identify as the child grows and develops (Rennie 2001). Depending on where the damage has occurred and the extent of the damage to the brain, the child may have other associated impairments. These include epilepsy, visual impairment, hearing impairment, communication, eating and drinking difficulties, emotional and/or behavioural difficulties and varying degrees of learning disability (Lacey and Ouvry 2000; Cartwright and Wind-Cowie 2005; Pawlyn and Carnaby 2008).

There are four main types of CP which result in the difficulties with movement and co-ordination that the child might have:

- *Hypertonic (spastic) CP*: Children with this type of CP have increased muscle tone. They may find their muscles becoming very stiff, especially when they try and move (e.g. when they reach out to a toy). This can reduce the amount of movement they have due to the hypertension in their muscles. It can also make them fearful to move as they may have difficulties in balancing.
- *Hypotonic (flaccid or floppy) CP*: Children with this type of CP have a decrease in muscle tone. The muscles are soft and floppy with little strength in them. Having hypotonic muscles means that the muscles do not support the joints and leads to the joints having an increased range of movement.
- *Athetoid CP*: Children with this type of CP have continuous and unwanted movements that they cannot control. Their limbs move in a slow writhing motion often described as snake-like movements. These movements increase when the child wants to complete an action. If the child wants to pick up a toy the arm and hand will writhe in all directions before landing on the toy.
- *Ataxic CP*: Children with this type of CP have lack of balance and demonstrate sharp and jerky movements. These movements describe all of their motion including the way they move their body or arm (e.g. when reaching out to touch an object), as well as movement of their whole body when they attempt to move around (e.g. start to crawl).

Exercise 12.1

Sitting in an easy chair, bend your arms up to rest on your chest. Clench your fists and tense your arm and shoulder muscles. Without releasing the muscle tension, attempt to move your arms away from your body. It is very difficult if not impossible to do so. Maintain the muscle tension for several minutes and then relax. Be conscious of how your muscles ache and the strain placed upon them in the few minutes you have been doing this exercise. Take some time and reflect upon your feelings. How might hypertonia affect someone's voluntary movement?

Having CP will affect how a child moves, movement being an essential basic ability to react to surroundings and explore and learn about the environment. Movement is also a way of expressing our personality, emotions and moods. Movement for a child with CP can cause pain, discomfort and distress and this can discourage the child from moving. Alternatively, lax and weak muscle tone can make movement extremely difficult and often the reward is not worth the effort. Assessment of the child's ability to move is essential to all plans for learning and care. A few simple questions can help identify difficulties in movement:

- How does the child move when placed on the floor?
- Are there any abnormal patterns of movement?
- What does the muscle tone feel like?
- Does the child use one side more than the other?

Unfortunately the more severe types of CP can result in the development of unusual body shapes. This is due to the tightness of the muscles changing the shape of the spine, limb alignments and body symmetry. Primitive reflexes that disappear as children develop normal movement patterns can be retained in children with CP and these also affect the shape and posture of the child. Long-term effects of gravity can pull the body into asymmetry and can 'flatten' the trunk and limbs. If the child uses one side of their body more than the other (e.g. always rolling to one side and not the other), their body will not develop symmetrically. This will make the development of balance, eye-to-hand co-ordination, perceptual skills and movements more difficult. It can also contribute to the development of muscle contractures, body and limb shape changes and hip dislocation (Stolk *et al.* 2000).

Exercise 12.2

Think about your body and the shapes it takes on when sitting, standing and lying down. How often is your position symmetrical? Symmetrical positions are often the most comfortable as our bodies are arranged equally and are balanced.

How long can you sit in a position that is not symmetrical before you make slight adjustments to your position? We are constantly moving, if only slightly, so as to allow blood to flow, ease aching muscles and take weight off joints that are under strain. This constant movement also helps our digestion and elimination processes, lung performance and circulation. Reflect upon someone with CP and assess how much voluntary movement they have. Consider how their movements might affect their body systems and the impact this may have on their health state.

There are many methods of assessing posture and body shape (Pountey *et al.* 1990; Goldsmith and Goldsmith 1996), but there are four simple questions that can be asked to aid identification of body asymmetry (Lacy and Ouvry 2000: 18).

- Does the body tend to stay in a limited number of positions?
- Do the knees seem to be drawn to one side, or outwards, or inwards?
- Does the head seem to turn mainly to one side?
- Is the body shape already asymmetrical?

If the answer is yes to any of these questions, postural management is essential to support the body and to protect body symmetry. Maintaining symmetry is important for the body systems to work to their optimum capacity. An asymmetrical body can reduce the space for body organs and even compress them. In the worst scenario, organs and systems can even be pushed out of their usual position. A compressed stomach will affect the process of digestion, reduce the space available for food and possibly cause reflux. Compression on the lower bowel will affect the normal muscle contractions (peristalsis), slow down food passing through the digestive system and cause constipation. A chair that supports the child in symmetry and alignment is needed to ensure that food eaten can

be processed effectively without causing the child digestive problems.

For a child with CP, having their body supported in symmetry becomes a 24-hour necessity. We spend approximately a third of our lives sleeping so even sleeping positions need to be considered in promoting postural management. Whatever activities are occurring, symmetry of position must be central to the activity. Our first challenge is to identify appropriate positions to support body symmetry that can be utilized as part of the daily activities for the child. Posture management becomes integral to the activity and is not carried out as specific therapy. A postural management programme is an approach that covers all activities and planned interventions that affect the individual's posture and ability to function. Each programme is planned specifically for each child and will encompass special seating, standing supports, exercises, night time postural support, possible surgery and multi-disciplinary therapy sessions (Gericke 2006).

Exercise 12.3

Think about a variety of play situations a child will enjoy. Identify two play activities that could be undertaken while the child's postural position is being managed in sitting up, lying on one side, lying on their back and standing.

Helping strategies

The following are some useful helping strategies:

- An asymmetrical body shape can affect the internal body systems. If the stomach and digestive tract are compromised, this may be managed by providing small nutritional meals more often, rather than attempting to provide a third of the daily requirements in three large meals. This strategy may help reduce reflux and aspiration.
- Treat a person's wheelchair with respect – people can spend long periods of time in their wheelchair, so that it almost becomes part of them. Avoid leaning on wheelchairs and 'kicking off' brakes.
- Be aware of the floor surfaces you are going over – some can be painful to people in a wheelchair.

Think about how the sensations of different floor surfaces can become part of the way the person can identify where they are and where they are going.

- Ensure that all activities are planned around the person being in as straight and aligned a position as possible. Remember the internal body systems and how they function.
- As the person will spend a large portion of their day in different positions, on the floor, on their side, sitting or standing, change the environment around them so that they can use their eyes and ears as much as possible. What are they able to see while on the floor apart from other people's feet?

Visual impairment

The Royal National Institute for the Blind (RNIB) has identified that every year 27.5 million people need to have regular eye tests. However, only 15 million people do so. This means that 12.5 million people do not have a regular eye test (Department of Health 2003). People with intellectual disability have higher levels of impaired vision compared to the general population (Welsh Health Survey 1995) with the RNIB (2009) estimating that at least 30 per cent of people with a learning disability are likely to have significant impairment of sight.

For children with complex care needs it is essential that they have regular eye tests to ensure that as practitioners we know exactly what they can see (Levy 2007). Even people who are registered as blind can have some useful vision. It is also necessary to monitor any changes as people grow older so that treatments can be accessed that may enhance vision or use of vision (Miller 2005). Optometrists and carers need to be aware of the high prevalence of vision defects and the importance of regular eye examinations in people with a learning disability (Woodhouse et al. 2003). Lack of clarity surrounding these exact numbers is due to the wide variety and types of visual impairment among children with learning disabilities. As damage to the brain is usually the cause of visual impairment in children with learning disabilities, there are many more kinds of visual difficulties that may develop. Children with learning disabilities may have:

- reduced visual acuity (clarity or sharpness of vision);

- visual field loss (may not be able to see above or below or to the sides);
- difficulty in hand-to-eye co-ordination;
- difficulty recognizing and matching objects;
- short- or long-sightedness;
- problems making accurate fast eye movements (scanning an object);
- problems keeping fixation on an object (they may have uncontrollable eye motions);
- each eye may have a different impairment.

Exercise 12.4

Sit in a busy room for ten minutes with your eyes closed. How do you know who is in the room with you? Who is coming and going? What activities are going on? How do you feel? Are you relying on your hearing more? This exercise offers a very small insight into what it is like without visual input. Without visual cues it is also difficult to keep track of time, and many people will think the ten-minute exercise takes a lot longer.

It is important to observe how the child uses their vision and/or if they have *any* useful vision. We need to observe what distance they can see, what colours they react to, and what size of objects they can see and at what distance. The following questions will help you gain knowledge of how a child is utilizing their vision. They are designed as support information to take to an optician; they are *not* intended to replace a formal visual assessment.

- What colours does the child respond to?
- When do they appear to focus on your face as you approach them?
- Do they react to toys held in front of them at 6 inches, 12 inches, 24 inches, 48 inches etc.?
- In what position do they hold their head? Is it tilted or turned to one side? Do they appear to be looking upwards/downwards at an object?
- What lighting do they respond to best? Light directed on the object? Daylight? Soft lighting? Do they respond to light stimulation in a sensory room?
- Does the child respond better when the object is placed on a contrasting background (i.e. a yellow teddy against a black jumper, a red plate on a white

placemat)? Visually busy patterns can hamper rather than enhance someone's vision.

- Are there times of the day when they respond better (i.e. first thing in the morning or after a bath when they are relaxed)? Try not to assess the child if they are tired or after a strenuous physiotherapy session.

This type of assessment will take time and require the child to be carefully observed in a variety of situations. A sensory room where light and colour can be controlled is a very useful resource during a visual assessment. If the child has low vision and experiences life in a blurred visual haze, the visual rewards and stimulation that encourage children to learn will not be present. Hence, many children with low vision 'switch off' and stop responding. Once the initial assessment is completed the sensory room can be utilized in many different ways to stimulate useful vision alongside the tactile and auditory skills that will be needed to supplement visual loss (Pagliano 1999). Non-visual ways of learning through touch, smell and hearing are essential to any child with low vision.

Helping strategies

- Use a sensory room to help identify when the person reacts to visual stimulation. Utilize all your knowledge about the person to maximize any vision assessment.
- Be aware of how differing eye conditions affect the person. Most people will have some useful vision, and changing the environment can help. Think about light and how this can be used; a simple strategy is to use an extra lamp to shine on a meal so that the person can see their food. Shadows can appear as dark holes, and will make walking across shadows cast on the floor very frightening. Harsh bright light can also cause problems for a person who has cataracts, causing them to squint and reduce their vision further.
- Colour and contrasting colours are often under-utilized when considering creating a pleasant homely environment which is useful to a person with low vision. Finding your way around can be very difficult when all the rooms and colour schemes blend in. Doorways can be made clear by having a contrasting door colour to the wall or

door surround. Walls can have a contrasting border along them to facilitate movement from area to area. Plates can be placed on a contrasting placemat so that the edge of the plate becomes clear. Edges to steps can also be highlighted in a contrasting colour.

- Think about the sensations and noises differing floor coverings make and how could you use this to help identify rooms. Lounge areas could be wool carpets; while kitchens could be vinyl floor covering and toilet areas could be tiled.
- Noises will also be used to orientate and identify areas. Sounds of the fish tank, the toilet flushing and cutlery being placed on the table, noises outside, a ticking clock, the fridge motor and the washing machine, can all help visually impaired people to identify where they are. Beaded curtains and wind chimes can be used on outside doors to identify that they *are* outside doors. Alternatively, constant noise such as the radio or television on all day can mask noises that act as auditory clues.
- Different shaped door handles can be used to identify different rooms.

Hearing impairment

There are an estimated 9 million deaf and hard of hearing people in the UK. There are about 20,000 children aged 0–15 years who are moderately to profoundly deaf. There are about 23,000 deaf-blind people. Some will be totally deaf and others will have some useful hearing (RNID 2003). People with learning disability have higher levels of impaired hearing compared to the general population (Welsh Health Survey 1995). Yeates (1991) identifies that the incidence of hearing loss is *much* higher in people with a learning disability: 37 per cent compared to 14 per cent of the general population, highlighting that hearing impairment in people with a learning disability is a significant issue. It is also recognized that children with CP are more likely to have a hearing impairment. For example, hypertonic quadriplegia and athetoid patterns of movement in all four limbs are associated with severe sensori-neural hearing impairment (Cogher *et al.* 1992). Inability to hear can have a major impact on independence and confidence, interaction and communication, so it is essential to minimize the impact of any hearing loss.

People with a learning disability may not be able to communicate a problem with their hearing. Changes in behaviour that may indicate a hearing loss can often be missed or misinterpreted. This is further complicated by the difficulties in recognizing the need for medical attention (Rogers *et al.* 1999). Mencap (1998) highlight that general practitioners find it difficult to identify when a hearing assessment is needed and are often dismissive of carers' concerns. Yeates (1991) notes that people with learning disabilities and hearing loss are a group that have experienced many problems accessing ordinary services, and that many consultants feel that people with learning disabilities cannot undergo hearing tests – the implication being that nothing can be done for them and that it will not make any difference if hearing loss is present in the individual. Questions to consider here include:

- Is the person not hearing?
- What are they not hearing?
- Are they unresponsive?
- Do they have a short concentration span?
- Do they have difficulties in co-ordinating their physical movements?
- Are they not responding to any auditory input?

To maximize hearing, audiologists recommend that people with learning disabilities, especially children, should receive a regular hearing assessment every two years, especially for those judged to be at higher risk. The examination is also the opportunity to look for any problems in ear health and to ensure that even a little hearing can be used beneficially. The answers to the following questions will help the audiologist in assessing the person more effectively. These may indicate that they might need help with hearing:

- How long is their concentration span?
- Do they respond differently to male and female voices?
- Do they respond better when eye contact is gained?
- When the television is on or music is playing do they sit close to the speaker?
- Do they respond to vocalizations?
- Do they respond to gestures such as pointing?
- Do they respond better in a quiet environment?

- Have they developed any unusual behaviours (i.e. bending of the outer ear, making noises to themselves, slapping the ear, poking the ear or banging the head)?

These questions are designed to help you gain knowledge of how a person is utilizing their hearing. They are to support information taken to an audiologist; they are *not* intended to replace a formal hearing assessment.

Exercise 12.5

Listen to a piece of music that you enjoy. Now turn off the treble and listen: the music will sound very different. This is similar to what people with a hearing impairment might hear when they have high frequency (Hz) hearing loss. Now listen to the piece again with the bass turned off. This is what a person might hear with low frequency (Hz) hearing loss. Music sounds different and may not be comfortable for the person with hearing loss to listen to. In fact some music can be quite painful depending on the hearing loss.

In helping a person utilize their hearing we need to concentrate on their being aware of sound, identification of the sound, where the sound is coming from, what they like to hear and what volume is needed for them to hear. A sensory room is an ideal place to help assess hearing skills as noise volume and location can be controlled and changed to assist the assessment and to stimulate residual hearing.

Exercise 12.6

Think of two activities that would help you understand how well a child can hear.

Helping strategies

- Always approach a hearing impaired person from the front, as they will not hear you approaching.
- Encourage them to utilize their hearing ability. A sensory room is a useful area to control sound for assessment and stimulation purposes.

- Remember that some frequency hearing loss can cause pain when hearing certain frequencies. Ensure you understand any hearing assessment and the implications it may have. Identify sounds that cause alertness and pleasure so that these can be used appropriately.
- Control everyday sounds so that any residual hearing can be utilized. Turning the television off or moving away from background noise may help.
- Hearing alarms should be supplemented by vibration and/or lights.
- Skill development needs to utilize touch and vision, showing and feeling rather than telling.

Communication

As professional carers we talk about normalization, person-centred planning, partnership working, multi-agency and multi-disciplinary teams and methods of working, planning and reviewing care. However thoughtfully prepared, care can often be about physical care based 'around' the child with PMLD. This type of care can be very time-consuming and physically tiring to the carer, becoming a routine of postural positioning and movement. It can lack the positive interactions that makes caring for someone else rewarding and worthwhile. Rewards for carers of people with PMLD are often of a long-term nature: skill development can take a long time, and carers can miss out on immediate feedback, which we all need to maintain positive interactions. Interactions can be judged as beneficial because we have made the person laugh or smile, but being told that I can make the person laugh or smile has further frustrated me due to the limited nature of the interaction, the child or person reacting to me rather than a two-way communication. Caldwell (1998) suggests that we need to 'get in touch' with people who appear locked in their own world. It is time we learnt 'new languages' based on the abilities and communication skills of the person with PMLD. Not all formal methods of communicating will be appropriate (Caldwell 2005), so first we need to observe how the person communicates. How do they communicate that they are thirsty? Want to move? Ask what is happening next? We need to learn each individual's 'language' and so become adept at learning to

communicate rather than teaching communication (see Chapter 9).

It is well known that there are barriers to communication. Some children with learning disabilities, especially if they have additional needs, may have experienced limited learning and life opportunities. This, in addition to other people's low expectations of someone with high support needs, creates additional communication difficulties. Practitioners may also feel they do not have the time or they may interpret communications to help meet their own needs, or be preoccupied and fail to focus on the individual (Bradley 2001). The person with PMLD will have all the needs of any person and additional needs dependent on how their physical, sensory and cognitive impairments affect their status. Each person is different and it is the difference that we need to concentrate on rather than the similarities. Each person will experience and perceive the world in a different fashion, a world that is very different to the visually- and sound-orientated world that other people experience.

Bradley (1994) identifies several challenges facing people with PMLD who want to be effective communicators:

- they may have visual impairments ranging from no useful sight to some useful vision;
- they may have a range of hearing impairments;
- they may not have reached a development level where speech is processed and has meaning;
- they may have physical impairments which affect speech or the physical co-ordination needed for gesturing or formal signing;
- they may be sensitive to touch or be wary of touch;
- they may communicate in idiosyncratic ways.

To interact meaningfully with a person who has PMLD it is important to learn about their world and how they communicate. It is the 'idiosyncratic' ways they communicate that are vehicles for effective two-way communication. It is extremely difficult for someone with PMLD to learn and utilize 'our' communication methods, whether these be oral, visual or tactile. It is far more effective for practitioners to learn how the person they care for communicates, 'tuning in' (Nind and Hewett 2001) to the person's unique face and body movements or pre-verbal communications, allowing us to recognize intentional communication signals. Without this 'tuning in' we fail to notice, recognize and interpret these signals. If these signals are not responded to, the person may give up trying to communicate, leaving us with only one-way communication. This 'tuning in' will mean, for professional carers, that they become multi-communicators, learning as many methods of communicating as the number of people they care for.

'Tuning in'

We need to observe closely, assess and interact by:

- use of eye contact, blinking – voluntary and non-voluntary – and eye gaze;
- reading facial expressions and small facial movements;
- recognizing intentional movements of the body which can be difficult when someone has CP;
- turn-taking in making noises, copying behaviours and responding to pulling faces;
- use of appropriate touch and physical contact;
- reading the person's body language, understanding what is intentional movement and what is not;
- utilizing personal space – this may mean recognizing that for a person in a wheelchair this includes their chair;
- making time and enjoying 'tuning in': this is fun time;
- focusing on the individual and not the activity.

Make a note of all your interventions and identify patterns of behaviour, facial expressions and noises. Remember the person with PMLD may have very little purposeful self-controlled movements. They may

rely on a subtle movement of the eyelid or a jerk of a toe. We must not miss these. A person with CP can function differently from day to day and sometimes hour to hour. We need to be able to recognize this and change strategies to accommodate these changes.

Children with PMLD will only communicate when they have a reason to do so. They may have had many experiences of their attempts at communicating being ignored or misunderstood. This leads to the child giving up trying and relying on family members or support workers to meet their needs. As professional carers we need to learn not to anticipate and meet every need as part of our daily care giving. It is important to think about what the person *can* communicate and create opportunities for them to do so. For example, instead of offering drinks on a regular basis so that the child is never thirsty, think about how we can use this situation to create an opportunity to communicate. Be creative, utilize every method possible. With the development of information technology and multi-media profiles containing audio recordings, video clips, photos and drawings we can capture any communications and attempt to make sense of them (Cavet and Grove 2005). *Creative Conversations* (Caldwell 2005) has many examples of how to be creative in developing communications with people with language difficulties. We have nothing to lose and everything to gain.

Helping strategies

- Learn and practise 'tuning in'.
- Monitor and record all actions and behaviours so that any intentional communications can be identified. Use assessment tools such as Disdat – a useful tool in helping to assess distress in people

Case study: *Seema*

Seema would sit in her wheelchair apparently unaware of her surroundings. She spent a lot of time sleeping. Her only enjoyment was eating and drinking and due to her CP she was totally dependent on her carer and the speed that the carer helped her with her meal. It was noted over time that if food was offered too soon Seema would lower her head slightly, as she had limited control of her head. If the food was given too slowly then Seema would grunt and lift her head. To communicate to Seema that it was mealtime her carer would take her to the table and then lift her head and make Seema's grunting noise, offering her some food. Food was delayed several seconds to encourage Seema to ask for her next spoonful. Within weeks Seema was controlling the speed she ate her meal and was developing a two-way conversation with her carers.

with severe communication difficulties (Regnard *et al.* 2007).

- Produce a communication tool that identifies how the person communicates. This may take the form of photographs capturing the person communicating, line drawings showing limited movements that indicate communications or a written description of the activity. Individuals will have their own unique tool (Murphy and Cameron 2002). These tools should be portable

and replaceable so that they can go with the person wherever they go.

- Do not give up. Pre-verbal intentional communications can be very difficult to recognize.
- Practise turn-taking. This is one of the basic elements of communication. Pat-a-cake and peek-a-boo are useful activities in encouraging turn-taking.
- Acknowledge and validate communication, no matter how basic.

Conclusion

Getting to know the individual very well, their skills and abilities, communication methods and how they interact with and perceive their environment are all essential if practitioners are to be effective in helping people with profound and multiple learning disabilities. This will mean taking time, often a long time, using keen observations, monitoring and recording all behaviours and working in partnership with all significant individuals and teams. Being creative in cultivating communications and being sensitive to attempts at communications can be and are rewarded by a two-way conversation and the development of enriching relationships. We must be mindful that regardless of the application of 'social' and 'medical' models, we are always dealing with a unique individual. A multi-dimensional assessment that takes account of medical and social constructions of disability is obviously important in understanding how people with PMLD perceive and adapt to everything in life. Being able to communicate effectively is essential in helping people with PMLD to make informed choices, to maintain their dignity and to achieve their potential. It is reassuring that in its three-year strategy *Valuing People Now* (Department of Health 2009) is laying an emphasis on people with 'complex needs' as people with PMLD have for too long been a neglected group.

References

Barr, O. (1999) Care of people with learning disabilities in hospital, *Learning Disability Practice*, 2: 29–35.

Bradley, A. (2001) *Understanding Positive Communications*. Kidderminster: BILD Publications.

Bradley, H. (1994) *Encouraging and Developing Early Communication Skills in Adults with Multiple Disabilities*. Focus Fact Sheet. London: RNIB Publications.

British Institute of Learning Disabilities (2009) *Hearing from the Seldom Heard: A New Resource*. www.BILD.org.uk (accessed 4 August 2009).

Caldwell, P. (1998) *Person to Person – Establishing Contact and Communication with People with Profound Learning Disability and Extra Special Needs*. Brighton: Pavilion Publishing.

Caldwell, P.A. (2005) *Creative Conversations: Communicating with People with Profound Learning Disabilities*. Brighton: Pavilion Publishing.

Cartwright, C., and Wind-Cowie, S. (2005) *Profound and Multiple Learning Difficulties*. London: Continuum International Publishing Group.

Cavet, J. and Grove, N. (2005) *Multimedia Technology for People with Profound and Multiple Impairment: An Evaluation of a Mencap Pilot Project Using Multimedia Profiling*. London: Mencap.

Cogher, L., Savage, E. and Smith, M.F. (1992) *Cerebral Palsy: The Child and Young Person*. London: Chapman and Hall Medical.

Department for Children, Schools and Families (2009) *Glossary of Terms*. www.dcsf.gov.uk/everychildmatters/_glossary/?i_ID=119 (accessed 21 August 2009).

Department of Health (1995) *The Health of the Nation: A Strategy for People with Learning Disabilities*. London: HMSO.

Department of Health (1998) *Signposts for Success in Commissioning and Providing Health Services for People with Learning Disabilities*. Wetherby: HMSO.

Department of Health (1999a) *Saving Lives: Our Healthier Nation*. London: HMSO.

Department of Health (1999b) *Once a Day*. Wetherby: HMSO.

Department of Health (2001) *Valuing People: A New Strategy for Learning Disability for the 21st Century*. London: DoH.

Department of Health (2003) *Registered Blind and Partially Sighted People Year Ending 31 March 2003, England.* London: DoH.

Department of Health (2009) *Valuing People Now: A New Three-year Strategy for People with Learning Disabilities.* London: DoH.

Emerson, E. (2009) *Estimating Future Numbers of Adults with Profound Multiple Learning Disabilities in England.* Lancaster: Centre for Disability Research, Lancaster University.

Emerson, E. and Hatton, C. (2004) *Estimating Future Need/Demand for Supports for Adults with Learning Disabilities in England.* Lancaster: Institute for Health Research, Lancaster University.

Foundation for People with Learning Disabilities (2005) *Linking Up: Emotional Support for Young People with Learning Disabilities.* London: The Mental Health Foundation.

Gericke, T. (2006) Postural management for children with cerebral palsy: consensus statement, *Developmental Medicine & Child Neurology,* 48(4): 244.

Goldsmith, J. and Goldsmith, L. (1996) *A Carers' Guide to the Management of Posture.* Ledbury: The Helping Hand Company.

Joint Committee on Human Rights (2008) *A Life Like Any Other?* House of Lords, House of Commons HL paper 40–1 HC 73–1. London: House of Lords.

Kelly, A. (2000) *Working with Adults with a Learning Disability.* Oxford: Speechmark Publishing.

Lacey, P. and Ouvry, C. (eds) (2000) *People with Profound and Multiple Learning Disabilities: A Collaborative Approach to Meeting Complex Needs.* London: David Fulton.

Levy, G. (2007) *Looking for Eye Problems in People with Learning Disabilities.* www.lookupinfo.org (accessed 4 August 2009).

Mencap (1998) *The NHS – Health for All?* London: Mencap.

Mencap (2007) *Death by Indifference.* London: Mencap.

Michael, J. (2008) *Health Care for All: Report of the Independent Inquiry into Access to Health Care for People with Learning Disabilities.* London: Department of Health.

Miller, O. (2005) *Visual Needs.* London: Continuum International Publishing Group.

Morris, J. (1999) *Hurtling into the Void: Transition to Adulthood for Young Disabled People with Complex Health and Support Needs.* Brighton: Pavilion Publishing/Joseph Rowntree Foundation.

Murphy, J. and Cameron, L. (2002) Let your mats do the talking, *Speech and Language Therapy in Practice,* Spring: 18–20.

Nind, M. and Hewett, D. (2001) *A Practical Guide to Intensive Interaction.* Kidderminster: BILD Publications.

Pagliano, P. (1999) *Multisensory Environments.* London: David Fulton.

Pawlyn, J. and Carnaby, S. (eds) (2008) *Profound Intellectual and Multiple Disabilities: Nursing Complex Needs.* Oxford: Wiley Blackwell.

Pountey, T.E., Mulchahy, C. and Green, E. (1990) Early development of postural control, *Physiotherapy,* 76(12): 799–802.

Race, D.G. (ed.) (2002) *Learning Disability: A Social Approach.* London: Routledge.

Regnard, C., Watson, B., Mathews, D., Reynolds, J., Gibson, L. and Clarke, C.L. (2007) Understanding distress in people with severe communication difficulties: developing and assessing the Disability Distress Assessment Tool (Dis Dat), *Journal of Intellectual Disability Research,* 51(4): 277–92.

Rennie, J. (ed.) (2001) *Learning Disability, Physical Therapy, Treatment and Management: A Collaborative Approach.* London: Whurr.

Richardson, M. (1997) Addressing barriers: disabled rights – the implications for nursing of the social construct of disability, *Journal of Advanced Nursing,* 25(6): 1269–75.

RNIB (2009) www.RNIB.org.uk (accessed 4 August 2009).

RNID (2003) *Facts and Figures on Deafness and Tinnitus.* London: RNID.

RNID (2009) www.RNID.org.uk (accessed 4 August 2009).

Robbins, D. (2001) *Transforming Children's Services: An Evaluation of Local Responses to the Quality Projects Programme.* London: Department of Health.

Roberts, K. and Lawton, D. (2001) Acknowledging the extra care parents give their disabled child, *Child: Care, Health and Development,* 27(4): 307.

Rogers, R., Mills, L. and Buckle, J. (1999) Providing equal access to primary care services, *Learning Disability Practice,* 2(1): 24–5.

Scottish Executive (2002) *Promoting Health, Supporting Inclusion: The National Review of the Contribution of all Nurses and Midwives to the Care and Support of People with Learning Disabilities.* Edinburgh: Scottish Executive.

Social Care Institute for Excellence (2008) *'Necessary Stuff': The Social Care Needs of Children with Complex Health Care Needs and their Families.* London: SCIE.

Stolk, J., Boer, T.A. and Seldenrijk, R. (eds) (2000) *Meaningful Care: A Multidisciplinary Approach to the Meaning of Care for People with Mental Retardation.* London: Kluwer.

Ware, J. (2003) *Creating a Responsive Environment for People with Profound and Multiple Learning Difficulties.* London: David Fulton.

Welsh Health Survey (1995) *Health Evidence Bulletins: Medical Conditions in People with Intellectual Disability.* Cardiff: HMSO.

Woodhouse, J.M., Adler, P.M. and Duignan, A. (2003) Ocular and visual defects amongst people with intellectual disabilities participating in Special Olympics, *Ophthalmic and Physiological Optics,* 23(3): 221–32.

Yeates, S. (1991) Hearing loss in adults with learning difficulties, *British Journal of Medicine,* 303(6800): 427–8.

13

Family care: experiences and expectations

Gordon Grant

Introduction

For families with children or adults with learning disabilities, caregiving typically begins at an early stage in the life course, continuing for many years, sometimes until the death of the caregiver. Over such a protracted period of time, parents and other family members face many challenges to their identities, to the structure and functioning of their support networks, to their capacity to maintain resilience in the face of daily stresses, and to their efforts to lead enriched lives outside the compass of their caregiving. Drawing from theoretical and empirical literature, and supported by case illustrations from the writer's own research, this chapter considers family experiences of caregiving and what family carers want from services. To begin, it is necessary to ask the question 'who is the family?' and to challenge some popular stereotypes about family care of children and adults with learning disabilities.

Who is the family?

Since policy and professional practice is increasingly aligned to the idea of working in partnership with families (Carers and Disabled Children Act 2000; Department of Health 2001a, 2001b, 2007, 2009; HM Government 2008) it seems reasonable to begin by asking 'who is the family'?

Despite major economic, political and social changes, the family as an institution has still endured but family structures, family forms and the boundaries of families continue to be reshaped. In post-industrial societies people are marrying later, having fewer children, and becoming parents later in life. Women are realizing improved educational opportunities, greater control over their fertility, and increased participation in paid employment. People are also living longer so intergenerational ties may have greater significance, especially to those family members in caregiving roles, with grandparents making more significant contributions (Hastings *et al.* 2002). More significant than these developments perhaps is a growing acceptance of the diverse patterns of family life. In post-industrial societies the family can be represented in terms of the subjective meanings of intimate connections as well as formal, objective blood or marriage ties. As a result, no particular family form has a monopoly in terms of producing moral, autonomous, caring citizens (Silva and Smart 1999).

This applies equally to bringing up family members who happen to have disabilities. In the context of changing definitions of 'family', for example, it is necessary to recognize the emergence of families of choice, parenting across households, as well as parenting by people with learning disabilities (Booth and Booth 1999) (see also Chapter 23). The new genetics, egg or sperm donorship will likely give rise to even newer family structures that have profound implications for forms of attachment, the enactment of reciprocity, and patterns of caregiving within families.

Clearly 'the family' is more than the sum of those individuals who live in the same home. Improvements in health and survival together with social and geographic mobility lead to the dispersal of families, though not necessarily to their fragmentation. Technologies like the internet, email, mobile phones and video links are contemporary means by which physical barriers to communication between family members can easily be accommodated, and responses to demands and crises dealt with. Such technologies represent means by which care and support 'from a distance' can be brought into play. However, they cannot replace requirements for 'hands-on' support and care where direct contact, intimacy or constancy are necessary. So how are caregiving families perceived?

Caregiving families: stereotypes and half-truths?

Stereotypes about families with children and adults with learning disabilities abound within professional and academic discourses, though some appear to be half-truths rather than positions substantiated by evidence.

Parents and family carers have been depicted as 'caught-in-the-middle' between their 'duty' to care and, at the same time, perpetuating dependency; the reality being that they have to deal with issues of being overprotective while confronting various social assumptions about disability (Power 2008). This leads to perceptions of such parents as being aloof, 'difficult to deal with' or even as perpetrators of the difficulties faced by their disabled children.

Then there are families seen as having agendas and needs that contrast with those of their children, rather than having mutual interests that are the natural product of interdependencies and reciprocities within the family. Here, families are represented as competitors with their disabled child for scarce professional resources. For instance, there is some evidence suggesting that professionals in key worker roles have a tendency to overstate differences in the needs and interests of parents and their disabled children (Williams and Robinson 2001).

A further stereotype concerns presumptions about the widespread existence of stress and burden in families (Olsson and Hwang 2003), linked to a pathological view of families as passive, unresourceful and lacking in agency. Reinforcing this view we see services that prioritize stress reduction in families or providing them with a break from the 'daily grind' of caring.

Then there are families depicted as being paralysed by time as a result either of wanting to remember earlier times before they were engulfed by the pile-up of caregiving demands, or being trapped by time and therefore unable to free themselves to do other things.

There is finally a perception that family care is maternal care, and that fathers are not that involved in caregiving. It is easy to see why this perception has emerged, most reported accounts of caring being based on the views and experiences of mothers. The recent national survey of fathers who have children with learning disabilities (Towers 2009) puts a very different complexion on this issue, and suggests that it is services that tend to exclude fathers, leaving their needs and contributions invisible, or worse, neglected.

> ### Exercise 13.1
>
> Think of two or three families you know within your own social circle or other families with disabled children you have encountered from work or placement experiences. Ask yourself:
>
> Which of the above stereotypes offers a way of characterizing each family?
>
> What aspects of family life do these stereotypes capture well?
>
> What aspects of family life do they fail to capture?

There is some truth in all of these stereotypes, but as such they only tell half the story. It is therefore important to consider theoretical perspectives that have contributed some understanding of the challenges families with children and adults with learning disabilities face, and how they deal with them.

Theoretical perspectives

Stress in families

Most prevalent within studies of families supporting children with disabilities are transactional stress-coping models (e.g. Lazarus and Folkman 1984; Orr et al. 1991). In these models people are seen as constantly appraising transactions with their environments; those seen as stressful (threatening or challenging) require coping to regulate distress or to manage the problem causing distress. The emphasis is very much on understanding the cognitive appraisals brought to situations, and the secondary and consequent appraisals of coping resources they can access to deal with these. Coping resources may be internal (e.g. skills, analytic ability) or external (e.g. finances, support networks).

There is a huge body of research based on this model which shows multiple sources of stress in families, including *child/individual-related* variables such as (challenging) behaviour, social skills, mental health, age, gender (Minnes *et al.* 2007; Plant and Saunders 2007; Neece and Baker 2008; Hsieh *et al.* 2009), *difficulty of caregiving tasks* (Plant and Saunders 2007), *carer-related* variables such as age, gender, ethnicity, socio-economic deprivation, coping strategies and self mastery (Grant and Whittell 2000; Salovita *et al.* 2003; Emerson *et al.* 2004; Macdonald *et al.* 2007; Paczkowski and Baker 2007; Trute *et al.* 2007; Towers 2009), and *external or contingent factors* like employment, relative poverty, concerns about the future and the structure of services themselves (Shearn and Todd 2000; Emerson et al. 2004; Hubert 2006; Bowey and McGlaughlin 2007).

The evidence also lends support to the belief that *mediators* of stress can be found in parental or carer appraisals of problems and difficulties, a disposition towards 'acceptance' or 'mindfulness', the capacity to embrace paradoxes, selective use of tailored coping strategies and, vitally, social support (Plant and Saunders 2007; Guralnick *et al.* 2008; Lloyd and Hastings 2008). These findings provide important clues about factors that need to be modelled into assessment frameworks by health and social care workers if families are to be afforded help and support consistent with the challenges they face and the personal and social resources at their disposal for dealing with them.

The extensive literature based on these models has latterly come to realize that stresses are far from unilaterally experienced and that coping has its rewards that can maintain people in potentially stressful situations for lengthy periods of time (Folkman 1997; Grant *et al.* 1998; Greer *et al.* 2006; Trute *et al.* 2007; Rapanaro *et al.* 2008). Hence the coexistence of rewards and stresses in family care is quite common. Moreover there is mounting evidence about family strengths and resilience, the ability of families to embrace paradoxes in their everyday lives, and what disabled children and their families say about their everyday lives (Helff and Glidden 1998; Larson 1998; Connors and Stalker 2003; Grant 2003).

Commenting on the literature about adults in general, Aldwin (1994) has suggested that there are at least four ways that stress can result in positive effects:

- *the inoculation effect*: created by the expansion of people's coping repertoires through experience;

- *the increase in mastery effect*: which has more to do with improved self-confidence, skill and sense of control in dealing with situations;
- *changes in perspectives and values emerging from threatening circumstances*: leading to a reordering of a person's value hierarchy and improved coping;
- *the strengthening of social ties* under certain circumstances.

Through such means it is claimed that individuals develop improved self-understanding since it is thought that this leads to an explanatory or organizing framework for individuals that evolves over time. If true this might suggest that individuals and families become better able to cope with things over the life course, even if they continue to live their lives under considerable pressures. However, evidence shows that services struggle to understand how parents experience 'time' (Todd and Shearn 1996), how supportive services can best be tailored to fit family routines, and how they should be addressing the multiplicity of demands and obligations families face within and outside of their caring (Stalker 2003). Even when family support services are in place offering the possibilities of valued short-term breaks, access can be unusually difficult, a process likened by some parents to 'jumping through hoops' (Doig *et al.* 2009).

Coping and resilience in families

The search for explanations as to why some people appear to cope better than others under conditions of threat or adversity has led to an interest in resilience in individuals and families (see also Chapter 21). Prompting much of this interest was the work of Antonovsky (1987). His theoretical and main empirical claim was that maintaining a sense of coherence (SOC) in a challenging or apparently disordered world makes the difference between staying psychologically healthy or succumbing to life's vicissitudes. SOC was defined by Antonovsky as a:

> global orientation that expresses the extent to which one has a pervasive, enduring though dynamic feeling of confidence that (1) the stimuli derived from one's internal and external environments in the course of living are structured, predictable and explicable; (2) the resources are available to meet the

demands posed by these stimuli; and (3) these demands are challenges, worthy of investment and engagement.

(Antonovsky 1987: 19)

Antonovsky equated these parameters respectively as comprehensibility, manageability and meaningfulness, though he viewed the motivational component of meaningfulness as most crucial.

Linked to the above, Hawley and DeHaan (1996) have attempted to integrate thinking about individual resilience to resilience as a family level construct. They suggest that:

> Family resilience describes the path a family follows as it adapts and prospers in the face of stress, both in the present and over time. Resilient families respond positively to these conditions in unique ways, depending on the context, developmental level, the interactive nature of risk and protective factors, and the family's shared outlook.

(Hawley and DeHaan 1996: 293)

A further perspective worth mentioning here is the notion of 'boundary maintenance' and 'boundary ambiguity' within families. Due largely to the work of Boss (1988), this is an attempt to understand situations where there is some uncertainty about whether a person is 'inside' or 'outside' the family system. The boundary issue arises in circumstances where there is either psychological presence in the face of physical absence, or psychological absence in the face of physical presence, the latter being of particular relevance in families supporting people with cognitive disabilities where there are accompanying behavioural difficulties. Uncertainty as to the person's absence or presence is considered to hinder the family's ability to adapt to changes brought on by cognitive decline and shifts in behaviour patterns. In such conditions family caregivers can become immobilized, and fail to reorganize to meet new demands. However, Boss's work has concentrated largely on families with relatives with dementia.

Drawing on these ideas Grant et al. (2007: 566) have attempted to develop a psycho-social model of resilience in families supporting children or adults with intellectual disabilities, suggesting that there are four interconnecting threads:

- the *search for meaning* in the face of apparently insurmountable odds or challenging circumstances seems to be a central feature of why and how resilience endures; it suggests that most external threats or demands are not intrinsically harmful. Rather it is the way they are perceived and appraised that is important;

- resilience makes demands on individual agency, and appears to require a strong survival instinct and capacity for development, underpinned by vision, stamina and a drive towards maintaining a *sense of control* over things that matter;

- the idea of continuity and progression over the life course and a capacity, where necessary, to reinvent oneself is linked to the above. This implies giving attention to the ways in which individuals *construct and maintain their identities*;

- finally there is the idea of the 'holding environment' constituted of familial, social, cultural and material resources that provides the context in which people continue to test and re-evaluate their identities as resilient, valued, contributing individuals, for it is this environment that generates opportunities and threats, while also moulding dispositions and values. How people *manage the boundaries* between themselves and their environments is therefore crucial to how they accomplish resilience.

Finally there is an argument to be made that families of disabled people are disabled by basically the same social barriers, prejudices and poorly conceived services as disabled people themselves (Dowling and Dolan 2001). In other words, the social model of disability (Oliver 1990) is just as relevant to an understanding of the everyday lives of families as it is to disabled people. A serious and very challenging consequence arising from this perspective is the persistence of poverty and inequality in the everyday lives of many families supporting children and adults with learning disabilities. For example, using compelling UK survey evidence Emerson et al. (2009) have shown that, when compared with other children, children with developmental delays appear to be more disadvantaged on every indicator of social and economic disadvantage examined. Two out of three children with developmental delays had been exposed to repeated disadvantage as measured by income, poverty, material hardship, social housing and receipt of means-tested benefits. The effect of repeated disadvantage on the risk of developmental delay remained after account was taken of parental education and occupational status. Compounding this situation, there is some evidence from Sweden that economic hardship is a major factor in parental well-being, and that this influence is independent of child variables (Olsson and Hwang 2008). The social and economic context in which parenting takes place therefore needs to be a key target for intervention in its own right.

Studies of children living in disadvantaged communities convey some similar messages about how families and children can prosper despite environmental threats. For example, Seaman *et al.* (2005) have shown that 'democratic' parenting styles – meaning styles typified by open communication concerning the time, place and nature of risks, and the associated rules for protecting children and promoting their prospects – are central to the accomplishment of resilience in their children. In communities characterized by a high degree of risk and lack of trust, parents in effect went about this by building social capital in various ways – by helping their children to exercise judgement and discretion, based on what was safe, bolstered by association with supportive peer networks, and by having a good knowledge of community resources. This has huge implications for the accomplishment of social inclusion by people with learning disabilities (Chapter 24) as well as for their protection from abuse and bullying (Chapter 16).

At the time of writing these appear to be the dominant theories and models informing family care research relevant to the lives of people with learning disabilities. It would be preferable to regard these perspectives as frameworks for practice. There will be further cross-references to them in the following section.

Exercise 13.2

Revisit the families you thought of in Exercise 13.1. Now ask yourself:

What are the typical everyday challenges each family faces?

How do they deal with these challenges?

What theoretical perspectives best explain how each family deals with the situation?

Discontinuities and the life course

Trajectories and clocks

For any family the life course is always filled with ambiguities as well as with things that are more patterned and predictable. Individuals and families have only partial control over the environments in which they live, work and spend their leisure time so there are inevitably tensions and uncertainties about the interactions involved.

For Heinz and Kruger (2001: 29), the life course is 'a major institution of integration and tension between individual and society that provides the social and temporal contexts for biographical planning and stock-taking as well as for ways of adapting to changes in public and private time and space'. Similarly, Clausen (1998: 196) suggests that the life course can be likened to a developmental process in which the individual moves from being a helpless organism to a more or less autonomous person that: '(a) takes place in a changing cultural, social structural and historical setting; (b) increasingly involves individual choices as to the action taken; and (c) almost always entails both continuities and discontinuities'.

With these definitions we get the idea of individuals following pathways full of twists and turns where key transition points may be reached that can be life changing. The birth of a child with lifelong disabilities in the family is perhaps a good example of a transition that may represent a major discontinuity for parents, or what has been called 'biographical disruption' (Bury 1982), yet in time it can also become transformative in more positive ways (Scorgie and Sobsey 2000).

Two metaphors are useful in helping to understand the processes involved – as clocks, and as journeys along trajectories.

Families face the ticking of different clocks and calendars that affect their choice-making and control over the entire life course. Most obvious are the *biological, physical and human development clocks of the disabled person and individual family members*. Then there are *social clocks representing the norms*, *values and rules* about times when life events are expected to occur (Mills 2000). Finally there are *calendars based on religious, family, employment or public service institutions*. Families therefore may not always find their own expectations, 'schedules' and arrangements fitting neatly with demands and expectations set by other clocks or calendars. Families may find themselves carrying on caring for a long time and therefore 'out of synch' with other families. In addition they may find it hard to balance their use of private and public time.

The life course can also be viewed as a journey along different time trajectories, each with their own routes and time demands. Journeying implies elements of agency, choice and control over the directions taken, though experiences and outcomes depend very much on perceptions of and responses to environmental demands encountered along the way. Below one trajectory is taken, the caregiving trajectory, to illustrate the kinds of transitions family carers are likely to face over the life course.

The caregiving trajectory

Journeying along the caregiving trajectory can be likened to moving from a position as relative novice to ultimate expert. 'Stages' in the caregiving journey have been highlighted (Nolan *et al.* 1996; Grant *et al.* 2003) that appear to signal important transitions. These have been described respectively as: 'building on the past' (before caregiving begins); 'recognizing the need'; 'taking it on'; 'working through it'; 'reaching the end'; and 'a new beginning'. Some central points about the continuities and discontinuities involved are now highlighted.

Some families may find themselves having to contemplate bringing up a disabled child before the child is born, either because of genetic testing or because of prior knowledge of family risk factors for disabling conditions. Either way, moral and ethical questions are raised. Family members may feel uncomfortable about sharing details of possible hereditary factors within a close network of family and friends, though genetic counselling may help with this (Pilnick *et al.* 2000). Although this 'building on the past' stage is really antecedent to 'hands-on' caregiving, it involves family members in information-seeking, planning and problem-solving, the results of which have

obvious life-changing potential. Many parents in this position are likely to be dealing with probabilities and uncertainties about the outcomes, and even where disabled children are born the prognoses parents are offered by experts are not always reliable.

Because learning disability can be the product of a huge range of aetiologies, determination of developmental delay may be neither immediate, accurate nor possible (see Chapters 3 and 10). Accordingly, parents can be left in a state of 'diagnostic limbo' for a long time, itself very disabling as Edelson's (2000) compelling autobiography attests. Though it appears to be central to achieving resilience (Grant *et al.* 2007), 'meaning-making' in these circumstances is remarkably difficult when, according to some commentators, 'parents must eventually focus attention on the present and future, maintain an accurate, undistorted view of the child's skills and abilities, hold a balanced view of the impact of this experience on themselves, and regulate their affective experience' (Pianta *et al.* 1996: 253). This is a tall order. Even at such an early stage, then, parents are thrust into a psychological time warp, having to rethink and make sense of suspected prognoses before they are in possession of all the facts.

The conditions under which disclosure of disability is eventually made are especially important to parental and family adjustment, as Chapter 11 has shown. It is little wonder that families at this stage struggle to establish a sense of coherence (SOC) (Antonovsky 1987) where their capacity to make sense of the situation is under such severe threat.

As families begin to 'take on' direct caregiving they are reported to improvise, and to discover the best ways of handling things very much by trial and error (Grant and Whittell 2000), for there are no books or 'handy recipes' for bringing up babies and young children, let alone those with disabilities. The Trevor family is a typical example. In this brief extract from an interview narrative, Mel Trevor is explaining the hit and miss nature of communicating with her 4-year-old daughter, Fiona:

Mel: The other hard thing is getting her to understand things. You have to repeat them over and over again. She picks up on most things quite easily but a lot of things she plays on it, and gets you quite frustrated and you don't know whether she is playing up or that she genuinely doesn't understand. That's the worst when you are sitting there and you are shouting at her and you're thinking, does she just not understand me, but when I questioned quite a few different people about it, they said to me to just treat her as if she did understand and would pick it up; even if she didn't, to just treat her normally anyway, to shout at her for doing something wrong.

Interviewer: So that is how you dealt with that?

Mel: Yes but I did get quite upset as to whether I was doing the right thing, should I shout at her or not? If I don't shout at her she'll get away with it, which she is very good at, playing the innocent . . . and [with Fiona] being the first [child] it was quite hard because you don't know what is normal.

Communicating meaningfully with a young child is basic to good care but the physical and psychological toll of doing so can be very taxing. During this phase it is common for families to spend lots of time information-seeking, yet setting limits on their caregiving to avoid burnout, while establishing structures and routines for managing things. It is something that helps to bring a degree of order and predictability into everyday life. It leads therefore to an 'increase in mastery effect', as previously described by Aldwin (1994).

'Working through it' connotes a proactive stance by families to maintain a sense of coherence (SOC) (Antonovsky 1987) in managing their affairs. It often coincides with a period during which families face a series of challenges to social and cultural norms, emphasizing the importance of social time (Mills 2000) – they may notice increasing differences in the emotional and intellectual development between their disabled child, siblings and other children. They will be reminded that theirs is likely to be a protracted period of caregiving – their disabled child continues to grow physically but as adulthood looms, ambiguous-looking issues of their child's adult citizenship status arise, for example about their autonomy, capacity and

legal rights (Zetlin and Turner 1985). Furthermore, family members, parents in particular, have their own identity needs to think about – as wage earners, as people with vocational interests, as parents to other children, as people with obligations to the extended family, and so on. An unbridled commitment to caring for their disabled child may leave these other identity needs neglected or compromised (Shearn and Todd 2000). At the same time, families typically report caregiving as being uplifting and rewarding as well as stressful, supporting Aldwin's (1994) assertions about the positive effects of challenges, and Larson's (1998) account of how parents manage paradoxes in their lives.

In 'reaching the end' of their caregiving careers, parents have reported increased reciprocities and interdependencies with their now adult children (Heller et al. 1997), supporting Aldwin's (1994) assertions about how, under certain circumstances, social ties can be strengthened and changes in values and perspectives arise that help to sustain coping.

In letting go to enable their adult child to live a more independent life in a home of their own, parents can find it difficult to plan ahead with this in mind. Plans can be fragile and prone to change, financial and legal matters far from clarified (Prosser 1997), with parents poorly supported about the options (Gilbert et al. 2008). During this stage of caregiving there is likely to be an accumulation of concerns and anxieties about what will happen after the death of the parents. Underlying this, parents can feel that others (statutory or not-for-profit agencies) will be unable to provide the standard of personalized support that they have given over a lifetime. Equally, many parents remain in a state of anxiety about predeceasing their sons or daughters, and what the consequences will be. Parents and families who suffer the death of a disabled child have been described as living in a state of 'silenced grief' (Todd 2007). When this happens professionals often withdraw their support to families too quickly, reinforcing a sense of loss.

The Crosby family

The Crosby family are fairly typical of others in this respect. David Crosby, 22 years of age, still lived at home with his parents, Margaret, 60, and Tom, 68. David, Margaret and Tom had for some time been discussing alternative permanent accommodation for David. Reflecting on the resolution of end-of-life issues, Margaret summed things up as follows:

> But I've always said, and a lot of parents say the same, I would rather grieve for David than have David grieving for me. I know then that David is safe. We've looked after him and he's safe and nobody can harm him; and he's not going to go into care where he's going to be ill-treated and perhaps be abused, because they're very vulnerable, so trusting and can easily be hurt. They're very feeling and understanding, and that's what really worries me.

This can lead to even very well-informed parents like Margaret and Tom again feeling trapped by time, aware of the balance of risks and benefits for David, yet paralysed all the same by indecision about future living options.

However, some older parents never complete 'launching' their offspring towards a more independent life because they do not wish to, for reasons to do with the feelings of intimacy, assertiveness and sense of control they experience (Tobin 1997). The question still has to be asked – in whose interests is this?

Even after relinquishing responsibility for direct hands-on caregiving, families typically continue to 'care about' their adult relative, and express a desire to maintain some involvement in their lives. Where care and support is shared with agencies, families may have important roles to play as arbiters of care standards since they will still retain more particularistic knowledge about their relative, knowing what works best for them. It is therefore important that families are not abandoned by services the minute that agencies take charge of things.

What families can expect from policy and services

Policy

Valuing People Now (Department of Health 2009) recognizes families as key partners in the delivery of the strategy yet acknowledges that much remains to

be done for real partnership working to be achieved. It reiterates the government's commitment to the national carers' strategy, *Carers at the Heart of 21st-Century Families and Communities* (HM Government 2008), emphasizing that all family carers should get support in their *own* right to enable them to live a life beyond their caregiving role and responsibilities. This ten-year strategy for carers encapsulates five key aspirations that by 2018:

- carers will be respected as expert care partners and will have access to integrated and personalized services they need to support them in their role;
- carers will be able to have a life of their own alongside their caring role;
- carers will be supported so that they are not forced into financial hardship by their caring role;
- carers will be supported to stay mentally and physically well and treated with dignity;
- children and young people will be protected from inappropriate caring and have the support they need to learn, develop and thrive.

Significant funding has been made available to implement the strategy, and the Standing Commission for Carers has been charged with ensuring that all family carers are included in the implementation of the new national carers' strategy. The strategy itself comprises many elements, three of which were launched as part of the New Deal for Carers: (1) a national information helpline and website through which carers can access information they need directly, or be referred on to more appropriate support; (2) a training programme, Caring with Confidence, to inform carers of their rights and the services available to them and help develop their advocacy and networking skills and (3) additional annual funding to councils in England for emergency care cover. Additionally the government is committing itself to rolling out personal budgets so that service users and family carers can purchase the support they need (see Chapter 22); there is to be piloting of ways to make primary and other health services more sensitive to carers' needs, investment in making it easier for carers to enter or re-enter employment, and a commitment to monitoring carer experience on a national level.

These are laudable aims and aspirations, *Valuing People Now* (Department of Health 2009) providing further details of how this is to be delivered within learning disability services. Less clear from the policy rhetoric is how this translates into the kinds of accessible, integrated, reliable, seamless, culturally congruent support that families and carers want. This is something to be monitored carefully.

Prospects for family-centred support

Fortunately there has been a lot of independent thinking and development work about what families and carers want from services. Particularly within child health and paediatric settings, but also internationally in learning disability services, there has been a valuing of family-centred practice (for example Hutchfield 1999; Law *et al.* 1999; Mackean *et al.* 2005; Moore and Larkin 2005). Though there is yet no universally agreed definition of family-centred practice, there is sufficient congruence in the conceptualizations, and emergent evidence, reviewed by Moore and Larkin (2005), to suggest that it concerns at its core a preparedness to acknowledge:

- family-identified needs, aspirations and priorities (outcomes);
- strengths, expertise, coping styles and contributions of individual family members and the family as an organic unit;
- the cultural and ethnic heritage of each family;
- partnership working with families based on mutual trust and respect;
- use of informal, community and formal supports for achieving family-defined outcomes;
- use of empowering help-giving styles that enhance self-determination and the prospect of positive child, family carer and family unit outcomes.

Parents are reported to want to work truly collaboratively with health care workers in making treatment decisions and on dynamic care plans that will work best for both child and family – yet they do not want the responsibilities of care, care management and advocacy responsibilities shifted on to them (Mackean *et al.* 2005). This is likely to be a challenge to the rolling out of plans for personal budgets where, by definition, more control and responsibility is exercised by service users and families. However, where family-centred practices are being implemented faithfully,

evidence suggests that parent satisfaction is associated with family-centred service delivery (Law *et al.* 1999) and family-centred practices are reported to be more helpful than professionally centred services within learning disability services (Wade *et al.* 2007). Evidence also suggests that parents receiving family-centred practices experience a greater sense of control (Trivette *et al.* 1996; Judge 1997) than peers receiving non-family-centred services. Further, over ten years ago, following a careful review of family-centred practice, Dunst *et al.* (1998: 4) showed that:

> practices that are family-centred, or which show a presumption toward family-centredness, are associated with a number of positive parent, family, and child benefits. Parents of children who experience practices that are family-centred in their orientation are more likely to report and demonstrate positive effects in terms of satisfaction with parenting, parent empowerment, parent and family well-being, personal self-efficacy, family cohesion, parent–child interactions, parent satisfaction with child progress, and other aspects of child, parent and family functioning.

This is indeed a major claim, albeit one based on North American experience, but the evidence is very compelling, bolstered further by Moore and Larkin's (2005) more recent review of international literature on family-centred practice.

Family-centred practice, as defined above, can be seen as a way of expressing how best to apply expectations for personalization to the family. From a practitioner perspective, this would appear to require:

- the embrace of family systems thinking as a complement to individualized casework or clinical work (*professional orientation*);
- an understanding of and sensitivity to reciprocities and patterns of mutual helping within the family (*family dynamics*);
- an understanding of how families frame life course demands so that services and supports can be made to fit family schedules, with greater predictability achieved (*life course perspective*);
- viewing families as potential or actual experts in the management of their own affairs and as

resources for dealing with them (*families as experts*);

- using the family and its network as a gateway to wider familial and community resources (*families as gateways*);
- recognizing and supporting the fulfilment of family member identity needs beyond caregiving and the achievement of 'life balance' (*home–work–leisure balance*);
- involving the family in all decision-making, including how to pace things (*inclusion and control*);

- embrace of practitioner help-giving styles that nurture self-determination by families (*empowerment practice*);
- respecting families and working with them as equals (*partnership working*).

Exercise 13.3

Going back to any of the case study families in this chapter, consider how you might frame support to them in terms of family-centred practice.

Conclusion

The posing of two apparently simple questions at the beginning of this chapter – how families do their caregiving, and what families want from services – has, perhaps inevitably, raised some fundamental but exciting challenges for practitioners. This is a particularly interesting juncture, even watershed, for families supporting children or adults with learning disabilities as the service system gears up for personalization, self-directed care and partnership working through *Valuing People Now* (Department of Health 2009) and *Putting People First* (Department of Health 2007). The many policy promises made to families are perhaps best expressed, at the family level, through a principled approach to family-centred practices. It is to be hoped that practitioners can indeed work as real partners with families and continue to share their experiences that add to the growing evidence base about family-centred practice.

Resources

www.carers.org.uk The Princess Royal Trust for Carers is the largest provider of comprehensive carer support services in the UK.

www.carersuk.org Carers UK was established by carers and sees itself as the voice of carers in the UK.

www.dh.gov.uk/ab/SCOC Provides the terms of reference for the Standing Commission for Carers.

www.familycarers.org.uk The National Family Carers Network links groups and organizations that support families that include an adult with a learning disability.

www.mencap.org.uk Mencap campaigns and provides support for people with learning disabilities and their families.

www.partnersinpolicymaking.co.uk/index.php Partners in Policymaking™ is a leadership training course for disabled adults and parents of disabled children.

References

Aldwin, C.M. (1994) *Stress, Coping and Development: An Integrative Perspective*. New York: The Guilford Press.

Antonovsky, A. (1987) *Unraveling the Mystery of Health*. San Francisco, CA: Jossey Bass.

Booth, T. and Booth, W. (1999) Parents together: action research and advocacy support for parents with learning difficulties, *Health and Social Care in the Community*, 7(6): 464–74.

Boss, P. (1988) *Family Stress Management*. Thousand Oaks, CA: Sage.

Bowey, L. and McGlaughlin, A. (2007) Older carers of adults with a learning disability confront the future, *British Journal of Social Work*, 37(1): 39–54.

Bury, M. (1982) Chronic illness as biographical disruption, *Sociology of Health and Illness*, 4: 167–82.

Clausen, J.A. (1998) Life reviews and life stories, in J.Z. Giele and G.H. Elder (eds) *Methods of Life Course Research: Qualitative and Quantitative Approaches*. Thousand Oaks, CA: Sage.

Connors, C. and Stalker, K. (2003) *The Views and Experiences of Disabled Children and their Siblings: A Positive Outlook*. London: Jessica Kingsley.

Department of Health (2001a) *Valuing People: A New Strategy* for *Learning Disability for the 21st Century*. London: Department of Health.

Department of Health (2001b) *Family Matters: Counting Families In*. London: Department of Health.

Department of Health (2007) *Putting People First: A Shared Vision and Commitment to the Transformation of Adult Social Care*. London: Department of Health.

Department of Health (2009) *Valuing People Now: A New Three-year Strategy for People With Learning Disabilities – Making it Happen for Everyone*. London: Department of Health.

Doig, L., McLennan, J.D. and Urichuk, L. (2009) 'Jumping through hoops': parents' experiences with seeking respite care for children with special needs, *Child: Care, Health and Development*, 35(2): 234–42.

Dowling, M. and Dolan, L. (2001) Families with children with disabilities – inequalities and the social model, *Disability and Society*, 16(1): 21–35.

Dunst, C.J., Brookfield, J. and Epstein, J. (1998) *Family-centred Early Intervention and Child, Parent and Family Benefits*. Final report submitted to the Pennsylvania Department of Public Welfare, Office of Mental Retardation, Harrisburg, Pennsylvania.

Edelson, M. (2000) *My Journey with Jake: A Memoir of Parenting and Disability*. Toronto: Between the Lines.

Emerson, E., Robertson, J. and Wood, J. (2004) Levels of psychological distress experienced by family carers of children and adolescents with intellectual disabilities in an urban conurbation, *Journal of Applied Research in Intellectual Disabilities*, 14: 77–84.

Emerson, E., Graham, H., McCulloch, A., Blacher, J., Hatton, C. and Llewellyn, G. (2009) The social context of parenting children with developmental delay in the UK, *Child: Care, Health and Development*, 35(1): 63–70.

Folkman, S. (1997) Positive psychological states and coping with severe stress, *Social Science and Medicine*, 45(8): 1207–21.

Gilbert, A., Lankshear, G. and Petersen, A. (2008) Older family-carers' views on the future accommodation needs of relatives who have an intellectual disability, *International Journal of Social Welfare*, 17(1): 54–64.

Grant, G. (2003) Caring families: their support or empowerment? in K. Stalker (ed.) *Reconceptualising Work with Carers: New Directions for Policy and Practice*. London: Jessica Kingsley.

Grant, G. and Whittell, B. (2000) Differentiated coping strategies in families with children or adults with intellectual disabilities: the influence of gender, family composition and the life span, *Journal of Applied Research in Intellectual Disabilities*, 13(4): 256–75.

Grant, G., Ramcharan, P., McGrath, M., Nolan, M. and Keady, J. (1998) Rewards and gratifications among family caregivers: towards a refined model of caring and coping, *Journal of Intellectual Disability Research*, 42(1): 58–71.

Grant, G., Nolan, M. and Keady, J. (2003) Supporting families over the life course: mapping temporality, *Journal of Intellectual Disability Research*, 47(4 & 5): 342–51.

Grant, G., Ramcharan, P. and Flynn, M. (2007) Resilience in families with children and adult members with intellectual disabilities: tracing elements of a psycho-social model, *Journal of Applied Research in Intellectual Disabilities*, 20: 563–75.

Greer, F.A. Grey, I.M. and McClean, B. (2006) Coping and positive perceptions in Irish mothers of children with intellectual disabilities, *Journal of Intellectual Disabilities*, 10(3): 31–48.

Guralnick, M.J., Hammond, M.A., Neville, B. and Connor, R.T. (2008) The relationship between sources and functions of social support and dimensions of child- and parent-related stress, *Journal of Intellectual Disability Research*, 52(12): 1138–54.

Hastings, R.P., Thomas, H. and Delwiche, N. (2002) Grandparent support for families of children with Down's syndrome, *Journal of Applied Research in Intellectual Disabilities*, 15: 97–104.

Hawley, D.R. and DeHaan, L. (1996) Toward a definition of family resilience: integrating life span and family perspectives, *Family Process*, 35: 283–98.

Heinz, W.R. and Kruger, H. (2001) Lifecourse: innovations and challenges for social research, *Current Sociology*, 49: 29–45.

Helff, C.M. and Glidden, L.M. (1998) More positive or less negative? Trends in research on adjustment of families having children with developmental disabilities, *Mental Retardation*, 36(6): 457–64.

Heller, T., Miller, A.B. and Factor, A. (1997) Adults with mental retardation as supports to their parents: effects on parental caregiving appraisal, *Mental Retardation*, 35: 338–46.

HM Government (2008) *Carers at the Heart of 21st Century Families and Communities: A Caring System on Your Side, A Life of Your Own*. London: The Stationery Office.

Hsieh, R.L., Huang, H.Y., Lin, M.I., Wu, C.W. and Lee, W.C. (2009) Quality of life, health satisfaction and family impact on caregivers of children with developmental delays, *Child: Care, Health and Development*, 35(2): 243–9.

Hubert, J. (2006) Family carers' views of services for people with learning disabilities from Black and minority ethnic groups: a qualitative study of 30 families in a south London borough, *Disability and Society*, 21(3): 259–72.

Hutchfield, K. (1999) Family-centred care: a concept analysis, *Journal of Advanced Nursing*, 29(5): 1178–87.

Judge, S.L. (1997) Parental perceptions of help-giving practices and control appraisals in early intervention programs, *Topics in Early Childhood Special Education*, 17(4): 457–76.

Larson, E. (1998) Reframing the meaning of disability to families: the embrace of paradox, *Social Science and Medicine*, 47(7): 865–75.

Law, M., Hanna, S., King, G., Hurley, P., King, S., Kertoy, M. and Rosenbaum, P. (1999) Factors affecting family-centred service delivery for children with disabilities, *Child: Care, Health and Development*, 29(5): 357–66.

Lazarus, R.S. and Folkman, S. (1984) *Stress, Appraisal and Coping*. New York: Springer.

Lloyd, T. and Hastings, R.P. (2008) Psychological variables as correlates of adjustment in mothers of children with intellectual disabilities: cross-sectional and longitudinal relationships, *Journal of Intellectual Disability Research*, 52(1): 37–48.

Macdonald, E., Fitzsimons, E. and Walsh, P.N. (2007) Use of respite care and coping strategies among Irish families of children with intellectual disabilities, *British Journal of Learning Disabilities*, 35(1): 62–8.

Mackean, G.L., Thurston, W.E. and Scott, C.M. (2005) Bridging the divide between families and health professionals' perspectives on family-centred care, *Health Expectations*, 8(1): 74–85.

Mills, M. (2000) Providing space for time: the impact of temporality on life course research, *Time and Society*, 9: 91–127.

Minnes, P., Woodford, L. and Passey, J. (2007) Mediators of wellbeing in ageing family carers of adults with intellectual disabilities, *Journal of Applied Research in Intellectual Disabilities*, 20(6): 539–52.

Moore, T. and Larkin, H. (2005) *More Than My Child's Disability: A Comprehensive Literature Review about Family Centre Practice and Family Experiences of Early Childhood Intervention Services*. Glenroy, Victoria: SCOPE.

Neece, C. and Baker, B. (2008) Predicting maternal parenting stress in middle childhood: the roles of child intellectual status, behaviour problems and social skills, *Journal of Intellectual Disability Research*, 52(12): 1114–28.

Nolan, M., Grant, G. and Keady, J. (1996) *Understanding Family Care: A Multidimensional Model of Caring and Coping*. Buckingham: Open University Press.

Oliver, M. (1990) *The Politics of Disablement*. London: Macmillan.

Olsson, M.B. and Hwang, C.P. (2003) Influence of macrostructure of society on the life situation of families with a child with intellectual disability: Sweden as an example, *Journal of Intellectual Disability Research*, 47(4/5): 328–41.

Olsson, M.B. and Hwang, C.P. (2008) Socioeconomic and psychological variables as risk and protective factors for parental well-being in families of children with intellectual disabilities, *Journal of Intellectual Disability Research*, 52(12): 1102–13.

Orr, R.R., Cameron, S.J. and Day, D.M. (1991) Coping with stress in children who have mental retardation: an evaluation of the double ABCX model, *American Journal on Mental Retardation*, 95: 444–50.

Paczkowski, E. and Baker, B.L. (2007) Parenting children with and without developmental delay: the role of self mastery, *Journal of Intellectual Disability Research*, 51(6): 435–46.

Pianta, R.C., Marvin, R.S., Britner, P.A. and Borowitz, K.C. (1996) Mothers' resolution of their children's diagnosis: organised patterns of caregiving representations, *Infant Mental Health Journal*, 17: 239–56.

Pilnick, A., Dingwall, R., Spencer, E. and Finn, E. (2000) *Genetic Counselling: A Review of the Literature*, Discussion Paper 00/01. Sheffield: Trent Institute for Health Services Research.

Plant, K.M. and Saunders, M.R. (2007) Predictors of care-giver stress in families of preschool-aged children with developmental disabilities, *Journal of Intellectual Disability Research*, 51(2): 109–24.

Power, A. (2008) Caring for independent lives: geographies of caring for young adults with intellectual disabilities, *Social Science and Medicine*, 67(5): 834–43.

Prosser, H. (1997) The future care plans of older adults with intellectual disabilities living at home with family carers, *Journal of Applied Research in Intellectual Disabilities*, 10: 15–32.

Rapanaro, C., Bartu, A. and Lee, A.H. (2008) Perceived benefits and negative impacts of challenges encountered in caring for young adults with intellectual disabilities in the transition to adulthood, *Journal of Applied Research in Intellectual Disabilities*, 21(1): 34–47.

Salovita, T., Italinna, M. and Leinonen, E. (2003) Explaining the parental stress of fathers and mothers caring for a child with intellectual disability: a double ABCX model, *Journal of Intellectual Disability Research*, 47(4/5): 300–12.

Scorgie, K. and Sobsey, D. (2000) Transformational outcomes associated with parenting children who have disabilities, *Mental Retardation*, 38: 195–206.

Seaman, P., Turner, K., Hill, M., Stafford, A. and Walker, M. (2005) *Parenting and Children's Resilience in Disadvantaged Communities*. London: National Children's Bureau and York: Joseph Rowntree Foundation.

Shearn, J. and Todd, S. (2000) Maternal employment and family responsibilities: the perspectives of mothers of children with intellectual disabilities, *Journal of Applied Research in Intellectual Disabilities*, 13: 109–31.

Silva, E.B. and Smart, C. (eds) (1999) *The New Family?* London: Sage.

Stalker, K. (2003) *Reconceptualising Work with Carers: New Directions for Policy and Practice*. London: Jessica Kingsley.

Tobin, S.S. (1997) A non-normative age contrast: elderly parents caring for offspring with mental retardation, in V.L. Bengston (ed.) *Adulthood and Aging: Research on Continuities and Discontinuities*. Berlin: Springer-Verlag.

Todd, S. (2007) Silenced grief: living with the death of a child with intellectual disabilities, *Journal of Intellectual Disability Research*, 51(8): 637–48.

Todd, S. and Shearn, J. (1996) Struggles with time: the careers of parents with adult sons and daughters with learning disabilities, *Disability and Society*, 11(3): 379–401.

Towers, C. (2009) *Recognising Fathers: A National Survey of Fathers Who Have Children with Learning Disabilities*. London: Foundation for People with Learning Disabilities.

Trivette, C.M., Dunst, C.J. and Hamby, D. (1996) Factors associated with perceived control appraisals in a family-centered intervention program, *Journal of Early Intervention*, 20(2): 165–78.

Trute, B. Hiebert-Murphy, D. and Levine, K. (2007) Parental appraisal of the family impact of childhood developmental disability: times of sadness and times of joy, *Journal of Intellectual and Developmental Disability*, 32(1): 1–9.

Wade, C.M., Mildon, R.M. and Matthews, J.M. (2007) Service delivery to parents with an intellectual disability: family-centred or professionally-centred? *Journal of Applied Research in Intellectual Disabilities*, 20(2) 87–98.

Williams, V. and Robinson, C. (2001) More than one wavelength: identifying, understanding and resolving conflicts of interest between people with intellectual disabilities and their family carers, *Journal of Applied Research in Intellectual Disabilities*, 14: 30–46.

Zetlin, A.G. and Turner, J.L. (1985) Transition from adolescence to adulthood: perspectives of mentally retarded individuals and their families, *American Journal of Mental Deficiency*, 89: 570–9.

Part Three
Adolescence and transitions to adulthood

Part Three of this book considers adolescence and transitions to adulthood. This is an especially important period for young people with learning disabilities and their families. It is a period when adult identities form that signal claims to rights, freedoms and independence as well as new responsibilities and risks. It is a period when familiar figures like siblings and friends begin to move away to pursue careers or set up home. Accompanying these transitions for those involved are growing sensitivities about typical and normative behaviour and the fulfilment of adult roles and identities. Steps towards a more independent life also bring with them challenges, risks and adult protection issues that can be life changing for both individuals and families. Young people also face transitions to adult service systems that may seek to support them in different ways, creating particular challenges for services to make experiences for them as seamless and free from disruption as possible. Chapters in this section provide the reader with an appreciation of how these issues are experienced in the everyday lives of people with learning disabilities, what services are doing to address them, and how health and social care practitioners can provide important help.

Beginning with some narrative accounts from adolescents and young people, Chapter 14 by Philippa Russell and Margaret Flynn provides first person accounts of the emergent identities of young people, their aspirations and the disabling barriers that they face. It draws the reader into a critical appreciation of a range of important issues, including:

- socially constructed barriers that young people with learning disabilities report and which impinge upon their development of self-concept;
- young people's aspirations for schooling, employment, friendships and social relations;
- barriers to the development of role models and the implications for young people's self-definitions;

- growing up in a culture of assessment, person-centred plans and reviews;
- the evolving structure of transition support services.

Chapter 15 by Jennifer Clegg, Elizabeth Murphy and Kathryn Almack is new to this second edition, and considers transition as a 'moment of change' at the point where a move from child to adult services lies in prospect. This is a critical time when a growing child's self-identity is changing more rapidly than before, bringing its own demands for parents in managing rights and risk, independence and interdependence. It is also a period when interagency collaboration has to be at a premium in enabling seamless service transition. The authors debate these issues by drawing upon extensive literature, including their own longitudinal study of young people leaving special schools. The chapter should help readers to appreciate:

- the significance of this transition 'moment';
- tensions in managing the emergent identities of young people;
- the experiences and perspectives of young people, families and professionals;
- ways of resolving moral dilemmas;
- requirements of seamless interagency work for effective transitioning.

In Chapter 16 Margaret Flynn and Hilary Brown encourage the reader to consider the wider contexts in which abuse takes place, critically appraising the more typical methods of prevention and pointing to examples of best practice. Drawing from serious case review evidence, and with the help of further case examples, the reader is enabled to reflect upon a range of issues surrounding constructions of personal safety, national policy and the prevention of abuse strategies. In particular the chapter supports a critical appreciation of the following factors:

- the social construction of personal safety and abuse;
- manifestations of abuse;
- lessons from serious case reviews;
- preventive strategies;
- implications for staff training and joined-up services.

Chapter 17 reviews the nature and causes of behaviour that challenges services, together with the main strategies employed in support of people who exhibit such behaviour. To assist the reader to develop a broad appreciation of the nature and causes of challenging behaviour Sally Twist and Ada Montgomery outline the mainstream approaches that may help the person with a challenging behaviour to lead a fulfilling and healthy lifestyle. The reader is assisted to understand:

- constructions of challenging behaviour, its causes, functions, modes of expression and prevalence;
- mental health and challenging behaviour;
- assessment of challenging behaviour;
- support and intervention;
- staff training and support;
- safety factors.

Chapter 18 by Alex McClimens and Helen Combes is the first of two addressing sexuality issues. In Chapter 18 the views and experiences of people with learning disabilities about sexuality and identity are discussed, drawing from group discussions and case studies. Moral dilemmas both for people with learning disabilities and those with a duty of care are identified, raising issues about education, rights and risk. The reader is invited to reflect on personal beliefs and values about sexuality, framed by an understanding of the legal and social context, in considering how to act. Readers will be helped to understand:

- the legal and historical context in which the sexual identities and freedoms of people with learning disabilities are set;
- the meanings of sexuality to young people and those assisting them;
- the issues concerning behaviour, risk factors, gender, contraception, parenting, relationships and consent;
- implications for social and health support service providers/carers.

Chapter 19 by Michelle McCarthy is new to this edition and focuses on the sexual lives of women with learning disabilities. It weighs evidence about how we come to know about the personal and sexual lives of these women. Three perspectives are emphasized in the chapter: recent history and societal changes necessary for the sexual lives of women with learning disabilities to have improved; experiences with respect to reproductive health, sexual abuse and women's personal lives; and finally the social context of women's lives because it is impossible to separate out women's sexual lives from the rest of their lives. The chapter will give the reader an appreciation of:

- typical sexual behaviour in 'mainstream' society as a yardstick;
- societal pressures on women generally and their ramifications for women with learning disabilities;
- risk factors in the sexual health of women with learning disabilities;
- the importance of the social context in shaping safe sexual experience.

In Chapter 20 Nigel Beail offers the reader some detailed examples of what happens to people with learning disabilities when they encounter the criminal justice system as either complainants, witnesses, accused or offenders. Drawing from the most recent research, the chapter introduces the reader to a series of case examples, enabling a critical appreciation of the support needs of people with learning disabilities at each stage of the process. In particular the following are critically examined:

- the historical view of criminality and learning disability;
- vulnerability of people to crimes committed against them;
- why people with learning disabilities come into contact with the criminal justice system;
- what happens to people with learning disabilities at different points in the criminal justice system and the difficulties they encounter;
- how people may be supported at each stage of the criminal justice system;
- mitigation factors;
- victim support;
- guidance for 'appropriate adults' and police officers.

Chapter 21 continues to draw from some narrative accounts by people with learning disabilities, including those from the Traveller community. Peter Goward and Linda Gething focus the reader's attention on the identification of factors that support both younger individuals and groups of people with learning disabilities in developing resilience, despite their encountering adversity. In particular the reader is invited to consider:

- the construction of scientific certainty and its limitations;
- the concept of resilience;
- the role of protective factors in relation to the individual, their support networks and the environment;
- the social construction of difference and the potential for reconstruction and renegotiation of social identities;
- the concepts of reciprocity and distributive competence;
- the accomplishment of resilience through shared action and the disabled rights movement.

Personalization is a central plank of health and social care policy in England and is core to the ambitions of *Valuing People Now*. In Chapter 22, another new addition to this edition, Martin Stevens reviews and critiques the personalization agenda, including 'cash for care' schemes, before introducing the latest evidence about the effectiveness of individual budgets for people with learning disabilities and their families. The rolling out of individual budgets is considered against the backcloth of person-centred planning approaches for which there are considered to be some distinct advantages but also, still, challenges. The chapter gives the reader an appreciation of:

- policy ambitions for personalization and challenges for its operationalization;
- the form of 'cash for care' schemes;
- the effectiveness of individual budgets;
- development challenges facing individual budgets and person-centred approaches.

A child becomes an adult when he realizes that he has a right not only to be right but also to be wrong.
(Thomas Szasz, *The Second Sin*, 1973)

Adolescents and younger adults – narrative accounts

Philippa Russell and Margaret Flynn

14

I was always being asked difficult questions, personal questions. Some of them were frightening. What was I going to do in adult life? I needed preparation for some of those questions. It seemed easier just not to answer. But really I had important things to say. I needed someone to break the questions down so that I could answer them. I felt quite frightened when someone asked me about my future. But I needed to talk about it, if only someone would understand. I think they went away saying he's got a learning difficulty, there's no point in talking to him.

> (John, looking back on his teenage years
> when a severe speech impediment and
> cerebral palsy made communication
> difficult except through the use of
> Makaton, in Russell 1998a: 24)

Introduction

The material on which this chapter is based is drawn from a variety of work – an anthology (Murray and Penman 2000) along with studies and focus groups which explore selected domains of young people's life experiences (e.g. Flynn 1998; Russell 1998a, Russell forthcoming). It is not proposed that these narratives and extracts from interviews promise authentic information about the experience of adolescence. More accurately, they are glimpses of young people's self-selected chronologies in which some experiences of adolescence are featured. The adolescence described may have been subject to the change arising from the young people's interaction with new experiences as they 'look back'. The first section summarizes what is known about the experience of adolescence. It presents two women's experience of school and their challenges to educational structures. The next section explores young people's concerns about the existence of a parallel

special school system and the absence of role models as they prepare to leave school. The enduring aspiration of employment against the pull of day services and the socially constructed shadows and silences surrounding medical realities and other matters of importance bring this section to a close. The next section considers the layered subject of people's friendships and relationships, bearing in mind that most of us recognize that a lack of friends is undesirable, regardless of the time spent with families. Finally, we look at identity matters – young people's self-definitions and the groups to which they assign themselves – which serve to affirm adolescents as somebodies. The aim is to consider how young people talk about and make sense of their adolescence, their experiences as children and young disabled people and the implications of these for their adulthood.

Context

Broadly, this chapter is concerned with the times in young people's lives which predate their being viewed as legally and ethically equal to make decisions for themselves. This life phase challenges beliefs about the appropriateness and scope of parental authority which links with an underlying uncertainty about the moral status of young people (e.g. Purdy 1992, and see also the following chapter in this volume). Adolescence marks the end of childhood and the beginning of adulthood as physical growth is completed and the skills required for adult roles and responsibilities are acquired. It is a period of enormous change as young people begin to have adult capacity, although their behaviour may occasionally be more childlike than adult. Not surprisingly, the age range defining adolescence varies according to the setting, the purpose of the definition and the individuals involved (Cotterell 1996; Blustein *et al.* 1999). It is noteworthy that research has consistently assembled evidence which demonstrates that the better we know people with learning disabilities, the more we discover that their aspirations, wants, values and pleasures fall within the range of desires common to most of us and that most young people aspire to what we recognize as an ordinary life (e.g. Kuh *et al.* 1986; Le Touze and Pahl 1990; Flynn and Hirst 1992; Lewis *et al.* 2007).

The subject of being with peers who do not have disabilities, and in turn inclusion in mainstream education opportunities or segregated special schools, exercises many young people and their families. While some positive aspects of segregated residential schools and colleges are acknowledged (e.g. Thomas *et al.* 1996), there are some remarkable barriers to be lowered and removed before local schools are assisted to become inclusive:

> I believe that we shouldn't be in special schools. Everyone should be together so we can mix and make new friends with all kinds of people. All people are different. We should not be sent far away and educated in places we don't want because of our differences. I have been to two special schools. In one, one of the teachers made a stuffed fish for us and two bunny rabbits. I took them home and I destroyed them because I didn't make them for myself. How do we learn to do things for ourselves if teachers do it for you? Why do we need schools if we don't learn anything for ourselves? I also went to a mainstream school and I had been there for five years when the Headmistress turned around and said 'What is this "mongol" person doing in my school?' My mother took her to High Court and we won and she lost. I was bullied at special school . . . Sending us to special school is not the best for us. We are still called names and bullied. We don't want special schools. We don't need special treatment. We want our human rights . . . I went on to college and work. Now I work on my stained glass. I am independent. I do my own things. I was brought up to be independent and disciplined. From my mother.
>
> (Anya Souza in Murray and
> Penman 2000: 78–9)

What I disliked was the 'pretend inclusion'. The school talked the talk, but I always felt second best. I had 'assessments' when other kids had tests. My mum was persuaded that I wasn't very well on 'SATs' days; I think the head teacher thought I would pull the results down. Most of the kids were fine. No bullying, nothing like that – but I felt really sad when I heard a teacher tell one of the mums that it was *'so good for the other children to have me in the school'*. I think he meant I was their charitable project for the year! I don't want to be a project, I want to be me!

> (Thomas, personal communication to Philippa
> Russell, at young people's focus group, 2009)

I didn't like being kept apart from the other children when I went to my primary school. I had to eat downstairs and everyone else ate upstairs. No one asked me what I thought about it or how I could have eaten with the other children . . . children know about the people who work with them better than the adults. I had a helper who wouldn't let me go in the playground. Now I write my helper's job description and we have got it sorted . . . I wanted to go to my local mainstream school. I am a part-time pupil there but only because the toilets are inaccessible. The leisure centre next door is fully accessible and they were happy for me to use their toilets – but that wasn't acceptable! So I go to mainstream part time but have to be driven 12 miles to a special school to use their toilet. By the time I have got there it is too late to come back . . . I go to and from school in a taxi. But I'd like to spend time after school with my friends like everyone else, to go to the library, to do homework together. I asked if I could bring a friend home with me but was told the insurance wouldn't allow it. I tried to argue there was plenty of room and the taxi must be insured for passengers anyway. The next thing I knew was that someone I didn't know was sharing the taxi with me and there wasn't room for my friends! I wasn't asking for much, only to use the taxi service better.

> (Lucy Mason and Maresa Mackeith
> quoted in Russell 1998b: 42–3)

Clearly there is more to inclusive education than opening doors and having the names of young people with disabilities on the registers. The challenge to the whole school system is to prepare all young people to participate fully in the lives of their communities.

Exercise 14.1

Think of the parents you know, who have young children with a learning disability.

How would you make sure that they understood all the options for the education of their child?

What information and advice would you offer, if they expressed strong preferences for a mainstream or for a special school?

All schools are required to have accessibility plans to improve accessibility and inclusion under the Disability Discrimination Acts 1995 and 2005 (Disability Rights Commission 2002c). What information would you give to families (and young people) about what to look for when assessing the accessibility of the school or college?

What sources of independent advice might be available in their communities? Most importantly, how would you convey a positive picture of the children's future and the importance of high-quality educational experiences in achieving good outcomes?

Some horizons of experience

Schools have unavoidable impacts on young people, not merely on their learning, but on their ways of behaving and their attitudes towards further education, work and adulthood. The organizational conclusion of adolescence may be attenuated by extending the ages at which young people leave school (typically at 19 years) and colleges (at ages up to 25 years) if they go directly from school. The preceding and following narratives illuminate the perplexing eligibility criteria and obstacles that prevailed as parents sought to identify the right kind of education for their children and challenge the perceptions of difference which impacted on their daughters' lives:

I am 24 years old . . . have problems with communication and co-ordination. I also have mild learning difficulties. I live at home with my parents and younger brother . . . In 1997 I went to Portland College, Mansfield, for two short assessment visits . . . It was a bit strange at first because it was my first time away from home. Fortunately that didn't last long because we were looked after by Care Tutors who were nice and friendly. I tried out different subjects such as Computers, English, Maths and Horticulture. They had a full programme of activities at weekends and evenings . . . There was also a lot of independence training which was very useful . . . I was delighted when they offered me a place on their Further Education Course for two or three years. That was the good bit. I then had to try and get funding to pay for the course. I applied to the Further Education Funding Council. I had to fill in a lot of forms and provide details of everything I had done since I left school. It seemed to take ages before I got a reply and unfortunately they turned me down. That, of course, was the bad bit. I was very disappointed. I appealed against the decision but they wouldn't change their minds. I am pleased that I have now been employed as a messenger in the postroom at Porterbrook House. I really enjoy the work and I have the same terms and conditions as all the other workers . . . I hope that I will have more good things than bad in the future.

(Sally Mason in Murray and Penman 2000: 213–14)

By the time I was 13 I was well into my secondary school. It was the Sheffield Maud Maxfield School for the Deaf. I am not deaf, and to this day I do not know why I was sent there. My looks had been very much improved, but the earlier name calling had left its mark. I was very insecure until I was about 15 years old. From the deaf school I was transferred to an open air school and it was here that I decided to change my name . . . I was a good dancer. This was achieved by going into Working Men's Clubs . . . My father in his mistaken wisdom tried to bribe young boys to dance with me by buying them drinks, but when my father disappeared, so did my partners. But I had a fighter's spirit and I danced on with my girlfriends as partners . . . In my young adult years there were still the knocks and bangs such as the man who admitted he'd only gone out with me for a bet . . . I met my future husband in a pub. He was not a dancer but he was a wonderful man. We got married . . . I was 24 years old. We had four very handsome boys . . . the experiences, good and bad, have made me who I am today. I am an ordinary woman who just happened to be born with a double hare lip and cleft palate.

(Anne Hunt in Murray and
Penman 2000: 32–3)

These narratives touch on many topics: the tenacity of a parallel, special education system and an enduring reluctance to educate children and young people with disabilities – or even with a hare lip and cleft palate – in local, mainstream schools; the arbitrariness of the ways in which classifications are made and the implications of this for children's education; the critical arena of self-expression in shaping young women's lives; and parental efforts to enable young people to sample ordinary experiences and preclude potential isolation.

In the late 1980s, a large, nationally representative sample of children and adults with disabilities was interviewed to assess the financial and social consequences of disability, including effects on employment and mobility, and to provide information about the use and need for health and social services (Martin and White 1988; Bone and Meltzer 1989; Martin *et al.* 1989; Smyth and Robus 1989). Seventy-nine young people with learning disabilities were interviewed to complement the main OPCS surveys (Flynn and Hirst 1992). This study confirmed that young people had not been emancipated from the 'day care' assumption which special school leavers often encounter; and that local adult and further education agencies addressed the need for scarcity of day services for adults with learning disabilities by providing courses for people with special needs. It also confirmed the widespread underemployment and unemployment of young people with learning dis-

abilities. It indicated also young women's generally impoverished employment status, when considered alongside that of young men, and arguably the absence of encouragement for them to be economically active (which resonated with such earlier research findings as Asch and Sacks 1983 and Hahn 1983).

What I really want is to meet an adult disabled person, I mean someone who is disabled and just getting on with their life. If I didn't read and watch TV programmes on disability, I would think I'd grow out of my disability and walk like everyone else when I was grown up! I am black, I live in a children's home and I am happy enough there. The people are good and they work hard to make sure I know about my culture, meet other people from West Africa. But I have a culture as a disabled person too. I'd like to meet a disability activist like I saw on TV last night. They say I need black role models. Great! But I think I need disabled role models even more because I don't see many disabled people getting onto the celebrity shows, getting jobs, having boyfriends. Trouble is, I just don't know how to meet disabled people. I grew up with people who were not disabled. Inclusive schools are fine, but nobody else uses a wheelchair. I'd like wheelchair sports, that sort of thing. But they don't think it's inclusive. Why can't the other kids use wheelchairs then, that would be equal.

('Sally', young woman in focus group,
personal communication to
Philippa Russell, 2009)

Such observations attest to the significance of wanting to learn from the insights, perspectives and experiences of older people who have had similar life experiences, and to construct self-images that are influenced by people whose lives appear enviable. They also attest to the importance of experienced mentors who may describe their situational influences and their ways of perceiving, explaining and understanding the preoccupations of adolescence.

The subject of employment as an enduring aspiration unifies the findings of many studies, focus groups and workshops examining the post-school opportunities and aspirations of school leavers with disabilities (e.g. Anderson *et al.* 1982; Flynn and Hirst

1992; Flynn 1998; Lewis *et al.* 2007). This aspiration cannot easily be set aside as the effects of not having a job reach far beyond unemployment, as these extracts from Flynn (1998: 2, 2, 3, 5, 7) demonstrate:

It's not very easy on Income Support because if you get employment you're only allowed £15.00 a week.

[You can't] retire [from a day centre] because you lose your place.

We work in environments where we're not paid . . . We don't want to be taken advantage of.

Mum wakes me at 8.30. I have breakfast with my mum. I get washed, clean my teeth and put the radio on. A big ambulance thing comes. It picks up three wheelchairs and a walker. I get to the centre at about 10.00. I sometimes go to [another centre] and go to the light room as well. At 10.30 we have coffee and a tea break. Then it's the light room until dinner time [mid-day until 1.30 pm]. After, I watch TV, play games on the computer . . . after tea break I get ready to go home. I wait for transport. People get dropped off then home at last.

Social services said we should have our education classes at the Technical College like everyone else. Now hardly anyone has education classes . . . you can't stay on a course at college for a very long time but some of us learn slowly. This does not mean we are not progressing . . . If you have a lot of disabilities you do not get to go to college . . . members would like to do courses that would help them to get a job . . . other members would like to do courses for leisure . . . in other words, our members would like the same opportunities as everyone else.

Such reflections, routines and experiences capture the terrains yet to be negotiated if young people with learning disabilities are to envisage themselves as employees. Chapter 27 has more to say on this theme. The insistent question, 'What do you want to do when you grow up?' is familiar to most young people whose prospective autonomy is taken for granted.

Answers may refer to living and working circumstances, travel, adventure, intimate relationships, marriage and parenthood. Such aspirations are known to have sustaining qualities. Although life in uncertain times may render us unwilling to think ahead, most of us anticipate that we will be instrumental in shaping our own futures. What the preceding quotations confirm are the starkly finite options available to young people with disabilities. Entering paid employment, leaving the parental home, having intimate relationships, getting married and perhaps having children are widely regarded as markers of adulthood. When such topics are 'silenced' (e.g. Fine 1995) the experiential conditions of young people's lives are effectively ignored:

When I was 14 I suddenly realised how little I knew about my disability. My parents did not want to discuss it and my teachers and friends were silent if I raised the issue. I wanted to know what the options were. How can you have a 'transition plan' if you don't know what jobs you could do? I began to watch things on TV, to read bits in the newspaper. I imagined dreadful things, I would get worse, I was really ill, I might die. I couldn't sleep at night and my schoolwork got worse. I felt really depressed. Then the school nurse talked to me and asked what I was worrying about. She was really helpful and practical. She told me about a group of young people in my town. She gave me information to read and told me about a national organisation for my disability. She also said I could ask to see the doctor on my own if I wanted – but I should tell my parents how I felt. In the end we wrote them a letter. I didn't want secrets. They were really upset to find I had been so worried. I went to see my paediatrician and he was wonderful, very helpful. I wish people would realise that we do want information about ourselves. We do want to meet other disabled people. We don't want to be seen as problems. I have my own health plan now and that's good.

(Peter in Russell 1998b: 52)

Realising that my disability may get worse. Nobody at home would talk about it. I never met any disabled people at my school. When

I was 14 they started saying, 'You can't' and I heard things. Now I know I might die young. That's awful. There are a lot of places for parents to get information, but no one seems to want to do that for me.

I want to know if I can have children. My parents don't want to know. They just say 'Look after yourself first.' But it matters doesn't it? Could I? And if not, why not?

I don't know much about sex education. They do it at school but lots of parents withdraw their children so it isn't much use. I may be disabled but I'm human like everyone else. And I can't just disappear down town to buy something to read.

I'd like to talk about incontinence. It's an awful subject isn't it? But it stops me going on school trips. I think it will stop me getting a job. What about girlfriends? Could I ring up the GP and get him to send me somewhere? I don't want my parents around.

(Young people in Russell 1998b: 92)

The example below is especially important. Young disabled people are now much more likely to be offered the possibility of elective surgery that might save their lives, might enable them to be a bit more mobile – or might not.

Yes, I really worry about the future. I know some people [with cystic fibrosis] do really well now. But some die. Some of the kids I've seen at my hospital have died. It's scary really. Of course there are lots of new operations and things. You can have a heart and lung transplant now if you are lucky. But are you lucky? It sounds silly, but I don't want someone else's heart. I might become someone else if I did! If I try and tell Mum how I feel, she cries and cries and says I am all she's got. Actually I want to meet other kids who have had the surgery, maybe I'm just being a baby. And even if I don't get operated on and I don't have long to live, I want to live a life to the full. I know two kids who have posthumous GCSEs – their families thought they shouldn't bother with course work and all that when they were

so ill, but they wanted to succeed. 'Jackie' said to us, 'if I get good grades, put the letter on my gravestone to show that someone special lived here'. I was terrified, talking about gravestones and all that, but Jackie *wants* to prepare for the future. Me, when I hear talk of gravestones, I reckon I'll have the surgery after all.

(Young person in focus group, Russell, 2009: 3. The young woman in question has had a successful heart/lung transplant and is off to university next year)

Such fundamental concerns bring to the foreground what is not being said to young people. It can be perceived as protective not to discuss the implications of people's medical conditions and disability. Yet such a hide and control stance can be endorsed by the wider context and wander into other topics of enormous significance to young people:

- 'The most important thing is loving each other, helping each other, emotional health.'
- 'You need to know every part of the body to help you explain.'
- 'No, I don't get embarrassed. Men and women are all the same in a way. Just different in others.'
- 'Parents tell you about having babies.'
- 'What matters is that you are as fit as you can be. But if you have a disability, you don't always get offered the health and well-being things. Me, I need help with my weight and I'd love a personal trainer at the gym. Being fat worries me much more than having a disability.'
- 'And that you don't just come out with things like that!'

Parents in some localities questioned whether sex education was necessary for their child's development, perhaps confirming the sense of censorship which appeared to characterize the sexuality of young adults. A local project found that the majority of parents interviewed did not know whether or how sex education was taught in the schools or how to teach some of the issues at home. Neither did they know whether menstrual cycle care featured in the curriculum for young women (Pearson *et al.* 1997):

Difficulties arose in one special school where they undertook no special health education, sex education or more neutrally, training in first aid. The families of some young people with learning disabilities wanted assistance with preparing their relatives for adulthood and the possibility of sexual relationships. Primary health care teams were anxious not to take a lead on this subject in order not to 'medicalise' sexuality. The local authority questioned why this and associated subjects should be seen as the unique responsibility of social care providers.

(Pearson *et al.* 1997: 68)

Sexuality has a central place in negotiating the transition to adulthood. The tasks of integrating sexual feelings and desires into a positive self-identity, which includes a positive sexual self, are complex. Values and norms about masculinity and femininity interact with family expectations about what constitutes acceptable behaviour, and yet, examination of these structured silences and shadows speaks of disproportionate exclusion, and more partitions to be dismantled (see also Chapters 18 and 19). Pearson *et al.* (1997) identified superficially neutral boundaries to controlling what it is that young people with learning disabilities may be taught, in school, by health care professionals and social care professionals. However, these have far-reaching consequences for young people and expose the dynamic of exclusion.

Improvements in the level and quality of personal, health and sex education for young people with learning disabilities (crucial as these are) will not in themselves guarantee social inclusion and positive personal relationships for young disabled people. A survey of the views of young disabled people between the ages of 16 and 24 (Disability Rights Commission and MORI 2002) found that over 35 per cent (regardless of their disability) expected to have more difficulties in making relationships in adult life and finding a partner than their non-disabled peers. Thirty-two per cent noted their difficulties in accessing a social life (which might be reasonably expected to generate the friendships and connections from which most people form closer individual relationships as adults). They commented on their over-dependence on parents and family members to facilitate social and leisure activities and the lack of freedom to just 'hang out' with their peers.

However, the survey clearly showed that the aspirations of young disabled people mirrored those for young people without a disability. The survey covered young people with a range of disabilities (including learning disability), and there was no difference in views expressed between the different disability groups represented. Key aspirations included:

- a well-paid job by the time the young people reached 30;
- the opportunity to travel;
- a home of their own;
- a partner and a family;
- to have attended university or to have continued education and training for a career.

Relationships mattered to those participating in the survey. Perhaps most worryingly, respondents in the 21–24 age range were twice as likely as those aged 16–20 to say they felt lonely a lot or all of the time. In effect, school and college had produced a range of friends and social activities which reduced or disappeared when young people dispersed to find work or to continue education or training outside their home areas. There was also a marked drop in confidence about the future as young people grew older. The survey found that one in three of the participants believed that they would be earning less than other people of their age by the time they were 30. Sixty-six per cent had problems with public transport (essential for a social life as well as potential employment).

The importance of access to a social life and employment in order to develop friendships was a key theme within the Disability Rights Commission survey (2002). A young woman (Russell 2003: 13) similarly observed with some sadness that:

. . . they talk about sex all the time at school, don't get pregnant, all that stuff. But they talk about it like learning to ride a bike. There's no point in learning to ride a bike if you don't understand the rules of the road and if there are no roads to ride on! It's a trick, nothing more. Me, of course I'd like a boyfriend. But I'd like some friends first – good mates teach you things, they look out for you. I'd feel safer if I got out more, learnt to hang out with the others. Otherwise all this stuff about condoms and HIV, it's stupid, isn't it? What I want is someone to help me get a life! No point in learning about sex and stuff, if you can't go anywhere without your mum tagging along behind you. Clubs, pubs, cinemas, just hanging out with your mates – I can't do it. Mum's there at 12.00 p.m. with the car and I'm Cinderella – but I never get to the ball!

Exercise 14.2

Recalling your own experience of adolescence, what were your preoccupations as a teenager and which, if any, were 'silenced'? What did being 'grown up' mean to you?

All adolescents think that their parents 'fuss' about safety when they are out and about on their own. How can we balance independence and maximum choice and control with the greater risks of hate crime experienced by many young disabled people?

Aspirations and realities

Our lives are not interesting. A fantastic life would be moving into a hostel on my own and staying there and having lots of money so I can retire into the country and not come back. I really want a girlfriend who is thinking about me now. I don't want people who help me. I like friends. I like an independent life. Now I just sit up and watch TV and listen until 5.00 in the morning. I go to sleep at 5.00 in the morning and 5.00 in the afternoon to make up my sleep. I like watching things about getting jobs . . . I've tried to get one before but things have stepped in my way . . . I like working with people . . . I'd love to go to sleep really tired after a hard day's work.

My life would be fantastic if I was happy, engaged and married; I could do sports when I wanted; read books; do crosswords and play snooker.

I'd like a conversation with me and my girlfriend. They can't tell me what to do with my life. I get picked on at the [day] centre and I haven't done anything. They get me mad sometimes. In the centre they think I talk too much. I would be really happy if people didn't get at me all the time. I like making coffee for people. I'd like lots of money to be able to buy my girlfriend an engagement ring. I'd like a job and I'd like to be boss.

I'd like to have a passport and travel, have a real gap year! I know a young woman who uses a wheelchair who did go off to South America. But my family nearly die when I suggest it. Not that I want to go to South America, I'd just like to go off on my own. The trouble is, when you are disabled like me, you never are on your own! All they say is 'you can't'. I'm tired of 'can't'. I think we talk much too much about risk.

I like training to move into a group home or flat with Adam. I like Adam's company. I would be really happy if we could get married and settle down . . . I think Adam would like a job. I'd like to go out with Adam for a meal. I'd like to see different countries because I read loads of travel books. I'd like to work in a coffee bar serving people. I like visiting places with Adam. I'd like a lot of money so I can go into an expensive shop like C&A and get lots of things from there.

It's about hopes and dreams, isn't it? School is really important. It's children's work, isn't it? Grown-ups go to work every day to earn their money. If you want to get a job, you have to go to work at school first, to learn lots of things. I want a good job, I want to get on in life. So I want a good school, then I've got a better chance, haven't I? I want to go to college, all that stuff, I'm tired of people saying 'can't'. But my school says 'you can', that's good. I feel they're fighting for me.

(Quotations from young people's focus groups in Russell 2003: 15–16)

Enduring friendships, and close and enjoyable relationships are recurring themes in the literature about adolescence. Concerns with belonging, being included, making and keeping friends and group affiliation are important sources of status and reputation (Cotterell 1996). Milardo (1992) proposed that friendship networks can be regarded as concentric circles, with very few in the centre (close friends or best friends) and friends and acquaintances in the outer circles. While school is a key location for meeting and making friends, out of school settings also play a part in developing closer friendships. Young people's confiding relationships were explored by Flynn and Hirst (1992). One in ten of the study sample claimed not to confide in anyone and over half confirmed that they confided in their mothers. The importance of families was similarly endorsed by young people in a focus group (Russell forthcoming), who stressed their (often reluctant) reliance on parents to act as supporters, advocates and, of course, chauffeurs.

When contrasted with young people who did not have disabilities, this signalled more reliance on their parents for emotional support than young people generally. This was particularly the case for young women. We concluded that confiding in parents, especially mothers, as opposed to other adults or special friends, was widespread and that this was clearly linked to being in the parental home. It also crucially linked with opportunity. Two parent focus groups (Russell forthcoming: 28) identified the lack of accessible and safe transport for after-school and weekend activities as a major barrier to independence for their children. The parents regretted what one family saw as:

> an old fashioned and interfering constant presence in our daughter's life. We are committed to giving her maximum independence, but that often means my husband or I picking her up from a club at 2.00 a.m. If we have to get up for work at 6.30 a.m. the next morning, that's a real burden for us. We do it for Lily's sake. But she worries about us and we know she sometimes won't go out when she wants to, because she thinks we are too tired.
>
> And yes, we've tried to book independent transport. But Lily didn't feel safe with the driver who turned up. So that idea came to a full stop and we're back as the taxi drivers. My husband even got pulled over by the police one evening – they thought he was a kerb crawler! He explained about Lily and how he had to hang around waiting for her. They were very nice about it. But it did not feel nice at the

time. And of course it's not nice for Lily, she deserves a young person's life – but most of her time she's stuck with two sixty pluses who'd really just like an early night, but who have to act as her 'best friends'!

The importance of young people's weekday activities in terms of offering possibilities for non-family relationships was confirmed, with just over two-thirds of the study sample referring to people who lived in their neighbourhoods. A few young people described adult figures such as teachers as their friends. Although many young women said that they saw their friends in their spare time, they were less likely to do so than their male peers. We expected the incidence of contact with friends to increase with age, reflecting greater freedom of movement as the young people got older. However, more of those in their early twenties were found to have limited social contact with their peers. The incidence of seeing friends also pointed to the particular isolation of young people with extensive support needs. The study suggested that it is more difficult to make new friends after leaving special school and to keep in touch with friends made at school (Flynn and Hirst 1992). However, the Disability Rights Commission and MORI's national opinion poll survey (2002) also found extensive problems in retaining old friends and making new friends in a cohort of young people aged 16–24, regardless of whether they had attended mainstream or special schools. One young woman of 23 who had attended a mainstream school and a local college commented in a personal communication that:

> Round here, most young people go away to work or college. They move on. I'd like to move on too. But where do I go? Yes, I'd like some new friends. But I can't afford taxis. My support worker doesn't work evenings. There aren't any safe buses and things to travel on. I thought it would get better when I left school. Actually it's worse. And I don't feel safe where I live . . . there are some nasty kids, I don't go out after dark any more. Really, I feel like an old lady. And I'm 20 years young.

Other young people have made similar comments:

> The name calling was painful. I got called

'spastic' and 'mongol'. They shouted at me 'cos I got learning difficulties and I don't read and write well. They said I was a dummy because I didn't get any homework. Well I went to my teacher and said I've got to learn to read and write, 'Help me!' She did and I've got a briefcase like the other kids for my papers now. I do homework just like them. If they call me spastic I just laugh.

I hear people talking about me to Mum. They're sorry for her, having me. She says, 'Don't worry – she's great!' She helped me to speak up for myself. She said, 'It's your life and you've got to say what you want.' I'm on the Student Council at school now, the first Disabled Student.

The word respite care. Actually I love my link family and I know Mum and Dad need a break. To be honest I need a break from them too! But the word respite I looked it up in a dictionary and it said, 'Relief from burden'. It worries me. Am I a burden? I don't want to be but I expect I am, and I needn't be. I said to Mum, 'If we had a wish list for the new bathroom, a better wheelchair, a wider front door, accessible shops, then I wouldn't be a burden to anyone.'

Being cared for! No one else is cared for when they are 13. I'd prefer to talk to someone about support and not care. I'm not the family dog! I want to be in charge.

(Russell 1998b: 91–3)

Identity matters

A key challenge for many young disabled people is that of developing an independent and confident identity amidst an ongoing procession of assessments, examinations and reviews. Russell (2003) found that many young people with disabilities or special educational needs were acutely aware of the constant assessments, reviews and target-setting which set them apart from their non-disabled peers.

In a series of focus groups with young disabled people (Russell 2003: 18), many participants described their anxieties about constant assessment. One pupil commented that: 'I'm sick of assessments all the time.

The other kids, they do tests and SATs and things, and I get assessments. Why? One of the lads, he said I was like a second-hand car. I must always be breaking down, to have all these people fussing over me. I felt really bad, sort of singled out.' Another noted that: 'It'd be OK if they assessed you, like, for things you could do. But all they want to do is find out what you're bad at! I'm sick of being a problem, I want them to help me find out what I'm good at.' A third talked angrily about assessment for the Disability Living Allowance:

> They sent someone to the house, like, and my mum and me, we had to go through all the things I couldn't do. My mum said, mind you don't look too good when he comes, we need the money. I think the money should be to help me move on, not to keep me stuck here. We do need the money, I can't use the bus and Mum hasn't got a car. So we just sat there and made a list of what I couldn't do.

But sometimes assessment is seen as having a positive purpose. One young person described how:

> the school really helped me make a video of my day, when I wanted help and what help I needed to learn. The good thing was that the video showed what I could do on my own. It made me feel in control. They were asking me what do you want to do, what job do you want, let's work together. That felt really good, like I really mattered. I felt I had something to show all those people at the review, like 'this is me and this is where I'm going'.

For many young people, getting the right support is crucial. One young man (Russell forthcoming) described angrily how, when he first attended a mainstream school, the learning support assistants decided it would be easier to group all those needing some support at lunchtime round one table. He was angry and upset that he and other pupils with disabilities or special educational needs were, as he put it,

> . . . sat around like little kids, when all we needed was some help in standing in the queue and carrying our trays back. We didn't want the staff to go and load the food up for us.

Half the time, we didn't want what they had chosen and then we got told off like little kids for not eating it up. And they kept mopping the table all the time – as if the other kids weren't spilling things too. The other kids, they took the micky and called us the 'rabbit table'. That's because our helpers made us eat salad all the time – no chips, no pudding. Talk about the Nazis! We're 15, for heaven's sake!

(Russell 2007: 17)

This boy, Paul, finally plucked up courage to tell a teacher about his humiliation. The response was positive – a round-table discussion, some very embarrassed learning support assistants and the end of segregated eating. Very importantly, Paul and his friends are now involved in recruiting their own personal assistants and in training them and other staff in the school to avoid a repeat of the 'rabbit table'. Paul, reflecting on the experience, commented that:

> . . . the staff, they did mean well but they saw us as babies! They made us feel like babies too. Funny thing is, when I went to a special school, they were the other way round – pushing us to do more for ourselves. But I guess we were pioneers at 'X' school. We were their first disabled students and they learnt on the job. What I've learnt is that you have to speak up – and if you do, people listen. That's inclusion but it's hard work.

(Russell 2007: 17)

Thus at a time when self-conceptions are emerging, some young people are highly attuned to being perceived as different and their daily interactions, and exposure to the views of others, yield opportunities for affirming these perceptions. Name-calling which hinges on young people's disabilities and appearance is harrowing at a time when positive self-images and group identification and solidarity should be developing. Young disabled people, becoming acutely attuned to the verbal bullying and harassment to which they are so often subject, also pick up undesired messages about the values and attitudes of those harassing them. At a time when young people spend time in public places and group settings, it is important to

feel part of a group which nurtures belonging and endorsement of their self-worth. But because of negative attitudes towards disability and difference, some young people feel devalued and isolated. They in turn may look to bullying and negative comments as a means of affirming their identity in their peer group to which they wish to belong.

Witnessing the sympathies extended to a parent and understanding why a father buys young men drinks so that his daughter will not be a wallflower speaks of a significant parental role in making the experience of connectedness possible for their children. It would be inaccurate to cast this role as cotton-wool protectiveness. It reveals a reassurance to their offspring that they are accepted in their families and that inclusion and membership are important. In being overtly supportive and pre-empting the possibility of rejection, they act as best they can to give their offspring the confidence to meet these new challenges.

The mother who asserted of her daughter, 'She's great!' declined to focus on her daughter's disabled identity and simultaneously reassured her acquaintance, and as significantly her daughter, that her sympathy was unmerited. This is a role that is also performed by teachers, as the teacher of the young woman with Down's syndrome demonstrates. She responded to her pupil's desire to be as her peers: a reader and a writer and to have homework as they did. While the name-calling persisted, this young woman had new resources to draw from in dealing with it.

Politicization arrives early for some young people with disabilities:

> What do we want from life? Like everyone else we want to have our own homes, our partners, we want to be healthy, we want to see our families and friends. Disability isn't an end, it's a beginning. We like to think 'can do' not 'this is a problem'. If you talked to us more, you would know that disabled people are real people with things to say. Please hear us!

> It's not just us who are disabled and make the problems. It's the big world out there. Just think, if we made it better out there, then all sorts of people would be better too – mums with pushchairs, old people, dogs and things

like that. I play sport, I go to school, I'm a scout and I help in a club for older people. We did citizenship in the National Curriculum the other day. That's me. I'm a citizen, not a problem!

(Young people in Russell 1998b: 93)

Exercise 14.3

You are the head teacher of a mainstream school. How do you deal with the peer ridicule, bullying and harassment as described in this chapter?

You are a teacher. How do you explore the subject of group identification with adolescents?

Conclusion

Listening to, and learning with, young people with learning disabilities breaks important ground. There are no shortcuts to realizing the practical, pragmatic and humane benefits of engaging children and young people in decision-making and in discussion about their identities and their lives.

Resources

www.transitionsupportprogramme.org.uk. Aiming High for Disabled Children, launched in May 2007, is the government's transformation programme for disabled children's services in England. One of the key issues identified in AHDC was the urgent need to co-ordinate services better for young disabled people in their transition to adult life. Therefore, a new Transition Support Programme was launched, with the aim of improving standards of transition in all local areas. The Transition Support Programme includes a Transition Support Team, based at the Council for Disabled Children in London. The Transition Support Team actively engages young people themselves as key partners in creating change at local and regional level. Further information and relevant publications are available from the team at www.transitionsupport programme.org.uk. Regular updates about the work of the team can be obtained by emailing tsp@ncb.org.uk.

References

Anderson, E.M. and Clarke, L. in collaboration with Spain, B. (1982) *Disability in Adolescence*. London: Methuen.

Asch, A. and Sacks, L. (1983) Lives without, lives within: the autobiographies of blind women and men, *Journal of Visual Impairment and Blindness*, 77(6): 242–7.

Blustein, J., Levine, C. and Nevelo-Dubler, N. (eds) (1999) *The Adolescent Alone: Decision Making in Health Care in the United States*. Cambridge: Cambridge University Press.

Bone, M. and Meltzer, H. (1989) *The Prevalence of Disability among Children*, OPCS Surveys of Disability in Great Britain, Report No. 3. London: HMSO.

Cotterell, J. (1996) *Social Networks and Social Influences in Adolescence*, Adolescence and Society Series. London: Routledge.

Disability Rights Commission (2002a) *Disability Discrimination Act 1995, Part 4, Code of Practice for Schools*. London: The Stationery Office.

Disability Rights Commission (2002b) *Disability Discrimination Act 1995, Part 4, Code of Practice for Post 16 Providers*, London: The Stationery Office.

Disability Rights Commission (2002c) *Code of Practice for Schools: DDA 1995, Part 5*. London: DRC.

Disability Rights Commission and MORI (2002) *Survey of Young Disabled People Aged 16–24*. Disability Rights Commission, Research and Evaluation Unit (available via the Disability Rights Website at www.drc-gb.org).

Fine, M. (1995) Silencing and nurturing voice in an improbable context: urban adolescents in public school, in M. Fine (ed.) *Disruptive Voices: The Possibilities of Feminist Research*. Ann Arbor, MI: University of Michigan Press.

Flynn, M. (1993) *Consultation with People with Learning Disabilities*. North Yorkshire Community Care Plan 1994–1995. Manchester: National Development Team.

Flynn, M. (1998) *Customer Research with People with Learning Disabilities*. York: City of York.

Flynn, M. and Hirst, M. (1992) *This Year, Next Year, Sometime . . .? Learning Disability and Adulthood*. Manchester: National Development Team.

Hahn, H. (1983) 'The Good Parts': Interpersonal Relationships in the Autobiographies of Physically Disabled Persons.

Wenner-Gren Foundation Working Papers in Anthropology. Stockholm: Wenner-Gren Center for Scientific Research.

Kuh, D., Lawrence, C. and Tripp, J. (1986) Disabled young people: making choices and future living options, *Social Service Research*, 15(4&5): 1–30.

Le Touze, S. and Pahl, J. (1990) *A Consumer Survey Among People with Learning Disabilities*. Canterbury: Centre for Health Services Studies, University of Kent.

Lewis, A., Parsons, S., Robertson, C., Ellins, J. and Davison, I. (2007) *My School, My Family, My Life: Telling it Like it Is. A Study Detailing the Experiences of Disabled Children, Young People and their Families in Great Britain in 2006.* Birmingham: Disability Rights Commission and University of Birmingham.

Martin, M. and White, A. (1988) *Financial Circumstances of Disabled Adults Living in Private Households*, OPCS Surveys of Disability in Great Britain, Report No. 4. London: HMSO.

Martin, M., Meltzer, H. and Elliot, D. (1989) *The Prevalence of Disability Among Adults*, OPCS Surveys of Disability in Great Britain. London: HMSO.

Milardo, R.M. (1992) Comparative methods for delineating social networks, *Journal of Social and Personal Relationships*, 9: 447–61.

Murray, P. and Penman, J. (eds) (2000) *Telling our own Stories: Reflections on Family Life in a Disabling World.* Sheffield: Parents with Attitude.

Pearson, M., Flynn, M., Maughan, J. and Russell, P. (1997) *Positive Health in Transition: A Guide to Effective and Reflective Transition Planning for Young People with Learning Disabilities.* Manchester: National Development Team.

Purdy, L.M. (1992) *In Their Best Interest? The Case Against Equal Rights for Children.* Ithaca, NY: Cornell University Press.

Russell, P. (1998a) *Making Connections: Challenges and Opportunities in Transition Planning.* London: Council for Disabled Children.

Russell, P. (1998b) *Having a Say! Disabled Children and Effective Partnership in Decision Making.* London: Council for Disabled Children.

Russell, P. (2003) Reports of consultation focus groups with parents and young people, in *Report of the Ministerial Working Party on the Future Role of Special Schools.* London: Department for Education and Skills Publications Unit.

Russell P. (2007) *Making the Disability Equality Duty a Reality.* London: Disability Rights Commission and Council for Disabled Children.

Russell, P. (2009) Young people's comments from series of focus groups organised as part of a local authority review of services for disabled children and young people [Note: permissions granted from the young people in the focus groups to use their unattributed quotes].

Russell, P. (forthcoming) 'Families In': Report of a European Union Study of the Lives of Families with a Child with a Learning Disability in Five Member Nations. (Contact prussell@ncb.org.uk for further information.)

Smyth, M. and Robus, N. (1989) *Financial Circumstances of Families with Disabled Children Living in Private Households*, OPCS Surveys of Disability in Great Britain, Report No. 5. London: HMSO.

Thomas, A., Legard, R. and Chetwynd, M. (1996) *Student Voices: The Views of Further Education Students with Learning Difficulties and/or Disabilities.* London: Social and Community Planning Research; Skill; National Bureau for Students with Disabilities; Further Education Funding Council.

15

Transition: a moment of change

Jennifer Clegg, Elizabeth Murphy and Kathryn Almack

Introduction

For young people with intellectual disabilities (ID) and their families, the point in the life cycle when they move from child to adult services has become known as *the* transition. Other possible points of psychological transition, such as going to school or leaving home, pale into insignificance because of the particular challenges presented by leaving children's services. Problems associated with this transition are not confined to Britain. One study in the US dubbed it 'the second shock' (Hanley-Maxwell *et al.* 1995), to follow the first shock parents experience on hearing their child's diagnosis. The significance of this transition was recognized in the government's 2001 White Paper, *Valuing People* (Department of Health 2001), which made continuity of care and support one of 11 key objectives for improving ID services.

As many chapters in this book show, intellectual disabilities can encompass individuals ranging from those with multiple and complex disabilities who have developmental ages in months rather than years, whose care needs are entirely met by others, to relatively able individuals who can live on their own and hold down paid employment. The chapter is illustrated by case studies of young people across this spectrum of ability.

Exercise 15.1

Why might it be problematic if the public sector services involved in this transition (Health, Education and Social Services for children, and also for adults) hold limited, and often differing, understandings of ID?

The situation of young people with ID is undoubtedly open to multiple interpretations. Public discourses range from (arguably naïve) statements in *Valuing People* that 'People with learning disabilities have been saying for a long time that we can speak up for ourselves' (Department of Health 2001: 24), to the Mental Capacity Act (2005) which specifies how to determine whether or not somebody with ID has the capacity to make a particular decision. Glaser and Strauss (1967) have pointed to the importance of examining the various 'definitions of the situation' brought to interactions by different parties. These interpretations relate not only to the assumed needs of the young person and those who care for him or her, but also to the appropriate means for having such needs met, and to the rights, responsibilities and roles of people with ID, of carers, of service providers and of the state. Such definitions are neither fixed nor immutable.

These complexities make it difficult for people to work out how they should act, and such confusion creates space for positivist principles to dominate the field. 'Normalization' is one such principle. Nearly 40 years ago Wolfensberger (1972) defined this principle as 'Utilization of means which are as culturally normative as possible, in order to establish or maintain personal behaviours and characteristics which are as culturally normative as possible' (p. 28) and described it as 'a captivating watchword standing for a whole new ideology of human management' (p. 27). More recent understanding of 'ideology' is that it is a style of explanation where beliefs and values are held not for their truth-value but to serve the interests of dominant groups (Honderich 1995). Normalization's key ideas were made memorable in O'Brien's (1987) five 'accomplishments' that services should enable people with ID to experience: Choice, Participation, Community Presence, Competence and Respect. These and related ideas, variously described as principles, values or (inaccurately) a philosophy, have had a powerful influence on services for people with ID across the developed world. They shaped the ideas on which *Valuing People* was based 30 years later: Choice, Inclusion, Independence and Rights; they also underpin the ten 'indicators' used by the Healthcare Commission (2007) to audit health care services for people with ID.

There has been extensive research into this transition, generally from the perspective of carers who remain most vocal about its difficulties. Todd and Shearn (1996) described how, as their child enters adult services, carers realize that their own lives are going to become increasingly distant from people who have non-disabled children, a realization that affects them profoundly. This is particularly significant given the findings of an international review of the subjective well-being of people caring for someone with ID at home: only in high-spending Sweden was their well-being similar to that of parents of children without ID (Cummins 2001). Clegg *et al.*'s (2001) transition study compared the perceptions of parents and staff, and the different cultures in child and adult services. While child services offered information about the person to adult services as required by law, most adult services had little interest in receiving it. Many staff in adult services did not trust the information they were given, and/or did not read it because they were committed to offering a fresh start to each person, in order to counter previous labelling. This 'fresh start' position also meant that staff in adult services expressed little interest in hearing about the young person from their parents; by contrast parents were keen to share their knowledge, and to receive the valued support they had previously obtained from school teachers.

Both the US (Furney *et al.* 1997) and Australia (Riches 1996) responded to transition difficulties by making significant changes to the policy contexts in which transitions occur. Until 2001 Britain continued to depend largely upon individual Disabled Persons Act (1986) workers to facilitate the transition process, but two initiatives changed that. *Valuing People* (Department of Health 2001) required Partnership Boards to take cross-agency responsibility for overseeing improvements in transition; and the former careers service for school leavers was replaced by a new service, Connexions. However, Connexions has attracted criticism recently for focusing on the most disadvantaged at the expense of promoting social mobility for the most able (Cabinet Office 2009).

In this chapter we examine the concepts and

perspectives that shape this transition, including the view that normalization continues to be the primary goal, and the belief that the principles are achievable if only people try hard enough. We do so by examining accounts given by people on the ground. We explore what it is about transition that is difficult, and for whom; and we examine what the research reveals about unresolved tensions embedded in transition.

Our examination of transition is shaped by an argument put forward by Gleeson (2009), that ID may be at a third moment of change. His argument that distinct and significant moments of change in ID reflect wider social transformations is fundamental to an understanding of this chapter.

According to Gleeson (2009), and historians such as Thomson (1998), the first moment of change occurred in the industrial era, when people with ID started to be conceptualized as a problem that required legal and institutional structures. Changing social conditions were making it harder for this group to cope in the community, but their problematization was also rooted in the moral and ideological environment of the time. The 'mentally defective' were considered to deserve care but also to need control: the 1913 Mental Deficiency Act allowed people with ID to be placed under care if they were at risk, but also if they constituted a risk to others. The development of large 'colonies' where care was provided to increasing numbers of people in asylums and sheltered farms was considered to be benevolent social engineering. Designed with the good intentions of providing care and meaningful occupation, they became too expensive in a political environment dominated by war and depression. Thomson concluded that these institutions went awry because 'Administrative practice blunted humanity, and under-resourcing and professional self-interests blocked alternatives' (1998: 147).

So the second moment of change involved the closure of these institutions. This was prompted by inquiries that revealed appalling conditions in the US, Australia and the UK, such as the Ely Hospital Inquiry (Department of Health and Social Security 1969). Gleeson (2009) argued that deinstitutionalization also reflected the emergence of neoliberal politics in the 1960s and 1970s, with its focus on restoring 'rights' and rescuing individuals from collective forms of care. Normalization ideals from the US were promulgated in international declarations and subsequently used to frame anti-discrimination legislation in many countries including the UK Disability Discrimination Act 2005. Policy documents such as the Warnock Report (1978) brought about a sea change in special education. Rather than separating children with ID and placing them into special schools, 'statements of educational need' specified the support such children needed in order to be schooled in mainstream settings. Similar thinking led to the development of the supported living accommodation which succeeded group homes: here, while people may be placed in accommodation with others, everybody has their own tenancy and levels of support designed to enable each person to live as independently as possible.

This second moment stretched over the last 40 years and many people continue to regard its ideals as an appropriate underpinning for service provision. However, there is a growing view that another, third moment is starting to take shape, spurred by growing disillusion with neoliberal policies that have failed to keep either the financial sector or climate change within safe limits. A key neoliberal assumption is that the origin of most problems is the failure of communication between individuals, which tends to result in professionals and agencies being exhorted to raise their game. However, increasing numbers of policy researchers (Cumella 2008) criticize this view: better communication alone cannot possibly transform all that is wrong with services. All agencies including the office of the National Director for Learning Disabilities (responsible for the *Valuing People Now* programme) agree that increased survival rates at birth and increased longevity is creating 1 per cent per annum growth in the population of people who have ID. A financial review commissioned by the Associate Directors of Social Services (Verita 2005) showed that significant new resources are required if services are to respond adequately not only to the increasing population but also to the raised expectations engendered by *Valuing People*. This gains further support from an analysis of funding at the transition to adult services for young people with complex disabilities excluding ID carried out by a team of health economists: Knapp *et al.* (2008) concluded that the considerable sums of money spent

on disabled young people are clearly not enough to meet government policy intentions.

The other main pressure for change comes from growing evidence that while normalization has improved the living conditions of people with ID significantly, it has had no impact on other desired outcomes such as social relationships. For example, Forrester-Jones *et al.* (2006) showed that 12 years after leaving hospital many people remain socially isolated. Emerson's (2005) survey found that 20 per cent reported no social contact with friends or family in the previous year, and 32 per cent reported that someone had been rude or offensive to them because of their intellectual disability. Burton and Kagan's (2006) policy analysis revealed that *Valuing People* ignored social class and social and cognitive disabilities, and took an excessively romantic view of 'the community' as a safe and accepting place. Users (Stewart 2009) and carers (Smellie 2009) highlight the gap between people with ID and society as their major concern.

So this third moment of change invites a standing back to reflect on the current pattern of service provision. There is a need to evaluate the ideas framing services, informed by a better understanding of the distinct needs and contributions of people with ID and those involved with them (Burton and Kagan 2006; Cumella 2008; Wilson *et al.* 2009; Counterpoint forthcoming[1]). In 2001 Gleeson and Kearns asked whether extreme polarization of ideas, such as 'social good–medical bad' and 'individual good–collective bad', coupled with severe moral judgements about people who question these ideas, may have become part of the problem. More recently Gleeson (2009) has argued that deinstitutionalization has too often been rendered as a moral struggle between therapeutic reform and institutional obduracy, in the process shattering the rights and responsibilities of parents. Clegg's (2008) analysis of the Sutton and Merton Inquiry found similar discounting of reasonable objections to closure made by parents and staff at Orchard Hill Hospital. A judgemental environment that inhibits questions and debate can prevent development for a while but ultimately ideologies are undermined by new ideas as they emerge.

In the rest of this chapter, we explore the conceptual basis of ID policy by drawing together published research on transition and data from our own longitudinal research project with a cohort of young people leaving special schools. Since readers will all have addressed the transition from school themselves, many quite recently, we will invite you to engage with the topic reflexively. However, our purpose in doing so is not to compare the lives of people with ID negatively against your experience, but to assist you to understand better the experiences not only of people with ID, but also of those who care for and work with them.

Our study: what is difficult about this transition, for whom?

We studied the process of transition to adult services for a cohort of 28 young people with moderate–profound ID over 18 months: before, during and after they left special schools and entered adult services (details in Clegg *et al.* 2008). All of the young people lived with their parents/carers prior to leaving school. Seven had been identified as displaying challenging behaviour; the young people with moderate disabilities all needed some help with personal care. Among the 16 severely/profoundly disabled people, some could name concrete experiences, others made choices by signs or pointing; four needed to be fed, bathed and toileted. We employed a range of methods to study the interfaces between all parties as they negotiated packages of care. Data were collected from the young people where possible, from parents, carers, specialist transition staff and senior policy staff: methods included face-to-face and telephone interviews and diaries, and were supported by documentary analysis.

We examined both process and outcomes concerning the way this transition turned out for the 28 young people and for their parents, and what they and transition workers (referred to here as TWs, and as female although there were a few men, to preserve anonymity) felt about these outcomes.

At the end of the first year after leaving school, 20 of these young people were continuing to live at home with their parents, attending a combination of day services and/or further education colleges. Three had moved into residential care homes and five young people were attending (or waiting to go to) residential further education colleges; three had unpaid work placements for up to one day per week.

Twenty-one parents felt that a good or acceptable outcome had been achieved for their young person: TWs agreed in all but one case. This positive outcome resonates with recent transition research from Australia (Rapanaro *et al.* 2008) which found that carers leavened the language of stress and burden by talk of fulfilment and growth. Of the remaining seven young people, parents considered outcomes for five were less than satisfactory although TWs assessed outcomes as good or reasonable. Parent opinions about the remaining two could not be determined. Nineteen parents felt their own situation had either improved or had not deteriorated. Of the remaining nine, negative outcomes included reports that changes in provision as their young people moved into adult services led to reduction in services and lack of resources which increased the burden of care for parents. We talked to all but two of the young people attending FE colleges and six of the nine young people accessing short breaks at the time of second interviews. All but one were positive about the experience, although some reported missing their child short break service. We observed five young people in residential care, day services or short break settings: one refused to eat and drink in their day centre and appeared unsettled, the

A smooth transition

Bethany's single-parent mother described her as having moderate–severe ID, no health needs and no challenging behaviour. She was not concerned about the transition beforehand because Bethany made friends easily. Bethany moved to a mix of days in FE college and a day service: there were some teething problems arranging transport. After the transition her mother felt that Bethany had settled well, matured and become more interested in her appearance. The main difference for Bethany's mother was that the shorter days and longer holidays taken by FE college meant that she had less time to herself. The TW found this mother to be very independent, and considered Bethany's needs to be well met.

A difficult transition

Andrew had profound ID, epilepsy and challenging behaviour; he was cared for at home by his widowed mother. She hoped that he would attend residential college and made a number of applications, but these were all refused: she felt that the school misrepresented Andrew in their assessments, and reported becoming depressed. Pursuing the possibility of residential college meant that Andrew missed opportunities for a gradual introduction to a local FE college. His subsequent late placement in an FE college, without preparation and without the company of peers from school, failed: according to the college he was too aggressive; according to his mother he would have been fine if they had done what she requested and placed him with a male teacher. Andrew was then placed in a day service: his mother felt he was being occupied rather than educated, bored and generally unhappy. Their TW found the case challenging because she was unable to deliver what Andrew's mother wanted for him, and was concerned that she took rejections by residential colleges personally. Andrew's mother reported that she had had to learn to lower her expectations, and that the transition period was worse than the year her husband died. She felt 'isolated, emotional, angry and unsupported'.

other four appeared very content in their surroundings.

While **outcomes** were generally positive, the **process** of transition was experienced as difficult and distressing by most parents. Sources of such distress included anxiety about the impact of changes on the young person, concerns about making the wrong decision and anxiety that the burden of care would become intolerable. These concerns were exacerbated by concerns about standards and availability of suitable provision, uncertainty about entitlements, bureaucratic difficulties, delays in decision-making and experiences of being rejected by services.

TWs also expressed dissatisfaction with the process and identified a range of constraints that hindered their ability to do their job well. A few TWs described coping with their workload, but most felt that their job and the process of transition were very difficult, if not impossible. During the 18 months of data-collection six of the original 12 TWs resigned, a further two had long-term periods of sick leave, and the remaining four all reported high levels of stress. Consequently, many families experienced times during transition when their TW changed and/or was on sick leave, and this situation exacerbated the difficulties facing other TWs in managing their own workload and covering the work of colleagues.

So, while outcomes were acceptable for most young people, the process left much to be improved. Even when parents and TWs told us that they were satisfied with the outcomes achieved and the young people we spoke with or observed were settled in

new environments, the process of transition was experienced as stressful by parents and TWs. We conclude that improving the transition for young people with ID does not rest on any particular staff group simply 'raising their game', and so we turn to an examination of the ideas that frame expectations about this transition. Do conceptual tensions make it difficult to identify and/or resolve transition difficulties? If so, what are these tensions, and how do the various parties to transition – young people, their parents, and TWs – respond to them?

What research reveals about unresolved tensions embedded in the second moment of change

The physical and organizational transition made by young people with ID as they move from child to adult services is often discussed as a transition to 'adulthood' as if this is an unproblematic claim. Yet adulthood is more than a description; it is a moral category which is invested with power. Typically, becoming an adult means that parental legal control is left behind and the person is granted self-determination. Entitlements acquired include the right to marry without the consent of others, to enter into contracts, to vote, to purchase alcohol, and, in general, for each person to live according to their own understanding of their best interests.

The extent to which it has been considered appropriate to invest young people who have ID with all the privileges, freedoms and responsibilities associated with adulthood has varied across time and place in a way which illustrates the three 'moments' outlined above. During the first moment even one of the strongest advocates of individual freedom, J.S. Mill, specifically excluded the 'feeble-minded' from the self-determination which he held to be the adult's inalienable right ([1859]1975). Historically, such exclusion from adult status was used to justify the imposition of patronizing and demeaning practices upon people with IDs, often based on custodial care and surveillance (Young 1990; Priestley 2003).

More recently, and characteristically of the 'second moment', government policy and professional practice have insisted that people with ID be granted full adult rights, including the same right to autonomy and self-determination as other non-disabled citizens. Those who questioned this new orthodoxy have been criticized as reactionary or 'disablist'.

We carried out our research in this second moment and much of the talk during interviews with parents and TWs was concerned with what it meant to be an adult in the context of significant ID (Murphy *et al.* in press). Our research data reveal the tensions embedded in second moment policies. For the most part professionals, particularly those who were qualified social workers, promoted 'second moment' solutions and decisions. They insisted that the young people must be granted the same self-determination which was the entitlement of young people without disability. They represented any erosion of such determination as evidence of moral culpability. They challenged any suggestion that the right to self-determination should be subject to an assessment of the young person's capacity for weighing alternatives or judging the likely consequences of their actions. This insistence on self-determination was coupled, in many cases, with a resistance to the idea that parents were well positioned to make a positive contribution to planning the young person's future. It was also associated with the view that the ideal was for young people to leave home, and to live independently, outside their family unit.

By contrast, most parents and those professionals employed through Connexions rather than through Social Services were much more equivocal about the young people's status as adults. Their ambivalence about the ascription of adult status to these young

people can be seen as a questioning of the certainties and orthodoxies of the second moment. Parents gave various reasons for equivocating about the young people's adult status, all of which highlighted the inability to conform to the expectations of the rational, independent, autonomous adult of the liberal convention. Some cited ongoing dependence.

> So [Jack's brother] was independent. He was gone. I didn't have to take him to the bus stop. I didn't have to wash him. I didn't have to say, you've got to have this treatment on your hair, you'd better get into bed now, you know. In a lot of ways you're still looking after a child but you've got to treat him with the respect of an adult.
>
> (Jack's mother)

Others were concerned that these young people lacked the capacity to make reasoned judgements about the potential consequences of their intended actions. Both parents and Connexions workers pointed to the young people's vulnerability and need for constant supervision.

> Colleges will say they can cope with anything but we're finding there's a significant number of people who drop out simply because . . . the support isn't there.
>
> (TW6)

Often these parents saw it as their responsibility (in some cases a burdensome responsibility) to make choices on behalf of their children. A few insisted that the young people's wishes should be respected even when they were at odds with their own. For example, William's father accepted his son's decision not to use the short breaks service even though this increased the burden of care on his wife.

> He used to go on short breaks and he took umbrage at it . . . just came and said, 'Don't want to go no more.' You can't force him to go . . . I mean at the end of the day you have to accept that they are 18, they've the right to vote, to have their own lives.

Most parents were more resistant to self-determination. One challenged head-on the assumption that just because her daughter had reached the age of majority she was able to make decisions for herself.

But once you get to 18 you're old enough to make your own decisions. So what's changed? Because she's still, I don't think she's ever going to be 18 . . . because you're physically 18 that's it. You know what you want to do with your life? Righty ho . . . I mean when she's one hundred and blooming eight she's still not going to be any better is she? Let's face it.

(Rebecca's mother)

They feared that, left to their own devices, the young people would make poor choices which had serious consequences both for the young people and for themselves as carers. Parents cast themselves as prioritizing the values of care and protection of vulnerable dependents over what they presented as a dogmatic insistence on self-determination at all costs. Many demonstrated an awareness of the wider public and policy context and potential questions/censure they face about the legitimacy of taking decisions on behalf of their young people. Yet one of their major concerns was the extent to which they felt confident that services would make appropriate judgements about 'the right thing' for their child and the extent to which resources would be available that would enable parents to feel confident in 'letting go':

Yes they are adults and they have a voice but sometimes William agrees things without understanding what is he agreeing, it's the carers and parents who actually know what it is because we've got it 24/7, not social services and that's the difference.

(William's father)

You see the problem with social workers who are trying to do their best for the people they're working with . . . who they don't know apart from what they see on paper and also they get a bit of a relationship between themselves and the client . . . so they make a decision based on what they see in front of them in terms of their paperwork and their overall impressions . . . and that is not necessarily a correct one . . . I personally work on the basis of my decisions being the least wrong possible.

(Louise's father)

Some parents suggest that out of all possible options, they are the people who have the fullest knowledge about their son or daughter and as such are best placed to make the right (or 'least wrong') decisions. Several suggested that the professionals involved did not have sufficient knowledge of the young people to be able to assess the risks and offer advice on the best course of action. The above quotes (from Almack et al. 2009) illustrate some of the moral complexities parents face when confronted with the dual imperatives to empower or protect their young person with ID.

Similar difficulties and differences of view were observed when we examined attempts to reverse first-moment exclusion of people with ID with second-moment 'inclusion' policy. Initially a complex social policy with ambitions to reshape the relationship between people with ID and society, inclusion soon became limited to three policy goals: mainstreaming, employment and independent living. In our research (Clegg et al. 2008) it was rare for the young people themselves to value mainstreaming, and parents/carers felt they had to defend the young people's limited engagement with mainstream social activities. Parents listed many practical barriers which prevented visits to community settings, describing ways in which they created a semblance of inclusion while avoiding disruption and embarrassment.

The only place you can really take him is to McDonalds and the drive through . . . My husband takes him to the pub a couple of nights a week but at half past five when the pubs are empty which isn't really what you'd call social is it, but when there's a crowd he doesn't want to leave . . . and people want to play pool and he wants to put the balls down.

(Tom's mother)

TWs also justified decisions to place young people in specialist day centres rather than in mainstream environments. These justifications were pragmatic: it should not be necessary to attend a specialist service in order to access physiotherapy, but it is. We interpreted such justifications as evidence that mainstreaming is not just a principle guiding service provision; it has become a moral imperative. The parents and TWs who found it difficult to support their young person to use mainstream settings acted as if they expect to be judged negatively, and possibly judged themselves negatively, for failing to make this aspect of inclusion a reality.

There was less tension associated with employment because, despite policy exhortation, only a small minority of respondents considered employment salient for this group. Four young men were keen to work but only two families considered it possible. Most parents regarded employment as an unobtainable ideal for their young person, and TWs agreed. Our findings concur with Scottish data showing the limited impact of employment policy, where only 1 per cent of relatively able individuals have paid employment with non-disabled people for more than 30 hours a week (Scottish Executive Statistics Release 2007).

The continuing advocacy of employment in *Valuing People Now* (Department of Health 2009) as the solution to what people with ID should do during the day is challenged by these data as a problematic underestimation of the support most of these young people require. The problem of identifying meaningful occupation after school-leaving remains: in our interviews no other concern was raised by parents as frequently as inactivity. Half the parents wondered whether their child would be able to find activities that engaged them after they left school. This was particularly true for those caring for young people with autism and more severe levels of disability, where many parents expressed concerns. One mother shown around a day centre feared that staff understanding of choice bordered on negligence:

> I did notice there were quite a few people just sitting round . . . and I did ask the question, 'What, you know, if Tom wouldn't join in, what would you do?' And the reply was, 'Well he's an adult, he has the right to make a choice, and if that's his choice that's what he's allowed to do.' Well Tom might be an adult in body but . . . he's got to be kept active otherwise he'll just, I don't know I think he'd go to sleep for a hundred years.
>
> (Tom's mother)

When Tom moved from school to day centre her concerns turned out to be more than justified. Failure to stimulate Tom left him sluggish and this was coupled with failure to provide the consistent staff he required in order to accept food and drink. As a result he became dehydrated and at risk of major seizures; and the day service's failure to exercise him meant that his ability to mobilize despite significant physical disability deteriorated markedly.

Further tension between inclusion and meaningful activity was identified by a TW who observed that specialist disability clubs had been closed without sufficient attention to how people with ID might become involved in mainstream clubs. Most of these young people required supported transport to collect and return them, and experienced facilitators willing to take responsibility for their well-being. These are only provided for activities run by specialist groups such as Nottingham Mencap or a special school's former pupils association.

Apart from the practical problems of finding sufficient support for those with moderate–severe IDs, there are also questions about whether simply inserting people with milder IDs into mainstream settings overcomes the discomfort experienced on both sides. It may simply expose everybody to negative experiences without the benefit of creating any social change. Hall (2004) found that many people with mild ID excluded themselves from mainstream social spaces they found intimidating, preferring to create refuges at the margins of society in clubs and church groups, and with family and friends. Similarly, Philo and Metzel (2005) argue that we need to think again about how society can cultivate spaces where people with ID experience a sense of place and connectedness.

When invited in 2005 to reflect upon her report, Warnock described inclusion policy as 'possibly the most disastrous legacy of the 1978 report' (Warnock 2005: 22). She was particularly concerned about the isolation and bullying experienced by many children with autism, and the disruption to the learning of the whole class caused by children with ID and challenging behaviours. Warnock defended the commitment to social justice that underpins mainstreaming, but argued different children have different needs and these are often best met in different environments.

To conclude, our transition research (see also Pilnick *et al.* in press) identified a number of tensions and dilemmas which inhibit all parties from finding a way forward: they are damned if they do and damned if they don't. It was evident that the various parties were struggling to identify the 'right thing to do' in a complex and fraught context, often with little sound information on which to base predictions about the likely outcomes and, indeed, with limited confidence that resources would be available to support whatever decision was eventually made. As school leaving dates drew closer some decision had to be made about each young person's future, but creative discernment was undermined by the rhetorical use of moral polarities that devalued alternative points of view and pushed some contributions outside the realm of the morally acceptable.

A third moment of change

The challenge, now, is to find a constructive way to create a third moment which retains the invaluable advances, protections and insights of the second moment and yet recognizes the concerns of people on the ground. Many parents and some TWs felt that rigid commitment to self-determination may simply leave vulnerable people exposed to risk and neglect, while engaging in impression management in order to avoid being considered morally culpable when they acted to protect what they believed to be their child's best interests.

A key characteristic of this moment of change, which questions liberal individualism and looks toward collective solutions to problems, is the doubt it casts on the idea that blueprints can or should be written for only one party to a relationship. In this transition, the key relationship is often between the young person and their family, usually their parents; but there is also a relationship, or at least a potential relationship, between people with intellectual disabilities and the rest of society that needs to be taken into account.

So if we are to find a constructive way to create a third moment, as Gleeson and Kearns (2001) argue, we must avoid reducing the debate to opposing moral polarities framed around notions of 'right' and 'wrong'. Such a reduction risks simply condemning those viewpoints with which we disagree as 'reactionary' and, in the process, failing to benefit from the positive contribution that they can make to discerning 'the right thing to do' in any individual situation. It also encourages a discussion that generates winners and losers. To move forward into the third moment, we need to learn to value doubt, dissent and heterodoxy and to build an inclusive landscape which sets aside doctrinaire assumptions. Making decisions about the future of a young person with severe ID is always likely to be difficult and, in some cases, may be very fraught. Good decisions are more likely to emerge from a context of tolerance where it is possible to transcend moral orthodoxies and engage reflexively with contributions made by others which challenge our own prior (and often taken-for-granted) assumptions.

In the case example below (detailed in Almack *et al.* 2009), Alec's mother points to how she and her husband have attempted to follow policy discourse concerning self-determination but have overruled

---

Case example: 'He hasn't got the bigger picture'

Alec's mother and father have made the decision for Alec to attend a residential college. Alec is very resistant to this idea and indeed to doing anything once he leaves school:

> I know all the new government guidance says we have to include our children with severe intellectual disabilities in the decision-making process but he was included in it to some extent that he was aware all the way through of what was happening and that he would be leaving school and there were all these options we'd looked at. But he wasn't going to make a decision except to stay at home and that wasn't acceptable. I have to say that actually his mental skills are very limited, he hasn't got the bigger picture and he'll just say what he wants to do at that moment in time. He has no capacity to see that residential college is an opportunity that won't come again and he actually needs to stagger the opportunities that are available to him so that he's not just sat in a day centre from now until the day he is 65 . . . I can't let him sit around at home, stopping me going to work, watching telly and videos all day long, becoming more and more isolated, eating more and more.

their son in taking a decision to opt for a residential college of further education. She suggests that his expressed choice, which is to do nothing other than 'sit around at home', puts him at increased risk of becoming isolated and jeopardizing his health by overeating. Alec's mother also refers to the potential constraints placed on her ability to lead her own life and to be in paid employment. The latter point is often overlooked in considerations of research into the life course experiences of parents/carers of people with ID. Todd and Jones (2003) suggest that while parents may be vigorous advocates for their sons and daughters they are more hesitant to express their own needs, and indeed many of the parents in our study struggled to articulate their own needs.

Exercise 15.2

The 'second moment' approach to determining a way forward is to insist that Alec's rights are the central, and perhaps the only, issue. We invite you to take a 'third moment' perspective by thinking more broadly. Please write a briefing note to the service manager summarizing the full range of issues raised by this situation from each person's perspective, as a basis for the more difficult task of developing a process of negotiation which respects and takes seriously the positions of all parties. You may wish to consider, for example, whether parents might find it more difficult to place their son or daughter outside their home but in the same town. If the only way parents can legitimate a decision for their child to leave home is by arguing that distant facilities are significantly better than anything available locally, that would be problematic for hopes of ending out-of-county placements. If this were a significant issue, service managers might be invited to consider what they could do to ease the situation.

Transition is a moment of uncertainty, amplified by a context of cultural change. The constructionist philosophers Deleuze and Guattari (1994) argue that 'Nothing positive is done, nothing at all, in the domains of either criticism or history, when we are content to brandish ready-made old concepts like skeletons intended to intimidate any creation' (Deleuze and Guattari 1994: 83). They argue that the creative act involves clearing a plane where new concepts can flourish, and that new concepts arise out of paradox. Thus the dilemmas many parents and some TWs struggled with during our research may themselves be the seeds of change. We suggest that the evidence points to the following implications for renewed professional practice in ID at this transition.

- Without additional resource to reduce unacceptably high rates of sickness among parents and TWs, change may be too difficult for people buckling under the burden of care.
- Professionals need to emerge from a rule-based approach to practice and the moral clarity associated with asserting client empowerment as a service goal, because this results in an underplaying of the constraints that people with ID experience, and because it excludes key members of their affective community from the picture.
- There is a need to develop a more textured understanding of need by juxtaposing awareness of the obdurate reality of the differences between people, in terms of their capacity for autonomy and self-protection, alongside a resistance to objectification and infantilization.
- Professionals supporting people with ID will have to develop, explore and examine new concepts that inform their practice; doing so will require that they learn how to tolerate and find their own way through moral uncertainty.
- It is vital to social development and furthering social justice for people with ID that policy-makers, who tend to be both risk-averse and uncertainty-averse, are willing to embrace uncertainty.
- The immense difficulty of promoting relationships between people with ID and local communities requires reflection before action. The geographers' concept of Belonging (Hall 2004) may be a more fertile starting point than current inclusion policies. Insights from community psychology (www.compsy.org.uk) such as how to work with the grain of local groups, rather than setting up new ones that collapse when funding is withdrawn, may also offer new ways forward.

Conclusion

Having a child with ID creates many challenges for parents, and these are amplified by the lack of culturally available narratives that tell them how to fulfil their role. Before the child with ID reaches the age of majority, narratives about childhood and parenting provide a reasonable fit. Problems start to multiply when the child leaves this status: the degree to which parents can draw on narratives of either childhood or adulthood become less relevant, while decisions made by parents become even more freighted with moral judgement. Such judgements come mainly from service workers but also from family members and other parents of young people with ID. Mixed feelings reported by some parents make the situation even more difficult: simultaneously not wanting to abandon their child and hoping for a future that is not entirely bound up in caring. A new approach needs to be constructed that achieves a better balance between the needs of people with ID and family members.

Our research focused on the degree to which the ideas driving service provision help or hinder the people facing this situation. The evidence underlines the fact that just saying something does not make it so: asserting adult status does not mean that each person has the capacity to make informed decisions about their best interests. Regarding employment as the solution to the problem of how people with ID spend their adult lives was shown to be unrealistic. A new approach needs to be constructed that achieves a better balance between opportunity, protection and control (see also Chapter 27). However, replacing current aspirations with other individualistic goals will not be enough. Sooner or later second-moment individualism is going to crumble. During 1989 Europe showed how change can be created by large numbers of people taking peaceful action. Whether ID experiences a bloody or a velvet revolution depends on the way we all respond, as well as the alternatives that we are able to imagine. Rather than continue to undermine key members of the affective community around people with ID, developing ways to talk to each other that maintain rather than destroy relationships would be a very good place to start.

Acknowledgements

Transition research supported by Big Lottery Fund grant No: RG/1/001044628. We thank the young people, families and staff who allowed us to accompany their transitions; special schools that supported the research; Nottingham Mencap steering group, Val Leyland, Anna Harvey and Jenny Lapish.

Note

1. Counterpoint was a round table of 30 international researchers from geography, history, nursing, philosophy, psychology, psychiatry and sociology, who met for three days to debate current conceptualizations of ID and explore new ideas and perspectives that may serve the needs of this population better. Papers and a summary of the plenary discussion will be published in the *Journal of Intellectual Disability Research*, 2010.

References

Almack, K., Clegg, J. and Murphy, E. (2009) Parental negotiations of the moral terrain of risk in relation to young people with learning disabilities, *Journal of Community and Applied Social Psychology*, 19(4): 286–99.

Burton, M. and Kagan, C. (2006) Decoding *Valuing People*, *Disability & Society*, 21: 299–313.

Cabinet Office (2009) *The Panel on Fair Access to the Professions*. http://www.cabinetoffice.gov.uk/strategy/work_areas/accessprofessions.aspx.

Clegg, J.A. (2008) Holding services to account, *Journal of Intellectual Disability Research*, 52: 581–7.

Clegg, J., Sheard, C. and Cahill, J. (2001) Severe intellectual disability and transition to adulthood, *British Journal of Medical Psychology*, 74: 151–66.

Clegg, J. Murphy, E., Almack, K. and Harvey, A. (2008) Tensions around inclusion: reframing the moral horizon, *Journal of Applied Research in Intellectual Disability*, 21: 81–94.

Cumella, S. (2008) New Public Management and public services for people with intellectual disability, *Journal of Policy and Practice in Intellectual Disability*, 5: 178–86.

Cummins, R. (2001) The subjective well-being of people caring for a family member with a severe disability at home: a review, *Journal of Intellectual & Developmental Disability*, 26(1): 83–100.

Deleuze, G. and Guattari, F. (1994) *What is Philosophy?* (trans. G. Burchell and H. Tomlinson). London: Verso.

Department of Health (2001) *Valuing People: A New Strategy for Learning Disability in the 21st Century*. London: HMSO.

Department of Health (2009) *Valuing People Now: A New Three-year Strategy for People with Learning Disabilities*. London: Department of Health.

Department of Health and Social Security (1969) *Report of the Committee of Inquiry into Allegations of Ill-treatment of Patients and Other Irregularities at the Ely Hospital, Cardiff*. London: HMSO.

Emerson, E. (2005) Adults with learning difficulties in England 2003/4. Survey report downloaded from www.dh.gov.uk/en/Publicationsandstatistics/DH_4120033.

Forrester-Jones, R., Carpenter, J., Coolen-Schrijner, P., Cambridge, P., Tate, A., Beecham, J. *et al.* (2006) The social networks of people with ID living in the community 12 years after resettlement from long-stay hospitals, *Journal of Applied Research in Intellectual Disabilities*, 19: 285–95.

Furney, K., Hasazi, S. and Destefano, L. (1997) Transition policies, practices, and promises: lessons from three states, *Exceptional Children*, 64: 343–55.

Glaser, B.G. and Strauss, A.L. (1967) *The Discovery of Grounded Theory: Strategies for Qualitative Research*, New York: Aldine Publishing Company.

Gleeson, B. (2009) Counterpoints of care: two moments of struggle. Paper presented to Counterpoint, a symposium organized by University of Nottingham.

Gleeson, B. and Kearns, R. (2001) Remoralising landscapes of care, *Environment and Planning D: Society and Space*, 19: 61–80.

Hall, E. (2004) Social geographies of learning disability, *Area*, 36: 298–306.

Hanley-Maxwell, C., Whitney-Thomas, J. and Pogoloff, S. (1995) The second shock: a qualitative study of parents' perspectives and needs during their child's transition from school to adult life, *Journal of the Association for Persons with Severe Handicaps*, 20: 3–15.

Healthcare Commission (2007) Investigation into the service for people with learning disabilities provided by Sutton and Merton Primary Care Trust, www.healthcarecommission.org.uk (accessed 20 December 2007).

Honderich, T. (1995) *The Oxford Companion to Philosophy*. Oxford: Oxford University Press.

Knapp, M., Perkins, M., Beecham, J., Dhansiri, S. and Rustion, C. (2008) Transition pathways for young people with complex disabilities: exploring the economic consequences, *Child: Care, Health and Development*, 34: 512–20.

Mental Capacity Act (2005) (c.9) www.opsi.gov.uk/ACTS/acts2005/ukpga_20050009_en_1.

Mill, J.S. ([1859]1975) *On Liberty* in *Three Essays*. Oxford: Oxford University Press.

Murphy, E., Clegg, J. and Almack, K. (in press) Constructing adulthood in discussions about the futures of young people with moderate–profound intellectual disabilities, *Journal of Applied Research in Intellectual Disability*.

O'Brien, J. (1987) A guide to lifestyle planning, in B. Wilcox and G.T. Bellamy (eds) *A Comprehensive Guide to the Activities Catalog*. Baltimore, MD: Paul H. Brookes.

Philo, C. and Metzel, D. (2005) Introduction to theme section on geographies of intellectual disability: 'outside the participatory mainstream'? *Health & Place*, 11: 77–86.

Pilnick, A., Murphy, E., Clegg, J. and Almack, K. (in press but available online). Questioning the answer: questioning style, choice and self-determination in interactions with young people with intellectual disabilities, *Sociology of Health & Illness*.

Priestley, M. (2003) *Disability: A Life Course Approach*. Cambridge: Polity Press.

Rapanaro, C., Bartu, A. and Lee, A.H. (2008) Perceived benefits and negative impact of challenges encountered in caring for young adults with intellectual disabilities in the transition to adulthood, *Journal of Applied Research in Intellectual Disabilities*, 21: 34–47.

Riches, V. (1996) A review of transition from school to community for students with disabilities in NSW, Australia, *Journal of Intellectual and Developmental Disability*, 21: 71–88.

Scottish Executive Statistics Release (2007) Adults with learning disabilities: implementation of 'The same as you?' www.scotland.gov.uk/stats (accessed 24 August 2007).

Smellie, I. (2009) The perspective of a local Mencap Society, *Mental Health Review Journal*, 14(2): 20–1.

Stewart, D. S. (2009) Making it happen for everyone: a reflection on changing services for adults with learning disabilities, *Mental Health Review Journal*, 14(2): 14–19.

Thomson, M. (1998) *The Problem of Mental Deficiency: Eugenics, Democracy and Social Policy in Britain c.1870–1959*. Oxford: Clarendon Press.

Todd, S. and Jones, S. (2003) 'Mum's the word!': maternal accounts of dealings with the professional world, *Journal of Applied Research in Intellectual Disabilities*, 16: 229–44.

Todd, S. and Shearn, J. (1996) Time and the person, *Journal of Applied Research in Intellectual Disability*, 9: 40–60.

Verita (2005) *Pressures on Learning Disability Services: The Case for Review by Government of Current Funding*. Report for Association of Directors of Social Services, www.Verita.net.

Warnock Committee (1978) *Special Educational Needs: The Warnock Report*. London: Department of Education and Science.

Warnock, M. (2005) *Special Educational Needs: A New Look*. Impact Paper No. 11. Macclesfield: Philosophy of Education Society of Great Britain.

Wilson, N., Meininger, H. and Charnock, D. (2009) The agony and the inspiration: professionals' accounts of working with people with learning disabilities, *Mental Health Review Journal*, 14(2): 4–13.

Wolfensberger, W. (1972) *The Principle of Normalization in Human Services*. Toronto: National Institute on Mental Retardation.

Young, I.M. (1990) *Justice and the Politics of Difference*. Princeton, NJ: Princeton University Press.

16

Safeguarding adults with learning disabilities against abuse

Margaret Flynn and Hilary Brown

Introduction

This chapter addresses adult protection or 'safeguarding', a term increasingly favoured by social care services in England and Wales. Experiencing abuse or neglect is to experience in the raw what it is like to be disempowered: it follows that you cannot exercise power in your life if you are not being appropriately protected from abuse or neglect. 'Abuse' can be seen as a vague, all-encompassing term, embracing crimes against property, as well as the violence, neglect, discrimination, humiliation, sexual assaults and mistreatment visited upon disabled children, young people and adults (Brown *et al.* 2000; Brown 2002). This chapter aims to encourage consideration of the wider context in which abuse occurs, an appreciation of the means of prevention and ways of 'learning the lessons'.

Far from being 'over-protected', people with learning disabilities are often chronically 'under-protected', being exposed to more dangerous situations than others, with less chance that abuses will be noticed and fewer opportunities to be rescued or supported than are offered to other citizens.

Policy

In recent years several serious incidents have demonstrated the need for immediate action to ensure that vulnerable adults, who are at risk of abuse, receive protection and support.

> The Government gives a high priority to such action . . . The circumstances in which harm and exploitation occur are known to be extremely diverse, as is the membership of the at risk group . . .
>
> Abuse is a violation of an individual's human and civil rights by any other person or persons . . . [it] may consist of a single act or repeated acts. It may be physical, verbal or psychological, it may be an act of neglect or an omission to act or it may occur when a vulnerable person is persuaded to enter into a financial or sexual transaction to which he or she has not consented, or cannot consent . . . can occur in any relationship and may result in significant harm to, or exploitation of, the person subjected to it . . . main different forms of abuse: physical . . . sexual . . . psychological . . . financial or material . . . neglect or acts of omission . . . discriminatory abuse . . .
>
> (Department of Health and the Home Office 2000: Foreword, paras 1.1 and 1.2, paras 2.5–2.7)

While public inquiries and undercover TV programmes have intermittently illuminated the nature and reach of abuse in the lives of vulnerable populations, we are attuned to our culture's ambient climate of minimizing and outright denial of abuse (e.g. MacIntyre 2003). As O'Connell Higgins (1994: 10) observed of the 'Holocaust deniers', 'If such uncertainty exists in the face of organised, abundantly documented evil, no wonder less centralised abuses are overlooked. Most of the traumatised bear no remaining physical manifestations of their abuse and have no witnesses'. Thus it is not surprising that abuse and safeguarding vulnerable populations are insistent, if recent, themes in government policy, not least as the consequences transcend individual suffering.

Exercise 16.1

What words and images do you associate with abuse?

Many 'classifications' focus on acts of abuse, but what matters most when it comes to appreciating its seriousness is to unpack the context within which it occurs, and to challenge the attitudes of individuals who abuse vulnerable people, and the indifference of those who stand on the sidelines. Usually it is clear that what is happening is wrong but even where the person's intent is not to harm, for example if they find themselves doing so because they are out of their depth, abusive or neglectful relationships need to be challenged and not colluded with. While different manifestations of abuse defy our efforts to record them and measure them over time, we know that we should be attentive and proactive if people's lives are not to be derailed.

'Vulnerability' is a much maligned concept but it is very much a part of the human condition and is made worse by naïve thinking about risks, decision-making or capacity. Although it is sometimes seen to be a stigmatizing label, we are all vulnerable at times when we do not know enough about a transaction, or if we have been misled or duped about another person's intentions towards us. Friends, family members, interest groups, advice agencies, advocates and ultimately the criminal justice system stand up for us all in these situations. Sometimes these interventions are very informal, a word here or a raised eyebrow there, but at other times they are more insistent or formal. It may go as far as removing someone who presents a threat from our home, or from the workforce serving our needs, and in dangerous circumstances this is necessary and appropriate.

In 2009 people who are employing their own staff using Direct Payments are regarded as self-sufficient entrepreneurs, and costly responsibilities that once resided within the public sector are being devolved to individuals and their families. *Transforming Adult Social Care* (Department of Health 2008b) is ostensibly signing up to the emancipatory aspirations of the disability movement. However, the principal lessons arising from self-directed care in mainland Europe include the *underestimation* of demand *and cost* and the creation of an unregulated, untrained and poorly paid workforce. Not only do the Resource Allocation System and self-assessments associated with Individual Budgets appear to operate independently of statutory Community Care Assessments, they assume that family caregivers will subsidize

their relatives (as individuals living with their families will receive half the funding available to people living outside the family home) and engage in the crucial – and unpaid – function of managing the Individual Budgets (ADASS 2009). Chapter 22 in the present volume summarizes more evidence about Individual Budgets within the context of moves to personalization in health and social care. It is worrying that neither Direct Payments Recipients nor Individual Budget holders benefit from the safeguarding mechanisms of regulated services.

Abuse steals lives

Steven Hoskin's body was found on 6 July 2006 at the base of the St Austell railway viaduct in Cornwall. In addition to the catastrophic injuries associated with falling 100 feet, a post-mortem examination found that Steven's body bore evidence of torture: cigarette burns, neck bruises from the dog collar and leash he had been dragged around in, a lethal dose of paracetamol tablets and alcohol, and bruises on his hands which finally caused him to fall to his death. All his life Steven had been terrified of heights.

Steven was a vulnerable adult whose needs were well known to the local NHS, social services and housing. But so too was Darren, the principal perpetrator of his murder. In 2007 Darren was sentenced to 25 years in prison.

Many months before his murder, Steven was 'targeted' by Darren. As the police noted, 'Darren had recognised the clear vulnerability of Steven Hoskin and "moved in" on him . . . he recognised the opportunity for accommodation . . . [He] was fully aware of Steven's vulnerability and took full advantage of these facts to control both Steven and the premises.' It appears that Darren was instrumental in Steven declining weekly assistance from social services, even though he did not read or write and struggled to manage money without help. A learning disability implies support needs throughout the life course, most particularly for adults without protective support networks, daily routines and/or the geographical proximity of families who are able and willing to assist. Steven's social network had reduced to Darren, his girlfriends and young people who were known to 'hang around' his bedsit. Their presence and noise nuisance led to neighbours complaining to the housing provider but this did not result in protective interventions. Some young people witnessed the violence and sexual bullying to which Steven was subject.

Darren was well known to all NHS services, including mental health services. His own history was chaotic: from being a runaway child, he became a violent and self-harming young man, leading a nomadic existence and making frequent suicidal gestures. He had convictions for arson and assault. Within eight years, he had five children with three partners, all of whom were teenagers and two of whom were ex-care leavers, known to be vulnerable themselves. The relationships were volatile and emergency protection orders were sought for the children following the hospitalization of one of his babies.

In the year and a half before Steven's murder, Darren made 24 calls to ambulance emergency call-out, at least eight of which were to Steven's bedsit. By January 2006, the ambulance service knew Darren was dangerous and had a 'warning marker' against him. Accordingly, they requested police attendance at all emergency visits. Although Steven was known to have a learning 'difficulty', the excessive use of emergency services by someone residing at his address did not result in an adult protection alert.

In the same timeframe, Darren made at least eight visits to accident and emergency services, seven visits to minor injury units, consulted his GP on 15 occasions and the out-of-hours GP service on 21 occasions. It does not appear that Darren's escalating use of NHS services, irrespective of his poor engagement with mental health services, evoked any concerted effort to bring it to a halt by finding out the reasons for such behaviour. Nor was his relationship with Steven explored.

Yet even the initial meeting of the Serious Case Review panel confirmed that there was no lack of information about Steven and his circumstances. With better interagency working, he would have been spared the destructive impacts of unrestrained physical, financial and emotional abuse in his own home.

All agencies have legal responsibilities, not only to prevent harm being caused by their own agents, but to safeguard vulnerable people against the harmful actions of third parties. What is striking about the responses of services to Steven's circumstances is that each agency focused on single issues within their own sectional remits and did not make the connections deemed necessary for the protection of vulnerable adults as proposed by *No Secrets* in 2000 (Department of Health and the Home Office 2000).

No Secrets was the first formal recognition that people with learning disabilities, mental health problems or difficulties associated with older age were at risk of abuse and that concerted efforts should be made across the usual agency boundaries and professional splits, to safeguard them. *No Secrets* urged the establishment of local multi-agency adult protection committees charged with ensuring joint working and information sharing to keep vulnerable adults safe. But in practice *No Secrets* – which was binding on social services but not on the other agencies – left a host of unanswered questions. Primary and secondary care personnel knew Steven was drinking to excess and they gave him the written contact details of the drugs and alcohol service. But Steven could not read and his alcohol abuse did not evoke the necessary 'alert' from any health care personnel. This is despite clear guidance from the British Medical Association that in the case of a vulnerable adult or child, protection must take precedence over confidentiality. If primary and secondary health care personnel had been attuned to Steven's learning disability and his vulnerability, arguably his visits could have been regarded as alerts.

At Steven's murder trial, Mr Justice Owens expressed his grave disquiet about the role of the adult social care service. It is worrying that this focus on social care has persisted since the Serious Case Review. The Review identified major failings in all services, including the police, children's social care, the NHS trust, the PCT, the ambulance service and housing (Flynn 2007).

Exercise 16.2

When an adult with a learning disability chooses not to be supported, what should happen?

Prevention

Prevention takes multiple forms. It makes sense to 'work upstream' rather than deal with the bleak consequences of abuse. There are some major risks, however, including the differential access to safeguarding processes of black and minority ethnic communities and people who 'self-fund' their own care outside community care assessments. Broadly, basic incident reporting confirms the vulnerability of older people to financial abuse. Refinement of this data would include follow-up and local 'case study' examples of excellence in safeguarding and, separately, practice which should discontinue or needs to improve.

However, prevention work is compromised by the failure to clarify the types and causation of the range of abuses we are dealing with and to develop robust strategies to address each. It is not enough to look at 'types' of abuse without considering the relationships and dynamics within which abuse occurs, individual motivation and the wider context. Evidence-based models are needed if sound preventative strategies are going to gain credibility. In particular there are disjunctions between action taken against potentially harmful and malevolent individuals, actions taken to support individuals who are too stressed or out of their depth to care in the way that they might wish, and actions taken to ensure that service provision is safe, well designed, appropriately resourced, and that the workforce is suitably trained and supervised and managed. It is helpful to think about the locus of the threat as either residing in an individual or in a system, but also to discriminate between those abuses which are deliberately planned and those that are not intended or inadvertent. This parallels the distinction within the legal framework between the *mens rea* and the *mens sana* – the act and the intent (see also Chapter 20 for a fuller discussion of this distinction in the context of people's experiences of the criminal justice system).

Brown (2002) put forward a three-stage model of prevention: primary prevention which includes the commissioning and design of safe services; secondary prevention that allows prompt identification and intervention; and tertiary prevention that acts to ameliorate and recompense individuals who have been harmed. *No Secrets* kick-started secondary pre-vention, and has fed back into primary prevention in the form of service design and quality assurance mechanisms, but it has done little in terms of impacting on remediation.

The primary prevention of different forms of abuse requires separately targeted and distinct strategies based on a proper and evidence-based understanding of their aetiology and a respect for organizational as well as individual factors that contribute to each subset of cases. Of course there is sometimes blurring across these distinct forms of abuse, as Steven Hoskin's murder reveals, but arguably the current lexicon of abuses could helpfully be conceived of in the following ways:

- hate crime, which takes place in public places, requires: bullying (including sexual bullying and cyber bullying) policies, public engagement, youth education, policing, and safe havens in the community;
- sexual abuse and predatory financial abuse: requires workforce regulation, very careful policing based on long-term intelligence, alert neighbours, health care, social care and housing professionals;
- parasitic abuse in which abuser(s) move in on a vulnerable person (perhaps presenting themselves as 'befrienders'). This type of abuse requires concerted intervention from housing providers, social care staff, emergency services, post offices, banks, local communities and shops;
- abuse in institutions and residential care settings: require sound commissioning, good policies especially around control and restraint, challenging behaviour, recruitment and supervision, and appropriate specialist knowledge on behalf of their staff;
- not all family homes are sanctuaries and abuse in family settings needs to be prevented by safe care planning and appropriate levels of support, regular review, alert health care input, public education and good links with domestic violence services;
- ethically challenging situations, for example whether to put a PEG tube in for someone with Down's syndrome with early signs of dementia, or whether and how to treat cancer in someone with dementia and learning disabilities: require consistent application of, and probably an

extension of the Independent Mental Capacity Advocacy.

The failure to take reasonable and appropriate steps to safeguard individuals from abuse or life-threatening events is in breach of Articles 2 and 3 of the European Convention of Human Rights. Adult protection activities should be triggered when someone is believed to be at risk of harm or abuse, not only at the point where there is demonstrable evidence of harm. To conform to human rights law, agencies have to be proactive in undertaking risk assessments to ensure that preventive action is taken wherever practicable. All agencies have legal responsibilities not only to prevent harm being caused by their own agents but to safeguard people against the harmful actions of third parties. It is disappointing therefore that *Valuing People Now* (Department of Health 2008) is solely concerned with 'hate crime' and has slipped into using this term as a catch-all, when it refers to a distinct subset of cases which usually take place in public spaces and can be fuelled by alcohol and a drive to earn peer approval, and which involve people being picked on because they are different, not because the victims are *who* they are but because of *what* they are. The selective amplification of 'hate crime' over much more prevalent forms of abuse and crimes is unhelpful.

Exercise 16.3

How does the typology proposed differ from that based on a definition of 'acts' without unifying explanation or context: physical, sexual, financial, psychological and institutional abuse?

Similarly, outcomes are complicated and need to be tailored to the situation. Deciding whether abuse occurred, and ticking a box that says not proven or substantiated, is not an end in itself since it does nothing to mitigate the situation. There should be interlocking 'layers' of safeguarding outcomes for the victim, the perpetrator, the service, the commissioning network, and for the policy/legislative agenda (Brown 2009); see Table 16.1.

Within the NHS the agenda must take on:

- the identification of 'at risk' patients;
- co-working to address the needs of intensive users of 999 calls;
- explicit investment in addressing the links between alcohol, violence, abuse and mental health;
- the number of accident-related injuries of adults 'at risk' and the resultant pathways;
- the number of complaints upheld which are on the

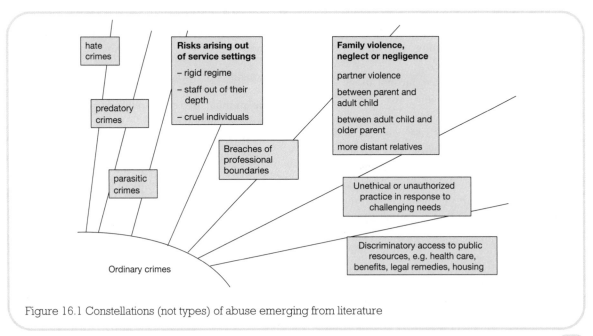

Figure 16.1 Constellations (not types) of abuse emerging from literature

For the victim	Immediate safety Long-term protection Redress Support for recovery
For the perpetrator	Criminal justice system Employment law/disciplinary Barring from workforce Other enforcement, e.g. injunction Extra help or enhanced care package if family member Extra help, training or supervision if staff person
For the service	Improved practice Increased funding Increased professional advice and consultation Scrutiny or regulatory action Regulatory enforcement Closure
For the commissioning network	Changes to contract Change of funding Reprovision of the service Change to interagency support
For national policy or legislative agenda	Serious Case Review, Serious Untoward Incident, Homicide Inquiry or public inquiry Acknowledgement of gaps in powers and duties

Table 16.1 Layers of outcome

neglect–abuse continuum, e.g. adults with dementia discharged from hospital in the early hours/inattention to eating, nutrition and pain control in secondary care;

- the proportion of drug and alcohol usage among 'at risk' populations who are not accessing treatment;
- A&E usage by adults 'at risk' who are known to have been subject to violence;
- the provision of support to victims of abuse through the Care Programme Approach, subsequent to disclosures in mental health services;
- investment in training and awareness raising at all levels.

For the police:

- the identification of 'at risk' citizens;
- co-working to address the needs of intensive users of 999 calls;
- convictions of perpetrators;
- investment in training and awareness raising at all levels.

For housing providers:

- the number of repeat referrals regarding homes 'targeted' and damaged;
- the number of injunctions to protect tenants from unscrupulous and abusive relatives, friends, 'befrienders' or lodgers;
- prompt responses to vulnerable tenants accruing rent arrears;
- prompt responses to the concerns of neighbours;
- investment in training and awareness raising at all levels.

A key indicator of preparedness, as opposed to outcome, would be for all sectors to indicate the financial resource invested. If safeguarding is *everyone's business* then all statutory agencies should be underwriting and investing in safeguarding activities.

> **Exercise 16.4**
>
> What outcomes would you envisage for adult social care services?

Learning the lessons

Emergent policies and legislation impacting on safeguarding tasks do not arrive with a curriculum and protected learning opportunities. It follows that learning about ways of safeguarding adults should be thought through. Local authorities generally offer 'core' awareness raising courses and investigation training for all sectors with the expectation that partner agencies will attend to subsequent training requirements. 'Train the trainers' courses feature significantly across most authorities.

Necessarily e-learning is attractive and has the advantage that it has extensive coverage, and can be used at any time, anywhere, at the learner's own pace. It offers important benefits for remote and rural personnel. At its best, traditional Problem Based Learning (which characterizes safeguarding training) based on cognitive educational theory involves group discussion which leads to the clarification of learning needs, for example. However, online, live discussion may be remote, in every sense, from the services in which people operate. Given that local authorities in England and Wales are expected to take the lead in safeguarding awareness raising, we remain to make better connections with training regarding domestic violence, risk assessment and management, health and safety as well as bullying in schools, for example. Training also needs to challenge the distancing that characterizes a consideration of abuse and abusing. Reporting of concerns is often delayed because people go into denial when it is someone they know whose behaviour is troubling them, or when they sometimes feel out of control themselves. Structured or 'distance' learning may help to familiarize practitioners with the language and the structures of the safeguarding community but they may not break through these internalized resistances to change or acknowledgement. Role plays and rehearsals may help to bring

the issues alive, and to give them the ambivalent and uncomfortable resonances that, in real life, accompany any interventions that have abuse as a backdrop.

In 2006 the Association of Directors of Adult Social Services (ADASS) published *Vulnerable Adult Serious Case Review Guidance: Developing a Local Protocol.* Unlike the Serious Case Reviews relating to children, in adult safeguarding Serious Case Reviews are voluntary and non-statutory. Paragraph 3 of the ADASS guidance states that the purpose of SCRs is 'not to reinvestigate nor to apportion blame', but rather:

3.1 to establish whether there are lessons to be learnt from the circumstances of the case about the way in which local professionals and agencies work together to safeguard vulnerable adults

3.2 to review the effectiveness of procedures (both multi-agency and those of individual organisations)

3.3 to inform and improve local inter-agency practice

3.4 to improve practice by acting on learning (developing best practice)

3.5 to prepare or commission an overview report which brings together and analyses the findings of the various reports from agencies in order to make recommendations for future action.

> (Association of Directors of Adult
> Social Services 2006: para. 3)

The Serious Case Review process has grown up with little beyond the ADASS guidance. In 2009 the term is being used to describe a wide range of reflexive processes, not all of which will lead to formalized agendas or action plans. Indeed, formalizing all reviews into a single protocol may lose the opportunity to conduct intermediate reflective learning or to register learning from such exercises. There is a necessary tension in the process of Serious Case Reviews between learning lessons for the future and raking back over the past. Serious Case Reviews of the kind deployed in relation to child abuse have an important element of holding individuals and agencies to account in a way that was not envisaged in *No Secrets.* This tension remains to be addressed because it cuts across both objectives, leaving organizations wary of contributing to the Serious Case

Review process and of sharing information freely in case they jeopardize their own reputations. This is even more moot in commercial organizations despite the fact that such providers dominate provision for some client groups in the social care field. Contract compliance has taken over from direct managerial control in this respect. These factors risk undermining the tasks of identifying gaps and designing stronger safeguards for the future. Finding fault and making sense do not sit well alongside each other.

Where the function is to determine accountability then this must be explicit from the outset so that individuals who are asked to contribute are allowed to be accompanied and/or legally represented and so that appropriate evidential requirements can be met. However, public inquiries should not become the most common form of review, not least as they are very time-consuming and expensive and there is remarkable similarity across their findings, e.g. poor practices sliding into abusive ones; the disengagement of governance processes from people's lives; the physical dangers of people becoming stuck in anti-therapeutic services; the disproportionate investment in restraining and over-sedating people; and absent management. There are plenty of intermediate mechanisms that should be in place that allow difficulties to be identified and fed in to training, organizational development and safeguarding practice, including:

- debriefing;
- clarifying what has happened and disseminating lessons to staff;
- revisiting the needs of vulnerable adults who may not have been helped to recover or seek redress;
- reinvestigating if management have not been held to account, or if individual wrongdoers have been allowed to evade responsibility;
- conducting a further root cause analysis of what went wrong and who was responsible;
- diagnosing the potential for strengthened safeguards;
- auditing implementation of new safeguards or improved practice;
- informing appropriate authorities of policy implications locally and nationally, including the need for legislative change or new guidance.

(Brown 2009)

Nevertheless there is scope for Serious Case Reviews to become case studies for learning and training purposes, not just in the localities in which they occurred but in the wider forum. They could be regarded as learning tools in situ. In respect of triggering and making sense of such reviews however, Brown (2009) observes:

> The 'seriousness' of cases referred to serious case review conflates a number of concepts: clarifying these helps to streamline referrals and underscore the function of the SCR process itself. In *No Secrets* . . . seriousness is discussed in terms of the impact of abuse on the vulnerable victim, the intent of the perpetrator, whether the abuse constitutes a criminal offence and whether there is a continued risk to the same vulnerable person or other potential victims.
>
> [In Kent] the severity of the abuse and its impact on the victim is a first stage in a screening process for SCR . . . [There, the process] also includes cases where there are major concerns about the perpetrator or perpetrators, for example, where the abuse has taken place in an institutional setting, is seen as part of an abusive culture, and/or has been perpetrated by multiple abusers, indicating that these might be forms of abusing that are seen to be more intractable or likely to be repeated. It is an additional consideration to take into account in the decision as to whether or not to commission an SCR and that is to do with whether the case gives rise to concerns about the way in which 'local professionals and services worked together to safeguard vulnerable adults'. In other words, a case might be serious because of the devastating effects it has had on an individual, or because of the complexity of the abusers and their motivation, but it should only be presented for review where it has proved too much for local safeguarding practice to deal with. A complex case that has been handled well could also prompt learning for local services but may not need to be the subject of an SCR . . . these cases increasingly present issues of multiple accountability and the need for parallel processing of related mechanisms, for example

the need to progress criminal prosecution alongside disciplinary action and supervisory input; the dovetailing of serious untoward incident and complaints procedures; and the examination of multi-agency decision making and action planning. Managing outcomes in relation to such a range of cases in terms of all these agendas has therefore escalated into a complex matrix of tasks where the aim is to resolve the issue as near to the person as possible and as informally as it is safe to do so. Alongside the operational imperatives is the need to channel learning from individual incidents into a wider service and professional context and network in ways that contribute to improved standards and governance.

(Brown 2009: 40–2)

Three illustrative case studies

The following case studies exemplify and amplify the phenomenon of abuse in three locations. They describe the circumstances of people we have met (Flynn and Brown 1997; Brown 2002) and people whose circumstances have been described to us by their relatives and support staff (Flynn and White-head 2005). Necessarily, people's names and identifying details have been changed.

Case study: *Doreen*

Doreen lives with her sister and large family in a depressed part of a large city. She attends a day centre and a residential respite service every three months. Staff from the respite service and the day service collaborate in working with Doreen. They are concerned that she is her sister's unpaid cleaner, cook and child minder and that she has very little money for 'spends', irrespective of her welfare benefits. Over time, staff encourage Doreen to be interested in her personal hygiene and help her to save from her modest income for deodorants, bath gel and shampoo. While puzzled that Doreen opts to leave her purchases in the day centre, and shower when she arrives each morning, they are so animated by the results and by Doreen's pleasure in her 'smellies' they turn their attention to her appearance. It takes many months for Doreen to save enough money to buy a new outfit and she goes shopping with two women staff with whom she gets on well. She is excited by her purchases and returns home animated. The following day Doreen is not wearing her new clothes and is evasive when staff ask her about them. It takes several days for Doreen to disclose that her sister returned them to the store 'to get the money back'.

Some context

Doreen is grateful that her younger sister, who is a single parent, has 'taken me in – otherwise I'd be in a home'. Doreen's sister does not welcome contact with staff from the day service or the respite service and has on occasion been verbally abusive to them. She views Doreen's welfare benefits as *her* money, not least as she describes herself as her sister's carer. Doreen has told staff that she would like her own home but she cannot discuss this with her sister as she fears it would make her angry.

Managing Doreen's safety

Irrespective of Doreen's abilities, she is not well placed to disentangle her interests from those of her sister's or to challenge the purview of her sister's decision-making. The mantra of 'choice' is not helpful in this situation as it offers no framework for discussing interdependence, belonging, intimidation or compliance that are at play. Furthermore, there appear to be no limits to the amount of domestic work expected of Doreen.

It is only when someone proactively intervenes to assert appropriate boundaries for Doreen that a space can be made within which she is free to exercise choice. Care managers have important roles in safeguarding vulnerable people and identifying one for Doreen marks a turning point in her life. The new care manager is not intimidated by Doreen's sister and has challenged her for gaining financially and using Doreen's skills rather than supporting Doreen. Having spent time with Doreen and staff who know her well and like her, she outlines the plan that Doreen should have her own tenancy with the support that she needs (most particularly regarding money management and risk of exploitative relationships). In the short term, to address Doreen's stress at what this means for her relationship with her sister, Doreen is spending more time in the independence unit of her respite service. Staff are removing the labels from Doreen's newly purchased clothes so that they cannot be exchanged and are supporting her to put an agreed sum every week into a Post Office savings account. They keep her savings book locked away in their care. They have a means of logging how she spends her money, tracking receipts and keeping a note of the staff who accompany her when she goes shopping 'for my bottom drawer!' Doreen benefits from being supported by women who are committed to changing her life for the better and helping her achieve her formerly unstated aspirations.

Case study: *Ben*

Ben lives in a residential service with five other people. He has a few words. He can name his favourite TV programmes and recognizes the actors and actresses. He indicates his wants by pointing and taking the hand of a member of staff. Ben is very overweight and has put on six stone since he moved into the service. He has a very affable nature and he laughs a great deal. What prompts his laughter is not always clear. A male member of staff calls Ben 'Fatso' and 'Hippo' and his mostly female colleagues do not challenge him. A member of staff in the day centre asked the unit manager why he thought that Ben was referring to himself as 'Fatso'. The manager said that it was 'just a joke'. A substantial change in Ben's demeanour is linked to the arrival of a new resident called Tim who begins to 'look after' Ben. Staff welcome Tim's help as Ben requires so much more of their time than other residents. There is insufficient continuity for them to ask why Ben has ceased to laugh and, as he is so large, his rapid weight increase goes unmonitored and unremarked. Several months after Tim's arrival a member of the waking night staff hears Ben screaming. She finds him naked and bleeding from his anus. Tim is in his bedroom, also naked and pleading with Ben to 'Shut up'.

Some context

Ben's very elderly mother is in a nursing home and has Alzheimer's. He has no siblings but a cousin has always taken an interest in him and she assisted her aunt in negotiating long-term help for Ben. Ben's cousin visits every couple of months and on each visit has expressed dismay to staff about his weight gain. She is told that it is Ben's 'choice' to eat lots of what he likes. Although she has complained to the local authority the independent inspection report indicates that she is being 'unduly overprotective' and states that '. . . Ben should be allowed to develop now that he is in an independent setting'. Ben's service relies heavily on transitional, agency staff. In terms of his support needs, Ben requires more help than his co-residents; the residential service's mission statement asserts that it aspires to 'maximizing potential . . . maximizing independence'; the local day service cannot accommodate Ben for more than three mornings a week. When Ben was initially admitted to the residential service, 'he was such a handful we got some medication for him'. Little is known of Tim's history prior to his transfer to the residential unit.

Managing Ben's safety

Ben is disadvantaged by being in a service with no appreciation of the importance of his health and safety. Unqualified staff have bought into the ideology of 'choice' and this acts to deflect them from paying proper attention to his weight gain, most particularly since Tim's arrival in the service. Ben's cousin is not regarded as a source of valuable information about Ben, or indeed as someone who is sufficiently committed to him to alert the service to her concerns. Nobody has asked her how the family sought to keep Ben safe in his previous life. Although Ben is registered with a local GP, support staff in the residential service are unaccustomed to collaborating with the GP or the practice nurse with and on behalf of residents.

Case study: *Michelle*

Michelle attended a day service which had a poor reputation. A member of staff, who was feared by many of his colleagues, ensured that Michelle came to work in his section. Although Michelle became agitated and increasingly reluctant to attend the day service, this was variously attributed to: her menstrual cycle; stubbornness; challenging behaviour; possible early-onset menopause and/or (most shamefully) 'attention seeking'. When a member of staff and a friend of Michelle from another part of the day centre walked into this man's 'office' they were shocked to see him hurrying to adjust his trousers and Michelle crying and rocking on a chair before him. He was verbally abusive to his unexpected visitors and concluded by telling them to 'f***ing knock in future'.

Some context

Michelle is a timid woman who has had many addresses since her parents signalled that they could not manage her as a young teenager. Many years in an institutional setting were followed by several years in a large hostel, two family placements combined with respite, a group home with a couple of people she had known from the hostel, a few months of living 'independently' in a supported tenancy (during which time she is believed to have been raped by a man who claimed to have been interested only in 'helping her') and at least three co-tenancies since. Although Michelle speaks she can rarely be persuaded to talk and becomes distressed if staff are persistent in their efforts.

Managing Michelle's safety

Michelle's abilities perplex the people who support her and those who manage the services she uses. Michelle can use local and national public transport; she can manage household routines; she can assist others in managing their household routines – and yet she is described as 'an innocent' when it comes to her own safety. She is supported by day centre staff with a very limited appreciation of what it takes to keep her and other people safe. Michelle has a loyal, if fairly new, friend, Mona, who appears close to her and seeks her out in the day service. It has the promise of being a mutual friendship as Michelle has been observed to talk to Mona.

Disquieting conclusions

Events in Doreen's, Ben's and Michelle's lives point to several sets of conclusions:

- Abuse can happen anywhere, even in services that are regularly inspected.
- The perpetrators of criminal and abusive acts may be close relatives, people who are paid to have a duty of care, other people with disabilities, and strangers.
- The people who know that a threshold has been crossed and subsequently alert authorities to criminal and abusive acts may be close relatives, people who are paid to have a duty of care, other people with disabilities, or strangers.
- It may be necessary to challenge unscrupulous relatives for regarding people's welfare benefits as payment for their caring, especially if their care is erratic or neglectful (Brown 2003).
- People who do not know how to relate well to colleagues are unlikely to be appropriate 'support' staff to people with learning disabilities. If currents of bullying, cruel joking, sexism, racism and homophobia are allowed to become established and go unchallenged there is no holding back the tide of abuse as it bears down on people who use the service.
- Although consequences are assigned to having such labels as 'highly dependent' and 'independent', these are neither necessarily protective nor prescriptive of the nature of assistance required.
- Support staff may develop ways of talking about their work which provide an unhelpful 'cover' for poor practice and which can lead to inherently harmful interpretations of 'choice' as cues for non-intervention (e.g. Flynn *et al.* 2003).
- Not everyone can alert others to their abuse, especially if it takes place within an ongoing

relationship, service or family culture. Even if someone else is raising the alarm on their behalf, it can be extraordinarily difficult to challenge the views of professionals or the bland findings of regulators.

It is tempting for service managers to identify 'the problem', take measures to ensure that it is unlikely to recur, and unwittingly draw the attentions of would-be abusers to other weaknesses in the service system. Not all staff working with people with learning disabilities have professional qualifications and training. They can be isolated in their work settings and from the larger communities of practitioners. It falls to managers to ensure that staff are supervised and have opportunities to work alongside experienced and competent practitioners if poor and idiosyncratic practices are not to take root and flourish. Moreover, long working hours and the non-involvement of unions render work settings/services vulnerable to abusive practices. Managers should be finding out what can be done to recruit and retain high-quality staff through structural routes such as negotiating improved terms and conditions, offering customized training opportunities (most particularly if services are offered to people with complex support needs), and ensuring that policies in respect of people's safety and health are credible and known to staff. This is a much more robust approach than one of bringing in poorly qualified staff, exposing them to challenges that they cannot meet and then rooting out individuals without changing the infrastructure which has led to the breach in standards.

A service's track record is revealing. Managers should take stock and be attuned to the histories and range of support needs of everyone in their service. How have known incidents of abuse and criminal acts been addressed to date? Do all service users have contact with individuals who are independent of the service and what measures are taken to ensure that these people are safe? How is poor practice dealt with and challenged? Is attention paid to the safe groupings of service users? Does the service have a history of using sedative medication and/or 'restraint' and 'punishment' to deal with difficult behaviour? Such questions should figure prominently in considerations of service management. Looking at a service's history is important, not merely as a means

to glean an approximation of events, but also as a means to understand the attitudes and assumptions of the narrators, to justify exclusions or restrictions and to identify sources of, and triggers to, improvement and reform.

Working to achieve safer services

Strategies to prevent abuse are often predicated on unsophisticated and/or muddled models of causation. They confound abuses that are deeply embedded within the structure of services with those which arise out of individual cruelty, exploitation or perversion on the part of an individual perpetrator. They advocate single approaches to identification of abuse which can lead to naïve 'scatter gun' approaches such as 'spot' inspections and the introduction of lengthy new procedures and/or checklists for quality. A more differentiated understanding of abuse leads to a more complex model in which different stages of prevention and levels of intervention can be mapped out.

Models borrowed from health promotion assist in this kind of analysis in that they are based on a separation of efforts designed to stop an illness occurring at all, from strategies designed to facilitate early identification, through to treatment and intervention to mitigate the effect of the illness and promote recovery. If applied to the prevention of abuse it can be seen that:

- primary prevention involves setting up a safe and well-ordered environment, screening unsuitable staff out of the workforce and paying attention to recruitment, registration, induction and supervision;
- secondary prevention involves alertness to signs and symptoms of abuse so that any concerns are picked up quickly and any further abuse 'nipped in the bud'; it is at this stage that the policies and procedures set out in No Secrets are most pertinent with their emphasis on early reporting and prompt investigation;
- tertiary prevention involves taking action to support and protect individuals who are known to have been abused and taking steps to return a service to a 'norm' of working within safe limits.

Not only is it important to act at all stages in this unhappy process, but it is also imperative to operate at all levels – to work with individual victims but also

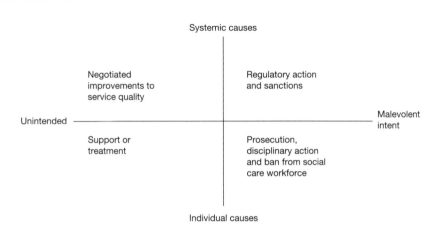

Figure 16.2 Assessing outcomes according to root causes

with staff teams and service policies. Commissioners and regulators of services need to take full responsibility for the perverse incentives they build into systems which are often more skilled at protecting business interests and reputations than the interests of vulnerable adults. Legal changes have proved necessary and helpful to address anachronisms and gaps in law and inadequacies in applying it within the criminal justice system. We remain to be challenged about the way that the needs of vulnerable groups are distorted in public policy and political discourse.

Exercise 16.5

Compare responses to the theatrical excesses in bank boardrooms in the UK and US in 2008–09, when financial markets plunged and surged and governments bailed them out, with their responses to 'loan sharks'/doorstop-payday lenders targeting those on welfare benefits and thin credit files who charge interest at 100 per cent to 20,000 per cent.

While the primary prevention of abuse is the ideal, the Steven Hoskin Serious Case Review and the three case studies demonstrate how challenging this is to achieve.

At the individual level

An introduction to being and feeling safe can arise from (or be compromised by) being part of a family.

This means that the contribution of schools, colleges, health and social care services is critical. At an individual level, there is neither a step-by-step formula nor an off-the-shelf solution. Prevention should reflect a stance, a willingness to see beyond such descriptions as 'mild learning disability in mainstream school', or 'deaf and moderately learning disabled', by considering people's histories, including their exposure to unsafe services and people; asking families how they have kept their relatives safe and reflecting with them how continuity of efforts between the family and services might be practised; exploring with support staff how they keep themselves and their loved ones safe; and considering how 'assertiveness training', for example, may be customized and made relevant to this young man or woman, as from today. The concerns have to be:

- to help people recognize and resist abusive acts and, as importantly, to seek help if they are victimized;
- to ensure that service users, relatives, visitors and staff understand the importance of their roles as 'lookouts' or 'alerters' with and on behalf of people who do not communicate their distress in readily understandable ways;
- to examine the unstated assumptions, unspoken prejudices and constraints of labels and ideologies and, rather than take them for granted, evaluate them in the light of the larger purpose of people's health, well-being and safety.

It matters that people know there are remedies beyond a service when bad things happen to them. In turn, there are growing examples of the police contributing to people's learning about personal safety.

At the service level

Policies are key preventive tools in reducing the likelihood of abuse and assault. They should be shaped by research findings and outline the parameters within which decision-making takes place. Services are likely to have developed approaches and policies regarding: the recruitment and screening of potential staff; complaints; personal development planning; confidentiality; risk-taking; sexuality; challenging behaviour; control and restraint; handling money; and administering medication, for example.

Staff training is one process for articulating a reliable understanding of abuse, and responsibility for preventing this resides with services. Staff should be attuned to signs of abuse and distress and, in hand with supervision, they should be orientated to listening to, and learning from, people with learning disabilities, and identifying the boundaries of effective and safe practice. They should be encouraged to revisit what is known of the struggle of adolescents as their competency and autonomy rise up forcefully – and put this alongside what is known of the person for whom they have lead responsibility.

Professional regulation is another tool in the abuse prevention kit. While it may appear remote from weak practice in an isolated service, it can be instrumental in ensuring that those responsible for abuse are prevented from working with vulnerable people. The overwhelmingly complicated experience of preventing abuse gives weight to: staff knowing what to do with their concerns and which referral routes to use; staff being attuned to the complementariness of their roles alongside those of other practitioners; making the complaints procedure known and accessible; knowing what information should be shared and what is confidential; anticipating and clarifying when intervention is justifiable; defining when, and in what circumstances, a police inquiry should be instigated; assisting people to identify the help and protection they require without jeopardizing action against perpetrators; and making sense of the lessons learned about enhancing the safety of vulnerable people.

At the government level

The external scrutiny of services, setting targets for developing professional skills in specialist and mainstream provision, clarifying channels of communication and routes through which action should be taken, and developing means to strengthen legal protection are critical means of raising standards within services for vulnerable people. Maximizing resources and setting appropriate measures of success and 'performance indicators' are necessary, as is the design of accountability structures that not only bring to justice those who abuse but confront those who have real power and responsibility for setting up and perpetuating unsafe services for people who, despite the rhetoric, depend on them.

If the Department of Health's (2008a, 2009) review of *No Secrets* is to promote ever greater investment in partnership working in safeguarding adults, then all 'partners' should be perceived as responsible. If the review is to achieve more effective practice in safeguarding adults, then all partners must play their full and proper role in achieving that improvement. This will include better trained staff, clear systems of performance monitoring and review, information sharing across and between statutory partners, and investment. The best testament to the memory of adults with learning disabilities who have died as a result of the criminal and abusive acts is that we learn the lessons.

Exercise 16.6

A rich relative has left many millions of pounds to a charity promoting the needs of vulnerable adults whose lives have been compromised by abuse with the proviso that it should be used 'to optimize the best outcomes'. How would you advise them to spend it?

Conclusion

Abuse actively undermines a person's autonomy, whether that is as a result of the deliberate targeting of a vulnerable person carried out in order to exploit them financially or sexually, or as the consequence of more pervasive neglect of their human rights, personal development, health or well-being. When abuse is at issue more, not less, intervention is needed to safeguard people, and this is as true for Direct Payments Recipients (Flynn 2005). People's independence is something to be nurtured and safeguarded. As with 'choice', however, it should not be seen as a rallying cry for abandonment or withdrawal: when people are left to sink or swim, too many sink.

References

Association of Directors of Adult Source Services (2009) The Current Legal Framework in the Light of Putting People First.

Association of Directors of Adult Social Services (2006) *Vulnerable Adult Serious Case Review Guidance: Developing a Local Protocol*. London: Association of Directors of Adult Social Services, http://www.adss.org.uk/publications/guidance/vulnerableadult.pdf (accessed 21 September 2008).

Brown, H. (2002) *Safeguarding Adults and Children with Disabilities Against Abuse: Integration of People with Disabilities*. Strasbourg: Council of Europe.

Brown, H. (2003) What is financial abuse? *Journal of Adult Protection*, 5(2): 3–10.

Brown, H. (2009) The process and function of serious case review, *Journal of Adult Protection*, 11(1): 38–50.

Brown, H., Wilson, B. and Kingston, P. (2000) Comment: unpacking 'discriminatory abuse', *Journal of Adult Protection*, 2(3): 17–18.

Department of Health (2001) *Valuing People: A New Strategy for Learning Disability for the 21st Century*. London: Department of Health.

Department of Health (2008a) *Safeguarding Adults. A Consultation on the Review of the 'No secrets' Guidance*. London: Department of Health.

Department of Health (2008b) *Transforming Adult Social Care*. London.

Department of Health (2008c) *Valuing People Now: From Progress to Transformation*. London: Department of Health.

Department of Health (2009) *Safeguarding Adults: Report on the consultation on the review of 'No Secrets'*. London: Department of Health.

Department of Health and the Home Office (2000) *No Secrets: Guidance on Developing and Implementing Multi-agency Policies and Procedures to Protect Vulnerable Adults from Abuse*. London: Department of Health and Home Office.

Flynn, M. (2005) *Developing the Role of Personal Assistants*. New Type of Worker Project Researched and Compiled for OPARATE – a Skills for Care Pilot Project examining new and emerging roles in social care. Leeds: Skills for Care.

Flynn, M. (2007) *The Murder of Steven Hoskin: A Serious Case Review. Executive Summary*. Cornwall Adult Protection Committee.

Flynn, M. and Brown, H. (1997) The responsibilities of commissioners, purchasers and providers: lessons from recent National Development Team Inquiries, in J. Churchill, H. Brown, A. Craft and C. Horrocks (eds) *There Are No Easy Answers – The Provision of Continuing Care and Treatment to Adults with Learning Disabilities who Sexually Abuse Others*. Chesterfield: Association of Residential Care and National Association for the Protection from Sexual Abuse of Adults and Children with Learning Disabilities, with the Social Services Inspectorate/ Department of Health.

Flynn, M. and Whitehead, S. (2005) *Bruises Easily? Keeping People Safe*. Manchester: National Development Team.

Flynn, M., Keywood, K. and Fovargue, S. (2003) Warning: health 'choices' can kill, *Journal of Adult Protection*, 5(1): 30–4.

MacIntyre, D. (2003) There should be a law against it, *Society Guardian*, 17 December.

O'Connell Higgins, G. (1994) *Resilient Adults: Overcoming a Cruel Past*. San Francisco, CA: Jossey Bass.

17

Promoting healthy lifestyles – challenging behaviour

Sally Twist and Ada Montgomery

Introduction

It is estimated that approximately 10 per cent of young adults with learning disabilities accessing services exhibit challenging behaviour (Emerson *et al.* 2001). The Mansell Report (Mansell 2007) found that while policy developments such as *Valuing People* (Department of Health 2001a) and *Our Health, Our Care, Our Say* (Department of Health 2006) have resulted in significant improvements in the lifestyles of people with learning disabilities in general, there has been less progress in the support and services available for people who present challenges to services. This chapter aims to provide a framework for understanding and responding to young people who present with challenging behaviour, to facilitate healthy and positive lifestyles for those individuals.

What is challenging behaviour?

A widely accepted definition of challenging behaviour is that described by Emerson (2001: 3): 'Culturally abnormal behaviour of such intensity, frequency or duration that the physical safety of the person or others is likely to be placed in serious jeopardy, or behaviour which is likely to seriously limit use of, or result in the person being denied access to, ordinary community facilities.' The essential elements of this definition are that the behaviour:

- is unacceptable by social standards, taking into consideration issues such as the person's age, social class and ethnocultural background;
- imposes a significant cost to the person – for example, physical harm to self, social rejection, exclusion from recreational, educational or employment opportunities;
- imposes a significant cost to others – for example,

physical harm, property damage, emotional distress.

This definition is the starting point in understanding challenging behaviour as it enables us to identify problematic behaviour that warrant further exploration.

Examples of challenging behaviour

Some examples of challenging behaviour include:

- verbal aggression;
- shouting;
- stripping;
- stealing;
- anal poking;
- self-injury;
- withdrawal from others;
- physical aggression;
- persistent screaming;
- inappropriate sexual behaviour;
- property damage;
- smearing faeces;
- disturbed sleep;
- non-compliance.

Prevalence of challenging behaviour

Most studies investigating the epidemiology of challenging behaviour have researched the prevalence of different types of challenging behaviour, that is, the number of people in the population under study who at that time exhibit challenging behaviour. The results of a study (Emerson *et al.* 2001) indicated that between 10 and 15 per cent of people with learning disabilities in contact with services presented with challenging behaviour, and that most exhibited two or more different types of challenging behaviour.

Correlational analyses of variables associated with different types of challenging behaviour indicate that an increased prevalence of such behaviour is seen in the following groups: men; people aged between 15 and 35 years; people with severe learning disability; people with additional disabilities (e.g. sensory impairment, communication difficulties); and people with specific syndromes and disorders, such as autism (Emerson 2001).

Understanding challenging behaviour

Exercise 17.1

Imagine the following scenario. You have a headache and would like some painkilling tablets. You find it difficult to talk to your carers. You have no direct access to painkilling tablets in your house, and you are unable to leave the house without support. How would you let other people know what is wrong?

How would you get your needs met? You might try to communicate non-verbally that you have a headache by pointing at your head. Now imagine that your best efforts at communicating your needs are not being understood by your carers. What would you do next? How would you get the attention of your carers? If the pain was getting very bad you might start to hit your head.

How would you feel if your carers then began to chide you, advise you to stop behaving in this way, ignore or isolate you? There are many ways you might behave or feel in this situation – for example, you might withdraw from everyone and hope the pain subsides; your behaviour might escalate until you significantly harmed yourself or someone else; and you might feel angry, upset or worried. Your reactions might vary depending on the situation – for example, whether this had happened before, your relationship with your carers, or how bad the pain was. Now try to imagine how you would feel if a carer spent some time trying to understand what was wrong, and after a period of time worked out what you were trying to communicate and gave you what you wanted.

Valuable learning points from the scenario in Exercise 17.1 are:

- Everyone has needs, many of which require the support of others. These include the need for food, clothing, shelter, physical, emotional and social care, opportunities to learn and develop skills and relationships, and access to community facilities, to name but a few. Individuals with learning disabilities have the same needs as people without learning disabilities; however, the way they express those needs may be different.

- Behaviour is a way of communicating our needs (see Chapter 9). A young person with learning disabilities may use challenging behaviour to communicate something to others, and it may be that using challenging behaviour is the most effective way for the person to communicate their needs at that time. Emerson (2001) argues that the task of understanding challenging behaviour involves investigating what the purpose of the challenging behaviour is for the person in their life – what does it do for the individual? This is often described as developing an understanding of the 'function' of the challenging behaviour.

- Challenging behaviour is not unique to people with learning disabilities. The exercise above did not necessarily describe someone with a learning disability; it could equally apply to someone finding it difficult to talk after dental surgery. In some situations behaviour can escalate and become problematic, often when we need support and others fail to understand and meet our needs. Unfortunately, the consequences of exhibiting challenging behaviour are often different for people with learning disabilities, compared to people without learning disabilities. For example, they may be subject to negative labelling, physical abuse, inappropriate medical or psychological interventions, exclusion or neglect (Emerson 2001).

- Challenging behaviour often has multiple contributory factors. The same behaviour may be expressing several different needs – for example, the need to communicate 'I have a headache', 'I need some painkillers' and 'I would like some emotional support or some activity to take my mind off the pain'. Similarly, different behaviours may be used to communicate the same need – for example, pointing at the head and hitting the head to tell people 'I have a headache' – and this may vary depending on personal and environmental factors. It should also be noted that no two individuals are the same, and although two people may exhibit virtually identical challenging behaviour they may be communicating very different needs. Similarly, two people engaging in different challenging behaviour may be expressing similar needs.

- The task of understanding what the person is trying to communicate using challenging behaviour may be difficult and time-consuming, but it is also likely to be very rewarding. Blunden and Allen (1987) noted that the term 'challenging behaviour' conveys that the behaviour presents a challenge to the carers rather than the person exhibiting the behaviour.

Exercise 17.2

Reflecting on what you have just read, think about your own behaviour. What behaviour have you exhibited that could be thought of as challenging? For example, being short-tempered with a friend, banging a door, regularly getting up in the middle of the night because you cannot sleep. List the behaviours, then write a brief explanation of why you exhibited each one.

The task of understanding challenging behaviour – being a detective

There are a multitude of possible needs that an individual may wish to communicate to others, which can make the role of attempting to understand and meet those needs a somewhat daunting one. It is important to remember that in most situations you will be aware of many of the needs of the individuals for whom you are caring, and in many cases the individual will find an effective way of communicating their unmet needs. However, there may be some situations where the individual uses challenging behaviour as a means of communication. Here, the role of the carer supporting the individual is rather like that of being a detective; trying to find clues to understand why the person is

behaving in the way they are (SETRHA and the Tizard Centre 1994).

Blocks to understanding challenging behaviour

Clements (1997: 84) cautions that 'making judgements and interpretations about other people and their needs is not a simple, scientific matter. It is a social process of construction and can be seriously flawed'. He identifies three potential blocks to effectively understanding challenging behaviour:

- lack of understanding of the complexity of human behaviour and the multiple contributing factors;
- making attribution errors about the function of the behaviour – one person's understanding of another person's behaviour will be influenced by a variety of factors, such as their relationship with the individual, their own emotional state, their past experiences and the power relationship between the two, and this may lead them to the wrong conclusions about the function of the challenging behaviour;
- the influence of personal attitudes and values, prejudices and stereotypes.

Therefore, it is important to take these factors into consideration when investigating what a person is trying to communicate by engaging in challenging behaviour.

Exercise 17.3

'Not waving but drowning': try and think of three examples of situations when you have misread the behaviour of friends or family members because of a snap decision or assumption you have made.

Responding to challenging behaviour

Clinical practice guidelines (British Psychological Society 2004; Royal College of Psychiatrists, British Psychological Society and Royal College of Speech and Language Therapists 2007) are available which provide a comprehensive framework for good practice in responding to challenging behaviour in adults with learning disabilities. The guidelines outline five stages: pre-assessment, assessment, formulation, intervention and evaluation.

Stage 1: Pre-assessment

Pre-assessment is completed to gather information that will guide the assessment process, and assist the risk screening process. Pre-assessment information should include:

- descriptions of the challenging behaviour;
- circumstances in which the behaviour occurs;
- frequency and severity of the behaviour;
- sensory impairments;
- how the person communicates;
- specific disabilities/impairments;
- medical problems;
- current medication;
- setting in which the person lives/works;
- previous interventions;
- risks to person or others;
- risk management strategies;
- mental capacity (see Department of Constitutional Affairs 2007);
- capacity to consent to interventions (see Department of Health 2001b, 2001c).

Stage 2: Assessment

Assessment should focus on the person and consider the interaction between the individual, their environment and the behaviours which are challenging (British Psychological Society 2004). Assessment should include:

Functional assessment

- *Detailed description of the behaviour.* For example, a description of the behaviour of someone who throws objects might be 'the young lady picks up objects from the mantelpiece and throws them across the room. She aims the objects at people or objects in the room.' Information about the sequence of the challenging behaviour can also assist in planning effective interventions. Although at times it may seem that challenging behaviour occurs 'out of the blue', this is not often the case. It is more likely that there is a sequence of behaviour that leads up to the challenging

behaviour. Returning to the example above, it might be observed that prior to throwing objects there is a sequence of build-up behaviour that begins with the young lady vocalizing loudly, followed by her holding her head in her hands, then by her moving to the mantelpiece and lifting up and replacing objects repeatedly.

Further useful information would include details about when the behaviour happens (date and time), where the behaviour happens (specific locations) and how often the behaviour happens. It may also be useful to know what the individual is doing when the behaviour occurs, who they are with and how they seem to be feeling.

This type of information can be gathered by people who are in regular contact with the individual, simply by observing the person in their usual surroundings and making a note of what happens. If more detailed information is required it may be useful to design a recording form, covering the areas described above. Validated assessments of challenging behaviour – for example, the Aberrant Behaviour Checklist (Aman *et al.* 1985) – can also be used to assess challenging behaviour and monitor change.

- *How does the challenging behaviour get in the way?* How does the challenging behaviour get in the way of the young person achieving their full potential for a positive and healthy lifestyle? For example, does the behaviour affect opportunities for developing positive personal relationships, participating in social, recreational, educational and occupational activities, empowerment and choice, or access to appropriate services? In the past, many young adults with learning disabilities who exhibited challenging behaviour were excluded or had limited access to ordinary community settings and lived in segregated and restrictive environments. O'Brien's (1987) interpretation of the philosophy of normalization and social role valorization in terms of five fundamental accomplishments for service delivery for individuals with learning disabilities (competence, community presence, community participation, respect and choice) can be a useful framework in the assessment of challenging behaviour.
- *What is the function of the challenging behaviour?* In some situations it may be a

relatively straightforward task to identify the function of the challenging behaviour, by detailed description or closer observation of the behaviour. However, in cases of severe and enduring challenging behaviour the task of identifying the function can be complex, and require a detailed analysis of the behaviour in question. Under these circumstances a multi-disciplinary team approach to assessment is recommended. It was noted earlier that a young person with learning disabilities may exhibit challenging behaviour to express a range of needs. Therefore, assessment by a range of professionals with expert knowledge can be valuable. In some cases the involvement of workers with specialist knowledge of challenging behaviour, such as the challenging behaviour team, a specialist behavioural nurse or a clinical psychologist may be necessary. Emerson (2001) provides a comprehensive review of descriptive and experimental methods for the functional assessment of challenging behaviour. He tabulates the advantages and disadvantages of different approaches, including structured interviews, antecedent–behaviour–consequences (ABC) charts, scatter plots and various experimental analyses, and interested readers are directed to this text for further information.

Assessment of the person

Knowledge of an individual's personal characteristics provides a better understanding of the person as a whole, and may help to determine the reasons why that person is exhibiting challenging behaviour. Obtaining information about the person's cognitive, sensory and physical impairments and how these impact on their skills and functioning can be helpful. For example, problems such as difficulties concentrating, understanding what people say or how they feel, finding it hard to cope with change, having to use a wheelchair or a hearing aid, or struggling to make friends may all contribute to situations that result in challenging behaviour. Information about the individual's personality characteristics can also help to assess challenging behaviour, and differentiate between behaviour that is 'normal' for that individual and behaviour that is 'challenging'.

Historical factors

It is helpful to know about an individual's personal history – what life events they have experienced, where they have lived, where they have gone to school, whether they have experienced any trauma, their family background, their role models, what values, attitudes, prejudices they have been subjected to – as these factors may influence their personal functioning and their reactions to future events. Life cycle factors are key to understanding in this connection. For example, consider a young woman who over the last few years has exhibited uncharacteristic challenging behaviour during the Christmas period. Finding out that the young woman's mother died on 24 December 2001, and that she dislikes changes to her usual routine (a common experience over the Christmas period with parties and suchlike), suggests that she may be likely to experience some distress during the Christmas period. This might help to explain the increase in challenging behaviour and, thereby, point to ways to support the individual through a potentially difficult time. Historical information about what interventions have been tried, what had worked, what has not, can also be useful.

Physical needs

A person may engage in challenging behaviour to communicate their physical needs. The scenario described in Exercise 17.1 illustrates that an individual may engage in challenging behaviour to communicate that they are in pain. There are many different reasons why someone may be experiencing pain – for example, toothache, in-growing toenails, muscular pain, menstrual pain, constipation or an ear infection. Other physical problems people may be experiencing include poor sleep, physical illness or food allergy.

Relationship/emotional needs

A young person may exhibit challenging behaviour as a way of communicating their feelings. Individuals with learning disabilities experience a range of emotions. However, as a result of their disabilities or their experiences they may find it difficult to recognize and express those feelings (see Chapters 9 and 15). Gathering information about loss or bereavement, changes of staff, changes of residents/friends, house/family dynamics, changes in routine and family problems can help to identify whether the individual is using challenging behaviour to communicate their unmet relationship or emotional needs.

Mental health issues

While reviews of the literature demonstrate that prevalence rates of mental health problems in adults with learning disabilities vary considerably, with reported rates of between 10 per cent and 80 per cent depending on the study variables, there is evidence to suggest that the rate of psychiatric disorders is higher among people with learning disabilities compared to the general population (see Campbell and Malone 1991; Borthwick-Duffy 1994 for reviews). Chapter 28 in the present volume reviews much of this evidence. Young adults with a diagnosis of learning disabilities and mental health problems are described as having a 'dual diagnosis'. A study (Moss et al. 2000) investigating the prevalence of psychiatric symptoms in adults with learning disability and challenging behaviour found that an increase in the severity of challenging behaviour was associated with a higher rate of psychiatric symptoms, and that self-injurious behaviour seemed to be related to higher levels of anxiety symptoms. Adults with mental health problems often present with behavioural disturbances, such as aggression, withdrawal, mood disturbances, self-injury or anti-social behaviour (Fraser and Nolan 1994). Thus, if a young adult with learning disabilities exhibits challenging behaviour, another important factor to consider is the possibility of unrecognized mental health problems, such as anxiety disorders, depression, schizophrenic or psychotic illness, or acute confusion (O'Hara and Sperlinger 1997) (see also Chapter 28).

Experiencing abuse

An individual may exhibit challenging behaviour to communicate that they are being abused or exploited in some way. Until recently the abuse of adults with learning disabilities had not been acknowledged or addressed in any systematic way. However, it is now widely accepted that such adults may be the victims of physical abuse, sexual abuse, psychological/emotional abuse, financial abuse and neglect (Brown 1997). Indeed, many individuals with learning disabilities may be at increased risk of abuse as a result of their personal vulnerability due to lack of knowledge of abuse, poor understanding or limited communication skills, and also because of the settings in which they live, work and socialize (Brown 1997). It is important that those caring for individuals with learning disabilities recognize that abuse occurs and that challenging behaviour may be a means of an individual communicating that abuse. Carers should be aware of the appropriate steps to take to address the problem (see Chapter 16).

Specific disabilities or diagnosis

When seeking to understand a person's challenging behaviour it is also important to be aware of specific disabilities or diagnoses and how these may contribute, for example: neuropsychiatric disorders such as epilepsy, attention-deficit hyperactivity disorder (ADHD), dementia; pervasive developmental disorders, such as autistic spectrum conditions; and phenotype-related behaviours, such as Prader Willi syndrome (Royal College of Psychiatrists, British Psychological Society and Royal College of Speech and Language Therapists 2007).

Environmental influences

Another important variable to be considered when trying to understand why a person is exhibiting challenging behaviour is their environment. Environmental factors to investigate include: size and layout (too big, overcrowded, too small, too much or too little furniture, too close to others?); access (access to other rooms, areas, outside, escape route, safe place, privacy?); noise levels (too loud, too quiet, source of noise, type of noise, continuous noise, sudden unexpected noise?); decoration (mirrors, ornaments, lighting, floor coverings, soft furnishings?); demands of the environment (too demanding or complex, over-stimulating, too much to understand or process, boring, does it require constant re-evaluation, too monotonous?); and activities (no outings, always at home, nothing to occupy self?). In addition, it may be important to investigate whether there has been a change in the environment.

Any of these factors could be experienced as stressful by an individual living, working or socializing in the environment, and could result in behaviour that is interpreted as challenging. For example, consider a situation where a young man with learning disabilities walked into his lounge, threw a chair through the window, then left and refused to return. When escorted back into the room by a staff member and encouraged to talk about what was wrong he became increasingly agitated and his behaviour escalated to screaming, verbal abuse, and attempting to throw an object towards the window. The young man was redirected to the kitchen for a cup of tea, where he was able to tell his carer why he became distressed. This was the first time the young man had been in the room since it was decorated. He became distressed when he saw the new orange curtains, as they reminded him of a residential establishment where he had lived as a child and where he had negative experiences.

This example illustrates how changes to the environment can cause distress for an individual and how, if that distress is not recognized, the behaviour can quickly escalate to challenging behaviour presenting significant risk of harm. One advantage for the carers in this situation was that when he was removed from the environment and supported to reduce his anxiety the young man was able to communicate the reasons for his distress. Developing an understanding why someone exhibits certain behaviours can be even more challenging for staff when the person is unable to communicate their distress directly.

Lack of opportunities for development

Most young people relish the opportunity to attend social events, develop friendships, take part in sports, learn new skills at college or work, or pursue an interest. It is possible, therefore, that a young person with learning disabilities may present with challenging behaviours because of their frustration and distress relating to the lack of opportunities available to them.

Stage 3: Formulation

A formulation is a hypothesis about why you think the challenging behaviour is happening based on the assessment information gathered, and should be written to guide interventions (British Psychological Society 2004).

Stage 4: Intervention

There are several texts providing detailed descriptions and evaluation of interventions for challenging behaviour (e.g. Donnellan *et al.* 1988; Carr *et al.* 1993; Zarkowska and Clements 1994; Emerson 2001) and clinical guidance (British Psychological Society 2004; Royal College of Psychiatrists, British Psychological Society and Royal College of Speech and Language Therapists 2007). A brief overview of interventions is provided below.

In theory, a comprehensive, multi-disciplinary assessment of a young person who exhibits challenging behaviour should provide a wealth of information, facilitate the development of hypotheses about the function of the behaviour, and support the development of an appropriate intervention. In practice, assessment is likely to show that the behaviour varies in frequency and intensity depending on different contextual factors, has different functions at different times and in different situations, and that there are several possible reasons why the individual might be exhibiting challenging behaviour. Thus, designing and implementing an effective intervention is rarely straightforward.

For example, analysis of a young man's challenging behaviour suggested that one reason he was hitting his head on the staff room door was that he was thirsty, as every time he engaged in this behaviour he was redirected by staff to the lounge and given a drink. The assessment raised concerns about the frequency with which the young man was requesting drinks, and prompted investigation of his physical health needs. It was also hypothesized that the young man might use the challenging behaviour to initiate social contact with members of staff, as the behaviour occurred less frequently when he was engaged with others. The assessment revealed that the young man had no effective, alternative ways of communicating these needs. This demonstrates that even in this simple example there are several areas for possible intervention, such as helping the young man to develop alternative means of communicating, exploring options for engagement in social relationships, and further medical investigation.

Accordingly it is recommended that interventions for challenging behaviour are:

- *Individually tailored*: an intervention based on a comprehensive assessment of the individual's challenging behaviour, personal characteristics and environmental factors. When planning interventions the key principles of rights, independence, choice and inclusion, outlined in the government White Paper *Valuing People* (Department of Health 2001a), should be considered. Thus, it may be appropriate to involve the individual, perhaps with the support of an advocate, in decision-making about interventions.

- *Evidence-based*: there is a growing body of research investigating the effectiveness of different interventions for challenging behaviour (see Emerson 2001; Beail 2003), and it may be useful to consult relevant studies when selecting an intervention. It should be noted that effective monitoring of challenging behaviour before, during and after the implementation of an intervention also allows 'practice-based' evaluation of the effectiveness of a specific intervention for that individual.

- *Multi-faceted*: in most cases a 'multi-component intervention package' (Emerson 1998: 143) will be necessary, which involves different approaches and multi-disciplinary involvement. In cases of severe challenging behaviour a multi-faceted approach is likely to include both reactive and proactive/preventative strategies for managing the behaviour.

- *Graded*: in terms of the restrictive and invasive nature of the intervention. Research indicates that physical restraint is frequently used in the management of severe challenging behaviour for adults with learning disabilities living in residential settings (Emerson *et al.* 2000). Recently published guidelines for the use of physical intervention for people with learning disabilities (Department of Health/Department for Education and Skills 2002) recommend that physical interventions should, wherever possible, only be used in the management of challenging behaviour when other strategies have been tried and found to be unsuccessful, or in emergency situations where the risk of not intervening outweighs the use of minimum force. Hence, good practice in developing interventions for challenging behaviour would dictate that the package of interventions should include a graded hierarchy of strategies, starting with the least restrictive or invasive interventions and moving towards the use of physical restraint or emergency medication only as a 'last resort'.

- *Clearly documented and evaluated*: strategies for intervention should be clearly documented and accessible to individuals involved in the young person's care, preferably in the form of care plans approved at a multi-disciplinary level. Care plans are likely to include a rationale for the chosen intervention package, clear guidelines explaining how the intervention will be implemented and plans for evaluation of the effectiveness of the intervention.

Outlined below are various approaches to intervention that could be implemented.

Reactive strategies

There will be some emergency situations when it will be necessary for a carer supporting a young person exhibiting challenging behaviour to take immediate action to reduce the risk of harm to the individual or others, or damage to property (Murphy *et al.* 2003). This type of intervention, known as a 'reactive strategy', often takes the form of restrictive physical intervention or emergency administration of medication. The British Institute of Learning Disabilities policy framework for physical interventions (Harris *et al.* 1996) describes three categories of physical intervention: direct physical contact between staff and client (e.g. holding); the use of barriers to limit freedom of movement (e.g. locked doors); and the use of material or equipment to restrict or prevent movement (e.g. arm splints). The Department of Health and Department for Education and Skills (2002) guidelines recommend that restrictive physical interventions should be used as infrequently as possible, that there should be clear policies and procedures for their use and that staff who may be required to intervene in this way should receive the appropriate training and support.

A distinction should be made between the use of reactive strategies to manage emergency situations and the planned use of these interventions as a 'last resort' to manage an individual's challenging behaviour. In this situation physical interventions should only be used when other less intrusive strategies have not worked.

Preventative strategies

The Department of Health and Department for Education and Skills (2002) outline primary and secondary prevention strategies for working with young people who exhibit challenging behaviour.

Primary prevention strategies include: ensuring that young people have suitable levels of support (i.e. that there are enough staff/carers and that those staff/carers have received appropriate training); ensuring that young people are supported to reduce conditions that may trigger incidents of challenging behaviour; care plans for challenging behaviour; and access to appropriate educational, occupational and recreational opportunities.

Secondary prevention strategies include:

- recognizing and knowing how to intervene at the first stages of a behavioural sequence that can develop into challenging behaviour (e.g. knowing that the first signs of anxiety include increased muscle tension, restlessness, signs of flushing and dilated pupils);
- skills in the use of de-escalation/diffusion and distraction techniques (e.g. de-escalation is a set of verbal and non-verbal skills that may help to reduce the level of arousal); verbal skills include speaking slowly, clearly and at low volume, being non-judgemental, listening carefully, clarifying the problem, answering truthfully and being supportive; non-verbal skills involve keeping your distance, making appropriate eye contact, showing that you are listening and being aware of your own body language – it should be relaxed, non-confrontational and open;
- developing multi-disciplinary care plans, use of medication and access to appropriate health care.

Behavioural interventions

In recent years, behavioural interventions have been perhaps the most widely used and most prolifically researched techniques in the treatment of challenging behaviour, particularly for adults with severe learning disabilities. This is an extensive area, and for further details readers are directed to Donnellan *et al.* (1988), Carr *et al.* (1993) and Emerson (2001). In a review of

103 outcome studies to establish best practice for interventions in challenging behaviour, Agar and O'May (2001) found evidence for the effectiveness of behavioural interventions for challenging behaviour, particularly when interventions were informed by functional assessment.

Emerson (2001) provides an excellent overview of the pros and cons of different behavioural approaches for challenging behaviour. Examples of behavioural approaches include: stimulus fading, non-contingent reinforcement, differential reinforcement of other behaviour (DRO), differential reinforcement of incompatible (DRI) or alternative (DRA) behaviour, extinction and punishment.

Medical interventions

Since physical and mental health problems can contribute to challenging behaviour it is essential that young people have access to appropriate health care services, in order that their heath needs are appropriately diagnosed and treated. One area of ongoing debate is the use of medication to treat challenging behaviour. Tyrer (1997) noted that:

> psychotropic drugs are widely used in people with learning disabilities and often with poor indicators . . . these drugs are often used when there is no evidence of psychiatric or medical illness. They are widely employed in patients who are behaviourally disturbed in order to control aggression and self-injurious behaviour.
>
> (Tyrer 1997: 205)

Medication can be an essential element of a multi-faceted intervention for challenging behaviour, and it is important we move towards providing a clear rationale and evidence base for the use of medication, and provide ongoing monitoring and evaluation of the effectiveness of medication on an individual basis.

Environmental interventions

Functional assessment may reveal certain environmental conditions (activities, people, approaches or situations) that trigger challenging behaviour which, if removed or avoided, are likely to result in fewer incidences of the behaviour (Clements 1997). For example, if it is hypothesized that a young person exhibits challenging behaviour when the environment is too noisy, then an intervention might involve an overall aim to provide quiet living and working environments, alongside a series of strategies to manage situations when high noise levels are unavoidable, such as access to quiet areas and distraction via engagement in activities or social interaction.

Clements (1997) identified several potential changes to the social system of which the young person is a part that may be effective in reducing the incidence of challenging behaviour; for example, promoting positive attitudes towards the individual, resolving potential conflicts within the social system, ensuring the individual has the opportunity to make choices, structuring the young person's time and planning activity appropriately for that person, improving engagement levels and adapting communication systems to the young person's needs.

Psychotherapeutic interventions

In recent years there has been a growth of interest in the use of psychotherapy with adults with learning disabilities to improve emotional well-being, enhance self-esteem and develop skills (such as assertiveness, relaxation, anger management and relationship-building). However, research investigating the effectiveness of different therapeutic approaches is in its relative infancy. If it is determined that a young person is exhibiting challenging behaviour as a way of expressing emotional distress it may be appropriate that they are offered a psychotherapeutic intervention. Examples of therapeutic approaches include:

- *Cognitive-behavioural interventions* (e.g. Stenfert Kroese *et al.* 1997) – self-management interventions which assume that emotional and behavioural problems are related to the young person's cognitive impairments and lack of skills, teach self-monitoring, self-instruction, self-control, problem-solving and decision-making alongside relaxation therapy and social skills training. Cognitive-behavioural therapy (CBT for short) is based on the premise that an individual's emotions and behaviour are influenced by their cognitions, and aims to effect change in the young person's distorted or negative thinking, beliefs and attributions, thereby resulting in positive changes to mood and behaviour.

- *Psychodynamic psychotherapy* – through the development of a relationship with the therapist, the individual develops an understanding of the defensive processes they use to manage psychological distress. Clients are encouraged to explore their early experiences and their emotional reactions to events.

- *Family therapy* – in contrast to cognitive-behavioural and psychodynamic approaches, family therapy intervenes at the level of the family. All family members are invited to sessions and encouraged to contribute to developing an understanding of problems in relation to difficulties experienced within family relationships. Fidell (2000) argues that systemic family therapy has obvious advantages for use with this client group, because of the stresses that the experience of having a learning disability places on the individual, the family and the organizations that support them.

In a recent commentary on the effectiveness of psychotherapy interventions for adults with learning disabilities, Beail (2003) argues that although the research is limited there is evidence that individuals make improvements in cognitive-behavioural and psychodynamic psychotherapy that are maintained at follow-up.

Stage 5: Evaluation

Interventions for challenging behaviour should be regularly reviewed and evaluated to ensure they are person-centred, effective and multi-disciplinary, and that they comply with legal requirements. For example, interventions should be reviewed to ensure they are evidence-based, least restrictive and in the young person's *best interests*.

Exercise 17.4

Planning strategies for supporting a young person who exhibits challenging behaviour can seem complicated and difficult, and you may feel as if you do not know where to start. In order to plan interventions for challenging behaviour you may need to develop skills in assessing the range of interventions required, considering what information will be needed to plan and implement those interventions, and how to evaluate the effectiveness of them. To illustrate this process, try the following example.

Think of what information you would need to know, what you would have to plan and organize, and what interventions you might use, when taking a young person who exhibits challenging behaviour (in the form of physically aggressive outbursts and stealing) to a local pub for lunch. Now think of what information you would need to know, what you would have to plan and organize, and what interventions you might use to accompany the same individual on a two-week holiday in Blackpool.

Staff/carer support and training

People who support individuals with learning disabilities and challenging behaviour may experience a range of distressing events, live or regularly work in environments where challenging behaviour is exhibited, be required to conduct assessments or interventions and support others who have experienced such events. Therefore, the needs of carers cannot be overlooked. Below we address the issues of personal safety, staff support and training.

Personal safety

When working with young people who exhibit challenging behaviour, staff and carers may be at risk of physical assault and may need to take steps to ensure their personal safety. The law is clear on self-defence. Everyone has a right to defend themselves, particularly in cases of physical assault on one's person. However, staff can find this difficult, as they may feel that taking steps to defend themselves is in conflict with what they see as their duty of care. The dilemma is that, in many cases, not responding can have serious consequences and carry a high risk of injury. So, if you are physically assaulted you are within your rights to defend yourself. The key legal issue is that your response must be in proportion to the risk presented to you. In other words, if a person were to nip you and you responded by hitting them, resulting in them falling to the floor, this would be

considered excessive use of force and could result in assault charges being made against you. Thus, the law allows you to defend yourself but requires that your response is reasonable and in proportion to the threat/risk that you face. The law also requires that you demonstrate a willingness to disengage, that you act with benevolence and in the other person's best interests, and that you act to maintain your own safety.

Challenging behaviour is by definition socially unacceptable, and in some severe cases can result in significant harm to others (e.g. physical or sexual assault), property damage or theft. In cases such as this it may be appropriate to involve the police and proceed with criminal investigation of the individual's actions. This type of intervention may be necessary to ensure the personal safety of people in contact with the individual.

Training

Wherever possible, staff working with people with learning disabilities and challenging behaviour should have the opportunity to attend a recognized and approved training scheme for managing challenging behaviour/violence and aggression. Training courses usually include learning about risk assessment, reactive and preventive management strategies, physical intervention, personal safety, and how to support and maximize the safety of the individual exhibiting the challenging behaviour. Research demonstrates that training can be effective in increasing an individual's understanding, skills and confidence in dealing with incidents of challenging behaviour that impose a significant risk, can increase knowledge and confidence in the use of distraction, diffusion and non-aggressive physical intervention techniques, and can enable carers to read situations with greater clarity, manage their responses in a controlled and responsible manner and resolve situations without incident or injury – thereby reducing the risks to everyone involved (Allen et al. 1997; Allen and Tynan 2000).

An assessment of challenging behaviour may highlight issues where the knowledge or skills of the staff is limited. In order to intervene effectively to reduce an individual's challenging behaviour, staff may benefit from support from professionals with expert knowledge of these issues. In addition to this, specific training on issues such as challenging behaviour, facilitating communication skills, specific physical or mental health problems, autism, dementia and the use of non-confrontational techniques is likely to be valuable for staff/carers who directly support the individual on a regular basis and who are largely responsible for implementation of care plans.

Staff support

Working with young people who exhibit challenging behaviour can be difficult, potentially dangerous and emotionally demanding. Research findings indicate that staff working in residential settings supporting individuals with learning disabilities and challenging behaviour feel significantly more anxious, less supported and have lower job satisfaction than staff supporting individuals who do not present with challenging behaviour (Jenkins *et al.* 1997). We feel it is important that people caring for young people with learning disabilities and challenging behaviour also have access to appropriate support. Examples of different types of staff support include: team meetings where information about assessment, formulation, intervention, care planning and evaluation can be discussed; advice, recommendations and support from members of the multi-disciplinary care team; clinical supervision; access to appropriate training; critical incident debriefing; ongoing staff support groups; and psychological consultancy.

Conclusion

This chapter is an overview of ways of understanding and responding to young people who exhibit challenging behaviour. It provides information to enable staff and carers to recognize behaviour that is challenging, develop hypotheses about why young people might behave in this way, and offer ideas for assessment and intervention. Overall, the chapter aims to support carers to feel more confident and knowledgeable when working with young people who communicate their distress through challenging behaviour.

Of course, how one evaluates the efficacy or otherwise of any form of behavioural intervention or therapy must be predicated upon a consideration of numerous factors. Not least among these are the ethics involved, the presumptions made about the behaviour in the light of the earlier assessment and the emerging results in terms of both actual and potential outcomes. Despite the professional's best efforts and intentions, sometimes interventions may not succeed in quite the way anticipated. For these reasons, evaluation is better understood not as an 'end stage' but rather as an integral and dynamic component that extends throughout the process of intervention. By such evaluative means, practitioners are better placed to respect not only the dynamic and holistic nature of human behaviour and understanding with which they are engaged, but also the person from whom it is derived.

Exercise 17.5

The aims of this exercise are to normalize challenging behaviour and give the reader the opportunity to work through the process of developing a strategy to change behaviour.

Readers are asked to think of something that they do that may be considered by others to be 'challenging' – that is, any behaviour that another person may find unacceptable, upsetting or difficult to understand. For example, swearing, nail biting, smoking, driving too fast. Once you have identified the behaviour that you do, apply the following process:

- Define the problem (e.g. swearing, smoking).
- Measure the frequency of occurrence (e.g. every second word, 20 per day).
- Analyse when the behaviour occurs (e.g. throughout the day, evenings only).
- Work out why the behaviour occurs (e.g. enjoyable, angry, worried, form of self-expression, habit).

- Identify times when the frequency of the behaviour increases or decreases (e.g. increased swearing when angry, increased smoking when at the pub).
- Generate positive objectives for reducing the behaviour (e.g. reduce swearing to get on better with people and present a more positive image of self, stop smoking to save money, improve health, live longer).
- Devise an intervention which consistently reinforces behaviour change (e.g. make a swear box and save money for a special treat, have a health check, get some nicotine patches, save up money usually spent on cigarettes).
- Identify reasons why behaviour reoccurs, and change intervention (e.g. forget to put money in swearbox so no money saved – put in IOUs; identify times when it is most tempting to have a cigarette, such as after a meal or in the pub, and plan to do something to keep busy at those times, and get some support from others in the same situation).

References

Agar, A. and O'May, F. (2001) Issues in the definition and implementation of 'best practice' for staff delivery of interventions for challenging behaviour, *Journal of Intellectual and Developmental Disability*, 26(3): 243–56.

Allen, D. and Tynan, H. (2000) Responding to aggressive behaviour: impact of training on staff members' knowledge and confidence, *Mental Retardation*, 38(2): 97–104.

Allen, D., McDonald, L., Dunn, C. and Doyle, T. (1997) Changing care staff approaches to the prevention and management of aggressive behaviour in a residential treatment unit for persons with mental retardation and challenging behaviour, *Research in Developmental Disabilities*, 18(2): 101–12.

Aman, M.G., Singh, N.N., Stewart, A.W. and Field, C.J. (1985) The aberrant behaviour checklist: a behaviour rating scale for the assessment of treatment effects, *American Journal of Mental Deficiency*, 89: 485–91.

Beail, N. (2003) What works for people with mental retardation? Critical commentary on cognitive-behavioural and psychodynamic psychotherapy research, *Mental Retardation*, 41(6): 468–72.

Blunden, R. and Allen, D. (1987) *Facing the Challenge: An Ordinary Life for People with Learning Difficulties and Challenging Behaviour*. London: King's Fund.

Borthwick-Duffy, S.A. (1994) Prevalence of destructive behaviours: a study of aggression, self-injury and property destruction, in T. Thompson and D.B. Gray (eds) *Destructive Behaviour in Developmental Disabilities*. Thousand Oaks, CA: Sage.

British Psychological Society (2004) *Psychological Interventions for Severely Challenging Behaviours Shown by People with Learning Disabilities: Clinical Practice Guidelines*. London: British Psychological Society.

Brown, H. (1997) Vulnerability issues, in J. O'Hara and A. Sperlinger (eds) *Adults with Learning Disabilities: A Practical Approach for Health Professionals*. Chichester: Wiley.

Cambell, M. and Malone, R.P. (1991) Mental retardation and psychiatric disorders, *Hospital and Community Psychiatry*, 42: 374–9.

Carr, E.G., Levin, L., McConnachie, G., Carlson, J.I., Kemp, D.C. and Smith, C.E. (1993) *Communication-Based Intervention for Problem Behaviour: A User's Guide for Producing Positive Change*. Baltimore, MD: Brookes.

Clements, J. (1997) Challenging needs and problematic behaviour, in J. O'Hara and A. Sperlinger (eds) *Adults with Learning Disabilities: A Practical Approach for Health Professionals*. Chichester: Wiley.

Department of Constitutional Affairs (2007) *Mental Capacity Act 2005: Code of Practice*. London: The Stationery Office.

Department of Health (2001a) *Valuing People: A New Strategy for Learning Disability for the 21st Century*. London: Department of Health.

Department of Health (2001b) *Consent: A Guide for People with Learning Disabilities*. London: Department of Health.

Department of Health (2001c) *Seeking Consent: Working with People with Learning Disabilities*. London: Department of Health.

Department of Health (2006) *Our Health, Our Care, Our Say: A New Direction for Community Services*. White Paper. London: Department of Health.

Department of Health and Department for Education and Skills (2002) *Guidance for Restrictive Physical Interventions: How to Provide Safe Services for People with Learning Disabilities and Autistic Spectrum Disorder in Health, Education and Social Care Settings*. London: DoH/DfES.

Donnellan, A.M., LaVigna, G.W., Negri-Shoultz, N. and Fassbender, L.L. (1988) *Progress without Punishment: Effective Approaches for Learners with Behavioural Problems*. New York: Teachers College Press.

Emerson, E. (1998) Working with people with challenging behaviour, in E. Emerson, C. Hatton, J. Bromley and A. Caine (eds) *Clinical Psychology and People with Intellectual Disabilities*. Chichester: Wiley.

Emerson, E. (2001) *Challenging Behaviour: Analysis and Intervention in People with Learning Difficulties*, 2nd edn. Cambridge: Cambridge University Press.

Emerson, E., Robertson, J., Gregory, N., Hatton, C., Kessissoglou, S., Hallam, A. and Hilery, J. (2000) Treatment and management of challenging behaviours in residential settings, *Journal of Applied Research in Intellectual Disabilities*, 13(4): 197–215.

Emerson, E., Kiernan, C., Alborz, A., Reeves, D., Mason, H., Swarbrick, R., Mason, L. and Hatton, C. (2001) The prevalence of challenging behaviours: a total population study, *Research in Developmental Disabilities*, 22(1): 77–93.

Fidell, B. (2000) Exploring the use of family therapy with adults with a learning disability, *Journal of Family Therapy*, 22(3): 308–23.

Fraser, W. and Nolan, M. (1994) Psychiatric disorders in mental retardation, in N. Bouras (ed.) *Mental Health and Mental Retardation: Recent Advances in Practices*. Cambridge: Cambridge University Press.

Harris, J., Allen, D., Cornick, M., Jefferson, A. and Mills, R. (1996) *Physical Interventions: A Policy Framework*. Kidderminster: BILD Publications.

Jenkins, R., Rose, J. and Lovell, C. (1997) Psychological well-being of staff who work with people who have challenging behaviour, *Journal of Intellectual Disability Research*, 41(6): 502–11.

Mansell, J.L. (2007) *Services for People with Learning Disabilities and Challenging Behaviour or Mental Health Needs*, Revised edn. London: Department of Health.

Moss, S., Emerson, E., Kiernan, C., Turner, S., Hatton, C. and Alborz, A. (2000) Psychiatric symptoms in adults with learning disability and challenging behaviour, *British Journal of Psychiatry*, 177: 452–6.

Murphy, G., Kelly, P.A. and McGill, P. (2003) Physical intervention with people with intellectual disabilities: staff training and policy frameworks, *Journal of Applied Research in Intellectual Disabilities*, 16(2): 115–25.

O'Brien, J. (1987) A guide to personal futures planning, in G.T. Bellamy and B. Wilcox (eds) *A Comprehensive Guide to the Activities Catalogue: An Alternative Curriculum for Youth and Adults with Severe Disabilities*. Baltimore, MD: Paul H. Brookes.

O'Hara, J. and Sperlinger, A. (1997) Mental health needs, in J. O'Hara and A. Sperlinger (eds) *Adults with Learning Disabilities: A Practical Approach for Health Professionals*. Chichester: Wiley.

Royal College of Psychiatrists, British Psychological Society and Royal College of Speech and Language Therapists (2007) *Challenging Behaviour: A Unified Approach. Clinical and Service Guidelines for Supporting People with Learning Disabilities Who Are At Risk of Receiving Abusive or Restrictive Practices*. London: British Psychological Society.

SETRHA (South East Thames Regional Health Authority) and the Tizard Centre, University of Kent (1994) *Understanding and Responding to Difficult Behaviour*. Brighton: Pavilion.

Stenfert Kroese, B., Dagnan, D. and Loumidis, K. (eds) (1997) *Cognitive-Behaviour Therapy for People with Learning Disabilities*. London: Routledge.

Tyrer, S. (1997) The use of psychotropic drugs, in R. Oliver (ed.) *Seminars in the Psychiatry of Learning Disabilities*. Glasgow: Bell & Bain.

Zarkowska, E. and Clements, J. (1994) *Severe Problem Behaviour: The STAR Approach*. London: Chapman & Hall.

18

(Almost) everything you ever wanted to know about sexuality and learning disability but were always too afraid to ask

Alex McClimens and Helen Combes

On the subject of sex, silence became the rule.

(Foucault 1990: 3)

Introduction

Dr James H. Bell, superintendent at the Virginia State Colony for Epileptics and Feebleminded, elected to have Carrie Buck, then 18 and an inmate at his institution, sterilized on eugenic grounds, following the discovery of her pregnancy. Her guardian objected and the case eventually went to the Supreme Court. In Buck vs Bell (1927) the court upheld the state's policy of sterilization of the mentally retarded (sic). After this ruling many other American states implemented similar laws. In his ruling Justice Oliver Wendell Holmes, referring to Carrie's mother and new daughter, who was also sterilized, concluded with this phrase: 'Three generations of imbeciles are enough.' Virginia's legislation was eventually repealed in 1974.

It's 2009. Otto Baxter, who has trisomy 21, and his mum, Lucy, have been using the media. They have appeared on television, radio and in print to discuss Otto's desire to have a sexual relationship, even if it means using the internet to find a partner and then having to pay for the pleasure. Nobody blinks. The debate is framed in terms of rights and choice.

Between Carrie Buck and Otto Baxter an attitudinal change has come about towards the sexuality of people living with the label of learning disability. In Carrie's time to have low intelligence was cause enough to be segregated, institutionalized and treated as a threat to society. The mere fact that she was capable of bearing children panicked the authorities into their extreme reaction.

When we began to write this chapter we decided to be honest with ourselves about the subject. We looked to our own lives and personal experiences – including our experience of working with individuals who have a learning disability. Since part of our argument is premised on the notion that sexuality is core to self-identity it is inevitable that some degree of auto-biography will have influenced our writing. This is not to suggest that we are promoting our own brand of white, middle-class professionalism about sexuality. Rather we are seeking to make a case for individuality, for difference and self-expression over conformity. To this end at all times we encourage readers to position themselves in the narrative, ask what they would do and how they would feel about the circumstances we describe. Only by adopting a self-reflexive stance can any of us hope to appreciate such a complex issue, which brings to the fore the ethical and moral dilemmas to be faced when working with people with learning disabilities. Our remit then is to examine sexuality and whether this term has any meaning for individuals with a learning disability and those involved in their care.

The research and background to this chapter has emerged through conversations we have had with people about sexuality, particularly with the people known to us through our research and clinical work. We have also been influenced by the published literature on sexuality and learning disability. We believe sexuality covers a wide range of issues – sexual behaviour, representations of gender, knowledge of risks, contraception, parenting and forming and maintaining relationships. Sexuality seems to be a developmental process, emerging and changing through our experience and contact with other people.

We use quotes from people with learning disabilities, which we believe enables us to consider how they feel about their sexuality and sexual identity. We have used real stories but different names throughout to protect the innocent.

The social and historical context

Historically people's understanding of the sexuality of people with learning disabilities seems to have been based on stereotypes (Bancroft 1989: 618): either people with learning disabilities were seen as child-like, with no sexual drive, or they were seen as animal-istic, driven by the desire to reproduce. This arguably led to a 'safety first' attitude from carers and families who sought to protect people with learning disabilities from any sexual contact or knowledge.

In practice the policy of segregation reinforced ignorance; men and women were cared for in separate environments and when sexual relationships were explored they were often enshrined in secrecy, known about anecdotally rather than from within a context of understanding. This ignorance in turn helped contribute to the high levels of abuse that exist within the field (McCarthy 1999) and when staff are placed in a context of fear, inertia can set in and the need to empower and enable gets lost in risk assessment. In 2007 the Family Planning Association found that 63 per cent of people with learning disabilities wanted to know more about sex and relationships . . . so what's stopping them?

Sex and the law

Throughout life, behaviour is regulated by laws, codes and rules. This is evident throughout care systems where relationships between carers and those they care for are subject to scrutiny. Much discussion is about sexuality and the rights and wrongs of sexually oriented behaviour. Throughout their working lives carers are confronted with their own personal prejudices and biases around sexuality. Legislative changes have challenged some widespread beliefs about the sexual activity of people with learning disabilities. The European Human Rights Act enshrined in law the rights of people with learning

disabilities to be bound by the same laws that govern all members of our society. Everyone has the right to consensual same-sex relationships, the right to peaceful assembly and to associate with others, the right to marry and to have a private family life and to freely express their ideas and views. As carers our role is to protect the human rights of vulnerable people, so long as this does not infringe the rights and freedoms of others (see Chapter 4).

Capacity and consent to sexual relationships

Within the United Kingdom the Human Rights Act (1998) reinforces the right to a family life and intimate relationships, free from prejudice and victimization. In England and Wales, the law pre-sumes that everyone has the right to make their own decisions, but the Mental Health Act allows this position to be challenged if the person cannot understand all of the information affecting their decisions, cannot retain information or cannot use the information (or communicate that) as part of the decision-making process. Regardless of the legal position, it is perhaps more likely that capacity will be questioned when the person has a learning disability.

The Sexual Offences Review Team reviewed the rights of people to have a private life free from exploitation and in 2003 the Sexual Offences Act enshrined in law the view that it is illegal for any sexual touching of a person with a mental disorder which impedes their choices if they:

- lack the capacity to agree to be touched;
- cannot communicate that choice or agree to being touched because of an inducement, threat or deception; or
- cannot give valid consent because the other person with whom they are in a relationship is in a position of trust with that person.

For a prosecution to take place it would have to be proved that the person committing the offence was aware of, and had taken advantage of, the other person's vulnerability. In sum, then, when judgements are being made about an expression of sexuality, it is important to see sexual relationships as (often) a reciprocal act between two consenting adults. Within care systems we have to be clear about how people arrive at the decision to say yes (or no) to a sexual relationship and how they go on to negotiate the terms for this relationship.

Same-sex relationships

If we backtrack again to the 1960s we would ask you to consider another group of people whose sexual expression was marginalized and hidden from society. Homosexuality between consenting adults aged 21 and over was illegal in England and Wales until 1967 and in Scotland until 1980. The age of consent to a homosexual relationship was finally lowered to 18 in 2000 and 16 in 2003. Over the last 40 years society's attitudes to homosexuality have changed, and now many public figures have 'outed' themselves; something that would have only been known about in private circles has become public knowledge. But has this understanding of a general change in the moral attitudes of our society been transferred to our care systems? Sell *et al.* (1995) found that 18 per cent of men and women in the UK report some homosexual attraction or behaviour since the age of 15. In Sweden

Lofgren-Martenson (2009) found that none of the parents of adults/children with learning disabilities they interviewed thought that their child may be interested in a same-sex relationship. And in interviews with care staff the researchers found that they did not identify any same-sex relationships between the people they cared for. Both groups stated that the person they care for had made close attachments with members of the same sex. The people with learning disabilities they interviewed were aware of same-sex relationships, but none of the people admitted to being attracted to people of the same sex themselves. Parents and carers attributed any interest in same-sex relationships to providing the person with an opportunity to test out and express sexuality rather than as a reflection of sexual preference; it was seen as an immature expression of sexuality.

Many people have conflicts about their sexuality, not only in terms of their sexual orientation, identity and preferences but also in understanding what is socially acceptable or even legally acceptable sexual behaviour. These issues are often not openly discussed within care settings despite an increase in the literature available to people. Many individuals have expressed their love of another same-sex person and have wondered how they can explore their desires without the support of their carers. One woman who worked with the second author would approach other women in bars only to find herself teased, ridiculed and beaten up by people who clearly recognized and exploited her vulnerability. Her parents despaired of asking people to protect her from this abuse. When a man expressed his love for another man the concern led to questions around capacity and vulnerability rather than how we might facilitate a mutually satisfying relationship between two consenting adults.

Teaching versus learning about sexuality

Of course it is important to ensure that people are aware of their rights and the risks entailed in sexual relationships. If there are aspects of sexuality that can be taught, then it is our duty to teach these things if we feel that people are either vulnerable or at risk. We would argue that aspects of our sexuality (as a process) are learnt through our relationships with others, whereas there are some issues we can teach through self help books, for example the different ways of having sex, maintaining sexual health and well-being. If our main concern is that someone is at risk of contracting chlamydia or AIDS then within our duty of care it is essential that we help the person to learn how to protect themselves against such risks. There is information available on the web about resources that have been specifically developed for people with learning disabilities (see www.sexual health.com; www.thpct.nhs.uk). The Family Planning Association (FPA) has funded research into the sexual needs of people with learning disabilities, and offers training to care staff about issues in relation to sexuality. The FPA has published a range of easy to access materials (including posters and DVDs) which challenge prejudices people may hold about people with learning disabilities having sex. Most sexual health clinics are able to offer a range of services to many diverse groups, and should not exclude people on the grounds of disability.

The question of whether we can teach people about their own sexuality is fraught with ethical and moral dilemmas. This is perhaps because other aspects of sexuality may well change through the relationships and conversations we have with other people. It is important to consider therefore whether one individual can decide what is, and is not, appropriate behaviour. To help to clarify these issues the authors ran a series of workshops about sexuality. We felt that it was important to help people to express their own feelings about their sexuality and to find out from those people where their ideas about their own sexuality had come from.

Set against this today we have internet dating sites for the general population (various) as well as specifically for people with learning disabilities (www.starsinthesky.co.uk). Otto Baxter is free to visit these sites, being restricted only by bandwidth.

These rights and responsibilities toward sexual expression have their attendant risks (McCarthy and Thompson 2008) and in our role as paid carers it is important that we grapple with finding a balance in these so that we can help the people we work with to arrive at informed decisions about their own sexual needs (see also the following chapter). Do you find questions about your own sexual attitudes and

behaviour too uncomfortable or probing? We would argue that before we can offer services to people with learning disability we need to examine our own positions to enable the delivery of non-discriminatory practice (Bywater and Jones 2007).

Let's talk about sex . . .

If we have a duty of care towards the people we work with it then follows that this must include some recognition of their rights and needs in terms of their sexuality. The question remains though, how exactly do we address this? We outline one attempt to engage people in an open discussion about their experiences of sex and their attitudes to sexuality.

Both of us had worked for some time with a group of adults with learning disabilities who attended a local day service. We were introducing research methods to the group with a view to future empirical work. In another part of their curriculum, these people were exploring popular culture and it was via this medium that we tried to instigate some discussion on how people present themselves in public. From this discussion, we made the link to expressing sexuality.

This was a mixed gender group of 20 adults with an age range between early twenties and late fifties. We first made the group aware of our intention to write about the topic and gave assurances about confidentiality and anonymity. Included in this exercise was a written note to parents and carers informing them of the subject matter. Two parents wrote back outlining their concern and asking that their son or daughter should not participate in the group. One member of staff also opted out of this stage.

Exercise 18.3

Should paid staff be allowed to opt out of sessions they feel uncomfortable with if sexuality is an integral part of our sense of self? What rules and regulations might organizations and services need to develop to enable people to opt into this work?

After a few sessions of general discussion, we moved on to a more focused topic. We discussed representations of men and women in popular magazines. Each of us had picked out a picture from a popular magazine and talked about why we felt attracted to, or interested in, that person. Building on this we asked the group to think back to their first experience of being attracted to someone else. We asked them to think about how this felt. We chose to explore 'first time' experiences for three reasons. We felt these early experiences might be more memorable and so spark discussion. We also thought that these formative experiences might have influenced how the individual then developed their own ideas and sexual identity. Finally, we reasoned that such memories might also be 'safe' in the sense that any current relationships were less likely to be implicated.

As the session progressed we charted the talk on a flip chart and gave everyone the opportunity to write down their own experiences on a short questionnaire at the end. We did this to give people who contributed less to the verbal debate the chance to have their say (although everybody did say something). This device also focused responses on six topics under two headings. Looking at 'the first time', we asked people to recall their first kiss, first date and first boy/girlfriend. Then, to check understanding, we asked people to say what they felt three words meant to them. These words were sex, love and friendship.

The discussion soon demonstrated that some pre-conceptions of people with learning disabilities as innocent, childlike or asexual were probably based on prejudice rather than any empirical observations. The group told us about a boyfriend who had 'a sexy arse' and of a girlfriend (described as a 'bird') who had 'big knockers'. Someone fancied their sister's husband, and two people, one of whom was in the group, were 'outed' as regularly having a snog behind the day centre equivalent of the bike shed.

The material generated by the questionnaire also revealed a range of awareness and experience. When asked to define 'sex', responses varied. Two individuals had this to say: 'I think it's rude. It means somebody touching you. I don't like to talk about it because it's vulgar', or similarly, 'Don't touch bodies. It would be rude. And I'd tell my mum and dad.' Another said, 'I've heard about it. So she can have a baby. It's cheeky and rude.' A different kind of answer emerged in 'Going out with girlfriend/

boyfriend. Go to their house when no one there. Go to bed together.'

When asked to describe their thoughts on 'love' we got these varied replies: 'I don't know. I've got no clue.' Or, 'Lotsa long time. Happy heart, beat faster' or 'It's nice. I love my mum.' On the subject of 'friendship' there was more commonality. Of the 13 written responses, four specifically mentioned 'talking' as a component of friendship while eight spoke of having a friend with whom they spent some time. This strong association of time spent talking underlines the value of relationships in general and highlights the need to engineer networks of relationships that can be used to support individuals with learning disabilities (see Chapter 24 on social inclusion).

These activities were then linked to popular television as the discussion moved on to how couples are seen in public life. The links between marriage, being in a couple and having children were seen as accidental rather than strictly necessary as we debated the Simpsons, the Beckhams, and Madonna and Guy Ritchie.

Reference to goings on in a soap opera brought age difference under scrutiny. What the group showed here was an appreciation of how things are as well as how things ought to be. A 10-year age gap between a group member in their fifties and their partner was dismissed as irrelevant yet a unanimous verdict of 'No' accompanied the question 'Can a 20-year-old go out with a 10-year-old?' The follow-up question about at what age it was OK to kiss someone you fancy brought responses within the range from 14 to 18.

One member of the group had seen two men in bed on a TV soap. Two group members offered examples of friends who were in lesbian couples, one of whom had children. We checked what people understood by the terms lesbian and gay. Lesbians, according to our respondents, loved other women and gay men loved other men. The consensus was that as long as people were happy and agreed then this was OK. The group members showed us that even when their immediate personal experience cannot accommodate these issues they could still refer to cultural resources to construct a position. On the evidence available from this small sample, that position is always one of inclusion and understanding.

During the course of these sessions various individuals asked to speak to us privately about their own sexuality. We have not been able to include their stories because these discussions took place beyond the scope of our public debate. One member of the main group wanted to write their story, knowing that it would be published. We are happy to include it here.

My first kiss!

It started one month after I started at senior school. Rebecca was the hottest girl at school at the time. She was going out with my friend Bill. Marge said, 'Why don't you [Rebecca] go out with S and I go out with Bill?'

One dinner time I was playing rounders and I hit a homer. At the end of dinner time me and Rebecca kissed each other on the lips and then the bell went to signal the end of dinner time. On the school bus home a couple of kids told me that she was a two-timing bitch. That night I couldn't stop thinking about her and that kiss. The next day she didn't turn up for school. Then I had all weekend to think about what had happened that Thursday. Monday came and she was at school. She told me it was over between us.

Playing mums and dads: Part 1

The work undertaken with the group is in no way definitive but it demonstrates that for these individuals sexuality and its expression was a live issue and that they were fully aware of themselves as sexual beings. Compare this group's construction of their sexuality with the experiences of other individuals with whom we have met and talked. The two case studies that follow demonstrate the gulf between innocence and experience. Whereas the group discussion had been based on genuine life lessons, none of these had transcended the emotional barrier that separates happy recollections from the harsh reality of loss, sorrow and regret. These emotions represent the flipside of adult sexuality. Both informants in the case studies are in their forties and the stories they relate bring into question the overall effect of the regulating agencies that exist to control our own access to our own bodies. Tricia begins by describing her feelings for an old flame. Harry then relates how a relationship went wrong.

Tricia relates her story with the benefit of 20 years' hindsight. Having read this passage it is worth thinking about whether Tricia is fully in control of her own sexual identity and destiny. There are clearly clinical considerations. Tricia is aware, for example,

---

Case study: *Tricia and John*

It were him I used to meet every night at half past eight. We used to stay in the house or go to the pub. His name was John and when I was at home and he used to come and pick me up some nights, can't remember if it was every night, I'll say some nights, at half past eight to go out . . . he'd come and sit and watch telly for a bit or we used to go to the pub, it were only a minute's walk from me mam's. He used to take me out Saturday and Sunday. Go to the pictures Saturday night. Sometimes Sunday too.

Yeah, we'd go to the pictures and then when he used to bring me back from the pub we used to have some lovin' dovin' in the passage, in the back passage, never in the house, always in the passage.

Me mam wanted me to marry him. She never said right out though. I had fits in them days but I got an idea when she died she wanted me to then. He were very nice, John. We never, y'know, like you shouldn't do. You know [mouthed silently] 's-e-x'. Even John wouldn't go right through everything. He were kind. If I'd stayed at home I'd have liked to settle down wi' John.

Now? Well, I'd love to get married. I've felt that way . . . Oh, for a long time. I don't know what I can do. I always wanted to marry John before I left home but there were my fits wi' epilepsy and I don't think I can have kids, wi' me women's problems. I'd have loved some. If I'd got married I'd have got some little children of my own who hadn't got homes. Adopt them. I'd like to see John again, though. He might be married now or have a girlfriend . . . there might be somebody else, I suppose.

that her epilepsy might have conspired against her, though quite how she is not sure. She also mentions that she has 'women's problems'. The vagueness of the term suggests more than a reluctance to engage in specific talk: it suggests an ignorance of what exactly these problems are and how they might be resolved. But Tricia is clear about one thing and that is her wish to get married and have children. Many of us can sympathize and empathize with that wish.

Playing mums and dads: Part 2

> Narratives about identity are therefore significant sites of power struggles in refiguring what it means to be human. What people with an intellectual disability offer everyone in society are stories of how to live as unique individuals in relation to one another. These stories challenge any dominant notion of social homogeneity.
>
> (Fullagar and Owler 1998: 446)

One of the dilemmas that frequently recurs when discussing the whole concept of learning disability is the humanity of the individuals who comprise this social group. This is seldom more apparent than when discussing sexuality. Myths still pervade the topic with individuals regarded as occupying either end of a spectrum that stretches from predatory animal instinct to childlike innocence. Such ingrained prejudice is difficult to counter with any appeal to reason or research. To address this, the following account makes a direct appeal to the emotions. The man who tells us part of his story has a learning disability. He also has two children. This fact makes him a father. Under any other circumstances this would have been a sad story. The tragedy is that the regulation of this aspect of his sexuality by governing agencies conspires to make a failure of his fatherhood.

When discussing inarticulate subjects, Booth and Booth point to the differences between interview research and narrative research (1996: 56). They see this as founded on the individual who has a story to tell. Harry, who we will soon meet, is just such an individual. Booth and Booth also posed a question in their paper about how exactly to overcome some of the silences that inevitably occur in the one-to-one interview situation. In this case, the option was quite simple: keep the tape machine running. To have interrupted the flow of confession would have denied Harry his moment. The extract that appears here is a distillation of hours of transcript that Harry contributed for previous life history research. The episode that he relates reveals how in one of the fullest expressions of sexuality available to modern western cultures, the parental couple bringing up children, any doubt over disability brings the normalizing machinery of the social services into action. Shotter (1993: 7), speaking about identity and belonging, describes a framework for 'becoming someone'. He suggests that:

> if one is to grow up and to qualify as a self-determining, autonomous person with one's own identity – to feel that one has grown up to be 'someone', someone who 'counts' in one's society – then, although one must grow up as a human being within that society, that in itself is not enough. For even as a participating member of it, one can still remain either dependent on other members of it in some way or under their domination in some other way. To be a person and to qualify for certain rights as a free, autonomous individual, one must also be able to show in one's actions certain social competencies, that is, to fulfil certain duties and to be accountable to others in the sense of being able to justify one's actions to them, when challenged, in relation to the 'social reality' of the society of which one is a member.

If we believe this then we must believe that Harry 'counts' in this sense. What follows is just part of his story.

Case study: *Harry and Rebecca*

I met Rebecca at work. She came for an interview job and . . . it were about a month or a month and a half and I asked her out. Then, since, y'know, we started being friends and started taking her out 'n that. When I asked her out she said, 'Yes, I would.' I asked her in a nice polite way and she said yes. That was when I was working on the forging.

I remember, once, taking her to catch the bus, outside the market, and she used to wave to me and she said, 'Don't wait for the bus, come back wi' me.' I used to say to her, 'I'll be alright.' This was when she was living wi' her mum and dad. Before she got caught, a long time before. I says, 'I can't', 'cos sometimes she never used to want me to go at night . . . I don't know . . . she's changed. I would have done but my mum and dad wanted me to come back. Things were different then.

Later she would stay at our house nearly every Friday. We used to go all o'er, everywhere. It were alright then. All things seem to change when you get . . . you're young, things pass on and you have to do different things in life, don't you? That's what it's all about. But when you have a date for the first time, you don't rush straight into things. You take one step at a time. That's what we did.

'Course it didn't stay that way for long. We just started going out like, as friends, and then, y'know, we shouldn't have rushed into it but . . . well, I may as well tell you; I've got a girl and a boy which I don't see. It upsets me that I don't see them but I think that in the long run they're better off where they are. They're getting looked after, getting clothes bought, and getting toys and presents at Christmas.

We'd never talked about it, never even occurred to us. These things happen; you make these mistakes and they just happen, don't they? But then you've got to do something about it, you can't blame the other person and say it's their fault; it takes two to tango. Both to blame. It just happened. No contraceptive. Should have done. We just never discussed it. Should have done.

We never lived together at all. I don't think we could live together . . . we'd always be arguing. I don't think Rebecca was bothered about living together. Because when people get married they always have so long then start having a divorce. I mean, everybody argues, no matter who it is. We all fall out in one way or the other. It's just a thing what goes off in life.

Things started to change then, after the kids arrived. We kept arguing. She wanted me to do something and I wouldn't do it. Like help. Most of the times I did but sometimes I didn't. I'd say something like, 'Oh, I'm tired.' That upset her a bit. That's why I only see her once a week now. She couldn't cope because the kids went into care. Well, Harry's in foster care and Sasha's been adopted. Everybody took to her straight away and they say what a nice girl she is but sometimes, if I talk about it, it upsets me and I just burst out crying sometimes. I know it isn't nice but that's the way it goes. The kids are looked after and that's all I can say.

I don't see the kids though, about eight years since I saw them last. I get photos, that's all. Rebecca sees them. What it is, the reason I don't get contact, is because they don't know who the father is of the kids. Social don't know. When they went into care they asked Rebecca about it but they didn't ask me. I felt hurt. When you see your kids it hurts you a bit, but when you don't see your kids it hurts you even more, deep down, than when you do see them. You understand? It's how it goes. It's hard. It's a shame when you don't see your kids. My lad's going away somewhere wi' the people who are looking after him, she told me. It's good that he gets a holiday.

But when they get older they'll come and look for me. Sasha might not 'cos it's too far, like. But Harry will. I don't know where they live though, do I? Rebecca knows.

Exercise 18.4

Ultimately we have to ask if things could have been any different for Tricia and Harry. We must surely conclude that information on contraception, women's reproductive health issues, parenting and nurturing might have benefited these people. What can we do to assist people in these very common circumstances? What other agencies might have usefully been involved? And crucially, how can we liaise successfully so that the outcomes are mutually satisfactory for all concerned?

You may also want to re-evaluate your responses to these questions after reading Chapter 19 which concerns the sexual lives of women.

In the next section we explore some of the issues that directly affect health care professionals when they try to plan care around the expression of sexuality by individuals with a learning disability. We approach this area from an oblique angle as we take in some of the relevant aspects of labels and labelling theory.

Labelling theory revisited

'Being sexual costs money. You need to buy clothes, to feel good about, and go places to feel good in' (Shakespeare 2000: 161). We asked our group to look through a variety of glossy magazines and to select images of people they felt attracted to. The photographs selected were chosen on the basis of the clothes that the people featured were wearing; pictures were chosen because the people were glamorous or pretty. A glance in the mirror will reassure the reader that one of the main areas by which people express their sexuality is in the way they choose to present themselves to the world. The mere fact that we get dressed in the morning says as much about ourselves as it does about the external environment. So we ask the reader to reflect: what governed your choice of clothing this morning?

There are many ways of dressing up or dressing down. The effect is the same. Some of the more obvious are hairstyling, make-up or accessories. These apply across the gender divide. Beyond this, there are semi-permanent adornments such as tattoos, body piercing, jewellery and eyewear. All of these were in evidence within the group. Fashion, lifestyle and, more specifically, brand awareness influence the acceptability of all of these adornments; none of them comes cheap. While neither of the authors are particularly label-conscious, both find themselves drawn to brands and packaging – neither would be seen outside without their Converse All-Stars, and to appear in public minus the iPhone is of course a social taboo. In addition, if other people discuss our sexual orientation it is essential (to us at least) that the label is the right one – not one given through assumptions. Labels identify and can give people a sense of belonging to a particular group.

The point here is that many people with learning disabilities may be as label conscious as their carers, both in terms of what clothes they wear and how they are described as people. To be denied the opportunity to express one's sexual identity – either through dress or through behaviour – may have a profound impact on our psychological and emotional well-being. And yet, given the structure of our society, many people with learning disabilities find themselves disenfranchized and unable to participate in shaping their sexuality as they might wish. For example, members of the group found it difficult to travel independently and had to rely on other people to help them. This clearly compromises their ability to make and maintain relationships.

Exercise 18.5

Where does this leave the health care professional? If, as we have hinted, economics is important for maintaining sexual identity, what kind of interventions will be successful? Is it necessary to include these issues as part of a plan of care? Look in the mirror and consider a poster of a contemporary pop diva or a boy band; could you see yourself dressed that way? Could you see a client you have cared for dressed that way?

For some individuals who have motor impairments the sense of self can likewise be affected. Morgan (1999) offers numerous examples of women who feel that the way their bodies are prevents them from participating in the ideal of woman that they see in the media. The act of walking in stiletto heels, for example, while thought of as glamorous by some and practised by many, would be either dangerous or impossible for most individuals with some varieties of cerebral palsy.

Yet because certain images predominate in the media, many of our clients, and probably just as many of their families and carers, must look on from the side as youth and beauty parade what passes for the norm, even though in the UK the average dress size is a 16 while on the catwalk it is an 8. Many men will be more familiar with a six-pack of beer than toned abdominal muscles. Few of us can approximate the images portrayed in the pages of the glossy magazines. Can we assist our clients to dress so that they strike a comfortable blend between fashion and function? What conversations might help people to understand these disparities? Can we ask personal shoppers to help the people we care for to discover how they want to present themselves, within the limits of their budgets?

Care planning: *reductio ad absurdum?*

One of the chief tasks for the health professional is to compile some plan of care. This plan is usually done in collaboration with the individual and such a plan must address certain core areas. Maslow ([1958] 1987) argued that psychological well-being and adjustment is contingent on the need to be able to survive and reproduce as well as to seek out relationships with others, to achieve all that we are able through responsibility and status. Once these esteem needs are met we have the potential for self-actualization through personal growth and fulfilment.

As well as the apparent social ramifications there remains a biological imperative here. All of us, for example, must eat and drink. And while we are not arguing that food and drink are in the same category as sex, how many of us are or have been guilty in the past of neglecting the sexuality of the individuals in our care?

If we consider for a moment that we also have a serious responsibility to protect the rights of the individuals we look after then this must include their sexuality. Consider the need to make the environment safe for those who occupy the home, the clinic or the centre. It is now common practice to undertake risk assessments about almost any activity of daily living.

Models of nursing, popular in the 1980s, made much of the so-called nursing process and we have assessed, planned and intervened with people in an endeavour to achieve a specified outcome. Within a medical/clinical model this may have had some utility, where cure, rather than living, is seen as the end point to caring. However, in translating this to a setting characterized as facilitating a valued life it arguably has little to offer. Notwithstanding this criticism, the Roper *et al.* (1996) model capitalized on a reductionist approach by which being human is equated to participation in the 12 activities of daily living: the need for air, food, drink, shelter, warmth, sleep, sex, safety, love, achievement, responsibility and status.

Exercise 18.6

In our experience two areas are often ignored in care planning: death and dying and expressing sexuality. Given that until we die we live as sexual beings, ignoring these activities appears to us to be flawed. Imagine that you are completing your own care plan around your own expressed sexuality. What topics might be included here? Would frequency and duration be part of the plan? Would the planning process reduce the element of spontaneity or limit the location? Who else might be involved and how would you go about making your preferences known? Would you be happy for these details to be written down, recorded and read by others?

Service responses

We feel that it is essential that services begin to see people with learning disabilities as sexual beings, but would challenge whether aspects of sexuality can be quantified in the same way as eating and drinking. Conversations about 'sexuality' and relationships should become part of our discourse. Person-centred care assumes change as part of the life cycle and challenges predominant models of care planning.

The groups with whom we have worked have valued having the time to talk about friendships, relationships and sex. People have told us about the frustrations they have with maintaining relationships, particularly when they live in care homes where it is difficult to meet people and to keep relationships private. If talking about sex ceased to be a taboo, then it may give people an opportunity to ask for space together or to explore concerns about sexual health. Conversations have to take place within a trusting relationship. Within new models of supported living and Direct Payments this may become feasible, with people being able to exercise more autonomy in determining the structure of their lives.

In addition to these personal (or group) conversations you may also feel it is important to discuss sexuality within person-centred planning meetings (see Chapters 22 and 25). Any person-centred approach should consider the changing nature of the person, including their developing sexual needs. There are always dilemmas when there are current concerns about risk or abuse. If you are concerned about health risks then an overriding duty of care would be to support someone in getting appropriate health advice. This advice would be available from a sexual health clinic. You may need to support the person to attend the clinic and to help them in disclosing sensitive and personal information. Advice and leaflets on contraception are available from a GP or family planning service. If as a carer you are concerned that someone has been raped, or that there is ongoing abuse, then the situation is more difficult. Most areas have adult protection procedures and guidance and these should be followed and supervision sought (see Chapter 16 on safeguarding). If your concern is a survivor of abuse then your duty is to help them to access appropriate help and advice from both the statutory and voluntary sector.

Conclusion

This chapter has tried to illustrate the importance of sexuality for human identity while maintaining a focus on the identity of people with learning disabilities. It has considered the historical context, with its emphatic denial of the sexuality of people with learning difficulties. Most of the chapter has been derived from the conversations we have had with people with learning disabilities about their identity, including sexual and significant relationships. These conversations have highlighted how important it is to people that their sexuality is recognized. We have also tried to consider the ethical dilemmas that may arise for staff working in human services. To this end we have tried to think about ways to raise these issues into people's conscious awareness. In the first instance these issues become part of our ordinary discourse (and not professionalized). This enables questions to be asked and prejudices to be challenged. Otherwise, silence will rule once again.

We are all sexual beings, and no one view should dominate another by suggesting that there are 'rules' that should be followed. The paradox of working with people with learning disabilities, however, is that they may well wish to talk with us about 'the rules'. Not to enter into this conversation would be to risk denying people their sexuality.

We have tried to emphasize the importance of sexuality to people's lives. It is a mistake to focus solely on sexuality at one stage of our life – sexual identities change throughout life and from person to person, encompassing chromosomal and physiological differences as well as sexual preferences.

The administration of care often means that people are categorized. However, to separate sexuality from the person is to deny a large part of the person's life and their potential for development and growth. Our duty of care means that we cannot ignore sexuality and should direct people to services that are available to help people to understand and make sense of their sexuality. We can also help people to discover how they want to present themselves to others. We would not wish to deny that sometimes there are risk issues related to sexuality. However, it is also important to remember that people have their own sexual identities which will develop *in spite of* service interventions.

We want to leave readers with a thought to take away. Sexuality as an area for discussion is rife with power relations, whether these are between men and women or between people with and without disabilities. This means that for health care professionals there is an urgent need to be aware that when we engage in any talk on the subject we are re-enacting these power relations. And whatever our gender or orientation, our professional alignment may lead people to see us as holding the power.

References

Bancroft, J. (1989) *Human Sexuality and its Problems*. Edinburgh: Churchill Livingstone.

Booth, T. and Booth, W. (1996) Sounds of silence: narrative research with inarticulate subjects, *Disability & Society*, 11(1): 55–69.

Bywater, J. and Jones, R. (2007) *Sexuality and Social Work*. Exeter: Learning Matters.

Christina, L., Stinson, J. and Dotson, L.A. (2002) Staff values regarding the sexual expression of women with developmental disabilities, *Sexuality and Disability*, 19(4): 283–91.

Craft, A. (ed.) (1994) *Practice Issues in Sexuality and Learning Disabilities*. London: Routledge.

Downs, C. and Craft, A. (1997) *Sex in Context*. Brighton: Pavillion.

Duffy, S. and Sanderson, H. (2004) Person-centred planning and care management, *Learning Disability Practice*, 7(6): 12–16.

Family Planning Association (2007) *Out of the Shadows* and *It's My Right!* http://www.fpa.org.uk/News/Press/Current/page1052.

Foucault, M. (1990) *The History of Sexuality, Volume 3: The Care of the Self*. London: Penguin.

Fullagar, S. and Owler, K. (1998) Narratives of leisure: recreating the self, *Disability & Society*, 13(3): 441–50.

Keywood, K. (2003) Supported to be sexual? Developing sexual rights for people with learning disabilities, *Tizard Learning Disability Review*, 8(3): 30–6.

Lofgren-Martenson, L. (2009) The invisibility of young homosexual women and men with intellectual disabilities, *Behavioral Science*, 27(1): 21–6.

McCarthy, M. (1999) *Sexuality and Women with Learning Disabilities*. London: Jessica Kingsley.

McCarthy, M. and Thompson, D. (2008) People with learning disabilities: sex, the law and consent, in M. Cowling and P. Reynolds (eds) *Making Sense of Sexual Consent*. Aldershot: Ashgate Publishing.

Maslow, A.H. ([1958] 1987) *Motivation and Personality*. New York: Harper & Row.

Morgan, S. (1999) *Body Image*. London: Routledge.

Roper, N., Logan, A.J. and Tierney, W.W. (1996) *The Elements of Nursing: A Model for Nursing Based on a Model of Living*, 4th edn. Edinburgh: Churchill Livingstone.

Sell, R.L., Wells, J.A. and Wypij, D. (1995) The prevalence of homosexual behavior and attraction in the United States, the United Kingdom and France: results of national population-based samples, *Archives of Sexual Behavior*, 24(3): 235–48.

Shakespeare, T. (2000) Disabled sexuality: towards rights and recognition, *Sexuality and Disability*, 18(3): 159–66.

Shotter, J. (1993) Becoming someone: identity and belonging, in N. Coupland and J.F. Nussbaum (eds) *Discourse and Lifespan Identity*. London: Sage.

Stein, J. and Brown, H. (1996) *Sexual Abuse of Adults with Learning Disabilities: The Quiz Pack*. Brighton: Pavillion.

Resources

www.changepeople.co.uk. Change: books and resources on pregnancy, health, abuse and related topics.

www.fpa.org.uk. Family Planning Association. To locate publications, go to shop, then learning disabilities publications.

19

The sexual lives of women with learning disabilities

Michelle McCarthy

Introduction

In this chapter, I aim to give an overview of what we know about the personal and sexual lives of women with learning disabilities. I also want to explore *how* we know what we know. For me personally, the time seemed right to give this overview, as it is some 20 years since I first started working in this field and, as such, it is a good time to take stock.

In order to consider what we know about the personal and sexual lives of women with learning disabilities today, we need to think about the past. It is not my intention to go back too far in history: the institutionalization and segregation of women with learning disabilities, often as a direct result of concerns about their sexuality and reproductive capabilities, has been ably documented elsewhere (Kempton and Kahn 1991; Potts and Fido 1991; see also Chapter 31 in this volume). But if we consider the more recent past and look at the information which has emerged about the sexual lives of women with learning disabilities, we can see certain patterns emerging.

During the 1990s, as a result of work done by myself (McCarthy 1993, 1999), as well as others (e.g. Millard 1994), the picture that emerged of the sexual lives of women with learning disabilities was, on the whole, very negative. Certainly the women with learning disabilities I had worked with reported sexual lives that were passive, i.e. sex was largely presented as something 'done' to them and it was often not enjoyed – certainly not on a physical level ('endured' would be more accurate in many cases). However, the women generally understood the importance of sex in developing and maintaining relationships with men and there was an acceptance of the status quo and an overriding sense of powerlessness. Somewhat more recently, in Scior's 2003 study, women with learning disabilities were still described in terms of their relationships with men as inhabiting 'powerless

positions which placed them at risk of exploitation' (2003: 787).

So, as we look back to that earlier work, we need to ask whether there has been a change in women's personal and sexual lives. And if there has been change, has it been for the better or worse?

The first thing to observe is that it is hard to know, because there is very little direct research on women with learning disabilities and their sexual lives. Why is this the case? There are a number of reasons. First, there are still relatively few researchers, women researchers, probably feminist researchers, who are interested in the lived experiences of women with learning disabilities, although certainly one of the pleasing changes over the past decade or so is that this number is definitely growing. We now have really important work on a number of aspects of women's lives, e.g. menstruation (Rodgers 2001a, 2001b), parenting (Tarleton *et al.* 2006; Baum and Burns 2007), gender identity (Burns 2000; Scior 2003), women living on and moving from locked wards (Owen 2004), women with learning disabilities using rape crisis services (Howlett and Danby 2007) and women's reproductive health (McCarthy 2002, 2009). The above are just those from the UK, but looking further afield, there is excellent work from women in other countries, e.g. from Ireland (Noonan Walsh 2002), Iceland and Australia (Traustadottir and Johnson 2000), to name but a few.

As I have indicated above, there are women who are doing good research with women with learning disabilities but inevitably not all are interested in sexuality. But where researchers are interested in sexuality, there are a number of barriers to doing such research. First, funding avenues are very limited, ethics committees can be obstructive (Brown and Thompson 1997; Hays *et al.* 2003) and the gatekeepers of learning disability services and/or parents can effectively prohibit women with learning disabilities from taking part. All of these things make it difficult to get access to women with learning disabilities in the first place in order to ask them about their experiences. But assuming all those barriers were to be overcome, you are still left with the ethical problems inherent in conducting research on such personal and sensitive areas of life (McCarthy 1998). You need, as far as possible, a context to make the experience meaningful to women with learning disabilities and some possibility of ongoing sources of support, if the women want and need it, not least because of the inevitable reports of sexual abuse which will emerge, whether you are directly asking about them or not. But my own experience, and indeed that of others (Scior 2003), has been that if you get the context right, then women with learning disabilities are, on the whole, not reluctant to talk about their experiences; indeed, many of them want to do so.

Exercise 19.1

What are some of the ethical issues when researchers want to explore the sexual lives of people with learning disabilities? How can these be overcome?

If, as I have argued above, we have little recent, and direct, research evidence about the sexual lives of women with learning disabilities, are there other ways we can find out what we need to know? I think so and if we want to know whether, and how, things have changed, we need to do three things:

1 consider, theoretically, what would need to have changed for the sexual lives of women with learning disabilities to have improved;
2 look at research from a wider context which will indirectly tell us about women's sexuality, e.g. studies of reproductive health, sexual abuse, women's personal lives;
3 look at research on women's social situation, because we cannot separate out women's sexual lives from the whole of the rest of their lives.

And it is these three things I want to attempt in this chapter.

What circumstances would need to have changed for the sexual lives of women with learning disabilities to have improved?

First, the sexual lives of all women would need to have improved, the theory being that if things have improved for women generally, some of this may transfer across to women with learning disabilities. Conversely, it is hard to imagine it the other way around, i.e. that circumstances could have got better for women with learning disabilities without other women having benefited from such changes too.

What, then, is the general picture for women? Actually it is quite hard to find research on the subjective sexual experience, i.e. how women *feel* about their sexual lives, as opposed to what they *do* sexually. You might think that you can simply judge what people feel by looking at what they do, i.e. they do what they enjoy and avoid what they do not like, but in fact it is much more complicated than that and research has always shown a complex set of motivations which guide people's behaviour (McCarthy 1999; Kaestle 2009). So, evidence on how women *feel* about their sexual lives is sparse. But as to what they actually *do*, there is more evidence, and the most comprehensive piece of research in the UK is the NATSAL 2000 (National Survey of Sexual Attitudes and Lifestyles) (Macdowall *et al.* 2002).

It tells us that in the UK, heterosexual[1] people:

- have more sexual partners than they used to, with average numbers of 12.7 for men and 6.5 for women;
- have sex at an earlier age (average age 16, for both men and women, but a third of British 15-year-olds have had sex);
- have higher numbers of concurrent (at the same time) partners, especially younger people;
- have more oral sex than previous generations, with women giving oral sex to men more than receiving it from them (that, incidentally, is a consistent pattern across many countries and cultures);
- have more anal sex than previous generations (although still a minority activity with some 11–12 per cent of people reporting this).

Other findings are that:

- the proportion of men who pay for sex has substantially increased (doubled in past ten years);
- overall consistent condom use had increased, but there were still pockets of high risk behaviour. In the UK there is clearly a great deal of unprotected sex, as we have relatively high teenage pregnancy rates, abortion rates, and high sexually transmitted infection (STI) rates (especially Chlamydia).

Can we deduce anything from this about whether women's sexual lives are generally better now than they were a decade or so ago? From these data, it is impossible to say, but the evidence does suggest that for young women particularly, their sexual lives are busier than they were. Whether this is also true for women with learning disabilities we cannot say, as we do not have the equivalent research.

Exercise 19.2

Why would heterosexual women report roughly half the numbers of sexual partners than heterosexual men?

The gap between first sexual experiences and 'settling down with one partner' is widening all the time. What might some of the implications of this be?

Moving away from actual sexual behaviour, what else would logically need to have changed for the sexual lives of women with learning disabilities to have improved?

There would need to be evidence of improvements in self-esteem and social status of women with learning disabilities. This has not happened, as far as I am aware. Again, there is little direct work on the topic of self-esteem and women with learning disabilities. So, we have to look elsewhere and extrapolate: for women generally, we know there is a challenge in remaining positive about self-image in the face of ever increasing pressures to conform to unrealistic and unhealthy ideals of how women should look (Wolf 1997; Orbach 2009). It is not hard to see that some of these pressures will filter across to women with learning disabilities too (McCarthy 1998). And in addition, some women have also to face negative societal images about disability. So, main-

taining a healthy self-image in the face of this is likely to be very hard for women with learning disabilities, certainly those who have any level of awareness of the media and popular culture (Christian et al. 2001). Along with the elderly, and those with certain physical disabilities, women with learning disabilities are the 'furthest away from cultural constructions of ideal female attractiveness' (Hassouneh-Phillips and McNeff 2005: 228), so they are particularly disadvantaged. The importance of self-esteem for women's sexuality and the maintenance of healthy partnerships with men cannot be overstated and is clearly shown by research on women with physical disabilities, with whom there are many parallels. Research has shown (Hassouneh-Phillips and McNeff 2005) that the women with the highest degree of physical impairments had the lowest self-esteem. They also were more socially isolated (which decreases chances of having emotional and practical sources of support from others). They tended to prefer to be in relationships with non-disabled men. This is due to societal devaluation of disability, i.e. being with a non-disabled man is seen as one of the few ways to affirm their own worth as women in a world which told them they were generally not valued. The exact same dynamic has been described in this country by Burns (1993) in her work with women with learning disabilities. Similarly a recent Swedish paper (Lofgren-Martenson 2004: 202) described the 'hierarchy of attraction' among young people with learning disabilities (those with moderate learning disabilities wanted relationships with those with mild learning disabilities and those with mild learning disabilities wanted someone without a learning disability). When women generally, and disabled women particularly, have a strong desire to be in a relationship with a man and a fear of being alone (perhaps related to not being able to manage alone because of the disability), then it has been shown clearly that these women are very vulnerable to abusive relationships (Burns 1993; McCarthy 1999).

If the sexual lives of women with learning disabilities had improved, we might expect this to be partly a result of better sexuality support now compared to the past. This would manifest itself in better trained staff, yet in the UK there are probably fewer specialist staff training now than a decade or so ago. Sexuality issues now are more likely to be subsumed in training on rights, on supporting individuals, and within the context of abuse. Without ongoing training and managerial support in directly handling situations related to sexuality, there is a tendency among staff (and indeed relatives too) to want to err on the side of caution. This can lead to a situation whereby 'staff members and relatives frequently act as "new obstacles or institutional walls" despite the fact that the old institutional obstacles have been removed' (Lofgren-Martenson 2004: 206). A recent study showed that staff members still perceive many kinds of sexual behaviour as being less appropriate for people with, as opposed to without, learning disabilities (Swango-Wilson 2008). It also found that the younger the staff members, the more accepting they were of sexual expression by people with learning disabilities (see also Cuskelly and Bryde 2004). So there is some hope for the future there, providing the younger staff members do not become more conservative as they age or become more jaded as they get more experience in learning disability services.

If there was better sexuality support available in learning disability services, then we would see more and better sex education for women with learning disabilities but there is no evidence for that. There are obviously pockets of very good practice here and there, but overall no evidence of improved sex education across the board. One study by Walter *et al.* (2001) on women with and without disabilities indicated that by far the most common sources of information about sexuality, for both groups, were direct experience (i.e. you learn about sex by doing it) and books/magazines. Formal sex education was way down the list. My own research with women with learning disabilities in the 1990s (McCarthy 1999) also showed clearly that direct experience, including the experience of being sexually abused, was the most common route for learning about sex.

Exercise 19.3

What would the components of a good quality sexuality support service be? When would be the right time to introduce sex education? Who is best placed to deliver it?

A final and most important thing that would need to have changed in order for an improvement in the sexual lives of women with learning disabilities to be apparent would be evidence of a reduction in levels of sexual abuse. Although it has been some years since a large-scale prevalence or incidence study was published, nevertheless sexual abuse remains a very current topic both within learning disabilities services and also in the media, legal and policy-making circles (see Chapter 16). Sadly, this is unlikely to change in the near future – over the years we have accumulated an abundance of evidence highlighting the factors which make women with learning disabilities, in particular, very vulnerable to sexual abuse. These include (not in order of importance):

- lack of formal and informal sex education and therefore a lack of awareness of what is usual, 'normal' or valued behaviour;
- social isolation and economic dependence, social vulnerability, not being 'streetwise' and questioning or suspecting other people's motivations;
- willingness to please and be accepted by those seen as having a higher social status;
- increased dependency on others;
- having to share services with men with learning disabilities who may have histories of perpetrating sexual abuse;
- difficulty in recognizing sexual abuse when it happens;
- difficulty in being believed if they do tell;
- a legal system out of tune with the experiences and needs of women with learning disabilities.

What research about sexual and reproductive health can tell us about women's sexual lives

Sexual health

One clear difference between now and a decade or so ago is that sexual health concerns and, in particular, issues relating to HIV, have largely disappeared from the learning disabilities literature. In the 1990s, although it was not commonplace, work was periodically published about women with learning disabilities and HIV prevention (McCarthy 1994, 1997) and also in relation to men with learning disabilities (Thompson 1994; Cambridge 1997). Today you find very little written on this specifically from within the learning disabilities field; this is partly a reflection of the wider health agenda where HIV/ AIDS issues have fallen out of the public sphere (despite not having gone away). Nevertheless, examples of good practice do periodically emerge in the literature and are worthy of mention, e.g. the Pearl Service in West London. This is a project to raise awareness and accessibility of a local sexual health clinic to people with learning disabilities (Davis 2008).

Lesbian sexuality

I indicated earlier that we still know next to nothing about lesbian sexuality for women with learning disabilities. My own research some time ago explored the attitudes of women with learning disabilities to lesbian sexuality (McCarthy 1999), but the women in my study had no same-sex experiences to draw on. Happily, there has been a significant contribution to knowledge and that is Abbot and Howarth's 2005 study, which they called *Secret Loves, Hidden Lives?* In it they describe how they struggled to find nine lesbians with learning disabilities in the whole UK to include in their research. They found confirmation of what has long been known, namely that lesbian sexuality is far more hidden in learning disability services than sexual relationships between men. Relationships between women were assumed to be platonic and largely unproblematic. The women they researched really did have 'secret loves, hidden lives', even more so than the men in this study. Of course it is debatable whether it is better to be overlooked (and therefore largely left alone) or acknowledged (but have people put obstacles in your way), as was more likely to be the experience of men in same-sex relationships.

Exercise 19.4

Identify the steps learning disability services could take so that women would know they could be supported whatever their sexual orientation.

Menstruation and menopause

Research in the past few years by Rodgers (2001a, 2001b) on women with learning disabilities generally, and more recently by Mason and Cunningham (2007) on women with Down's syndrome, found a pervasive feeling of negativity among women with learning disabilities regarding their periods. They found that women often lacked knowledge and understanding of menstruation and that, as girls, they were not prepared for the onset of menstruation.

At the other end of women's reproductive life cycle, my own research on the menopause showed similar findings (McCarthy 2002). I found that many women with learning disabilities were not prepared for the menopause, and although they realized they were experiencing certain physical changes in their bodies, they generally lacked awareness as to what these meant. Recent research by Willis (2008) found very similar findings. The implications of such research are that, in the twenty-first century, girls and women with learning disabilities are still being left in positions of ignorance about their bodies. This only serves to highlight their difference from other women and is wholly unnecessary.

Contraception

My most recent piece of research was looking at the way contraception is prescribed to women with learning disabilities (McCarthy 2009a, 2009b). While there were some positive findings, i.e. some women with learning disabilities were making their own choices about whether to use contraception and which method, in general this was not the case. Most women felt that the important decisions about whether to start and stop contraception and which methods to use were made by other people. My research confirmed what we have long known about the disproportionately high use of Depo-Provera (DP) with women with learning disabilities. In my view, there is not enough attention paid to this within learning disability services, although the risks (e.g. of osteoporosis in women with learning disabilities who use DP in the long term) are increasingly being highlighted in the medical literature (Zurawin and Paransky 2003; Dizon *et al.* 2005; Watson *et al.* 2006). Of particular concern is that many women with learning disabilities use this method, and/or other methods, for *very* long periods of time. A recent Canadian study (Dizon *et al.* 2005) reviewed all cases of girls and young women with learning disabilities referred for menstrual and contraceptive advice in a particular area: in 42 per cent of cases, DP was the only option offered and in another 36 per cent of cases it was a choice between DP and the pill. Many of the girls in this study were so young that they had not even started their periods, but were referred because their families were worried at the prospect of the onset of menstruation.

My own recent research found a number of cases of girls with learning disabilities as young as 12, 13 and 14 starting on contraception and also that once girls or women with learning disabilities started to use contraception they tended to stay on it, regardless of their individual circumstances. I also found at the other end of the age range women in their mid- to late forties still being prescribed DP, despite ample evidence, well known to the medical profession, that women's fertility declines sharply after 35. Of course, women can and do get pregnant after this age, but some of the women in my study were not even sexually active. I have described such prescribing practices as 'overkill' (McCarthy 2009b), which is an emotive term but a justified one in the circumstances. My conclusions from this research are that the sexuality, and especially the reproductive capacity, of women with learning disabilities are still often seen as a threat to be contained. Furthermore, when we focus on pregnancy prevention over and beyond anything else, then this compromises women's health and their dignity.

Sterilization

With regards to sterilizations of people with learning disabilities, research by Stansfield *et al.* (2007) makes interesting reading. They reviewed all the cases referred to the UK Official Solicitor's Office for sterilization over an 11-year period. They found that of a total of 73 people referred, 72 had a learning disability, only three of whom were men. Few women with learning disabilities were thought to be sexually active and the authors say that 'sterilization was not being used to enable a positive sexual relationship free from the worries of pregnancy, but rather for fear

of the unexpected' (Stansfield *et al.* 2007: 577). In other words, a 'just in case' attitude prevails here, as it does with contraception. However, with surgical sterilization, there is at least a degree of legal scrutiny. But when a woman with learning disabilities is put on contraception for most or all of her reproductive life, this is arguably a chemical sterilization, yet it has no legal scrutiny.

The social lives of women with learning disabilities

In the introduction, I said that it is highly unlikely that women with learning disabilities would have experienced positive changes in their sexual lives without other aspects of their lives changing for the better too. So, this raises the question, are their lives more generally satisfying? To answer this we would need to look at a number of areas, such as accommodation, work and leisure opportunities, but space does not permit that here (although these areas are all covered elsewhere in the book). Friendships and social networks are of particular relevance and are covered in detail in Chapter 24 by Roy McConkey, but here I want to draw brief attention to the ways in which friendships (or lack thereof) impact on women's ability to develop more intimate personal relationships.

Before we look at research evidence, it is worth noting that one very welcome development in recent years has been the establishment of specialist dating/relationship agencies for people with learning disabilities, the most high profile of which is *Stars in the Sky* (www.starsinthesky.co.uk), but there are others (e.g. Jenner and Gale 2006). Although such services have been some of the most obvious, visible and welcome initiatives in the past decade, they still reach only a minority of people with learning disabilities and, for the majority, the research on friendships and social networks is rather depressing. A good example is Emerson and McVilly's study (2004), which reported findings from a large population-based study. This indicated overall low levels of friendship activities for adults with learning disabilities and these were very modest kinds of activities such as having a friend visit their house or visiting a friend's house. It also showed that most activities with friends occurred in public places, with little or no opportunity for privacy. This obviously has implications for the development of intimate relationships. The findings also showed clearly that the main determinants of the form and content of people's friendships were the settings in which they lived and the efforts made by staff, rather than the individuals' personal characteristics (i.e. their skills, behaviours and interests).

Further research by McVilly *et al.* (2005) suggested that women with learning disabilities tended to feel more lonely than men with learning disabilities. This was partly because women felt the lack of friends with whom they could talk intimately, whom they could trust and be open and honest with about problems. Men with learning disabilities, on the other hand, felt friendship was more about shared activities and practical support and these were evidently easier to find.

An interesting study was by LeRoy *et al.* (2004) in the US and Ireland. It was important because it looked at the life experiences of older women with learning disabilities, a group that the authors themselves described as 'the least studied and understood members of the disability population' (LeRoy *et al.* 2004: 430). The study did not look at the women's intimate or sexual relationships, but did look at the important relationships the women had: paid staff were the most significant people in the lives of most of the women and they relied on them for practical and emotional support. Family ties remained very important to the women, even though they often had little contact on a daily, weekly or monthly basis. The women's friends were all other service users and they had difficulty maintaining links with friends who lived in different homes, relying as they did on staff for transport and help with keeping in touch with people.

Study after study suggests that personal relationships are one of the key areas requiring attention if people with learning disabilities are to live ordinary and valued lives in community settings. Services always recognize this in their mission statements, which commonly suggest that enhancing the quality of life of people with disability is a priority. Yet in practice, promoting and supporting personal relationships, and in particular friendships, is often neglected.

Conclusion

In this chapter, I have sought to demonstrate that in the absence of direct research which explores in detail with women with learning disabilities what their sexual lives are like, it is still possible to gain insights into this topic. Looking at the personal and sexual lives of other women, including those with other forms of disabilities, is certainly instructive. Researching around the topic, so to speak, by looking at areas of tangential interest, also throws light on the subject, as we saw when we examined the evidence on reproductive health or friendships.

Having said that, it is important not to overlook the need for direct research evidence. The fact is that many women with learning disabilities have active sexual lives. In order for others to support them, we need to be well informed about their needs. There is only one real way to do that and that is to talk to women with learning disabilities themselves – to ask them what they are doing, how they feel about it and whether they need the help of anyone else either to maintain things the way they are if they are happy, or, if not, to try to change things for the better.

Note

1. Here I am referring to heterosexuals only, to provide context to what I am saying about women with learning disabilities; one thing which has not changed over time is that we still know very little about lesbian sexuality and women with learning disabilities.

References

Abbot, D. and Howarth, J. (2005) *Secret Loves, Hidden Lives?* Bristol: The Policy Press.

Baum, S. and Burns, J. (2007) Mothers with learning disabilities: experiences and meanings of losing custody of their children, *Tizard Learning Disability Review*, 12(3): 3–14.

Brown, H. and Thompson, D. (1997) The ethics of research with men who have learning disabilities and abusive sexual behaviour: a minefield in a vacuum, *Disability and Society*, 12(5): 695–707.

Burns, J. (1993) Invisible women – women who have learning difficulties, *The Psychologist*, 6(March): 102–5.

Burns, J. (2000) Living on the edge: women with learning disabilities, in J. Ussher (ed.) *Women's Health: Contemporary International Perspectives*. Leicester: BPS Books.

Cambridge, P. (1997) How far to gay? The politics of HIV in learning disability, *Disability and Society*, 12(3): 427–53.

Christian, L., Stinson, J. and Dotson, L. (2001) Staff values regarding the sexual expression of women with developmental disabilities, *Sexuality and Disability*, 19(4): 283–91.

Cuskelly, M. and Bryde, R. (2004) Attitudes towards the sexuality of adults with an intellectual disability: parents, support staff, and a community sample, *Journal of Intellectual & Developmental Disability*, 29: 255–64.

Davis, R. (2008) Excellence network teams use early intervention to improve users' lives, *Community Care*, 8 May: 17–18.

Dizon, C., Allen, L. and Ornstein, M. (2005) Menstrual and contraceptive issues among young women with developmental delay, *Journal of Paediatric and Adolescent Gynaecology*, 18(3): 157–62.

Emerson, E. and McVilly, K. (2004) Friendship activities of adults with intellectual disabilities in supported accommodation in northern England, *Journal of Applied Research in Intellectual Disabilities*, 17(3): 191–7.

Hassouneh-Phillips, D. and McNeff, E. (2005) 'I thought I was less worthy': low sexual and body esteem and increased vulnerability to intimate partner violence in women with physical disabilities, *Sexuality and Disability*, 23(4): 227–40.

Hays, S., Murphy, G. and Sinclair, N. (2003) Gaining ethical approval for research into sensitive topics: 'two strikes and you're out?' *British Journal of Learning Disabilities*, 31(4): 181–9.

Howlett, S. and Danby, J. (2007) Learning disability and sexual abuse: use of a woman-only counselling service by women with a learning disability: a pilot study, *Tizard Learning Disability Review*, 12(1): 4–15.

Jenner, P. and Gale, T. (2006) A relationship support service for people with learning disabilities, *Tizard Learning Disability Review*, 11(2): 18–25.

Kaestle. C. (2009) Sexual insistence and disliked sexual activities in young adulthood: difference by gender and relationship characteristics, *Perspectives on Sexual and Reproductive Health*, 41(1): 33–9.

Kempton, W. and Kahn, E. (1991) Sexuality and people with intellectual disabilities: a historical perspective, *Sexuality and Disability*, 9(2): 93–111.

LeRoy, B.W., Walsh, P.N., Kulik, N. and Rooney, M. (2004) Retreat and resilience: life experiences of older women with intellectual disabilities, *American Journal of Mental Retardation*, 109(5): 429–41.

Lofgren-Martenson, I. (2004) 'May I?' About sexuality and love in the new generation with intellectual disabilities, *Sexuality and Disability*, 22(3): 197–207.

McCarthy, M. (1993) Sexual experiences of women with learning difficulties in long-stay hospitals, *Sexuality and Disability*, 11(4): 277–86.

McCarthy, M. (1994) Against all odds: HIV and safer sex education for women with learning difficulties, in L. Doyal, J. Naidoo, and T. Wilton (eds) *AIDS: Setting a Feminist Agenda*. London: Taylor and Francis.

McCarthy, M. (1997) HIV and heterosexual sex, in P. Cambridge and H. Brown (eds) *HIV and Learning Disability*. Kidderminster: BILD.

McCarthy, M. (1998) Interviewing people with learning disabilities about sensitive topics: a discussion of ethical issues, *British Journal of Learning Disabilities*, 26(4): 140–5.

McCarthy, M. (1999) *Sexuality and Women with Learning Disabilities*. London: Jessica Kingsley Publishers.

McCarthy, M. (2002) Going through the menopause: perceptions and experiences of women with intellectual disabilities, *Journal of Intellectual and Developmental Disability*, 27(4): 281–95.

McCarthy, M. (2009a) Contraception and women with intellectual disabilities, *Journal of Applied Research in Intellectual Disabilities*, 22: 363–9.

McCarthy, M. (2009b) 'I have the jab so I can't be blamed for getting pregnant': contraception and women with learning disabilities, *Women's Studies International Forum*, 32(3): 198–208.

McCormack, B., Kavanagh, D., Caffrey, S. and Power, A. (2005) Investigating sexual abuse: findings of a 15-year longitudinal study, *Journal of Applied Research in Intellectual Disabilities*, 18: 217–27.

Macdowall, W., Wellings, K., Nanchahal, K., Mercer, C.H., Erens, B., Fenton, K.A. *et al.* (2002) Learning about sex: results from Natsal 2000, *Journal of Epidemiology and Community Health*, 56 (supplement 2): A1–A26.

McVilly, K.R., Stancliffe, R.J., Parmenter, T.R. and Burton-Smith, R.M. (2005) 'I get by with a little help from my friends': adults with learning disabilities discuss loneliness, *Journal of Applied Research in Intellectual Disabilities*, 19: 191–203.

Mason, L. and Cunningham, C. (2007) An exploration of issues around menstruation for women with down syndrome and their carers, *Journal of Applied Research in Intellectual Disabilities*, 21(3): 257–67.

Millard, L. (1994) Between ourselves: experiences of a women's group on sexuality and sexual abuse, in A. Craft (ed.) *Practice Issues in Sexuality and Learning Disabilities*. London: Routledge.

Noonan Walsh, P. (2002) Women's health: a contextual approach, in P. Noonan Walsh and T. Heller (eds) *Health of Women with Intellectual Disabilities*. Oxford: Blackwell.

Orbach, S. (2009) *Bodies*. London: Profile Books.

Owen, K. (2004) *Going Home? A Study of Women with Severe*

Learning Disabilities Moving Out of a Locked Ward. London: St George's Hospital Medical School.

Potts, M. and Fido, R. (1991) '*A Fit Person To Be Removed': Personal Accounts of Life in a Mental Deficiency Hospital.* Plymouth: Northcote House Publishers.

Rodgers, J. (2001a) The experience and management of menstruation for women with learning disabilities, *Tizard Learning Disability Review,* 6(1): 36–44.

Rodgers, J. (2001b) Pain, shame, blood and doctors: how women with learning difficulties experience menstruation, *Women's Studies International Forum,* 24(5): 523–39.

Scior, K. (2003) Using discourse analysis to study the experiences of women with learning disabilities, *Disability and Society,* 18(6): 779–95.

Stansfield, A., Holland, A.J. and Clare, I.C.H. (2007) The sterilization of people with intellectual disabilities in England and Wales during the period 1988 to 1999, *Journal of Intellectual Disability Research,* 51(8): 569–79.

Swango-Wilson, A. (2008) Caregiver perception of sexual behaviours of individuals with intellectual disabilities, *Sexuality and Disability,* 26(2): 75–81.

Tarleton, B., Ward, L. and Howarth, J. (2006) *Finding the Right Support: A Review of Issues and Positive Practice in Supporting Parents with Learning Difficulties and their Children.* London: Baring Foundation.

Thompson, D. (1994) The sexual experiences of men with learning disabilities having sex with men: issues of HIV prevention, *Sexuality and Disability,* 12(3): 221–42.

Traustadottir, R. and Johnson, K. (eds) (2000) *Women with Intellectual Disabilities: Finding a Place in the World.* London: Jessica Kingsley.

Walter, L., Nosek, M. and Langdon, K. (2001) Understanding the sexuality and reproductive health of women with and without physical disabilities, *Sexuality and Disability,* 19(3): 167–76.

Watson, K., Lentz, M. and Cain, K. (2006) Associations between fracture incidence and use of depot medroxyprogesterone acetate and anti-epileptic drugs in women with developmental disabilities, *Women's Health Issues,* 16(6): 346–52.

Willis, D. (2008) A decade on: what have we learned about supporting women with intellectual disabilities through the menopause? *Journal of Intellectual Disabilities,* 12(2): 9–23.

Wolf, N. (1997) *The Beauty Myth: How Images of Beauty Are Used Against Women.* London: Vintage.

Zurawin, R. and Paransky, O. (2003) The role of surgical techniques in the treatment of menstrual problems and as contraception in adolescents with disabilities, *Journal of Pediatric and Adolescent Gynaecology,* 16: 51–6.

20

Supporting people with learning disabilities within the criminal justice system

Nigel Beail

Introduction

People with learning disabilities may initially come into contact with the criminal justice system as a suspect or a complainant. If charged, the suspect becomes a defendant in court and then, if found guilty, continues as an offender with disposal needs such as prison, special hospital, probation or a community order. Sometimes the court may make an additional Treatment Order. Victims of crime become complainants and attend court as witnesses for the prosecution. People with learning disabilities may also witness a crime and be required to give statements and then appear in court for the prosecution or the defence. However, by whatever means they come into contact with the criminal justice system they may find the experience frightening, bewildering and stressful. In recent years research concerning offenders has increased considerably but interest in complainants or witnesses has only received modest attention. This chapter will look at the various stages of the criminal justice process and examine the support needs of people with learning disabilities who come into contact with it. The chapter will draw on the most recent research on offenders and witnesses with learning disabilities in relation to the criminal justice system, with accounts of some personal experiences.

Links between criminality and learning disability?

The belief that there is a link between criminality and learning disability persisted throughout the first three-quarters of the twentieth century. However, real evidence for such a link has never been proven (Lindsay 2009). Indeed, Holland *et al.*'s (2002) and Lindsay's (2009) reviews found little evidence to support the view that learning disability predisposes

people to engage in criminal behaviour. There would appear to be very little in the way of reliable evidence concerning the prevalence of offending among people who have learning disabilities. McBrien (2003) identified 14 published studies conducted in the UK during the 1990s, which reported prevalence rates among offender populations. She identifies significant problems in interpreting these studies. They were carried out in a range of settings at different stages of the criminal justice process. For example, some studies were carried out in custody, some at the court stage, some in prisons and some with those on probation. The size of the populations studied also varied considerably. Interpretation was further hampered by the fact that there was no consistent approach to the identification of learning disability. The assessment approaches included self-report (whether the person feels they have reading problems, learning difficulties or attended special school), historical information (known user of learning disability services), the Quick Test (Ammons and Ammons 1966) and short forms of standardized intelligence tests. None of the studies carried out assessments that would be appropriate to make a formal diagnosis of learning disability. The prevalence rates ranged from 1 per cent using *ICD-10* criteria (WHO 1992) in a prison survey to 21 per cent using self-report from those entering a remand prison. However, further assessment of that group on a short form of a standardized intelligence test found no one with an IQ score below 70. A more recent study of 102 prisoners in Australia reported only 2 per cent to have full-scale IQ scores below 70 (Holland and Persson 2007). Thus, it is questionable what these studies are actually telling us.

McBrien (2003) has also reviewed studies which have investigated the prevalence of offenders among populations of people with learning disabilities. She found only five surveys, of which only two had been published. These studies only concerned people with learning disabilities who were known to services. The problem with this approach is that many people with learning disabilities are not known to services. Also, no assessments were carried out of those known to services. McBrien excluded two studies, as their prevalence rates were unclear. Of the others the rates ranged from 2 to 9.7 per cent.

People with learning disabilities are at greater risk of having a range of crimes committed against them, compared to other sections of the population. Studies have found higher incidence of physical and sexual assault and robbery, theft and burglary (Wilson and Brewer 1992; Brown *et al.* 1995). There are also laws which have the aim of protecting people with learning disabilities from exploitation. For example, under the Sexual Offences Act 1956 it is an offence for a man to have unlawful sexual intercourse with a woman who is a 'defective'. Men with 'severe mental handicap' are given protection under the Sexual Offences Act 1967. The terms used in these Acts reflect the language usage at the time. Today, whether or not the person has capacity to consent to sexual acts is a matter for the court. Expert evidence on the person's learning disability may be submitted but the issues concerning the degree of a person's learning disability is determined by the jury.

Identifying those with learning disabilities when they come into contact with the criminal justice system

It is important that people with learning disabilities are identified when they come into contact with the criminal justice system. This has been affirmed in the Bradley Report: a government-commissioned review of people with mental health problems or learning disabilities in the criminal justice system. Due to their significant limitations in learning and social functioning they are disadvantaged and therefore vulnerable. They may have limited or no understanding of legal procedure, they are more likely to be acquiescent, suggestible and compliant in police interrogations or interviews and, as such, they are at risk of making false confessions or statements. Those convicted and given custodial sentences may cope

poorly within the prison system and may be vulnerable to bullying and abuse by more able inmates (Talbot 2008). Also, in the UK, people with learning disabilities are officially seen as vulnerable and are entitled to certain legal protections under the Police and Criminal Evidence Act 1985 and the Youth and Criminal Justice Act 1999. Further, for offenders, learning disability may be used in mitigation. This is a particularly important issue in some states of America where the death penalty is imposed for capital crime, as the Supreme Court ruled that this was inhumane for people who have learning disabilities (Beail and Edwards 2004).

When a person is arrested the police officer tells them, 'You are under arrest' and then cautions them: 'You do not have to say anything. But it may harm your defence if you do not mention, when questioned, something which you later rely on in court. Anything you do say may be given in evidence.' This is a long statement, which many people with learning disabilities may not understand. However, they may not tell the police officer that they do not understand. Once arrested the person has to be taken to a police station and presented to the custody officer. The custody officer's job is to look after people who are under arrest. In order to support persons who have learning disabilities who come into contact with the criminal justice system we need to identify them as soon as possible. What can be achieved will depend on the organization of interagency working. It is the custody officer who is most likely to observe that a person has learning limitations. Many areas now have nurses and social workers working in a liaising role between the police and health and social services. They are more familiar with the signs of learning disability and can help custody officers develop skills to detect the presence of such disability. They can provide a clinical opinion and advise the police whether further assessment is needed.

Some useful questions to ask are:

- Did you attend a special school?
- Did you have extra help in school?
- Do you have any difficulties reading and writing?

These are crude screening questions but can help identify vulnerability.

Mr A was arrested and taken to the police station. The custody officer had concerns about his understanding and asked the court liaison nurse to interview him. She shared the officer's concerns about his learning ability and also asked Mr A about his educational history. This revealed that he had attended a special school. However, further enquiries made through the local community learning disability service produced no reports or documents to state that he had a learning disability. Many people with learning disabilities are not in contact with or supported by specialist learning disability services and may not have an adequate assessment of their disability. This was the case for Mr A and so he was then referred to the local clinical psychology service for a full diagnostic assessment. As Mr A was over the age of 16 his consent to the assessment was sought. This is a legal requirement and no one can give consent for any assessment or treatment for a person over 16 years other than that person. Mr A consented to the assessment. The outcome was a formal diagnosis of learning disability. The psychological assessment also raised concerns about Mr A's mental health and vulnerability to abuse. A report was compiled and recommendations were made for treatment and management as an alternative to continuing in the criminal justice system.

The decision concerning whether or not the person continues in the criminal justice system is usually taken by the Crown Prosecution Service (CPS). This is a separate organization from the police. The role of the police is to gather all the evidence. It is the lawyers, who are Crown Prosecutors and work for the CPS, who decide whether the person should be charged with a criminal offence and whether the case should go to court.

In some situations the alleged offender may not be capable of consenting. Here, the health care professional should consult with colleagues and others involved in the person's life and consider what is necessary for their health and well-being, and what will be in their best interests. In such circumstances the discussions concerning the decision-making process must be fully documented.

Victims of crime who have learning disabilities also need their disability to be identified.

In a large-scale sexual abuse inquiry by several police forces, the police contacted former attendees of several residential schools by letter. The former pupils were all now adults in their twenties and the police were not aware that some of them had learning disabilities. Mr B received one of these letters. As he was unable to read, his care worker read the letter. The letter was asking Mr B if he was aware of any abuse taking place when he was at school. The care worker did not feel confident to deal with this matter on her own and so contacted a social worker at the local community team for adults with learning disabilities. The social worker contacted the clinical psychologist for learning disability services due to her experience in working with sexual abuse victims. The psychologist visited Mr B at his home and explained that he had been sent a letter by the police and what was being asked. Mr B said he had not been abused and did not know anything about it. However, the psychologist continued to visit Mr B at home as he may want to ask more questions about the letter, may have been disturbed by it or may have been denying past abuse. When the psychologist paid a second visit, Mr B said he wanted to see her in private and then disclosed a catalogue of abuse that had taken place over a number of years. With Mr B's consent the psychologist contacted the police who were keen to interview Mr B. His learning disability was explained so that the police were aware that they needed to make special provision for the interview.

Mr B was known to services and therefore information regarding his learning disability could be communicated to the police. Mr A, however, was not known. When he was taken to the police station the custody officer raised concerns and discussed these with the court liaison nurse. However, the method they used was similar to that employed in the studies reviewed by McBrien (2003). A criticism of these methods is that they have varying results and do not provide for an immediate formal diagnostic assessment. Thus some form of quick screening procedure is needed that is reliable and valid. Unfortunately there are no well-established methods currently available for non-psychologists to administer. Some have used the Ammons Quick Test (Ammons and Ammons 1966). This is a quick and easy test to apply and does provide an estimate of IQ. However, it is very dated and has not been restandardized or updated. Thus IQ estimates may now be less reliable than desired. However, the test is only likely to be used if custody officers and interviewing officers have some skills in identifying the presence of learning disability in the first place. This involves checking that the person retains and understands information given, and when interviewing does not rely on yes/no responses. Police officers need to be aware that people with learning disabilities have a tendency to answer yes/no questions in the affirmative and may also fail to disclose their disability.

When a person is placed under arrest, the custody officer tells them their rights. In addition to their right to remain silent, the person also has the right to consult a solicitor, the right to have somebody informed of their arrest and detention, the right to consult a copy of the *Codes of Practice* (Home Office 1995) and to obtain a copy of the custody record. After advising detainees of their rights the custody officer gives them a leaflet explaining their rights. It is here that the police should check a detainee's understanding. The liaison nurse or social worker can play a significant supporting role here. If they are inexperienced in the field of learning disability they can contact the local community service for people with learning disabilities for further advice and support. This is important because people with learning disabilities may not understand the right to remain silent. The leaflet explaining their rights while being detained is complicated and cannot be understood by most detainees. People with learning disabilities are particularly disadvantaged as their reading skills are also limited or absent. Due to memory difficulties the information is not retained and therefore not comprehended. It is probably not encoded because it is too complicated (Gudjonsson 1992). Thus, it is only if the learning disability is identified that people with learning disabilities receive fair treatment.

Mr A was offered treatment as an alternative to continuing his journey through the criminal justice system. However, after attending four sessions with a clinical psychologist, where he did not engage, he refused further sessions and ended the treatment. This information was fed back to the court liaison service, but Mr A had broken contact with them. A few weeks later a solicitor in another jurisdiction contacted the psychologist who formally assessed and diagnosed Mr A's learning disability. Mr A had been arrested and charged for another offence but this time his learning disability had not been identified. Thus the police, without anyone else present, interviewed Mr A. It was the solicitor, who was not appointed until

after the police interview, who identified possible learning disability and made further enquiries.

Being interviewed by the police

In the UK the Police and Criminal Evidence Act (PACE) *Codes of Practice* (Home Office 1995) have important provisions for interviewing special groups. They state: 'A juvenile or a person who is mentally disordered or handicapped, whether suspected or not, must not be interviewed or asked to provide or sign a written statement in the absence of the appropriate adult unless . . . delay will involve an immediate risk of harm to persons or serious loss of or damage to property.' Thus, it is important that the police are aware that the person has a learning disability so that PACE is not violated. When Mr A was arrested for the second time his learning disability was not identified and therefore PACE guidance was not followed. When this happens the defence lawyers may argue that the statement produced from the interview with the detainee is not admissible in evidence.

The person chosen to fulfil the appropriate adult role may be a relative or 'someone who has experience of dealing with mentally disordered or mentally handicapped persons but is not a police officer or employed by the police'. Thus professionals who work with people with learning disabilities may fulfil this role. The police should inform the appropriate adult that he or she is not simply acting as an observer but: 'first, to advise the person being questioned and to observe whether or not the interview is being conducted properly and fairly, and secondly, to facilitate communication with the person being interviewed'. In order to assist, the appropriate adult needs to be familiar with the detainee's expressive and receptive communication skills and be aware of their response style to open and progressively closed questions.

In the UK, detained suspects are told their rights again prior to being interviewed and the interview is audio-recorded.

Mr C was interviewed by two police officers about allegations concerning sexual acts with underage children. Mr C was able to tell the police that he had learning disabilities and they contacted the clinical psychologist who had been working with him. They asked the psychologist to sit in on the interview and advise on their questioning. Mr C's sister agreed to act as appropriate adult and his social worker was also in attendance. After introductions and checking Mr C understood his rights the police began interviewing him about the allegations. As these unfolded his sister became agitated and then burst out and called Mr C a range of expletives and needed to be restrained by a police officer and social worker and removed from the interview room. The interview then proceeded but the psychologist had to continue in the role of appropriate adult for Mr C as the social worker had to stay with his sister. Clearly on this occasion Mr C's sister was not able to fulfil the role of appropriate adult for her brother.

Research on the role of the appropriate adult (Medford *et al.* 2003) found that they contribute very little to police interviews.

For example, Mr D was arrested following allegations of rape. The police followed PACE as Mr D was blind but they had not identified that he also had learning disabilities. He was interviewed five times by the police on the same day with very short breaks between the interviews. His appropriate adult was his support worker. During these interviews the appropriate adult made one intervention, which was to correct a police officer's spelling of the detainee's name. Medford *et al.*'s (2003) study of 501 interviews, of which appropriate adults were present at 347, found that family members contributed more than social workers and volunteers and that their presence had several effects. In the case of adult suspects it increased the likelihood of a legal representative being present and of the legal representative taking a more active role. Also, less interrogative pressure was noted in interviews where an appropriate adult was present.

Victims and witnesses with learning disabilities should also be interviewed with an appropriate adult or registered intermediary present. Mr B, who agreed to be interviewed by the police, asked the psychologist to act as appropriate adult during his interviews with them. This turned out to be important, as the police officers had never interviewed a witness with learning disabilities before. During the interview they asked several leading and closed questions which caused the appropriate adult to intervene. Mr B also had physical difficulties, which caused tiredness. It was the appropriate adult who checked this with Mr B and ended the sessions. Mr B provided new and corroborating

evidence and in particular important evidence that identified the abuser. The police told him that he would most likely be needed as a witness in court. As the matter progressed the appropriate adult for Mr B was also asked to provide a statement on the interviews and was informed that she would also be needed as a witness. This is something that people who take on the role of appropriate adult are often not aware of. It is therefore important that any person who acts in this role should make notes concerning the interview and file them carefully.

Victims of crime and witnesses of crime may be interviewed at the police station, in a special interview suite, at home or elsewhere. The Crown Prosecution Service also has Witness Care Officers who provide a single point of contact for witnesses and support them to give best evidence. Interviews are usually recorded by hand and the police officer writes a statement for the complainant or witness. However, The Youth Justice and Criminal Evidence Act 1999 makes provision for complainant and witness interviews to be video-recorded. Also a Registered Intermediary may be appointed to support the witness throughout any interviews and when giving evidence in court. They can help the witness understand and answer questions and may advise on the best way for the victim to give evidence; such as through a video link or by the use of screens in open court. A Registered Intermediary is a professional such as a speech and language therapist or a clinical psychologist who has undergone special training. The final decision as to whether a Registered Intermediary can be used to help in court is made by the judge or magistrate.

Being charged

Once the police have finished interviewing a suspect they will consider what action needs to be taken. If the police do not think that the person arrested and interviewed carried out the crime they will release them. If they think the suspect did commit the crime and it is a first and minor offence the police may give the suspect a formal caution. This involves the police talking to the suspect about the crime and about what might happen if they do it again. The term 'being cautioned' means that the suspect is not charged and will not have to attend court. However, the police keep a note of the offence on file.

If the police decide they need to make further enquiries they may let the suspect go home on police bail. This means that they will have to return to the police station on another day. However, if the crime the person is suspected of is serious and may place others at risk then the suspect may be detained further. A suspect can be held for interviewing for six to eight hours. If the interviewing officers need more time, the case has to be reviewed by an inspector. The inspector can extend the period of detention up to 24 hours. Then, after further review, a superintendent can extend the period for a further 12 hours. Thereafter the police must release the suspect on bail, charge them or seek a further period of detention from a magistrate. Whatever action the police take, the person with a learning disability will need help and support in understanding what is happening.

If the police feel they have enough evidence they will present this to the CPS who decide which criminal offences the suspect should be charged with. Once the decision has been made to prosecute a suspect the police will charge the suspect. The police will tell the person, 'I am charging you with [and then tell them the offence].' Once charged the person will have their fingerprints and a photograph taken. Depending on the seriousness of the crime the person may be released on bail or detained further on remand at a prison until the matter comes to court. Throughout this process a person with a learning disability will need some support. They will need things explained to them in terms they can understand and they also may need emotional support.

Reliability of statements

If the police and the Crown Prosecution Service decide to take a matter to court, defendant, complainant and witness statements will be produced and relied upon. Of concern is the reliability of statements made by people with learning disabilities. Such people are generally more suggestible than people of average ability. This is due to their impaired memory capacity, which makes them more vulnerable to suggestibility, acquiescence and confabulation. They are susceptible to suggestion, particularly to giving in to leading questions. Further, they are less able to cope with the uncertainty and expectations of questioning. However, a review of the available evidence concluded that

people with learning disabilities can provide accurate accounts of events they have witnessed when interviewed appropriately (Kebbell and Hatton 1999). The research suggests that people with learning disabilities can provide accurate accounts, particularly when questioned using open questions about central information rather than closed questions about peripheral information.

The police interviewed Mr D for over four hours. In that time there were four breaks, but only for a few minutes at most. His appropriate adult made no interventions regarding the police questioning. During the fifth interview Mr D confessed to rape and the interview was terminated. Mr D's solicitor had concerns about the conduct of the interview and the way that the confession was extracted. He also had concerns about Mr D's level of intellectual functioning. Mr D was formally evaluated by a clinical psychologist and found to have learning disabilities. A psychologist was also appointed to evaluate the recordings of the police interviews. In his evidence, the psychologist showed that Mr D had been consistent in his version of events throughout the interviews. The confession was made finally to an account of events given throughout the interview by the police. He resisted police officers' attempts to discredit his account but then after four hours accepted their account of events. His confession was him saying 'yes' to the interviewing officers' version of events. Thus Mr D was able to resist the officers' attempts to alter his account as he remembered it but could not resist material introduced by them. Hence he became suggestible and acquiescent when questioned about a version of events he did not recall.

Suggestibility has been assessed by the Gudjonsson Suggestibility Scales (GSS) (Gudjonsson 1997). These were developed to assess an individual's response to 'leading questions' and being told their answers are wrong ('negative feedback') when being asked to report a factual event from recall. The original scale was devised as a result of the conceptual framework developed to assess the reliability of evidence by way of psychological procedure in the case of Mary – a woman who had learning disabilities – who was the main witness in a criminal trial (Gudjonsson and Gunn 1982). Gudjonsson (1992) argues that, unlike other tests of suggestibility, the GSS are particularly applicable in legal contexts, such as police interviews with crime witnesses and interrogation of criminal suspects. However, the current version of the scale has significant problems when employed with people who have learning disabilities (see Beail 2002; White and Willner 2005; Willner 2008) and should be used with caution.

Guidance for appropriate adults, Registered Intermediaries and police officers

In order to assist the person with a learning disability the appropriate adult should use their knowledge of the person to help avoid certain hazards in the interview. The police and Registered Intermediaries would also improve the accuracy of the statements they produce by following these guidelines, which have been summarized by Tully and Cahill (1984). Interview participants should avoid:

- the person acquiescing to leading questions which contain a suggestion as to the answer being sought;
- the interviewer using undue pressure, leading the witness to confabulate (filling in parts they had not witnessed or could not recall);
- repeated questioning on a particular point causing the person to guess or deviate from what they had already said in response to open questions; repeated questioning suggests to the interviewee that they have not given the right answer and so they shift in response to this negative feedback and pressure;
- the interviewer offering compromised descriptions to the witness having difficulty recalling peripheral information – for example, if it had been established that a person in a witnessed event was wearing a jacket but not its colour, the interviewer may suggest a sort of colour; however, that colour may fit with facts known to the interviewer and not the witness;
- the interviewer offering limited alternatives to the witness or defendant;
- information given in free recall being ignored because it does not fit with the interviewer's assumption of what happened;
- the interviewer misunderstanding or failing to

check their understanding of the interviewee's responses.

Going to court

In court proceedings the defendant sits in the dock throughout. Prior to the hearing, professionals who have been supporting the defendant need to make some assessment of how the person with learning disabilities will cope in court. This should be discussed with the prosecution or defence lawyers so that they can take any concerns to the judge with any recommendations to help the defendant. This may include someone being close by or sitting by the dock, or frequent breaks to give time for information about the proceedings to be explained to the defendant.

Witnesses go into court to give their evidence when they are called or they may give their evidence under the provisions of the Youth Justice and Criminal Evidence Act 1999. Under this Act the court will make some provision to accommodate witnesses with learning disabilities. This includes the appointment of a Registered Intermediary, video evidence, giving evidence by video link. There are provisions to allow someone who knows the witness well to sit with them during the proceedings. For those who go into open court, screens may be erected to shield them from the defendant and wigs may be removed. For witnesses with learning disabilities the court may provide a separate place to sit and allow the presence of support staff or advocates.

In court, each witness is interviewed by the prosecuting counsel and the defence counsel. A study of court transcripts of cases where the complainant has been a person with a learning disability found that lawyers frequently asked questions containing negatives and double negatives, multiple questions, and questions with complex vocabulary and syntax. Leading and closed questions were also frequently used, especially in cross-examination (Kebbell et al. 2000). Such an approach is not conducive to eliciting the best possible accounts from adult witnesses with learning disabilities. If a Registered Intermediary is appointed then they may point out the difficulties with this style of questioning. However, lawyers will use methods of questioning either to secure a conviction or to get their client off. Thus they will use such questioning styles according to how they think they can enhance or reduce the credibility of the witness. While professionals who support people with learning disabilities may not approve of such tactics, the lawyers' only answer is that they are doing their job.

The judge can have an impact on a lawyer's questioning style and therefore witness accuracy. The judge has a general duty to ensure that the trial is conducted fairly and has the discretion to intervene to stop any questioning that is likely to result in the court being misled. However, a study of court transcripts by O'Kelly *et al.* (2003) found that judges did not intervene to modify the examination process. Indeed they found no differences between the treatment of witnesses with or without learning disabilities. O'Kelly *et al.* argue that judges should intervene to ensure that all witnesses are able to give the most complete and accurate evidence possible.

Learning disability as a mitigating factor

Increasingly, learning disability is being accepted as a mitigating factor in crime. A behaviour or its consequences (*actus rea*) do not define crime; the person's state of mind (*mens rea*) when they engage in the behaviour is also a significant defining factor (such as intention, recklessness and so on). Thus the court may require evidence regarding the defendant's learning disability and its impact on their behaviour. When the person with a learning disability is a victim of crime the court may also need evidence regarding the degree of their learning disability. This is especially the case when a sexual crime has been committed. The trial will therefore involve the evidence of expert and professional witnesses. Expert witnesses are professionals who prepare reports for the court on the instructions of the prosecution or the defence. Professional witnesses are those who know the defendant or victim with learning disabilities through their work and are asked to provide statements or reports or release their case notes to the court. If case notes are required then the solicitor should make a written request for the defence or Crown Prosecution Service to the professional's employer. The professional needs to consider whether releasing the notes would be harmful to their client. If the professional considers

that it would not be in their client's interest then they can refuse to release them. The client also has the right to refuse. However, the lawyer may disagree and apply to the court for an order for them to be released. If this happens the professional and their client would be called to a court hearing to explain why they believe the notes should not be released. The judge will then make an order on the basis of what he or she has heard from the client, the professional and the lawyer. If the judge orders that the notes be released, the professional must do so or be held in contempt of court.

In court proceedings where a decision regarding the person's level of learning disability is to be made, expert testimony may be submitted in evidence. The criteria for the admissibility of expert testimony were stated by Lord Justice Lawton in the case of *R* v. *Turner* (1975), as follows: 'An expert's opinion is admissible to furnish the court with scientific evidence which is likely to be outside the experience and knowledge of the judge or jury.' Commonly, scientific evidence likely to be outside the judge's or jury's experience or knowledge concerns the assessment of intelligence and social functioning by a clinical psychologist. This expert evidence may be supported by evidence from professionals who work with the client. They are able to inform the court on the person's history and current day-to-day functioning and support needs.

In the past the courts have held very rigid views on what constitutes mental impairment. In the case of *R* v. *Masih* (1986), expert testimony was given regarding IQ. In this case the defendant's IQ was found to be 72, which falls at the lower end of the 'borderline' range. In Lord Lane's view, expert testimony in a borderline case was not as a rule necessary and was therefore excluded. The judgment went on to state that an IQ of 69 or below was required for a defendant to be formally classified as being 'significantly mentally impaired' (Gudjonsson 1992). This judgment was made according to a very rigid definition of mental impairment with no account being taken of test error or the individual's level of social functioning. Clinical psychologists should always report the range within which the person's IQ falls and not a single figure. This makes an allowance for individual variation in test performance from day to day and for errors made in testing. A diagnosis of learning disability should also only be made when an examination of social functioning (adaptive behaviour) is also made. Today the courts place less reliance on cut-off scores such as 70 and have broadened the criteria for admissibility of psychological evidence.

In the case of *R* v. *Raghip* (1991) the Court of Appeal placed less reliance on arbitrary cut-off IQ scores and recognized the importance of evidence from other psychological tests and areas of functioning. These may include assessments of the person's social and moral reasoning, memory, suggestibility, acquiescence and tendency to confabulate. The psychologist may also screen for any mental health problems and advise on whether a psychiatric opinion is needed. Where mental health difficulties are apparent, the lawyer may seek the opinion of a psychiatrist. This may be important, as there are provisions under the Mental Health Act 1983 and 2007 to detain and treat offenders who have learning disabilities. The court may also hear evidence regarding the potential risk of future offending. This would be established by an expert in risk assessment in relation to offending (for a discussion see Johnson 2002 and Lindsay and Beail 2004).

Expert evidence may be heard to establish facts outside the experience or knowledge of the jury. Thus information on intelligence as measured on a fully standardized intelligence test such as the Wechsler Adult Intelligence Scale-IV would be admissible but not opinion on whether someone is mentally impaired or learning disabled. Therefore, the final decision as to whether a person has a learning disability can only be taken by the court. However, in *R* v. *Robbins* (1988) the Court of Appeal decided that the direction of the judge permitting the jury to decide whether the complainant had a severe mental impairment without expert evidence was unobjectionable. Therefore, expert evidence may not always be sought.

Disposal: custody or diversion

People with learning disabilities are vulnerable and would be especially so in an institution such as a prison. *The Reed Report* (Department of Health 1992) stated that offenders with mental disorder should be diverted from prison and that those with learning

disabilities should as far as possible be placed in the community rather than in institutional settings. The report went on to state that the conditions should be of no greater security than is justified by the degree of danger the offender presents to themselves and others – hence the need for skills in risk assessment and management.

Within services for people with learning disabilities judgements are often made regarding the alleged offender's state of mind without involving the criminal justice system. For example, professional staff supporting a person with a learning disability who has committed an act that could be seen as an offence may decide that the person did not know that what they did was illegal, or could not anticipate the consequences of their behaviour. As such, many acts which would normally be seen as criminal are seen as 'challenging behaviour'. In such circumstances the police are often not contacted. There are also some police forces that do not proceed with a prosecution against a person with learning disabilities because formal assessment suggests that it is unlikely that they had *mens rea* for the alleged offence or would not be able to plead. However, the frequency of this is unknown. There are also areas where the police work in liaison with health and social care professionals to divert alleged offenders away from the criminal justice system towards a needs assessment and development of a package providing management and treatment in the community or in special provision.

In other cases the matter does go to court. However, there is very little data on the frequency with which this occurs. If the defendant is found guilty the court has several options. They could send the offender to prison, but if evidence is presented on the learning disability and mental state then the court may alternatively use the provisions under the Mental Health Act to detain the person for assessment and/or treatment.

There are now numerous services which specialize in the in-patient assessment and treatment of offenders with learning disabilities (see Lindsay *et al.* 2002; Taylor *et al.* 2002 for examples). However, the assessment of risk may be such that the court may request further reports from professionals and the probation service to establish whether the offender could be rehabilitated in the community. There is some evidence emerging to show that offenders with learning disabilities can be treated and managed successfully in the community. This will involve a package of support from a multi-disciplinary team (Clare and Murphy 1998) including individual or group therapy such as psychodynamic psychotherapy (Beail 2001) or cognitive behavioural therapy (Murphy *et al.* 2007; Lindsay 2009). However, despite recommendations for community placements with treatment, the evidence base for this approach is in its early days (Beail 2004; Lindsay 2009).

Victims of crime may also need support and treatment after court appearances. One of the difficulties for victims is that the treatment process for the post-traumatic stress they may experience may be seen as interference to their recall of the actual event. Thus, many victims have to wait until after the trial before they can undergo active psychological treatment. After Mr B had finished being interviewed by the police he was very distressed by the experience and wanted to talk to someone about it. Fortunately the police provided supportive counselling up until the trial but advised that active psychotherapy should not start until afterwards. A wider range of psychological therapies are now available to people with learning disabilities but the evidence base is still in its infancy (Beail 2003, 2004; Prout and Nowak-Drabik 2003; Willner 2005).

Exercise 20.1

The local police have contacted you. They have a young man at the police station that they would like to question regarding certain offences. However, they are concerned that the man may have learning disabilities, as he does not seem to understand what they are saying to him.

How can you assist the police in the short term to determine whether the young man may have a learning disability?

If he has a learning disability, what is he entitled to under PACE?

What factors do those supporting him during a police interview need to be aware of?

What alternatives to continuing in the criminal justice system exist in your area for people with learning disabilities?

One of the witnesses to the alleged crime is known to local learning disability services. What support can you provide locally and what other supports may be available to them?

Conclusion

The focus of this chapter has been the support needs of people with learning disabilities when they come into contact with the criminal justice system. For most people, being accused of a crime or being a victim or witness to crime is a stressful experience. For people with learning disabilities it is even more so. This has been officially recognized and the criminal justice system is beginning to respond. PACE recognized the vulnerability of people with learning disabilities and made provision for support during interviews. Also, victims' needs are now being addressed under the Youth Justice and Criminal Evidence Act 1999, the publication of guidance on achieving best evidence (Home Office and Department of Health 2002) and a public policy statement by the Crown Prosecution Service (2009). Booklets with pictures and text reflecting the procedures used by the police and by the courts have been produced to use with people with learning disabilities (Hollins *et al.* 1996). However, the significant issue of identifying those that need support has not been addressed and still needs attention. Key questions still need to be asked:

- Are the police officers in your area given any training in identifying vulnerability factors such as learning disability?
- Do the local police have the support of court liaison nurses and social workers?
- Does the community learning disability team have the capacity to respond to urgent requests for help and support when a person with a learning disability has been arrested or become the victim of a crime?
- Can your service arrange for a formal diagnostic assessment by a clinical psychologist should this be needed?

- Do you have access to psychiatric services to assist with assessment of any mental health needs under the Mental Health Act 1983 and 2007?

Whether we are dealing with offenders, victims or witnesses there will be resource issues. If the police want to carry out interviews, are any members of the service willing and able to act as appropriate adults? Is there a Registered Intermediary in your area? Can you provide resources to support victims, offenders or witnesses through the court process? Can you put together packages of support to provide management and treatment for any offenders diverted from a custodial sentence? Also, can you provide the victims of crime and the witnesses of crime with counselling and psychotherapy to address any post-traumatic reaction? These are the practical questions commissioners, service managers and providers need to ask and to assess themselves on.

The research base on people with learning disabilities and the criminal justice system is growing and has done so considerably in the last few years. There have been several special issues of journals devoted to forensic issues and learning disabilities and a book devoted to offenders with learning disabilities has also been published (Lindsay *et al.* 2004). This growing literature has largely focused on offenders and less so on victims and witnesses. But despite the growth in research there are still more questions than answers and research endeavours must continue to help inform clinical practice and social care.

References

Ammons, R.R. and Ammons, C.H. (1966) The quick test (QT) provisional manual, *Psychological Reports*, 11: 111–61.

Beail, N. (2001) Recidivism following psychodynamic psychotherapy amongst offenders with intellectual disabilities, *The British Journal of Forensic Practice*, 3: 33–7.

Beail, N. (2002) Interrogative suggestibility, memory and intellectual disability, *Journal of Applied Research in Intellectual Disabilities*, 15: 129–37.

Beail, N. (2003) What works for people with mental retardation: critical commentary on cognitive-behavioural and psychodynamic psychotherapy research, *Mental Retardation*, 41: 468–72.

Beail, N. (2004) Approaches to the evaluation of outcomes in work with developmentally disabled offenders, in W.R. Lindsay, J.L. Taylor and P. Strurmey (eds) *Offenders with Developmental Disabilities*. Chichester: Wiley.

Beail, N. and Edwards, W. (2004) Rigidity and flexibility in diagnosing mental retardation in capital cases, *Mental Retardation*, 42: 480–3.

Brown, H., Stein, J. and Turk, V. (1995) The sexual abuse of adults with learning disabilities, *Mental Handicap Research*, 8: 3–24.

Clare, I.C.H. and Murphy, G.H. (1998) Working with offenders or alleged offenders with intellectual disabilities, in E. Emerson, C. Hatton, J. Bromley and A. Caine (eds) *Clinical Psychology and People with Intellectual Disabilities*. Chichester: Wiley.

Crown Prosecution Service (2009) *Supporting Victims and Witnesses with a Learning Disability*. London: CPS Policy Directorate.

Department of Health (1992) *The Reed Report*. London: HMSO.

Gudjonsson, G.H. (1992) *The Psychology of Interrogations, Confessions and Testimony*. Chichester: Wiley.

Gudjonsson, G.H. (1997) *The Gudjonsson Suggestibility Scales Manual*. Hove: Psychology Press.

Gudjonsson, G.H. and Gunn, J. (1982) The competence and reliability of a witness in a criminal court, *British Journal of Psychiatry*, 141: 624–7.

Holland, S. and Persson, P. (2007) *Intellectual Disability in the Victoria Prison System: Characteristics of Prisoners with an Intellectual Disability Released from Prison 2003–2006*. Melbourne: Victoria Department of Justice.

Holland, T., Clare, I.C.H. and Mukhopadhyay, T. (2002) Prevalence of 'criminal offending' by men and women with intellectual disability and the characteristics of 'offenders': implications for research and service development, *Journal of Intellectual Disability Research*, 46(Suppl. 1): 6–20.

Hollins, S., Clare, I.C.H. and Murphy, G.H. (1996) *You're Under Arrest*. London: Gaskell.

Home Office (1995) *Police and Criminal Evidence Act Codes of Practice*. London: The Stationery Office.

Home Office and Department of Health (2002) *Achieving Best Evidence: Guidelines for Vulnerable and Intimidated Witnesses*. London: HMSO.

Johnson, S.J. (2002) Risk assessment in offenders with intellectual disabilities: the evidence base, *Journal of Intellectual Disability Research*, 46(Suppl. 1): 47–56.

Kebbell, M.R. and Hatton, C. (1999) People with mental retardation as witnesses in court, *Mental Retardation*, 3: 179–87.

Kebbell, M.R., Hatton, C. and Johnson, S.D. (2000) *Witnesses with Learning Disabilities in Court: Full Report of Research Activities and Results*. Unpublished manuscript: University of Birmingham.

Lindsay, W.R. (2009) *The Treatment of Sex Offenders Who Have Developmental Disabilities: A Practice Workbook*. Chicester: Wiley-Blackwell.

Lindsay, W.R. and Beail, N. (2004) Risk assessment: actuarial prediction and clinical judgement of offending incidents and behaviour for intellectual disability services, *Journal of Applied Research in Intellectual Disabilities*, 17: 229–34.

Lindsay, W.R., Neilson, C.Q., Morrison, F. and Smith, A.H.W. (1998) The treatment of six men with a learning disability convicted of sex offences with children, *British Journal of Clinical Psychology*, 37: 83–98.

Lindsay, W.R., Smith, A.H.W., Law, K., Quinn, A., Anderson, A., Smith, T. *et al.* (2002) A treatment service for sex offenders and abusers with intellectual disability: characteristics of referrals and evaluation, *Journal of Applied Research in Intellectual Disabilities*, 15: 166–74.

Lindsay, W.R., Taylor, J.L. and Sturmey, P. (eds) (2004) *Offenders with Developmental Disabilities*. Chichester: Wiley.

McBrien, J. (2003) The intellectually disabled offender: methodological problems in identification, *Journal of Applied Research in Intellectual Disabilities*, 16: 95–106.

Medford, S., Gudjonsson, G.H. and Pearse, J. (2003) The efficacy of the appropriate adult safeguard during police interviewing, *Legal and Criminological Psychology*, 8: 253–66.

Murphy, G., Powell, S., Guzman, A.M. and Hayes, S.J. (2007) Cognitive behavioural treatment of men with intellectual disabilities and sexually abusive behaviour: a pilot study, *Journal of Intellectual Disability Research*, 51: 902–12.

O'Kelly, C.M.E., Kebbell, M.R., Hatton, C. and Johnson, S.D. (2003) Judicial intervention in court cases involving witnesses with and without learning disabilities, *Legal and Criminological Psychology*, 8: 229–40.

Prout, H.R. and Nowak-Drabik, K.M. (2003) Psychotherapy with persons who have mental retardation: an evaluation of effectiveness, *American Journal of Mental Retardation*, 108: 82–93.

Taylor, J.L., Novaco, R.W., Gilmer, B. and Thorne, I. (2002) Cognitive-behavioural treatment of anger intensity in offenders with intellectual disabilities, *Journal of Applied Research in Intellectual Disabilities*, 15: 151–65.

Talbot, J. (2008) *No one Knows: Experiences of the Criminal Justice System by Persons with Learning Disabilities and Difficulties*. London: Prison Reform Trust.

Tully, B. and Cahill, D. (1984) *Police Interviewing of the Mentally Handicapped: An Experimental Study*. London: The Police Foundation.

White, R. and Willner, P. (2005) Suggestibility and salience in people with intellectual disabilities: an experimental critique of the Gudjonsson Suggestibility Scale, *Journal of Forensic Psychiatry and Psychology*, 16(4): 638–50.

WHO (World Health Organization) (1992) *ICD-10: International Classification of Diseases and Related Health Problems*, 10th revision. Geneva: WHO.

Willner, P. (2005) The effectiveness of psychotherapeutic interventions for people with learning disabilities, *Journal of Intellectual Disability Research*, 49: 445–8.

Willner, P. (2008) Memory as an artefact in the assessment of suggestibility, *Journal of Intellectual Disability Research*, 52: 318–26.

Wilson, C. and Brewer, N. (1992) The incidence of criminal victimisation of individuals with intellectual disability, *Australian Psychologist*, 27: 114–17.

Independence, reciprocity and resilience

Peter Goward and Linda Gething

21

Introduction

This chapter argues that the modern era's emphasis on scientific knowledge has inadvertently disadvantaged certain sections of society, most notably those people with a learning disability. Within this context people are seen as vulnerable and at risk, thus overlooking their capacities, talents and ability to survive adversity. Using examples from the lived experiences of Sophie, John and Jo-boy, the different types of protection that accrue from daily living and contribute to a sense of resilience are explored. Importantly, a link is made between putative differences, positive experiences, self-esteem and resilience. Using examples of 'parenting' the chapter closes by identifying reciprocity, the ability to 'give' as well as 'take', as a means through which such positive experiences can be socially generated.

One of the key features of the modern era is a collective faith in science and certainty. Modernity's central quest is to find out the true and indisputable facts about things. If science cannot immediately discern the meaning then the answer is to look harder, with increasingly complex instruments. In many cases this stance has proved immensely successful and rendered enormous benefits. We, and I suspect you, are very grateful that biologists took the time to painstakingly dissect the human body to understand better how it functions, that medical scientists began to understand disease and provide inoculations and treatments, that public health pioneers mapped out the pattern of illness around the 'Broad Street' pump that led to better public health, and that finally the mysteries of DNA and the genetic code are being broken. As students in the health and social care arena you will have first-hand experience of the effects of the modernist allegiance to science and quantification in such things as quality assurance mechanisms, wherein the assumption is that benchmarks and standards inevitably lead to quality care.

> ### Exercise 21.1
>
> Identify five ways in which science has had a beneficial effect on your health and well-being.
>
> Identify five ways in which you think science has negatively affected how you live your life.

The theories and notions that have underpinned illness and vulnerability were, and to some extent still are, hugely consequential to our capacity to conceptualize and deliver treatment, care and support. For example, Darwin's theories on natural selection contributed to the idea that some people, and indeed some cultures, were superior to others and therefore that some people and collectives were naturally inferior socially, physically or intellectually. The works of Bowlby, Harlow, Freud, Piaget and others generated ideas that appeared to suggest that if a child was not brought up in a certain way, if things did not occur in a prescribed order or if adversity intervened at a crucial phase, then dire consequences would inevitably ensue. Arguably, scientific interventions such as medication and surgery were found to be ineffective for people with intractable, chronic or psychologically/intellectually based 'illness'. When this challenged medical and scientific superiority the 'evidence' was metaphorically 'brushed under the carpet' of sanatoriums, colonies and asylums and the people therein labelled 'at risk' and 'vulnerable'.

The past experience of people with learning disability is clearly illustrated by Ryan and Thomas (1987). They describe the dominant influence of medicine over the lives of many people with learning disability, perceived to be far in excess of any medical problems that they may have presented. This contributed to an ideology of people with learning disability as being sick, helpless and needing to be taken care of. Perceiving people as sick, incurable and dependent has led to behaviour that confirms these perceptions. Hence an expectation of underachievement is likely to compound the problems of people with a learning disability. Changing attitudes is never easy at the best of times and even when it does occur it often moves so slowly that the pace is barely perceptible. Perceptions of people with a learning disability in the past still prevail in whole or in part in contemporary society. The Mencap report *Death by Indifference* (2007) catalogues an appalling and tragic series of events that highlights the dangers of seeing 'us' as different from 'them' that no amount of resilience can counter unaided.

Valuing People Now (Department of Health 2009) is the latest in a line of social and health care policy reforms that incrementally seek to promote equality and enrich the health and well-being of people with difficulties and disabilities. It is sufficient at this point to highlight the ways in which policy can positively impact on the lives of Sophie, John and Jo-boy, helping them feel supported and hence able to exploit and enhance appropriate patterns of resilience and recovery. For example John and Jo-boy, as members of travelling communities, would be keen to see more culturally sensitive services that recognized the need for more wayside stopping places, flexibility in retaining housing while travelling extensively, and a greater degree of understanding as to the needs for education of all travelling children, including those with special needs (Department of Health 2009). Similarly, Sophie would be interested in how she could be helped to be supported to '. . . work, pay taxes, vote, do jury service, have children, and participate in community activities or faith groups' (Department of Health 2009).

Increasingly, feminist and postmodernist challenges have been posed to the all-pervasive centrality of scientific truth and many of the stances that were previously seen as immutable, unchallengeable and 'taken for granted' are now being reappraised. Thus the notion that everyone who has suffered from maternal deprivation, been late with potty training or in any way deviates from the norm will throughout their life suffer the consequences in terms of risk and deficiencies is being increasingly, albeit slowly, replaced by an emphasis on competency and resilience.

The notion of resilience

Resilience is not the polar opposite of risk and therefore a resilient person is not one who has never experienced any difficulty. Rather, a resilient person can be conceptualized as someone who has experienced adversity and not only survived but become more hardy in the process; what Radke-Yarrow *et al.* (1990) refer to in their title as 'hard growing' children. If a person has never been faced with a problem or has never been exposed to any sort of risk then they could not claim to be resilient, for how would they know? This is similar to me not being able to claim that I do not suffer from altitude sickness because I have never been up a mountain.

Facing and overcoming some sort of a problem is therefore an inherent component of resilience and led early theorists to label resilient children as 'invulnerable' and 'invincible' because of their ability to thrive in the face of adversity. While an attractive notion, such children are not, unlike the frying pan, Teflon-coated. Nor are they like the cartoon coyote who tries to capture the roadrunner and in the process gets pulverized by a falling rock but gets back up and is miraculously intact.

Being resilient does not mean that people do not feel pain or that they are inured to suffering but that there are factors that, in a way not yet fully understood, appear to act as buffers that protect a person against 'going under'. This metaphor is apposite as the buoyancy that not going under suggests is evident in the title of Wolin and Wolin's book, *The Resilient Self: How Survivors of Troubled Families Rise Above Adversity* (1993). Similarly, Jacelon (1997: 123) notes that 'resilience is the ability of people to spring back in the face of adversity'; Dyer and McGuiness (1996: 276) define resilience as 'a global term describing a process whereby people bounce back from adversity and go on with their lives'; and finally Richardson (2002: 319) identifies that 'the resiliency process is a life-enriching model that suggests that stressors and change provide growth and increased resilient qualities and protective factors'.

Throughout this chapter we will use the experiences of people with learning disabilities to inform and illustrate various points. Sophie is 23 and a very active member of her self-advocacy group. Her story as told to her group will be used to illustrate sections of this chapter. While her experience is unique to her it may also mirror that of some other people with a learning disability.

Sophie has experienced more than her fair share of adversity. She remembers children making fun and laughing at her in the street. She also remembers children pushing her around and on one occasion she had to go to hospital because a boy had thrown a stone at her and it had cut her eye. However, what she recalls with the most passion is her sadness at not being allowed to play with other children. She spent many hours watching them play through her bedroom window. After the stone-throwing incident her father refused to let her join in their games.

Sophie has thrived in the face of adversity. She has faced her frustration and her experience of loneliness and now has a social network that is not significantly different from her peers. She has a gregarious nature and an infectious laugh that draws people to her like a magnet. However, Sinason (1992) warns us that the smile is often a guise. There are potential dangers of overestimating people's powers of recovery. We should therefore be cautious in allowing the promotion of resilience to lead to overlooking the importance and impact of people's suffering.

The nature of protection

Dyer and McGuiness (1996: 277) observe that the pathway towards becoming resilient is a dynamic and iterative one that 'is highly influenced by protective factors'. Rutter (1985), in discussing the nature of protection, suggests that there may be some difference in the way that differing factors generate protection and thus resilience. The distinction he makes is between prophylactic factors that serve to prevent untoward impact, a little like body armour protects people from bullets, and palliative factors which attempt to minimize and limit the damage following adverse impact. Garmezy (1985), in noting the buffering effect of protective factors, categorizes them under three broad headings: personality or dispositional factors, family-related factors and social or environmental factors. While the categorical systems proposed by Rutter and Garmezy at first sight seem very different they are compatible once the factors themselves are unpackaged.

Dispositional factors

Dispositional factors are the most extensively researched and therefore numerically the greatest category and include such diverse elements as sociability, autonomy, intellectual capacity, creativity, internal locus of control, high energy levels, gender, ordinal position among siblings or being an only child and ethnicity. As all of these factors are to a greater or lesser degree present from birth, or at least from a very early age, they can be equated with the prophylactic qualities described above. They are the factors that help construct a shield, perhaps even before the child is able to purposively affect his or her environment, and as such there is an inbuilt element of chance. I had no control or ability to affect which gender I was born to, how many brothers and sisters came before me, or how outgoing, intelligent or placid I appeared to others. Cederblad *et al.* (1995), who studied nearly 600 people over a 40-year period, place particular emphasis on a placid, 'easy going' temperament and intelligence as being important as children develop into resilient adults. She concludes that this is because they 'increase the coping capacity of an individual . . . If a person is high on sociability . . . he/she can also get a little help from his friends' (p. 18). This would seem to place people who have learning difficulties at a disadvantage.

Exercise 21.3

Try and remember what you were like as a small child or, if you are able, talk to your parents and get their views. How many of the dispositional protective factors did you appear to possess? In what ways, if at all, do you think they helped you in later life?

While Sophie has a learning disability that for many would be sufficient to view her as vulnerable, she also has a range of dispositional protective factors on which to draw. These include that she is female, is sociable and outgoing, has no physical markers of difference and is active and physically robust. However, the potential these have for offering protection is negated by the absence of other, more socially related issues such as prejudice, discrimination and the resultant exclusion and lack of opportunity to make meaningful contributions.

For a person with a learning disability, life's losses may be profound. From birth, issues of loss may affect the person because of the very nature of their difference. Many of the difficulties that people experience are because they are treated differently from the norm and perhaps partly because of their being sheltered from challenging opportunities.

Sophie recounts that when she was 6 her mum died from cancer. She has only known this fact for the past three years. She remembers being sent away on holiday as a treat for her birthday. When she arrived home her mother was gone. When she asked where her mother was she was often told 'she has gone to a better place'. Her family, although loving and caring, had assumed that she was incapable of understanding her mother's death. This is not an uncommon experience for people with a learning disability, as noted by Hollins (1995). She suggests that families comfort themselves with the hope that the person with the learning disability has not noticed. An additional problem created by this conspiracy of silence is that the person with the learning disability has no one to confide in. Sophie says that she did not feel able to talk about her mother's whereabouts or share her feelings of sadness.

The very nature of the learning disability experience exposes individuals to what could be perceived as adverse life events. They experience oppression similar to that experienced by other oppressed groups. This is located in barriers that deny opportunities in family, work, leisure, education and so on (Oliver 1990). Oppression can also take the form of negative labelling, stereotyping, sexual abuse and violence.

However, as we can see from the experiences of Jo-boy, not all is as it seems. His experiences of being a member of an ethnic group which is frequently marginalized illustrates how dispositional protective factors can help maintain self-esteem and create a sense of well-being even though they are outside our control.

This particular day I was getting a lift from Jo, an Irish Traveller who was on his way to pay his road tax when he pulled up at a shop to get his son, Jo-boy, a soft drink. At the same time a small gang of youths was passing and shouted 'Why don't you p . . . off, we don't want dirty filthy f . . . . . pykies around here.' I asked why neither Jo nor Jo-boy seemed perturbed by this unsolicited invective and they explained that they felt the same about the 'Gadje' (members of settled society). From their perspective their dirt was on the outside and could easily be washed off, unlike members of sedentary society whose habits polluted the internal self. Jo-boy, as an example, described how the Gadje saw cats as clean because they licked their fur, but for many Gypsies and Travellers were dirty because they licked their fur with their tongue and so brought pollution into their bodies, unlike hedgehogs who, for very obvious reasons, didn't do much licking with their tongue and so dirt was kept on the outside, thus preserving inner purity.

In this way I was helped to understand how ethnicity and cultural mores could provide dispositional protection even, or especially, in relation to factors that are outside of our choosing or ability to influence. As well as ethnicity being seen as a resilience-promoting factor, similar dynamics can be seen in employment and work-related activities (McLaren and Challis 2009).

Family-related factors

In these factors there is the possibility of interactions that are supportive and helpful in times of adversity and so the protection is of the buffering, palliative kind. Writers such as Beardslee and Podorefsky

(1988), Baldwin *et al.* (1993) Egeland *et al.* (1993), Grant *et al.* (2007) and Mo Yee Lee *et al.* (2009) all note that being required to help and take on responsibility, clear rules and sanctions, shared values and celebrating family events are all significant contributors to the development of resilience in the face of adversity. McCubbin *et al.* (1998) and also Antonovsky and Sourani (1988) observe that family factors are most effective when they work collaboratively rather than in isolation and thus form a unified 'family schema' or 'a sense of coherence'. In supporting this coherent approach Szalacha *et al.* (2007) observe: 'Ironically, in our focus on those aspects likely to be particularly salient in the lives of children of colour, we find that the factors that can protect them from risks associated with perceived discrimination are rooted in race and ethnicity.' Support for this stance can be seen in the following example.

John Finn was a Gypsy Traveller who had learning difficulties and exhibited challenging, impulsive behaviour. Because of some bad experiences with health and social care services his family, like many other Traveller families, avoided contact with the wider community and 'looked after our own [family schema] in a way that fits in with what we does [sense of coherence]'. John had his chores to do and was expected to contribute to the family economy by helping his dad collect scrap. While doing this he functioned as part of the family work unit and, because Traveller communities generally shun waged labour and place less value on literacy and numeracy, he was an accepted and valuable part of the team. Gypsy and Traveller communities are usually closely knit, kin-based collectives but are frequently dispersed across a wide geographical area. So when John 'lost it' as his mum described it and became overly boisterous, or when his family needed some respite, he was taken, along with his own trailer (caravan), to one of his relatives and their family several miles away where he helped them and contributed to their income. Over time this pattern was repeated until eventually John circled back to his 'Ma' who was by now rested and refreshed. At no time during such periods of community respite care was John ever out of contact with his family. He was always within his culture and not exposed to ridicule or culturally insensitive practices and, as with any other family member, when it was his birthday the whole extended community

celebrated with John wherever his 'home' was at the time.

Similarly, Sophie's experiences support the notion that taking on responsibilities and early exposure to helping are all protective and help generate a degree of resilience. After the death of her mother, Sophie lived with her father and two older brothers. They have a very close and loving relationship and have a great influence over her decisions. She will often punctuate her conversations with, 'Well Dad says . . .' or 'Russell doesn't think . . .' or 'David thinks that I should . . .' In many ways she appears to have taken on the traditional female role of housekeeper within the family. She takes great pride in this role and appears to have gained confidence and self-esteem from the skills that she has developed. She will say, 'I make a great cup of tea' and 'Dad says that I can iron a shirt just as good as Mum'. Whenever a conversation involves household duties, Sophie takes the opportunity to boast about her adeptness.

Exercise 21.4

How does your family, however you determine it, require family members to be helpful; set and maintain rules and standards; celebrate significant family milestones such as birthdays?

Try and think of how these things have influenced the way that you are now and imagine how different you would have been if they had not occurred.

Social factors

Of all the protective factors this is the least well described. Although Wamboldt and Wamboldt (1989) discuss the possible impact of myths, stories and customs, this appears to be from a position in which the myths and stories are told by the powerful and successful. The heroism of living a life filled with the potential for ridicule, discrimination, oppression and putative failure, as experienced by many minority groups including those based on ethnicity, religiosity, sexual orientation or physical and intellectual difficulties, has yet to find its way into modern myths and stories. Possibly the only social factor to be given any serious consideration in the bulk of the literature is the presence of alternative caregivers including individuals of significance from outside the family (Luthar and Zigler 1991). Those old enough to remember the film *To Sir with Love* will recall the resilience that Sydney Poitier, as a respected teacher, helped his pupils attain. Younger readers may relate more easily to the similar storylines of films such as *Dangerous Minds*.

Exercise 21.5

Did you ever have someone outside your family who, in some way, helped shape your life? In what ways do you imagine things would be different if they hadn't been there?

Perhaps because the main epistemological thrust for studies into risk and vulnerability has been rooted in medical and developmental psychology, understandably the psychological gaze falls first on the individual and their intrapsychic and interpersonal processes. This may partly account for the lack of overt attention on social protective factors. Also, in the study of children and their development, the salient collective is the family unit and it is not until later that a wider social vista becomes influential and therefore visible in research findings.

However, as the role of health as opposed to illness, and competencies instead of deficiencies, has become more central, then issues concerning social inclusion and connectedness have grown in importance. This is particularly apparent in the work of Griffiths *et al.* (2009) who describe friendships, support networks, community connectedness and access to local community services as being important social factors. Arguably, within the fields of sociology and anthropology, there has been a much richer discussion relating to social influences on health and resilience, including the damaging effects of social exclusion. One of the richest sources of debate is located within the literature on ethnicity and the social construction of difference.

Miri Song (2003), in describing how minority ethnic identities can be constructed, reconstructed and negotiated, identifies that a minority status does not inevitably lead to risk and vulnerability. Protection and resilience are thought to be achieved through

recognizing that power and control are distributed unequally and that by celebrating difference the resultant increase in esteem leads to resilience.

People with learning disabilities have many things in common with people from ethnic minority groups in that both collectives can experience discrimination, disempowerment and yet can also show remarkable resilience in the face of the adversity caused by perceptions of what being different means.

Them and us

Miri Song (2003: 45) writes that 'A distinct ethnic identity is central to a group's efforts to differentiate themselves from other groups.' This idea echoes the work of the Norwegian anthropologist Frederick Barth, who highlighted the importance of 'the ethnic boundary that defines the group, not the cultural stuff that it encloses' (Barth 1969: 15). The notion of a boundary presupposes that there are those who are within the boundary and those who are without. As the boundary is not a physical thing but a socially constructed one it therefore requires regular reiteration of the differences between those inside or outside in order to maintain it. Both Barth and Song focus on race and ethnicity to describe how it is possible for minority groups to gain esteem and cultural kudos through showing resilience in the face of discrimination and oppression. For example, in some young ethnic collectives being 'bad' is seen as 'good' and therefore offers protection through enhancing feelings of belonging to the group, by accentuating the difference between the 'cool' us and them – the prosaic white majority (Song 2003).

Jenkins (1998) draws a parallel between ethnicity and incompetence (learning difficulties) through the shared sense of exclusion by a hegemonic society in that 'Categorisations of incompetence and "racial" categorisations are often dimensions of hierarchical schema of human adequacy and acceptability: as sexual partners, mates, affines, colleagues, neighbours and so on' (Jenkins 1998: 2). Having mates, colleagues and partners is not only something that people usually take for granted but is a means whereby we gain social support in times of trouble. Other chapters in this book describe in more detail some of the positive and negative effects that personal and social networks, culture, leisure and employment have on the lives of people with learning disabilities (see Chapters 24, 26 and 27). Therefore here it is enough to identify that this applies equally to people with learning disabilities. However, this does not mean that if people choose to adopt different ways of associating and different ways of choosing and forming friendships and relationships then this is in some ways inferior or less meaningful than patterns constructed by the social majority.

It is therefore possible for people with learning difficulties to gain the self- and minority group esteem that Song's subjects have by recognizing and reframing difference in a positive way. However, to do this there needs to be a recognition of the power imbalance inherent in Jenkins's notion of a categorization of human adequacy. If higher levels of esteem contribute to a felt sense of resilience then people need the opportunity to gain esteem through positive life experiences.

In Chapter 23 of this book, Llewellyn and McConnell draw our attention to the fact that support is not always supportive as it depends on how it is perceived by the recipient. They describe how 'competence inhibiting' support can take over, thereby undermining confidence and recreating dependence.

To the observer, the interdependency that exists between Sophie and her family is evident. However, this is rarely acknowledged by any of the parties concerned. They exercise control over Sophie while at the same time relying on her contribution to the household. This of course could be, as reflected in the findings of Oakley (1974), the result of a lack of value placed on housework by society in general. But Mitchell (1997) claims that families often find difficulty with the concept of adulthood in their sons and daughters with learning disability.

Giving and receiving care is something that most individuals experience at various stages in their life. Many individuals with learning disability like Sophie find that their experience is unique as many of their relationships throughout their lives can be defined as caring. They are extensively defined by others as dependents, vulnerable, people in need of care and protection. The notion of care can be disabling as the person in receipt of care is often assumed to be passive and dependent (Morris 1993).

Care and protection can present themselves in many guises but on a day-to-day level can often result in things being done for the person, preventing their autonomy and independence. This may arise from negative attitudes and low expectations but it can also arise from benevolence and wanting to be helpful. The consequences are that people are often deterred from taking risks and making mistakes and are also denied the opportunity to achieve success.

Sophie tells us about her schooldays:

I used to go to Nana's for tea after school 'cause Dad was at work. I was really naughty at Nana's; I threw my tea on the floor. She'd get cross and shout at me; that made me more upset. You see I used to see Granddad behind Mr Khan's shop; he was watching me. I knew how to cross the road. I pressed the button and waited for the green man, and then I'd see Granddad and feel really mad.

Any sense of achievement and independence that Sophie felt due to this accomplishment was shattered by seeing her grandfather watching her. Other examples where the sense of achievement is negated are when tasks are 'finished off' by the well-meaning individual. The fastening of the missed button, straightening the slightly crooked tie, putting the last hair in place, and so on . . .

Opportunities to take control and make decisions can also be limited for the person with a learning disability: 'The freedom to exercise choice is seen as a motivating force that assists learning and is vital to the concept of self' (Jackson and Jackson 1998: 22). The disabling effects of limited choice are illustrated in the following personal (LG) experience.

I don't usually arrive early for work. I park my car on a plot of waste land that serves as a car park and is well managed by the very helpful car park attendant who directs us into our spaces so that every square inch of the waste land can be utilized effectively. Last week I arrived uncharacteristically early, the car park was empty; there was no helpful attendant to direct me to my space. Where should I park? The decision was overwhelming and I was left feeling incompetent. This would also have been the conclusion of any bystanders who had the time to watch me shunting backwards and forwards across the car park before I eventually chose a space and left my car – still with the slight doubt that I was not in the right place.

The above examples show that all people including those with 'special needs' need to feel special and gain esteem by doing the very ordinary everyday things others take for granted but which are often placed out of their reach. However, this does not always happen and there are many reasons given for why people with learning disabilities may feel socially excluded and not very special. One that is particularly relevant to the notion of protection and resilience is that relating to 'tragedies'.

Learning disability has often been portrayed as a family 'tragedy'. People comment on the negative picture given to them as prospective parents of a child with Down's syndrome. All parents develop expectations of their child's future based on their own experience. Therefore, at the time of diagnosis of their child's disability parents can find their cosy expectations of becoming mothers and fathers shattered. This can lead them to perceive a child with a learning disability as a 'tragedy' in the family, which can contribute to the child being perceived and treated as different. This difference is not necessarily the positive sense of difference that Miri Song discusses, but a negative one that focuses on passivity, helplessness and incompetence.

Oliver (1990) makes the claim that policies and practices that are concerned with doing things for people, rather than enabling them to do things for themselves, are maintained by the ideology of personal tragedy theory. The language of dependency, impairment, burden and multiple needs represents those who are dependent as less than complete individuals. Disability becomes the sole or major identifier of the person, thus erasing individual traits and abilities and negating the possibility of individual growth, development and change.

Viewing people as useless and unable to take care of themselves decreases the power of individuals to take control over their lives and essentially increase dependency. Morris (2001) observes that those who cannot take care of themselves are not allowed to take their place in society; this inevitably leading to social exclusion. Segregated schools, leisure facilities and further education opportunities are still commonplace and the majority of people with learning disabilities are unemployed and too many live in relative poverty (see Chapter 27).

For many people with learning disabilities the findings of Morris (1993: 164) are a mirror of their experience. She found that the lived experiences of, and the meanings they attach to, social exclusion for young people with learning disabilities was:

- not being listened to;
- having no friends;
- finding it difficult to do the kinds of things that non-disabled young people do, such as go shopping, go to the cinema, go clubbing, etc.;
- being made to feel that they have no contribution to make, that they are a burden;
- feeling unsafe, being harassed and bullied;
- not having control over spending money, not having enough money.

Sophie can certainly identify with the young people in Morris's study. She will begin many sentences with, 'I am not allowed to . . .' Her family, although loving and supportive, have found it difficult to move from protecting her as a child to allowing her to have the independence of an adult. They have struggled to protect and keep her safe while denying her the opportunities to take risks. Families can be crucial in enabling the achievement of independent lives and developing confidence and self-esteem. Although Sophie has a well-defined and valued role within her family this has not been extended beyond the family. The close relationship that she is experiencing appears to be hindering her from becoming a self-reliant individual. She will also make the comment that 'they will miss me if I left home'. Williams and Robinson (2001) demonstrate that many people with learning disabilities take responsibilities within the family and help to support their parents. However, no one appeared to recognize this situation as *mutual* care. An acknowledgement of mutual care would not only bolster self-esteem but begin to redress any power imbalance through the enactment of reciprocity.

The notion of reciprocity

The essence of reciprocity is captured by Finch and Mason (1993) who state that 'Reciprocity provides the glue that holds the community together. I help you,

you help me, and everyone is happy.' The mutuality that is central to reciprocity is echoed by Jordan (1996: 165), who defines it as 'the notion that meaningful communication and economic exchange require respect for the social value of each member, and willingness to obey very basic principles, such as taking turns . . .'. Tones and Green (2004) link reciprocity to health promotion through its ability to generate empowerment, suggesting that empowerment has to do with the relationship between individuals and their [social as well as physical] environment; the relationship is reciprocal.

From the above it can be seen that for reciprocity to make people 'happy' it is dependent on 'taking turns'. Therefore, by inference, not 'taking turns' would make people sad and disempowered.

Exercise 21.6

Have you ever found yourself in a situation in which you are passive and somebody else is doing everything for you, being extremely nice to you and accepting nothing back in return?

How did you feel 'early on' in this period?

Did your feelings change over the course of the event?

How did you think the other person felt?

Sophie describes a situation where she experiences a degree of reciprocity through having a defined role and the feeling that her family would miss her presence. This clearly bolsters her self-esteem by making her feel valued and thus helping her face adversity (i.e. to be resilient). She has the responsibility for most of the household tasks and provides support to her father and brothers. Yet they see themselves as the carers of Sophie. Because she is identified as a victim or burden the emphasis appears to be on her incapacity and not her capabilities. She does not appear to contribute to the decision-making within the household and will constantly defer to her father's and brothers' opinions. This could be seen as a carefully orchestrated attempt by her family to maintain the boundary between 'us' (the family) and 'them' (everyone else) in a laudable but ultimately unhelpful desire to protect Sophie.

However, Margalit (2003) stresses the importance of reciprocity in fostering a wider range of interpersonal relationships and its close relationship with the experience of resilience. The notion of dependency associated with learning disability can create a power imbalance in relationships where reciprocity exists but is not acknowledged or allowed to extend beyond family members. Hudson (2003) notes that overly controlling parental autonomy where the person is not allowed to make decisions, take responsibility and develop a degree of independence and control are factors that can impede the transition to adulthood. Part of being an adult usually includes relationships with people outside of the family, accessing their help and support but also being open, helpful and supportive to them. Thus, for Sophie, the lack of contact with a broader range of people outside the family could be seen as limiting her ability to meet others and form the sorts of friendship and personal relationship that most other young women take for granted, including having a family of their own (see Chapter 23).

The evidence from parenting

As noted earlier, resilience can only exist in the presence of adversity. Feldman (1986) is clear that being born to parents at least one of whom has a learning difficulty is an adverse condition. This finding was the result of studying the interactions of 12 mothers with learning difficulties and their 2-year-old children.

Despite the significant lack of consensus on what behaviours are consistent with a successful meeting of the above criteria, the assumption is that it is the parents' learning difficulties, rather than their socioeconomic status and social exclusion, or a whole range of other factors, that generate such putative dangers. Feldman concludes that such children run the '. . . risk of developmental delay, cultural-familial retardation, maltreatment and neglect . . .' (1986: 777).

Similarly, McGraw and Sturmey, in their study of the difficulties clinicians face in the early detection of parents who have learning difficulties, noted that 'Half of the learning-disabled parents known to services are being reported for abuse and neglect and a quarter are having a child removed from their home' (1993: 113). However, more encouragingly they also found that the 'pregnancies appeared to give them [the parents] a sense of pride and increased self-esteem' (1993: 107). They also observed that while some parents were likely to be more restrictive and punishing, 'some children appear to have resilience to damaging, negative environments and manage to thrive despite their exposure to such poor care' (1993: 110). This they attributed to 'interactions with other people from inside and outside of the home environment', which prompted McGraw and Sturmey to highlight the 'importance of long-term social support for such children and their families' (1993: 110).

This more positive outlook is replicated and enhanced by Tim and Wendy Booth (1998). In recognizing that resilience is generated by (usually iterative) exposure to adversity, they recognized that it is likely to take time to manifest itself, unlike vulnerability which is more immediately evident. The Booths focused their attention on adults who had been brought up by parents of whom at least one had a learning disability. This enabled them to obtain a more balanced picture as the angst generated immediately after adversity had been tempered by time and the opportunity for reflection. Their findings supported the notion that external support was a key factor in developing individual and family resilience and highlighted two aspects in particular. The first was a network of supportive relationships which, in their study, included school friends, helpful neighbours, support workers and people from agencies such as school, church or health care services. The second was a sense of participation and involvement such as working, being part of the local community, belonging to clubs and joining in with ceremonies and celebrations. The key feature in this was that the person felt able to draw support from the community but also that they could contribute something.

Booth and Booth (1998: 98) refer to the combination of the two aspects identified above as 'distributive competence' which 'attests to the fact that parenting is mostly a shared activity and acknowledges the interdependencies that comprise the parenting task'. The notion that a shared approach to managing life's vicissitudes through a network of external support in which those supported are active contributors is an important one. Its importance is not to be measured only by externally judged indicators of success such as whether health visitors think that

parents are 'good enough' or that the child is thriving. It must also be gauged more subjectively by the parents and their offspring on the basis of their happiness, their felt sense of success and the effects on their levels of esteem. This resonates with findings about the quality of life and healthy ageing in people with learning disabilities (see Chapter 34). As discussed earlier, esteem is a crucial mediator between protective factors and resilience; hence anything that lowers self-esteem is unlikely to be maximally protective and therefore would fail to act as an effective buffer between the person, risk and vulnerability.

Many parents reading this will be familiar with the importance of sharing responsibilities and of having support from a range of people in the process of bringing up children. How refreshing it is when a neighbour offers to help do the shopping, how glad we are when a niece babysits, and how comforting when the health visitor assures us that it's normal for a baby to cry. However, in all of this we, as parents, know that we will assume a central role in the child's upbringing and will be able to influence the intensity, volume and nature of the support offered. In this way we can gain a great deal of pleasure and self-esteem when we see our efforts rewarded in the first smile, the first word and the first teetering attempt at walking, and know that we were central to it happening. However, this is not always the case for some parents.

Learning disability is often the sole reason why children are removed from their parents (O'Hara 2003). Parents with a learning disability constantly live with this fear and therefore have additional pressures to those of family life and bringing up children. There can be a complexity of services involved and the possibility of encounters with people who have negative preconceived ideas about people with learning disability being parents is a reality. Guinea (2001) found that the pressure that these parents experienced was primarily environmental and not associated with any lack of competence in parental skills. In her study most parents lived close to their extended families, and they provided much of the external support. Such social support may be positive but, as identified by Llewellyn and McConnell (2002), it can also prevent mothers from creating social networks. They found that many mothers did not have friends or support from their neighbours and were in reality socially isolated.

Conclusion

The White Paper *Valuing People* (Department of Health 2001) reinforces the importance of social inclusion, choice, advocacy, rights and independence. For Bates and Davis (2004) social inclusion means ensuring that people with learning disabilities have access to the same range of social roles and activities as their non-disabled peers.

With today's increasing awareness of human rights, people with a learning disability are challenging the history of exclusion and are establishing their rights as citizens. People First of Canada has found a new way to build a national and international organization in which education is the key strategy (McColl and Bickenbach 1998). Most major towns and cities in the UK have an established People First group. Such groups are speaking to university students, professionals, employers, government officials and families about their experience of discrimination and the changes that need to occur. They are also participating in research and speaking at conferences. A key to their struggle is to replace the old patterns of exclusion and segregation with the right to social inclusion and participation.

Goodley (2000) states that this movement of self-advocacy captures resilience in the face of adversity. People with a learning disability are speaking for themselves and are challenging the labels that define them as incapable. As Goodley confirms, 'they are not passive recipients of oppression, they are active resilient social members'. In a similar vein, Masten and Powell (2007) reach the conclusion that 'resilience usually arises from the operation of ordinary adaptive processes, rather than rare or extraordinary ones . . .'.

Sophie has all the hopes and dreams of many young women including being able to have a job, to have somewhere nice to live, to get married and have children. Through the telling of her story she has demonstrated resilience, particularly as much of the power and control in her life is not within her command. John and Jo-boy will continue to be part of a rich and supportive community and in doing so will contribute meaningfully to their community's resilient way of life.

Hopefully these stories, and the countless others that have never been captured, alongside the academic legitimation provided by a range of leading academics, will provide an impetus for future practitioners and researchers to carry on exploring the parameters of 'hard lives worth living'.

References

Antonovsky, A. and Sourani, T. (1988) Family sense of coherence and family adaptation, *Journal of Marriage and the Family*, 50: 79–92.

Baldwin, A.L., Baldwin, C., Kasser, T. *et al.* (1993) Contextual risk and resiliency during late adolescence, *Development and Psychopathology*, 5: 741–61.

Barth, F. (1969) *Ethnic Groups and Boundaries: The Social Organisation of Cultural Difference*. London: George Allen & Unwin.

Bates, P. and Davis, F.A. (2004) Social capital, social inclusion and services for people with learning disabilities, *Disability and Society*, 19(3): 195–207.

Beardslee, B. and Podorefsky, D. (1988) Resilient adolescents whose parents have serious affective and other psychiatric disorders: importance of self-understanding and relationships, *American Journal of Psychiatry*, 145(1): 63–9.

Booth, T. and Booth, W. (1998) Risk, resilience and competence: parents with learning difficulties and their children, in R. Jenkins (ed.) *Questions of Competence*. Cambridge: Cambridge University Press.

Cederblad, M., Dahlin, L., Hagnell, O. and Hansson, K. (1995) Intelligence and temperament as protective factors for mental health: a cross-sectional and prospective epidemiological study, *European Archives of Psychiatry and Clinical Neuroscience*, 245: 11–19.

Department of Health (2001) *Valuing People: A New Strategy for Learning Disability for the 21st Century*. London: Department of Health.

Department of Health (2009) *Valuing People Now: A New Three-year Strategy for Learning Disabilities*. London: Department of Health.

Dyer, J. and McGuiness, T. (1996) Resilience: analysis of the concept, *Archives of Psychiatric Nursing*, X(5): 276–82.

Egeland, B., Carlson, E. and Sroufe, L. (1993) Resilience as process, *Development and Psychopathology*, 5: 517–28.

Feldman, M. (1986) Research on parenting by mentally retarded persons, *Psychiatric Clinics of North America*, 9(4): 777–96.

Finch, J. and Mason, J. (1993) *Negotiating Family Responsibilities*. London: Routledge.

Garmezy, N. (1985) Stress resistant children: the search for protective factors, *Journal of Child Psychology and Psychiatry*, book supplement No. 4. Oxford: Pergamon.

Goodley, D. (2000) *Self-advocacy in the Lives of People with Learning Difficulties*. Buckingham: Open University Press.

Grant, G., Ramcharan, P. and Flynn, M. (2007) Resilience in families with children and adult members with intellectual disabilities: tracing elements of a psycho-social model, *Journal of Applied Research in Intellectual Disabilities*, 20: 563–75.

Griffiths, R., Horsfall, J., Moore, M., Lane D., Kroon, V. and Langdon, R. (2009) Building social capital with women in a socially disadvantaged community, *International Journal of Nursing Practice*, 15(3): 172–84.

Guinea, S.M. (2001) Parents with a learning disability and their views on the support received: a preliminary study, *Journal of Learning Disabilities*, 5(1): 43–56.

Hollins, S. (1995) Managing grief better: people with developmental disabilities, *The Habilitative Mental Healthcare Newsletter*, 14(3).

Hudson, B. (2003) From adolescence to young adulthood: the partnership challenge for learning disability services in England, *Disability and Society*, 18(3): 259–76.

Jacelon, C. (1997) The trait and process of resilience, *Journal of Advanced Nursing*, 25(1): 123–9.

Jackson, N. and Jackson, E. (1998) Choice-making for people with a learning disability, *Learning Disability Practice*, 1(3): 22–5.

Jenkins, R. (1998) Culture, classification and (in)competence, in R. Jenkins (ed.) *Questions of Competence*. Cambridge: Cambridge University Press.

Jordan, B. (1996) *A Theory of Poverty and Social Exclusion*. Cambridge: Polity Press.

Lee, M., Greene, G., Hsu, K., Lisw, A., Lisw, D., Fraser, J. *et al.* (2009) Utilizing family strengths and resilience: integrative family and systems treatment with children and adolescents with severe emotional and behavioral problems, *Family Process*, 48(3): 395–416.

Llewellyn, G. and McConnell, D. (2002) Mothers with learning difficulties and their support networks, *Journal of Intellectual Disability Research*, 46(1): 17–34.

Luthar, S. and Zigler, E. (1991) Vulnerability and competence, *American Journal of Orthopsychiatry*, 61(1): 6–22.

McColl, M.A. and Bickenbach, J.E. (1998) *Introduction to Disability*. London: Saunders.

McCubbin, H., Futrell, J., Thompson, E. and Thompson, A. (1998) Resilient families in an ethnic and cultural context in H. McCubbin, E. Thompson, A. Thompson and J. Futrell (eds) *Resiliency in African-American Families*. Thousand Oaks, CA: Sage.

McGraw, S. and Sturmey, P. (1993) Identifying the needs of parents with learning disabilities: a review, *Child Abuse Review*, 2: 101–17.

McLaren, S. and Challis, C. (2009) Resilience among men

farmers: the protective roles of social support and sense of belonging in the depression-suicidal ideation relation, *Death Studies*, 33: 262–76.

Margalit, M. (2003) Resilience model among individuals with learning disabilities: proximal and distal influences, *Learning Disability Research and Practice*, 18(2): 82–6.

Masten, A. and Powell, J. (2007) A resilience framework for research, policy and practice, in S. Luthar (ed.) *Resilience and Vulnerability: Adaptation in the Context of Childhood Adversities*. New York: Cambridge University Press.

Mencap (2007) *Death by Indifference*. London: Mencap.

Mitchell, P. (1997) The impact of self-advocacy on families, *Disability and Society*, 12(1): 43–56.

Morris, J. (1993) *Independent Lives*. London: Macmillan.

Morris, J. (2001) Social exclusion and young disabled people with high levels of support needs, *Critical Social Policy*, 21(2): 161–83.

Oakley, A. (1974) *Sociology of Housework*. Oxford: Blackwell.

O'Hara, J. (2003) Parents with learning disabilities: a study of gender and cultural perspectives in East London, *British Journal of Learning Disabilities*, 31: 18–24.

Oliver, M. (1990) *The Politics of Disablement*. London: Macmillan Press.

Radke-Yarrow, M. and Sherman, T. with the collaboration of Mayfield, A. and Stilwell, J. (1990) Hard growing: children who survive, in J. Rolf, A.S. Masten, D. Cicchetti, K.H. Neutchterlein and S. Weinstraut (eds) *Risk and Protective Factors in the Development of Psychopathology*. Cambridge: Cambridge University Press.

Richardson, G. (2002) The metatheory of resilience and resiliency, *Journal of Clinical Psychology*, 58(3): 307–21.

Rutter, M. (1985) Resilience in the face of adversity, *British Journal of Psychiatry*, 147: 598–611.

Ryan, J. and Thomas, F. (1987) *The Politics of Mental Handicap*. London: Free Press.

Sinason, V. (1992) *Mental Handicap and the Human Condition*. London: Free Association Books.

Song, M. (2003) *Choosing Ethnic Identity*. Cambridge: Polity Press.

Szalacha, L., Erkut, S., Coll, C., Fields, J., Alarcon, D. and Ceder, I. (2003) Perceived discrimination and resilience, in S.S. Luthar (ed.) *Resilience and Vulnerability-Adaptation in the Context of Childhood Adversities*. Cambridge: Cambridge University Press.

Tones, K. and Green, J. (2004) *Health Promotion: Planning and Strategies*. London, Sage.

Wamboldt, F. and Wamboldt, S. (1989) *Family Myths: Psychotherapy Implications*. New York: Haworth Press.

Williams, V. and Robinson, C. (2001) 'He will finish up caring for me': people with learning disability and mutual care, *British Journal of Learning Disabilities*, 29: 56–62.

Wolin, S.J. and Wolin, S. (1993) *The Resilient Self: How Survivors of Troubled Families Rise above Adversity*. New York: Villard Books.

22

Personalizing learning disability services

Martin Stevens

In a remarkably short space of time, personalization has moved from being a term mainly associated with website design (see, e.g. Bonnett, 2001) to occupying a place at the very heart of emergent British social work policy, philosophy and even legislation.

(Ferguson 2007: 388)

Introduction

Personalization of public services has been a key goal of policy for much of the life of the Labour government since it was elected in 1997. This chapter will cover aspects of personalization in relation to social care services for adults with learning disabilities. To set the scene, the chapter starts with a discussion of definitions of personalization. This is followed by a brief outline of the general policy backdrop to personalization, which includes the role of 'choice' in public services. The emergence of 'cash for care' schemes, in which people are given money in order to purchase care services, is described and some of the benefits and drawbacks evidenced in research and from the wider literature are discussed. Personalization has been thought potentially to produce increased risk of abuse by giving more choice and control over who provides services. Consequently the degree to which safeguarding practice and policy (see also Chapter 16) plays in developing personalized services is discussed.

A critical perspective on specific policy around people with learning disabilities follows. Particular issues are emerging around developing personalized approaches for the sizeable minority of people with learning disabilities whose behaviour can be seen as difficult or challenging. 'Person-centred planning' is one of the major approaches promoted by the Department of Health as a means to develop support packages for people with learning disabilities. We describe this approach and present some of the

evidence and debates it has generated. Despite the challenges presented, potential benefits of developing more personalized approaches are given throughout the chapter.

Definitions of personalization

Ferguson (2007) notes that it is difficult to define personalization beyond a superficial level as there is no detailed or precise definition. The superficial definition relates to individualized approaches to developing responses to people's needs and increasing their choice and control. However, it is also linked to an increase in personal responsibility for choosing and managing support services. The Social Care Institute for Excellence's (SCIE) 'rough guide' to personalization (Carr and Dittrich 2008) gives the following description, which includes these elements:

> Personalisation means starting with the **individual as a person** with strengths and preferences who may have a network of support and resources, which can include family and friends. They may have their own funding or be eligible for state funding. Personalisation reinforces the idea the individual is best placed to know what they need and how those needs can best be met. It means that people can be **responsible for themselves** and **can make their own decisions** about what they require, but that they should also have information and support to enable them to do so.
>
> (SCIE 2008: 3, emphasis added)

This sense of promoting individual responsibility as well as providing more choice over services is further emphasized in a longer-term goal to:

> . . . work with people who use social care services to help them transform their lives by:

- ensuring they have more control;
- giving them more choices and helping them decide how their needs can best be met;
- giving them the chance to do the things that other people take for granted; and
- giving the best quality of support and protection to those with the highest levels of need.

(Department of Health 2005: 16)

In policy documents, definitions of personalization also include these separate elements. For example, in the Green Paper of 2005, *Independence, Well-being and Choice*, the first paragraph of the 'vision' stressed contribution as well as control:

> Our society is based on the belief that everyone has a contribution to make and has the right to control their own lives. This value drives our society and will also drive the way in which we provide social care.
>
> (Department of Health 2005: 16)

This emphasis continues and appears in broad-reaching policy documents, such as *Building Britain's Future* (HMG 2009a), which outlines the overall activity planned in response to the recession. In the foreword, access to services is connected to contributing to society:

> We will ensure that citizenship is earned by those who give something back to the communities in which they choose to make their home. And we will fight to ensure that every British family has full access to the next generation of high-quality, personalised, public services.
>
> (HMG 2009a: 8)

This lack of precision creates problems both in terms of implementation and in critically analysing the development: how are analysts to focus their attention when the target is only loosely defined? Also, this issue creates anomalies where associated terms (such as Resource Allocation Systems or RAS) are not mentioned in legislation and yet are driving practice.

Policy background

The personalization of public services has been one of the cornerstones of the reform of public services for the Labour government, particularly in the early part of the 2000s. Personalization has moved to the centre stage since the publication of *Improving the Life Chances of Disabled People* (Prime Minister's Strategy Group 2005), which strongly promoted the concept and made explicit reference to Individual Budgets, a key vehicle for delivering personalized services. Also in 2005, the Department of Health published an influential Green Paper, *Independence, Well-being and Choice: Our Vision for the Future of Social Care in England*. Moreover, personalization has been a central feature of policy documents from a number of other government departments and agencies (Cutler *et al.* 2007).

Personalization of social care services was the subject of a cross-department 'concordat' (HMG 2007). Local Authority Circulars (key methods of implementing central government policy at a local level) published in 2008 and 2009 (Department of Health 2008, 2009a) made it clear that local authorities were to implement personalization, and identified specific funding to be specially dedicated to support them in doing so.

Most recently, another Green Paper, published in 2009, *Shaping the Future of Care Together* (Department of Health 2009b), reiterated some of these messages about the centrality of personalization when developing options for funding social care in the long term. This set out a plan for a National Care Service, retaining the commitment to personalization: a service underpinned by national rights and entitlements but also personalized to individual need.

The increased breadth of this policy agenda is illustrated in the authorship and ownership of these policy documents, which have, since the White Paper *Our Health, Our Care, Our Say* (Department of Health 2006), all been published as Her Majesty's Government documents, as opposed to being published as Department of Health initiatives.

Conceptions of choice

Underpinning these policy developments are different conceptions of choice as a guiding principle.

The period following the Second World War has been characterized as 'state collectivist paternalism' (Stewart 2005: 306). Services for people with learning disabilities were provided by mainly local authorities and the NHS, but choice was not explicitly championed.

However, from the 1970s, and particularly during the Thatcher government (from 1979 to 1990), choice became an important feature of policy. It was mainly limited to purchasing care in a 'free market' with choices, in theory, open to people with learning disabilities about the provider of their care, housing and social or leisure services and occupation.

With the election of the Labour government came a promise of increasing focus on addressing social exclusion and child poverty. However, such aims were in tension with, and subservient to, a strong emphasis on a similar economic approach, in which market forces and consumerism, by individuals or their proxies, remained the keys to improving the quality of services (Scourfield 2007). Individuals and families continued to be conceptualized as the key agents of change; individual characteristics and behaviour were seen as the key source of problems to be solved by the application of services.

Consequently the 'New Right' concept of choice remained largely unchanged (Scourfield 2007) and unchallenged. Choosing different providers remained the dominant model. People whose abilities to make choices were limited by cognitive impairment or features of social exclusion possessed limited consumer power and were least able to exercise these kinds of choices. Further, there are large numbers of people who do not choose to access services, but are drawn into the system: people who are sectioned under the Mental Health Act, for example, for whom 'choice' is limited.

However, the focus on choice and control also came from disabled people: the 'disability movement', mainly involving people with physical disabilities, led a campaign for a radical revision of 'care', which highlighted these issues. They argued that disabled people had rights to choice and control over their lives (Glasby and Littlechild 2006; Morris 2006). Given the importance of the relationship with those providing, especially intimate, personal care, choosing who undertook these tasks was of prime importance:

> [I] will have one or two carers providing care rather than lots of different ones provided by the previous care agency to cover care hours.
>
> (Person with learning disability quoted by Glendinning et al., 2008b: 54)

While the language of choice and control may appear similar to that of consumerism, a different set of ideas underpinned the campaign. Calls for increased autonomy (Morris 2006; Ellis 2007; Boyle 2008; Beresford and Haslar 2009) by disabled people focused primarily on choice of lifestyle and a right to particular levels of support, with much less emphasis on consumerism as a means to improving services:

> To support a system in which the individual who needs the help has the power to determine how that help is delivered is not to support an individualist right-wing agenda. Rather, it is about promoting collective responsibility for protecting individual rights.
>
> (Morris 1997: 59)

Perhaps the sharpest distinction between the neoliberal choice agenda and the impetus behind the disability movement's campaign can be seen in the emphasis on society as the key agent both in terms of generating and ameliorating disability. This lies at the heart of the social model of disability (Oliver 1996) that underpinned much of the disability movement's campaigns (Renshaw 2008).

'Cash for care' schemes

The main practical change called for by the disability movement was to receive money instead of care services, which were felt to be inflexible and unreliable (Morris 1997, 2006). In what can be seen as the 'original cash for care model' (James 2008: 25), the Independent Living Fund (ILF) was established in 1988, and continues to operate today, although it has undergone several changes in scope. The ILF is administered through the Department for Work and Pensions; people with high-level needs are given money to purchase support, to supplement other community services. However, eligibility criteria are higher than for access to publicly funded social care services. For example, to be eligible for ILF, a person needs to get at least £320 worth of support a week or £16,640 a year from social services (for more details see Independent Living Fund website) (www.ilf.org.uk/making_an_application/eligibility).

The ILF was followed in 1996 by the introduction of Direct Payments, which were enabled by the Community Care Act 1996. For the first time, local authorities were permitted to offer people money instead of services (Scourfield 2005). Direct Payments users were able to arrange and pay for their own services, often employing Personal Assistants to undertake personal care and to support them in living ordinary lives. Initially offered only to disabled people of working age, the Community Care Act 1996 was amended in 2000, to enable people aged over 65 and parents of disabled children to access Direct Payments. In 2001, local authorities were required (as opposed to just being permitted) to offer Direct Payments to all people eligible for social care services, by the Health and Social Care Act (Taylor 2008). Such 'Cash for Care' schemes, as they are broadly known, have been developed in many European countries as well as the United States (Ungerson 2004).

Despite the increasing pressure to offer Direct Payments, and the evidence of positive responses from people using services, take-up remained slow. Overall, Direct Payments users represented about 1.5 per cent of the total number of people using community care services (Davey et al. 2007). However, 3.6 per cent of people with learning disabilities were using Direct Payments, which was the third highest group, although this is still at a very low level (Cambridge 2008), especially when compared with physically disabled people 6.2 per cent of whom were using Direct Payments (Davey et al. 2007). Specific arrangements had been made for proxies such as parents to be allowed to enable a person with learning disabilities to access such funding through a Trust Fund if the person was unable to consent to or manage the process, which increased take-up in this group (Williams 2006). Partly as a consequence of low take-up of Direct Payments, the idea of Individual Budgets was proposed, which aimed to offer increased choice and control to people who did not want to take full responsibility for managing their own care as required by Direct Payments or were not able to do so (Department of Health 2005).

A central feature of Individual Budgets was that people (or their proxies) should be made aware of the amount of money allocated for their support. In addition to Direct Payments, Individual Budgets could be managed in a number of different ways, including through third parties in arrangements less formal than Trusts. Increased flexibility in the kinds of goods and services to be used to support people in reaching goals was permitted, such as the ability to pay family members who provided care or support. It is important to note that the law is framed in terms of entitlement to having needs met, rather than receiving financial payments. Potentially this makes the amounts allocated to individual or personal budgets uncertain in times when constraints on public money are likely to be increasing. Individual Budgets were also intended to integrate funding from a number of public sources (Supporting People; Independent Living Fund; Integrated Community Equipment Services; Access to Work and Disabled Facilities Grants) (Glendinning et al. 2008b).

In 2006–07, Individual Budgets were piloted in 13 local authorities across the country. A major evaluation was commissioned (Glendinning et al. 2008b), which investigated outcomes using a randomized trial approach, in which people were randomly allocated to receive an Individual Budget (if they consented) or to receive traditional service approaches. In addition, a range of perspectives were obtained on process and implementation issues such as training issues (Manthorpe et al. 2008a) and safeguarding (Manthorpe et al. 2008b). The summary findings of this research are presented in Box 22.1.

Box 22.1: Findings of the Individual Budgets National Evaluation

- Individual Budgets were typically used to purchase personal care, assistance with domestic chores, and social, leisure and educational activities.
- People receiving an Individual Budget were more likely to feel in control of their daily lives, compared with those receiving conventional social care support; people with learning disabilities reported the greatest increased feelings of control.

- People with a learning disability spent significantly more on leisure activities compared with other client groups. This included one-off payments for a rock concert and football tickets and use of recurrent payments for Sky subscriptions, gym membership, going to the cinema and meals out.
- Satisfaction was highest among mental health service users and physically disabled people and lowest among older people.
- Little difference was found between the average cost of an Individual Budget and the costs of conventional social care support, although there were variations between user groups.
- Individual Budgets appear cost-effective in relation to social care outcomes, but not with respect to psychological well-being; there were differences in outcomes between user groups.
- For *people with learning disabilities*, there was potential for a cost-effectiveness advantage in terms of social care outcomes. When looking at the psychological well-being outcome, standard care arrangements look slightly more cost-effective than Individual Budgets.
- Staff involved in piloting Individual Budgets encountered many challenges, including devising processes for determining levels of Individual Budgets and establishing legitimate boundaries for how Individual Budgets are used.
- Individual Budgets were seen as:

  ☐ a reinvigoration of social work values in supporting people to identify and reach a wide range of goals; or
  ☐ potentially eroding social work skills through fragmentation of the role and fears that social work would be limited to crisis interventions, safeguarding and high-end complex casework.

- There were particular concerns about safeguarding vulnerable adults.

- Despite the intention that Individual Budgets should include resources from different funding streams, staff experienced numerous legal and accountability barriers to integrating funding streams; at the same time there was frustration that NHS resources were not included in Individual Budgets.
- Individual Budgets raise important issues for debate, including the appropriate principles underpinning the allocation of resources to individuals and the legitimate use of social care resources.

(Glendinning *et al.* 2008a)

The promised flexibility over how budgets can be used raises questions about the boundaries of publicly funded social care and suggests the need for wider debate about how this is to be established, even if this is only in the sense of developing methods for decision-making on a case-by-case basis. Social workers and other care co-ordinators will need some clarity over such issues so they will have an idea about how far they will be supported in working with people to develop creative responses to their situations (Glendinning *et al.* 2008b).

Despite the mixed evidence from the evaluation, Individual Budgets, in a new guise of 'Personal Budgets', lie at the heart of the 'transformation of social care' initiated by the English government (HMG 2007; Department of Health 2009d):

> Personal budgets should be available for everyone who wants them, to give them more choice and control over their care.
>
> (Department of Health 2009d: 27)

It is important to stress that all forms of personalized budget schemes have been found to produce benefits in terms of less institutionalized services (Cambridge 2008), which is of key importance for people with learning disabilities. The Individual Budgets evaluation also identified that the process was often seen positively:

> We made a plan together with my broker. I quite enjoyed doing it because we did it together. I did some drawings and pictures of

what I wanted to do and found it very interesting.

> (Service user with a learning disability quoted by Glendinning *et al.* 2008b: 159)

However, it also seems clear that support is needed for people using services and their families to manage budgets and decision-making, so that the implications are fully understood.

Safeguarding

Safeguarding people who use social care services has received increasing attention as they are often at risk of abuse, mistreatment or neglect. Policies to improve adult safeguarding practice illustrate the greater focus on risk more generally in society. People with learning disabilities may be thought more at risk of abuse and neglect than other groups. For example, people with learning disabilities were over-represented in the proportions of referrals to adult protection services in two local authorities (Mansell *et al.* 2009), suggesting the importance of safeguarding in this area. They were particularly likely to be referred after being sexually abused.

Moves to increase choice for disabled people may carry the risk of increased use of unregulated and poor quality services, further heightening concerns about safeguarding. The evaluation of Individual Budgets found that practitioners were concerned about the potential for increased risk associated with personalization. The increased use of Personal Assistants, who are not subject to any scrutiny or regulation, and the increased role for families in managing Individual or Personal Budgets, were thought to increase risk of financial abuse and poor quality care (Manthorpe *et al.* 2008a, forthcoming). Other commentators have also predicted that one consequence of personalization may be that people using services and their families will have to take on risks previously managed by the state (James 2008). Furthermore, Cambridge (2008) points to the difficulties of implementing person-centred planning, with its reliance on family networks, for people who have experienced abuse within the family.

Government is aware of such concerns. For example, Skills for Care, the government-funded training agency for social care, published a 'toolkit'

(Skills for Care 2008) to support the employment of Personal Assistants, which includes advice about how to seek help if people are being abused by them. The report of the consultation on *No Secrets* (Department of Health 2009c) identified this area as a key area for developing policy following the high level of concern raised by respondents.

Personalizing learning disability services

Cambridge (2008) identifies three stages of personalizing learning disability services: first, the initial drive to close long-stay hospitals and develop community-based alternatives in the late 1980s; second, the mainstreaming of care management through the 1990s and finally 'the promotion of social inclusion . . . through person-centred planning and direct payments' (Cambridge 2008: 92).

Policy developments in England, Scotland and Wales (Department of Health 2001; Scottish Executive 2004; Learning Disability Implementation Advisory Group 2006) set out strategies for learning disability services. Rights, Independence, Choice and Social Inclusion were strong themes in all of these (Department of Health 2001; Prime Minister's Strategy Unit 2005), in line with policy documents relevant to community care more generally. These themes were reflected in the aim to maximize the use of general or ordinary public services in order to overcome some of the problems of exclusion that people with learning disabilities have faced (Gosling and Cotterill 2000; Stevens 2004; Department of Health 2005).

Valuing People (Department of Health 2001), the English policy document, announced a wide-ranging set of policy goals and initiatives. The most relevant in relation to personalization were commitments to increase:

- support for people moving on from long-stay hospitals;
- supported living opportunities for people living with older parents;
- choice over accommodation;
- the range of services supporting people to find meaningful activities, including access to employment;

- locally based specialist services for people with severe challenging behaviour.

Central to all these aims are various forms of person-centred or individual life planning for people with learning disabilities in which the needs of the individual are identified and the person is fully involved in making plans for living arrangements and support. Funding was identified in order to support these developments, as was a focus on different forms of partnership working (Department of Health 2001; Learning Disability Advising Group 2001; Scottish Executive 2004; Welsh Assembly Government 2004). Local authorities in England and Wales were required to set up Learning Disability Partnership Boards, in order to implement person-centred planning (Robertson *et al.* 2005). *Valuing People Now* (Department of Health 2007, 2009d) promised renewed support for person-centred planning, as:

> Experience shows us that the best way for local authorities to develop services that achieve social inclusion is to ... prioritise making support for person-centred planning available to people in receipt of traditional day services – and direct payments and individual budgets.
>
> (Department of Health 2007: 30)

For the purposes of this chapter it is valuable to examine person-centred planning in more detail because it remains such an important approach to arranging services for people with learning disabilities, although the research evidence is mixed.

Person-centred planning

While the notion of person-centred planning first came to prominence in public policy in *Valuing People*, the ideas of promoting more individualistic services for people with learning disabilities had been emerging for many years within UK policy and practice (Dowling *et al.* 2007). For example, the goals of individual programme planning, a process which has a long history in learning disability services, sound remarkably similar:

> These involve the client, in conjunction with other significant people, in planning for the future, with the aim of improving quality of life.
>
> (Alexander and Hegarty 2001: 17)

Alexander and Hegarty (2001) describe individual programme planning as being 'person centred' and being closely related to what the person wants. More widely, person-centred planning has been developed in the United States for about 30 years (Mansell and Beadle-Brown 2004). However, person-centred planning represents a number of departures from these previous methods (see Table 22.1).

From	To
Individual programme planning	Person-centred planning
• Participative	• Person in control
• Professional convened planning groups	• 'Circle of support' selected by person using services, including family and friends
• Deficit model	• Focuses on whole quality of life from person's perspective
• Professional communication styles	• Accessible presentation of information
• Service-driven solution	• Solutions including family, community and services
• Standardized planning approach	• Fluid and continuous planning process
• Professional co-ordination	• Co-ordination through independent facilitator prompting circle of support members

Table 22.1 Person-centred planning compared with previous approaches

While *Valuing People Now* (Department of Health 2007; HMG 2009b) recognized that progress in implementing person-centred planning has not been smooth, it linked this approach to the broader personalization agenda. However, it acknowledged that developments in services across a broad range, including transport, leisure, education, health, housing, community safety and the criminal justice system will be crucial to realizing the goals. Person-centred approaches, and the use of personal budgets or direct payments, are cited throughout as the way to make plans, for example in planning support needed for employment, accessing leisure facilities or when supporting parents with learning disabilities (HMG 2009b).

Person-centred planning, as outlined in both policy documents (Department of Health 2001; HMG 2009b), involves starting with the individual and their family. The guidance to person-centred planning (Department of Health 2002) highlighted the importance of obtaining multiple perspectives on 'what is important to the person from their own perspective' (Department of Health 2002: 11). Fundamentally the approach involves gathering the views of the person and his or her family and social network, along with the understandings of relevant professionals (social workers, occupational therapists, doctors and nurses, among others). Primacy is given to the individual and family members' perspectives, informed by professional knowledge.

In theory, a facilitator or person-centred planning co-ordinator works with the individual and family to identify their 'circle of support' (Department of Health 2002: 38), relevant networks and professionals, and helps to gather these views. Many of the members of the circle of support are invited to a person-centred planning meeting, where the aim is to produce a plan to commission, provide and organize services 'rooted in listening to what people want, to help them live in their communities as they choose' (Department of Health 2002: 16).

Dowling *et al.* (2007), in a review of the literature, identify a number of reasons why progress on developing person-centred planning approaches has been slow, including: the complexity of changing funding and service structures; shortages of staff and a lack of clarity about the approach. Further, in common with other areas of personalization, a tension has been noted between the goals of using more informal services and the increased focus on risk and safeguarding (James 2008). General levels of resources have been felt to be insufficient to implement person-centred planning and specifically for small-scale local services (Dowling *et al.* 2007).

Mansell and Beadle-Brown (2004) identify three factors related to the particular characteristics of people with learning disabilities that make implementing person-centred planning, which relies on developing and maintaining effective 'circles of support', difficult and expensive. First, people with learning disabilities very often have limited social networks, which are dominated by family and staff, with very few friends. Second, the high proportions of people with high levels of communication difficulties makes the development of relationships with staff more difficult, which can make eliciting and understanding goals and needs challenging. Third, many people with learning disabilities also have problems with aggression or self-injure, also making empathy and understanding needs and desires more difficult. Mansell and Beadle-Brown (2004) also point out that levels of reciprocity and mutual interdependence in modern society will make developing the kind of relationships needed to implement person-centred planning problematic.

The first major study of person-centred planning, which involved 95 people in four local authority sites, was completed in 2005 (Robertson *et al.* 2005, 2007). The study found that certain sub-groups were less likely to have plans: people with mental health or emotional problems; people with autism; people with high levels of mental health problems; and people with restricted mobility. These findings suggest that coverage issues identified by Mansell and Beadle-Brown (2004) in relation to previous versions of individualized planning continue to be a problem. How person-centred planning interacts with care management practice has also been identified as a barrier, given the influence of budgetary controls over purchasing decisions, which run counter to the principles of the approach.

Mansell and Beadle-Brown (2004) argue that resource constraints, organizational efforts to control budgets, skill shortages or simple lack of staff numbers can mean that planning processes become paper exercises, which do not lead to improvements in outcomes for people with learning disabilities. They conclude that a focus on legal entitlements, different ways of funding, including greater use of Direct Payments, and developing the workforce to improve support for people with learning disabilities to reach goals would be of greater benefit. However, Emerson and Stancliffe (2004), in a direct response to Mansell and Beadle-Brown, point to evidence about the positive impact of individualized planning, and conclude that person-centred planning could therefore represent a means of increasing such benefits.

Robertson et al. (2007), reporting on the research described above, identify a further set of barriers. First, sensitive topics such as sexuality and sexualized behaviour tend to be ignored in person-centred plans. Second, there is some evidence that options covered by plans are not significantly different from existing service uptake. Third, gaining the support of people outside family or practitioner networks to engage with the process is a major barrier to developing plans and reaching their goals. Finally, Robertson et al. (2007) report evidence that implementation of plans is patchy, partly because of a lack of services available: this was the most important barrier to people being able to achieve the goals identified in plans.

However Dowling et al.'s (2007) review also noted some positive signs. While overall evidence at the time was limited, there was no doubting the value given to the approach by practitioners and groups of service users. Furthermore, there is some emerging evidence about potential benefits. Robertson et al. (2005) report that person-centred planning does produce a range of positive benefits, at no extra cost, for people with learning disabilities in relation to:

- community involvement;
- contact with friends;
- contact with family;
- choice.

There are mixed views about the overall potential for the approach. Dowling et al. (2007) conclude that the approach may be sustained, in the light of the strong policy backing, practitioner support and links with other developments, such as Direct Payments. Others argue that the evidence is not strong enough for widespread implementation (Emerson and Stancliffe 2004; Mansell and Beadle-Brown 2004). These authors argue that any benefits arising from person-centred planning techniques arise more out of increased control over the use of resources (e.g. in the form of Direct Payments), rather than the planning process.

Challenging behaviour

Many people with learning disabilities behave in ways that are described as challenging, such as aggressive or self-injurious behaviour, although estimates of prevalence vary, largely depending on how it is defined (Hayden and Stevens 2004; Lowe et al. 2007). Two major prevalence studies in the UK used similar definitions and methods and produced estimates of between 10 per cent and 15 per cent of people with learning disabilities (Emerson et al. 2001; Lowe et al. 2007) falling into this group.

Developing personalized support plans and services that can address these behavioural challenges has been problematic. Challenging behaviour has been identified as a risk factor in terms of abuse (Emerson 2001) and is associated with greater likelihood of people living in institutional settings (Lowe et al. 2007). Both of these factors make personalized approaches more difficult. Developing circles of social support becomes problematic for people living in residential care, because of the increased likelihood of isolation and poorer family relationships. Given the general fears about risk and personalized services discussed above, the increased risk factor is likely to make professionals and possibly family members more conservative in their approach to developing support packages.

Stevens (2005) found, in a study of challenging behaviour in learning disability services, that staff were seen by people with learning disabilities using the services as protective and able to distribute just consequences against people who challenge:

> But we managed to sort that, there's been many a time that David's been told [by staff members] he's going be out of here if he keeps doing things like this.
>
> (Person with learning disabilities, quoted by Stevens 2005: 969)

This study also suggested that support for people living in the community was needed in relation to the behaviour of others. Staff working with people with learning disabilities who live with or spend time with others who present challenging behaviour will need to understand the complexities of how to support people (see Chapter 17). This task is made more complex by the need also to establish appropriate boundaries in relation to the roles that staff are able to play so that people are enabled to manage relationships as much as possible themselves. This creates an extra complexity in terms of providing personalized services, particularly in the use of Personal Assistants, and points to a need to develop specific skills for this new workforce.

Choice in where and with whom you live may be thought a central indicator of progress towards personalized services in which people exercised choice and control. However, despite some progress, many people with learning disabilities still have little control over these key aspects of their lives (Commission for Social Care Inspection 2004). Enabling people to have more direct control over living arrangements may generate benefits in terms of the types and intensity of behaviours, as Clements *et al.* (1995) argue. Not only would this reduce the interaction between incompatible personalities, which may generate and maintain some of the problematic behaviour (Stevens 2005), but would mean less time spent in institutional settings (Emerson 2001). Such environments have been seen to foster problematic behaviours (Emerson *et al.* 2000). This is one of the stated aims outlined in *Valuing People* (Department of Health 2001) as well as being very much in line with policy direction more generally. However, supporting people who challenge and their families to make decisions is likely to require specialist co-ordination skills (Cambridge 2008).

Conclusion

To summarize, personalization can be seen as being driven by two conflicting perspectives. First, to put it extremely, it can be viewed as an attempt to develop market-driven responses to developing social care services. From this perspective, individuals and their families are conceptualized as making rational purchasing decisions about which services to buy in a free market, divorced from their social contexts. Fundamentally this is an individualistic perspective which focuses on individuals and their families as key agents. Alternatively, again to put it extremely to highlight the comparison, personalization is a way of increasing choice and autonomy for people with all kinds of disabilities and needs, over basic elements of life. This is facilitated by user choice over who provides what kinds of support and when and how.

Critically, however, this second perspective adopts a social model of disability that focuses on civil rights and removing social barriers as opposed to making up for individual deficits (Oliver 1996). Society is conceptualized as the key agent in this perspective. Various forms of cash for care schemes emerged as policy partly as a result of the campaign from the disability movement that argued for the social model and partly through the support of a government that was driven by a faith in markets.

Person-centred planning has been strongly promoted as an approach to identifying individual aspirations and needs. While there are examples of benefits, questions have been raised about whether this can be undertaken with the majority of people with learning disabilities who are eligible for social care services and how far it is possible to address the full range of their support needs.

The role to be played by social workers in supporting people with learning disabilities to make the best of opportunities to develop plans and access supports to increase choice and control is uncertain. It is quite possible that they will be working primarily with people with extremely high needs, in complex family and social situations, or where abuse is suspected. However, supporting people to make such choices can be thought to require good social work tasks of seeking to secure well-being, enabling people to fulfil their potential and working in partnership with people, their families and local communities (General Social Care Council 2008). Further, social workers will need to operate within current statutory frameworks, which require them to assess prospective users and carers, ensure that assessments comply with binding guidance and check that they have needs that meet relevant eligibility criteria.

Exercise 22.1

Devise a plan to use a personal budget to support these two people:

1 Beatrice is in her early thirties. She has Down's syndrome and mild to moderate learning disabilities. She has lived with her parents all her life. Her parents are in their late seventies and in reasonable health: they do not have any other children. Since she left boarding school Beatrice has been at a day service for five days a week. Beatrice has been expressing dissatisfaction at the day service over recent months and is increasingly reluctant to go. Her parents have stated that they would not be able to cope if Beatrice did not go to the day service.

2 Richard is 25 years old and has severe autism and learning disabilities. He has lived in a group home for the past three years. He has always had occasional but very violent outbursts, often in response to loud noise. However, the outbursts have been more frequent over recent months and the home manager has become increasingly concerned about the risks to other service users. She has expressed the view that Richard is not well placed in the home, where noise levels are often high because of other service users' behaviour.

Consider the following issues when thinking about devising a support plan:

- Who would be involved?
- What elements might go into a support plan for this person?
- Would Personal Assistants be appropriate for this person?
- What reliance would you place on family support?
- How would you manage the potential conflict of interest between family members and the person with learning disabilities?
- What safeguarding issues may be present?
- What conditions might you set?
- How might you review this plan?

References

Alexander, M. and Hegarty, J. (2001) Measuring client participation in individual programme planning meetings, *British Journal of Learning Disabilities*, 29(1): 17–21.

Beresford, P. and Haslar, F. (2009) *Transforming Social Care: Changing the Future Together. Report of the findings from an event bringing together service users and policymakers to feed into the Government's Green Paper Consultation.* London: Shaping Our Lives, www.shapingourlives.org.uk/documents/TransformingSocialCareReport.doc (accessed 23 July 2009).

Boyle, G. (2008) Autonomy in long-term care: a need, a right or a luxury? *Disability & Society*, 23(4): 299–310.

Cambridge, P. (2008) The case for a new 'case' management in services for people with learning disabilities, *British Journal of Social Work*, 38(1): 91–116.

Carr, S. and Dittrich, R. (2008) *Personalization: A Rough Guide.* London: Social Care Institute for Excellence, www.scie.org.uk/publications/reports/report20.asp (accessed 3 August 2009).

Clements, J., Clare, I. and Ezelle, L.A. (1995) Real men, real women, real lives? Gender issues in learning disabilities and challenging behaviour, *Disability and Society*, 10(4): 425–35.

Commission for Social Care Inspection (2004) *Valuing People – Much Achieved, More to Do: A Summary Report of Inspections Carried Out During 2003/2004 of 12 Councils' Social Care Services for People with Learning Disabilities.* London: Commission for Social Care Inspection.

Cutler, T., Waine, B. and Brehony, K. (2007) A new epoch of individualization? Problems with the 'personalization' of public sector services, *Public Administration*, 85(3): 847–55.

Davey, V., Fernández, J-L., Knapp, M., Vick, N., Jolly, D., Swift, P. et al. (2007) *Direct Payments: A National Survey of Direct Payments Policy and Practice*. London: Personal Social Services Research Unit, London School of Economics and Political Science, http://www.pssru.ac.uk/pdf/dprla.pdf (accessed 3 August 2009).

Department of Health (2001) *Valuing People: A New Strategy for Learning Disability for the 21st Century*. London, www.archive.official-documents.co.uk/document/cm50/5086/5086.htm (accessed 3 August 2009).

Department of Health (2002) *Valuing People: A New Strategy for Learning Disability for the 21st Century. Towards Person-Centred Approaches, Planning with People: Guidance for Implementation Groups*. London: Department of Health, www.dh.gov.uk/en/Publicationsandstatistics/Publications/PublicationsPolicyAndGuidance/DH_4009374 (accessed 3 August 2009).

Department of Health (2005) *Independence, Well-being and Choice*. London: Department of Health, www.dh.gov.uk/en/Publicationsandstatistics/Publications/PublicationsPolicyAndGuidance/DH_4106477 (accessed 3 August 2009).

Department of Health (2006) *Our Health, Our Care, Our Say: A New Direction for Community Services*. London: HMSO, www.dh.gov.uk/en/Publicationsandstatistics/Publications/PublicationsPolicyAndGuidance/DH_4127453 (accessed 3 August 2009).

Department of Health (2007) *Valuing People Now: From Progress to Transformation*. London: HMSO, www.dh.gov.uk/en/Consultations/Liveconsultations/DH_081014.

Department of Health (2008) Local Authority Circular LAC (DH) (2008) 1: Transforming Social Care. London: HMSO, www.dh.gov.uk/en/Publicationsandstatistics/Lettersandcirculars/LocalAuthorityCirculars/DH_081934 (accessed 3 August 2009).

Department of Health (2009a) Local Authority Circular LAC (DH) (2009) 1: Transforming Social Care. London, HMSO, www.dh.gov.uk/en/Publicationsandstatistics/Lettersandcirculars/LocalAuthorityCirculars/DH_095719 (accessed 3 August 2009).

Department of Health (2009b) *Shaping the Future of Care Together*. London: HMSO, www.dh.gov.uk/en/Publicationsandstatistics/Publications/PublicationsPolicyAndGuidance/DH_102338 (accessed 30 July 2009).

Department of Health (2009c) *Safeguarding Adults: Report on the Consultation on the Review of 'No Secrets'*. London: HMSO, www.dh.gov.uk/en/Consultations/Responsestoconsultations/DH_102764 (accessed 30 July 2009).

Department of Health (2009d) *Valuing People Now: A New Three-year Strategy for People with Learning Disabilities, 'Making it Happen for Everyone'*. London: HMSO, www.dh.gov.uk/en/Publicationsandstatistics/Publications/PublicationsPolicyAndGuidance/DH_093377 (accessed 30 July 2009).

Dowling, S., Manthorpe, J. and Cowley, S. (2007) Working on person-centred planning: from amber to green light? *Journal of Intellectual Disabilities*, 11(1): 65–82.

Ellis, K. (2007) Direct payments and social work practice: the significance of 'street-level bureaucracy' in determining eligibility, *British Journal of Social Work*, 37(3): 405–22.

Emerson, E. (2001) *Challenging Behaviour: Analysis and Intervention in People with Severe Intellectual Disabilities*. Cambridge: Cambridge University Press.

Emerson, E. and Stancliffe, R.J. (2004) Planning *and* action: comments on Mansell and Beadle-Brown, *Journal of Intellectual Disabilities*, 17: 23–6.

Emerson, E., Robertson, J., Gregory, N., Hatton, C., Kessissoglou, S., Hallam, A. *et al.* (2000) Treatment and management of challenging behaviours in residential settings, *Journal of Applied Research in Intellectual Disabilities*, 13(4): 197–215.

Ferguson, I. (2007) Increasing user choice or privatizing risk? The antinomies of personalization, *British Journal of Social Work*, 37(3): 387–403.

General Social Care Council (2008) *Social Work at its Best: A Statement of Social Work Roles and Tasks for the 21st Century*. London: General Social Care Council, http://www.gscc.org.uk/NR/rdonlyres/4EDB6D7E-C18C-4A38-8BEA-D271E9DFFC06/0/RolesandTasksstatementFINAL.pdf (accessed 30 July 2009).

Glasby, J. and Littlechild, R. (2006) An overview of the implementation and development of direct payments, in J. Leece and J. Bornat (eds) *Developments in Direct Payments*. Bristol: The Policy Press.

Glendinning, C., Challis, D., Fernández, J-L., Jones, K., Knapp, M., Manthorpe, J. *et al.* (2008a) *Evaluation of the Individual Budgets Pilot Programme: Executive Summary*. York: Social Policy Research Unit, http://php.york.ac.uk/inst/spru/research/summs/ibsen.php (accessed 27 July 2009).

Glendinning, C., Challis, D., Fernández, J-L., Jones, K., Knapp, M., Manthorpe, J., *et al.* (2008b) *Evaluation of the Individual Budgets Pilot Programme: Final Report*. York: Social Policy Research Unit, http://php.york.ac.uk/inst/spru/research/summs/ibsen.php (accessed 27 July 2009).

Gosling, V. and Cotterill, L. (2000) An employment project as a route to social inclusion for people with learning difficulties?, *Disability and Society*, 15(7): 1001–18.

Hayden, C. and Stevens, M. (2004) Identifying the extent of challenging behaviour in adult learning disability services, *British Journal of Social Work*, 34(6): 811–29.

Her Majesty's Government (2007) *Putting People First: A Shared Vision and Commitment to the Transformation of Adult Social Care*. London: HMSO, www.dh.gov.uk/en/Publicationsandstatistics/Publications/PublicationsPolicyAndGuidance/DH_081118 (accessed 3 August 2009).

Her Majesty's Government (2009a) *Building Britain's Future*. London: HMSO, www.hmg.gov.uk/buildingbritainsfuture.aspx (accessed 3 August 2009).

Her Majesty's Government (2009b) *Valuing People Now: A New Three-year Strategy for People with Learning Disabilities*. London: HMSO, www.dh.gov.uk/en/Publicationsandstatistics/Publications/PublicationsPolicyAndGuidance/DH_093377 (accessed 25 November 2009).

James, A. (2008) A critical consideration of the cash for care agenda and its implications for social services in Wales, *Journal of Adult Protection*, 10(3): 23–34.

Learning Disability Advisory Group (2001) *Fulfilling the Promises: A Report of an External Learning Disability Advisory Board.* Cardiff: Welsh Assembly Government.

Learning Disability Implementation Advisory Group (2006) *Proposed Statement on Policy and Practice for Adults with a Learning Disability.* Cardiff: Welsh Assembly Government, http://wales.gov.uk/docrepos/40382/dhss/socialservices/reportsenglish/implementation-group-consul1.pdf?lang=en (accessed 3 August 2009).

Lowe, K., Allen, D., Jones, E., Brophy, S., Moore, K. and James W. (2007) Challenging behaviours: prevalence and topographies, *Journal of Intellectual Disability Research*, 51(8): 625–36.

Mansell, J. and Beadle-Brown, J. (2004) Person-centred planning or person-centred action? Policy and practice in intellectual disability services, *Journal of Applied Research in Intellectual Disabilities*, 17: 1–9.

Mansell, J., Beadle-Brown, J., Cambridge, P., Milne, A. and Whelton, B. (2009) Adult protection: incidence of referrals, nature and risk factors in two English local authorities, *Journal of Social Work*, 1: 23–8.

Manthorpe, J., Stevens, M., Rapaport, J., Harris, J., Jacobs, S., Challis, D. *et al.* (2008a – Advance Access)) Safeguarding and system change: early perceptions of the implications for adult protection services of the English Individual Budgets pilots – a qualitative study, *British Journal of Social Work*, doi:10.1093/bjsw/bcn028.

Manthorpe, J., Jacobs, S., Rapaport, J., Challis, D J., Netten, A P., Glendinning, C. *et al.* (2008b – Advance Access). Training for change: early days of Individual Budgets and the implications for social work and care management practice: a qualitative study of the views of trainers, *British Journal of Social Work*, Advance Access, published online on 7 March 2008 doi:10.1093/bjsw/bcn017.

Manthorpe, J., Stevens, M., Rapaport, J., Harris, J., Jacobs, S., Moran, N., *et al.* (forthcoming) Individual budgets and adult safeguarding: parallel or converging tracks? Further findings from the evaluation of the individual budget pilots, *Journal of Social Work*.

Morris, J. (1997) Care or empowerment? A disability rights perspective, *Social Policy and Administration*, 31(1): 54–60.

Morris, J. (2006) Independent living: the role of the disability movement in the development of government policy, in C. Glendinning and P.A. Kemp (eds) *Cash and Care: Policy Challenges in the Welfare State.* Bristol: The Policy Press.

Oliver, M. (1996) Defining impairment and disability: issues at stake, in C. Barnes and G. Mercer, *Exploring the Divide.* Leeds: The Disability Press.

Prime Minister's Strategy Unit (2005) *Improving the Life Chances of Disabled People.* London: The Stationery Office, www.cabinetoffice.gov.uk/strategy/work_areas/disability.aspx (accessed 3 August 2009).

Renshaw, C. (2008) Do self-assessment and self-directed support undermine traditional social work with disabled people?, *Disability & Society*, 23(3): 283–6.

Robertson, J., Emerson, E., Hatton, C., Elliott, J., McIntosh, B., Swift, P. *et al.* (2005) *The Impact of Person Centred Planning.* Lancaster: Institute for Health Research, University of Lancaster.

Robertson, J., Hatton, C., Emerson, E., Elliott, J., McIntosh, B., Swift, P. *et al.* (2007) Reported barriers to the implementation of person-centred planning for people with intellectual disabilities in the UK, *Journal of Applied Research in Intellectual Disabilities*, 20(4): 297–307.

Scottish Executive (2004) *Same as You? A Review of Services for People with Learning Disabilities*, Edinburgh: Scottish Executive, www.scotland.gov.uk/ldsr/docs/tsay-00.asp (accessed 3 August 2009).

Scourfield, P. (2005) Implementing the Community Care (Direct Payments) Act: will the supply of Personal Assistants meet the demand and at what price? *Journal of Social Policy*, 34(3): 469–88.

Scourfield, P. (2007) Social care and the modern citizen: client, consumer, service user, manager and entrepreneur, *British Journal of Social Work*, 37(1): 107–22.

Skills for Care (2008) *We Help People Who Employ their Own Personal Assistants: A Toolkit to Help People Employ their Own Personal Assistants.* Leeds: Skills for Care, www.skillsforcare.org.uk/entry_to_social_care/recruitment/PAtoolkit.aspx (accessed 3 August 2009).

Stevens, A. (2004) Closer to home: a critique of British government policy towards accommodating learning disabled people in their own homes, *Critical Social Policy*, 24(2): 233–54.

Stevens, M. (2005) Moral positioning: service user experiences of challenging behaviour in learning disability services, *British Journal of Social Work*, 36(6): 955–78.

Stewart, A. (2005) Choosing care: dilemmas of a social market, *Journal of Social Welfare and Family Law*, 27(3): 299–314.

Taylor, N.S.D. (2008) Obstacles and dilemmas in the delivery of Direct Payments to service users with poor mental health, *Practice*, 20(1): 43–55.

Ungerson, C. (2004) Whose empowerment and independence? A cross-national perspective on 'cash for care' schemes, *Ageing and Society*, 24(2): 189–212.

Welsh Assembly Government (2004) *Consultation Draft, Journal 2004: Welsh Assembly Government Adults and Older Persons with Learning Disabilities, Guidance on Service Principles and Service Responses.* Cardiff: Welsh Assembly Government.

Williams, V. (2006) *How Can Local Authorities Increase the Take-up of Direct Payment Schemes to Adults with Learning Disabilities?* OutLine 3, Research in Practice for Adults, Totnes, www.ripfa.org.uk/publications/outlines/outlinesPDF/3.pdf (accessed 31 July 2009).

Part Four
Adult identities and community inclusion

In the fourth part of the book we continue to follow the life cycle by moving from adolescence towards a focus on adulthood. When this shift occurs it is relative and differs from person to person, family to family and culture to culture. For example, in many Gypsy and Traveller communities it is common for people to take on adult responsibilities from around 14 years of age, whereas in sedentary societies it appears permissible to avoid adulthood at least until 18, or even later.

The nature of adulthood is similarly variable as some people view the move towards adulthood as a 'loss', as giving things up. Such people speak of lost innocence, the passing of youth and the end of freedom. However, others view it more positively and welcome an adult's ability to take responsibility, make decisions and contribute to the society of which they are a part.

Central to this more positive view of adulthood, and a significant factor in social inclusion, is the ability and opportunity to engage with work and leisure pursuits; to broaden the scope of social networks, friends and acquaintances; and to establish independent and culturally congruent patterns of living.

Grappling with such issues of potential loss and the prospect of increasing autonomy can be rewarding, but it is also challenging and daunting for everyone, irrespective of gender, culture, ethnicity or social class. Not so many years ago some people, such as those with learning disabilities, were excluded from this challenge and consigned to a lifetime of near total dependency and isolation from the 'mainstream' society. Although marked progress has been made in recent years, the chapters within this section demonstrate that there is still a long way to go and give some indication of how you can help.

In Chapter 23 Gwynnyth Llewellyn and David McConnell challenge the presumption that people with learning disabilities cannot be adequate parents by showing how in many ways the joys and problems of child rearing are shared by all parents, with or without disability. However, like all families, those in the featured stories are unique and face different and diverse challenges. As the chapter unfolds we see repeated examples of how parents with a learning disability have not only to contend with new babies and growing children but also the barriers that arise from stereotypical views and misconceptions within society and service agencies regarding their capabilities as parents. The narratives demonstrate resilient qualities in these parents, despite the many challenges they face every day. The chapter will help the reader to understand:

- the major themes and areas of concern that arise from the literature on parents with learning disabilities;
- the range of challenges and the diversity of potential solutions;
- the scope of coping strategies and the efficacy of factors that promote resilience;
- the implications for practitioners and service delivery in providing appropriate and sensitive support to parents with learning disabilities.

Chapter 24 by Roy McConkey highlights the central place of friendships in people's lives. People with learning disabilities can too often experience socially impoverished lives for many reasons. This can manifest in a lack of close and enduring friendships. This chapter reviews the importance of social ties in people's everyday lives to their sense of well-being and connectedness, and it considers ways of helping people to nurture and maintain friendships. Dilemmas about intimacy are discussed. The reader is encouraged to consider:

- the extent of loneliness, its origins and causes, and the effects on the lives of people with learning disabilities;

- the rewards and benefits that friendships bring to people's lives;
- the personal, social and attitudinal issues involved in promoting and sustaining relationships and friendships;
- the role of support workers in supporting people to widen their social networks and deepen their friendships.

Person-centred planning (PCP) is the focus of Chapter 25 by Jacqui Brewster and Paul Ramcharan. In exploring the important differences between individual programme planning (IPP) and PCP, Jacqui Brewster and Paul Ramcharan identify the importance of locating power and control with the individual and his or her family. By teasing out the relationship of needs and wishes it is suggested that PCP opens up care to encompass not only individuals but also neighbourhoods and communities alongside service provision. Utilizing examples, the authors provide insights into how PCP might be operationalized within the present policy context. Through this the reader is helped to gain a greater understanding of:

- what being person-centred entails;
- listening and hearing what people with learning disabilities want and value;
- ways of eliciting support from family, friends and associates within PCP;
- the strengths and potential weaknesses of PCP.

In Chapter 26, Ghazala Mir draws attention to the systematic discrimination that contributes to the higher levels of ill health in some minority ethnic communities. She shows that belonging to such a community can confer a degree of strength, support and resilience. Using examples from the lives of people with learning disabilities from South Asian and African Caribbean backgrounds, the chapter identifies a deficit in the level of cultural competency demonstrated by some health and social care professionals. In exploring the relationship between integrated and specialist services for those from minority ethnic communities, a parallel is drawn with similar debates relating to specific or generic services for people with learning disabilities, which in turn raises the question of the needs of people from an ethnic minority with a learning disability. In pointing to some possible answers, the chapter seeks to provide the reader with an appreciation of:

- the challenges of access to services faced by people from BME communities, and examples of 'good practice';
- the ingredients of 'cultural competence';
- the importance of advocacy and the role played by key individuals and support groups;
- the importance of targets and monitoring systems in relation to cultural competence in health and social care workers, and equality issues in service provision;
- the strengths and weaknesses of policy in addressing diversity issues.

The importance of work, supported employment and leisure is the focus of Chapter 27, which is new to this edition. Margaret Flynn, Keith McKinstrie and Richard Parrott begin by reviewing the evolution of alternatives to day centre services for adults with learning disabilities. Policy ambitions for ratcheting up the number of people with learning disabilities in employment are spotlighted, in particular the heavy dependency on supported employment initiatives. Evidence for the claims about supported employment is critically reviewed. An organizational case study is presented to illustrate what can be accomplished at the local level. In this chapter the reader is encouraged to consider:

- the importance and meaning of work for adults with learning disabilities;
- the role of national policy in setting the conditions for helping more people into employment;
- 'winners and losers' in securing and retaining employment;
- pathways to employment and professional roles and responsibilities.

In Chapter 28, Chris Hatton and John Taylor explore the nature of mental health and grapple with fundamental questions about the nature of mental health and mental illness. In doing so there is a recognition that life circumstances, life events and a range of other factors can challenge, but also strengthen, mental equilibrium. People with learning disabilities, because of prejudice and stereotyping, are as likely, if not more so, to encounter a range of potentially challenging circumstances as anyone else. Additionally the factors that may support the resilience of people with learning disabilities may be less accessible. This chapter will assist the reader to appreciate better the problematic nature of mental health and the significant obstacles that people who have a learning disability as well as a mental health problem can face in accessing support and appropriate assistance. In particular the reader's attention is drawn to the following:

- mental health and its relationship to people with learning disabilities;
- the barriers to recognizing mental health problems and accessing services for people with learning disabilities;
- diagnostic and assessment issues;
- the range of possible interventions including biological and psychosocial treatment modalities.

In Chapter 29, another chapter new to this edition, Jane Hubert reviews the circumstances of a small but very neglected group of people: men with severe intellectual disabilities and mental health problems in long-term care. Until very recently the men whose lives are depicted were still locked up in a long-stay hospital. Based on fine-grained ethnography over years, the lives of these men before and after they were moved are characterized. The brief but graphic portrayals of their lives demonstrate how care environments, despite improvements, can still suppress the identities of these men as humans and offend their dignity. The chapter will help readers to understand:

- the ease with which it is possible to 'other' adults with complex disabilities;

- how even contemporary care environments can suppress people's identities as human beings;
- the conditions under which care staff may find themselves 'complying';
- steps that can be taken to improve the living conditions of the men.

In Chapter 30, Paul Ramcharan and Malcolm Richardson suggest that, since the 1960s, policy has adopted different strategies to promote community inclusion for people with learning disabilities. These strategies, they assert, have consecutively sought to reproduce: the characteristics of communities; the characteristics of everyday community living and normal lives and a level of personal choice and autonomy akin to members in the wider community; and, more recently, the application of a common framework of human rights for citizens. Each of these strategies has strengths and weaknesses which are exposed. The reader is helped to appreciate:

- the complexities of using social engineering to promote social inclusion;
- the nature of 'community';
- the interdependence of social and economic policy in manufacturing the conditions favouring community cohesion;
- the powerful roles of intermediaries in the lives of people with learning disabilities in shaping access and opportunities for social engagement;
- the scope of professional endeavour in enabling social inclusion.

No matter how old a mother is she watches her middle-aged children for signs of improvement.
(Florida Maxwell-Smith, *Measure of My Days*, 1968)

23

You have to prove yourself all the time: people with learning disabilities as parents

Gwynnyth Llewellyn and David McConnell

Introduction

This chapter is about people with learning disabilities being parents. Before you read further, take a moment to think about how society regards parents and parenting on the one hand and on the other how people with learning disabilities are usually portrayed.

For some people, parenting by people with learning disabilities is controversial. This is not surprising. In our society, parenting is an important marker of adulthood and social status. Being a parent implies maturity and responsibility (see Chapters 11 and 13). In contrast, the popular view of people with learning disabilities is that they are childlike or childish. This implies that they are unlikely to become adult and therefore not capable of taking on adult roles like parenting. This stereotypical view about people with learning disabilities makes it hard for others to imagine they could be parents. It is as if people with learning disabilities, being viewed as children themselves, could not be responsible for their own children. This pessimistic view has led to many challenges for people with learning disabilities becoming or wanting to become parents.

The stories of five families headed by parents with learning disabilities are central to this chapter. Their narratives illustrate the challenges and the achievements typically found in the lives of parents with learning disabilities. Their stories also speak to the particularity of each parent and their family's circumstances. From their individual and collective experience we can begin to understand the place of parenthood in achieving successful, quality lives.

Prior to introducing the family narratives we identify major themes in the literature concerning parenting by people with learning disabilities. The emphasis placed on particular topics at different times illustrates the changing nature of beliefs about whether people with learning disabilities should or could be parents. From the narratives we draw lessons that challenge the presumption that people with learning disabilities cannot be adequate parents. We invite you to explore the literature and resources noted in the final section of the chapter. The resources section is arranged around the major themes discussed in the next section.

A word of caution is necessary in relation to the literature about parenting by people with learning disabilities. First, various terms are used to describe parents, reflecting the differences in acceptable terminology across countries. These terms include mentally retarded or intellectually handicapped parents, parents with intellectual disability and parents with learning disabilities or learning difficulties. Second, the parents included in research studies rarely represent all parents with learning disabilities. For practical reasons, parents studied are generally those already known to social care or disability agencies. We therefore know much less about parents with learning disabilities who have not been identified and referred to the service system. Third, although the literature refers to parents with learning disabilities, in reality studies typically only include mothers. There is a very large gap in the literature where we know almost nothing about fathers with learning disabilities.

Themes in the literature on parenting for people with learning disabilities

Preventing conception

Until the middle of the twentieth century concern about people with learning disabilities becoming parents was a major reason for segregating young men and women with learning disabilities from the rest of the community. Young women with learning disabilities were often placed in institutional 'care' on the presumption that they were or would become promiscuous. Within the institutional walls men and women were separated from each other. Young women and to a lesser extent men with learning disabilities were routinely sterilized to prevent another generation of 'feeble-minded' people. This eugenic fear that people with learning disabilities would reproduce a large number of genetically inferior offspring was eventually discredited (see Chapter 2). Research has demonstrated that the majority of children born to parents with learning disabilities do not experience learning disabilities themselves.

References for review articles are included in the first section of the resources section at the end of the chapter. The most recent of these is an authoritative position paper written by a multi-national and multi-disciplinary group of scholars comprising the International Association for the Scientific Study of Intellectual Disability (IASSID) Special Interest Research Group on Parents and Parenting with Intellectual Disabilities. Based on international scientific consensus, the position paper reviews the current state of knowledge in the field and identifies some important directions for future research. This position paper is included in a special journal issue devoted entirely to the topic of parenting with intellectual disabilities.

The question of competence

As institutions closed, the possibility of people with learning disabilities becoming parents again came under close scrutiny. As younger people with learning disabilities were now out and about in their local community there was growing concern that they too, in similar vein to their peers, may want to become parents. One of the first questions to be asked was whether they would be able to be adequate parents. Interestingly, a study conducted by Mickelson as early as 1947 concluded that many people with learning disabilities were capable of looking after their children (Mickelson 1947). This study was the first of many to investigate this question of parental competence, also covered in the review articles.

Parents' ability to learn

During the 1970s the emphasis changed from questioning parental competence to questioning whether parents had the capacity to learn. Alexander Tymchuk and Maurice Feldman in North America pioneered the use of applied behavioural techniques to teach parenting tasks to parents with learning disabilities. These techniques include the opportunity to learn skills in the situation where these will be applied; use of illustrated material and demonstration; and practise opportunities with positive reinforcement. Together the studies on parent learning demonstrated that parents with learning disabilities can and do learn childcare, home safety, child health and parent–child interaction skills. Over the next two decades parent education programmes broadened the skills to be taught and expanded the range of techniques for learning (see the second section of resources, page 327).

A focus on children

At around the same time parent education programmes were being developed, interest was growing in how the children of parents with learning disabilities fared. Earlier, as we have seen, the primary concern was that the children would inherit defective genes (the 'nature' argument). With the demise of the eugenics movement, attention was redirected to the quality of care that their parents provided (the 'nurture' argument). In the earlier research parental neglect was defined primarily as poor household organization and low standards of cleanliness. Commentators explained parents' deficiencies in this area due to their knowing no better (an act of omission) rather than purposeful neglect of their children. Although household cleanliness remained a key factor in determining neglect, by the late 1980s inadequate stimulation had become the defining feature.

The key question at this time was: what are the outcomes for children reared by parents with learning disabilities? Investigators focused mostly on outcomes for younger children. The clear message from these studies is of substantial variation among children of parents with learning disabilities with most children meeting age-norm expectations. More recent research has looked into a broad range of factors that may help explain this variation. Early experience, including pregnancy and birth outcome, is one influential factor. The parents' social support network appears to be another: links have been made between perceived social support, parenting practices and child problem behaviours. A third factor is the presence of at least one consistent and supportive adult in children's lives, an indicator of resilience also found in the lives of children in other potentially vulnerable situations (see the third section of resources, page 327).

Despite this evidence, family and children's court studies in Australia, the United States and the United Kingdom suggest that parents with learning disabilities are 15 to 50 times more likely than other parents in the community to have their children removed and placed in care. These studies also demonstrate that allegations of abuse by parents with learning disabilities are rare. Children are removed more often on the grounds that they are 'at risk' of harm due to neglect, that is, their parents' presumed inability to provide a safe, healthy and nurturing environment. Many authors have noted that the prejudicial belief that people with learning disabilities cannot learn is a major factor in court decisions to remove children. Another factor influencing court decisions is the lack of support services that are able and/or willing to support parents in their parenting role (see the fourth section of resources, page 327).

Support to parents in their parenting role

The well-documented relationship between social support and maternal health led researchers to explore the influence of support on outcomes for parents with learning disabilities and their children. The findings from quantitative and qualitative studies demonstrate substantial variations in the type of support offered and the way it is provided. As Tucker and Johnson (1989) noted, support to parents with learning disabilities fell into one of two types: competence-promoting or competence-inhibiting. People offering the competence-promoting type of support helped parents to learn and achieve by themselves. In contrast, those offering competence-inhibiting support 'did for' the parent rather than helping the parent to do for themselves. Competence-inhibiting support denied parents the opportunity to learn, undermined their confidence and made their situation worse. A key factor in determining the effectiveness of support is how parents perceive the support they are offered. Several practice tools for assessing the nature, type and frequency of support and programmes for helping parents develop support networks are now available (for examples, see the fifth section of resources, page 327).

Service delivery

With the growing number of referrals of parents with learning disabilities to health and social care agencies in the 1990s, the emphasis changed to issues of service delivery and practice. The key question became which services, either community-based or specialist disability, are most appropriate to meet the needs of parents with learning disabilities and their children? Building up to a recent series of reports in the United Kingdom and elsewhere, most commentators favour parents with learning disabilities being included in community-based services and offered specialist disability services only when appropriate adaptations could not be made (see the sixth section of resources, page 328). Principles to guide development and delivery of support include the following:

■ services need to be *family-centred* in contrast to a parent-only or child-only focus;

- services need to emphasize *prevention* as a priority rather than crisis intervention;
- services need to take a *strengths-based* rather than deficit approach to intervention;
- services need to be *tailored* to meet the individual support needs of each parent and family;
- services need to provide support for parents with learning disabilities *over the long term*;
- services need to provide *flexible support*, recognizing that the intensity of support required waxes and wanes as children develop and life circumstances change.

Some parallels can be seen in these principles with family-centred thinking outlined in Chapter 13.

Parent voices

A new development in the literature pays attention to parents' voices in order to understand their experiences of parenting. The seminal work of Tim and Wendy Booth in the United Kingdom gave credit for the first time to parents with learning disabilities as experts on their own lives. The increasing recognition and documentation of parents' voices provides a dramatic counterpoint to the mostly negative portrayal of their lives in the literature and popular press (see the seventh section of resources on page 328).

Recent developments

Over the last decade, research about parents with learning disabilities seems to have reached a 'critical mass'. Although there are many questions that warrant research attention, researchers, policy-makers and practitioners have begun to think more about 'knowledge translation' – that is, the challenge of bridging the gap between research and practice. The endorsement by many countries of the 2006 United Nations Convention on the Rights of Persons with Disabilities will likely force the issue. The UN Convention affirms the right of persons with disabilities to marry and found a family in Article 23 (1). Further, in Article 23 (1) and (2), states are bound to 'take effective action and appropriate measures to eliminate discrimination against persons with disabilities in all matters relating to marriage, family, parenthood and relationships . . .' and '. . . render appropriate assistance to persons with disabilities in the performance of their child-rearing responsibilities'. In Australia, for instance, we are implementing and evaluating a national strategy called *Healthy Start* to translate knowledge and build systems capacity to support parents with learning disabilities and their children. The website for *Healthy Start*, which contains many references, practice points and other valuable resources for working with parents with intellectual disabilities, is www.healthystart.net.au.

The family stories that follow are constructed from interview material we have gathered over many years and our personal knowledge of the parents and their families. Wherever possible the parents' own words are used. We ask you to place yourself imaginatively in their shoes. While reading each family story, note down particular issues that strike you. Before going on to the next story, note down how the issues raised illustrate more generally societal beliefs about parenting or learning disabilities, service philosophies or practices.

A little joy: *Lynne's story*

The first story is Lynne's. She is 38 years old. Her 5-year-old daughter Joy was removed by child protection services shortly after her birth. Lynne did not have the opportunity to take her daughter home. Only recently could she bring herself to part with the cot that stood ready but unused. Three or four times a year Lynne travels nine hours by train to be with her daughter for several hours. This occurs on scheduled access visits that are supervised by child protection staff.

On loss

I nearly lost Joy. I had an infection and very high blood pressure, and she was born very early. I didn't know what the heck was going on. I had tubes in my nose, and there were doctors and nurses around watching me like a hawk. I said, 'Can I visit my daughter?' They said 'No, you are too sick and she is too sick as well.' They were telling me to sleep, to go to sleep, but I just wanted to see her. I don't know how long I was in intensive care. When I finally got to see her I just broke down. She was so small. There were tubes in her nose. I was scared and sad when I saw her. I felt hopeless. I just wished I could do more for her. She was fighting for her life.

Craig and his family wanted me to 'get rid of the kid', but I wanted to have a go. I wasn't planning to get pregnant, I just did. He denied being the father. He wouldn't put his name down on the birth certificate. He didn't want anything to do with her. If I had my time over I wouldn't get involved with a person like that. We met when I was working at a sheltered workshop. We started off as friends at first, but he turned out to be a ratbag. I thought we were friends, but it was a funny friendship. He was basically just using me for sex. He wouldn't take no for an answer. In a way I am blaming myself for that.

Little Joy spent quite a few months in hospital. I just hated leaving her there. I went back and forwards from the hospital to visit her each day. When they said yeah, you can take your daughter home, I was so excited, and scared, all at the same time. Little Joy and I took a taxi from the hospital to Karitane, a place where you can live while you learn how to take care of your baby. We spent two weeks there. They treated me just like everyone else, and everyone was a big help to little Joy, and it was OK. They said I could take my daughter home, but they were worried because I was alone.

The staff at Karitane wanted to organize some support for me so I could take Joy home. They called DOCS [social services] because there are not many services around so that people with disabilities can take their kids home. The DOCS workers came, they said yeah I could take my daughter home, and I thought OK, they are really nice people. But the more they came out they started to look down on me as a disability person.

To be treated like a disability person is to be treated like you got something wrong with you. As if I am dumb as anything, a total idiot. I don't know how to behave like a disability person. I only behave like a normal person. Sometimes I make mistakes, but who doesn't? To me there is no such thing as disabilities really. To me that is just a tag. I want to be treated just like everyone else, like a normal person, a person who can do things and learn things. To me everyone is normal, no matter what they got wrong with them, I mean, the way I see it, no one is perfect.

Looking back, I think DOCS knew what they were doing right from the word go. They told me I could take my daughter home, but they were probably thinking, 'we are going to take her baby away, here is why, because her family don't want nothing to do with her, they want nothing to do with her child, she has no family support at all, she is a disability person, and what with her epilepsy, she hasn't a hope in heck of being able to look after her baby'. I asked them to give me a go; they said, 'No, our boss won't let us.' I even asked the boss. She said, 'No, because our main concern is the baby, and look we are not saying you are an unfit mother or anything, it is just that our first priority has to be the baby.' They reckoned I wouldn't cope, but how could they know? All I needed was a chance and someone to help me.

What ended up happening was the fire alarm went off twice on one day and DOCS were putting the pressure on me. That is when I went to the bathroom, locked the door and just broke down. In other words, I cried, I went hysterical. Well who wouldn't? I said look, take her, I don't want her. I said that but I didn't really mean it. They took her then and there. They took little Joy away from me. I took it very hard. I was feeling numb, scared and confused. To be frank I think the way they did it was hitting below the belt, and wasn't called for really. They called the police! They probably thought 'we will get the police just in case things turn nasty'. Don't worry; I didn't threaten them or anything like that.

On trial

At first I was allowed to see little Joy every week, but it had to be supervised at the DOCS office. I was going back and forth to the court. I wanted to have a go at being a mum. I am a trier not a quitter. After three or four months they stuck Joy and me in a refuge together. The refuge was noisy with other people's troubles; I don't think it was a good place for Joy and me. We didn't fit in. I mean I am no Einstein, but for crying out loud, you don't put a parent in a refuge to learn parenting skills!

Then what happened was, I got taught so many different ways how to care for Joy it was confusing. I was trying my best to have a go at being a mum. But I was on tenterhooks, and thinking 'what are they going to do next?' I was going back and forth to court, and what with hearing all the problems in the refuge, and with DOCS coming and putting the pressure on me, it was all too much. I snapped. And that is when DOCS took Joy to the foster carers where she has been ever since. The day they took her away, for the second time, I couldn't bear to see her go. I just had to turn my back. They said, 'You sure you don't want to give her a goodbye kiss or anything like that?' I said, 'Just take her away.' I wish I had given her that kiss now.

The court case went on for more than one year. There were tests, tests and more tests. I saw a psychologist. She made me put blocks together and say what was missing from the pictures. I think the questions were dumb. She said she was on my side. But when she got in the stand she said something like 'Lynne is a lovely person, but because of her disability I don't think she can manage without a lot of support.' And she didn't think that kind of support would be there for me. DOCS won the case. I was upset, but I was glad it was over. I mean I had been suicidal. I had wanted to destroy myself. It might sound weird, but just coming out of that court case knowing I didn't actually kill myself has made me stronger. I survived.

On love

Joy is now 4 turning 5 years old. The foster carers moved away, so Joy is a nine-hour train trip from home. I love Joy. And I will admit I miss her like anything. Sometimes she calls me mummy, but mostly she calls the foster carers mummy and daddy. That makes me feel sad really. The last time I saw her she came running up behind me and put her arms around me. I said, 'I love you Joy.' The woman who was supervising the access visit said she knows who her mother is, which I am glad about really because I wasn't sure if she knew who her mother was or not.

I have nothing against the foster carers. They are spoiling her. I can see why. Joy is the baby of all the kids, and they get on really well together. There have been some very difficult times though. I remember the first time I met the foster carers. It was during the court case. Apparently they didn't want Joy at first, but they took her anyway. The first thing they said to me was, 'She is good', and they said, 'We love her to death and treat her as part of the family.' I thought, 'What? My daughter? In your dreams. You are not going to adopt her sweetie!'

I told myself, 'Lynne, don't you dare put her up for adoption.' A lady said to me I might as well. I thought no, I can't. I mean I just can't. I would never forgive myself. She might come back and say, 'Why did you give me up for adoption? What happened? Mum, why? I mean you are supposed to be my mother.' I couldn't do it. I mean OK, this might sound stupid, but I would rather lose the roof over my head than I would my daughter.

On hope

I live for my visits with Joy. Deciding what we might do together is the hardest part. I don't know the town very well, and what the possibilities are. But we always have fun together. Sometimes we go to a park or to the movies, but we always seem to end up at Kids World. There have been hard times. Like when Joy told me she didn't want to see me the next day. I think she was going to miss out on doing something with her friends. I said that was OK, even though it hurt like heck. And not only that, another time Joy asked me to read her a book. She ended up reading it to me! I was so embarrassed. When I got back home I enrolled in a literacy course to improve my reading and writing. Now I am a much better reader. I can almost read a whole book to Joy!

The fight goes on. But do you know what? DOCS has just agreed to unsupervised access! This means that I can spend time with Joy without anyone looking over my shoulder. And they gave me some encouragement a few weeks back. They said, 'Lynne, you are not so tense, you are more comfortable with Joy'. DOCS have treated me better since I dropped the appeal.

And what if they returned Joy now? Well I would welcome her with open arms. I would hug her. I might never let her go! I think I would be an overprotective mother. I'd make sure she gets to school safely and on time for that matter. But getting her back would take a miracle. I will always love little Joy. So if she says 'Mum, let's live together', I will say OK. A lady told me that when she is 18 years old she has to move on from the foster carers and she can live where she wants. Maybe she will want to live with me.

Cutting the cord: *Debbie's story*

The second story comes from Debbie. She has four children, all boys, the youngest of whom is 9 months of age. Debbie is happily married to Glen, who has a good job and makes a good living. She has a wide network of friends, a home of her own, and loves being a mother. Now life is good. But this was not always the case. When we first met Debbie in 1995 she was struggling to be free from a controlling mother and abusive partner.

On school and work

I had a hard life. In high school I was teased and bullied. One day some older students threw chairs at me. I had to get stitches in my head. My mother took me out of school. I was sent to a special school. It was like a workshop. I learned reading, writing and maths. I even learned to tell the time. I was 15½ before I could tell the time!

When I left school I got a job in a 'disability workshop'. I mostly did office work, which I really liked doing. But if you ask me, it was a bit of slave labour. The best thing about that job was meeting Marie. She was my supervisor. We got on really well together. She became my best friend, and we used to go out together after work. Marie was with me when I met my husband Glen, and she was the maid of honour at my wedding.

I just started going to TAFE [Technical and Further Education College]. I'm getting my reading and writing better. We also do maths and get to use the computers. At TAFE my teacher is helping me to write the story of my fourth son's birth. One day, when all the kids are at school, I might want to go back to work.

About my mother

My mother made my life miserable. She never thought I could do anything. She'd never let me do things in the kitchen when I was growing up. I was never allowed to have my own money, she used to keep it and control what I could spend it on. She did this even when I was on my own looking after Nathan! She made all my decisions for me. I was never in control of my own life. My sisters always had their own money and they were allowed to do things. I was the one she saw as stupid and dumb. She never thought I'd be able to look after myself, or look after my children.

When I got pregnant with Nathan she was on at me to get an abortion. She told me I'd never be able to look after a baby. When I refused to have an abortion she told me she'd ring up welfare and put my baby up for adoption. She couldn't do that, because I had to agree to it. After Nathan was born and after I had kicked my partner out, I was on my own for just two days when 'the welfare' turned up at the door to check that everything was going all right. I'm sure my mother phoned them and told them to go and check on me. But I proved her wrong. For five years I looked after Nathan by myself. People used to say to me, 'You do a good job with your son.'

Whenever I got pregnant mum always gets on at me to have an abortion. Only once was she happy when I told her I was pregnant. When Glen and I had Zachary, my third son, she was pleased, because he was Glen's and she realized he was sticking around. When I fell pregnant with our next son, though, it was the same old story. She said we couldn't afford it and I couldn't cope with four kids. Glen said he would really tell her what he thought if she ever said that in front of him! She doesn't understand that Glen and I raise these kids together. I don't have to cope on my own!

On meeting her husband

I was pregnant with my second child when I met Glen. He told me it didn't matter. I had a hard time believing him. Lots of people I knew also thought he was just using me for sex and would leave when the baby was due. But Glen treated me properly, and he said he was ready for a family. He took on a 5-year-old and me being pregnant, and he was all excited that he was going to become a dad. Even though the baby wasn't his. I moved into Glen's house and he was with me when the baby was born. He cut the cord! Then he had the video camera on Jacob, he was just hysterical. I named my son after him: Jacob Glen. Glen cried when I told him that's what I was going to call the baby.

The week we got engaged so many things happened. It was one good thing after another. First I got my driver's licence. Then Glen proposed to me. And he did it in the right romantic way. He took me out to dinner in the city and we stayed at a hotel with a spa bath. He even got the photographer in the restaurant to take photos of him proposing! The only bad part was I was pregnant with our son, and I was sick! I couldn't eat my dinner! But it was such a lovely night.

Glen is a wonderful husband. I wouldn't be able to manage with these kids without him. He helps me with the kids and does things for me. Sometimes we ask one of our friends to babysit so we can go out for dinner together. We have been on holidays once without the kids since we got married. They stayed with Glen's mum and dad so we could go to his best mate's wedding in Melbourne. We had a great time, but I missed the kids so much, I was glad to get back to them.

We didn't plan to have four. When I told Glen I thought I was pregnant the last time he just said, oh well, if you are you are and we'll just manage. We had to sell the house and buy another one. Now we live in a much bigger house with more room for the kids to play.

On being a mother of a child with a disability

Recently two of our sons were diagnosed with a disability. It is hard having a disabled child. Jacob has behavioural problems, and they told us that Zach had autism. Glen said he didn't have autism, because he was very interactive with us and with his brothers. He told the doctor that, and it turned out he was right. But he is behind with his development. Jacob and Zachary are both going to have speech therapy, and Zach is starting to say words now. We have noticed with our fourth son that he is much further ahead than Jacob or Zach were – so we can see what the doctor is talking about.

With any kid it's not easy being a mum. My eldest, Nathan, has trouble at school because he gets bullied. We have to go up to the school to talk to the principal. I love all my kids, and I love being a mum. It is so exciting watching them grow and learn and do new things all the time.

Living up to expectations: *Kylie's story*

This is Kylie's story. Kylie is 20 and has three children; however, the first two are in care. Kylie and her partner Vuna married before the birth of their third child, William. Their relationship has a turbulent past but they have managed to turn things around. William is a happy baby who is meeting all his developmental milestones.

On feeling bad

My first boy Edward was born three years ago. I was 17. Things weren't great then. Vuna and I hadn't been together for long and DOCS [social services] made me live in a place for teenage mums, a place called Glen Mervyn. The place was okay but I felt everyone was telling me what to do and deep down questioned whether I could look after my son. Things got worse when I found out I was pregnant again. Edward was only six months old when this happened. So being a mum at 17, having a baby and another on the way was really hard.

When Edward was born I wanted to go back to live with my family. Things were not great between Vuna and me. DOCS said no and came and took Edward off me. That was heartbreaking because he was my first son and I loved him. Others couldn't see that. They only saw me as having a disability and as someone who couldn't do things.

I had a hard upbringing and nobody was really there for me when I was growing up. Growing up like this makes learning and going to school hard. So I didn't do well at school. When I was in Year 8 (13 years old) I had to go to a special school. Even though I had to go to this school, I didn't see myself as having a disability. I just think I have some problems learning. When people say I have a disability they think I can't do a lot of things and that is definitely not true. This makes me feel bad. See on the inside I just feel normal and I just want people to treat me that way. In many ways when people treat me like I can't do things they are the ones that create problems for me. Their attitudes really suck and make me angry and frustrated. Because people have thought I can't do things I have lost confidence in myself.

If it wasn't bad enough having Edward taken away from me, when my second son, Gilead, was born, DOCS came into the hospital and took him from me. I had him on the Friday. The DOCS workers came in that same day and said they were coming back on the Monday to take Gilead into care. What these workers did was the cruellest thing. I had to stay in a hospital ward with all these other mothers who had their babies and who were celebrating, knowing that in two days' time my baby was going to be taken away from me. These workers had no idea. Because they just saw me as a person with a disability they assumed I didn't have feelings or that I cared about things. They knew stuff all. My heart broke the day my son was born. My heart is still broken. On the Tuesday I went to court. I wanted to go back to the hospital to say goodbye to my son and the DOCS workers said, 'Don't bother; he won't be there.' I just broke down and cried. They didn't try and comfort me; they just walked away.

After that I had a hormone implant. I didn't want to go through the pain of having any more children removed from me again. But a month after having the implant I fell pregnant. When the doctor told me I felt shocked. I was happy but I was also scared – scared they would come and take this baby too. Vuna and I decided we were going do things differently. We got married and got everything ready for William. I did a child care course as part of 'work for the dole', a government programme for people without jobs. Vuna did a father's programme.

On hope and trust

On 10 March 2003, William was born. Vuna and I thought everything was fine. The doctor said I could go home within 24 hours. I was ready to go and the social worker came and said, 'No, no, no, you can't go until DOCS has come.' I just thought, 'Oh no, not again.' I wanted to throttle her. First they said the reason why they were calling DOCS was because they were worried I wasn't feeding William enough. DOCS and the hospital staff put me on a one-week trial to see if I was a good enough mother. Vuna got the idea of us keeping a book and writing down every time I fed, bathed or changed William. When the week was up they had a meeting. Now they said that they were concerned I was doing things for William by the clock and that I wasn't bonding to my baby. I couldn't win. Because DOCS had removed our other children we were in a 'lose, lose' situation. We couldn't do anything right.

We went to court and we bumped into Margaret, a social worker who trains family support workers about parents with disabilities. She sat and talked with us. And she became our advocate. After the first court hearing Vuna and I talked and we decided we just needed to get help. So we rang people we felt understood us. At first I found it so hard to talk to people and tell them how I felt and what I thought. Because up until this time nobody seemed to care that my heart was breaking, and because I felt shy and uncomfortable. I had no self-esteem left. Margaret and Renee, my outreach worker from Glen Mervyn, helped me put words to my feelings and encouraged me to tell people. Up until then I had just drawn the curtain and didn't want to let anyone in.

DOCS backed off. They gave us a chance. And things are different this time around. Even though I am only 20 I am a lot more mature now than when I was 17. When William was born, DOCS weren't prepared to believe I was different. They just judged me on how I was three years ago. Glen Mervyn was different. The staff were prepared to put their past ideas about me aside and support me. It is important to remember that people change – even people with learning problems!

On help from other people

This time round, people believed in me. Even when I felt I couldn't do things, my worker Renee from Glen Mervyn and Margaret and Vuna told me I could. I saw they got really excited and were proud of me when I tried to do things and that made me feel good about myself. Vuna and the workers work with me. They don't just do things for me nor do they tell me what to do. They don't lecture me. They help me solve problems and reassure me that all mothers need support and help. It is not just me because I have learning problems. They also don't act like they have all the answers and they listen to my ideas.

When they need to explain things they do it in a way that I can understand. Sometimes they draw pictures. They also take my questions seriously and don't treat me like I am dumb for asking questions. They also don't try to teach me things before I needed to know them. When the time is right and William is starting to do new things, the workers help me out with the information I need, like what food to feed William at what stage and things like that.

Their sense of humour also helps. Renee and Margaret make fun of things, which relaxes me. This helps me to be more myself. They also make mistakes, which helped me. Margaret, Renee and Vuna sometimes have trouble doing things or forget things. Showing me that they aren't perfect makes me feel better about myself and makes me realize I can do some things better than them.

I have other supports too. I have a good local doctor. I feel I can talk to her and she gives me time. If William gets sick I know I can rely on her to help me. She loves William and cares about us as a family. Vuna and I have also joined a church. The church community helps me believe in myself. They don't treat me like I am dumb or different. They treat me just like anybody else. They also encourage me and tell me I am a good mum.

Vuna has stood by me through thick and thin and is a really good dad. Vuna does more for me than I do for him and I love him for this. William makes it easier too. He has a lovely little nature. He is very clever and meets all his milestones. This makes me feel I am doing the right thing. He seems to be really enjoying being part of our family.

I feel like things have all fallen in my lap now and I am happy. If only those people who didn't believe in me could see me now. Our next goal is to have our other boys returned to us . . . then we can be the family and parents we want to be.

Taking one day at a time: *Joy and Shirley's story*

The next story comes from Joy and her mother Shirley. Joy lives with Shirley. Their lives are intertwined. Andrew, Joy's teenage son, is beginning to assert his independence and they are careful to give him the space he needs. Joy and Shirley are private people, even shy. Nevertheless they are involved in a range of community activities and make important contributions through their volunteer work.

On starting a family

Shirley: Joy didn't plan to get pregnant. She and David had been friends for quite a while and I think they were planning to get married, maybe in a year or so. The staff at the workshop didn't think that they could possibly cope with the demands of a baby. But I supported Joy's decision to go ahead with the pregnancy. My philosophy is that slow learners like Joy and David should be given a chance, and with encouragement and family support, there is no reason why they can't succeed.

Joy: David never had a family. He grew up in institutions and group homes. Me and Mum wanted to be his family, so David moved in with us. It was hard though because he didn't know how to be part of a family. We were living here when Andrew was born. It was good having Mum here to help. Mum and me took it in turns.

Shirley: Andrew was born early and he had a lot of problems. Joy was so good with him, and so eager to learn. We had to see the doctor regularly and we had all kinds of therapists coming here. Joy made every effort to follow all their instructions. I was here to help and to offer guidance, but really Joy grew into the responsibility. Joy really matured. I always say that watching Joy at the time was like watching a rose bud open. Becoming a mother is the best thing that could have happened for Joy.

Joy: We lived with Mum then we got our own place. It was just down the road. I looked after Andrew. David wasn't much help. But Mum was there to help me when I needed it. I could call her every day. David never did much of the looking after, and he also had trouble with his temper. He used to get angry and shout a lot. When he got angry I took Andrew and we went for a walk until he calmed down. But then one day David got angry and hit me. Andrew was 5 then, and he called Mum on the phone and told her. Mum came and got me and Andrew and we came back to live with her. This is where we have been ever since. We don't see David much any more.

Shirley: Joy and I share the load. She is not a burden at all. Like I do the washing and Joy does the ironing and we share the cooking. For a few years my mother was living here too. She was old and frail and we looked after her together. We had four generations all living under the same roof! Joy also does the grocery shopping. Before Andrew came along Joy was very shy. She didn't want to go outside the door on her own, not even to the shop. Now she is more confident. They all know her down the shops. She is always running in to someone she knows. It might be someone she used to know from the workshop, or it might be someone from church, or it might be one of our neighbours. We have good neighbours. We look out for each other here.

On volunteering

Joy: When Andrew was in junior school I used to go there twice a week to do reading with the children in kindergarten and first class. I also helped in the library. I like to sort things. But now Andrew is at high school. The only volunteering I can do there is in the canteen. But I am not good with handling money.

Shirley: Joy helps out a lot down at the church now. Like, every second Friday there is a group called MOPS, mothers of preschoolers. I was asked to help look after the babies, so Joy comes with me and we look after them together. There are about 15 little babies there. We like looking after them, but looking after older children is too much responsibility. There are so many rules, spoken and unspoken about how to handle and how to talk to children, and the rules have changed. It is hard for both of us to get used to the new rules. But babies are easier to handle. Joy is good at rocking the babies to sleep in their prams. The other mums there really trust Joy.

Joy: On Sundays we go to church. I like the music. Andrew goes to Sunday school. He also goes to night church. Sometimes he is a steward. That's the person who collects the offering. He doesn't want me to go with him on Sunday nights. He wants to be more independent now. I like going to church, but I don't always understand the Bible very well. Mum says that doesn't matter. The important thing is just being there. And I like the music.

Shirley: On a Saturday morning Joy also helps the little ones at T-Ball. That is before her own game. Joy and Andrew play in a team together. I usually go down and help prepare the morning tea. They call me 'the cook'.

Joy: I heard about T-Ball from a lady down the street. Me and Andrew walked down to the field. We were standing there watching when Harry (the coach) asked us if we would like to come and join in. I didn't know if I could play it. We have been playing for seven years now. Me and Andrew we love playing it. We even went to Japan to play in a tournament! We might even go to New Zealand to play. That is what the coach said, if we can get the money.

On friendship

Joy: Every week I go to a group at the church. We do craft activities together. I do my fabric painting. I like listening to the other women talk. They talk about all sorts of things, like what is happening in the world, and what they heard on the news. They tell jokes too. They make jokes about men and sex! There is one mum there who has a daughter with a disability. I knew her from the workshop. But I don't speak much. I tell them about T-Ball. But I don't talk much when I'm down there. I haven't got much to say. Mum says it is because we are one-to-one people.

Shirley: We do a lot of things together. It's all about sharing experiences.

Juggling work and family: *Robert and Julie's story*

Robert and Julie tell the final story. They are well-known activists who have championed the cause of self-advocacy for people with learning disabilities in Australia and particularly in New South Wales. They have three children; the eldest is 13 years and the youngest is 9. Robert and Julie have recently separated yet they continue to 'work as a team' when it comes to the children. Their children always come first.

On getting married and starting a family

Julie: My life could have been so different! I grew up in a country town and my parents were very protective. My life was pretty much restricted to home, the disability workshop, and occasionally tagging along with my brother and his girlfriend. I think life would have been more of the same if it wasn't for a teacher at the local community college. I was doing a typewriting course, and I had to write a story. The teacher read my story and took a real interest in me. She talked to me about another life, and encouraged me to join a social group. This group became Self-Advocacy: an organization to help people with learning disabilities speak up for themselves. I met Robert there.

Robert: Julie approached me, and she liked me a heck of a lot, you could see it. We got to be good friends and one thing just led to another. Julie and I got to talking: we talked about Julie moving to Sydney and us getting a flat together, we talked about getting married then having children. But it didn't work out quite the way we planned. Julie got pregnant. I asked her, 'What do you want to do?' and she said, 'I want to have the child.' I said, 'We will do the right thing then and get married.' This friend of ours got some information for us about abortion and started talking to us about it. We told him that we were getting married and we were having the baby. He said, 'OK, I'll support you in any way you like.' He was the best man at our wedding.

Julie: Other people were no support at all. Some workers were telling me not to have the baby. It was very upsetting. But Robert and I talked about it. I also talked to my mum. She was worried about how we would manage, but she decided to support us. She said, 'We need to discuss wedding plans.' We got married in my home town.

Robert: It was a great wedding, 140 people came. Julie and I decided together who was going to do what. Julie got the dresses organized for the bridesmaids and I got the suits for the groomsmen. Julie's mum and my best man helped out a lot. We got married in a church. I remember Julie kicking off her high heels as she walked down the aisle! [I think the hairdresser had given her some champagne.] We held the reception at a local club. One of Julie's old school teachers was the MC [Master of Ceremonies]. I made a speech, my brother made a speech and my best man made a speech. Julie met the rest of my family and they got on like a house on fire.

On learning to be a parent

Julie: Our baby came early. They had to do an emergency C-section. I remember waking up and she wasn't there. My first reaction was, 'What have you done with my baby?' Until I saw my baby girl I was panicking. It was the worst thing I have ever gone through. She was so small, just 3 pounds and 3 ounces. And she had a heart murmur. But she is OK now. Now she is fine, growing up a real young lady. We learned heaps at the hospital. But then we had to go to a special live-in clinic to learn parenting skills. We didn't like it there. They showed us different ways of looking after our baby, different to what the hospital had showed us, and it was confusing. We preferred the ways we learned at the hospital.

Robert: You don't learn how to be a dad growing up in institutions. My parents gave me up when I was just 3 years old. I had a lot of problems. I was born with hydrocephalus, with a harelip, cleft palate, webbed fingers and other deformities. I had lots of operations. I was in and out of hospital. I think it was very stressful for my parents and the doctor suggested that they put me in an institution and forget about me. Most of my childhood was spent within the walls of an institution. I learnt a lot of things there. I learnt to be wary of people. But I was basically raised by nurses. I never had a role model. For most of my life I have never had a father.

Julie: Friends and family helped us a lot, especially my aunty. She has always been there for us. Robert had a falling out with his family, so we never see much of them. We learned a lot from listening to and watching other people. But that is not to say we have simply followed directions. Robert and I listen and carefully consider the advice we get. Often it is conflicting! Then we try out different strategies before deciding what works best for us. For example, people told us lots of different things to do when our baby was teething. We tried different things before we found the best solution. We have also learned a lot from experience. Like everyone else, we have learned from our mistakes.

On sharing responsibility

Robert: We now have three beautiful children: Amanda-Lee (13), Bradley (11) and Cassandra (9). None of our children has learning disabilities, but they do need a bit of extra help in school. Bradley likes school, and he does his homework. Amanda-Lee doesn't! Cassie now goes to a special school. She was born with heaps of medical problems. Like, she had to have a colostomy bag. They have now done surgery and fixed it up, but we are still toilet training her. We use a star-chart system to encourage her.

Julie: Robert and I have always shared the responsibility for the children. We make the decisions together. And between us we have managed to have a career as well. When we first met, we were both involved in Self-Advocacy; we helped set it up. And since Self-Advocacy got funding, one or both of us has had a job there. At first I stayed home to look after the kids, and Robert went to work. But we swapped roles after Cassie was born.

Robert: I think we were both shocked when we learned about Cassie's medical problems. Julie had a bit of a breakdown. We talked about it and decided that the best thing to do was for me to resign from my job. Cassie needed constant care, and we decided that I should be the one to give it. Julie applied for my position and got it. She has been working for Self-Advocacy ever since.

On separation

Robert: Julie and I separated about two years ago. It was a hard decision, and one that I think surprised a lot of people. But it was the right decision for our family. So many people have problems with their children because they are divorced. I am not going to let that get me down, and it hasn't and it won't. I try to think positive all the time.

  Julie and I share the care: we still work together as a team when it comes to the children. I moved out and found a place in the same area. The kids live with me four days each week, from Mondays through to Thursdays. Julie picks them up from school on a Thursday and they stay with her over the weekend.

  Julie and I regularly talk about the kids, and she knows she can call me any time. Like sometimes, if Julie has to go into work early, she will call me up and I will pick the kids up and walk them to school. And we still do stuff together as a family. Like sometimes Julie wants to take the kids to the pool. It is hard when there is just one of you because Cassie has to go to the toilet every hour. So sometimes I go with Julie: one of us looks after Cassie, while the other keeps an eye on the other two. Julie and I agree that the kids come first.

On work

Julie: I love my work. With Robert and I sharing custody I am able to keep working. It is a stretch though. I have to be very organized and stick to routines. I almost never have nothing to do! I have a duty statement that is three pages long! I have to support individual consumers, train staff about the rights of people with learning disabilities, and visit workplaces. When people come in and we ask them who they would like as their advocate, they usually ask for me! I like making a difference in people's lives. Sometimes they are people who haven't had an opportunity, or feel they cannot go against their parents, or people who are wanting to do something more in their lives. I help them brainstorm all the possibilities and I help them develop a consumer action plan. I want to be the next Manager of Self-Advocacy. That is my goal. I have even done a course on work assessment and training. I am one of only two people with learning disabilities in New South Wales who have completed that course!

Robert: Nowadays I only do casual work. I do it when I get a call, when I am asked to do it, maybe once, twice, three times a month. It depends. I know a heck of a lot of people, and a lot of people know me! I get asked to give talks and training – disability awareness training mostly. It's because people don't know how to talk to you. They think you are different. I have given talks at courts, workplaces, schools, universities and loads of other places. I loved teaching the children, but I have never given a talk at the school my kids go to. Amanda-Lee gets teased for having a father like me. I try to help people see that everybody has a disability – mine is just easier to see. And nobody should think that disability is not their business. Anything can happen, like a car accident. I also want to show that people with disabilities can do things. They can be parents!

On keeping up with the kids

Robert: It is tough being a parent though. I am quite strict with my kids. Being a good parent is about setting limits for children. I will not take any crap from them. But it is also important to listen. I will listen to them, I will question and I will find out. It is important to find out before we take actions. I never hit my children or yell at them (well, maybe sometimes I yell). They know the tone of my voice.

I try to teach them. There are different ways of behaving and some are more accepted in the community. But sometimes they embarrass themselves, sometimes they embarrass me with their manners!. But they are good kids really. I also think it is important to know what is happening in their lives. Like if one of the kids gets a bruise, I want to know how it happened. I'll call Julie, and if necessary the school.

Years ago, my daughter was touched the wrong way. I reported it and the school did nothing. So I went to DOCS (social services). Then something was done about it. The school punished the boy. I took my daughter to hospital and to have counselling. It is important that people see that I am a responsible father. You have to prove yourself all the time. People are always watching you because you have got a disability.

I think it is safe to say that our children don't see us as parents with learning disabilities. To them we are just Mum and Dad. Julie and I have proven that together, and with the right support, people with learning disabilities can raise a normal happy family. We have also proven that people with learning disabilities can have successful careers and run an organization together!

Lessons from parents' lives

We draw three major lessons from the family stories. The first is that parents with learning disabilities are as diverse a group of parents as you could hope to find. Some years ago, Taylor (1994) suggested that practitioners must treat parents with learning disabilities as individuals and not as members of a category. Earlier Budd and Greenspan (1984) had reached a similar conclusion. They observed that, 'If few generalizations can be made about parenting abilities of "mentally retarded" women, then each family deserves to be examined on an individual basis for specific child-rearing strengths and weaknesses' (1984: 488).

The learning disabilities label continues to evoke a stereotyped response. This seduces us to focus on the qualities that labelled people are thought to have in common. The stories in this chapter emphasize how parents with learning disabilities are different from each other in many ways: in their personalities, life experiences, living situations, the people in their lives, and the ways in which they learn and adapt to parenthood. Importantly, parents with learning disabilities, similar to other parents, change and develop as they respond to the dynamic and ever-changing demands of their children growing up. A useful exercise to do now is to reread the stories to identify significant differences. Try to pay attention to each family's particularity.

Exercise 23.2

The following questions will help guide your review:

What do parents say about their childhood experiences?

Who do the parents talk about as being supportive and 'there for them' as a parent?

There are ups and downs in each family's life. What significant turning points do the parents identify?

The second lesson is that, as a group, parents with learning disabilities face predictable challenges. These challenges come from the 'place' of people with learning disabilities in society. This place is one of being thought less able, less capable than others. Parents with learning disabilities face low expectations about their abilities, capacity and potential to take on parenting. These low expectations translate for many parents with learning disabilities into an ever-present threat that the welfare authorities will step in and remove their children. In addition, many parents with learning disabilities live in difficult socio-economic and personal circumstances. These may include being on social security benefits and living in less than desirable neighbourhoods with little opportunity to access appropriate or useful support to raise their children.

There are many challenges facing parents with learning disabilities illustrated by the family stories in this chapter. The motion picture *I am Sam* (Nelson 2001), in similar vein, presented the challenges facing Sam, a single father with learning disabilities, as he fought to retain custody of his daughter. Taken together family stories and movies such as *I am Sam* can alert practitioners to the socio-political context, the 'bigger picture', in which parents with learning disabilities raise their children.

The next exercise is to think about the societal factors that present significant barriers to people with learning disabilities being parents. The family stories bring these challenges 'alive'. You may also reflect on material in the earlier chapters of this book to identify some of these barriers.

Exercise 23.3

Identify several major challenges faced by people with learning disabilities wanting to be parents.

What barriers arise out of others' low expectations and how do these barriers affect parents' lives?

Competence-promoting support has been shown to be more effective. What are the features of competence-promoting support and competence-inhibiting support? Provide examples of both types of support from the family stories.

The third lesson that we can draw from the family stories is that parents with learning disabilities share remarkable achievements in common. In becoming a parent and raising children they contribute to society and in so doing defy others' expectations. They achieve this under circumstances that would deter or defeat the sturdiest of people wanting to become parents. These achievements confront and overturn the stereotyped view that people with learning disabilities should not or could not be parents.

The family stories demonstrate a shared resilience among these parents in the face of adversity, confirming earlier accounts about resilience (see Chapter 21). A dominant theme is each parent's ongoing struggle to show that they too are just like everyone else. They struggle against the oppression of the disability label; they work hard to show that they are no different or less than others. Their battle against the disability label emerges frequently in their talk of doing things 'normally'. Having a white wedding and getting married emerge as symbols of their achievement in meeting societal expectations of a normal rhythm of adult life. Parents with learning disabilities also struggle against the systemic barriers which flow on from beliefs that learning disability means (less than). They achieve, for example, by succeeding in the face of child protection scrutiny and intervention.

The family stories also demonstrate achievements at an individual level, for example in overcoming parental control or learning new skills never thought possible. Parents with learning disabilities also achieve by taking on and seeking out opportunities unlikely to come their way in the natural course of things. The final exercise requires the reader to locate shared and individual achievements evident in these stories. The questions guide this task.

Exercise 23.4

Are there major achievements in common in these family stories? If so, what are these and how did each parent reach their achievements?

Identify new activities that parents have taken up or skills learnt or tasks undertaken in response to being parents.

Labels such as learning disability suggest a static condition, yet the family stories suggest ongoing development and change. Identify at least one instance of change in each story and draw out the circumstances in which this change occurred.

Conclusion

There have always been some people with learning disabilities who became parents. The eugenics movement and the era of institutionalization, however, generated a pervasive belief that people with learning disabilities must not be allowed to take on the role of parenting. Contradicting this belief, people with learning disabilities became parents and more are doing so and achieving successful, quality lives, as the narratives in this chapter demonstrate. Research across several continents has contributed to our understanding of the challenges faced by these parents in 'having to prove themselves all the time'. No one in any place would suggest seriously that the task of parenting is an easy one. All parents need support to raise healthy, happy children in safe environments. Some parents benefit from additional support. All parents benefit from having at least one person who believes in and works with them to help achieve their goals for themselves and their children. The lessons we have drawn here from the family stories and the literature serve to illustrate the way forward for practitioners in providing support and services to parents with learning disabilities.

Resources

Literature reviews

IASSID Special Interest Research Group on Parents and Parenting with Intellectual Disabilities (2008) Parents labelled with intellectual disability: position of the IASSID SIRG on parents and parenting with intellectual disabilities, *Journal of Applied Research in Intellectual Disabilities*, 21: 296–307.

Special Issue on Parents and Parenting with Intellectual Disabilities (2008) *Journal of Applied Research in Intellectual Disabilities*, 21(4).

Parent learning

Llewellyn, G. (1997) Parents with intellectual disability learning to parent: the role of experience and informal learning, *International Journal of Disability, Development and Education*, 44(3): 243–61.

Llewellyn, G., McConnell, D., Honey, A., Mayes, R. and Russo, D. (2003) Promoting health and home safety for children of parents with intellectual disability: a randomised controlled trial, *Research in Developmental Disabilities*, 24: 405–31.

Wade, C., Llewellyn, G. and Matthews, J. (2008) Review of parent training interventions for parents with intellectual disability, *Journal of Applied Research in Intellectual Disabilities*, 21: 351–66.

Outcomes for children

Aunos, M., Feldman, M. and Goupil, G. (2008) Mothering with intellectual disabilities: relationship between social support, health and well-being, parenting and child behaviour outcomes, *Journal of Applied Research in Intellectual Disabilities*, 21: 320–30.

McConnell, D., Mayes, R. and Llewellyn, G. (2008) Women with intellectual disability at risk of adverse pregnancy and birth outcomes, *Journal of Intellectual Disability Research*, 52: 529–35.

Child protection and court studies

Booth, T., McConnell, D. and Booth, W. (2006) Temporal discrimination and parents with learning difficulties in the child protection system, *British Journal of Social Work*, 36: 997–1015.

McConnell, D., Llewellyn, G. and Ferronato, L. (2006) Context contingent decision-making in child protection practice, *International Journal of Social Welfare*, 15: 230–9.

Maternal health and social support

McConnell, D., Mayes, R. and Llewellyn, G. (2008) Prepartum distress in women with intellectual disabilities, *Journal of Intellectual and Developmental Disability*, 33: 177–83.

Traustadóttir, R. and Sigurjónsdóttir, H.B. (2008) The 'mother' behind the mother: three generations of mothers with intellectual disabilities and their family support networks, *Journal of Applied Research in Intellectual Disabilities*, 21: 331–40.

Service delivery and family support

Clayton, O., Chester, A., Mildon, R. and Matthews, J. (2008) Practitioners who work with parents with intellectual disability: stress, coping and training needs, *Journal of Applied Research in Intellectual Disabilities*, 21: 367–76.

Mildon, R., Wade, C. and Matthews, J. (2008) Considering the contextual fit of an intervention for families headed by parents with an intellectual disability: an exploratory study, *Journal of Applied Research in Intellectual Disabilities*, 21: 377–87.

Voices of parents

Mayes, R,. Llewellyn, G. and McConnell, D. (2006) Misconception: the experience of pregnancy for women with intellectual disabilities, *Scandinavian Journal of Disability Research*, 8: 120–31.

Strike, R. and McConnell, D. (2002) Look at me, listen to me, I have something important to say, *Sexuality and Disability*, 20(1): 53–63.

Websites

www.afdsrc.org. Australian Family and Disability Studies Research Collaboration.
www.bild.org.uk. British Institute of Learning Disabilities.
www.disabledparentsnetwork.org.uk. Disabled Parents Network.
www.dppi.org.uk. Disability, Pregnancy and Parenthood International.
lookingglass.org/index.php. Through the Looking Glass.
www.supported-parenting.com. Supported Parenting.

References

Budd, J. and Greenspan, S. (1984) Mentally retarded mothers, in E.A. Blechman (ed.) *Behaviour Modification with Women*. New York: Guilford Press.

Mickelson, P. (1947) The feeble-minded parent: a study of 90 family cases, *American Journal of Mental Deficiency*, 51: 644–53.

Nelson, J. (2001) *I Am Sam*. New Line Cinema.

Taylor, S.J. (1994) Children's division is coming to take pictures: family life and parenting in a family with disabilities, in S.J. Taylor, R. Bogdan and Z.M. Lutfiyya (eds) *The Variety of Community Experience: Qualitative Studies of Family and Community Life*. Baltimore, MD: Paul H. Brookes.

Tucker, B.M. and Johnson, O. (1989) Competence-promoting versus competence-inhibiting support for mentally retarded mothers, *Human Organisation*, 48: 95–107.

Promoting friendships and developing social networks

24

Roy McConkey

Introduction

Many people with learning disabilities lead lonely lives. In this chapter you will read the evidence for this, think about why this is so, ponder the consequences of it and consider what can be done about it.

Building relationships is a daunting task. Support staff might teach a person the necessary communication and social skills; they may organize leisure activities for them and perhaps even arrange social gatherings such as parties, but as Firth and Rapley (1990: 21) noted, 'It is not possible to provide friendship, or to make friends for other people . . . friendships can only be chosen.' Thus staff cannot rely on their usual 'organizing strategies' when it comes to enabling people with learning disabilities to find and cement their own friendships. They need to adopt different strategies, but often these fall outside their present roles and job descriptions.

Promoting friendships has its risks. What if the person in your care chooses the 'wrong' people – as you see it? Could they be taken advantage of? Will they get hurt if the friendship is not reciprocated? All the same fears that your parents probably had about your choice of friends when you were a teenager going on 40! Yet you and they managed to find a way through and so too can staff and parents who are responsible for people with learning disabilities. But it means 'positive risk taking' rather than trying to eliminate risk, as so often happens in service policies and procedures (HM Government 2009).

People with learning disabilities are often faced with stigmatized, discriminatory and hurtful attitudes from other members of the community including health professionals, employers and neighbours. Thus societal attitudes can act as a strong barrier to social inclusion, especially if they remain unchallenged. Often, specialist services have left it to family carers and people themselves to confront negative attitudes, but should they not be proactive in challenging discriminatory practices (Sayce 2003)?

The rewards that come from having a network of friends are great. It means having the company of others, laughter and adventure, people to give you advice and guidance, practical help, emotional support and protection and, above all, friends to whom you can show love and affection and who will do the same for you. Quality of life studies constantly stress the importance of friendships and this is no less so for people with learning disabilities (Schalock and Alonso 2002). Indeed, it could be argued they have even more need for friends than those without a disability, as their lives are often more impoverished in other ways (see Chapters 6, 17, 19, 23, 26–29, 33). To deny them opportunities for friendships only compounds their disability. Yet as we shall see, this is precisely what happens in many of our support services.

Friendships and people with learning disabilities

Of all the assessments done on people with learning disabilities, the one least likely to be carried out is an examination of their friendships! But if you did take the time to enquire, you would probably confirm the evidence from a growing number of research studies, namely that people with disabilities have few close friends, whatever their age or wherever they live.

Children and teenagers

Children and teenagers with developmental disabilities have a high risk of being excluded from peer friendships (Webster and Carter 2007). For example, Smyth and McConkey (2003) interviewed the parents of over 50 school leavers from two special schools for pupils with severe learning difficulties in Northern Ireland. Three in five of the young people (58 per cent) were reported to have no friends of their own.

Of those reported to have friends (16 students in all), 12 were from the same school or centre the young person attended but only one young person had a weekly meeting with these friends outside the school setting; more often it was fortnightly (three), monthly (four) or occasionally (four). Of the four students reported to have non-disabled friends (11 per cent), only one person met his friend weekly, usually in clubs or pubs. In all, 90 per cent of parents would like their son or daughter to be more involved with friends of their own age and they mentioned the need for more clubs (10) and for more sports and leisure activities (six).

Adult persons living with family carers

McConkey et al. (1981) interviewed over 200 parents in Dublin city who had a son or daughter living with them at home – average age 23 years. Previous Irish studies with non-disabled samples of comparable age found that three-quarters of young people regularly shared their leisure time with friends. But of those who had learning disabilities, only two in five spent any time with a friend and as many as one in five were reported to have no one with whom they shared their leisure time. Some of the comments made by the young people sum up their plight: 'I need a friendship. I wish I had a companion I could go out with and chat to. I have nobody and it hurts me.' 'I would like to have friends although my mammy might not like friends coming in all the time to the house.' Similar findings have been reported by Jobling and Cuskelly (2002) from Australia and by Rosen and Burchard (1990) in the US.

People in residential settings

Robertson et al. (2001) obtained information on the social networks of over 500 people (average age 45 years) living in three types of residential accommodation which had been nominated by key informants as being 'good exemplars' of that type of provision. Staff, family members and other people with learning disabilities featured in the networks of most people, but fewer than one-third had a person from outside these categories in their network. The median size of each person's networks was two persons (once staff were excluded) but a quarter only had one or no persons in

their networks. This pattern held irrespective of the type of setting the person resided in, although people living in less institution-like services had larger social networks and they were more likely to have a relative or non-disabled person in their networks.

These findings are echoed in the systematic literature review undertaken by Verdonschot et al. (2009).

Charting friendships

It is easy to dismiss these findings by thinking they do not apply to the people with whom you work. But how do you know unless you take the trouble to find out? Two findings I can almost guarantee.

First, the people they name will often be staff and fellow service-users. Probe a little deeper and you may find that the amount of time and the types of contact they have with their so-called 'friends' is very different to what you expect and get from your own friends. Also, if you were to ask the people they name about their friendships, many may never mention the person who gave you their name in the first place. An unreciprocated friendship is no friendship at all (see Chapter 30).

Second, most people will tell you about the friend or friends they used to have. This starts with teenagers and goes on throughout people's lives. The fewer friends one presently has, the more precious become the memories of those you once knew. Probe further and you may discover that some friendships were broken because service personnel decided that a person had to move from a hospital, home, school or centre with no consideration given to the social networks the person had forged and no support given to them to maintain contact with old friends (McConkey et al. 2003).

So what can be done to help people to form and sustain friendships? First we need to appreciate the complex web of processes that underpins the development of human friendships (Duck 1992).

How friendships develop

Despite the centrality of friendships to human well-being, there is no prescription for their successful development. You will know from your experience that some friendships spring up rapidly from an

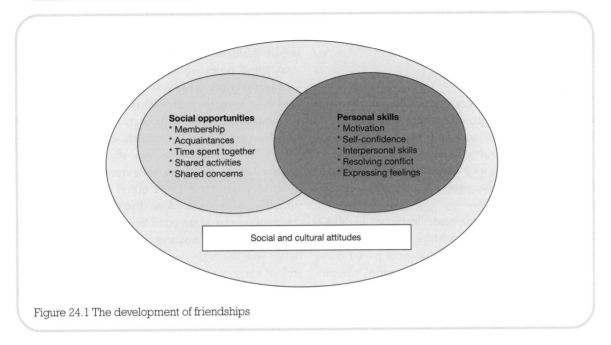

Figure 24.1 The development of friendships

initial meeting while others evolve over a long period of time. Some of your friends have a lot in common while others are very different from each other. You may have friendships that have lasted for years, whereas others have faded after a short time.

But underlying this variation there do appear to be some common elements in the development of friendships. As Figure 24.1 shows, these fall into two groups: the social opportunities and the personal skills and attributes required by the individual. However, these groupings are interlinked and interactive. For example, self-confidence grows as people avail themselves of social opportunities, yet some self-confidence is needed to join with others in social activities.

We can use this framework to understand better why people with learning disabilities can find it so difficult to make and keep friends – particularly with people who are not learning disabled.

Social opportunities

Membership

Babies are born into a world of social opportunities: first within their family but gradually extending into the wider society as they attend crèches and playgroups and become 'members' in other social

groupings, such as neighbourhood playmates, schools and youth organizations. These opportunities introduce the person to others and others to the individual. Although such introductions are first determined by the child's carers, later their siblings, peers and the person themselves will begin to make their own introductions.

However, from an early age, children with learning disabilities can become segregated from their non-disabled peers. This may be for the best of reasons, such as special schools that offer teaching and support better suited to their disabilities. Nonetheless, a consequence is that their opportunities to belong to the same social groupings as other children is often curtailed (Koster et al. 2009). This pattern is then continued into the teenage and adult years.

Acquaintances

Acquaintances can start to develop from within our membership groupings. This is a crucial step in the growth of friendships as our close friends are likely to emerge from acquaintances or else it is through our acquaintances that we are introduced to others who may become our friends (Firth and Rapley 1990).

Building acquaintances is dependent on factors such as physical attractiveness, similarity in appearance and ease of communication, which may be perceived by others to be lacking in people with disabilities.

Time spent together

Some friendships may develop rapidly but more usually it is a case of 'getting to know one another' by spending time together. This is the time for testing out if you share interests, values and attitudes; for example, as you gossip about others, recount past experiences and make suggestions for activities you might do together.

The fact that people with learning disabilities develop close personal friendships with their peers in special schools, centres and residences is testimony to the importance of spending time together. However, this contact is often denied to non-disabled people as their meetings with disabled people tend to be restricted to social greetings on the streets (McConkey 1987). Nevertheless, when they do get the opportunity to spend time together, notably when people with learning disabilities are placed in ordinary work settings, then increased numbers of friendships are reported (Jobling and Cuskelly 2002).

Shared activities

Various shared activities help to forge closer relationships, especially if they involve the sharing of feelings and emotions such as those engendered by sports, drama and religious celebrations (McConkey *et al.* 2009). Equally, participation in a variety of social pursuits helps to build a network of acquaintances and creates more opportunities for friendships.

This brings us to a real vicious circle. The more acquaintances and friends you have, the easier it is to join in a range of social pursuits which in turn help to consolidate and sustain friendships. But the opposite is then also true. Fewer acquaintances means fewer opportunities to engage in social pursuits. Indeed, the lives of people with learning disabilities tend to be dominated by watching television and listening to music (Smyth and McConkey 2003).

Shared concerns

Friendships are often nurtured through working together on common concerns. Membership of self-help groups and residents' associations can bring people together, as can the sharing of adversities such as discrimination and grief (Ward 1998). The latter may impel people to share many feelings, thoughts and values which otherwise they might not have done and in so doing they discover their 'soulmates'.

However, people with learning disabilities are usually perceived as a concern in their own right rather than people who can share emotions and support other people in their times of need. This mutuality factor more than others explains why staff usually cannot be considered friends of their clients in the fullest sense of the word 'friends', although it may happen in some instances and certainly does occur when staff leave the work setting and relinquish the role of caregiver.

As you reflect on the above contexts for growing friendship, it quickly becomes apparent how important it is for people with learning disabilities to be given opportunities to be in the company of other people – both disabled and non-disabled. This is the foundation on which acquaintances and friendships develop. It's as simple as that. Yet for many decades in the last century people were denied these opportunities – paradoxically on the grounds that it was in their best interests. A more haunting question remains: is social exclusion still happening in the twenty-first century under the pretext of protection?

Personal skills and attributes

Social opportunities are not sufficient on their own. People need to contribute actively to the process of making friends.

Motivation

'Without a desire to develop a relationship, no relationship is likely', wrote Firth and Rapley (1990: 15). Lack of motivation may be because people want to be alone; they may feel they have sufficient friends already; or they could be ambivalent about what a relationship may bring – unwilling to risk rejection or undertake obligations. However, people's motivation is strongly affected by their past experience. Those who have experienced repeated or traumatic rejection may themselves openly reject people who offer friendship (Vanier 1991). Also, people with autistic spectrum disorders can show little interest in other people. Likewise, some people may have mental health problems such as depression and as a result are hard to get to know (see Chapter 28).

A challenge for staff and families is therefore to keep people motivated to be sociable, for them to find laughter and fun in the company of other people and for them to experience having their particular 'wants' met through, and with, other people.

Self-confidence

This is needed throughout all social activities, from greeting people to keeping in contact with them. People who are shy, retiring or taciturn therefore have difficulty in making friends. Self-confidence is also influenced by people's upbringing and their past experiences as well as their feelings and beliefs about themselves – 'I'm ugly: nobody will want to be my friend.' Ironically, successful social interchange builds self-confidence, but how does this get started if there is little self-confidence in the first place?

Once again, a key role for staff and family carers is to promote and encourage the person's self-confidence by accentuating their positive features and compensating for their weaknesses. However, this often goes against the culture of helplessness that pervades their lives – they need to have things done for them!

Interpersonal skills

This covers a multitude of abilities including 'body language', communication skills, social conventions, and judging people's moods and attitudes and acting accordingly. Young children are often excused for their lack of interpersonal skills but only up to a point. It takes a great deal of observation, imitation and feedback to master all the subtle skills that oil our interactions with other people and convey our willingness for friendships. However, these skills take longer to develop when people have disabilities and indeed many may never be realized. In these instances, the more able communicators have to be prepared to adjust their communications but many find this hard to do (McConkey et al. 1999).

Resolving conflict

For some people the problem is not making friends, it is keeping them. The skills involved in avoiding and resolving conflict are difficult for people to learn if they are not able to 'put themselves in another's shoes'. Often they cannot appreciate or anticipate the hurt they might cause to their erstwhile friend through misjudged words or actions.

Such insights cannot be directly taught, but people do benefit from reflecting on their experiences in one-to-one sessions or through role-playing with video playback so that they can be helped to identify the specific behaviours that may be causing the problems (O'Reilly and Glynn 1995).

Expressing feelings

Many people are poor at expressing their feelings to others. They may be reluctant to give praise, to say sorry, to express their hurt, even to say thanks. This failure may cause relationships to stagnate and even break down. However, as in other domains of their life, people with learning disabilities can benefit from sharing their emotional difficulties, although surprisingly this often does not feature among the priorities of staff working in services – possibly because these behaviours are thought to be *part* of their disability (Arthur 2003).

The complexity of the skills required to make and sustain friendships is all too apparent. Little wonder children take some ten years before they become adept at these skills. It is not surprising that people with learning disabilities may struggle to acquire some or all of these high-level social skills. However, this difficulty is *not* an inherent feature of their disability. Rather, the lack of social opportunities that many have experienced allied with the dearth of educational programmes focused on communication and interpersonal skills are far more to blame.

Exercise 24.1

Pick a friend you know well. Use the above framework to identify his or her strengths when it comes to making friends. What do you feel are his or her main weaknesses?

Now repeat this for a person with learning disabilities you know well. What are his or her strengths when it comes to making friends? What do you feel are his or her main weaknesses? How might these be overcome?

Social and cultural attitudes

Friendship formation is also influenced to a greater or lesser degree by the prevailing social and cultural attitudes within the communities in which people live. This is most obviously felt in so-called 'divided societies' in which Jews, Muslims, Catholics or Protestants will find many subtle and sometimes not so subtle influences that affect their choice of friendships. Arguably, these influences are just as potent in a society that separates people into the 'able' and the 'disabled'. In many senses, people with a learning disability are still outsiders within our society, with few people in their social networks. They continue to experience discrimination and hurtful attitudes from their fellow citizens (see Box 24.1).

Box 24.1: Hurtful attitudes reported by people with learning disabilities (McConkey 1994)

- Name-calling from children
- Teenagers who try to take money off you
- People who stare at you in shops
- Trouble from GPs; they talk to the staff but not us
- Trouble from churches; no one talks to us or makes us welcome
- Bad neighbours – always complaining and blaming us for things which are not our fault
- Staff in centres who smoke in your face and boss you around
- People who mean well but get it all wrong – 'patronizers'
- Youngsters knocking on your door and running away
- Parents who mean well but who treat us like children
- Shop assistants who don't take time to listen if we can't make ourselves understood

Research studies undertaken in various countries have identified several truisms about society's attitudes (McConkey 1994). The majority of people – usually around 75 per cent – have had no personal contact with people who have learning disabilities. Hence their images of them are likely to be stereotyped and possibly mistaken. Locating people with disabilities in community settings is no guarantee that they will meet and get to know local people. Fewer than 10 per cent of people living close to a day centre had met any of the attenders. People anticipate many more problems for themselves than is borne out by the reality of the experience. This has been shown in studies with neighbours of group homes, employers, teachers, nurses, therapists and GPs (e.g. McConkey 1994).

Personal contact with people who have learning disabilities has consistently been found to lead to more positively disposed attitudes; rather than putting people off, it appears to win them over. Hence the priority should be to create even more opportunities for people to meet. Some neighbourhoods are more welcoming than others to groups of people with learning disabilities. Taking time to determine the characteristics of neighbourhoods through community consultations would help services seek out those districts where the risks of active opposition are lower and the chances for social integration higher.

But the most crucial conclusion about attitude change is also the most hopeful. It is so much easier to change attitudes to specific individuals than it is to an indeterminate group of people known as the 'handicapped'. This is why media campaigns, political lobbying and information leaflets have all proven to be relatively ineffective in changing societal attitudes. Far more powerful is the opportunity to meet and get to know people as people, not as patients, residents or service-users. Moreover, such meetings should take place in ordinary locations such as pubs, churches and shopping malls rather than in special centres (McConkey 1994).

The need for go-betweens

However, these encounters will not happen if left to chance. 'Go-betweens' are needed. As the name implies, their strength derives from knowing both parties. They know the needs, interests and talents of the person with a learning disability but, unlike them, they are connected with various community networks. They are well placed to identify possible connections either with individuals or groups. But for this to happen, a go-between has to be prepared to ask! Schwartz (1992) identifies this simple task as one of the most crucial weapons in the armoury of community integrators. Equally he notes the reluctance of some professional staff and carers to ask favours of others. Why? Maybe they feel no one can quite measure up to the task or that there are too many risks involved – hence they have to continue shouldering the responsibility. More worryingly, perhaps they feel that there are no benefits to befriending a person with learning disabilities. Interestingly, family carers and voluntary helpers seem much more adept at naming these benefits than are paid staff (Stainton and Besser 1998).

The next stage is that of introductions. The go-between needs to put the strangers at their ease by facilitating the conversation, modelling interactions, finding joint activities for them to do and, when the opportunity arises, discreetly withdrawing for a time so that they take on the responsibility for maintaining the interaction.

Finally, the go-between needs to be supportive of the blooming partnership by keeping in touch with both, checking how things are going and making discreet suggestions, while subtly praising them for how well they are coping with the challenge.

The contribution of go-betweens to the lives of people with disabilities has been best captured in the work of Edgerton et al. (1984) who describe the crucial role of people they termed 'benefactors' in helping people with learning disabilities discharged from long-stay hospitals to socially integrate into local communities; although this dependence decreased over time as people merged into society.

Without the active support of 'go-betweens' the social isolation of people is likely to persist (Hall and Hewson 2006). Yet rarely are these connecting tasks written into the job descriptions of professional workers; nor are people recruited for their 'relationship-building' skills. Paradoxically, most of us acquire these skills and utilize them in our personal lives so perhaps their deployment in the service of people with learning disabilities could be readily promoted if only the will to do so was there from service managers and administrators.

Friendly with whom?

This is an apposite juncture at which to think a little more about a challenging issue: namely, are people with a disability 'happier with their own kind' or should they find friendships predominantly with non-disabled people?

In the heyday of the normalization movement, a premium was placed on people with learning disabilities being integrated into mainstream society. Specialist, segregated settings only served to devalue their humanity and perpetuate the low status that society placed on such individuals. Implicitly the message was: don't congregate people with disabilities.

This was also the wish of some people with learning disabilities – especially those who were more mildly affected. Edgerton et al.'s (1984) research, for example, identified a strong wish to lose the label of 'mentally retarded' and to pass as non-disabled within their community.

With hindsight, this idealistic thinking was naïve for a number of reasons. Not least, it discounted the express wish of many people with learning disabilities who value their friendships with similar people (e.g. Bayley 1993). Many of the advances in social policy have resulted from marginalized groups banding together, promoting solidarity and advocating their rights. This has been equally true for the disabled movement, led predominantly by those with physical and sensory disabilities, but it is also emerging for people with learning disabilities (Ward 1998). Social integration has been very slow to evolve. People who have moved into dispersed community housing still have few non-learning disabled people in their social networks and those who report most satisfaction with their existing level of relationships tend to be those with a greater proportion of other learning disabled people in their networks (Gregory et al. 2001).

In our society, intimate relationships tend to occur among people who are matched in terms of age, background and interests. Indeed, legal prohibitions exist preventing men having sexual intercourse with women who have 'mental impairment'. These are likely to be ignored if both parties are deemed to have a learning disability and are thought capable of giving consent. Hence those seeking an intimate relationship are more likely to find it among friends who are similarly labelled. I will return to this issue later.

In sum, a more reasonable stance is to promote both types of friendship; it is not an either-or situation. However, there is an important provision: it depends on the person. In a group home, for instance, one person may be reluctant to socialize with the other residents as they are keen to escape what they see as the stigmatizing label of learning disability. However, other residents may prefer to be in the company of their fellow housemates as they may feel threatened and uneasy in the company of people who are more able communicators than they are. Hence the importance of person-centred planning which takes account of people's talents and preferences and the need to find ways of providing a range of opportunities suited to that particular person's needs and aspirations.

Nurturing friendships

In this section we examine various strategies that can be used with people who have learning disabilities to widen their network of acquaintances and to nurture their friendships. Before exploring these in more detail, three basic principles need to be stressed:

- Friendships cannot be made for other people; people choose their friends. At best we can build up a network of acquaintances out of which friendships may develop.
- Friendships usually grow out of shared interests and activities and from among people already known to the person. This is the starting point.
- Choice and self-determination are key elements in friendships. Hence you need to constantly consult and listen to the people you are trying to help. We must not impose our values and desires onto another.

Befrienders

These three principles are at odds with the popular idea in services and with family carers of finding a person (usually a volunteer) to befriend a person with learning disabilities. Experience suggests that such schemes can be done and that they do offer benefits

for both parties (e.g. Walsh *et al.* 1988), but they are risky for a number of reasons.

The matching of 'friends' is often done by a professional worker or scheme co-ordinator; hence the person with learning disabilities has very limited scope for choosing and developing their own friendships. The 'friendship' that develops runs the risk of being artificial in the sense that the able-bodied person is invariably cast in the role of helper and supervisor. Through time this can place quite a strain on the relationship. If the able-bodied person is no longer able or willing to continue, there is the added problem of finding a replacement while dealing with possible feelings of disappointment and loss in the person left behind.

In sum, the befriender approach is another example of adopting a specialist solution to a disability issue. Therein lies the biggest risk of all: a befriender absolves everyone else — busy support staff and social workers for example — from their responsibilities for nurturing friendships.

The four-stranded approach

Newton *et al.* (1994) start from a different perspective entirely. Their proposition is that the focus of all staff involved with disabled persons should not be on the person with the disability *per se* but rather on the relationships between the person and the other members of their communities. (Note that the term 'communities' can include a family community, a service community such as a day centre or a work community as well as neighbourhood communities.) Newton *et al.* identified four interrelated elements to nurturing relationships (see Figure 24.2). These are examined in turn below.

Social support

Among the many definitions of social support in the literature, the original conceptualization by Cobb (1976) is particularly apposite for those of us working with individuals who have a learning disability. He viewed social support as telling people they are cared for and loved, showing them they are valued and esteemed and helping them to find a place in a network of communication and mutual obligation. The goal of social support is to make people feel good about themselves and to feel needed.

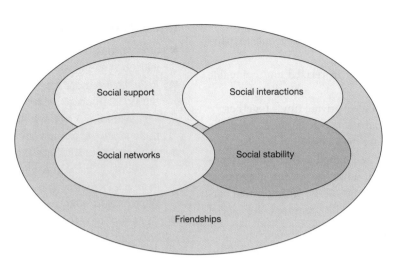

Figure 24.2 Nurturing friendships (Newton *et al.* 1994)

Numerous studies have documented the stress-buffering and health-promoting influences of social support across a wide variety of societal groups and it is a concept that has been extensively investigated with parents of children with disabilities (Sarason and Sarason 1985).

The practical outworking of social support can take different forms such as material support (e.g. providing them with money and loan of equipment); emotional support (e.g. listening if they have problems); information support (e.g. naming other people they could contact); and instrumental support (e.g. practical assistance such as escorting a person on a bus).

Of course many staff in services will recognize this as a summary of their job descriptions but there is a crucial difference. People with learning disabilities need to be seen as sources of support to others and not just as receivers of support. It is the mutuality of support that is a hallmark of friendships. This is the basis on which many advocacy groups function.

Social interactions

Here the focus is on what happens when two or more people meet and jointly engage in activities, be it conversing, celebrating a birthday, attending a meeting or painting a room. As noted earlier, people with learning disabilities can experience particular difficulties in holding their own in such settings.

However, certain settings are more conducive for promoting social interactions than others (see Box 24.2). As you read through the list you might consider why these have been chosen rather than other activities such as watching television or listening to music – the most commonly reported pastimes of people with learning disabilities.

Box 24.2: Activities for developing relationships (Firth and Rapley 1990)

- Going to the cinema, theatre and concerts
- Snooker, pool and darts
- Singing and acting
- Shared hobbies and classes (e.g. pottery, cooking)
- Rambling and hill-walking
- Folk/old-time dancing
- Disco dancing
- Camping
- Holidays
- Visiting museums and attractions
- Going to the pub or meal out
- Religious events
- Tenants' associations
- Self-advocacy groups
- Team sports
- Part of a team helping others in need

Some of the common features you might have noted are:

- *couples*: there are opportunities for people to 'pair-off' for the activity;
- *relaxation*: people meet in relaxed and enjoyable situations;
- *privacy*: people can have private times together;
- *shared feelings and values*: people are given the opportunity to share their views and beliefs;
- *common cause*: it was noted earlier how friends are often forged in adversity or for a common cause – advocacy groups can be an important setting to acquire the skills required for social interaction.

Of course some of the above features can still be incorporated into watching television and listening to music, for example by having privacy at home for friends to do this together or by talking together about films and TV programmes with a strong emotional content.

Another approach has been to provide education programmes that aim to develop the communication and social skills of people with learning disabilities. Although research reports are broadly positive, there is less convincing evidence of their widespread application in practice (Chadsey-Rusch 1992). One reason is that the support staff who are in the best position to provide this guidance (namely those who are with the individual most frequently and consistently) are also those who are least likely to be trained in the skill development of the people they support. Rather, social skills courses, if they are provided at all, tend to be run by specialist staff in 'classrooms' with possibly little carry-over into the person's everyday life.

An alternative strategy for promoting better communication is to focus on the more able person and encourage them to adapt their interactions to become better attuned to the person with the disability (Purcell *et al.* 2000). Box 24.3 summarizes how people should change the way they talk to people with learning disabilities. Equally, able communicators – including staff – must become more adept at using sign systems such as Makaton with people with limited verbal skills (see Chapter 9).

Box 24.3: Adapting communication (Purcell *et al.* 2000)

- *Slow down*: leave more time for client initiations and responses.
- *Respond*: be more responsive to clients during interactions, with more use of non-verbal feedback in particular, such as head nods, facial expression and gestures.
- *Fewer questions*: reduce their use of closed questions (e.g. Do you want tea?) and increase the use of open questions (e.g. What do you want to drink?).
- *Comment*: increase the use of comments about yourself, what is happening and so on.
- *Simplify*: reduce the complexity and amount of the verbal language you use, with shorter sentences and simpler words.
- *Attention*: get and maintain the person's attention on shared activities through use of gestures and verbal prompts.

Social networks

A social network is composed of people who socially interact. This broad definition is useful as it reminds us that we all belong to many different networks and we enter and leave various networks in the course of any day.

That said, our networks vary in terms of size, intimacy and longevity. But for most people with learning disabilities, their networks tend to be smaller, more dense (the same people feature) and have more unreciprocated relationships. As we noted earlier, many learning disabled individuals are overly reliant on one or two people (usually a family or staff member) for companionship, and in fact there are some who are friendless. Some have argued that the advent of dispersed community housing has resulted in more loneliness for tenants, with fewer opportunities to join with others in communal pursuits compared to residential homes and long-stay hospitals (Srivastava 2001).

One solution has been the concept of a community for people with disabilities living together with able-bodied helpers on a life-sharing basis. The Camphill communities begun by Rudolf Steiner or the L'Arche communities founded by Jean Vanier are two examples of international practices also found in Britain and Ireland (Jackson 1999). These 'intentional communities' have been the subject of much debate. However, recent research found that these residents had greater satisfaction with their friendships and relationships than those living in dispersed community housing, although the size of their networks were similar (Gregory *et al.* 2001).

Another approach attracting much interest of late is that of creating 'circles of support' or a 'circle of friends' (Neville *et al.* 2000). There is no prescription for the form and format these take as they will be guided very much by the wishes and needs of the person with a learning disability as identified in their person-centred plan (see next chapter). That said, there are some common strands in such circles. They might include family members such as siblings and cousins, alongside neighbours and acquaintances, coworkers for people in jobs, members of clubs, churches and suchlike who know the person. The size does not matter; a few interested people can make a start. The circle does *not* have to include professional workers although they can have a key role as facilitators or gobetweens, as noted earlier.

It is likely that the depth of friendship will vary across the members of the circle. Some may be prepared to be intimately involved, others will continue as acquaintances, but they will be better informed than previously. The circle might meet from time to time to explore with the person and each other the contributions they are making to each other's lives. Activity plans might develop as to how the circle could change or develop. 'In all circles of support people are encouraged to dream' (Neville *et al.* 2000: 151).

Circles of friends can find expression in different ways. For example, Key Ring is a housing provider for people with learning disabilities that works by building up mutually supportive networks among the tenants living within a geographical area as well as linking them into the communities where they live (Simons and Watson 1999). Likewise, new forms of day provision often operate on the basis of creating social networks for their clients by slotting them into educational, employment and recreational opportunities in the community (Towell 2000).

Social stability

The final element is probably the least investigated among people with learning disabilities, namely the continuity and stability of their social relationships. Undoubtedly there are many examples of lifelong friendships but we have an imperfect understanding of why this happens for some and not for others. Equally, change is a feature of everyone's friendships and sometimes this can be good for all concerned. Yet there have been few studies on the impact on people with learning disabilities when they lose friends.

The dimension of social stability is particularly challenging for services as the lower paid staff they employ have a high turnover rate. This makes it very difficult for staff to assist people to sustain any relationships that have been forged. This reality is unlikely to change for the foreseeable future, which again emphasizes the need to promote friendships among service-users and to build circles of support beyond service staff.

Exercise 24.2

Pick one person with learning disabilities whom you know well. Make a list of the different ways you think their social networks might be widened. What would staff need to do differently to make this happen?

Intimate relationships

As friendships flourish, some will grow into more intimate relationships (see also Chapters 18 and 19). This raises particular issues for support services (Simpson *et al.* 2006) and the topic is worthy of a more exhaustive discussion than space permits here. Nonetheless a few pointers can be provided.

Such relationships are likely to have stood the test of time. Staff need to respect the person's choice and help both people to enjoy and develop their friendship. This will mean treating the people as a couple when it comes to planning activities, giving them times for privacy and taking pleasure in the benefits which the friendship brings to them rather than becoming preoccupied with the risks, which professional staff are wont to do.

Staff may need to help them work through the problems or difficulties that such a relationship will encounter from time to time. In particular, they may need assistance with the 'negotiation' skills needed to repair disputes and disagreements such as trying to see the other's viewpoint, being prepared to listen to their hurt, apologizing and finding ways of showing respect and love for their partner. Equally, staff need to be aware of their limitations. A point may come when it is necessary to encourage the couple to seek help from specialist workers or organizations, such as Relate.

Throughout, support staff need to have from their employers:

- clear policy and practice guidelines;
- time given over at team meetings to discuss the implementation of the guidelines;
- staff supervision to deal with the issues that arise.

Conclusion

A few themes have re-echoed throughout this chapter. Friendships can take a long time to grow, opportunities need to be offered and a plentiful supply of encouragement may be required.

Friendships can take many forms. We need to look beyond the immediate contacts in people's lives and try to build a circle of support for each person that will root them more firmly within their local community and society (McConkey *et al.* 2009).

Friendships enrich people's lives. New styles of person-centred services are needed along with new ways of defining staff roles and responsibilities.

Nevertheless, many services remain as they always have been because we mistakenly continue to try to isolate, care for or 'fix' the individual with the disability rather than nurturing relationships with other people (McConkey *et al.* 2009). In modern parlance, we need to be in the business of creating 'social capital' in the neighbourhoods and communities in which people with learning disabilities live (Bates and Davis 2004). Who knows what would result if relationships became the focus of all our endeavours? Now is the time to find out.

References

Arthur, A.A. (2003) The emotional lives of people with learning disability, *British Journal of Learning Disabilities*, 31: 25–30.

Bates, P. and Davis, F.A. (2004) Social capital, social inclusion and services for people with learning disabilities, *Disability & Society*, 19(3): 195–207.

Bayley, M. (1993) The personal friendships of people with learning difficulties, *Social Care Findings*, 39.

Chadsey-Rusch, J. (1992) Towards defining and measuring social skills in employment settings, *American Journal on Mental Retardation*, 96: 405–18.

Cobb, S. (1976) Social support as a moderator of life stress, *Psychosomatic Medicine*, 38: 300–14.

Duck, S.W. (1992) *Human Relationship*, 2nd edn. London: Sage.

Edgerton, R.B., Bollinger, M. and Herr, B. (1984) The cloak of competence: years later, *American Journal of Mental Deficiency*, 88: 345–51.

Firth, H. and Rapley, M. (1990) *From Acquaintance to Friendship: Issues for People with Learning Disabilities.* Worcester: British Institute of Mental Handicap.

Gregory, N., Roberston, J., Kessissoglou, S., Emerson, E. and Hatton, C. (2001) Factors associated with expressed satisfaction among people with intellectual disability receiving residential supports, *Journal of Intellectual Disability Research*, 45: 279–91.

Hall, L. and Hewson, S. (2006) The community links of a sample of people with intellectual disabilities, *Journal of Applied Research in Intellectual Disabilities*, 19: 204–7.

HM Government (2009) *Valuing People Now: A New Three-year Strategy for Learning Disabilities.* London: Department of Health.

Jackson, R. (1999) The case for village communities for adults with learning disabilities: an exploration of the concept, *Journal of Learning Disabilities*, 3: 110–17.

Jobling, A. and Cuskelly, M. (2002) Life styles of adults with Down syndrome living at home, in M. Cuskelly, A. Jobling and S. Buckley (eds) *Down Syndrome across the Life Span.* London: Whurr.

Koster, M., Nakken, H., Pijl, S.P. and van Houten, E. (2009) Being part of the peer group: a literature study focusing on the social dimension of inclusion in education, *International Journal of Inclusive Education*, 13: 117–40.

McConkey, R. (1987) *Who Cares? Community Involvement with Mental Handicap*. London: Souvenir Press.

McConkey, R. (1994) *Innovations in Educating Communities about Learning Disabilities*. Chorley: Lisieux Hall.

McConkey, R., Walsh, J. and Mulcahy, M. (1981) The recreational pursuits of mentally handicapped adults, *International Journal of Rehabilitation Research*, 4: 493–9.

McConkey, R., Morris, I. and Purcell, M. (1999) Communications between staff and adult persons with intellectual disabilities in naturally occurring settings, *Journal of Intellectual Disability Research*, 43(3): 194–205.

McConkey, R., McConaghie, J., Mezza, F. and Wilson, J. (2003) Moving from long-stay hospitals: the views of Northern Irish patients and relatives, *Journal of Learning Disabilities*, 7: 78–93.

McConkey, R., Dunne, J. and Blitz, N. (2009) *Shared Lives: Building Relationships and Community with People Who Have Intellectual Disabilities*. Amsterdam: Sense Publishers.

Neville, M., Baylis, L., Boldison, S.J., Cox, A., Cox, L., Gilliand, D. *et al.* (2000) *Building Inclusive Communities*. Rugby: Circles Network.

Newton, J.S., Horner, R.H., Ard, W.R., LeBaron, N. and Sappington, G. (1994) A conceptual model for improving the social life of individuals with mental retardation, *Mental Retardation*, 32: 393–402.

O'Reilly, M.F. and Glynn, D. (1995) Using a process social skills training approach with adolescents with mild intellectual disabilities in a high school setting, *Education and Training in Mental Retardation and Developmental Disabilities*, 30: 87–98.

Purcell, M., McConkey, R. and Morris, I. (2000) Staff communication with people with intellectual disabilities: the impact of a work-based training programme, *International Journal of Language and Communication Disorders*, 35: 147–58.

Roberston, J., Emerson, E., Gregory, N., Hatton, C., Kessissoglou, S., Hallam, A. *et al.* (2001) Social networks of people with mental retardation in residential settings, *Mental Retardation*, 39: 201–14.

Rosen, J.W. and Burchard, S.N. (1990) Community activities and social support networks: a social comparison of adults with and without mental retardation, *Education and Training in Mental Retardation*, 25: 193–204.

Sarason, I.G. and Sarason, B.R. (1985) *Social Support: Theory, Research and Application*. Dordrecht: Martinus Nijho Publishers.

Sayce, L. (2003) Beyond good intentions. Making anti-discrimination strategies work, *Disability & Society*, 18: 625–42.

Schalock, R. and Alonso, M.A.V. (2002) *Handbook on Quality of Life for Human Service Practitioners*. Washington, DC: American Association on Mental Retardation.

Schwartz, D.B. (1992) *Crossing the River: Creating a Conceptual Revolution in Community and Disability*. Cambrdge, MA: Brookline Books.

Simons, K. and Watson, D. (1999) *The View from Arthur's Seat: Review of Services for People with Learning Disabilities – A Literature Review of Housing and Support Options Beyond Scotland*. Edinburgh: Scottish Executive Central Research Unit.

Simpson, A., Lafferty, A. and McConkey, R. (2006) *Out of the Shadows: A Report on the Sexual Health and Wellbeing of People with Learning Disabilities in Northern Ireland*. London: FPA.

Smyth, M. and McConkey, R. (2003) Future aspirations of parents and students with severe learning difficulties on leaving special schooling, *British Journal of Learning Disabilities*, 31: 54–9.

Srivastava, A. (2001) Developing friendships and social integration through leisure for people with moderate, severe and profound learning disabilities transferred from hospital to community care, *Tizard Learning Disability Review*, 6(4): 19–27.

Stainton, T. and Besser, H. (1998) The positive impact of children with intellectual disability on the family, *Journal of Intellectual and Developmental Disability*, 23: 57–70.

Towell, D. (2000) Achieving positive change in people's lives through the national learning disabilities strategy: lessons from an American Experience, *Tizard Learning Disability Review*, 5(3): 30–6.

Vanier, J. (1991) *Community and Growth*. London: Longman & Todd.

Verdonschot, M.M.L., de Witte, L.P., Reichrath, E., Buntinx, W.H.E. and Curfs, L.M.G. (2009) Community participation of people with an intellectual disability: a review of empirical findings, *Journal of Intellectual Disability Research*, 53: 303–18.

Walsh, P.N., Coyle, K. and Lynch, C. (1988) The partners project: part 1, *Mental Handicap*, 16: 122–5.

Ward, L. (1998) *Innovations in Advocacy and Empowerment for People with Intellectual Disabilities*. Chorley: Lisieux Hall Publications.

Webster, A.A. and Carter, M. (2007) Social relationships and friendships of children with developmental disabilities: implications for inclusive settings. A systematic review, *Journal of Intellectual & Developmental Disability*, 32: 200–13.

25

Enabling and supporting person-centred planning

Jacqui Brewster and Paul Ramcharan

Introduction

Person-centred planning (PCP) was seen in *Valuing People* (Department of Health 2001a) and related guidance (Department of Health 2001b) as a central strategy through which people with learning disabilities gained more control and pursued better lives based upon their own hopes, dreams and aspirations. While *Valuing People Now* (Department of Health 2009) moves towards a personalization agenda set out in *Putting People First* (Department of Health 2007; see Chapter 22 this volume), it recognizes that services should 'have person-centred plans for everyone they support and . . . use these to review and improve the support they provide to individuals to ensure that agreed outcomes continue to be met' (Department of Health 2007: 54). In this agenda best outcomes can be produced only where person-centred approaches are accompanied by individualized funding, '. . . resource flexibility, supported decision-making, brokerage and care management [to succeed in] implementing self-directed support' (Beadle-Brown 2006: 5).

For those involved in the lives of people with learning disabilities, including direct support and other staff, it is therefore important to know something about the roots of person-centred planning, to know what evidence there is to support it, to have a working knowledge of how it operates and, further, to know the criticisms and limitations of the approach. This chapter aims to provide a basic grounding in these ideas but does so recognizing that there is now substantial information, resources and training around person-centred planning and that at the time of writing new guidance is pending.

PCP as a trend towards individualization?

From the levels of professional control which characterized lives in the large institutions (see Chapter 2), community care has seen a succession of models in which this control has gradually transferred from professionals to people with learning disabilities. Sanderson (2002) states that PCP has not simply appeared but has naturally 'evolved' from the 'most progressive' philosophies and care practices of the last three decades. PCP is part of a wider move towards person-centred approaches within medical, health and social welfare. In their seminal work on person-centred planning Robertson *et al.* (2005) suggest that:

> PCP may be best considered as an evolutionary step in the long-standing trend towards the increasing individualization of supports and services.
>
> (Robertson *et al.* 2005: iii)

So what exactly has been the latest 'mutation' in this evolution? Below we seek to demonstrate this movement by comparing PCP with its predecessor, Individual Programme Planning (IPPs), which featured as a central strategy during the All Wales Strategy (Welsh Office 1983), the first UK national policy to seek to build services based broadly upon normalization principles.

The All Wales Strategy saw people with a learning disability and their families being *involved* in preparing, implementing and reviewing individual programme plans. As Felce *et al.* (1998: 16) note:

> Co-ordination . . . was to be done by multi-disciplinary teams . . . each person . . . was to have a nominated key worker . . . to act as a single point of contact for individuals, families and generic services alike.

Contrast this with the official UK definition of PCP:

> Person Centred Planning is a process for continual listening and learning, focusing on

what is important to someone now and in the future, and acting upon this in alliance with their family and friends.

(Department of Health 2001b: 12)

To understand how these two systems differ we compare them in Table 25.1 along five well-established dimensions (Sanderson 2000; Department of Health 2001a, 2001b).

Dimension of PCP	The IPP process	The PCP process
1 Person at the centre		
Person's place in planning process	Involved as participant	Control
The planning group	Professionally convened	Person, advocates and supporters, i.e. circle
Membership of group	Professionals with user/carer	Chosen by the person, relationship-oriented
Ethos of planning meeting	Participative	Person in control and ownership
2 Family members and friends as partners in planning		
Ethos	Participation of carer and user in identifying professionally assessed need	Partnership with family, friends and community. Professionals invited as necessary
Resolution of conflict	Professional knows best	Creative management of conflict through negotiation. The person and his/her circle knows best
3 Using the person's gifts, capacities and aspirations to judge the relevant support they need		
Ethos	Takes a deficit perspective in assessing needs	Is artful, creative and innovative in responding to wishes and dreams
Approach	Quantitative, concentrating on training the person to be more independent and keeping them safe	A qualitative approach concentrating on total quality of life from the person's perspective
Information-holding and collecting	Information and decisions held by professionals and presented in ways that can be inaccessible to the person. File on shelf	Information presented in ways which are accessible and meaningful to the person and accessed by those involved in the planning
4 Planning for action		
Focus	Service- and professionally oriented. Assumes services can meet all needs	A shared commitment to action in family, relationships and community as well as in services to support these changes
Resources mobilized	Service resources to promote inclusion	A focus on mobilizing those with a commitment to the person, i.e. communities of interest

Dimension of PCP	The IPP process	The PCP process
Provision	'Off-the-shelf' service packages	Demand for a made-to-measure response from services and others
5 The planning process		
Meetings	IPP meeting and six-monthly review	Plan is not the outcome. Circle of support meets as often as necessary. A continuous process of listening and responding to wishes as the person grows
Co-ordination	Professional co-ordinates the service response through purchaser	A continual process with the circle facilitator prompting relevant parties to act. This may also involve assessment for services under the NHS and Community Care Act 1991
Service orientation	Person as recipient of what is available	Reflects what is possible. Still limited by service availability, but able to push for new services to cover an unmet need. A variety of formats running from the artistic and personal history right through to formal plans for action
Product	A completed and locally standardized pro forma usually split into specific sections to reflect quality of life issues and specialist health and other needs	

Table 25.1 Comparison of the IPP and PCP process along the five PCP dimensions

Here are some summary dichotomies which may help you to understand the differences between IPPs and PCPs summarized in Table 25.1: a movement from participation to control; professionally led versus personally owned process; professional assessment compared to creatively produced outcomes; a plan held by professionals to one owned by the person; services that are supplied in ready-made-up off-the-shelf form compared to creative services demanded by the person to achieve their own goals; a process of regular review compared to a continuous process of change. While we await pending guidance on PCPs, the original guidance published soon after *Valuing People* (Department of Health 2001b: 12) defines PCP as follows:

A process of continually listening and learning, focusing on what is important to someone now and in the future, and acting upon this alliance with their family and friends. The listening is used to understand a person's capacities and choices. Person-centred planning is the basis for problem-solving and negotiation to mobilise the necessary resources to pursue a person's aspirations. These resources may be obtained from someone's own network, service providers or from non-specialist and non-service sources.

Use the case study below to compare what differences the two approaches may have in relation to Jane.

Case study: *Jane*

Jane is a young woman of 19 years who has just left school. She lives at home with her parents and her 10-year-old brother. Jane loved school, had many friends, and is a real extrovert. Her favourite subjects at school were music and art. Jane has Down's syndrome and when she was at school lost a lot of time due to her asthma and epilepsy. She and her family have recently moved to another part of the country due to her father's new job. The whole family are trying to find their feet. Jane has enrolled on a special needs literacy and numeracy course at the local further education college but she is unhappy there and wants to do something else. She tells her newly appointed social worker that she is sick of feeling 'poorly'. When asked what she wants, Jane is very clear . . . she wants a job where she can help people; she has always wanted to sing on stage; she wants a boyfriend and some space away from her little brother.

Exercise 25.1

Think about Jane's wishes and aspirations for the future and her practical day-to-day needs. Write a description of how you would see a planning meeting for Jane under the IPP process and then under a PCP process. Which do you feel would produce a better outcome and why? Who might lead the process? Who else would be involved? Which process would you prefer if you were to make a plan for a time of change in your own life?

One of the very real issues is that the PCP system still requires professionals, usually a care manager, to provide decisions under the provisions of the NHS and Community Care Act 1991. The early guidance on PCP exhorts care managers to ensure under the provisions of the NHS and Community Care Act that 'people's goals and choices are powerfully reflected in care planning and design, and in the purchase and review of services' (Routledge and Sanderson 2001: 45). Moreover, control over the level of funding to each person must be related not just to their needs but, given limited overall funding, to the comparative needs of other people with learning disabilities, leading Felce (2004: 28) to argue that 'strategic planning provides a resource climate within which PCP and decision-making can take place'. At the same time the most systematic examination of PCPs has found cost neutrality (Robertson *et al.* 2005), and similar cost-neutral models around assessment for direct payments have also been claimed (see Duffy 2005), making the likelihood of government support for the personalization agenda significantly stronger.

Above we have set out some of the basic assumptions around person-centred planning in contemporary policy in the UK. It is now necessary to seek to bring person-centred planning to life by examining how it operates as a process.

Person-centred tasks

Person-centred care is based on a number of assumptions (see Sanderson 2000 for a review). It is

> A life philosophy – an aspiration about being human, about pursuing the meaning of self, respecting difference, valuing equality, facing the anxieties, threats and guilts in our own lives, emphasising the strengths in others and celebrating uniqueness and our own 'personhood'.
>
> (Sheard 2004: 2)

This highlights the importance of working with people in a way which recognizes and acknowledges their unique identity as people of value whatever label they have been given because of their 'difference'. Such care and support is important for everybody – we all need support in life, we all need to feel recognized, 'celebrated', loved and respected for what we do and who we are. The means through which a person-centred approach can be accomplished are set out below.

Celebrating uniqueness and learning to value the person

- **A person-centred approach means helping people to recognize their unique qualities and abilities,** looking beyond impairments, showing people that we recognize their gifts, enjoy being with them and treat them with respect and dignity.

To recognize a person's qualities assumes at least two things. First, that we are able to communicate with that person, and second, that we know the person well enough to be able to recognize their own unique gifts and talents. Often this will involve not only meeting and knowing the person, but knowing others who care about and for them. The people who care about and for the person, who support them and know them best, can be called a 'circle of support' (see Perske and Perske 1988; Brandon 1991), and that circle may change over time. Service workers working in a PCP system are therefore less likely to be on their own in knowing the person and can learn a lot more about the person through those in the circle.

- **Learning about the person implies knowing them, listening to them, learning from them and their circle and then, as a group, being there to see changes in their life experiences.**

One of the strengths of learning with the person and their circle is that, particularly for those whose communication we find hard to understand, we can learn about the best ways to communicate with them. We can learn from the circle how to share a system of communication with those who know the person best and be inventive about the best ways to learn from them.

But *what* should we be learning from the person? If we think about our own relationships we expect those around us to know the things we like, our dreams, nightmares and so forth. It is no different for people with learning disabilities. Perhaps the central difference is that in order to provide a consistent approach, the circle needs to meet as a group to share their understanding with the person.

- **The circle should meet to ensure that they share a view about the person based upon the person's own preferences, whether verbalized or reported as their responses to previous experiences.**

At the centre of the person-centred process is listening to the person and/or observing the things which give them pleasure as well as the things that drive them crazy; talking to people about the things they love, the things that comfort them when they are down, the things that make them feel cherished; and sharing activities which reflect the things that they love.

- **Circles should focus on dreams, aspirations and wishes.**

Essential lifestyle planning does not only look at hopes, dreams and aspirations through storytelling, discussion and sharing histories. It also focuses on the mundane everyday 'stuff of life' that contributes to quality of life. This experience means that people respect your 'non-negotiables' (Smull and Burke-Harrison 1992) and that they provide competency-enhancing support (Booth and Booth 1994) without creating dependency.

Exercise 25.2

Take a few minutes to think about the place of a chosen routine in your own life. Write down the answers to each of these questions.

Morning routines: what do you do when you get up in the morning? Dress straight away or slob about in your nightwear for a while? Jump out of bed immediately with a smile on your face or does it take lots of caffeine to get you going? Take a bath or a shower? What shower gel, toothpaste, cosmetics, teabags etc. do you use? Is it important to leave the house tidy before you leave or are you not bothered?

Other rituals: what are your comfort rituals when you've had a bad day? Glass of wine, hot bath, go to the gym, go out for dinner, phone a friend? Which side of the bed do you sleep on?

Now compare and contrast these answers with those of a friend. What do your rituals say about the things in life that are important to you?

In *Positive Rituals and Quality of Life*, Michael Smull (2004) reiterates the importance of finding out what people want their days to be like:

> Our efforts need to begin with these daily rituals. We have found that some of the people referred to us because of 'non-compliant' or aggressive behaviour simply have daily rituals that were not recognised. Our obsession with implementing program plans and continuous

Type of PCP	Cues to use and predominant focus	Approach
Essential lifestyle planning (Smull *et al.* (undated)	Where the circle does not know the person well Where it is difficult to understand what the person wants	Listening to the person's story, getting to know their unique skills and qualities, how they communicate, what support is needed for them to stay fit and healthy and to make plans about who will do what, when and how. It may involve storytelling, learning logs, discussion of incidents, routines and rituals. It is perhaps the most comprehensive PCP approach
MAPS (Forest and Lusthaus 1989)	When a person can communicate their dreams Where the person already has support to work towards their dreams	The group: finds a way together; explores the person's story and history; explores what the 'best life' would be; explores nightmares and worries; brainstorms who the person is and who she or he wants to be. By picture-building it provides a way of planning action
Personal futures planning (see Mount and Zwernik 1988; Mount 2000)	To give an overview of the person's life as it is To focus on the future and on dreams	Provides a means of drawing up maps of key areas in the person's life, for example a community map, health map or a choices map. It specifically addresses areas of concern. It outlines personal accomplishments and provides tools to implement six key tasks associated with planning a personal future
PATH (see O'Brien *et al.* 1993)	To develop and plan for action and change	A way of developing a series of actions that can achieve a person's dream. It helps identify who does what, when they do it and how they do it. The approach also explains the role of the circle facilitator

Table 25.2 A summary of person-centred planning approaches

training has resulted in ignoring, suppressing, and trying to replace rituals that are positive, individual adaptations to the rhythms of life.

Smull points out that the routines of many people living in residential care settings may change according to which member of staff is on duty. He also points out that our comfort rituals are not just something we allow ourselves when we have been 'good' – we will still have that bottle of wine even if it was our fault that we had a bad day, whereas people with learning disabilities are often expected to 'earn' these

Case study: *George*

George has lived in service settings from being a teenager after the death of his parents. George has moved many times and he has never had a key worker move with him. Now George is elderly and physically frail. Through a support group George was recently invited to talk about himself and his past and express this by making a personal poster using paint and magazine images. George shared with the group that he was the son of a Northumbrian farmer and he moved the group with stories of feeding chickens, fetching eggs and bringing the sheep in with a beloved sheepdog. The care worker attending with George was fascinated. Despite having worked with George for six months and having a great deal of information in the form of care plans and risk assessments, she had not got to know George as a person with a past and a future.

indulgences. The sense of control over my rituals is therefore a vital part of experiencing a life that is 'good to and for me'. So it is for all individuals.

- **It is vital to consider how present life experiences respect routine, ordinary and day-to-day choices.**

As well as present life circumstances and future dreams, our personal identity is also shaped by our past. Helping people explore their biography can be a powerful means of self-expression and an important ingredient in appreciating constituents of successful ageing and adaptation (see Chapters 32 and 34).

Life story work, personal posters, art work, poetry, diaries, scrapbooks and photo albums can be powerful ways of helping people express their identity (see Chapter 1). As Atkinson and Walmsley (1999) point out, life history work can serve several purposes: understanding personal identity; recapturing ownership of one's life; comparing the past with present circumstances; dealing with the experiences of a difficult history; and planning ahead. Exploring the past is often a necessary step towards planning for the future and it can sometimes be painful and take a long time.

However, we all have things which we share with very few people, if anybody at all. Often this privacy has been denied people with learning disabilities and very personal details may have been shared in public settings without their express permission. People may not want to tell us everything about their lives and we must also be aware that for many people with learning disabilities there may be some very painful memories from a lifetime of exclusion, isolation, loneliness, and sometimes abuse. Some people may find it cathartic to share this information, others may

find it all too painful or difficult to share, or may not have the words. We must therefore be sensitive about asking people to share memories with us, watch for signs that the person may be distressed and give support and/or get further support to help the person where necessary.

- **Exploring the past is very often as important as knowing the present and dreaming about the future.**

Being person-centred requires that any circle of support collectively understands the core of a person's ideals, values and emotional strengths and frailties and to be 'mapping' inclusion. Personal futures planning (see Mount and Zwernik 1988; Mount 2000) and MAPS (see Falvey *et al.* 1997) focuses on these issues of direct action to support the person to make such inclusion meaningful to them (see Table 25.2), though not to the exclusion of other approaches.

In considering a person's life we might address: where the person wants to spend their days; the clothes they choose to wear or the fragrance they use; the possessions they enjoy; the way they decorate their home; and the people the person wishes to share these things with. We also need to know more about the person's health needs and how they choose to stay healthy. This may involve creating a map of their choices in relation to community and health, as in personal futures planning, or planning how to accomplish what they choose. A central task of being person-centred therefore involves ensuring that plans for a person's future are inclusive and that their identity is, over time, seen as an included rather than an excluded identity.

Person-centred interaction

So far consideration has been given to the parameters of person-centredness and how these are translated into forms of PCP. But there is also a 'how': the ways in which people are brought together and how they treat one another.

Welcoming family and friends

Family and friends provide an abundance of shared memories and experiences and a depth of emotion which means that they often care in a way which is different to the paid caregiver. Our relationships with family and friends help us to form a view of ourselves as lovable and loving human beings. A person-centred approach to care welcomes family and friends as individuals with special knowledge and insight into the person. It warrants a more honest and open way of working with families and supports these relationships in enthusiastic and non-judgemental ways. Many families have found person-centred planning to be an empowering and effective way to create plans for the future and many organizations are now working to help families take control and plan in partnership with service providers and the much wider community (see www.familiesleading planning.co.uk).

Interaction based on demonstrable respect, partnership and power sharing

The way we speak to a person, including the words we use, our tone of voice, the inflection used and the body language that accompanies our verbal expression, strongly reflect the way we see that person and the level of respect we have for them.

Exercise 25.3

Consider the difference between these two interactions:

'My mum used to make porridge.'

'Did she? We don't have time this morning. We're going to be late for day care if we don't hurry up.'

'My mum used to make porridge.'

'Did she John? My mum did too. What was it like? Tell me about it as we get ready to go out. We could make some tomorrow if you like.'

Identify the differences between the two. Which is better and why?

A person-centred approach to care recognizes that people with learning disabilities often have problems communicating. It approaches all attempts at communication, be they making noises, walking away, singing, laughing, crying, or getting angry and aggressive, as a serious attempt to express self, to participate, to make choices and to be a social person.

Care where the carer shares of themselves

David Brandon (1989) describes how staff often lose their way when working with people and become overwhelmed by the demands of the organization they work in. Brandon describes this as 'learning a few crude techniques' and losing the 'easy giving of self'. This 'easy giving of self', Sheard (2004) argues, is often undervalued in our services, yet the people who give of themselves in this way make a huge and positive impact on the lives of those with whom they are involved (Sanderson 2002). 'Person-centred teams' (Sanderson 2002) exist where individuals are recognized within the team for the unique qualities and skills they bring to the people they support. Teams will then develop their own person-centred team plan which mirrors the values and processes of person-centred planning. Within such teams staff give of themselves and are valued for who they are and what they do.

PCP in practice

A number of person-centred approaches have been developed. You might want to look at MAPS (Forest and Lusthaus 1989), PATH (O'Brien et al. 1993), personal futures planning (Mount and Zwernik 1988), essential lifestyle planning (Smull and Burke-Harrison 1992) and life review (Kropf and Greene 1993). Table 25.2 summarizes aspects of the different approaches to PCP. Column 2 of Table 25.2 also helps to identify cues for the use of different approaches.

Five characterizing features of PCP were identified and compared to the previously existing IPP system in Table 25.1, while some of the main approaches to PCP are outlined in Table 25.2. As has already been said, there are many different planning styles, each looking at who the person is, their unique gifts, skills and needs, along with their personal history. Each style also finds out what is important to the person while identifying the people who love and care for the person. Each different style also explores how the person can take part in their community and how they can be helped to live a life outside the service system.

PCP meetings should be conducted using language and communication methods which are meaningful, accessible and enjoyable for the person, making the meeting friendly and uplifting, i.e. which are qualitatively different from those generally heard in service settings.

The PCP process starts with the creation of a 'circle of support' around the person. The circle will involve people who love and care for the person, chosen by the person themselves, and it is the circle who will help the person to make plans for change in their lives based on the things the person sees as important.

A facilitator will typically co-ordinate the group in the above activities, mobilize change and ensure that the group monitors how things are going over time. Meetings should take place in a setting chosen by the person and the facilitator should also ensure that meetings are conducted in an atmosphere of support, enthusiasm and positive respect. The facilitator's role is therefore essential (see Mount 1991; Joyce 1997) and professionals may not be in that role. Instead, Kilbane and Sanderson (2004) suggest four main roles which professionals may assume in the person-centred planning process.

1 *Introducing* people and their families to person-centred planning and demonstrating and explaining how the process might help.
2 *Contributing* to the person-centred plan as a facilitator, a member of the circle or as somebody whom the circle calls upon to help with an aspect of the plan.
3 *Integrating* person-centred approaches in their day-to-day work with people by providing information and education and wider experiences of the process.

4 *Safeguarding* person-centred planning. This will mean advocating for the person, ensuring plans are of a good quality, determined by the person and their circle, and actually put into practice.

PCP has the potential to change the very fabric of people's lives by placing at their disposal the resources, skills and commitment of those people who are closest to the person. However, there may, as outlined in the final section to follow, be some real difficulties with the PCP approach.

Evidence for and criticisms of PCP

The major commitment to PCP outlined earlier in this chapter would suggest that there is a significant evidence base supporting its adoption in policy. However, like normalization before it, the acceptance of PCP seems to have occurred without a great deal of questioning or criticism. Normalization was accompanied by a substantial number of personal stories of its success and efficacy but very little systematic empirical research.

> It epitomised the way forward for the design of services: anything progressive could be achieved only by adopting the normalisation principle. It had moved from being ridiculous and naïve to become the accepted wisdom. To criticise it was tantamount to heresy.
>
> (Chappell 1997: 47)

Perhaps less cynically Dowling *et al.* (2007) suggest that successful implementation is supported not only through policy exhortation but via case studies and practitioner commitment as well as well-founded evidence.

In relation to PCP, Sanderson *et al.* (2000: 1) have pointed out that 'there is a wealth of material on person-centred planning that is hidden from the usual places where we search for information'. Generally speaking, during the normalization period materials such as these were published in-house or used primarily in workshops controlled by a small group of recognized leaders who were able using these means to 'control' the brand and the marketing. An argument can be made that recognition of training among a small number of UK providers whose PCP training is recognized as a 'passport to practice' leads to suspicions that the information they provide may not necessarily be the best place to find independent information. For the most part we are therefore left with anecdotal reports or with largely descriptive, process-oriented accounts that offer rather mixed results (Parley 2001). Whatever their merits, there are now many sites producing highly significant and important sources of knowledge, information, stories, examples and approaches (see for example Martin and Carey 2009), which should be viewed by students and practitioners alike.

So, what research evidence is there to support PCP? The question remains as to whether PCP helps to create conditions that positively and materially alter the (quality of) lives of service users and families. Ten years ago Rudkin and Rowe (1999), reviewing data from five studies, concluded there was no quantitative evidence to support the use of life-style planning in general or in any individual form. Medora and Ledger (2005), in a study of 26 people with varying support needs, found that lifestyle planning enabled people to express preferences and make choices and, further, reinforced a sense of ownership and inclusion. Holburn *et al.* (2000) developed validated measures of PCP processes and outcomes, and later Holburn *et al.* (2004) pointed to better outcomes in service satisfaction, autonomy, choice, daily activities and relationships and faster resettlement to the community in their study of 18 pairs matched by PCP and Individual Service Plans (ISPs).

However, the most significant study, which was funded under the Learning Disability Research Initiative (LDRI), designed to support the implementation of *Valuing People* (see Grant and Ramcharan 2007), has been the work of Robertson *et al.* (2005), the findings of which have now been widely reported (Robertson *et al.* 2006, 2007a, b; Wigham *et al.* 2008). The research sought to evaluate, every three months over two years, the impact of PCP for the first 25 people in four diverse localities which had received expert support from one part of the research team to develop policies, procedures and practices for implementation of PCP. Outcomes measured related to adaptive behaviour, community activities, service type and volume, social networks, risk, choice, health, mental health and medication. The outcomes

represent those likely to be achieved in a best case scenario given the expert help with implementation.

This study found that PCP could produce significantly better outcomes but that 'there are powerful inequalities in both access to and the efficacy of PCP in relation to participant characteristics, contextual factors and elements of PCP process' (Robertson *et al.* 2007a: 232). Indeed, of the final 93 people with learning disabilities recruited to the study, only 65 had a plan at the end of the study period, indicating significant differences in access to PCP as well as to its outcomes. In summary, the study found that: those less likely to access PCPs were people with mental health problems, emotional or challenging behaviours, those with autism, higher health need and restricted mobility; access to a plan was more likely where there had been more person-centred ways of working prior to the introduction of PCP, with committed facilitators and allocated key workers and when a person lived close to their family home. PCP had a positive effect on people's lives leading to benefits in community involvement, contact with friends and family and in relation to choice; however, there was no impact on social networks, employment, physical activity and medication and negative impacts on risks, physical health and behavioural/emotional needs (see Robertson *et al.* 2005, 2007a, b; Wigham *et al.* 2008).

The importance of this study cannot be over-emphasized but its findings have also led some to ponder how far PCP can go in producing better lives for all people with learning disabilities. Burton and Kagan (2006) have suggested that in neo-liberal social policy initiatives such as *Valuing People*, 'a kind of inadvertent trick takes place where the least impaired people are used in the imagery to stand for all others ... yet the life circumstances of many of those with lesser impairments is ignored' (Burton and Kagan 2006: 305). *Valuing People Now* seems to recognize these limitations, its subtitle being 'Making it happen for everyone': an acknowledgement that PCP has perhaps not worked for everyone (Department of Health 2009: para. 2.1: 52). While recognizing the importance of service co-ordination and wider planning, PCP and the personalization agenda still represent the primary vehicle for the future, leading to suspicions that not enough innovation has been tied into the system to create better lives for all. So what problems might be associated with PCP into the future?

As indicated in the central part of this chapter, PCP may seem a simple idea but it is a complex and time-consuming process (Kilbane and Thompson 2004; Medora and Ledger 2005). Associated with this is the view that so much focus is placed upon the creation of a plan itself that there is not much time left to pursue actions in innovative ways (Mansell and Beadle-Brown 2004; Routledge and Gitsham 2004; Cambridge and Carnaby 2005). This is exacerbated where circles of support have to be built because no natural informal social and supportive networks exist for the individual (Mansell and Beadle-Brown 2004). The era of IPPs had a similar problem given their resource-intensive nature, leading to a very low take-up (Felce et al. 1998: 56). Conflicts additional to work demands are also likely to emerge, for example with professional responsibilities and work cultures (Kilbane and McLean 2008), the tensions between organizational and individual planning (Duffy 2004), the professional focus on risk as informal experiences increase (James 2008) and the absence of leadership and commitment (Cambridge and Carnaby 2005) and well-trained staff (LeRoy et al. 2007). Additionally, reflecting on the service context, Dowling et al. (2007) point further to slow-changing service cultures, immutable service and funding structures, high staff turnover and maintaining professional power as recalcitrant issues standing in the way of progress in implementing PCPs.

But within a PCP framework the demands on staff are mirrored by those on families and other members of a person's circle of support. Sanderson and Smull's approach (2005) indicates a high expectation on families but also that, for those who have families, they are likely to be the most consistent thread in their lives. Compared with professionals, families have been identified as having more drive and motivation (Gregson 2007) and to be more creative in their problem-solving (LeRoy et al. 2007).

For many family carers already struggling with recalcitrant services, fighting while tired and stressed for a person's rights, the idea of accommodating the interests of other parties in a co-ordinated circle may represent just one step too far. Indeed, spending copious resources on training people to do planning using specific tools and approaches, a requirement of the PCP system, may create an 'activity trap' where those unable to undertake such training may feel sidelined. The study by Robertson et al. (2005) measured the outcomes of PCP in areas for which they had provided significant PCP training. Much more is therefore yet to be learned about the potential of PCP in naturally existing circumstances. More also needs to be done to examine not just PCP but PCP in tandem with other features of personalization such as direct payments and self-directed support.

Conclusion

When talking to a student recently about her experiences of what she found to be a very difficult placement in a group home, it was discovered that she dealt with the problems by talking to members of staff, making suggestions for change, challenging negative attitudes and by making sure, as she put it, that she made a positive difference each day, in some small way. We can all make these 'differences', and as Packer (2000: 30) puts it '. . . every little bit counts. Small ripples can make big waves, but only if enough of those involved in direct care are prepared to be proactive in spite of these limitations, and to accept the psychological conflict this involves.'

We might also challenge 'old service models' by questioning how services are designed, by getting involved in supporting people with learning disabilities through self-advocacy activities or by attending service planning or Partnership Board meetings and advocating the rights of service users. Adopting a person-centred approach in the face of traditional services is not easy and requires us to find others to talk to who understand, as well as looking after our own physical and psychological health.

We need to be aware of the barriers to adopting person-centred approaches and helping people create person-centred plans and to reflect on these approaches in a positive but well-informed way, while continuing to work towards a more positive future for people with learning disabilities.

In replying to the criticisms of PCP raised by Mansell and Beadle-Brown (2004), O'Brien (2004: 15) states that we must guard against cynicism and pessimism and see PCP as an opportunity to help people live better lives:

> There is no need nor justification to look at person centred planning through rose-coloured glasses. There is good reason to look with clear eyes at the possibilities for a significantly greater measure of choice and inclusion and to make an energetic commitment to the hard work of making those possibilities real at whatever scale the local and national environment can support.

References

Atkinson, D. and Walmsley, J. (1999) Using autobiographical approaches with people with learning difficulties, *Disability and Society*, 14(2): 203–16.

Atkinson, D. and Williams, F. (eds) (1990) *Know Me As I Am*. London: Hodder & Stoughton.

Beadle-Brown, J. (2006) Person centred approaches and quality of life, *Tizard Learning Disability Review*, 11(3): 4–11.

Booth, T. and Booth, W. (1994) *Parenting Under Pressure: Mothers and Fathers with Learning Disabilities*. Buckingham: Open University Press.

Brandon, D. (1989) Professional behaviours, in D. Brandon (ed.) *Mutual Respect*. London: Good Impressions Publishing.

Brandon, D. (1991) *Direct Power: A Handbook on Service Brokerage*. Preston: Tao.

Burton, M. and Kagan, C. (2006) Decoding *Valuing People*, *Disability and Society*, 21(4): 299–313.

Cambridge, P. and Carnaby, S. (2005) Introduction and overview, in P. Cambridge (ed.) *PCP and Care Management with People with Learning Difficulties*. London: Jessica Kingsley.

Chappell, A.L. (1997) From normalisation to where? in L. Barton and M. Oliver (eds) *Disability Studies: Past, Present and Future*. Leeds: The Disability Press.

Department of Health (2001a) *Valuing People: A New Strategy for Learning Disability for the 21st Century*. London: Department of Health.

Department of Health (2001b) *Valuing People: A New Strategy for Learning Disability for the 21st Century. Towards Person Centred Approaches. Planning with People: Guidance for Partnership Boards*. London: Department of Health.

Department of Health (2007) *Putting People First: A Shared Vision and Commitment to the Transformation of Adult Social Care*. London: Department of Health.

Department of Health (2009) *Valuing People Now. A New Three-year Strategy for People with Learning Disabilities: Making It Happen for Everyone*. London: Department of Health.

Dowling, S., Manthorpe, J. and Cowley, S. (2007) Working on PCP: from amber to green light? *Journal of Intellectual Disabilities*, 11(1): 65–82.

Duffy, S. (2004) In control, *Journal of Integrated Care*, 12(6): 7–13.

Duffy, S. (2005) Transforming the allocation of resources for care, *Journal of Integrated Care*, 13(1): 1–11.

Falvey, M.A., Forest, M., Pearpoint, J. and Rosenberg, R.L. (1997) *All My Life's a Circle. Using the Tools: Circles, MAPS and PATHS*. Toronto: Inclusion Press.

Felce, D. (2004) Can PCP fulfil a strategic planning role? Comments on Mansell and Beadle-Brown, *Journal of Applied Research in Intellectual Disabilities*, 17: 27–30.

Felce, D., Grant, G., Todd, S., Ramcharan, P., Beyer, S., McGrath, M. *et al.* (1998) *Towards a Full Life: Researching Policy Innovation for People with Learning Disabilities*. Oxford: Butterworth Heinemann.

Forest, M. and Lusthaus, E. (1989) Promoting educational equality for all students: circles and maps, in S. Stainback, W. Stainback and M. Forest (eds) *Educating all Students in the Mainstream of Regular Education*. Baltimore, MD: Paul H. Brookes.

Grant, G. and Ramcharan, P. (2007) *Valuing People and Research: The Learning Disability Research Initiative. Overview Report*. London: Department of Health.

Gregson, K. (2007) PCP in Hampshire: creating sustainable approaches, *Learning Disability Practice*, 10(2): 20–3.

Holburn, S., Jacobson, J., Vietze, P., Schwartz, A. and Sersen, E. (2000) Quantifying the process and outcomes of person-centred planning, *American Journal on Mental Retardation*, 105: 402–16.

Holburn, S., Jacobson, J., Schwartz, A., Flory, M. and Vietze, P. (2004) The Willowbrook Futures Project: a longitudinal analysis of person-centred planning, *American Journal on Mental Retardation*, 109: 63–76.

James, A. (2008) A critical consideration of the cash for care agenda and its implications for social services in Wales, *Journal of Adult Protection*, 10(3): 23–34.

Joyce, S. (1997) *Planning On: A Resource Book for Facilitators*. Ontario: Realizations.

Kilbane, J. and McLean (2008) Exploring the history of person centred practice, in J. Thompson, J. Kilbane and H. Sanderson (eds) *Person Centred Practice for Professionals*. Maidenhead: Open University Press.

Kilbane, J. and Sanderson, H. (2004) 'What' and 'how': understanding professional involvement in person-centred planning styles and approaches, *Learning Disability Practice*, 7(4): 16–20.

Kilbane, J. and Thompson, J. (2004) Never ceasing the exploration: understanding PCP, *Learning Disability Practice*, 7(3): 28–31.

Kropf, N.P. and Greene, R.R. (1993) Life review with families who care for developmentally disabled members: a model, *Journal of Gerontological Social Work*, 21(1/2): 25–40.

LeRoy, B., Wolf-Branigin, K., Israel, N. and Kulik, N. (2007) Challenges to the systematic adoption of PCP, *Best Practices in Mental Health*, 3(1): 16–25.

Mansell, J. and Beadle-Brown, J. (2004) Person-centred planning or person-centred action: policy and practice in intellectual disability services, *Journal of Applied Research in Intellectual Disabilities*, 17: 1–9.

Martin, A. and Carey, E. (2009) Person centred plans: empowering or controlling? *Learning Disability Practice*, 12(1): 32–7.

Medora, H. and Ledger, S. (2005) Implementing and reviewing PCP: links with care management, clinical support and commissioning, in P. Cambridge (ed.) *PCP and Care Management with People with Learning Difficulties*. London: Jessica Kingsley.

Mount, B. (1991) *Dare to Dream: An Analysis of the Conditions Leading to Personal Change for People with Disabilities*. Manchester, CT: Communitas.

Mount, B. (2000) *Personal Futures Planning: Finding Directions for Change Using Personal Futures Planning. A Sourcebook of Values, Ideals and Methods to Encourage Person Centred Development*: Manchester, CT: Capacity Works.

Mount, B. and Zwernik, K. (1988) *It's Never Too Early, It's Never Too Late: A Booklet about Personal Futures Planning*. St Paul, MN: Governor's Planning Council on Developmental Disabilities.

O'Brien, J. (2004) If person centred planning did not exist, *Valuing People* would require its invention, *Journal of Applied Research in Intellectual Disabilities*, 17: 11–15.

O'Brien, J., Pearpoint, J. and Forest, M. (1993) *PATH: A Workbook for Planning Positive Possible Futures*. Toronto: Inclusion Press.

Packer, T. (2000) Facing up to the Bills, *Journal of Dementia Care*, 8(4): 30–3, Care. 9(1): 26–8.

Parley, F.F. (2001) Person-centred outcomes: are outcomes improved where a person-centred care model is used? *Journal of Learning Disabilities*, 5(4): 299–308.

Perske, R. and Perske, M. (1988) *Circles of Friends: People with Learning Disabilities and their Friends Enrich the Lives of One Another*. Nashville, TN: Abingdon Press.

Ramcharan, P. and Grant, G. (2001) Views and experiences of people with intellectual disabilities and their families. (1) The user perspective, *Journal of Applied Research in Intellectual Disabilities*, 14: 348–63.

Ray, M. (1999) Developing person centred standards for care homes, *Journal of Dementia Care*, 11(6): 16–18.

Robertson, J., Emerson, E., Hatton, C., Elliot, J., McIntosh, B., Swift, P. et al. (2005) *The Impact of Person Centred Planning*. Lancaster: Institute for Health Research, Lancaster University.

Robertson, J., Emerson, E., Hatton, C., Elliot, J., McIntosh, B., Swift, P. et al. (2006) Longitudinal analysis of the impact and cost of person-centered planning for people with intellectual disabilities in England, *American Journal on Mental Retardation*, 111(6): 400–16.

Robertson, J., Emerson, E., Hatton, C., Elliot, J., McIntosh, B., Swift, P. et al. (2007a) Person-centred planning: factors associated with successful outcomes for people with intellectual disabilities, *Journal of Intellectual Disability Research*, 51(3): 232–43.

Robertson, J., Emerson, E., Hatton, C., Elliot, J., McIntosh, B., Swift, P. et al. (2007b) Reported goal setting and benefits of person centred planning for people with intellectual disabilities, *Journal of Applied Research in Intellectual Disabilities*, 20(4): 297–307.

Routledge, M. and Gitsham, N. (2004) Putting PCP in its proper place? *Tizard Learning Disability Review*, 9(3): 21–6.

Routledge, M. and Sanderson, H. (2001) *Valuing People: A New Strategy for Learning Disability for the 21st Century: Towards Person-Centred Approaches. Planning with People: Guidance for Implementation Groups*. London: Department of Health.

Rudkin, A. and Rowe, D. (1999) A systematic review of the evidence base for lifestyle planning in adults with learning disabilities: implications for other disabled populations, *Clinical Rehabilitation*, 13: 363–72.

Sanderson, H. (2000) *Person Centred Planning: Key Features and Approaches*. York: Joseph Rowntree Foundation.

Sanderson, H. (2002) A plan is not enough: exploring the development of person centred teams, in S. Holborn and P. Vietze (eds) *Person Centred Planning: Research, Practice and Future Directions*. Baltimore, MD: Paul H. Brookes.

Sanderson, H. and Smull, M. (2005) *Essential Lifestyle Planning for Everyone*. London: Helen Sanderson Associates.

Sanderson, H., Kilbane, J. and Gitsham, N. (2000) *Person-centred Planning (PCP): A Resource Guide*, www.valuingpeople.gov.uk/documents/PCPResource.pdf.

Sheard, D. (2004) Person centred care: the emperor's new clothes? *Journal of Dementia Care*, 12(2): 22–5.

Smull, M. (2004) *Positive Rituals and Quality of Life*, www.paradigm-uk.org (accessed 10 May 2004).

Smull, M., Sanderson, H. and Allen, B. (undated) *Essential Lifestyle Planning: A Handbook for Facilitators*. Manchester: North West Training and Development Team.

Smull, M.W. and Burke-Harrison, S. (1992) *Supporting People with Severe Reputations in the Community*. Alexandria, VA: National Association of State Directors of Developmental Disabilities Services Inc.

Welsh Office (1983) *All Wales Strategy for the Development of Services to Mentally Handicapped People*. Cardiff: Welsh Office.

Wigham, S., Robertson, J., Emerson, E., Hatton, C., Elliott, J. McIntosh, B. et al. (2008) Reported goal setting and benefits of person centred planning for people with intellectual disabilities, *Journal of Intellectual Disabilities*, 12(2): 143–52.

26

Culture and ethnicity: developing accessible and appropriate services for health and social care

Ghazala Mir

Introduction

The health of people from minority ethnic communities is of growing concern as a social policy issue. Research has shown that higher levels of ill health, limited access to health and social care and disadvantage are related to health determinants such as housing and employment (Acheson 1998; Department of Health/HM Treasury 2002). Higher levels of poverty are also implicated in the greater incidence of long-term conditions within these communities (Nazroo 1997). Studies of disability have highlighted later diagnosis, poor levels of information to service users and low take-up of service provision alongside systematic discrimination in the allocation of welfare benefits (Chamba *et al.* 1999; Ahmad 2000).

The notion of 'cultural competence' has been promoted to address these inequalities and involves sensitivity to cultural differences and respect for diverse values (Acheson 1998; Betancourt *et al.* 2003). Evidence suggests that 'cultural competency' among service professionals is often disturbingly inadequate and professional uncertainty about how to meet the needs of service users from minority ethnic communities is widespread (Acheson 1998; Betancourt *et al.* 2003). For example, stereotypical views of South Asian families 'looking after their own' and barriers in communication often result in services failing to meet minimum acceptable standards (Chamba *et al.* 1998). It is not surprising, therefore, that South Asian family carers are reported to suffer from high levels of stress and poorer mental and physical health than their white peers (Hatton *et al.* 1998).

The younger age profile of people within some, particularly South Asian, communities has been highlighted as an important factor in the future planning of services for people with learning disabilities and their family carers (Emerson and Hatton 2008). Demand for primary health care services is already high within these communities (Nazroo 1997), yet there remains a considerable level of unmet need for health and social care services generally (Aspinall and Jackson 2004).

This chapter is based on a review commissioned by the Department of Health to accompany *Valuing People*, the English learning disability strategy (Mir *et al.* 2001) and an Equality Impact Assessment of *Valuing People Now*, the revised strategy for implementation over the next three years (Department of Health 2008, 2009).

Access to health and social care

The importance of service support for minority ethnic families has been highlighted by a number of studies demonstrating problems with access. These include poor awareness of existing services, lack of bilingual staff, culturally inappropriate activities and diet, and racial discrimination, all of which contribute to low take-up and poor service development (Baxter 1998; CVS Consultants 1998; Hatton *et al.* 1998; Bignall and Butt 2000).

A 'colour-blind' approach, or assertion that 'we treat everyone the same', is often operated within health and social care organisations. Such statements may indicate that the needs of minority ethnic communities have either not been considered or have been ignored (Alexander 1999). This results in underdeveloped policies and an absence of mechanisms by which needs can be explored and service development effected. This approach also fosters stereotypes and racist attitudes which may influence the use of discretionary decision-making and deprive communities of their rights to services (Ahmad 2000).

A second response has been that of specialist services provided solely for minority ethnic communities. These have acted as valuable access points, positively influencing take-up and offering innovative ways of providing support (Mir and Tovey 2003). However, specialist services can promote a surrogate form of racism if they are inadequately funded and used to absolve mainstream services of responsibility (Ahmad 2000). Limited resources can result in these services failing either to address diversity within minority ethnic communities or to link with mainstream provision that provides a wider range of opportunities (Mir et al. 2001).

Mainstream services are likely to be better resourced than specialist services and the ideal solution for unmet needs may be a quality mainstream service that is sensitive to the needs of all users. However, the cultural needs of some minority ethnic service users are currently more likely to be met in specialist provision, suggesting a continuing need for specialist services alongside improvements in general provision (Mir et al. 2001).

Service providers within mainstream services sometimes feel that, as a matter of policy, integrated services must be pursued. This is expressed as a statement of principle, however, rather than as a view based on the wishes of service users themselves (Mir et al. 2001). Among people with learning disabilities and family carers, both kinds of provision are valued and strong views are expressed in favour of both (CVS Consultants 1998; Tait et al. 1998). Specialist services are felt to be easily accessible and to offer familiar, appropriate and comfortable environments. Integrated services, on the other hand, offer wider opportunities and the ability to meet a wider range of people. The key issue appears to be the quality of the services available: where inclusive services are sensitive to cultural and religious needs, there is likely to be no need for specialist services. For that to occur, mainstream services and organisations need to address their own shortcomings (whether or not specialist provision exists) in order to improve access and provide appropriate facilities. At the same time, resources will be needed to develop separate provision where this provides a more effective service. The need for specialist services will remain to a greater or lesser

extent so long as they represent the only available means of addressing issues of identity and access for people from minority ethnic communities. These arguments echo debates about whether services for people with learning disabilities should similarly be specialist or integrated into mainstream provision (Mir et al. 2001). Evidence suggests that decisions about the extent and nature of any specialist services need to be made at a local level in consultation with service users and family carers.

It is also important to consider how to inform communities of the existence and relevance of services to the needs of minority ethnic communities. Non-traditional publicity about services via community centres, community radio and TV may be more effective than traditional methods, especially as not all family carers or people with learning disabilities are literate. Face-to-face communication and visual media may also be effective means of passing on information orally (Mir 2008).

Translated literature provided in a vacuum and not linked to staff who can respond to individual queries is not entirely useful, however, if language remains a barrier to applying for services. Moreover, some concepts such as 'carer' are not as meaningful in some communities as they have become within the ethnic majority; attempts to promote these within communities need to ensure that roles and expectations are clearly explained (Baxter et al. 1990).

Access to emotional support may be just as important as help with practical issues. Many people with learning disabilities from minority ethnic communities experience isolation as a result of family restrictions and a lack of opportunity for social contact (Butt and Mirza 1996; Bignall and Butt 2000). Racism and harassment in everyday settings may further increase feelings of isolation and emotional stress (Butt and Mirza 1996). Studies show that the initial diagnosis and continuing effects of impairment or long-term illness have a strong impact on many already disadvantaged families, and there is evidence of high levels of stress among South Asian carers (Azmi et al. 1996; Emerson et al. 2004). However, concerns about worrying others may often lead to both parents and family members concealing their distress from each other (Ahmad 2000).

Socio-economic disadvantage and financial insecurity may add significantly to the stress that carers experience (Chamba *et al.* 1999). Caring obligations affect employment opportunities and consequently reduce family income. This situation is compounded by the additional costs which may be associated with caring for a disabled person, for example in relation to transport, clothing and heating (Baldwin 1994). While such issues can affect all carers, social inequalities in income mean that the financial impact of caring may be even greater for minority ethnic families (Chamba *et al.* 1999; Emerson 2007).

The simultaneous disadvantage experienced by individuals in relation to race, disability and gender has been termed 'double disadvantage' or 'triple jeopardy' (Baxter *et al.* 1990; Butt and Mirza 1996). The interaction of multiple kinds of discrimination produces its own particular effect on individuals and social groups, which is more than the sum of its parts (Begum 1995). Such factors are implicated in the securing of equality with others in relation to outcomes (see Chapter 6).

Developing the social model of disability to address such multiple disadvantage is important as a means of questioning established patterns of service delivery and providing insights into how these interacting dimensions of inequality in health and social care might be addressed (Mir and Tovey 2003).

Good practice examples

Examples of good practice have varying levels of impact on the relationships between people from minority ethnic communities and service providers. At lower levels of engagement this can involve raising awareness and one-way information from service providers, who retain control of what is offered, to service users. Higher levels of engagement involve the development of a dialogue with minority ethnic communities, recruitment of staff from these communities and forums where shared decision-making, shared values and accountability can be developed (see Mir *et al.* forthcoming).

Raising awareness

Refugees, who have different needs to people established in the UK, are even less aware of services and entitlements than other minority ethnic groups, and creative ways of outreach need to be found. In Kensington and Chelsea, outreach workers used a video-recording to communicate information about registering with a GP. The video used images and drama to overcome the problem of catering for a potential 80 to 90 different languages (Lewis 1996).

A touring exhibition in Bradford run by South Asian staff aimed to increase awareness of short-term breaks. Venues included the Bradford Mela, the city centre, mosques, community centres, temples, street corners and open events. Photographs (especially of South Asian users with South Asian staff) were used as well as a video in Urdu. Publicity included a local South Asian radio station, the local press and South Asian publications (Mir *et al.* 2001). The initiative demonstrated that families do respond when contact methods are relevant to their background and experiences. It considerably improved South Asian referrals to the services and increased disability awareness within local communities through positive media images of disabled people, which are often absent from both minority and majority media (Begum *et al.* 1994).

Developing dialogue/influencing change

The Parvaaz Project secured funds for a South Asian Development Officer to work with families and other agencies to effect change in mainstream services. The job involved holding seminars and meetings and creating awareness among South Asian parents about entitlements, benefits, rights and equipment that could be beneficial to them. The Development Officer worked with national and local organisations to help them become more sensitive and responsive to the needs of South Asian people with learning disabilities and their carers (Mir *et al.* 2001).

Westminster Primary Care Trust set up a Black and Minority Ethnic Health Forum, an arms-length advisory group which aims to influence both Westminster and Kensington and Chelsea Primary Care Trusts. The Forum holds regular meetings with local groups and the two boroughs' Primary Care Trusts, hospitals, Mental Health Trusts and Social Services Departments. Using its links with more than 300 community groups and voluntary agencies in the local area, the Forum has created a new way for the Trust to listen to the experiences of local black and ethnic minority people. Community groups are involved in planning and executing the process and have used information from these communities to influence planning decisions within the Trust (Mir 2008).

Policy responses to inequality

The White Paper *Valuing People* (Department of Health 2001) raised considerable awareness about the needs of minority ethnic communities but failed to set targets that could meet these needs or monitor how effectively implementation of the White Paper included people from minority ethnic communities. A number of initiatives were launched to promote inclusion, primarily:

- A subgroup of the Learning Disabilities Task Force focused on ethnicity and this was instrumental in securing priority for work on ethnicity within the Learning Disability Development Fund through which national work on implementation was resourced. The subgroup later evolved to become the National Advisory Group on Learning Disabilities and Ethnicity.
- A toolkit to help Learning Disability Partnership Boards to include minority ethnic communities within their work (VPST/Department of Health 2004).
- An Ethnicity Training Network and an information network along with regional networks on learning disabilities and ethnicity managed through the Valuing People Support Team regional leads.
- A leadership training programme for Partnership Board teams to improve services within local areas.

Despite these initiatives, the Learning Disability Task Force expressed repeated concerns about the unmet needs of people with learning disabilities from minority ethnic groups and their family carers (Learning Disability Task Force 2003, 2004). Two national surveys monitoring Partnership Board progress (Care Services Improvement Partnership 2005; Hatton 2007) indicated continued exclusion from work to implement the White Paper, with only half of Boards responding to the survey itself. Of those that did respond around half had done nothing to carry out legally required assessments of how their policies impacted on minority ethnic communities

(Department of Health 2009). Partnership Boards did report, however, that prioritization of ethnicity in learning disability resource allocation had significant impact on their ability to be inclusive (Department of Health 2008; see also Caton *et al.* 2007).

Valuing People Now (Department of Health 2009) aimed to impact on groups that had benefited least from *Valuing People* (Department of Health 2001), including minority ethnic communities, yet it also failed to set specific targets in most of the policy areas it addressed and consultation events to formulate the revised strategy were themselves not inclusive (Department of Health 2008). The omission of specific targets was of particular concern in relation to health, given the high levels of poor health in minority ethnic populations, and this continued exclusion is likely to widen rather than address these health inequalities. Within studies that had significantly informed *Valuing People Now*, such as the Disability Rights Commission Formal Investigation (Disability Rights Commission 2006), the complex barriers faced by people from minority ethnic communities had been highlighted. Yet, the policy objectives for work to improve the health of people with learning disabilities make no reference to ethnicity (Department of Health 2008).

While urging Learning Disability Partnership Boards (responsible for implementing *Valuing People*) to comply with the Race Relations (Amendment) Act 2000 and proactively ensure race equality in service provision, the policy itself has most often failed to address these very issues in ways that can make a significant impact on service provision. The pockets of good practice stimulated by resourcing work on ethnicity within the Learning Disability Development Fund are unlikely to be replicated elsewhere until leadership is taken more effectively in this area by policy-makers.

Exercise 26.1

Think of your contact with people with learning disabilities and their carers from a cultural background other than your own. How confident did you feel about how to interact? Do you feel that you were able to understand and respond to their needs? What would increase your confidence and ability to respond in a culturally competent way?

Advocacy and networks of support

Where families play a major part in the care of people with learning disabilities the importance of responding to the needs of family carers has been highlighted. The concerns of minority ethnic carers are often not taken seriously, for example when reporting developmental delay and abuse (Mir and Tovey 2003). Advocacy support can play an important role in such situations by ensuring that people with learning disabilities and their carers are heard and that they receive feedback about promised action to meet their needs (Morris 1998). Advocacy support has also been identified as a particular issue for people with challenging behaviour who may be placed out of their locality and disconnected from their own community, with little practical or emotional help (Downer and Ferns 1993; Lewis 1996). 'Key workers' may take on the role of advocate as well as providing information and a gateway to services (Mukherjee *et al.* 1999) and are associated with fewer unmet needs. Their availability is often ad hoc, however, and depends on the initiative of individual professionals; not all professionals identified as key workers may truly take on this role (Joseph Rowntree Foundation 1999).

A general shortage of advocates has been identified, however (Lewis 1996), and an acute shortage of minority ethnic advocates in particular (Mir *et al.* 2001). Efforts to recruit minority ethnic advocates are often unsuccessful and may be related to inappropriate publicity. However, there may be other factors too, related to the ability and motivation to volunteer. Atkinson (1999) points out that lack of funding is a barrier to the recruitment of advocates and that

secure funding makes it possible to invest in training, support and payment. Payment for such services and accredited training may be particularly important for people from disadvantaged communities who face greater barriers to employment and education. The skills that such volunteers bring to organizations are often central to the success of work with minority ethnic communities and cannot effectively be carried out without them. Such a pivotal role would appear to need more effective resourcing.

At the same time, it should not be assumed that families will necessarily want support from someone from their own community. Some families may prefer White advocates to keep some distance between themselves and the professionals with whom they have contact (Mir *et al.* 2001).

As a concept, advocacy is not necessarily understood or accepted by all communities (Mir *et al.* 2001). The model of advocacy offered can therefore do much to encourage or deter take-up of advocacy services by people with learning disabilities and their carers.

Exercise 26.2

Read the following case study and try to identify why the attempt to work with minority ethnic communities was not successful.

The case study below highlights the need for organizational training about disability and ethnicity, which may not be internally available and needs to be sought from further afield. Minority ethnic community organizations cannot offer expertise for

Case study: *Advocacy (1)*

An inner-city advocacy group found that the employment of a South Asian worker on a part-time contract did not result in any significant increase in caseload of service users from minority ethnic communities that had historically been very low. The appointed worker had no previous experience of disability work and her appointment did not attract individuals who required advocates to the service. The organization's model of citizen advocacy promoted self-referral and advocates felt accountable solely to the person with learning disabilities.

Local minority ethnic community groups were not set up to focus on disability generally or learning disabilities specifically and were unable to make referrals. They perceived minority ethnic families as hostile to advocacy for cultural reasons and through failure to understand or accept the clinical diagnosis of learning disability. Consequently, no further work was considered viable and the worker was replaced with a member of staff whose remit did not include a focus on minority ethnic communities.

Case study: *Advocacy (2)*

Sheffield Citizen Advocacy identified low take-up of services by South Asian service users and established a joint project with the Youth Service to increase the confidence, independence and participation of young South Asian women with learning disabilities through a range of activities. It recognized the need to work with families in the first instance and appointed a South Asian worker who was supported by other staff with broader experience of advocacy work. Home visits were used to strengthen and refine her existing familiarity with families' beliefs and cultures. Family members were invited to attend alongside the young women if they wished, building a relationship of trust with workers. Family carers' participation in the group helped them appreciate the skills the young women already had and were developing. They also gained opportunities for support from other parents and consequently increased their own support network. The project thus provided access to a range of opportunities for both young people and carers without undermining the family structures and values of the community to which they belonged.

all issues relating to these communities and those that focus specifically on both disability and ethnicity are best placed to facilitate service development. Their experience is vital to identifying and supporting individuals who might benefit from an advocacy service. Without actually speaking to people with learning disabilities or their carers from minority ethnic communities, assumptions about their reasons for not using a service are likely to be inaccurate.

The model of advocacy operated by this project also worked against the development of an appropriate service. Self-referral precludes attempts to enhance take-up through direct approaches to individuals or families for whom advocacy is a new concept. In addition, where advocates focus solely on empowering individuals without considering the needs or roles of family members, this can be difficult for families to accept and may provoke or exacerbate conflicts. For communities that place a high value on collectivity and interdependence, this approach undermines the principles on which family structure is based. Minority ethnic communities are not necessarily resistant to the idea of advocacy and a number of self-advocacy groups have been set up by people from these communities themselves (Mir *et al.* 2001). However, the role of the advocate may need to include work with families rather than be independent of them. Considering the importance of family to many people with learning disabilities (Bignall and Butt 2000; Ward 2001), outcomes which do not alienate family members will most often accord with the wishes and interests of individuals with learning

disabilities themselves (see Chapter 13 in relation to family-centred support).

Case study 2 demonstrates an approach which runs counter to the argument that family carers' needs and views should not influence how people with learning disabilities decide to lead their lives. Such an argument can be both simplistic and potentially detrimental to the well-being of people with learning disabilities.

Exercise 26.3

Discuss why the above case study provides successful advocacy input.

As highlighted, members of South Asian communities often perceive kinship-based groups as an important source of identity and support (Priestley 1995; Ahmad 2000). Family expectations about the social roles of people with learning disabilities are consequently significant in decision-making affecting individuals.

The roles of women and girls, in particular, are interpreted differently in different communities and across generations. Parents who restrict the activities of their daughters may feel they are safeguarding them from situations in which they are vulnerable to abuse or more exposed to unacceptable behaviour, such as mixed gender environments. Parents may also feel under social pressure from within their communities to uphold such restrictions and to maintain the existing boundaries of appropriate behaviour between (particularly younger) men and women (Kelleher and Hillier 1996; Dwyer 1998). There may be a feeling within some communities that traditional values and beliefs are undermined by services which attempt to encourage young women to spend more time out of their homes in environments that are considered unsuitable (Dwyer 1998; Jacobson 1998).

Negative attitudes to disability have not been specifically addressed within minority ethnic communities (Hatton *et al.* 2002), while within the ethnic majority such attitudes have been strongly challenged. Thus greater stigma may be attached to disability in cultures where the social model of disability has not been promoted (Mir and Tovey 2003). Indeed in some minority ethnic communities people may attempt to keep the existence of disabled family members a secret (Westbrook *et al.* 1993; Mir and Tovey 2003).

Young disabled people feel such prejudice must be dealt with if individuals are to receive enough support to develop more independent lives (Bignall and Butt 2000). Family carers, too, suffer from negative attitudes and are often left unsupported by their extended families as well as services (Katbamna *et al.* 2000). Negative attitudes are compounded by the lack of access to facilities and opportunities highlighted earlier. Failure by service providers to offer adequate support to individuals and families can reinforce the notion that disability is 'tragic' – people are more likely to move away from this conception of disability when they have information that promotes a positive approach and when they are able to manage their circumstances without struggling (Mir and Tovey 2003).

Restrictions by family members are often interpreted as oppressive by service professionals, and stereotyped images of individuals suffering from 'culture clash' may be reinforced when staff feel obstructed by family members. Where services are modified to address the issues raised by families, however, access can usually be improved and family members value the opportunities provided. Whereas respecting an individual's independence is important, a focus on independence has sometimes proved to be a convenient pretext for undermining minority cultures (Mir *et al.* 2001). The key to widening opportunities available to people from minority ethnic communities lies in respecting cultural identity rather than in persuading individuals and families that the majority culture is necessarily better. At the same time, respecting cultural diversity should not be confused with supporting oppressive family practices (Bignall and Butt 2000). Pursuing a balanced approach is not easy for professionals but lack of balance can alienate service users, families, or both. It can be helpful for professionals to seek advice from relevant community organizations, where expertise in culturally appropriate interventions is most often found (Mir *et al.* 2001).

Partnerships and shared decision-making

Minority ethnic community groups can act as a gateway to support services. However, studies show that links between local authorities and minority ethnic community groups in a number of areas are often poor. There is evidence of inadequate consultation over needs and services through such groups, despite the knowledge that available services are not being used. The drive for partnership working assumes to some extent that groups of service users will already be established or easily formed. This may only be true of some areas in which minority ethnic communities live and partnership activity may involve facilitating the development and progression of community groups (Mir *et al.* 2001).

Community organisations may need support initially to form and then to become involved in planning and managing services, and perhaps to secure contracts to offer services themselves. Such groups often provide a range of services that do not mesh well with the structures of local authorities or other purchasing agencies. The bidding process works against small organisations and they may need assistance to apply for such contracts effectively. Public bodies are now required to promote equality through service contracts that require funded organisations to ensure the involvement of all ethnic groups at all levels (Home Office 2000). The former Commission for Racial Equality (now part of the Commission for Equality and Human Rights) recommends that such contracts should be evaluated and monitored by people who are representative of the local population (CRE 2003).

Appropriate skills and attitudes have commonly been found within services run by and for people from particular communities themselves. This suggests that partnerships and interaction with such community-based services will be an important element of any strategy. However, cultural sensitivity is only one element of quality in service provision, and many service users feel that what is actually being provided is more important than who is providing it. An emphasis is also needed on well-resourced schemes offering a variety of activities and opportunities. Schemes that are subject to cuts in funding are limited not only in the scope of their activities but also in their ability to build on previous work (Mir et al. 2001).

Recruiting people to reflect the make-up of the population served can also improve cultural competence within service provision. Individuals who have relevant skills and knowledge in this area can pass these on to colleagues through informal and formal training and help challenge any stereotypes or negative attitudes that may exist within service teams (Mir et al. 2001). It should not be assumed, however, that people will automatically have such skills just because they are from a minority ethnic community. The grade at which appointments are made is likely to be a factor in the level of support that people might need to develop this kind of role (Robinson 2002).

Increased employment of people from some minority ethnic communities has the added benefit of addressing the higher unemployment levels they experience. This strategy communicates a powerful message of social inclusion to people from these groups, including service users. Both employment and social inclusion are linked to health status and health inequalities (Mir and Din 2003).

Once people from minority ethnic communities form part of the workforce it is important to ensure

they are properly supported to do the work for which they have been employed. If they are expected to take on a casework role, it will be important to make sure they are not the only members of staff dealing with service users from minority ethnic groups (Betancourt et al. 2003). Otherwise, service users from these groups may not have access to the full range of opportunities open to everyone else (Mir et al. 2001). If staff are expected to take on a strategic role, they will need to be employed at an appropriate grade and have the authority and connections to make sure a strategy can be implemented.

The agenda for research and practice

Developing the social model

Research on learning disabilities and ethnicity has emphasized unmet need and the consequent implications for social policy and practice. However, the theoretical implications of this research have been less well developed. The historical approach to disability has been to see it as a personal tragedy, with solutions through medical intervention. A social model of disability stresses that the impact of impairment is 'mediated, to a degree, by social and cultural circumstances' (Mercer and Barnes 2000: 83; see Chapters 2 and 35 for a fuller discussion). Thus, attitudes towards people with learning disabilities can have a greater impact on individuals than the learning disability itself and can affect access to a range of opportunities.

The potentially disabling effects of specific attitudes and professional practices require explicit recognition. The social model allows us to analyse and explain the experiences of service users and carers with reference to social injustice and discrimination rather than as personal misfortune alone. However, the model requires further development to recognize multiple disadvantage and to reflect accurately the experience of people with learning disabilities from minority ethnic communities (see Mir and Tovey 2003).

Monitoring and reviewing services

This chapter has highlighted a need for conceptual shifts in the values underlying service provision to allow more inclusive approaches. Inconsistency in the approaches adopted by services in different geographical areas, or even within the same locality, have been highlighted (Mir and Tovey 2003), indicating a need for national leadership to set quality standards in service provision for people from these communities.

At a local level, for example, flexible ways of involving service users and carers and enabling them to express their views, if necessary in languages other than English, need to be developed (Mir 2008). At a broader level, statistical information about people from minority ethnic groups is needed to deliver services equitably. Proactive attempts to identify families currently unknown to services have been recommended, for example through GP surgeries (Allgar *et al.* 2008). Monitoring service take-up and minority ethnic staff numbers increases organizational awareness of gaps in provision and can lead to targeted action by commissioners (Audit Commission 2004; Sultana and Sheikh 2008). However, monitoring procedures are often inadequate for such purposes (Butt and Mirza 1996; Mir *et al.* 2001; Sultana and Sheikh 2008).

Exercise 26.5

You are managing a service in an area with a substantial mix of ethnic groups. How would you ensure that your staff were organized to provide an appropriate standard of care? How would you make sure that services meet the needs of people from all cultures?

The extent of unmet need within minority ethnic communities has, understandably, led to an emphasis on difficulties faced by people with learning disabilities and their families, with far less documentation of factors influencing positive features of their experience. Within service provision, examples of good practice are increasingly being identified as role models for future service development. There is a need to build on these and consider how the expertise developed, particularly in community-based services, can be linked into other parts of learning disability provision. The development of formal links between voluntary and statutory services could contribute to staff training and service development and is likely to raise the quality of provision in both areas (Mir and Din 2003). At the level of family and other non-professional networks, examples of good practice have yet to be explored and disseminated.

Valuing People Now (Department of Health 2009) identifies a need for helplines and information services for carers to focus more on families from minority ethnic communities. Other aspects of the policy on partnership with families of people with learning disabilities that relate to empowering carers would appear to be even more necessary and involve a higher level of engagement through which minority ethnic carers and service users are able to influence change.

Monitoring and review processes continue the cycle of organization and service development by feeding into the evidence base about minority ethnic communities, leading to greater awareness, further engagement and continued action. This cycle and the actions outlined in this briefing support organisations to develop a culture of inclusion, based on an understanding that the inequalities currently experienced by people from minority ethnic communities are both avoidable and unjust (Department of Health 2002).

Conclusion

In referring to 'minority ethnic communities', there is a risk of implying homogeneity where none exists. The traditions and cultural heritage of different communities inevitably differ, as do their experiences of disadvantage, service provision and racism in different ways, though many of these experiences may be similar. This chapter argues for sensitivity and appropriate responses to the needs of communities for which service providers have responsibility, drawing on common themes as well as the views and experiences of particular groups.

The literature itself focuses more on the needs of people with learning difficulties from South Asian communities than those from African Caribbean backgrounds; little literature is available about the needs of those from other groups, such as the African and Chinese communities, refugees or Travellers. These gaps in the literature indicate areas to which further attention needs to be given.

The need for cultural competence has been significantly promoted by national policy documents on learning disability (Department of Health 2001, 2009; VPST 2005). Pockets of change around the country have been stimulated by prioritizing work on ethnicity over a two-year period through the Learning Disability Development Fund. This priority has now been discontinued, however, so there is a need for targeted support to help to break the pattern of piecemeal approaches in addressing current inequities in service provision. The appointment of a programme lead in this area (Department of Health 2009) is hopefully a helpful beginning for this process.

Given that highlighting needs has, in itself, failed to result in policy that influences widespread and consistent changes in practice, the agenda for future research and practice must focus on what many government departments have failed to do: providing models for inclusive services and ways of measuring take-up by people from minority ethnic communities. It is key to future progress that strategies and service models ensure that the needs of people from minority ethnic communities are considered throughout learning disability services and are consistently built into service developments.

One way forward might be to implement and evaluate small-scale service innovations as demonstration projects that could be replicated on a national scale. Using research in this way could help develop existing services in localities and add to knowledge about what works in practice – rather than simply repeating the findings of unmet need from previous studies. This would not only be a more effective use of research but would also, importantly, be of immediate benefit to people from minority ethnic communities who are helped by interventions that are developed and evaluated in the process. This helps avoid replicating social disadvantage through research, in which people from socially disadvantaged groups are often exploited by the process and may receive little, if any, benefit for their contribution (Barnes 1996).

Research that works hand in hand with practice may come closer to bridging the gap that often exists between research recommendations and the service developments that would translate these into practice. At best such studies could provide a stimulus to effective interventions being adopted on a wider scale and higher national standards of cultural competence.

References

Acheson, D. (Chair) (1998) *Independent Inquiry into Inequalities in Health*. London: The Stationery Office.

Ahmad, W. (ed.) (2000) *Ethnicity, Disability and Chronic Illness*. Buckingham: Open University Press.

Alexander, Z. (1999) *The Department of Health: Study of Black, Asian and Ethnic Minority Issues*. London: Department of Health.

Allgar, V., Mir, G., Evans, J., Marshall, J., Cottrell, D., Heywood, P., Emerson, E. and Mir, G. (2008) Estimated prevalence of people with learning disabilities: template for general practice, *British Journal of General Practice*, 58(551): 423–8.

Aspinall, P. and Jackson, B. (2004) *Ethnic Disparities in Health and Health Care: A Focused Review and Selected Examples of Good Practice*. London: Department of Health/London Health Observatory.

Atkinson, D. (1999) *Advocacy: A Review*. Brighton: Pavilion Publishing/Joseph Rowntree Foundation.

Audit Commission (2004) *The Journey to Race Equality: Delivering Improved Services to Local Communities*. London: Audit Commission.

Azmi, S., Hatton, C., Caine, A. and Emerson, E. (1996) *Improving Services for Asian People with Learning Disabilities: The Views of Users and Carers*. Manchester: Hester Adrian Research Centre/Mental Health Foundation.

Baldwin, S. (1994) Needs assessment for people from Black and minority ethnic groups, *Care in Place*, 1(2).

Barnes, C. (1996) Disability and the myth of the independent researcher, *Disability and Society*, 11(1): 107–10.

Baxter, C. (1998) Learning difficulties, in S. Rawaf and V. Bahl (eds) *Assessing Health Needs of People from Minority Ethnic Groups*. London: Royal College of Physicians/Faculty of Public Health Medicine.

Baxter, C., Poonia, K., Ward, L. and Nadirshaw, Z. (1990) *Double Discrimination*. London: King's Fund Centre/Commission for Racial Equality.

Begum, N. (1992) *Something to be Proud of*. London: Waltham Forest Race Relations Unit.

Begum, N. (1995) *Beyond Samosas and Reggae: A Guide to Developing Services for Black Disabled People*. London: King's Fund.

Begum, N., Hill, M. and Stevens, A. (eds) (1994) *Reflections: The Views of Black Disabled People on their Lives and Community Care*. London: Central Council for Education and Training in Social Work.

Betancourt, J.R., Green, A., Carrillo, J. and Ananeh-Firempong, O. (2003) Defining cultural competence: a practical framework for addressing racial/ethnic disparities in health and health care, *Public Health Reports*, 118(4): 293–302.

Bignall, T. and Butt, J. (2000) *Between Ambition and Achievement: Young Black Disabled People's Views and Experiences of Independence and Independent Living*. Bristol: The Policy Press/Joseph Rowntree Foundation.

Butt, J. and Mirza, K. (1996) *Social Care and Black Communities*. London: HMSO.

Care Services Improvement Partnership (2005) *Improving Services for People with Learning Disabilities from Minority Ethnic Groups: Report to the Learning Disabilities Task Force with Recommendations for a Report to the Minister from the Valuing People Support Team*. London: Valuing People Support Team.

Caton, S., Starling, S., Burton, M., Azmi, S. and Chapman, M. (2007) Responsive services for people with learning disabilities from minority ethnic communities, *British Journal of Learning Disabilities*, 35(4): 229–35.

Chamba, R., Ahmad, W. and Jones, L. (1998) *Improving Services for Asian Deaf Children*. Bristol: The Policy Press.

Chamba, R., Ahmad, W., Hirst, M., Lawton, D. and Beresford, B. (1999) *On the Edge: Minority Ethnic Families Caring for a Severely Disabled Child*. Bristol: The Policy Press.

Cinnirella, M. and Loewenthal, K.M. (1999) Religious and ethnic group influences on beliefs about mental illness: a qualitative interview study, *British Journal of Medical Psychology*, 72: 505–24.

Commission for Racial Equality (2003) *Race Equality and Public Procurement: A Guide for Public Authorities*, http://www.equalityhumanrights.com/uploaded_files/PSD/26_race_equality_public_procurement.pdf (accessed September 2009).

CVS Consultants/Asian People with Disabilities Alliance (1998) *Ethnicity and Learning Difficulties: Moving Towards Equity in Service Provision*. London: CVS Consultants.

Department of Health (2000a) *A Quality Strategy for Social Care*. London: Department of Health.

Department of Health (2000b) *Implementation of Health Act Partnership Arrangements*. London: Department of Health.

Department of Health (2000c) *The NHS Plan*. London: The Stationery Office.

Department of Health (2001) *Valuing People: A New Strategy for Learning Disability for the 21st Century*. London: Department of Health.

Department of Health (2008) *Valuing People Now: 'Making it Happen for Everyone'. Equality Impact Assessment*. London: HMSO.

Department of Health (2009) *Valuing People Now: A New Three-year Strategy for Learning Disabilities*. London: Department of Health.

Department of Health/HM Treasury (2002) *Tackling Health Inequalities: Cross Cutting Review*. London: Department of Health/HM Treasury.

Disability Rights Commission (2006) *Equal Treatment: Closing the Gap. A Formal Investigation into Physical Health Inequalities Experienced by People with Learning Disabilities and/or Mental Health Problems*, London: DRC.

Downer, J. and Ferns, P. (1993) Self-advocacy by black people with learning difficulties, in P. Beresford and T. Harding (eds) *A Challenge to Change: Practical Experiences of Building User-led Services*. London: National Institute for Social Work.

Dwyer, C. (1998) Contested identities: challenging dominant representations of young British Muslim women, in T. Skelton and G. Valentine (eds) *Cool Places*. London: Routledge.

Emerson, E. (2007) Poverty and people with intellectual disabilities, *Mental Retardation and Developmental Disabilities Research Reviews*, 13(2): 107.

Emerson, E. and Hatton, C. (1998) Residential provision for people with intellectual disabilities in England, Wales and Scotland, *Journal of Applied Research in Intellectual Disabilities*, 11: 1–14.

Emerson, E. and Hatton, C. (2008) *People with Learning Disabilities in England*. Lancaster: Centre for Disability Research, Lancaster University.

Emerson, E. and Robertson, J. (2002) *Future Demand for Services for Young Adults with Learning Disabilities from South Asian and Black Communities in Birmingham*. Lancaster University: Institute of Health Research.

Emerson, E., Robertson, J. and Wood, J. (2004) Levels of psychological distress experienced by family carers of children and adolescents with intellectual disabilities in an urban conurbation, *Journal of Applied Research in Intellectual Disabilities*, 17(2): 77–84.

Ganguly, I. (1995) Promoting the health of women of non-English-speaking backgrounds in Australia, *World Health Forum*, 16: 157–63.

Hatton, C. (2007) *Improving Services for People with Learning Disabilities from Minority Ethnic Communities: Report on the Second National Survey of Partnership Boards*. Lancaster: Institute for Health Research, Lancaster University.

Hatton, C., Azmi, S., Emerson, E. and Caine, A. (1997) Researching the needs of South Asian people with learning difficulties and their families, *Mental Health Care*, 1: 91–4.

Hatton, C., Azmi, S., Caine, A. and Emerson, E. (1998) Informal carers of adolescents and adults with learning disabilities from South Asian communities, *British Journal of Social Work*, 28: 821–37.

Hatton, C., Akram, Y., Shah, R., Robertson, J. and Emerson, E. (2002) *Supporting South Asian Families with a Child with Severe Disabilities: A Report to the Department of Health*. Lancaster University: Institute for Health Research.

Home Office (2000) *Race Relations (Amendment) Act 2000*. London: Home Office.

Jacobson, J. (1998) *Islam in Transition: Religion and Identity among British Pakistani Youth*. London: Routledge.

Joseph Rowntree Foundation (1999) *Implementing Key Worker Services: A Case Study of Promoting Evidence-based Practice*. York: Joseph Rowntree Foundation.

Katbamna, S., Bhakta, P. and Parker, G. (2000) Perceptions of disability and relationships in South Asian communities, in W. Ahmad (ed.) *Ethnicity, Disability and Chronic Illness*. Buckingham: Open University Press.

Kelleher, D. and Hillier, S. (eds) (1996) *Researching Cultural Differences in Health*. London: Routledge.

Learning Disability Task Force (2003) *Making Things Happen: First Annual Report of the Learning Disability Task Force*. London: Learning Disability Task Force.

Learning Disability Task Force (2004) Report: Rights, independence, choice and inclusion, http://www.valuingpeople.gov.uk/documents/TaskForceReport2004.pdf.

Lewis, J. (1996) *Give Us a Voice*. London: Choice Press.

Mason, D. (2000) *Race and Ethnicity in Modern Britain*. Oxford: Oxford University Press.

Mercer, G. and Barnes, C. (2000) Disability: from medical needs to social rights, in P. Tovey (ed.) *Contemporary Primary Care: The Challenges of Change*. Buckingham: Open University Press.

Mir, G. (2008) Effective communication with service users, *Ethnicity and Inequalities in Health and Social Care*, 1:1.

Mir, G. and Din, I. (2003) *Communication, Knowledge and Chronic Illness in the Pakistani community*. Leeds: Centre for Research in Primary Care, University of Leeds.

Mir, G. and Tovey, P. (2003) Asian carers' experiences of medical and social care: the case of cerebral palsy, *British Journal of Social Work*, 33(4): 465–79.

Mir, G., Tovey, P. and Ahmad, W. (2000) *Cerebral Palsy and South Asian Communities*. Leeds: Centre for Research in Primary Care, University of Leeds.

Mir, G., Nocon, A. and Ahmad, W. with Jones, L. (2001) *Learning Difficulties and Ethnicity*. London: Department of Health.

Mir, G., Lawler, J. and Godfrey, M. (forthcoming) *Women, Faith and Social Cohesion*. York: Joseph Rowntree Foundation.

Modood, T., Berthoud, R., Lakey, J., Nazroo, J., Smith, P., Virdee, S. *et al.* (1997) *Ethnic Minorities in Britain: Diversity and Disadvantage*. London: Policy Studies Institute.

Morris, J. (1998) *Still Missing?* London: The Who Cares Trust/Joseph Rowntree Foundation.

Mukherjee, S., Beresford, B. and Sloper, P. (1999) *Unlocking Key Working: An Analysis and Evaluation of Key Worker Services for Families with Disabled Children*. Bristol: The Policy Press.

Nazroo, J. (1997) *The Health of Britain's Ethnic Minorities*. London: Policy Studies Institute.

Priestley, M. (1995) Commonality and difference in the movement: an 'Association of Blind Asians' in Leeds, *Disability and Society*, 10: 157–69.

Robinson, M. (2002) *Communication and Health in a Multi-ethnic Society*. Bristol: The Policy Press.

Sultana, K. and Sheikh, A. (2008) Most UK datasets of routinely collected health statistics fail to collect information on ethnicity and religion, *JRSM*, 101(9): 463.

Tait, T., Chavannes, M., Dooher, J. and Miles, M. (1998) *A Study to Consider the Accommodation Support and Care Needs of Individuals with Learning Disabilities from the Asian Community in the City and County of Leicester*. Leicester: de Montfort University/The Housing Corporation.

VPST (Valuing People Support Team)/Department of Health (2004) *Learning Difficulties and Ethnicity: A Framework for Action*. London: VPST/DoH.

VPST (2005) *The Story So Far . . . Valuing People. A New Strategy for Learning Disability for the 21st Century*. London: VPST.

Ward, C. (2001) *Family Carers: Counting Families In*. London: Department of Health.

Westbrook, M.T., Legge, V. and Pennay, M. (1993) Attitudes towards disabilities in a multicultural society, *Social Science and Medicine*, 36: 615–23.

27

Work, supported employment and leisure

Margaret Flynn, Keith McKinstrie and Richard Parrott

Introduction

In this chapter an account is given of alternatives to day centres that have for so long been the mainstay of daytime activity for adults with severe and profound learning disabilities. Efforts to develop more contemporary, community-inclusive forms of day activity have slowly been supplanting the more traditional, segregated day centre provision, spurred by *Valuing People* (Department of Health 2001). This has brought some increasing investment in supported employment, and to some extent in social firms which are market-led businesses that aim to create quality jobs for people severely disadvantaged in the labour market. These developments are intended to be more attuned to the aspirations of working-aged people with learning disabilities. But are they? And what new challenges have they brought? We chart the mixed evidence about the successes so far of supported employment in particular, and comment on the fresh challenges laid down by *Valuing Employment Now* (Department of Health 2009a), the government's latest bid to help prepare more people with learning disabilities for employment. Finally, we provide an organizational case study written from a local authority perspective about the implementation of work, supported employment and leisure activity in a northern English city.

Alternatives to day centres

In addition to segregating people unnecessarily, day centres have proved themselves for decades to be poor conduits for preparing people with learning disabilities for sheltered, supported or full employment. With the recent publication of *Valuing Employment Now* (Department of Health 2009a) there at last appears to be a principled commitment to helping people with learning disabilities realize their potential

for paid work. The statistics are stark but the promises now at least transparent:

- Achieving equality for all disabled people by 2025, as set out in *Improving the Life Chances of Disabled People*. This includes the chance for all disabled people to get a job. We know that 65 per cent of people with learning disabilities would like a paid job.
- A dedicated employment strategy for people with learning disabilities because they have not benefited from the progress made for disabled people generally. While the employment rate of disabled people in Britain overall has risen steadily, that of people with learning disabilities is much lower – just 10 per cent for people receiving adult social services. This represents a waste of talent and opportunity for people with learning disabilities, employers and our wider economy and society.
- A strategy focusing on people with moderate and severe learning disabilities, because they have benefited least from previous initiatives.
- The default must be that everyone will have the chance to get a job. But there should be choice about what work people do, just as for non-disabled people.
- By 'work', we mean real jobs in the open labour market that are paid the prevailing wage, or self-employment. We do not mean volunteering or work experience, unless this is part of a genuine pathway to real work. This is about doing a good job that the employer and the employee value.
- Our aspiration is for as many people with learning disabilities as possible to work at least 16 hours a week, because this is the point at which most will be financially better off and achieve greater inclusion.
- People with profound and complex disabilities should not be excluded from the world of work. We know from international evidence that it

is possible for everyone to make an economic contribution. This strategy is also relevant to those who aspire to employment but, for example for health reasons, may genuinely not be able to work full time.

- Delivering real change will need leadership at all levels.

(Department of Health 2009a: 13–14)

So what had been happening to make these goals a priority at this time?

Work alternatives managed by statutory providers of day services

When *Caring for People: Community Care in the Next Decade and Beyond* (Department of Health 1989) had been digested by local authority social services departments, there was an understandable sense of urgency about developing new work-related initiatives for clients of working age. Joint Investment Plans between social services departments and health authorities included employment targets, and Welfare to Work strategies espoused the philosophy of giving people with learning disabilities the chance to work. Action plans identified who should take forward 'work'-related initiatives, but not necessarily how. As a consequence, development was patchy throughout the 1990s, with some statutory service providers establishing satellite work projects and others contracting with outside agencies to do it for them.

Where local authorities took the lead, 'workers' were commonly not paid a wage, and their 'work' not focused on commercial outputs. Training to nationally accredited standards, such as NVQs, has become commonplace, but there has been little evidence to suggest that employers are eagerly awaiting an annual crop of horticulturalists, kitchen assistants and bookbinders with basic qualifications and a smidgen of non-commercial work experience. The unpaid work trainees of 15 plus years ago are still unpaid work trainees today. Further, many are still attached to day centres, giving them, their parents and carers a sense of security alongside a sense of the satisfaction and pride that arises from being a 'worker'.

Day service staff invited to supervise new work schemes are unlikely to turn into business entre-

preneurs as a result. They are still day service employees. Encouraged by their 'eternal trainees' and yet reined in by local authority risk aversion, they run work schemes as if they were day centres.

Work alternatives managed by voluntary sector organizations

Voluntary sector organizations have always provided alternatives to statutory day services and, because of their freedom from some public sector constraints and a tendency towards innovation and pioneering at the margins, they have developed a vast array of work alternatives over many years.

Until recently, the idea of self-sufficiency and commercial viability has rarely been considered, and service providers have been at the mercy of local and national political trends in grant-giving for their survival. Many did not survive, while others have spent so much time raising money for short-term survival that there is neither the energy nor the capacity for longer-term planning. As with the statutory sector, wage payments to 'workers' have been rare.

The 'workers' who turn up on the doorstep of voluntary sector providers are likely to have been through the statutory services first. They may have voted with their feet, or they may have been pushed, or something in between the two. If boredom, personality clashes or parental dissatisfaction cause further turbulence, they have been forced to move on to the next time-limited training programme or work project with vacancies. Even in localities with Case Register assisted tracking of people with learning disabilities, the exercise of identifying outcomes for them bears some of the hallmarks of enthusiastic trainspotting. This circular movement of bodies has little to do with career planning or development – these are not options.

Exercise 27.1

From people with severe learning disabilities you know, list what typical jobs they do.

Now ask yourself if these jobs reflect their (i) genuine interests, (ii) skills, (iii) career aspirations.

Supported employment

According to *Valuing Employment Now* (Department of Health 2009a: 101), supported employment is:

> a well-evidenced way of helping people with learning disabilities (and other disabled people) to access and retain open employment, through the core components of: vocational profiling; job finding; job analysis and placement; job training; and follow-along services.

In the UK context, it is accepted that welfare rights advice is also an essential factor in successful supported employment.

Supported employment agencies proliferated in the UK in the late 1980s and early 1990s (Lister *et al.* 1992; Pozner and Hammond 1993). If a person with a learning disability wanted a job, then an appropriate agency would offer advice and support in identifying a suitable area of work, in applying for the job, in attending the interview and, where necessary, in providing on-the-job support. A career opportunity opened up for local authority and voluntary sector employees in 'job coaching' and the art and science of 'training in systematic instruction' was imported from the US and applied to all manner of job tasks (Powell 1991).

Supported employment continues to provide support to many learning disabled people annually, often utilizing government aid schemes such as 'Workstep' (formerly the Supported Employment Programme, SEP) to subsidize the wage of the disabled worker, and European funding programmes to pay for the agency employees and additional support costs. Referrals come through word of mouth and, typically, those referred have had enough of moving around the system, or are re-entering the public world after a bad day care experience and a period of withdrawal. The high cost of supported employment needs to be weighed against the economic and social benefits of helping learning disabled people to find and keep jobs (Corden 1997; O'Bryan *et al.* 2000).

Two significant external factors have contributed to the slippage and stalling of supported employment in the UK in recent years. First, the European funding regimes that have propped up many agencies have been contingent on 'progression' towards employment, enabling many agencies to thrive on placing people in voluntary work, or 'training' programmes, without ever getting them into employment. This mimics the 'train then place' stance of day services and defeats the innovatory 'place then train' characteristic associated with supported employment.

Second, the prevailing nature of supported employment has been 'person-centred' and agencies have learned a lot about how to work with clients, but not nearly as much about how to work with employers. Not surprisingly, the number of learning disabled people entering paid employment on the same basis as their non-disabled peers remains very low.

Supported employment: weighing the evidence

With supported employment being such a central plank in helping people to enter and retain employment, it seems sensible at this juncture to reflect what the most recent evidence has to say about the effectiveness of supported employment.

In their recent literature review of supported employment for the cross-government learning disability employment strategy team, Beyer and Robinson (2009) have been able to assess both benefits and weaknesses. On the benefits side, and there are many, supported employment seems to offer positive outcomes:

- it is a proven way, when used properly, of getting people into work;
- it is better than the sheltered alternatives;
- wages in supported employment tend to be higher than in sheltered alternatives;
- there are well-established procedures, with good outcomes, for teaching people with learning disabilities the relevant skills for the workplace;
- people are generally more satisfied with supported employment than sheltered options;
- the case for work experience for young people while at school is strong;
- the cost-benefit of supported employment increases over time in comparison to sheltered options; but natural support approaches, which put employers and co-workers at the forefront of induction and training, with support from skilled job coaches, appear to offer the prospect of greater cost-benefit outcomes.

The review also pointed to developmental challenges. It showed that even though supported employment can place people with severe learning disabilities in jobs, it is still used disproportionately with people with moderate and mild learning disabilities. More men are using supported employment than women and they generally work longer hours than women. There is therefore an important equality issue here.

It has been found that people lose jobs more for social- than task-based reasons, suggesting that support strategies are needed to ensure that people are socially embedded in the workforce. There is strong and independent evidence suggesting that people are far from fully integrated with work peers in different employment settings (Wistow and Schneider 2003; Cramm *et al.* 2008; Jahoda *et al.* 2008). It is argued that efforts to support employers to work with their supported employees, including creating their own job coaching roles, is likely to have potential for better outcomes.

The job coach role is critical to the success of supported employment but it appears to involve a number of skills that are not generally part of the repertoire of social care workers, nor of Disability Employment Advisers, Connexions Advisers or the range of Personal Advisers in government schemes. From the Beyer and Robinson (2009) review, it is evident that fidelity to a viable model of supported employment is essential, so that job coaches, and any natural supports like co-worker training or organized peer support, are underpinned by relevant skill sets. At the moment supported employment, as practised, is far too variable. Further, for people with severe learning disabilities job coaching and natural supports need to be sustained for lengthy periods to secure positive outcomes for individuals as well as a return on investment.

Personal factors like motivation appear to be implicated in the success of supported employment. For example, Hensel *et al.* (2007) found that those who secured employment were more motivated by status aspiration and judged themselves as significantly less happy than those who did not gain employment at first interview, suggesting that those more dissatisfied with their life might be more inclined to change it, if given the opportunity. This replicates a similar finding reported earlier by Rose *et al.* (2005).

It is also worth bearing in mind that wider social and cultural factors may be influential in the success of supported employment initiatives. For example, Spanish research (Vila *et al.* 2007) examining integration in the workplace illustrates that family, training (prior to and during integration), monitoring of the worker, and work setting were all relevant and contributing aspects of the process. Work–life balance issues in supported employment are yet to come under the spotlight in the UK.

It is notable that few European countries appear thus far to have made the substantial investments necessary to effect wholesale change from (sheltered) workshop to community-based supported employment practice. There have clearly not been sufficient incentives to make this happen. It remains to be seen whether *Valuing Employment Now* will deliver in this respect. The test will be to see how far beyond the present baseline of 10 per cent of people with learning disabilities in employment the bar can be raised towards the employment goal set for the year 2025.

There are still some questions to be asked about what constitutes success in the supported employment of people with learning disabilities. In the study by Schneider and Wistow (2003) the securing of a job was only the first step. Retaining the job was also necessary, but there were very important issues beyond this:

> The general picture of our respondents' experience of working life is of task-based roles, following a routine, not doing particularly skilled work, and having low levels of autonomy and responsibility. All of the jobs are 'entry level', sometimes called secondary sector jobs, characterised by low wages, low skill levels, poor working conditions, little job security, and few if any possibilities for advancement . . . We found that many people wanted more autonomy in work, which implies that training and job enhancement programmes should be put in place to achieve this progression.
>
> (Schneider and Wistow 2003: 23)

Like other workers, then, people with learning disabilities, having tasted work, want to feel that they can progress in work and develop careers for themselves.

This has huge implications for the sustainability and customizing of workplace support for people.

Social firms

In the late 1990s, the NHS Surrey Oaklands Trust was successful in a grant application to a European transnational fund (Helios) for money to explore the extent to which social firms were operating in the UK. A social firm, as defined by the European Confederation of Co-operatives and Social Business, is a business that creates employment for disabled people through the market-oriented production of goods. The term 'social firm' was not in common usage in the UK in the late 1990s, although many community businesses and co-operatives fitted the description well. The result has been the development, over the last ten years, of a social firm movement, spearheaded by Social Firms UK, a practitioner-led organization that now boasts 300 organizational members, according to its website.

For some local authority social services departments who were struggling with rising numbers in day centres, increasing numbers of part-time attendees and serious annual budget deficits, the rhetoric of social firms came as music to their ears. Service managers were tasked with setting social firms up as income-generating alternatives to traditional day centre activity, typically without any additional budget to do so. Despite interest from the Department for Work and Pensions, and from HM Treasury, and a general policy chorus in favour of modernizing day services by skirting day centres and exploring employment and learning opportunities in non-specialist contexts, no significant social firms have yet developed out of day service structures. 'Pack-it' in South Wales is the single example of a successful packaging and distribution social firm, with a turnover in excess of £1 million, that can claim to have local authority roots. The reality has been that the cultural divide between low-risk, non-commercial day centres and high-risk, economically viable social firms has been too great.

Why would local authority employees swap their favourable terms and conditions of employment to set up businesses with a high chance of failure and a workforce of people with learning disabilities who perceive their 'work' as taking place in day centres? Why would parents and carers, for whom the only imaginable alternative to the day centre they have known for years is a bigger day centre, opt for losing out on welfare benefits in the faint hope that their sons and daughters with learning disabilities might survive for a few months on a minimum wage in a doomed enterprise before being flung penniless on the scrap heap? These questions do not require written answers . . .

Despite such overwhelming obstacles to social firm development from within statutory structures, the tide bringing 'social enterprise' to the UK is so strong that social firms are being set up by individuals who have the support of a government-backed enterprise sector, and a vision of a future in which disabled and non-disabled people can live and work alongside each other without anyone being surprised about it.

Summary

- The statutory sector's work-related initiatives and strategies have barely dented the day care assumption or such employment simulations as unpaid jobs and (unduly long-term) training.
- Local authority employees do not have a track record of becoming effective business entrepreneurs attuned to self-sufficiency and commercial viability.
- Securing grant funding plagues the endeavours of those seeking employment for people with learning disabilities.
- Supported employment, as it was originally conceived, is stalling, irrespective of its track record in finding jobs and maintaining people

in employment, because of European funding requirements.

- Social firms have inherited the promise once associated with supported employment and face similar challenges.

Micro enterprises and self-employment

Self-employment has been emerging much more recently as a further option for people with disabilities and it seems possible that its reach may yet be extended through the rolling out of personal budgets (see Chapter 22). According to some commentators, the definition of work should 'include those activities that people with disabilities undertake in the management of daily living, including the employment of personal assistants, and the creation of employment opportunities for others' (Pavey 2006: 226). This would also add interesting new prospects for independence and control in people's lives. In its favour self-employment respects the capacity and assets of people with learning disabilities, their interests and strengths. As Beyer and Robinson (2009) suggest, a small business is a way of gaining income from a hobby or a personal interest. In this respect it may provide more scope for meeting vocational interests than can be accomplished by the prevailing job market, especially one facing the present global recession. Beyer and Robinson's (2009) review suggests, however, that the penetration of the micro-enterprise model into the UK has been limited and is unlikely to make a major impact on total numbers of people entering employment.

Exercise 27.3

See what information you can find out about social firms and micro-enterprises in your local area.

Assess how useful this information is for people with learning disabilities on your caseload.

How will these goals be achieved?

Valuing Employment Now (Department of Health 2009a) is refreshingly explicit about how employment

prospects for people with learning disabilities are to be achieved. It proposes:

- a changed culture that presumes the employability of people with learning disabilities;
- joint working to create employment paths for individuals;
- better work preparation at school, college and adult learning;
- use of personal budgets;
- increased high-quality job coaching;
- simplification of the benefits system and removal of disincentives to employment;
- promotion of self-employment;
- help for employers to appreciate the business case;
- improved transport for people to get to work;
- addressing barriers where people live;
- better support for those who are most excluded;
- people with learning disabilities and families leading the way;
- better data on performance management.

This is rightly a heady agenda, demanding much from close, cross-agency working. But, as ever, there is a sting in the tail. Quoting *Valuing Employment Now* (Department of Health 2009a: 13–14):

> The economic climate also means that there will be little opportunity for new investment. The strategy focuses on more effective use of existing resources, including education, adult learning and employment support. Local authorities will also be encouraged to refocus some of their current spend on adult day services onto supported employment, and to use their new responsibility for funding 16–19 learning (16–25 for those subject to a learning difficulty assessment) to review and align provision.

It seems appropriate, therefore, at this juncture to invite a local authority commentary on the practicalities of implementing this strategy.

A view from Sheffield (Keith McKinstrie and Richard Parrott)

Day time opportunities, in their broadest sense, play a key role in people having purposeful lives within their community as well as developing a range of friendships, activities and relationships. They also provide reliable support to family carers, assisting them to lead fulfilling lives in their own right.

Drivers for change

The *'What?'* shaping the local authority agenda is defined by national policy which prompts the move from people having day services in day centres to supporting people in work, learning and leisure activities in their own communities. *Valuing People* (Department of Health 2001) set out a series of expectations for more opportunities for people to do the things they want to, including learning new skills through further education, spending time with friends, and the chance to get a 'real' job. However, some groups of people missed out in the drive to more community-based day time opportunities. Summarizing progress in *The Story So Far*, Greig (2005) wrote that although there had been progress in many areas, people with more complex needs and people from the black and ethnic minority communities were not benefiting as much as other people with learning disabilities.

In 2007 the Social Care Institute for Excellence (SCIE) published *Having a Good Day*, which was based on an extensive review of policy and practice in the UK by the Foundation for People with Learning Disabilities and the Norah Fry Research Centre (Cole and Williams 2007). 'Successful provision' was seen as people with learning disabilities spending their days:

- working;
- in education or training;
- volunteering;
- participating in leisure activities, arts and hobbies;
- socializing with friends.

Arguably it highlights a danger – that the majority of people with learning disabilities who are not working are the new leisure class: a 'retired' population with time to pick and choose how to spend their days.

It noted that all people, irrespective of the support they need, should be:

- undertaking activities that have a purpose;
- being in ordinary places doing things that most members of the community would be doing;
- doing things that are right for them personally;
- receiving support that meets their individual and specific requirements and overcomes inequalities;
- meeting local people, developing friendships and a sense of belonging.

National policy has also shaped the *'How?'* for local authorities. The personalization agenda with its shift in choice and control to the individual, the strategy that the Learning and Skills Council espoused in *Learning for Living and Work* (2006) and the cross-government strategy *Progression Through Partnership* (HM Government 2007) all contribute to the mechanisms for local authorities to deliver change.

The challenge for local authorities

It is well documented that over the last ten years an increasing number of adults with learning disabilities have required social care services, including day time opportunities. This is projected to continue for the next ten years (Emerson and Hatton 2008). The range of needs is wider than ever, with more people having the most complex needs, with profound and multiple learning disabilities, with autism, including those from black and ethnic communities.

People with a learning disability and their families also have higher expectations about their rights to be supported in an independent life – that they can have services and support of their choice, at a time they wish and that those services will work in partnership with them to meet their needs and enable them to live full lives as citizens.

Meanwhile, resources are not keeping pace with increasing demand. In 2005 the Association of Directors of Social Services (2005) reported that the single greatest area of pressure on social services budgets was the increasing demand on learning disabilities services, due to more children with major disabilities surviving into adulthood and more adults surviving into older age. Adults with a learning disability now represent the second highest level of social care expenditure. (Gross expenditure by councils on social care for adults was around £15 billion in 2006–07. Of this expenditure, around £3.29 billion (21.9 per cent) was spent on adults aged 18–64 with learning disabilities – including Supporting People funding.) The impact of the current economic downturn is likely to compound this pressure.

The challenge for the local authority is to commission, develop and encourage day time opportunities that meet the increasing and changing needs and expectations of people with learning disabilities and their families within the context of resources being unable to keep pace with increasing demand.

The journey

Day time opportunities are provided in a wide range of statutory, private and third sector organizations. They are commissioned in a range of ways, including local authority directly provided services, local authority contracts with local voluntary sector organizations and social care-funded individual or 'spot' purchasing arrangements with voluntary sector organizations and independent providers. In addition an increasing number of people access day time opportunities using direct payments, Independent Living Fund (ILF) awards, Trusts or third party payments.

Many local voluntary sector organizations also provide day time opportunities for people who do not access social care funding. These opportunities may be funded by other means, i.e. charities, Lottery or regeneration funding. Increasingly people are accessing a range of day time opportunities from a range of providers rather than receiving all their support from one service.

For many years people with learning disabilities have been saying that they, like most of the population, want to work. Economic inclusion is social inclusion. But in reality, most people with a learning disability face the major systemic barriers to getting and keeping a job that have always prevailed, as reported earlier in this chapter.

National policy emphasizes the importance of work for people with a learning disability, recognizing that the number of people with a learning disability in work remains very low. In 2001, *Valuing People* expected Learning Disabilities Partnership Boards to develop strategies to increase employment for people with a learning disability. *Valuing People Now* (Department of Health 2009b), and *Valuing Employment Now* (Department of Health 2009a) have significantly raised the policy expectation, with challenging government targets for the number of people with a learning disability in work over the next

decade and beyond. This has been reinforced through Public Service Agreement 16 and the new National Performance Indicator NI 146, which requires local targets for increasing the number of adults with a learning disability known to Councils with Adult Social Services Responsibilities (CASSRs).

Day time opportunities, further education, volunteering and other socially inclusive activities can all help people gain the skills and confidence they need to get a job and/or access 'mainstream' activities in the community. Similarly there is recognition that volunteering, while for some people a valued end in itself, for others can be a vital stepping stone on their way to paid employment, by developing skills and confidence, and building a curriculum vitae. It is essential that the best of 'day time opportunities' incorporate each of these aspects and that the links are acknowledged and strengthened.

The strategy

A cornerstone of any strategy for day time opportunities and employment is that it is owned by the whole of the local authority. It cannot be the sole responsibility of specialist learning disability services. Without shared ownership between the local authority and its partner organizations, day time opportunities are regarded as the business of 'social services'.

In developing a variety of day time opportunities across the local authority it must be recognized that some people with a learning disability and their carers still value aspects of services in specialist learning disability settings. People with complex needs may need access to specialist facilities, including for example accessible toilets in which people may be assisted to change continence pads and have showers. Some services will need to be based in buildings that are of high quality and offer a valued environment.

Much success in improving people's day time activities has been achieved 'one person at a time' through person-centred approaches (Chapter 25) and the use of individual budgets (Chapter 22) to arrange bespoke day time activities. It is for the local authority to encourage partner organizations, and others in the private and voluntary sectors where there is no contractual link, to develop a range of services corresponding to the perceived needs and preferences of people with learning disabilities in the community, to increase the range of options. The local authority is uniquely placed to form alliances with like-minded service providers to support them in their thinking, and at the same time reinforce the commercial and other possibilities of a developing on 'market place' where people are increasingly influential as the holders of economic power.

The local authority has the leadership responsibility for making sure that the voices of people with learning disabilities are heard and responded to; it should be familiar with the barriers to people's inclusion, ensuring that these inform commissioning and partnership arrangements across the authority. Opportunities can only increase if these partnerships are nurtured and developed, with a common vision driving change.

Example of increasing day time opportunities

The needs analysis of one local authority shows that over the next ten years there will be a significant increase in the number of people with a learning disability and complex needs. Taking on the *Valuing People* principle of 'all means all', it was recognized that access to community facilities for people with complex needs was highly restricted as there were no accessible changing facilities in the parts of the city people chose to use.

The initial step was for workers in the specialist learning disabilities service to obtain the endorsement of the Learning Disabilities Partnership Board, and crucially the Chief Executive of the Council, for a 'changing places campaign'. Working to the City Council agenda, part of the approach was to emphasize that the initiative would make the city a more attractive place for people to come and visit and should therefore be promoted as part of the city's tourism strategy.

Potential sites for changing places were then identified collaboratively with an officer from the parks and countryside department, and a number of sites across the local authority were targeted by accessibility, transport links, leisure and sports facilities, recreation and pastimes.

The influence of the Council was harnessed so that all new planning applications for buildings with public access should have changing places included as standard, as should any significant redevelopments. It was also proposed that changing places should be included as part of the standard tourist information for the City. Officers within the City Council, but outside the specialist service, used their networks with the commercial sectors across the City to get 'the message' across, to help them recognize the economic potential of improving their facilities.

Key factors that enabled the local authority to be influential in expanding the range of mainstream day time opportunities for people with some of the most complex needs groups were the importance of committed and informed individuals within, and endorsement from the top of, the organization. The outcome of this 'local authority' as opposed to 'learning disability' approach has so far resulted in a number of mainstream venues, including the Town Hall, a hospital, an international sports venue, sports arenas, cricket club, and shopping centre all becoming accessible to the general public, including those adults with learning disabilities and complex needs.

An approach to increasing employment for adults with a learning disability

As with day time opportunities, a cornerstone of any strategy for employment is that the responsibility is not limited to specialist learning disability services. The report of the government's Working Group on Learning Disabilities and Employment (2006) concluded that responsibility for making sure all people can access employment is community-wide, not simply one for health and social care.

This was reinforced when we were consulting on our Learning Disability Employment Strategy with employers. A key message was: 'We support the plan, but we don't want you talking to us about learning disability one week, someone else about mental health the next week, someone else again about another marginalized group the week after – we want a single, efficient and co-ordinated approach.' However, the starting point was that, to date, the driving force had been with learning disability services. Meeting the employers' requests on our own would be a significant challenge.

The catalyst for a new approach was the new National Performance Indicator NI 146 – increasing the proportion of people with a learning disability in paid work. The Learning Disability Partnership Board proposed – and the Local Strategic Partnership agreed – that NI 146 should be one of the top 35 priorities within the Local Area Agreement. Work for people with a learning disability is now seen as an equalities issue for the whole community, requiring a mainstream and co-ordinated approach across a range of public, private and voluntary organizations and, most importantly, local employers.

The expertise in supporting groups of people into work who are furthest away from the labour market lies with mainstream employment services. In Sheffield we have based the delivery of our Learning Disability Employment Strategy with the Council's Lifelong Learning and Skills Section. This co-ordinates the city's overall strategy on employment and skills. It has formally established links with employers in all sectors. It has links with the city's supported employment delivery partners. It has links with the key funding partners including the Department for Work and Pensions. It can influence the Area Based Grant elements of funding for employment. As a City Pathfinder it can comment on procurement and bids in employment programmes, influencing spend and objectives. It supports the city's Skills Strategy, helping make sure that learning disability developments play a role in delivering jobs that help meet the city's needs. Importantly, it has also provided a base for delivering the related Local Area Agreement priority on increasing employment for people with mental health problems, allowing for co-ordination of effort, planning, resources, communications and much more.

Thoughts

Transforming social care is a long-term project and it remains early days. By enhancing the capacity of mainstream services to perceive and meet their responsibilities for the whole community, and improving access to the public space, the local authority aims to improve social and economic inclusion so that health and social care resources can be focused where they are most needed.

However, this change cannot happen at the required pace without clear leadership. Experience confirms that mainstream agencies do not deliberately or cynically create barriers for disabled people. Rather, they involve and are led by people who are highly motivated to improve access and quality for disabled 'customers'. They are also keen for advice, ideas and support from people with a learning disability, their families and learning disability professionals so they can travel on this journey together.

Exercise 27.4

Reflect upon the importance of employment to people with learning disabilities in helping them to achieve independence, self-esteem and social inclusion.

In enabling this to happen, now ask what are the roles and contributions of:

- your profession?
- your employing agency?
- civil society?

Conclusion

Some wonderfully dynamic examples of supported employment, social firms and micro-employment have engaged the imaginations of people with learning disabilities, families, care managers and service planners. However, while the aspiration of employment has been endemic in research reports glimpsing the worlds of adults with learning disabilities for at least two decades, progress in translating utopian enthusiasm into real jobs is slow and the barriers are stubborn. Work in Sheffield confirms that if we are to be inclusive, it is important to attend to the realities of people's physical support needs and 'changing places', as an example, are essential. In the worlds of adults with learning disabilities the boundary between what is regarded as work and non-work activity/support is hazy as changes in one domain have a significant impact on the other.

It remains to be seen whether or not adults who are supported to be Direct Payments recipients, for example, will be able to fulfil employment aspirations. Will the commissioning of supported employment services persist if adults with learning disabilities are not brought up to see themselves as prospective employees? Don't they and their families collectively have to assert this aspiration at a time when individually they are encouraged to see themselves as individual entrepreneurs? Knowing adults with learning disabilities who enjoy 'real jobs' we know that they take pride in the fact that their work achieves something, it involves their effort and persistence (even though there may be pleasurable elements in it) and the circumstances under which activities are undertaken matter a great deal. Such adults, while still in the minority, have a crucial role in inspiring the next generation of employees.

Resources

www.base-uk.org. British Association for Supported Employment.

www.euse.org. European Union of Supported Employment.

www.scotchbonnet.org.uk. Scotch Bonnet Catering.

www.socialfirms.co.uk. Social Firms UK.

References

Association of Directors of Social Services (2005) *Spending Pressures in Learning Disability Services*. London: ADSS.

Beyer, S. and Robinson, C. (2009) *A Review of the Research Literature on Supported Employment: A Report for the Cross-government Learning Disability Employment Strategy Team*. Cardiff: Welsh Centre for Learning Disabilities and Carol Robinson Consulting.

Cole, A. and Williams, V. (2007) *Having a Good Day: A Study of Community-based Day Activities for People with Learning Disabilities*. SCIE Knowledge Review 14, London: Social Care Institute for Excellence.

Corden, A. (1997) *Supported Employment, People and Money: Social Policy Reports, Number 7*. York: The University of York, Social Policy Research Unit.

Cramm, J.M., Tebra, N. and Finkenflugel, H. (2008) Colleagues' perception of supported employee performance, *Journal of Policy and Practice in Intellectual Disabilities*, 5(4): 269–75.

Department of Health (1989) *Caring for People: Community Care in the Next Decade and Beyond*. London: DoH.

Department of Health (2001) *Valuing People: A New Strategy for Learning Disability for the 21st Century*. London: DoH.

Department of Health (2009a) *Valuing Employment Now: Real Jobs for People with Learning Disabilities*. London: DoH.

Department of Health (2009b) *Valuing People Now: A New Three-year Strategy for People with Learning Disabilities*. London: DoH.

Emerson, E. and Hatton, C. (2008) *Estimating Future Need for Adult Social Care Services for People with Learning Disability in England*. Lancaster: Centre for Disability Research, University of Lancaster.

Greig, R. (2005) *Valuing People: The Story So Far. London*: Department of Health.

Hensel, E., Kroese, B.J. and Rose, J. (2007) Psychological factors associated with obtaining employment, *Journal of Applied Research in Intellectual Disabilities*, 20(2): 175–81.

HM Government (2007) *Progression Through Partnership: Strategy for Learners with Learning Disabilities*. London: The Stationery Office.

Jahoda, A., Kemp, J., Riddell, S. and Banks, P. (2008) Feelings about work: a review of the socio-emotional impact of supported employment on people with learning disabilities, *Journal of Applied Research in Intellectual Disabilities*, 21(1): 1–18.

Learning and Skills Council (2006) *Learning for Living and Work: Improving Education and Training Opportunities for People with Learning Difficulties and/or Disabilities*. Coventry: LSC.

Lister, T., Ellis, L., Phillips, T., O'Bryan, A., Beyer, S. and Kilsby, M. (1992) *Survey of Supported Employment Services in England*. Manchester: National Development Team.

O'Bryan, A., Simons, K., Beyer, S. and Grove, B. (2000) *Economic Security and Supported Employment for the Policy Consortium on Supported Employment*. Manchester: National Development Team and Joseph Rowntree Foundation.

Pavey, B. (2006) Human capital, social capital, entrepreneurship and disability: an examination of some educational trends in the UK, *Disability and Society*, 21(3): 217–19.

Powell, T.H. (1991) *Supported Employment: Providing Integrated Employment Opportunities for Persons with Disabilities*. New York: Longman.

Pozner, A. and Hammond, J. (1993) *An Evaluation of Supported Employment Initiatives for Disabled People*, Employment Department Research Series No. 17. Sheffield: Department of Employment.

Rose, J., Saunders, K., Hensel, E. and Kroese, B.S. (2005) Factors affecting the likelihood that people with intellectual disabilities will obtain employment, *Journal of Intellectual Disabilities*, 9(1): 9–23.

Schneider, J. and Wistow, R. (2003) *Supported Employment in the UK: A Profile of Providers and Service Users*. Durham: Department of Health Learning Disability Research Initiative, University of Durham.

Vila, M., Pallisera, M. and Fullana, J. (2007) Work integration of people with disabilities in the regular labour market: what can we do to improve the processes? *Journal of Intellectual and Developmental Disability*, 32(1): 10–18.

Wistow, R. and Schneider, J. (2003) Users' views on supported employment and social inclusion: a qualitative study of 30 people in work, *British Journal of Learning Disabilities*, 31(4): 166–74.

Wistow, R. and Schneider, J. (2007) Employment support agencies in the UK: current operation and future development needs, *Health and Social Care in the Community*, 15(2): 128–35.

Working Group on Learning Disabilities and Employment (2006) *Opportunities for People with a Learning Disability. A Report to Ministers and the Learning Disability Task Force*. London: Department for Work and Pensions.

28

Promoting healthy lifestyles: mental health

Chris Hatton and John L. Taylor

Introduction

Interest in mental health problems among people with learning disabilities has increased exponentially in the past 30 years, from a starting position of almost complete professional and research indifference. This 'therapeutic disdain' (Bender 1993) has been described as being caused by a lack of interest in the problems of people seen as different; people with learning disabilities being considered not able enough to benefit from psychological therapies; and therapists' reluctance to offer therapy to people who are unattractive because of their disabilities.

The picture is now quite different, with an explosion of interest in the mental health needs of people with learning disabilities. The quantity of research in this area is increasing, although still at a rudimentary level compared to mainstream mental health research. Professional interest in terms of developing effective interventions with people with learning disabilities and mental health problems is also increasing, although the published evidence base here is still largely at the level of case studies, case series and small trials and there are still huge inequalities in access to effective mental health services experienced by people with learning disabilities (Clark 2007; Nocon and Sayce 2008; Chaplin 2009).

In this chapter we will introduce issues relating to the causes and prevalence of mental health problems among people with learning disabilities, and the identification, assessment and treatment of these problems.

What is mental health?

Exercise 28.1

Quickly write down your own idea of what you mean by mental health and mental health problem. Ask other people to do the same exercise and compare your definitions.

- Are your definitions consistent?
- How would they distinguish a mentally healthy person from a person with a mental health problem?
- How would your definition apply to people with learning disabilities?
- What problems are there with your definition?
- How easy or difficult was it to try and write a definition?

Terms like mental health, mental illness, mental disorder and psychopathology are commonly used as if everyone has a common understanding of what they mean. However, the fundamental question of what mental health is, and how it may be distinguished from mental illness, is still being hotly debated with no consensus in sight (Sims 1988).

In this chapter we will take a broadly holistic view of mental health, where 'Health is a state of complete physical, mental and social well-being and not merely the absence of disease or infirmity' (World Health Organization 1946). This definition emphasizes health as positive well-being within a broad social context, rather than health as being the absence of disease within an individual. This definition is helpful in two ways: it emphasizes well-being as the crucial indicator of health rather than physical signs of brain disease, and it emphasizes the social context within which mental health is experienced.

Applying a generic mental health framework to people with learning disabilities

As other chapters in this book have demonstrated, the living circumstances of people with learning disabilities as a group can be quite different to the general population, with welfare services often having a greatly increased role in the lives of people with learning disabilities. These differences can have a profound impact on the degree and nature of mental health problems experienced by people with learning disabilities, and also on the way that services understand and respond to mental health problems with people with learning disabilities.

Living circumstances, life events and other risk factors

Exercise 28.2

Quickly write down your ideas about which life circumstances are risk factors for mental health problems and which are protective factors. Do you think people with learning disabilities are more or less likely to experience each of the life circumstances you have written down?

As a group, people with learning disabilities are more likely to experience several living circumstances and life events associated with an increased risk of mental health problems in the general population, including birth trauma, stressful family circumstances, poverty, unemployment, stigmatization, lack of self-determination, and a lack of meaningful friendships and intimate relationships (Hastings *et al.* 2004; Martorell *et al.* 2009; Emerson and Hatton forthcoming). The cumulative effect of living in such circumstances, in terms of being placed at the bottom of social and economic hierarchies, can be crucial in triggering mental health problems; particularly important are feelings of humiliation (feeling put down or devalued), entrapment (feeling imprisoned in a punishing situation for some time), loss (death or separation from important other people) and danger (feeling the threat of a potential future loss) (Brown 2000; Wilkinson and Pickett 2009). Certainly, people with learning disabilities do report experiencing stigma, linked to feelings of being different, negative beliefs about themselves and their social attractiveness, and reassurance seeking (Dagnan and Waring 2004; Jahoda *et al.* 2006; Hartley *et al.* 2008; Mac-Mahon and Jahoda 2008).

People with learning disabilities may also be at greater risk of developing mental health problems due to psychological factors such as a reduced capacity for coping productively with stressful circumstances, poorer memory and poorer problem-solving and planning skills (van den Hout *et al.* 2000).

Accessing services

Exercise 28.3

Quickly write down your ideas about how most people with mental health problems get help.

- How is the person's mental health problem recognized?
- How do people get access to services?
- Which services do they access and what help do they get?
- Is this likely to be the same for people with learning disabilities?

There is considerable debate about how people with learning disabilities and mental health problems are to be best supported, with consistent findings that learning disability services have a limited understanding of mental health problems, with people with learning disabilities frequently receiving poor or no services to treat their mental health problems (Bhaumik *et al.* 2008; Lunsky *et al.* 2008; Chaplin 2009).

Services for people with learning disabilities and people with mental health problems are largely separate and have quite distinct service cultures, with relatively few specialist mental health services for people with learning disabilities (Bailey and Cooper 1997: Hassiotis *et al.* 2000). For example, support staff in social services may be quite hostile to seeing a person's behaviour as symptomatic of a mental health problem rather than a form of 'challenging behaviour' (Costello 2004), an issue compounded by overlapping definitions and a lack of clarity in how mental health problems and challenging behaviours relate to each other (Myrbakk and von Tetzchner 2008a; Felce *et al.* 2009). 'Diagnostic overshadowing' (Reiss *et al.* 1982) may also occur, where carers and professionals misattribute signs of a mental health problem (for example, poor self-care as a result of depression) as being due to a person's intellectual disabilities.

Typical referral pathways to mental health services, through a GP due to a person having problems fulfilling social roles (e.g. as spouse, parent, employee) (Goldberg and Huxley 1980), may also be less accessible to people with learning disabilities. First, people with learning disabilities are less likely to be in social roles where problems would be apparent. Second, environments for people with learning disabilities may be so restricted that a mental health problem may not be activated or displayed (e.g. a specific phobia). Third, some mental health problems may not manifest themselves in behaviours that are seen as problematic by carers or professionals (e.g. depression manifesting in social withdrawal and loss of energy) (Edelstein and Glenwick 2001). In contrast, people with learning disabilities may be referred to mental health services when their behaviour is construed as a problem by other people rather than being a problem for the person themselves (e.g. anger in response to restrictions on autonomy and choice).

Finally, training programmes helping care staff to work effectively with people with learning disabilities and mental health problems are relatively rare (Quigley *et al.* 2001; Costello *et al.* 2007), although innovative programmes are being developed and evaluated (Costello *et al.* 2007; McGillivray *et al.* 2008; Raghavan *et al.* 2009).

Identifying mental health problems

Exercise 28.4

Imagine you are trying to interview a person speaking a language different to yours about their mental health problems.

- How would you tell them what you were doing?
- How would you communicate important ideas?
- How would you understand what the person was telling you?

Most professionals working in services for people with learning disabilities are likely to be working with a person with additional mental health problems

(Quigley *et al.* 2001). It is vital that professionals have the awareness and skills to identify potential mental health problems (Oliver *et al.* 2005), although there are difficult questions arising from the process of identification.

Question 1: do standard psychiatric diagnostic criteria apply to (some or all) people with learning disabilities?

Over the past 30 years, persistent problems in the general identification of mental health have led to the development of internationally recognized standard psychiatric classification systems such as the Diagnostic and Statistical Manual of Mental Disorders (American Psychiatric Association 1994) and the International Classification of Diseases Classification of Mental and Behavioural Disorders (World Health Organization 1993). While these classification systems may have increased the reliability of psychiatric diagnoses for the general population, it is unclear how applicable they are to people with learning disabilities (Sturmey 1999).

First, it is possible that these ways of classifying mental health problems may not be applicable to the experiences of people with severe and complex learning disabilities, who frequently have little or no symbolic language skills (Sturmey 1999; Cooper *et al.* 2007a; Dagnan 2007). For example, can a person with no symbolic language experience auditory hallucinations, or have the cognitive skills necessary to conceptualize and plan a suicide attempt?

Second, these classification systems are categorical; to reach a threshold for a mental health problem, a person needs to experience a pattern of symptoms at a certain level of frequency and severity. Many people with learning disabilities may show clear signs of a mental health problem, but not show a sufficient range of signs to trigger a diagnosis of a mental health problem (Moss *et al.* 1996a; Langlois and Martin 2008). There are also broader questions about how useful categorical diagnostic systems are in guiding clinical work with people with mental health problems.

Third, these classification systems contain some assumptions that might be difficult to apply to people with learning disabilities. For example, these systems often diagnose a mental health problem as a change from the usual, when a person with learning disabilities may have had unrecognized mental health problems for months or years. These systems also assume a usual level of functioning that may be difficult to apply to people with learning disabilities; for example, criteria for depression include a diminished ability to think or concentrate.

Within the ICD-10 system, there have already been modified diagnostic criteria produced for people with mild learning disabilities (World Health Organization 1996) and people with moderate to severe learning disabilities (Royal College of Psychiatrists 2001). However, both of these modifications have been the subject of some debate (Einfeld and Tonge 1999; Cooper 2003) and are based on informal expert consensus methods with limited validity.

Question 2: is it possible to accurately assess mental states in people with learning disabilities?

Identifying a mental health problem almost always involves gaining some access to the mental state of the person (Sims 1988). Many mental states, whether perceptions, emotions or beliefs, can really only be accessed by the person describing what their mental state is; inferring a mental state from a person's behaviour can be highly questionable.

Research evidence suggests that most people with learning disabilities and good functional communication skills can give accurate descriptions of their own mental states, as long as interview schedules are sensitively adapted (Finlay and Lyons 2001; Dagnan and Lindsay 2004). There are many examples of self-report mental health measures that have been successfully developed or adapted for people with mild or moderate learning disabilities (see below). However, there is little or no research evidence demonstrating that asking people with more severe and complex learning disabilities about their mental states produces reliable or valid responses (Ross and Oliver 2003a).

Some of these problems in gaining descriptions of mental states seem to be a function of the person's skills; for example, many people with learning disabilities have difficulties in recognizing and describing emotions, often using restricted or idiosyncratic emotional vocabularies (Rojahn et al. 1995a). Many of the ideas involved when assessing mental states are also abstract and complex (for example, distinguishing

between a voice, a thought and a dream), and therefore difficult to understand.

Question 3: to what extent can we use information from other people to assess mental health problems in people with learning disabilities?

Many measures to assess mental health problems in people with learning disabilities have been designed to be used with an informant (typically a paid carer or a family member) rather than with the person themselves (see below). There is some convergence between the self-reports of people with mild or moderate learning disabilities and informants using highly structured clinical interview schedules, with informants more likely to pick up behavioural signs and unlikely to reliably report mental state (Moss et al. 1996b). However, people with learning disabilities and carers are less likely to agree using less structured interviews concerning emotional distress (Bramston and Fogarty 2000).

Question 4: to what extent can we use observational information to assess mental health problems in people with learning disabilities?

Many mental health problems are considered to have distinctive patterns of behaviour associated with them, although relying on behavioural observations alone is unlikely to reliably identify most mental health problems. For example, self-reports and behavioural observations often do not agree (Rojahn et al. 1995b). Moreover, the frequent reporting of 'atypical' behavioural symptoms in people with severe and complex learning disabilities suggests that reliable behavioural markers of mental health problems are unlikely in this group (Ross and Oliver 2003a).

Informed consent and capacity

Consent to treatment is an important ethical issue for clinical professionals (Sturmey and Gaubatz 2002). Many people with learning disabilities, particularly those living in institutional settings, have been subject to various forms of abuse, including dangerous interventions that have resulted in injury and harm. Although some people with learning disabilities can understand the elements necessary for participation in treatment, many cannot (Arscott *et al.* 1999). In any case, many people with learning disabilities living in institutional or hospital settings have been placed there because they are judged to be legally incompetent (see also Chapter 4). In such cases it is unclear who can consent either to treatment or participation in treatment outcome research. However, this is probably not very different for people without learning disabilities (e.g. Featherstone and Donovan 2002). Therefore, we need to avoid the situation where discriminatory decisions to exclude people with learning disabilities from potentially beneficial treatments are made on the basis of erroneous assumptions about their capacity to give consent compared with members of the general population. A balance is required in order to protect potentially vulnerable individuals and to promote self-determination.

According to the Lord Chancellor's Department (1999), valid consent requires: (a) that clients are provided with sufficient accurate information concerning the treatment; (b) that they have capacity to make a decision about accepting treatment and to understand the consequences of the decision; and (c) that their decision to accept treatment is voluntary. Capacity involves the ability to comprehend information about the treatment, to be able to assimilate and recall the information, and to be able to make a decision about accepting the treatment being offered (Wong *et al.* 1999).

Making information about treatment understandable and accessible to people with cognitive limitations is challenging for clinicians, but not insurmountable (Arscott *et al.* 1999). One helpful approach is to include a psycho-educational preparatory phase following which participants will be better informed and able to give or withhold valid consent (e.g. Taylor *et al.* 2002a). However, the extent to which consent-giving by people with learning disabilities can ever be totally free, and so voluntary, given issues around acquiescence and suggestibility, is questionable. This is a debate that needs to be brought into the open so that clinicians, clients and their supporters can be clear about the ethical issues in this difficult area of work.

If consent cannot be given and the client would have benefited from a particular treatment, then another ethical dilemma is the denial of the benefits of particular treatment interventions to people for whom adequate consent cannot be obtained. In England and Wales this issue is addressed in the Department of Health (2001) guidance document, *Seeking Consent: Working with People with Learning Disabilities*. This guidance suggests that individuals who do not have the capacity to give consent can be given treatment if it is judged to be in the person's best interests. However, given the history of harmful fads and fashions in treatments for people with learning disabilities (Mostert 2001; Sturmey *et al.* 2004), we cannot assume that well-intended treatments are always helpful, neutral or harmless. In the absence of good evidence to support particular interventions we should be cautious about offering them to people with learning disabilities who may have difficulty in resisting them.

How many people with learning disabilities experience mental health problems?

Exercise 28.5

What proportion of people with learning disabilities and the general population do you think will experience the following mental health problems?

Depression
Anxiety
Psychosis/schizophrenia
Dementia

What were the reasons behind your guesses?

Gaining accurate information on the prevalence of mental health problems among people with learning disabilities is challenging (Kerker *et al.* 2004), with research on problems such as personality disorder particularly sparse (Pridding and Proctor 2008). Recent studies with population-based samples (rather than samples of people in contact with specialist services) using over-inclusive screening measures suggest rates of psychopathology around 40 per cent for children and adolescents with learning disabilities (Einfeld *et al.* 2006; Emerson and Hatton 2007) and rates of psychopathology between 20 per cent and 40 per cent for adults with learning disabilities (Taylor *et al.* 2004a; White *et al.* 2005; Cooper *et al.* 2007b), with higher rates reported when behaviour problems are included within the definition of psychopathology. This compares to a prevalence rate of approximately 25 per cent for similar mental health problems in general population adults (Goldberg and Huxley 1980); although it is widely stated that psychopathology is more prevalent among adults with intellectual disabilities we believe this conclusion is premature.

More specifically:

- *Depression*: reported prevalence of depression varies widely (Stavrakaki 1999), with population-based studies reporting rates of 6.6 per cent to 8 per cent (White *et al.* 2005; Cooper *et al.* 2007b), but studies focusing on depressive symptoms reporting very high rates from 44 per cent to 57 per cent (Meins 1995; Marston *et al.* 1997). People with mild/moderate learning disabilities display the range of depressive symptoms found in the general population, although the validity of the 'atypical' symptoms reported for people with severe/profound learning disabilities is questionable (Ross and Oliver 2003a).
- *Anxiety*: both population-based studies and specific anxiety studies suggest high levels of anxiety disorders in adults with learning disabilities (22 per cent to 27 per cent; Stavrakaki and Mintsioulis 1997; White *et al.* 2005), although rates of anxiety excluding specific phobias have been reported to be much lower (e.g. 3.8 per cent; Cooper *et al.* 2007b). The validity of diagnoses of anxiety is particularly questionable for people with severe/profound intellectual disabilities (Matson *et al.* 1997).
- *Psychosis*: there is substantial evidence that rates of psychosis are substantially higher among people with learning disabilities (White *et al.* 2005; Cooper *et al.* 2007b, 2007c; Morgan *et al.* 2008), although estimated rates of psychosis vary from 1.2 per cent to 6 per cent. Once again, the absence of reliable self-report makes the diagnosis of psychosis in people with severe/profound intellectual disabilities difficult.
- *Dementia*: the prevalence of dementia is much

higher among older adults with learning disabilities compared to the general population (21.6 per cent vs 5.7 per cent aged 65+; Cooper 1997). People with Down's syndrome are at particularly high risk of developing dementia, with an age of onset 30–40 years younger than the general population (Holland *et al.* 1998).
- *Substance misuse*: general research suggests low levels of alcohol and drug use among adults with learning disabilities (e.g. Lund 1985), although alcohol use may be higher in more independent living circumstances (Robertson *et al.* 2000b).
- *Anger and aggression*: studies conducted across three continents using broadly similar designs and methods have found the prevalence of aggression among people with learning disabilities to be between 10 per cent and 16 per cent in community populations, and 35 per cent to 47 per cent in institutional and specialist service settings (Taylor 2002; Taylor and Novaco 2005).

Assessing mental health problems in people with learning disabilities

The development of reliable and valid mental health screening measures for people with learning disabilities is in its early stages, with a proliferation of measures and little evidence on the reliability or validity of any of them (Beail 2004; Dagnan and Lindsay 2004; Novaco and Taylor 2004). Different measures vary according to:

- whether they are measures developed for the general population and then used or adapted for people with learning disabilities, or whether they are specifically designed for people with learning disabilities;
- whether they are designed as self-report measures to be completed by people with learning disabilities (almost always in an interview format), or whether they are designed to be completed by informants about the person with learning disabilities (in either a questionnaire or interview format);
- whether they are designed primarily for people with mild/moderate learning disabilities, people with severe/profound learning disabilities, or the whole range of people with learning disabilities;

- whether they are designed to act as a screen across a wide range of mental health problems, or whether they focus in more detail on a particular mental health problem;
- how much training and knowledge of mental health issues is needed to use the measure;
- the length of time they take the professional, person with learning disabilities and/or the informant to complete.

Information on a wide range of mental health measures is presented in Tables 28.1 and 28.2. When working in more depth with a person, it can also be useful to develop individual measures for the most important aspects of that person's experience (Finlay and Lyons 2001; Dagnan and Lindsay 2004).

Promoting good mental health in people with learning disabilities

Exercise 28.6

Imagine a person with a particular mental health problem.

- What interventions might work for this person?
- How would you decide which intervention(s) to try?
- If this was a person with mild learning disabilities, would the range of possible interventions be different? Why?
- What adaptations, if any, would you have to make to an intervention to make it work for a person with mild learning disabilities? Why?

As with mental health interventions for the general population, interventions with people with learning disabilities can be broadly put into three categories:

1 *Biological interventions*, typically medication.
2 *Psychological interventions*, typically behavioural approaches, cognitive-behavioural therapy and psychodynamic psychotherapy.
3 *Social interventions*, which may involve changing the life circumstances of the person and working with families and staff systems.

Before discussing particular mental health interventions, it is important to note that evidence for the effectiveness of any mental health intervention for people with learning disabilities is sparse and very rarely at the level of well-designed randomized controlled trials. For any professional engaged in a mental health intervention with a person with learning disabilities, there is needed both creativity in designing and conducting interventions and rigour in assessing the effectiveness of the intervention for the individual.

Biological interventions

Although there is a large evidence base concerning the effectiveness of psychotropic medications (medication designed to alter some aspect of psychological functioning) in the general population, there is very little systematic evidence concerning their use with people with learning disabilities (Thompson *et al.* 2004). In the absence of systematic evidence, clinical recommendations suggest using similar medication strategies for people with and without learning disabilities, particularly in terms of prescribing specific medications for specific, diagnosed mental health problems (Rush and Frances 2000). However, there is substantial evidence showing that particular psychotropic medications are often over-prescribed for people with learning disabilities, inappropriately prescribed for challenging behaviours rather than diagnosed mental health problems and prescribed in complex and dangerous combinations (Robertson *et al.* 2000a; Haw and Stubbs 2005).

- *Antipsychotic medication*: older, neuroleptic antipsychotics are frequently prescribed for people with learning disabilities (25–57 per cent of people living in NHS settings; 20–50 per cent of people living in community-based residential services; 10 per cent of people living independently or with family members; Robertson *et al.* 2000a). They are usually prescribed to reduce challenging behaviour, despite strong evidence that they have no specific impact on challenging behaviour beyond sedation, have long-term and irreversible side-effects (Robertson *et al.* 2000a; Thompson *et al.* 2004), and are administered to people who have little understanding of their impact (Crossley and Withers 2009). There is very little evidence

Screening tools for multiple mental health problems

Measure	General population measure or specific for people with learning disabilities?	Completed with person with learning disabilities?	Completed with informant?	Areas assessed	Details of measure
Reiss Screen for Maladaptive Behavior (Reiss 1988a, b)	Specific	No	Yes	Total Aggressive behaviour Psychosis Paranoia Depression (behavioural signs) Depression (physical signs) Dependent personality disorder Avoidant behaviour Autism	36 items Adequate reliability Adequate sensitivity Poor specificity (Sturmey and Bertman 1994; Myrbakk and von Tetzchner 2008b)
Diagnostic Assessment for the Severely Handicapped (DASH) (Matson et al. 1991)	Specific	No	Yes	Total Anxiety Depression Mania Autism Schizophrenia Stereotypies/tics Self-injury Elimination disorders Eating disorders Sleep disorders Psychosexual disorders Organic syndromes Impulse control/miscellaneous	Designed for people with severe learning disabilities 83 items Adequate reliability Some evidence for adequate sensitivity (Bamburg et al. 2001) Poor specificity (Myrbakk and von Tetzchner 2008b)

Psychopathology Instrument for Mentally Retarded Adults (PIMRA) (Matson et al. 1984; Senatore et al. 1985)	Specific	Total Schizophrenic disorder Affective disorder Psychosexual disorder Adjustment disorder Anxiety disorder Somatoform disorder Personality disorders	Yes	Yes	56 items Adequate reliability Questionable sensitivity and specificity (Sturmey et al. 1991; Masi et al. 2002)
PAS-ADD Checklist (Moss et al. 1996c)	Specific	Total Affective/neurotic disorder Organic condition Psychotic disorder	No	Yes	29 items Adequate reliability Reasonable sensitivity Questionable specificity (Moss et al. 1998; Hatton and Taylor 2008)
Mini PAS-ADD (Prosser et al. 1997)	Specific	Total Anxiety and phobia Depression Expansive mood Obsessions and compulsions Psychoses Dementia Autistic features	No	Yes	86 items Good reliability Good sensitivity Questionable specificity (Prosser et al. 1998; Deb et al. 2001; Myrbakk and von Tetzchner 2008)
Symptom Checklist 90 (revised) (SCL-90-R) (Derogatis 1983; Kellett et al. 1999)	General (adapted)	Global severity index Positive symptom distress index Positive symptom total Somatization Obsessive–compulsive Interpersonal sensitivity Depression	Yes	No	Adapted by using an assisted completion format 90 items Good reliability Adequate sensitivity and specificity (Kellett et al. 1999)

Table 28.1 Assessment measures: multiple mental health problems

continued

Measure	General population measure or specific for people with learning disabilities?	Areas assessed	Completed with person with learning disabilities?	Completed with informant?	Details of measure
		Anxiety Hostility Phobic anxiety Paranoid ideation Psychoticism			
Brief Symptom Inventory (Derogatis 1993; Kellett et al. 2003, 2004)	General (adapted)	Global severity index Positive symptom distress index Positive symptom total Somatization Obsessive-compulsive Interpersonal sensitivity Depression Anxiety Hostility Phobic anxiety Paranoid ideation Psychoticism	Yes	No	Adapted by using an assisted completion format 53 items Good reliability Adequate sensitivity, questionable specificity (Kellett et al. 2003, 2004; Endermann 2005)
Developmental Behaviour Checklist – Adults (Mohr et al. 2005)	Specific	Total Self-absorption Disruption Anxiety Depression Communication disturbance Problems in social relating	No	Yes	106 items Some evidence on sensitivity and specificity (Torr et al. 2008) Good reliability and validity (Mohr et al. 2005)

Detailed diagnostic assessments for multiple mental health problems

| Psychiatric Assessment Schedule – Adults with Developmental Disability (PAS-ADD) (Moss et al. 1997) | General (adapted) | To ICD-10 criteria: Schizophrenia Depression Phobic anxiety disorders Other anxiety disorders Autism screen | Yes | Yes | Comprehensive adaptation of Schedules of Clinical Assessment in Neuropsychiatry (World Health Organization 1992) Extensive rewording and redesign for use with both person with learning disabilities and an informant Uses ICD-10 standard psychiatric classification system for diagnosis (World Health Organization 1993) Semi-structured interview; core 145 questions Adequate reliability and validity (Moss et al. 1996a, b, 1997; Costello et al. 1997; Deb et al. 2001) |
| Mood and Anxiety Semi-Structured (MASS) Interview | Specific | To DSM-IV criteria. Anxiety disorders (GAD, panic disorder, OCD, anxiety disorder not otherwise specified) | No | Yes | Semi-structured interview (30–60 minutes); 35 symptom items with behavioural descriptions |

Table 28.1 Assessment measures: multiple mental health problems

continued

Measure	General population measure or specific for people with learning disabilities?	Areas assessed	Completed with person with learning disabilities?	Completed with informant?	Details of measure
(Charlot et al. 2007)		Major depressive disorder Mania			Good reliability Adequate sensitivity and specificity (Charlot et al. 2007)
Psychopathology checklists for Adults with Intellectual Disability (Hove and Havik 2008)	Specific	Derived from DC-LD criteria (Royal College of Psychiatrists 2001) Dementia Psychosis spectrum Depression Mania Anxiety disorders (agoraphobia; social phobia; specific phobia; generalized anxiety; panic anxiety) Obsessive-compulsive disorder Problem behaviour (verbal aggression; physical aggression; destructive behaviour; self-injurious behaviour; sexually inappropriate behaviour; opposition behaviour; demanding behaviour; wandering behaviour)	No	Yes	Psychopathology checklists 218 items Problem behaviour checklists 52 items Adequate reliability Adequate sensitivity, poor specificity (Hove and Havik 2008)

Table 28.1 Assessment measures: multiple mental health problems

Measure	General population measure or specific for people with learning disabilities?	Areas assessed	Completed with person with learning disabilities?	Completed with informant?	Details of measure
Hospital Anxiety and Depression Scale (Zigmond and Snaith 1983)	General (adapted)	Depression (7 items) Anxiety (7 items)	Yes	No	14 items (7 for depression, 7 for anxiety) Adapted with wording changes and standardized response format (Dagnan et al. 2008) Good reliability, encouraging validity (Dagnan et al. 2008)
Zung Depression Scale (Zung 1965; Kazdin et al. 1983; Prout and Schaefer 1985; Lindsay et al. 1994; Dagnan and Sandhu 1999)	General (adapted)	Depression	Yes	Yes (for adapted version; Gordon et al. 2007)	20 items Original measure used (Prout and Schaefer 1985) Adapted with wording changes and fewer response options (Kazdin et al. 1983; Lindsay et al. 1994; Dagnan and Sandhu 1999) Good reliability, encouraging validity (Powell 2003; Gordon et al. 2007; Dagnan et al. 2008)

Table 28.2 Assessment measures: specific mental health problems

continued

Measure	General population measure or specific for people with learning disabilities?	Areas assessed	Completed with person with learning disabilities?	Completed with informant?	Details of measure
Beck Depression Inventory (Beck et al. 1961) Beck Depression Inventory II (Beck et al. 1996)	General (adapted)	Depression	Yes	No	21 items Original measure used (Prout and Schaefer 1985) Adapted with wording changes and fewer response options (Kazdin et al. 1983; Helsel and Matson 1988; Nezu et al. 1995) Good reliability and validity (Powell 2003; Lindsay and Skene 2007)
Glasgow Depression Scale (Cuthill et al. 2003)	Specific	Depression	Yes	Yes – carer supplement	20 items Carer supplement 16 items Good reliability (Dagnan et al. 2008) Good sensitivity and specificity (Cuthill et al. 2003)
Mental Retardation Depression Scale (Meins 1995, 1996)	Specific	Depression	No	Yes	9 items Adequate reliability and validity (Meins 1995, 1996)

Measure					
Self-report Depression Scale (Esbensen et al. 2005)	Specific	Depression	Yes	No	32 items Adequate reliability and validity (Esbensen et al. 2005)
Zung Self-Rating Anxiety Scale (Zung 1971; Lindsay et al. 1994)	General (adapted)	Anxiety	Yes	No	20 items Adapted with wording changes and fewer response options (Lindsay et al. 1994) Adequate reliability, encouraging validity (Ramirez and Lukenbill 2008)
Beck Anxiety Inventory (Beck and Steer 1990; Lindsay and Lees 2003)	General (adapted)	Anxiety	Yes	No	21 items Adapted (Lindsay and Lees 2003) Adequate reliability and validity (Lindsay and Skene 2007)
Glasgow Anxiety Scale (Mindham and Espie 2003)	Specific	Anxiety	Yes	No	27 items Good reliability Good sensitivity and specificity (Mindham and Espie 2003)
Mood Interest and Pleasure Questionnaire (Ross and Oliver 2002, 2003b)	Specific	Mood: Interest and pleasure	No	Yes	Designed for people with severe learning disabilities 25 items Good reliability, adequate validity (Ross and Oliver 2002, 2003b)

Table 28.2 Assessment measures: specific mental health problems

continued

Measure	General population measure or specific for people with learning disabilities?	Areas assessed	Completed with person with learning disabilities?	Completed with informant?	Details of measure
Positive and Negative Syndrome Scale (PANSS) (Kay et al. 1989; Hatton et al. 2005)	General	Psychotic experiences: positive symptoms, negative symptoms, general symptoms	Yes	No	28 items Good reliability Good validity on positive symptoms and general symptoms, inadequate validity on negative symptoms (Hatton et al. 2005)
Psychotic Rating Scales (PSYRATS) (Haddock et al. 1999; Hatton et al. 2005)	General	Psychotic experiences: auditory hallucinations, delusions	Yes	No	17 items Good reliability Good validity on auditory hallucinations, unknown validity on delusions (Hatton et al. 2005)
Novaco Anger Scale (NAS) (Novaco 2003; Novaco and Taylor 2004)	General (adapted)	Anger: disposition and experience in the cognitive, arousal and behavioural domains	Yes	No	48 items Original measure (Novaco 2003) Adapted for people with mild-borderline learning disabilities and to be administered as a structured interview (Novaco and Taylor 2004) Good reliability and validity

Measure	Type	Description			Details
Provocation Inventory (PI) (Novaco 2003; Novaco and Taylor 2004)	General (adapted)	Anger: Reactivity across a range of potentially provoking situations	Yes	No	25 items Original measure (Novaco 2003) Adapted for people with mild-borderline learning disabilities and to be administered as a structured interview (Novaco and Taylor 2004) Good reliability and validity
Ward Anger Rating Scale (WARS) (Novaco 1994; Novaco and Taylor 2004)	General	Anger: a two-part scale regarding (a) verbal and physical behaviours associated with anger and aggression; and (b) anger attributes displayed during the previous 7 days	No	Yes	25 items Original measure (Novaco 1994). Good reliability and validity (Novaco and Taylor 2004; Steptoe et al. 2008)
Imaginal Provocation Test (IPT) (Taylor et al. 2004b)	General (adapted)	Anger: an idiographic measure of anger reactivity in terms of emotional and behavioural responses and attempts to regulate these	Yes	No	10 items (administered in two parallel forms) Original measure (Novaco 1975) Adapted for use with people with LD Good reliability and validity and sensitive to change following intervention (Taylor et al. 2004c)

Table 28.2 Assessment measures: specific mental health problems

concerning the use of atypical antipsychotics with people with learning disabilities. Although some studies suggest they may reduce some aggression and self-injury, there are conflicting findings and associated side-effects such as sedation and weight gain (Thompson *et al.* 2004).

- *Antidepressant medication*: rates of antidepressant prescriptions with people with learning disabilities are much lower (14 per cent in NHS settings; 6 per cent in community-based residential services) and more closely associated with diagnoses of depression (Robertson *et al.* 2000a). However, older antidepressants such as monoamine oxidase inhibitors and tricyclics are reported to be mixed in their effectiveness, with dangerous side-effects (Thompson *et al.* 2004). Newer SSRIs have been reported to be effective in small studies of people with learning disabilities and depression (Thompson *et al.* 2004).

- *Antiepileptic medication*: rates of epilepsy are high among the population of people with learning disabilities, and antiepileptics are frequently prescribed (46 per cent in NHS settings; 36 per cent in community-based residential services; Robertson *et al.* 2000a).

- *Hypnotic and anxiolytic medication*: a wide range of medications can be used to reduce symptoms of anxiety and panic, although their use is not widespread among people with learning disabilities (11 per cent in NHS settings; 9 per cent in community-based residential services; Robertson *et al.* 2000a) and there is little evidence concerning their effectiveness (Thompson *et al.* 2004).

Psychological interventions

Research evidence concerning the efficacy of psychological interventions for people with learning disabilities and mental health problems is small but increasing (Taylor *et al.* 2008; Gustafsson *et al.* 2009). Existing evidence consists of a small number of case studies using behavioural interventions with symptoms of mental health problems, a larger body of case series and occasional trials using cognitive-behavioural therapy for a range of mental health problems, and uncontrolled trials using psychodynamic psychotherapy with mental health problems. While it is clear that people with learning disabilities

can benefit from psychological interventions (Taylor *et al.* 2008), it is unclear how many people could benefit or what approaches work best for whom (Beail 2003). Psychological interventions have typically focused on five domains of mental health problem: depression, anxiety, psychosis, anger and offending.

- *Depression*: there is a small but increasing body of case studies, case series and small trials evaluating cognitive-behavioural therapy with people with mild/moderate learning disabilities and depression (Jahoda *et al.* 2006), reporting improvements in self-reported depressive symptoms and behaviour maintained at follow-up (Lindsay *et al.* 1993; Dagnan and Chadwick 1997; Lindsay and Olley 1998; Lindsay 1999; McCabe *et al.* 2006; McGillivray *et al.* 2008).

- *Anxiety*: case studies and case series have demonstrated the potential feasibility of cognitive and behaviour therapies in reducing anxiety among people with learning disabilities (Dagnan and Jahoda 2006), including behavioural interventions such as relaxation (Dixon and Gunary 1986; Lindsay and Baty 1986; Lindsay *et al.* 1988, 1989; Morrison and Lindsay 1997), anxiety management training (Lindsay *et al.* 1989) and cognitive-behavioural therapy (Lindsay *et al.* 1997; Lindsay 1999).

- *Psychosis*: less evidence is available concerning psychosocial interventions for people with learning disabilities and psychosis, with case studies of behavioural treatments (Stephens *et al.* 1981; Mace *et al.* 1988) and case studies and case series of cognitive-behavioural treatments (Leggett *et al.* 1997; Haddock *et al.* 2004; Kirkland 2004; Oathamshaw and Haddock 2006; Barrowcliff 2008) demonstrating both feasibility and the potential for improvements in outcomes.

- *Anger*: more intervention studies have been conducted concerning cognitive-behavioural interventions to reduce anger in people with learning disabilities, mainly using adaptations of the Novaco approach to anger management (Taylor and Novaco 2005). A series of studies involving either wait list or randomized comparison groups have demonstrated the effectiveness of cognitive-behavioural anger treatments in community settings (Rose *et al.* 2000, 2005; Willner *et al.* 2002; Lindsay *et al.* 2004a) and more secure settings (Taylor *et al.* 2002b, 2004b, 2005).

- *Offending*: Lindsay *et al.* (2004b) have comprehensively covered the field of offending by people with learning disabilities, with additional specific reviews of psychological interventions with offenders with learning disabilities (Lindsay and Taylor 2005). Individual and group cognitive-behaviour therapy with sex offenders with learning disabilities has shown considerable promise (see Lindsay 2002), as has cognitive-behavioural group work with fire-setters and arsonists (Taylor *et al.* 2002b, 2004d, 2006).

Psychodynamic psychotherapeutic interventions

There have been several suggestions that psychodynamic psychotherapy can be useful for people with learning disabilities and mental health problems (Beail 2003, 2004). Recent UK uncontrolled trials of routine clinical practice have demonstrated promising results for psychodynamic-interpersonal therapy with adults with mild/moderate learning disabilities,

including adults with mental health problems (Beail and Warden 1996; Beail 2000) and adult offenders (Beail 2001).

Social interventions

Given the life circumstances that put people with learning disabilities at potentially greater risk of developing mental health problems, it would be expected that social interventions would be developed to reduce social and environmental risk factors and increase resilience (Emerson and Hatton 2007). However, interventions at this level have very rarely been conducted with people with learning disabilities, beyond the involvement of broader interpersonal systems such as families or staff members around the person. Interventions designed to improve people's living arrangements have rarely been designed with mental health as an outcome, and broader policy changes such as deinstitutionalization have rarely been evaluated in terms of their impact on mental health. There is clearly a great potential for social interventions to improve the mental health of people with learning disabilities.

Case study: *James*

As mentioned in the introduction to this chapter, one possible reason that people with learning disabilities have not historically been offered psychological therapies to help with their mental health problems is the belief that these approaches would not be effective as clients are not clever enough to understand or engage in talking therapies. This issue has been raised in connection with cognitive-behavioural therapy generally and the cognitive component of cognitive-behavioural anger treatment for people with learning disabilities specifically (Rose *et al.* 2000; Willner *et al.* 2002). So, can people with learning disabilities successfully engage in work on the content of thoughts/cognitions that play a role in maintaining mental health problems?

James is a 22-year-old man with mild learning disabilities (WAIS Full Scale IQ of 66) and borderline personality disorder. He has a history of depression, self-injurious behaviour, sexually aggressive behaviour and physical violence. James attended special schools but was excluded on several occasions because of assaults on other students. As a 17-year-old James was sexually abused by an older male friend of his family. His mental health and behavioural problems deteriorated after this time. The frequency of James's self-injury increased and he complained of mood swings and difficulty in controlling his temper. When he was 20 years old he was prescribed antidepressant medication for low mood, poor appetite, sleep problems and flashbacks to his own sexual abuse. Unfortunately, soon after, James overdosed on his medication and was admitted to the acute mental health ward of a specialist learning disability hospital. After only a short time in this environment James was displaying sexually predatory behaviour towards less able patients, refusing his medication and being physically aggressive towards staff, and required physical restraint. Consequently he was sectioned under the Mental Health Act 1983 and transferred to a low secure forensic ward in the hospital.

James continued to be disturbed and aggressive and he was assessed as a potential candidate for individual anger treatment. Self-rated anger assessments specially modified for clients with learning disabilities were used to assess the level of James's anger problems and to guide the treatment. The Novaco Anger Scale (NAS) (Novaco 1993) is a measure of anger disposition that assesses the cognitive, arousal and behavioural components of an individual's experience of anger. The Provocation Inventory (PI) (Novaco 1993) is a measure of anger reactivity across a range of anger-provoking situations. James's scores on these assessments were significantly higher than the means for his reference group, and his scores on the cognitive sub-scale of the NAS and the unfairness/injustice sub-scale of the PI were particularly elevated.

The cognitive-behavioural anger treatment used with James was developed especially for clients with mild learning disabilities and severe or chronic anger control problems (Taylor and Novaco 2005). It incorporates cognitive restructuring, arousal reduction and behavioural skills training components in equal measures. James completed all 18 sessions of anger treatment (six sessions Preparatory Phase and 12 sessions Treatment Phase) within the planned time period and without incident. His approach towards the treatment was positive and generally enthusiastic. His response to the different components of the intervention was also positive. James learned how to control the physiological component of anger arousal through a combination of breathing control, progressive muscular relaxation, distracting imagery and self-instructions. He was able to show limited ability to deal successfully with angry situations using role-play, although his coping skills in terms of problem-solving lagged behind his understanding of these issues, and this was reflected in ongoing difficulties outside the therapy sessions.

In terms of the cognitive component of the therapy, James was able to learn to identify the automatic thoughts (usually negative and unhelpful) that accompanied angry incidents. As the treatment progressed he was able to spontaneously generate alternative and more adaptive cognitions in response to such incidents. In treatment James engaged in cognitive restructuring with relative ease, and in so doing he demonstrated an ability to take the perspective of others by putting himself in another's position in relation to particular situations. Figure 28.1

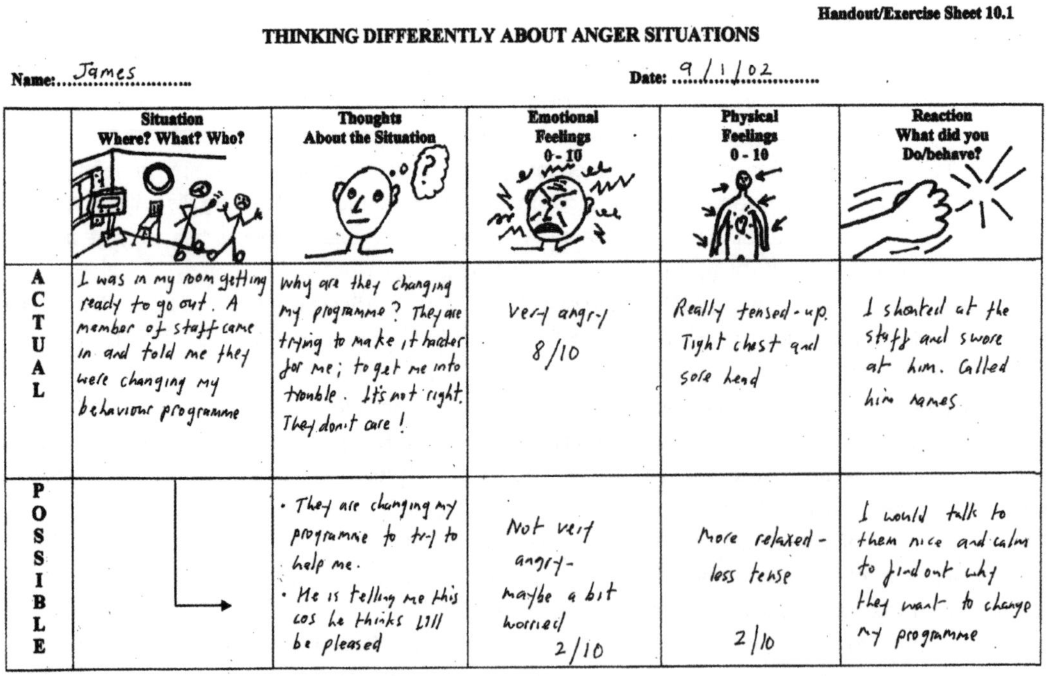

Handout/Exercise Sheet 10.1

THINKING DIFFERENTLY ABOUT ANGER SITUATIONS

Name: James Date: 9/1/02

	Situation Where? What? Who?	Thoughts About the Situation	Emotional Feelings 0 - 10	Physical Feelings 0 - 10	Reaction What did you Do/behave?
ACTUAL	I was in my room getting ready to go out. A member of staff came in and told me they were changing my behaviour programme	Why are they changing my programme? They are trying to make it harder for me; to get me into trouble. It's not right. They don't care!	Very angry 8/10	Really tensed-up. Tight chest and sore head	I shouted at the staff and swore at him. Called him names.
POSSIBLE	→	• They are changing my programme to try to help me. • He is telling me this cos he thinks I'll be pleased	Not very angry - maybe a bit worried 2/10	More relaxed - less tense 2/10	I would talk to them nice and calm to find out why they want to change my programme

Figure 28.1 Generating alternative thoughts

provides an example, from within a treatment session, of how James was able to use an incident that occurred between sessions to generate alternative thoughts about a particular situation (being told that his behaviour programme was about to be changed). He could see that thinking about this situation differently would lead him to feel less angry, be more in control and so react in a more adaptive and productive manner. The 'possible' or alternative thoughts–emotional feelings–physical feelings–reaction chain generated by James in response to the activating situation was then used in the session by James to practise coping more effectively with anger; first in imagination (using stress inoculation technique while relaxed) and then in practice (using role-play). James was then encouraged to practise thinking differently about situations between sessions using daily anger logs so that this skill is moved temporally closer to real situations.

It can be seen from this example that people with (mild) learning disabilities can make the link between cognitions/thoughts and feelings/reactions and unlink the automatic connection between events and feelings/reactions. Thus people with learning disabilities *can* engage in and benefit from the cognitive component of cognitive-behavioural therapy. James's pre-post treatment and follow-up scores on the self-rated anger assessments support this view. The cognitive sub-scale of the NAS came down following treatment and remained lower at eight-month follow-up. James's scores on the unfairness/injustice sub-scale of the PI followed a similar pattern. While James's behaviour on the ward continued to cause staff concern, their staff-rated anger scores converged with James's self-ratings and reflected his progress in the anger treatment.

Conclusion

As this chapter has shown, the picture concerning people with learning disabilities and mental health problems is changing, from one of almost total professional indifference to rapidly increasing professional interest and concern. However, some of the most basic issues concerning the conceptualization, assessment and management of mental health problems in people with learning disabilities have yet to be resolved. The social contexts within which people with learning disabilities live further complicate the picture. Treating mental health problems seriously in people with learning disabilities has the potential to liberate many people with learning disabilities from debilitating distress and to enable them to lead fulfilling lives. However, the history of services for people with learning disabilities teaches us that professional interest can be a mixed blessing; professional interest in mental health problems also contains the potential for unnecessary labelling, further stigma, restrictive service interventions and unnecessary medication. It is our responsibility to ensure that we work towards the former rather than being complicit in the latter.

References

American Psychiatric Association (1994) *Diagnostic and Statistical Manual of Mental Disorders*, 4th edn. Washington, DC: American Psychiatric Association.

Arscott, K., Dagnan, D. and Stenfert Kroese, B. (1999) Assessing the ability of people with a learning disability to give informed consent to treatment, *Psychological Medicine*, 29: 1367–75.

Bailey, N.M. and Cooper, S.-A. (1997) The current provision of specialist health services to people with learning disabilities in England and Wales, *Journal of Intellectual Disability Research*, 41: 52–9.

Bamburg, J.W., Cherry, K.E., Matson, J.L. and Penn, D. (2001) Assessment of schizophrenia in persons with severe and profound mental retardation using the diagnostic assessment for the severely handicapped (DASH-II), *Journal of Developmental and Physical Disabilities*, 13: 319–31.

Barrowcliff, A.L. (2008) Cognitive-behavioural therapy for command hallucinations and intellectual disability: a case study, *Journal of Applied Research in Intellectual Disabilities*, 21: 236–45.

Beail, N. (2000) An evaluation of outpatient psychodynamic psychotherapy amongst offenders with intellectual disabilities, *Journal of Intellectual Disability Research*, 44: 204.

Beail, N. (2001) Recidivism following psychodynamic psychotherapy amongst offenders with intellectual disabilities, *British Journal of Forensic Practice*, 3: 33–7.

Beail, N. (2003) What works for people with mental

retardation? Critical commentary on cognitive-behavioural and psychodynamic psychotherapy research, *Mental Retardation*, 41: 468–72.

Beail, N. (2004) Methodology, design, and evaluation in psychotherapy research with people with intellectual disabilities, in E. Emerson, C. Hatton, T. Thompson and T.R. Parmenter (eds) *The International Handbook of Applied Research in Intellectual Disabilities*. Chichester: Wiley.

Beail, N. and Warden, S. (1996) Evaluation of a psychodynamic psychotherapy service for adults with intellectual disabilities: rationale, design and preliminary outcome data, *Journal of Applied Research in Intellectual Disabilities*, 9: 223–8.

Beck, A.T. and Steer, R. A. (1990) *Manual for the Beck Anxiety Inventory*. San Antonio, TX: The Psychological Corporation.

Beck, A.T., Ward, C.H., Mendelsohn, M., Mock, J. and Erbaugh, J. (1961) An inventory for measuring depression, *Archives of General Psychiatry*, 4: 561–71.

Beck, A.T., Steer, R.A. and Brown, G.K. (1996) *Beck Depression Inventory: 2nd Edition Manual*. San Antonio, TX: The Psychological Corporation.

Bender, M. (1993) The unoffered chair: the history of therapeutic disdain towards people with a learning difficulty, *Clinical Psychology Forum*, 54: 7–12.

Bhaumik, S., Tyrer, F.C., McGrother, C. and Ganghadaran, S.K. (2008) Psychiatric service use and psychiatric disorders in adults with intellectual disability, *Journal of Intellectual Disability Research*, 52: 986–95.

Bramston, P. and Fogarty, G. (2000) The assessment of emotional distress experienced by people with an intellectual disability: a study of different methodologies, *Research in Developmental Disabilities*, 21: 487–500.

Brown, G.W. (2000) Medical sociology and issues of aetiology, in M.G. Gelder, J.L. Lopez-Ibor Jr. and N.C. Andreasen (eds) *New Oxford Textbook of Psychiatry*. Oxford: Oxford University Press.

Chaplin, R. (2009) New research into general psychiatric services for adults with intellectual disability and mental illness, *Journal of Intellectual Disability Research*, 53: 189–99.

Charlot, L., Deutsch, C., Hunt, A. and McIlvane, W. (2007) Validation of the Mood and Anxiety Semi-structured (MASS) Interview for patients with intellectual disabilities, *Journal of Intellectual Disability Research*, 51: 821–34.

Clark, L.L. (2007) Learning disabilities within mental health services: are we adequately preparing nurses for the future? *Journal of Psychiatric and Mental Health Nursing*, 14: 433–7.

Cooper, S.A. (1997) High prevalence of dementia among people with learning disabilities not attributable to Down's syndrome, *Psychological Medicine*, 27: 609–16.

Cooper, S.A. (2003) (ed.) Diagnostic criteria for psychiatric disorders for use with adults with learning disabilities (DC-LD), *Journal of Intellectual Disability Research*, 47: Supplement 1.

Cooper, S.A., Smiley, E., Finlayson, J., Jackson, A., Allan, L., Williamson, A. et al. (2007a) The prevalence, incidence and factors predictive of mental ill-health in adults with profound intellectual disabilities, *Journal of Applied Research in Intellectual Disabilities*, 20: 493–501.

Cooper, S.A., Smiley, E., Morrison, J., Williamson, A. and Allan, L. (2007b) Mental ill-health in adults with intellectual disabilities: prevalence and associated factors, *British Journal of Psychiatry*, 190: 27–35.

Cooper, S.A., Smiley, E., Morrison, J., Allan, L., Williamson, A., Finlayson, J. et al. (2007c) Psychosis and adults with intellectual disabilities: prevalence, incidence, and related factors, *Social Psychiatry and Psychiatric Epidemiology*, 42: 530–6.

Costello, H. (2004) Does training carers improve outcome for adults with learning disabilities and mental health problems? PhD thesis, King's College, University of London.

Costello, H., Moss, S., Prosser, H. and Hatton, C. (1997) Reliability of the ICD-10 version of the Psychiatric Assessment Schedule for Adults with Developmental Disability (PAS-ADD), *Social Psychiatry and Psychiatric Epidemiology*, 32: 339–43.

Costello, H., Bouras, N. and Davis, H. (2007) The role of training in improving community care staff awareness of mental health problems in people with intellectual disabilities, *Journal of Applied Research in Intellectual Disabilities*, 20: 228–35.

Crossley, R. and Withers, P. (2009) Antipsychotic medication and people with intellectual disabilities: their knowledge and experiences, *Journal of Applied Research in Intellectual Disabilities*, 22: 77–86.

Cuthill, F.M., Espie, C.A. and Cooper, S.-A. (2003) Development and psychometric properties of the Glasgow Depression Scale for people with a learning disability: individual and carer supplement versions, *British Journal of Psychiatry*, 182: 347–53.

Dagnan, D. (2007) Commentary: the prevalence, incidence and factors predictive of mental ill-health in adults with profound intellectual disabilities, *Journal of Applied Research in Intellectual Disabilities*, 20: 502–4.

Dagnan, D. and Chadwick, P. (1997) Assessment and intervention, in B. Stenfert Kroese, D. Dagnan and K. Loumidis (eds) *Cognitive-Behaviour Therapy for People with Learning Disabilities*. London: Routledge.

Dagnan, D. and Jahoda, A. (2006) Cognitive-behavioural intervention for people with intellectual disability and anxiety disorders, *Journal of Applied Research in Intellectual Disabilities*, 19: 91–7.

Dagnan, D. and Lindsay, W.R. (2004) Research issues in cognitive therapy, in E. Emerson, C. Hatton, T. Thompson and T.R. Parmenter (eds) *The International Handbook of Applied Research in Intellectual Disabilities*. Chichester: Wiley.

Dagnan, D. and Sandhu, S. (1999) Social comparison, self-esteem and depression in people with learning disabilities, *Journal of Intellectual Disability Research*, 43: 372–9.

Dagnan, D. and Waring, M. (2004) Linking stigma to psychological distress: testing a social-cognitive model of the experience of people with intellectual disabilities, *Clinical Psychology and Psychotherapy*, 11: 247–54.

Dagnan, D., Jahoda, A., McDowell, K., Masson, J., Banks, P. and Hare, D. (2008) The psychometric properties of the hospital anxiety and depressions scale adapted for use with people with intellectual disabilities, *Journal of Intellectual Disability Research*, 52: 942–9.

Deb, S., Thomas, M. and Bright, C. (2001) Mental disorder in adults with intellectual disability. I: Prevalence of functional psychiatric illness among a community-based population aged between 16 and 64 years, *Journal of Intellectual Disability Research*, 45: 495–505.

Department of Health (2001) *Seeking Consent: Working with People with Learning Disabilities*. London: Department of Health Publications.

Derogatis, L.R. (1983) *SCL-90-R: Administration, scoring and procedures: Manual II*. Towson, MD: Clinical Psychometrics Research.

Derogatis, L.R. (1993) *Brief Symptom Inventory: Administration, Scoring and Procedures Manual, 3rd edn*. Minneapolis, MN: National Computer Systems.

Dixon, M.S. and Gunary, R.M. (1986) Fear of dogs: group treatment of people with mental handicaps, *Mental Handicap*, 14: 6–9.

Edelstein, T.M. and Glenwick, D.S. (2001) Direct-care workers' attributions of psychopathology in adults with mental retardation, *Mental Retardation*, 39: 368–78.

Einfeld, S.L. and Tonge, B.J. (1999) Observations on the use of the ICD-10 Guide for Mental Retardation, *Journal of Intellectual Disability Research*, 43: 408–13.

Einfeld, S.L., Piccinin, A.M., Mackinnon, A., Hofer, S.M., Taffe, J., Gray, K.M. *et al.* (2006) Psychopathology in young people with intellectual disability, *Journal of the American Medical Association*, 296: 1981–9.

Emerson, E. and Hatton, C. (2007) Mental health of children and adolescents with intellectual disabilities in Britain, *British Journal of Psychiatry*, 191: 493–99.

Emerson, E. and Hatton, C. (forthcoming) Socio-economic position, poverty, and family research, *International Review of Research in Mental Retardation*.

Endermann, M. (2005) The Brief Symptom Inventory (BSI) as a screening tool for psychological disorders in patients with epilepsy and mild intellectual disabilities in residential care, *Epilepsy & Behavior*, 7: 85–94.

Esbensen, A.J., Seltzer, M.M., Greenberg, J.S. and Benson, B.A. (2005) Psychometric evaluation of a self-report measure of depression for individuals with mental retardation, *American Journal on Mental Retardation*, 110: 469–81.

Featherstone, K. and Donovan, J. (2002) 'Why don't they just tell me straight, why allocate it?' The struggle to make sense of participating in a randomised controlled trial, *Social Science & Medicine*, 55: 709–19.

Felce, D., Kerr, M. and Hastings, R.P. (2009) A general practice-based study of the relationship between indicators of mental illness and challenging behaviour among adults with

intellectual disabilities, *Journal of Intellectual Disability Research*, 53: 243–54.

Finlay, W.M. and Lyons, E. (2001) Methodological issues in interviewing and using self-report questionnaires with people with mental retardation, *Psychological Assessment*, 13: 319–35.

Goldberg, D.P. and Huxley, P. (1980) *Mental Illness in the Community: The Pathway to Psychiatric Care*. London: Tavistock.

Gustafsson, C., Ojehagen, A., Hansson, L., Dandlund, M., Nystrom, M., Glad, J. *et al.* (2009) Effects of psychosocial interventions for people with intellectual disabilities and mental health problems: a survey of systematic reviews, *Research on Social Work Practice*, 19: 281–90.

Haddock, G., McCarron, J., Tarrier, N. and Faragher, E.B. (1999) Scales to measure dimensions of hallucinations and delusions: the psychotic symptom rating scales (PSYRATS), *Psychological Medicine*, 29: 879–89.

Haddock, G., Lobban, F., Hatton, C. and Carson, R. (2004) Cognitive-behaviour therapy for people with psychosis and mild intellectual disabilities: a case series, *Clinical Psychology & Psychotherapy*, 11: 282–98.

Hartley, S.L., Hayes Lickel, A. and MacLean Jr, W.E. (2008) Reassurance seeking and depression in adults with mild intellectual disability, *Journal of Intellectual Disability Research*, 52: 917–29.

Hassiotis, A., Barron, P. and O'Hara, J. (2000) Mental health services for people with learning disabilities: a complete overhaul is needed with strong links to mainstream services, *British Medical Journal*, 321: 583–4.

Hastings, R.P., Hatton, C., Taylor, J.L. and Maddison, C. (2004) Life events and psychiatric symptoms in adults with intellectual disabilities, *Journal of Intellectual Disability Research*, 48: 42–6.

Hatton, C. and Taylor, J.L. (2008) The factor structure of the PAS-ADD Checklist with adults with intellectual disabilities, *Journal of Intellectual and Developmental Disabilities*, 33: 330–6.

Hatton, C., Haddock, G., Taylor, J.T., Coldwell, J., Crossley, R. and Peckham, N. (2005) The reliability and validity of general psychotic rating scales with people with mild and moderate intellectual disabilities: an empirical investigation, *Journal of Intellectual Disability Research*, 49: 490–500.

Haw, C. and Stubbs, J. (2005) A survey of off-label prescribing for inpatients with mild intellectual disability and mental illness, *Journal of Intellectual Disability Research*, 49: 858–64.

Helsel, W.J. and Matson, J.L. (1988) The relationship of depression to social skills and intellectual functioning in mentally retarded adults, *Journal of Mental Deficiency Research*, 32: 411–18.

Holland, A.J., Hon, J., Huppert, F.A., Stevens, S. and Watson, P. (1998) Population-based study of the prevalence and presentation of dementia in adults with Down's syndrome, *British Journal of Psychiatry*, 172: 493–8.

Hove, O. and Havik, O.E. (2008) Psychometric properties of Psychopathology checklists for Adults with Intellectual

Disability (P-AID) on a community sample of adults with intellectual disability, *Research in Developmental Disabilities*, 29: 467–82.

Jahoda, A., Dagnan, D., Jarvie, P. and Kerr, W. (2006) Depression, social context and cognitive behavioural therapy for people who have intellectual disabilities, *Journal of Applied Research in Intellectual Disabilities*, 19: 81–9.

Kay, S. R., Opler, L.A. and Lindenmayer, J.P. (1989) The positive and negative syndrome scale (PANSS): rationale and standardisation, *British Journal of Psychiatry*, 155 (Suppl. 7): 59–65.

Kazdin, A.E., Matson, J.L. and Senatore, V. (1983) Assessment of depression in mentally retarded adults, *American Journal of Psychiatry*, 140: 1040–3.

Kellett, S., Beail, N., Newman, D.W. and Mosley, E. (1999) Indexing psychological distress in people with intellectual disabilities: use of the Symptom Checklist-90-R, *Journal of Applied Research in Intellectual Disabilities*, 12: 323–34.

Kellett, S., Beail, N., Newman, D.W. and Frankish, P. (2003) Utility of the Brief Symptom Inventory in the assessment of psychological distress, *Journal of Applied Research in Intellectual Disabilities*, 16: 127–34.

Kellett, S., Beail, N., Newman, D.W. and Hawes, A. (2004) The factor structure of the Brief Symptom Inventory: intellectual disability evidence, *Clinical Psychology and Psychotherapy*, 11: 275–81.

Kerker, B.D., Owens, P.L., Zigler, E. and Horwitz, S.M. (2004) Mental health disorders among individuals with mental retardation: challenges to accurate prevalence estimates, *Public Health Reports*, 119: 409–17.

Kirkland, J. (2004) Cognitive-behaviour formulation for three men with learning disabilities who experience psychosis: how do we make it make sense? *British Journal of Learning Disabilities*, 32: 1–6.

Langlois, L. and Martin, L. (2008) Relationship between diagnostic criteria, depressive equivalents and diagnosis of depression among older adults with intellectual disability, *Journal of Intellectual Disability Research*, 52: 896–904.

Leggett, J., Hurn, C. and Goodman, W. (1997) Teaching psychological strategies for managing auditory hallucinations: a case report, *British Journal of Learning Disabilities*, 25: 158–62.

Lindsay, W.R. (1999) Cognitive therapy, *The Psychologist*, 12: 238–41.

Lindsay, W.R. (2002) Research and literature on sex offenders with intellectual and developmental disabilities, *Journal of Intellectual Disability Research*, 46 (Suppl. 1): 74–85.

Lindsay, W.R. and Baty, F.J. (1986) Behavioural relaxation training: explorations with adults who are mentally handicapped, *Mental Handicap*, 14: 160–2.

Lindsay, W.R. and Law, J. (1999) Outcome evaluation of 161 people with learning disabilities in Tayside who have offending or challenging behavior. Presentation to the BABCP 27th annual conference, University of Bristol, July.

Lindsay, W.R. and Lees, M.S. (2003) A comparison of anxiety and depression in sex offenders with intellectual disability

and a control group with intellectual disability, *Sex Abuse*, 15: 339–45.

Lindsay, W.R. and Olley, S. (1998) Psychological treatment for anxiety and depression for people with learning disabilities, in W. Fraser, D. Sines and M. Kerr (eds) *Hallas' The Care of People with Intellectual Disabilities*, 9th edn. Oxford: Butterworth Heinemann.

Lindsay, W.R. and Skene, D.D. (2007) The Beck Depression Inventory II and the Beck Anxiety Inventory in people with intellectual disabilities: factor analyses and group data, *Journal of Applied Research in Intellectual Disabilities*, 20: 401–8.

Lindsay, W.R. and Taylor, J.L. (2005) A selective review of research on offenders with developmental disabilities: assessment and treatment, *Clinical Psychology and Psychotherapy*, 12: 201–14.

Lindsay, W.R., Michie, A.M., Baty, F.J. and MacKenzie, K. (1988) Dog phobia in people with mental handicaps: anxiety management training and exposure treatments, *Mental Handicap Research*, 1: 39–48.

Lindsay, W.R., Baty, F.J., Michie, A.M. and Richardson, I. (1989) A comparison of anxiety treatments with adults who have moderate and severe mental retardation, *Research in Developmental Disabilities*, 10: 129–40.

Lindsay, W.R., Howells, L. and Pitcaithly, D. (1993) Cognitive therapy for depression with individuals with intellectual disabilities, *British Journal of Medical Psychology*, 66: 135–41.

Lindsay, W.R., Michie, A.M., Baty, F.J., Smith, A.H.W. and Miller, S. (1994) The consistency of reports about feelings and emotions from people with intellectual disability, *Journal of Intellectual Disability Research*, 38: 61–6.

Lindsay, W.R., Neilson, C. and Lawrenson, H. (1997) Cognitive-behaviour therapy for anxiety in people with learning disabilities, in B. Stenfert Kroese, D. Dagnan and K. Loumidis (eds) *Cognitive-behaviour Therapy for People with Learning Disabilities*. London: Routledge.

Lindsay, W.R., Allan, R., Parry, C., Macleod, F., Cottrell, J., Overend, H. *et al.* (2004a) Anger and aggression in people with intellectual disabilities: treatment and follow-up of consecutive referrals and a waiting list comparison, *Clinical Psychology and Psychotherapy*, 11: 255–64.

Lindsay, W.R., Taylor, J.L. and Sturmey, P. (eds) (2004b) *Offenders with Developmental Disabilities*. Chichester: Wiley.

Lord Chancellor's Department (1999) *Making Decisions. The Government's Proposals for Making Decisions on Behalf of Mentally Incapacitated Adults*. London: The Stationery Office.

Lund, J. (1985) The prevalence of psychiatric morbidity in mentally retarded adults, *Acta Psychiatrica Scandinavia*, 72: 563–70.

Lunsky, Y., Bradley, E., Durbin, J. and Koeg, C. (2008) A comparison of patients with intellectual disability receiving specialised and general services in Ontario's psychiatric hospitals, *Journal of Intellectual Disability Research*, 52: 1003–12.

Mace, F.C., Webb, M.E., Sharkey, R.W., Mattson, D.M. and Rosen, H.S. (1988) Functional analysis and treatment of bizarre speech, *Journal of Behavior Therapy and Experimental Psychiatry*, 19: 289–96.

McCabe, M.P., McGillivray, J.A. and Newton, D.C. (2006) Effectiveness of treatment programmes for depression among adults with mild/moderate intellectual disability, *Journal of Intellectual Disability Research*, 50: 239–47.

McGillivray, J.A., McCabe, M.P. and Kershaw, M.M. (2008) Depression in people with intellectual disability: an evaluation of a staff-administered treatment program, *Research in Developmental Disabilities*, 29: 524–36.

MacMahon, P. and Jahoda, A. (2008) Social comparison and depression: people with mild and moderate intellectual disabilities, *American Journal on Mental Retardation*, 113: 307–18.

Marston, G.J., Perry, D.W. and Roy, A. (1997) Manifestations of depression in people with intellectual disability, *Journal of Intellectual Disability Research*, 41: 476–80.

Martorell, A., Tsakanikos, E., Pereda, A., Gutierrez-Recacha, P., Bouras, N. and Ayosu-Mateos, J.L. (2009) Mental health in adults with mild and moderate intellectual disabilities: the role of recent life events and traumatic experiences across the life span, *The Journal of Nervous and Mental Disease*, 197: 182–6.

Masi, G., Brovedani, P., Mucci, M. and Favilla, L. (2002) Assessment of anxiety and depression in adolescents with mental retardation, *Child Psychiatry and Human Development*, 32: 227–37.

Matson, J.L., Kazdin, A.E. and Senatore, V. (1984) Psychometric properties of the psychopathology instrument for mentally retarded adults, *Applied Research in Mental Retardation*, 5: 881–9.

Matson, J.L., Gardner, W.I., Coe, D.A. and Sovner, R. (1991) A scale for evaluating emotional disorders in severely and profoundly mentally retarded persons: development of the Diagnostic Assessment for the Severely Handicapped (DASH) Scale, *British Journal of Psychiatry*, 159: 404–9.

Matson, J.L., Smiroldo, B.B., Hamilton, M. and Baglio, C.S. (1997) Do anxiety disorders exist in persons with severe and profound mental retardation? *Research in Developmental Disorders*, 18: 39–44.

Meins, W. (1995) Symptoms of major depression in mentally retarded adults, *Journal of Intellectual Disability Research*, 39: 41–5.

Meins, W. (1996) A new depression scale designed for use with adults with mental retardation, *Journal of Intellectual Disability Research*, 40: 220–6.

Mindham, J. and Espie, C.A. (2003) The Glasgow Anxiety Scale for people with an Intellectual Disability (GAS-ID): development and psychometric properties of a new measure for use with people with mild intellectual disability, *Journal of Intellectual Disability Research*, 47: 22–30.

Mohr, C., Tonge, B.J. and Einfeld, S.L. (2005) The development of a new measure for the assessment of psychopathology in adults with intellectual disability, *Journal of Intellectual Disability Research*, 49: 469–80.

Morgan, V.A., Leonard, H., Bourke, J. and Jablensky, A. (2008) Intellectual disability co-occurring with schizophrenia and other psychiatric illness: population-based study, *British Journal of Psychiatry*, 193: 364–72.

Morrison, F.J. and Lindsay, W.R. (1997) Reductions in self-assessed anxiety and concurrent improvements in cognitive performance in adults who have moderate intellectual disabilities, *Journal of Applied Research in Intellectual Disabilities*, 10: 33–40.

Moss, S., Prosser, H. and Goldberg, D. (1996a) Validity of the schizophrenia diagnosis of the psychiatric assessment schedule for adults with developmental disability (PAS-ADD), *British Journal of Psychiatry*, 168: 359–67.

Moss, S., Prosser, H., Ibbotson, B. and Goldberg, D. (1996b) Respondent and informant accounts of psychiatric symptoms in a sample of patients with learning disability, *Journal of Intellectual Disability Research*, 40: 457–65.

Moss, S., Prosser, H., Costello, H., Simpson, N. and Patel, P. (1996c) *PAS-ADD Checklist*. Manchester: Hester Adrian Research Centre, University of Manchester.

Moss, S., Ibbotson, B., Prosser, H., Goldberg, D., Patel, P. and Simpson, N. (1997) Validity of the PAS-ADD for detecting psychiatric symptoms in adults with learning disability (mental retardation), *Social Psychiatry and Psychiatric Epidemiology*, 32: 344–54.

Moss, S., Prosser, H., Costello, H., Simpson, N., Patel, P., Rowe, S., Turner, S. and Hatton, C. (1998) Reliability and validity of the PAS-ADD Checklist for detecting psychiatric disorders in adults with intellectual disability, *Journal of Intellectual Disability Research*, 42: 173–83.

Mostert, M. P. (2001) Facilitated communication since 1995: a review of published studies, *Journal of Autism and Developmental Disorders*, 31: 287–313.

Myrbakk, E. and von Tetzchner, S. (2008a) Psychiatric disorders and behaviour problems in people with intellectual disability, *Research in Developmental Disabilities*, 29: 316–32.

Myrbakk, E. and von Tetzchner, S. (2008b) Screening individuals with intellectual disability for psychiatric disorders: comparison of four measures, *American Journal on Mental Retardation*, 113: 54–70.

Nezu, C.M., Nezu, A.M., Rothenberg, J.L. and Dellicarpini, L. (1995) Depression in adults with mild mental retardation: are cognitive variables involved? *Cognitive Therapy and Research*, 19: 227–39.

Nocon, A. and Sayce, L. (2008) Primary healthcare for people with mental health problems or learning disabilities, *Health Policy*, 86: 325–34.

Novaco, R.W. (1975) *Anger Control: The Development and Evaluation of an Experimental Treatment*. Lexington, MA: D.C. Heath.

Novaco, R.W. (1993) Stress inoculation therapy for anger control: a manual for therapists. Unpublished manuscript, University of California, Irvine.

Novaco, R.W. (1994) Anger as a risk factor for violence among the mentally disordered, in J. Monahan and H. Steadman (eds) *Violence and Mental Disorder: Developments in Risk Assessment*. Chicago, IL: University of Chicago Press.

Novaco, R.W. and Taylor, J.L. (2004) Assessment of anger and aggression in male offenders with developmental disabilities, *Psychological Assessment*, 16: 42–50.

Oathamshaw, S.C. and Haddock, G. (2006) Do people with intellectual disabilities and psychosis have the cognitive skills required to undertake cognitive behaviour therapy? *Journal of Applied Research in Intellectual Disabilities*, 19: 35–46.

Oliver, M.N.I., Miller, T.T. and Skillman, G.D. (2005) Factors influencing direct-care paraprofessionals' decisions to initiate mental health referrals for adults with mental retardation, *Mental Retardation*, 43: 83–91.

Powell, R. (2003) Psychometric properties of the Beck Depression Inventory and the Zung Self Rating Depression Scale in adults with mental retardation, *Mental Retardation*, 41: 88–95.

Pridding, A. and Proctor, N.G. (2008) A systematic review of personality disorder amongst people with intellectual disability with implications for the mental health nurse practitioner, *Journal of Clinical Nursing*, 17: 2811–19.

Prosser, H., Moss, S., Costello, H., Simpson, N. and Patel, P. (1997) *The Mini PAS-ADD: An Assessment Schedule for the Detection of Mental Health Needs in Adults with Learning Disability (Mental Retardation)*. Manchester: Hester Adrian Research Centre, University of Manchester.

Prosser, H., Moss, S., Costello, H., Simpson, N., Patel, P. and Rowe, S. (1998) Reliability and validity of the Mini PAS-ADD for assessing psychiatric disorders in adults with intellectual disability, *Journal of Intellectual Disability Research*, 42: 264–72.

Prout, H.T. and Schaefer, B.M. (1985) Self-reports of depression by community based mildly mentally retarded adults, *American Journal of Mental Deficiency*, 90: 220–2.

Quigley, A., Murray, G.C., McKenzie, K. and Elliot, G. (2001) Staff knowledge about symptoms of mental health in people with learning disabilities, *Journal of Learning Disabilities*, 5: 235–44.

Raghavan, R., Newell, R., Waseem, F. and Small, N. (2009) A randomized controlled trial of a specialist liaison worker model for young people with intellectual disabilities with challenging behaviour and mental health needs, *Journal of Applied Research in Intellectual Disabilities*, 22: 256–63.

Ramirez, S.Z. and Lukenbill, J. (2008) Psychometric properties of the Zung Self-Rating Anxiety Scale for adults with intellectual disabilities (SAS-ID), *Journal of Developmental and Physical Disabilities*, 20: 573–80.

Reiss, S. (1988a) *Reiss Screen for Maladaptive Behavior*. Worthington, OH: IDS.

Reiss, S. (1988b) The development of a screening measure for psychopathology in people with mental retardation, in E. Dibble and D. Gray (eds) *Assessment of Behavior Problems in Persons with Mental Retardation Living in the Community*. Rockville, MD: National Institute of Mental Health.

Reiss, S., Levitan, G.W. and McNally, R.J. (1982) Emotionally disturbed mentally retarded people: an underserved population, *American Psychologist*, 37: 361–7.

Robertson, J., Emerson, E., Gregory, N., Hatton, C., Kessissoglou, S. and Hallam, A. (2000a) Receipt of psychotropic medication by people with intellectual disability in residential settings, *Journal of Intellectual Disability Research*, 44: 666–76.

Robertson, J., Emerson, E., Gregory, N., Hatton, C., Turner, S., Kessissoglou, S. *et al.* (2000b) Lifestyle related risk factors for poor health in residential settings for people with intellectual disabilities, *Research in Developmental Disabilities*, 21: 479–86.

Rojahn, J., Lederer, M. and Tasse, M.J. (1995a) Facial recognition by persons with mental retardation: a review of the experimental literature, *Research in Developmental Disabilities*, 16: 393–414.

Rojahn, J., Rabold, D.E. and Schneider, F. (1995b) Emotion specificity in mental retardation, *American Journal of Mental Retardation*, 99: 477–86.

Rose, J., West, C. and Clifford, D. (2000) Group intervention for anger in people with intellectual disabilities, *Research in Developmental Disabilities*, 21: 171–81.

Rose, J., Loftus, M., Flint, B. and Carey, L. (2005) Factors associated with the efficacy of a group intervention for anger in people with intellectual disabilities, *British Journal of Clinical Psychology*, 44: 305–17.

Ross, E. and Oliver, C. (2002) The relationship between mood, interest and pleasure and 'challenging behaviour' in adults with severe and profound intellectual disability, *Journal of Intellectual Disability Research*, 46: 191–7.

Ross, E. and Oliver, C. (2003a) The assessment of mood in adults who have severe or profound mental retardation, *Clinical Psychology Review*, 23: 225–45.

Ross, E. and Oliver, C. (2003b) Preliminary analysis of the psychometric properties of the Mood Interest and Pleasure Questionnaire (MIPQ) for adults with severe and profound learning disabilities, *British Journal of Clinical Psychology*, 42: 81–93.

Royal College of Psychiatrists (2001) *DC-LD: Diagnostic Criteria for Psychiatric Disorders for Use with Adults with Learning Disabilities/Mental Retardation* (Occasional Paper OP 48). London: Gaskell.

Rush, A.J. and Frances, A. (2000) (eds) Expert consensus guidelines series: treatment of psychiatric and behavioural problems in mental retardation: special issue, *American Journal on Mental Retardation*, 105: 159–226.

Senatore, V., Matson, J.L. and Kazdin, A.E. (1985) An inventory to assess psychopathology in mentally retarded adults, *American Journal of Mental Retardation*, 89: 459–66.

Sims, A. (1988) *Symptoms in the Mind: An Introduction to Descriptive Psychopathology*. London: Bailliere Tindall.

Stavrakaki, C. (1999) Depression, anxiety and adjustment disorders in people with developmental disabilities, in N. Bouras (ed.) *Psychiatric and Behavioural Disorders in Developmental Disabilities and Mental Retardation*. Cambridge: Cambridge University Press.

Stavrakaki, C. and Mintsioulis, G. (1997) Anxiety disorders in persons with mental retardation: diagnostic, clinical, and treatment issues, *Psychiatric Annals*, 27: 182–9.

Stephens, R.M., Matson, J.L., Westmoreland, T. and Kulpa, J. (1981) Modification of psychotic speech with mentally retarded patients, *Journal of Mental Deficiency Research*, 25: 187–97.

Steptoe, L.R., Lindsay, W.R., Murphy, L. and Young, S.J. (2008) Construct validity, reliability and predictive validity of the dynamic risk assessment and management system (DRAMS) in offenders with intellectual disability, *Legal and Criminological Psychology*, 13: 309–21.

Sturmey, P. (1999) Classification: concepts, progress and future, in N. Bouras (ed.) *Psychiatric and Behavioural Disorders in Developmental Disabilities and Mental Retardation*. Cambridge: Cambridge University Press.

Sturmey, P. and Bertman, L.J. (1994) Validity of the Reiss Screen for maladaptive behaviors, *American Journal of Mental Retardation*, 99: 201–6.

Sturmey, P. and Gaubatz, M.D. (2002) *Clinical and Counselling Practice: A Case-guided Approach*. New York: Allyn and Bacon.

Sturmey, P., Reed, J. and Corbett, J. (1991) Psychometric assessment of psychiatric disorders in people with learning difficulties (mental handicap): a review of the measures, *Psychological Medicine*, 21: 143–55.

Sturmey, P., Taylor, J.L. and Lindsay, W.R. (2004) Research and development, in W.R. Lindsay, J.L. Taylor and P. Sturmey (eds) *Offenders with Developmental Disabilities*. Chichester: Wiley.

Taylor, J.L. (2002) A review of the assessment and treatment of anger and aggression in offenders with intellectual disability, *Journal of Intellectual Disability Research*, 46 (Suppl. 1): 57–73.

Taylor, J.L. and Lindsay, W.R. (2007) Developments in the treatment and management of offenders with intellectual disabilities, *Issues in Forensic Psychology*, 6: 23–31.

Taylor, J.L. and Novaco, R.W. (2005) *Anger Treatment for People with Developmental Disabilities: A Theory, Evidence and Manual-based Approach*. Chichester: Wiley.

Taylor, J.L., Novaco, R.W., Gillmer, B. and Thorne, I. (2002a) Cognitive-behavioural treatment of anger intensity in offenders with intellectual disabilities, *Journal of Applied Research in Intellectual Disabilities*, 15: 151–65.

Taylor, J.L., Thorne, I., Robertson, A. and Avery, G. (2002b) Evaluation of a group intervention for convicted arsonists with mild and borderline intellectual disabilities, *Criminal Behaviour & Mental Health*, 12: 282–93.

Taylor, J.L., Hatton, C., Dixon, L. and Douglas, C. (2004a) Screening for psychiatric symptoms: PAS-ADD Checklist norms for adults with intellectual disabilities, *Journal of Intellectual Disability Research*, 48: 37–41.

Taylor, J.L., Novaco, R.W., Gillmer, B.T. and Robertson, A. (2004b) Treatment of anger and aggression, in W.R. Lindsay, J.L. Taylor and P. Sturmey (eds) *Offenders with Developmental Disabilities*. Wiley: Chichester.

Taylor, J.L., Novaco, R.W., Guinan, C. and Street, N. (2004c) Development of an imaginal provocation test to evaluate treatment for anger problems in people with intellectual disabilities, *Clinical Psychology and Psychotherapy*, 11: 233–46.

Taylor, J.L., Thorne, I. and Slavkin, M. (2004d) Treatment of fire-setters, in W.R. Lindsay, J.L. Taylor and P. Sturmey (eds) *Offenders with Developmental Disabilities*. Chichester: Wiley.

Taylor, J.L., Novaco, R.W., Gillmer, B.T., Robertson, A. and Thorne, I. (2005) Individual cognitive-behavioural anger treatment for people with mild-borderline intellectual disabilities and histories of aggression: a controlled trial, *British Journal of Clinical Psychology*, 44: 367–82.

Taylor, J.L., Robertson, A., Thorne, I., Belshaw, T. and Watson, A. (2006) Responses of female fire-setters with mild and borderline intellectual disabilities to a group-based intervention, *Journal of Applied Research in Intellectual Disabilities*, 19: 179–90.

Taylor, J.L., Lindsay, W.R. and Willner, P. (2008) CBT for people with intellectual disabilities: emerging evidence, cognitive ability and IQ effects, *Behavioural and Cognitive Psychotherapy*, 36: 723–33.

Thompson, T., Zarcone, J. and Symons, F. (2004) Methodological issues in psychopharmacology for individuals with intellectual and developmental disabilities, in E. Emerson, C. Hatton, T. Thompson and T.R. Parmenter (eds) *The International Handbook of Applied Research in Intellectual Disabilities*. Chichester: Wiley.

Torr, J., Iacono, T., Graham, M.J. and Galea, J. (2008) Checklists for general practitioner diagnosis of depression in adults with intellectual disability, *Journal of Intellectual Disability Research*, 52: 930–41.

van den Hout, M., Arntz, A. and Merckelbach, H. (2000) Contributions of psychology to the understanding of psychiatric disorders, in M.G. Gelder, J.L. Lopez-Ibor Jr. and N.C. Andreasen (eds) *New Oxford Textbook of Psychiatry*. Oxford: Oxford University Press.

White, P., Chant, D., Edwards, N., Townsend, C. and Waghorn, G. (2005) Prevalence of intellectual disability and comorbid mental illness in an Australian community sample, *Australian and New Zealand Journal of Psychiatry*, 39: 395–400.

Wilkinson, R.G. and Pickett, K.E. (2009) *The Spirit Level: Why More Equal Societies Almost Always Do Better*. London: Penguin.

Willner, P., Jones, J., Tams, R. and Green, G. (2002) A randomised control trial of the efficacy of a cognitive behavioural anger management group for clients with learning disabilities, *Journal of Applied Research in Intellectual Disabilities*, 15: 224–35.

Wong, J.G., Clare, I.C.H., Gunn, J. and Holland, A.J. (1999) Capacity to make health care decisions: its importance in clinical practice, *Psychological Medicine*, 29: 437–46.

World Health Organization (1946) Constitution of the World Health Organization, *Official Record of the World Health Organization*, 2: 100.

World Health Organization (1992) *Schedules of Clinical Assessment in Neuropsychiatry, Version 1*. Geneva: World Health Organization.

World Health Organization (1993) *The ICD-10 Classification of Mental and Behavioural Disorders*. Geneva: World Health Organization.

World Health Organization (1996) *ICD-10 Guide for Mental Retardation*. Geneva: World Health Organization.

Zigmond, A.S. and Snaith, R.P. (1983) The hospital anxiety and depression scale, *Acta Psychiatrica Scandinavia*, 67: 361–70.

Zung, W.K. (1965) A self-rating depression scale, *Archives of General Psychiatry*, 12: 63–70.

Zung, W.K. (1971) A rating instrument for anxiety disorders, *Psychosomatics*, 12: 371–9.

29

Retrieving lost identities: men with severe intellectual disabilities and mental health problems in long-term care

Jane Hubert

Introduction

As seen in the previous chapter, men and women with severe or profound intellectual disabilities, and mental health problems and challenging behaviour, are among the most vulnerable people in Britain and yet the evidence base about how best to support them remains weak. Many have lived socially and physically excluded lives in long-stay hospitals since childhood (see Chapters 2, 5 and 31). In spite of 60 years of government policy of care in the community, many of these old hospitals have only fully closed in very recent years, with the last hospital finally closing in April 2009. The imminent closure of an old long-stay hospital in southern England provided an opportunity to document the experiences of a group of men who had lived most of their lives in a closed institution, and to follow their transition into smaller units in the 'community'.

Those who were the last to leave the wards of the old institutions were mainly people considered to be the most difficult to place in a community environment – men and women with severe and complex disabilities, mental health problems, challenging behaviour, and those who were perceived as 'dangerous' (Collins 1992; Hubert 2000). A number of people still live on the old hospital sites, but in new, often purpose-built, 'campus' homes. In many of these an institutional culture has continued, and residents are said to have a poorer quality of life than those living in residential homes in the community (e.g. Emerson *et al.* 2000, but see also Chapter 5 in the present volume). Because of these negative findings, it is now planned to close most of these 'campus' homes by 2010, and to resettle the 3000 or so men and women living in them.

The research

An ethnographic research project was carried out at St George's, University of London, with 20 men living in a large locked ward of a long-stay hospital, before it was closed. The research also involved follow-up visits to the men in their new homes. All of the men had severe or profound intellectual disabilities and challenging behaviour, and most of them had psychiatric diagnoses and autism.

The fieldwork consisted of participant observation (Dewalt and Dewalt 2002) in the ward (over 250 hours) and in their new homes. Little was known about the men as individuals, and the aims of this study were to get to know them by sharing their lives, albeit to a limited degree, and to describe them as individuals, as far as possible documenting their lives from their own perspectives, and thereby attempting to retrieve and restore their individual identities (see Chapter 1 describing how narrative approaches can assist efforts to unlock the hidden identities of people separated from 'mainstream' society).

As young children, all the men had lived at home with their families. When their behaviour became too difficult for their parents to manage, or for other family reasons, they were placed in children's hospitals on a long-term basis. At the time they were admitted, the majority of them from 4 to 8 years old, they were often described simply as 'difficult to manage children', but after 30 or 40 years of life in institutions most of them fulfilled the popular stereotype of 'mad' people in institutions. They roared and screeched, banged their heads on the walls or with their fists, flung themselves at the walls and floor, tore their clothes, spread faeces and urine, and injured themselves or each other.

Over the years the men had become socially invisible, and this invisibility had led to a loss of social identity, because they had no social role in the world outside. Their lives were spent within the confines of the locked ward. This was their home, but it bore little resemblance to a normal home. It consisted of three large, bare, high-ceilinged rooms, more like a community hall than a place to live. Apart from these rooms, only the toilets were accessible to the men. The doors to the dormitory area, bathrooms, office and garden were all locked. The key that opened the door into the ward also opened all the internal doors. To the staff who worked there it was also the key that opened the door to the outside world. They could unlock the door and step out of the ward into their lives, but for the 20 men in the ward, who had no keys, there was no other life.

Because most of the men in the ward were unable to communicate by means of speech, they were considered to be essentially unknowable, and few members of staff had built up meaningful reciprocal relationships with them as individuals. The men's social invisibility, and the empty, constricted lives that they lived, had led to a degree of dehumanization, and this was increased by representing them as sexual predators. In addition, most members of staff paid little attention to the men's hygiene and dress, and ignored ways of behaving which ensured that these men would be perceived as 'beyond the pale' in the outside world, perhaps thereby justifying the decision to physically exclude them.

Communication

The majority of the men had no speech; a few could say some words, but all of them spent a considerable amount of time trying to communicate their feelings and needs. There was seldom any response to these attempts to communicate, and the men were thus rejected as interactive social beings. Most of the men used many other ways of communicating, such as touch, gesture and non-verbal sounds. The lack of response to the men's non-verbal communication

was apparent in day-to-day life on the ward, but there was also another level at which this lack of acknowledgement of communication was evident. All the men had severe challenging behaviour, but there was little attention paid, if any, to the possible reasons why the men behaved as they did (see Chapter 17 which considers assessment and support of people with challenging behaviours). For example, one man frequently spread urine and faeces over himself and around the walls and floor. When the researcher asked him what the matter was, he stopped what he was doing, and asked quietly, 'Where's Daddy?'

Loss of family identity

This man, and others in the ward, indicated clearly that they missed their families, even after some thirty years in the institution. One man would interrupt his violent behaviour to sit on the researcher's feet, take her hand to stroke his head, and say 'Mummy'. These responses indicated emotions and memories that tended to be ignored in the locked ward.

Although the men indicated that they still felt themselves to be sons, and to belong to a long absent family, they had, as part of their overall loss of identity, gradually lost their familial and kin identity. Except for the few who had a parent or other relative closely involved in their lives, they were not perceived as sons, or brothers, or nephews or uncles. Their identities were constructions by other people – care staff and health professionals who had come into the ward over the years. Their personal histories had been lost, to be replaced by other people's records made for other people's purposes (see Chapter 2 for a full discussion of the role of social construction in 'othering' people).

However effectively they had been shut away from the outside world, and irrespective of whether their parents still visited them, they continued to show their awareness of themselves as a member of a family. For example, Leroy constantly pulled anyone he could towards the locked door of the dormitory area. If he was allowed in he hunted for his best clothes – a shirt and suit – and wanted to be changed into them. He had done this for years, because he used to wear them for his father's visits. In fact his father had retired to the Caribbean without him, many years earlier, but Leroy continued to try to get him back, maintained the link with him, and perhaps tried to will him to come and see him, by trying to dress up for him.

Exercise 29.1

Consider for a moment what it would be like for you to be (i) locked up, (ii) separated for decades from your family, (iii) deprived of a confidante who could communicate with you, let alone understood you.

Write down your thoughts and feelings.

Consider all the possible reasons why people have been treated this way for so long.

Loss of gender identity

One of the most significant consequences of the physical and social exclusion of these men was their loss of gender identity and roles. There seemed to be little acknowledgement of their individual desires, needs, hopes and fears as adult men, or of the possibility that they might have normal sexual feelings for each other. They were largely perceived as dangerous, or at the very least unpredictable, and in many cases this had been used as the justification for controlling them within a locked environment.

For example, one man, David, was always naked. If he was given clothes he simply tore them up, and his nudity had become accepted on the ward. But in 'normal' society nudity in public is not acceptable. The ward may not have seemed a very normal environment, but, in addition to the residents, there were many care staff and health professionals who came into the ward.

Because David was always naked, he was not perceived, or treated, as a social adult, nor as an adult man. His sexuality was denied and he was, in a sense, desexed and degendered. Because the staff no longer perceived David as an adult man, it seemed to be assumed that the men he lived with did not do so either.

As part of the research, parents and relatives who were still in contact were visited at home. After visiting his parents, the researcher talked to David about them, and about the house where he had lived as a child:

> I said that I expected that he missed them. He stopped roaring and looked at me as I spoke, and then suddenly said, out of the blue, 'Bless you'. I had never heard him say anything spontaneously before that was not a one-word demand . . . No one around us disputed what he had just said. But those two appropriate words, dredged up from somewhere, indicated that he had understood, and emphasised the fact (usually ignored) that he had feelings as well as needs, and that he had memories, too.
>
> (From field notes)

David's story was true of the men in the ward. As they grew up within the confines of a children's hospital, and then a locked ward, they were not helped to develop into men whose adulthood and gender were acknowledged and respected. On the contrary, they had, over the years, been allowed (and sometimes encouraged) to develop ways of behaving that led them further and further into the category of 'other'.

Emotional needs

The emotional well-being of the men went largely unnoticed from day to day. If they became too disturbed, the response tended to involve increased medication. Many of the men appeared depressed and anxious, some even seemed to be scared, but there was a general disregard of individuals' anxieties.

This neglect of the men's conspicuous physical and psychological suffering had become an integral part of the ethos of the ward. However, it is known that the traumas experienced by men and women in closed institutions, such as early separation from parents, living in emotionally and physically deprived environments, and emotional, physical and sexual abuse, are likely to cause many problems (see also Chapters 28 and 31). These legacies of the past could have been addressed for many of the men in this study – it is now widely accepted that individual and group psychotherapy can be effective with people 'who prove highly challenging to the services and to society as a whole' (Royal College of Psychiatrists 2004: 14). However, the anxieties and fears of these men had remained unacknowledged and untreated (Hubert and Hollins 2006).

Closure of the ward

Although it had been government policy for many years to close the old long-stay hospitals, the process has been slow and long drawn out. The last people to be resettled were mainly those with complex disabilities, including mental health problems and challenging behaviour.

Research comparing life in the community with institutional life has generally shown that on most counts community-based services are better than institutions (Emerson and Hatton 1994; Kozma *et al.* 2009). However, in the areas of challenging behaviour and psychotropic medication there have been mixed or worse results (IASSID Special Interest Group on Comparative Policy and Practice 2009). This is supported by Mansell (2006) who concludes that people with higher support needs tend to have worse outcomes than those with fewer support needs. Thus people with severe and profound intellectual disabilities and challenging behaviour are at the greatest disadvantage in the building of their new lives in the community.

The transition

The transition of the men to the 'community' had been planned for a number of years, but in the event it was repeatedly delayed, and there was a prolonged period of turmoil and loss. There was a series of short-term managers, and many other changes of care staff on the ward. The atmosphere became increasingly fraught, to some extent because the staff felt insecure, since their own futures were not assured. For those who had worked for some time in the ward, or in the institution as a whole, there was already a significant sense of loss.

Three men moved individually into separate homes in the community. One group of men moved into a purpose-built 'campus' home on the hospital site. Two other groups moved into houses in the community. Although the move into a campus home was the least traumatic for the men, ten years later their home is still in the middle of a derelict site, which has been awaiting planning permission and the building of a new housing estate.

Life in the new homes

There are many aspects of day-to-day life that can be used to measure whether the outcomes for people moving into the community have been successful (Hubert and Hollins, submitted). These include:

- having a degree of autonomy, i.e. the freedom to make decisions on a day-to-day basis, and to take part in life-changing decisions;
- involvement and participation in domestic life and day-to-day activities;
- participation in community and family life: contact and relationships with people outside the home;
- opportunities to develop individual skills and competency;
- access to health care, and to specialist input when necessary, including mental health specialists;
- the size of the unit and the ratio of staff to residents;
- the organizational structure of the home, the extent of institutional practices, and the existing 'rules' of the house;
- what daytime activities are offered and provided;
- the degree of encouragement given to maintain or develop family relationships, and relationships with others beyond the residents and staff;
- the extent to which each individual's adulthood is acknowledged, including acceptance of sexual needs and preferences;
- the extent to which there is active encouragement to communicate, by whatever means an individual offers.

(Hubert and Hollins, submitted)

Exercise 29.2

The outcomes listed above are not exhaustive. From your reading of this and the previous chapter, consider what other outcomes might be considered important for this group of men, and why.

Then look at what *Valuing People Now* says about the aspirations of and for people with learning disabilities. How might this change your thinking about this group of men, and why?

Many of these outcomes will depend on the level and nature of staff training, staff experience and attitudes, and on the attitudes, beliefs and actions of the home manager.

In the present study it is clear that the lives of the men in the campus home and the two community group homes have improved in many ways. The houses are smaller, and there are only up to seven residents in each. Food is prepared in the kitchens, rather than being imported from Cornwall overnight. The men have access to their bedrooms and, some of the time, access to the garden. Access to the kitchen varies from house to house. Thus their lives approximate, to some extent, to other people's lives in the community – but there is a vital difference: they remain locked in.

Life in the three new homes varies, and in two of the three houses the quality of life has varied significantly at different times under different managers.

The campus home

In the new campus home, where there has been only one home manager since the move, the quality of life of the men has improved in a number of ways, and remains stable. In particular, the men are encouraged to communicate, and their various means of communication are responded to. Their individual skills are being recognized, and some attempts are being made to develop these skills; even those with the most severe intellectual disabilities are involved, for example, in art and craft work of various kinds.

The men have access to their own rooms and to the office. They are involved in the preparation of snacks and meals, and residents and members of staff sit together to eat. Because they are still on the old hospital site most of them spend some time every weekday in the day centre they had attended in the past, and in a new centre set up for those with autism.

The men living in the campus home are now treated more as social beings and as individuals, and the nature and extent of their day-to-day activities reflected this. However, it is clear that the improvements in the quality of life of the men, and the perception that others have of them, emanated from the beliefs and style of leadership of the home manager, who had been there since the home opened. It is not clear that the positive developments in the house

would survive without someone there to constantly instil and fulfil the same aims and philosophy.

In spite of the efforts of the home manager, there seemed to be little input from psychologists or other professionals to try to understand the men's challenging behaviour. For example, the man who had always stripped off his clothes in the locked ward was still naked, some nine years later. The fact that he would not wear clothes seriously affected his quality of life, not only because it affected other people's perceptions of him as a social adult within the home, but also because he could not leave the house and enter the outside world, and thus was unable to interact with the wider community.

The campus home is undeniably a mini-institution in that the men live a communal life, and they live behind locked doors and gates. They do have more day-to-day choices than they had before, but the degree to which the men now have control over their own lives is limited. They are not involved in major decisions about the direction of their lives, any more than they were able to choose who they would live with, probably for the rest of their lives. The life-changing decisions are made by other people, and will continue to be, because it is assumed that the men do not have the capacity to contribute to such decisions.

Houses in the community

Two other groups of men moved into houses in the community. The quality of life for the men in these two houses has varied widely at different times since they moved in. Both have had a frequent turnover of home managers, and the attitudes and style of each manager have governed the nature of the life in the houses.

In House A, the bright paint and soft furnishings appeared very welcoming. However, the lives of the men who lived there were still restricted. The kitchen was locked the whole time, and at mealtimes the top half of the stable door would be unlocked for as long as it took to hand out a plate for each man, and then locked again. The men sat silently as they ate, while members of staff stood around the room. They seldom spoke to the men, except to tell them what to do, and conversations were often held across their heads.

There were few planned daytime activities. Six months after they had moved only two men had planned activities, once a week, away from the house, and no day activities were brought into the house.

At House B there were also problems with a frequent turnover of home managers, acting managers, and care staff. To begin with, the house was in a bad state of repair, and there was little colour in the house. The bedrooms were bare and beds unmade. The men had been unable to use the garden throughout the summer because of loose tiles on the roof. Mealtimes, which were the only time that the men were brought together, were almost silent.

The only man who had been on no medication in the locked ward was now on antipsychotic drugs, because his tendency to spread urine and faeces was not tolerated in the new house. In the locked ward, when he was in a good mood, he was bright, communicative and funny. Now he shuffled around the house, looking at the floor, or sat for hours on the side of his bed, immobile.

Under some of the managers, the atmosphere in this house improved. As in House A, the quality of life of the men has varied, and presumably will continue to vary, according to the attitude and actions of the house manager, and the resulting ethos of the house. Of the three homes, the campus home, in spite of its location on the old hospital site, remained the most stable environment.

Exercise 29.3

Reflecting on your own experience as well as what you have just read so far, consider all the possible reasons for variations in the quality of care in apparently similar care homes.

Why does staff turnover seem to be so problematic?

What are the consequences for the men described in this chapter?

What should be done?

Discussion

The quality and stability of the lives of the men improved in a number of material ways, but there were fundamental issues that had not substantially changed, especially in the homes in the 'community' (Hubert and Hollins, submitted):

- The quality of the men's lives was highly dependent on the attitude and level of dedication of those in direct charge of the homes, and as a result also on the quality and training of care staff employed in them.
- In two of the three homes there had been a constant turnover of staff, including home managers, thus there was little continuity in staff knowledge of the men or in relationships with them.
- Only the long-term manager of the campus home was aware of the existence of the vignettes drawn up by the researcher about each man. In the other homes the succession of different managers meant that the vignettes had been long forgotten.
- The men still lived largely institutionalized lives; they were still, in a sense, just contained, rather than developing their own individual lives.
- Some of the staff working in the homes continued to have an 'institutional' approach; they did not interact with the men as one adult to another, but retained a patronizing adult–child relationship.
- We found no evidence that the men were being enabled to develop new relationships outside the confines of the homes. Their social world still consisted of co-residents and staff.
- There was limited input from professionals other than to adjust medication reactively, rather than to tackle the anxieties, trauma and memories that are likely to underlie the men's challenging behaviour. Thus the men continued to behave in ways that made them socially unacceptable.
- Only one man had discontinued medication; for the others similar doses of psychotropic medication continued.

(Hubert and Hollins, submitted)

Conclusion

To a great extent the men still lived within the old paradigm of social exclusion and denial of individual identity and autonomy. The findings show that the men lived predominantly institutionalized lives, and continued to be physically and socially excluded from the social world around them. They did have more choices from day to day than before, but they were excluded from decision-making at a more fundamental level.

The men's lives were better than they had been in material terms, but within the structure of the system there was only a very limited possibility to actually change their lives. There appear to be few fundamental changes in professional and social attitudes, and as a result men such as these continue to live socially excluded and forgotten lives. Despite no longer being in a long-stay hospital, the men continue to live in environments that strip them of personal identities and associations they still cherish after decades. Their lives have improved in some important material ways but not, so far, in a manner that allows them to express their core identities as human beings.

References

Collins, J. (1992) *When The Eagles Fly: A Report on Resettlement of People with Learning Difficulties from Long-Stay Institutions*. London: Values into Action.

Dewalt, K.M. and Dewalt, B.R. (2002) *Participant Observation: A Guide for Fieldworkers*. Alta Mira, CA: Alta Mira Press.

Emerson, E. and Hatton, C. (1994) *Moving Out: Relocation from Hospital to Community*. London: HMSO.

Emerson, E., Robertson, J., Gregory, N., Hatton, C., Kessissoglou, S., Hallam, A. *et al.* (2000) Quality and costs of community-based residential supports, village communities, and residential campuses in the United Kingdom, *American Journal of Mental Retardation*, 105: 81–102.

Hubert, J. (2000) The social, individual and moral consequences of life in long-stay institutions, in J. Hubert (ed.) *Madness, Disability and Social Exclusion: The Archaeology and Anthropology of 'Difference'*. London: Routledge.

Hubert, J. and Hollins, S. (2006) Men with severe learning disabilities and challenging behaviour in long-stay NHS hospital care: qualitative study, *British Journal of Psychiatry*, 188: 70–4.

Hubert, J. and Hollins, S. (submitted) Leaving the institution? A follow-up of men with severe intellectual disabilities and challenging behaviour, *Journal of Policy and Practice in Intellectual Disabilities*.

IASSID (International Association for the Scientific Study of Intellectual Disabilities) Special Interest Group on Comparative Policy and Practice (2009) Proposed position statement on deinstitutionalisation and community living. Unpublished report.

Kozma, A., Mansell, J. and Beadle-Brown, J. (2009) Outcomes in different residential settings for people with intellectual disability: a systematic review, *American Journal on Intellectual and Developmental Disabilities*, 114(3): 193–222.

Mansell, J. (2006) Deinstitutionalisation and community living: progress, problems and priorities, *Journal of Intellectual and Developmental Disability*, 31(2): 65–76.

Royal College of Psychiatrists (2004) *Psychotherapy and Learning Disability* (Council Report CR116). London: Royal College of Psychiatrists.

30

Engaging communities of interest

Paul Ramcharan and Malcolm Richardson

Introduction

In Chapter 2 it was shown that prior to industrialization the majority of people lived in family homes in their communities. Chapter 1 also shows that this community existence was not always comfortable and, indeed, was sometimes very challenging. By far the majority of people with learning disabilities lived on the margins of society carrying the varying labels of the era: possessed, changelings, vagrants, village idiots and so forth. In the absence of paid work and family the fate of people with learning disabilities must have been harsh and their lives very difficult. But the solution of the early industrial era to develop large institutions was no less inhumane, as attested to in Chapter 2 of this volume.

In the UK the movement of people into the community from the large institutions starting in the 1960s therefore brought with it new problems, for never before had community living, social justice, community acceptance and well-being been achieved *together* as a matter of course for people with learning disabilities.

The assumption that community inclusion is a necessary end in itself has been addressed in both meaningful attempts at social engineering and in social policy initiatives now for over half a century. Although it cannot be exhaustive, this chapter seeks to capture in broad terms the ways in which policy and services have sought to accomplish community inclusion since the early 1960s when the UK commitment to deinstitutionalization, resettlement and community inclusion began. By examining the emergence of different policy, service-related and academic strands contributing to community inclusion some of the assumptions about community will be examined.

It will be argued that since the 1960s policy and attempts at social engineering aimed at community inclusion for people with learning disabilities have consecutively sought to reproduce:

- the characteristics of communities;
- the characteristics of everyday community living and normal lives;
- a level of personal choice and autonomy akin to members in the wider community; and
- more recently and in prospect, the application of a common framework of human rights for citizens.

These will be used as main section headings in this chapter, with the nature of each being examined and their successes and limitations considered. It will be argued that different approaches, while producing small 'lifestyle' changes, are yet to affect fundamentals of community inclusion such as housing and employment.

Reproducing the characteristics of communities

When the UK Hospital Plan detailing the figures for deinstitutionalization of people with mental illness was published in 1961, the political and social policy context was significantly different to that today. There was a post-Second World War optimism and, based upon significant social research, a view that communities would be far warmer, nurturing and caring environments than institutions.

Of particular note, the work of Willmott and Young (1960) in the East End of London showed how, within local communities, there was a strong reciprocal bond upon which people relied for mutual aid. For example, one person might take children from several families to school, another might look out for the elderly gentlemen living at Number 17, and local church members might fundraise through a fete. Within the boundaries of many such community localities, employment, leisure, spiritual and other collectives might operate to make the connection between its residents yet stronger. One central thesis from early work such as this was that communities were warm places where there existed mutual reliance, a sense of belonging and a system of mutual care and support. In such communities the currency of exchange was the recognition that 'if I rely on you today then, at some point, you can rely on me in the future', i.e. what goes around, comes around.

Exercise 30.1

In small groups consider the community in which you live. Are there similarities between your community and the East End communities of the 1960s described by Willmott and Young?

If your community is different then why is this so?

Following early moves towards deinstitutionalization both the Seebohm Report (1968) and Barclay Report (1982) emphasized a 'community development model' for social work practice. Seebohm recognized that as a concept 'community' is often related to locality, but also that with better transport and services distributed outside communities to which people travelled, locality was not always the defining feature of such communities:

> Although community has traditionally rested upon geographical locality, and this remains an aspect of many communities, today different members of a family may belong to different communities of interest as well as the same local neighbourhood. The notion of a community implies the existence of a network of reciprocal social relationships, which among other things ensure mutual aid and give those who experience it a sense of well-being.
>
> (Seebohm Report 1968: 147)

One can see how, based upon this view of community, the inclusion of people with learning disabilities as they left the institutions would be best accomplished by accessing the care and support *taken to be present* within such communities.

The work of Philip Abrams (see Bulmer 1986) on 'neighbourhoodism' was central in this respect. Abrams further hypothesized that forms of care can differ depending upon the *personnel* involved and in

Setting	Personnel		
		Professionals	**Non-specialists**
	Institution	Institutional treatment	Institutional care
	Community	Community treatment	Community care

Figure 30.1 Representation of Abrams's framework for forms of care

what *setting* the care is provided (Figure 30.1). In this typology professional care in institutions leads to an 'institutional treatment' model, but where that care is provided by non-specialists it becomes an 'institutional care' model. In contrast, in the community, professional care will yield a 'community treatment' model and lay or non-specialist inputs will produce a 'community care' model – i.e. care *by* the community.

For Abrams it was absolutely vital to transfer as much care to the community as possible, to deprofessionalize relationships, set people free from service dependency and build caring neighbourhoods and communities. Both Abrams and Seebohm saw the means through which such community care could be developed as being through building neighbourhood groups, good neighbour schemes, participation in local voluntary organizations and in developing 'communities of interest'. But, as it turned out, the early community development approaches of the 1970s were short-lived for a number of reasons, not many of which were related to people with learning disabilities.

The resettlement of people with mental illness tested resources, not least given a fight over whether funding in the community should flow to those with recognized illness, often the 'unworried unwell', or to the 'worried well' whom Goldberg and Huxley (1980) estimated made up one quarter of the adult population at any one time. The immensity of the task of working with communities around the needs of people with mental health problems (in addition to diagnosed mental illness) and people with learning disabilities also was so great as to pose a challenge rather akin to 'drinking the ocean'.

Moreover, reliance on the support of the community was hard to find and people with mental illness resettled into communities were often faced by a strong NIMBY (not-in-my-backyard) lobby. These experiences cast some doubt on the inherent warmth of communities and their engagement in the lives of people with disabilities. Indeed Willmott and Young's work had also shown that many people, particularly those in the younger adult age bracket, were leaving tight-knit communities for looser-knit suburban life, leading to the argument that 'Community turned out to be a function of shared adversity, something that those who were benefiting from the prosperity of the 1960s chose to escape' (Chapman 1999: 40).

The capacity of some families and individuals to survive independently means that 'mutual reliance' was seen as surplus to requirements. A recent study also argues that in contemporary communities such mutuality is often based on a materialist philosophy in which providing care is seen as a 'good' over which to barter directly. In this model a person provides care (for example after-school care or looking after children) to a similar level to the person with whom they are sharing tasks (Ramcharan et al. 1994). As many families in this study pointed out, the cost to neighbours and others in the community was too high where additional support was required from neighbours to look after their relative with a disability and the most they could rely upon was 'help in an emergency'. Moreover, as many pointed out, people with learning disabilities still tended to go to schools and day services in segregated settings with the result that their paths with peers and others in the community seldom crossed and no opportunity structure for mutuality existed.

Evidence from a secondary analysis of socializing patterns in the US General Household Survey between 1974 and 1996 (Guest and Wierzbicki 1999) also indicate a slow but continual decline in social ties, a small growth in non-neighbourhood socializing and highest levels of socializing among older people, those with children and the most disadvantaged. Moreover, Bridge et al. (2004), in their review of neighbouring, suggest that: 'Neighbourliness involves distance and privacy as well as closeness and conviviality.'

The contrasts between the 'warm' view of community upon which early post-war policy was based and the later view are summarized in Table 30.1.

The experience of the 'warm' community of early theorizing and policy was an important starting point, but the evidence suggests that it is not easy to reproduce and may be illusory in much of contemporary society. For people with learning disabilities there was also a policy shift to consumerism and to incorporate normalization.

The 'warm' community	The (post)modern community
Reciprocity on the grounds of neighbourliness	Reciprocity on the grounds of equal exchange of services or goods
A sense of identity out of belonging to a mutually supportive community	A sense of identity and belonging only with those who share interests
Stronger together supporting all members	Stronger together with those with whom one shares an identity based upon personal interest
Commitment is voluntary and there is a volunteering commitment	Commitment based upon personal choice and personal gain
A sacrifice of some privacy – spontaneity to meeting up	A maintenance of privacy – meetings are planned

Table 30.1 A comparison of elements of the 'warm' and the '(post)-modern' community

Exercise 30.2

Prior to reading the next section use the two scenarios to populate the boxes where indicated in ways that will help June to become part of the local community using both scenarios. What are the problems? Repeat this exercise at the end of the next section of the chapter. What have you learned?

Scenario 1 – June is in her fifties and has been resettled to a house in the grounds of the hospital where she lives with 12 other people with learning disabilities. June is shy and spends time doing crochet chains which she hands to people as gifts. June uses hospital day services and visits family irregularly.

Scenario 2 – June has been resettled to a small home in the community with three other people who came from the same hospital as she did. June uses the Adult Training Centre locally but does also go to a local leisure centre once a week to swim.

	Professional resources and services required in support	Non-specialist care/support required
Scenario 1		
Scenario 2		

Reproducing characteristics of community living and normal community lives

It should be noted that the shift in emphasis from deinstitutionalization to the reproduction of ordinary community lives was also prompted because the rate of deinstitutionalization for people with learning disabilities was at first very slow. As pointed out in Chapter 5 of this volume, after publication of *Better Services for the Mentally Handicapped* (Department of Health 1971), efforts at resettlement were managed by health and social services and involved a move to a varied assortment of independent living, hostels, some smaller group homes and to adult placement or fostering services. Many of those resettled early were people with 'mild' disabilities who continued to use services provided by the very hospitals from which they had come. And the majority of people with learning disabilities were still in the old institutions at this time.

The 1980s also saw the emergence of normalization with its emphasis on socially valued roles, as well as a number of pilot schemes involving smaller group living arrangements (Lowe and de Paiva 1991), which set the scene for the development of housing for people with learning disabilities over the next 40 years. However, by the 1980s social policy was itself undergoing huge transformation with the rise of consumerism (Burton and Kagan 2005). In this model those in receipt of welfare were being recategorized as individuals in receipt of services with rights as consumers. It was always likely given these developments that in Abrams's terms a 'community treatment' rather than a 'community care' model would flourish. A further consideration was that the government had to manage not simply the transfer of people with learning disabilities from the institutions but the transfer of service workers and professionals to new community teams too.

The emergence of individual planning and services developed around individually assessed need appeared in the 1983 All Wales Strategy (AWS) with an exhortation to *involve* people with learning disabilities in all aspects of planning, managing and implementing services (Felce *et al.* 1998). At the same time the advent in the 1980s of normalization dictated an approach to building an ordinary life (King's Fund 1980), where the growth of community services aimed to fulfil individual need with a focus on smaller non-institutionalized residential settings, increased employment opportunities and a focus on developing friendships and networks in community settings. However, in the early 1980s community services in Wales were found to be 'unplanned, fragmented, poorly co-ordinated and without adequate mechanisms to involve individuals and their families in decision-making' (Felce *et al.* 1998: 49). Indeed,

> The function of services in relation to the community was not spelt out clearly enough. Hence the operationalisation of something as vague as 'mobilising community resources' . . . had no ready template . . . The new tangible services developed were the clearest mani-festation of this activity, though they were often the result of 'top-down' planning processes.
>
> (Felce *et al.* 1998: 67)

The aim of community inclusion cited in the AWS and virtually every policy since has lacked guidance or models to accomplish such inclusion and ordinary lives. Yet during the AWS period the experience of adults with learning disabilities remained far from this ideal.

For example, the dominant model of segregated Adult Training Centre (ATC) provision in which all day activities were based saw only a gradual move to satellite systems in which people participated in inclusive community-based activities. Yet in a survey 11 years after implementation (Beyer *et al.* 1994), over two-thirds of person-hours were still spent at the ATCs and of these over half the activities were arts and crafts or contract work. The contract work itself involved menial work such as packing bags (for example with screw and dowels for DIY furniture) and for which a measly pocket-money rate was paid so as 'not to affect welfare benefit payments'. During the AWS period only 5 per cent per annum of people attending ATCs went on to open employment places, giving rise to questions about whether the training in such centres actually worked. Pockets of opportunity in alternative day opportunities and open employ-ment were also achieved and, for the latter, employers estimated that integration into the general workforce for over half of these workers was 'excellent' (Beyer *et al.* 1995).

The situation today is not much better and it is interesting to note that *Valuing Employment Now* (Department of Health 2009) estimates that only

10 per cent of people with learning disabilities are in paid work. Setting a goal of 45 per cent employment (the same as 'other' disabled people) by 2025, the document says the present employment rate '. . . represents a waste of talent and opportunity for people with learning disabilities, employers and our wider economy and society' (Department of Health 2009: 11). The strategy does not add any additional funding but seeks to work through Partnership Boards to reallocate day service funding to supported employment and provides a 13-point plan for creating a value system and infrastructure among service providers and employers aimed at accomplishing the target (Department of Health 2009: 14–17). See Chapter 27 in this volume for more details.

The conclusion seems to be that if employment is central to achieving community inclusion then for many people with learning disabilities there is likely to be a significant wait in prospect. A second conclusion is that top-down community treatment models of service provision, even if seemingly co-ordinated, do not necessarily lead to significant change even over substantial periods of time, leaving for many a life course unlikely to achieve open employment and its associated outcomes relating to income, quality of living and wider social networks.

The experience of residential options also proves instructive. Like employment, housing represents an *opportunity structure* through which the wider benefits of community living were supposed to have been accessed and experienced. Consensus from a significant number of studies indicates that small-scale group homes dispersed in the community provide best outcomes for residents (Emerson *et al.* 2000). So, for example: leisure activities have been found to be greater and more varied in smaller community settings (Mansell 1994; Golding *et al.* 2005); larger social networks have been found in smaller settings as compared to the large institutions (Stancliffe and Keane 2000; Golding *et al.* 2005); while leisure, social network and community activities were found to be greater in group homes than in cluster housing (Emerson *et al.* 2000; Emerson and McVilly 2004). But as Robertson *et al.* (2001a, b) say, the data indicate changes to be small when set against the expectation of full inclusion into the community.

Two further unspoken and yet hugely important assumptions have been important in the history of community care services for people with learning disabilities at least up to the establishment of the personalization agenda. These are the focus on changing the individual rather than the community and, associated with this, a 'graduation model' (Taylor 2001). In the 'graduation model' the preoccupation is with ensuring the person has the skills to 'graduate' to the right to a new life.

For example, early resettlement favoured people with 'mild' learning disabilities, with more leaving the institutions early. Yet even within this view there are things that are simply never questioned. Indeed one can ask in relation to the 'graduation model' why it is that, virtually without complaint from government or academics, people with learning disabilities are in a completely different queue for housing from the rest of society. Why are group homes acceptable for people with learning disabilities but not for others?

Once again there is an implicit and yet unspoken assumption that at some point distant, people with learning disabilities will graduate to 'real' housing and 'real lives'. In this respect Reinders (2008) asks, 'Why maintain a hierarchy of (human) being that is premised by the faculties of intellect and will? Why not ask how to conceive of our own common humanity regardless of any state or condition . . .' (Reinders 2008: 53).

In a society based on such hierarchy, many people with learning disabilities never graduate. Instead they are caught in a lifetime of segregated services with the 'promised land' always that vital step away.

The person must have the right behaviour and right skills to work, to move into less restricted, more integrated homes or into the open employment market. And this explains why there has been so much emphasis on behaviour management and social skills training within services and as a research outcome measure. It is an approach implicitly built upon an 'equality of opportunity' model with the idea that merit and achievement are the only rightful arbiters of access to position and, consequently, economic resources. And since equality of opportunity gives differential access to resources, and since people with learning disabilities are nearer to the bottom of the 'merit ladder', their quality of life and those of their children is passed on intergenerationally.

We shall consider the 'capability' and human rights models later as a counter to the equal opportunity position. However, to acquire equal opportunity seems to require two additional conditions. First, people should be provided equal access to education and to employment and society should take away the obstacles that disable them through inaccessibility. This is the position of the social model of disability. The second is the need for support to make these accomplishments a reality.

> ## Exercise 30.3
>
> First reconsider your answers to the previous exercise.
>
> Additionally, consider what ordinary lives mean in terms of housing, employment, relationships, leisure and health. If people with learning disabilities had such ordinary lives would they accomplish community inclusion? If not, why not?

Professional support – with a twist: experiences from North America

While the UK largely adopted what Abrams identified as the *community treatment* model during the 1980s and 1990s there were pockets of significant and innovative work in North America pointing to new strategies for organizing support to accomplish a *community care* model. Four of these with particular relevance today were outlined in the seminal publication *Making Friends: Developing Relationships between People with a Disability and Other Members of the Community* (Roeher Institute 1990) and these are summarized and discussed further below.

1 One-to-one or matching

The key example here is citizen advocacy in which an ordinary citizen is recruited by a citizen advocacy organization to provide both instrumental (practical) and affective (friendship) long-term support, and through this to introduce the person to new social networks. Understandably this is a time-consuming strategy with citizen advocates hard to recruit and no guarantee of success. Notably, citizen advocacy was given additional funding in *Valuing People*.

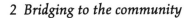

2 Bridging to the community

This involves someone working out of a voluntary sector organization as a 'connector' or 'guide' whose role it is to build 'associational maps' of the community, introduce the person to new places and opportunities, guide the person to new relationships and establish links with valued members of the community before fading out. The underlying assumptions of this approach are identified as a focus on gifts, trust and a belief that people have not been included because no one has asked the community for such inclusion. In this model we can see the ideals of diversity and positive regard, non-discrimination and support sufficient for, but not so cloistering as to prevent, self-determination and choice (Amado 1993).

There may indeed be something singularly important about this 'being there' model since as Reinders (2008) says,

> Not many people in our society believe that spending time with an intellectually disabled person will contribute to the 'quality' of their lives; therefore it is also true that not many people would know what it is to be a friend of such a person. This is not necessarily their fault. Even though disability is claimed to be 'out of the closet' it is still true that many people with intellectual disabilities live in protected environments. It takes an effort to reach out and meet them.
>
> (Reinders 2008: 7)

Taylor and colleagues have produced some important accounts featuring such self-determination and in many cases the expectation is that the community is confronted to accept difference by people with learning disabilities simply 'being there' (e.g. Taylor *et al.* 1987, 1995; Taylor and Bogdan 1989).

3 Community development (with self-advocates)

In this model the Roeher Institute (1990) saw self-advocates as playing a central role in supporting the development of links with the community. While it is possible to view a significant proportion of the work of self-advocacy groups as seeking to accomplish these outcomes through claiming rights, community education, participation in service planning and setting up parliaments (see Chapter 7), community development has not featured as a key stated policy for most self-advocacy groups.

However, Goodley notes that it is perhaps limiting to think that self-advocacy takes place only in self-advocacy groups, is fixed or, indeed, is fixed by government policies. Rather the movement shows resilience in so far as the identities and roles chosen by self-advocates are constantly reworked (Goodley 2005: 342). In other words this is about choosing how they want to construct their own identity. It is about 'border-crossing' (Peters 1996) from the disability identity to an 'included' identity, rather than an approach in which their identity is professionally defined and which dictates how people should behave and what skills they should pursue.

More recent legislation and policy have further contributed to supporting disabled people to 'be there'. For example, the Disability Discrimination Acts 1995 and 2005 have the potential over time to significantly improve the accessibility of environments and change how businesses act towards people with disabilities and what responsibilities public authorities must assume. The right to accessible environments championed by the disability lobby and social model theorists has meant that community initiatives have more power to back up their claims for change to make local communities more accessible.

Additionally, community development itself has become significantly more technical since its early days in the 1970s. For example, the Kansas-based community toolbox which readers are encouraged to visit (http://ctb.ku.edu) has significant resources concerned with:

- understanding community context (e.g. assessing community assets and needs);
- collaborative planning (e.g. developing a vision, mission, objectives, strategies and action plans);
- developing leadership and enhancing participation (e.g. building relationships, recruiting participants);
- community action and intervention (e.g. designing interventions, advocacy);
- evaluating community initiatives (e.g. programme evaluation, documentation of community and systems change);

- promoting and sustaining the initiative (e.g. social marketing, obtaining grants).

The approach recognizes the differences between communities, targets initiatives, builds bridges, attempts bonding and, crucially, addresses how funding can be sourced both through grants and local partnerships. This has resonance with the emergent literature on social capital which Putnam (1998) suggests is achieved where people have:

- formal and informal engagement;
- links with institutions which are public-regarding and private-regarding;
- the building of bonds of trust to repair cleavages;
- immediacy in response to new connections;
- durable, intense and multi-stranded networks and social ties through neighbourhoods or new media.

It might be argued that contemporary approaches to social capital and community development need to target people with learning disabilities perhaps by building links to the self-advocacy movement which, in some cases, is already linking with the community in innovative and productive ways.

The values underlying community development models have also changed from the early days incorporating values that challenge the equality of opportunity model. Kenny (2006) suggests these values as a set of common commitments to:

- powerless people and social justice;
- citizenship and human rights;
- collective action;
- diversity;
- change and involvement in conflict;
- liberation, open societies and participatory democracy;
- accessibility of human services programmes; and,
- empowerment and self-determination.

And, indeed, the fourth area identified by the Roeher Institute lies in the area around reproducing change through extending personal choice and autonomy and, as such, falls into the next section of this chapter.

Reproducing personal choice and autonomy of the wider community

4 Using social networks and circles to build friends

The centrality of friendship to quality of life and the real problems in developing and supporting such friendships has been considered in Chapter 24 of this volume. Bayley (1997) shows how such friendships can contribute to fundamental human needs such as intimacy, nurturance, reassurance of worth, guidance as well as reliable assistance leading to social inclusion (categories taken from Weiss 1975). However, drawing on O'Brien and Lyle's (1987) five accomplishments he also argues that people with disabilities need support additional to friendships to be able to exercise choice and to pursue their hopes, dreams and aspirations. In other words, the gap between a person's choice and a life that is self-determined relies on additional support (Boyle 2008).

There are now also a significant number of studies which demonstrate that, where competence is distributed among a group, life quality is better (Lunsky and Benson 2001; Odom *et al.* 2004). Similar studies are emerging in relation to people with learning disabilities. Cross-culturally, for example, Nuttall (1998) has shown how by taking the name of a 'spirit child' (a deceased and distant relative) newborns (including those with learning disabilities) among Greenland Eskimos create a system of distributed competence for the child's welfare which draws distant family into the child's life. Booth and Booth (1998) in their study of children with at least one parent with a learning disability show that they fare better where there is a wider group supporting them.

Where such 'distributed competence' does not exist naturally to support both choice, and pursuit of choices, one strategy has been to develop 'purposive networks' (Wenger 1992). In the US the early 'circles of support' (Willer *et al.* 1993), developed around people with acquired brain injury, were of this purposive nature:

> The overriding purpose of these circles is to build inclusive communities, to enable people with disabilities to participate fully in their community, to contribute their talents, to

receive support and to be accepted as valued community members by building onto, or replicating natural networks in the community.

(Rowlands 2002: 56)

It is really important to emphasize that in this early work on circles of support, which is at the centre of PCPs, they were originally seen as community-based and professionals were seen neither as owners nor facilitators. It was about involving a network that knows or gets to know the person and will be there on an ongoing basis to play an active part in their lives. It can be argued that there has been at least some shift in emphasis or, put more cynically, colonization of person-centred planning by professionals compared to the early work around circles of support. But have they achieved community inclusion where other strategies have failed?

The latest research evidence is equivocal (see Chapters 22 and 25) and indicates that although PCP for those who have a plan led to benefits in community involvement, contact with family and friends and choice, there was little impact on social networks. The results also indicate differences across different groups and contexts, indicating that the potential and applicability of PCP may be limited (Robertson *et al.* 2007). It might be argued for those who do benefit from PCP in terms of community inclusion that the benefits are about 'lifestyle' changes. They have had little effect so far in helping to improve housing or employment outcomes for people.

The community in prospect

In this chapter an historical review of community involvement and inclusion as well as resultant policy responses since the 1960s, at the point of deinstitutionalization, have been outlined. Although change has occurred around inclusive education, day services and supported employment, and more fundamentally around housing, these have not challenged the architecture of exclusion. The majority of people with severe learning disabilities are still in segregated schools, most, albeit in smaller settings, living with other people with disabilities, with a huge majority not employed and showing few signs of becoming so.

In the introduction to this chapter it was argued that community living, social justice, community acceptance and well-being have yet to be achieved as a matter of course for people with learning disabilities. In these respects improvements in community living and presence and some indicators of positive lifestyle change must be set against signs that the community is still as unaccepting of people with learning disabilities as it has always been. For example, anti-social behaviour orders (ASBOs) empower the community to seek such orders for behaviours people in the community see to be of threat, and it appears that people with learning disabilities are much more likely to have an ASBO applied than others in society (Ramcharan *et al.* 2006). Acceptance of difference is still unlikely especially where the community is empowered to police itself. This still leaves open questions of social justice and well-being which are considered below.

Earlier it was argued that equal opportunity cannot be achieved by disabled people and people with learning disabilities where:

- environments, community and infrastructure are inaccessible;
- the level of support is insufficient to allow competition on an equal basis.

Yet even where environments have been made more accessible and support provided, the accomplishment of community inclusion remains illusory for many people with learning disabilities. Talking of those with the most profound disabilities, Reinders argues that:

> Our humanity is an endowment, not an achievement. Therefore the fact that profoundly disabled humans cannot claim achievement because of their absence of purposive agency does not affect their humanity in any way.

(Reinders 2008: 50)

In this view there is a necessity for social justice and distributive justice as *outcomes* which recognize society's commitment to producing the good life for all citizens independent of equality of opportunity. The UK has its own Human Rights Act (see Finnegan and Clarke 2005) and is signatory to the UN Convention on the Rights of People with Disabilities

(CRPD) which incorporates other UN conventions on civil and political as well as economic, social and cultural rights. The Convention was opened for signature on 30 March 2007 (the date the UK became signatory) and was ratified on 3 April 2008 (with the UK ratifying on 8 June 2009). Under various Articles the CRPD offers significant mechanisms to protect rights as humans, to produce equality under the law, to support participation in the political process and other areas that affect their lives. Rights to freedom of association and movement alongside the right to free speech, freedom of religion and thought are supplemented by a number of economic, social and cultural rights such as those shown in Box 30.1.

Despite the potential of the CRPD, Lecomte and Mercier argue (2009: 66) that 'the impact of the Convention on countries that already have disability legislation in place ... seems to be minimal'. Although there are reporting procedures to the UN under the CRPD in which countries should show incremental improvements, it is hard to see how countries such as the UK will not fare better than countries in which disability is a focus for some of the more severe infringements to fundamental and inalienable rights such as to life, freedom from torture, servitude or forced labour.

The potential of human rights frameworks and the application of a human rights-based approach to the fulfilment of rights in everyday life is yet to be tested and it is certainly the case that we are only now at the starting blocks in this regard. However, not everyone is convinced that a human rights-based approach will indeed deliver better lives:

> By raising issues of equal rights and social justice advocacy movements have successfully altered the course of public policy ... But it is important to realise that these have been in the domain of citizenship and have left unaffected the domain of personal intimacy ... Apart from the institutional barriers that can be removed by public policy, there are cultural barriers that are entrenched in people's hearts and minds. This is the reason why we need to think beyond rights and justice.
>
> (Reinders 2008: 6)

Box 30.1: Some Articles from the UN Convention on the Rights of People with Disabilities

Article 19

States Parties to this Convention recognize the equal right of all persons with disabilities to live in the community, with choices equal to others, and shall take effective and appropriate measures to facilitate full enjoyment by persons with disabilities of this right and their full inclusion and participation in the community, including by ensuring that:

(a) Persons with disabilities have the opportunity to choose their place of residence and where and with whom they live on an equal basis with others and are not obliged to live in a particular living arrangement.

(b) Persons with disabilities have access to a range of residential and other community support services, including personal assistance necessary to support living and inclusion in the community, and to prevent isolation or segregation from the community.

(c) Community services and facilities for the general population are available on an equal basis to persons with disabilities and are responsive to their needs.

Article 27

States Parties recognize the right of persons with disabilities to work, on an equal basis with others; this includes the right to the opportunity to gain a living by work freely chosen or accepted in a labour market and work environment that is open, inclusive and accessible to persons with disabilities. States Parties shall safeguard and promote the realization of the right to work.

Article 28

States Parties recognize the right of persons with disabilities to an adequate standard of living for themselves and their families, including adequate food, clothing and housing, and to the continuous improvement of living conditions, and shall take appropriate steps to safeguard and promote the realization of this right without discrimination on the basis of disability.

Value that supports community inclusion	Focus	Support structure	Nature of outcome
Autonomy and choice	Hopes, dreams, aspirations	Family, circles of support, social networks and professionals where necessary	Trust, love, reciprocity
Diversity	Recognizing worth, acceptance of difference, positive regard	'Being there'; a focus on changing community attitudes	Heterogeneity across communities; 'border-crossing' from excluded to included identity
Ordinary lives	Housing, education, work, leisure	Facilitating access and providing support for lives like the rest of society	An opportunity structure supporting everyday relationships; social networks common to the community
Community development and social capital	Bridging, bonding, accessing, funding inclusive initiatives	Community initiatives, fading out	Extended networks and communities of interest
Human rights	Protecting and fulfilling rights	A human rights-based approach	Equality with other citizens around civil, political, economic, social and cultural rights
Human capability and well-being approach	Supporting the acquisition of resources to maximize potential	A focus on self-actualization and fulfilment of well-being	Distributive justice and well-being as a human

Table 30.2 Values that support community inclusion, their focus, support structure and outcomes

The argument leaves us with yet another conundrum. If a human rights approach is insufficient to establish community involvement as an outcome, to what other frameworks can we look? Nussbaum (2000, 2006) argues that unequal political and social circumstances create inequality for the poor, for women and for people with disabilities. In contrast to socialist arguments proposing the need for equality of outcome, goods and services she provides a metric for distributive justice and a framework for measuring well-being. The metric for distributive

justice places a responsibility on the state to ensure that material and institutional resources are provided to support well-being as defined by the capability of life, health, bodily integrity, imagination and thought, emotions, practical reason, affiliation, regard for other species, play and control over one's own environment (Nussbaum 2007). It is in fulfilling such life needs to the maximum possible that, for Nussbaum, the good life is experienced. Perhaps most appealing in this approach is the recognition that:

Our humanity is an endowment, not an achievement. Therefore the fact that profoundly disabled humans cannot claim achievement because of their absence of purposive agency does not affect their humanity in any way.

(Reinders 2008: 50)

This means it is possible to commit resources independent of any personal achievement. The problem, however, is whether it will ever be politically expedient to commit resources in this way and whether communities can accept and live with diversity.

Exercise 30.4

In Table 30.2 some of the key values supporting the development of community are summarized. See if you can think of additional strategies, policies, service and support structures through which each might be accomplished.

References

Amado, A.N. (ed.) (1993) *Friendships and Community Connections between People with and without Developmental Disabilities.* Baltimore, MD: Paul H. Brookes.

Barclay, P. (1982) *Social Workers: Their Roles and Tasks.* London: Beresford Square Press.

Bayley, M. (1997) *What Price Friendship? Encouraging the Relationships of People with Learning Difficulties.* Wooton Courtenay: Hexagon Publishing.

Beyer, S., Kilsby, M. and Lowe, M. (1994) What do ATCs offer? A survey of Welsh day services, *Mental Handicap Research*, 7: 16–40.

Beyer, S., Kilsby, M. and Willson, C. (1995) Interaction and engagement of workers in supported employment: a British comparison between workers with and without learning disabilities, *Mental Handicap Research*, 42: 115–40.

Booth, T. and Booth, W. (1998) Risk, resilience and competence: parents with learning difficulties and their children, in R. Jenkins (ed.) *Questions of Competence: Culture, Classification and Intellectual Disability.* Cambridge: Cambridge University Press.

Boyle, G. (2008) Autonomy in long-term care: a need, a right or a luxury? *Disability and Society*, 23(4): 299–310.

Bridge, G., Forrest, R. and Holland, E. (2004) *Neighbouring: A Review of the Evidence*, www.neighbourhoodcentre.org.uk.

Bulmer, M. (1986) *Neighbours: The Work of Philip Abrams.* Cambridge: Cambridge University Press.

Burton, M. and Kagan, C. (2005) Decoding *Valuing People*: social policy for people who are learning disabled, *Disability and Society*, 21(4): 299–313.

Chapman, T. (1999) Stage sets for ideal lives: images of home in contemporary show homes, in T. Chapman and J. Hockey (eds) *Ideal Homes? Social Change in Domestic Life.* London: Routledge.

Department of Health (1971) *Better Services for the Mentally Handicapped.* Cmnd 4683. London: HMSO.

Department of Health (2009) *Valuing Employment Now: Real Jobs for People with Learning Disabilities.* London: Department of Health.

Emerson, E. and McVilly K.R. (2004) Friendship activities of adults with intellectual disabilities in supported accommodation in Northern England, *Journal of Applied Research in Intellectual Disabilities*, 17(3): 191–7.

Emerson, E., Robertson, J., Gregory, N., Kessissoglu, S., Hatton, C., Hallam, A. *et al.* (2000) The quality and costs of village communities, residential campuses and community based residential supports in the UK, *American Journal on Mental Retardation*, 105: 81–102.

Felce, D., Grant, G., Todd, S., Ramcharan, P., Beyer, S., McGrath, M. *et al.* (1998) *Towards a Full Life: Researching Policy Innovation for People with Learning Disabilities.* Oxford: Butterworth Heinemann.

Finnegan, P. and Clarke, S. (2005) *One Law for All? The Impact of the Human Rights Act on People with Learning Difficulties.* London: Values into Action.

Goldberg, D. and Huxley, P. (1980) *Mental Illness in the Community: The Pathway to Psychiatric Care.* London: Tavistock Publications.

Golding, L., Emerson, E. and Thornton, A. (2005) An evaluation of specialized community-based residential supports for people with challenging behavior, *Journal of Intellectual Disabilities*, 9(2): 145–54.

Goodley, D. (2005) Empowerment, self advocacy and resilience, *Journal of Intellectual Disabilities*, 9(4): 333–43.

Guest, A. and Wierzbicki, S. (1999) Social ties at the neighbourhood level: two decades of GSS evidence, *Urban Affairs Review*, 35(11): 1943–52.

Kenny, S. (2006) *Developing Communities for the Future.* Melbourne: Thompson.

King's Fund (1980) *An Ordinary Life.* London: King's Fund.

Lecomte, J. and Mercier, C. (2009) The emergence of human rights of persons with intellectual disabilities in international law: the cases of the Montreal Declaration on international disabilities and the United Nations Convention on the Rights of Persons with Disabilities, in F. Owen and D. Griffiths (eds) *Challenges to the Human Rights of People with Intellectual Disabilities.* London: Jessica Kingsley.

Lowe, K. and de Paiva, S. (1991) *NIMROD: An Overview.* London: HMSO.

Lunsky, Y. and Benson, B.A. (2001) Association between perceived social support and strain, and positive and negative outcome for adults with mild intellectual disability, *Journal of Intellectual Disability Research*, 45(2): 106–13.

Mansell, J. (1994) Specialised group homes for persons with severe or profound mental retardation and serious problem behavior in England, *Research in Developmental Disabilities*, 15(5): 371–88.

Nussbaum, M. (2000) *Women and Human Development: The Capabilities Approach*. Cambridge: Cambridge University Press.

Nussbaum, M. (2006) *Frontiers of Justice: Disability, Nationality, Species-Membership*. Cambridge, MA: Belknap Press.

Nussbaum, M. (2007) Twentieth anniversary reflections: human rights and human capabilities, *Harvard Human Rights Journal*, 20: 21–4.

Nuttall, M. (1998) *States and Categories: Indigenous Models of Personhood in Northwest Greenland*, in R. Jenkins (ed.) *Questions of Competence: Culture, Classification and Intellectual Disability*. Cambridge: Cambridge University Press.

O'Brien, J. and Lyle, C. (1987) *Framework for Accomplishment*. Decatur, GA: Responsive Systems Associates.

Odom, S.L., Klingerman, K. and Jakowski, M. (2004) Investigating inclusion: a review of research methods for individuals with intellectual disability, in E. Emerson, C. Hatton, T. Thompson and T.R. Parmenter (eds) *The International Handbook of Applied Research in Intellectual Disabilities*. Chichester: Wiley.

Peters, S. (1996) The politics of identity, in L. Barton (ed.) *Disability and Society: Emergent Issues and Insights*. Harlow: Addison Wesley Longman.

Putnam, R. (1998) Foreword, *Housing Policy Debate*, 9(1): v–viii.

Ramcharan, P., McClimens, A. and Roberts, B. (2006) People with learning difficulties should not get ASBOs, *Community Care*, 20 June.

Ramcharan, P., Whittell, B. and Grant, G. (2004) *Advocating for Work and Care: The Experience of Family Carers Seeking Work*. Sheffield: University of Sheffield.

Reinders, H.S. (2008) *Receiving the Gift of Friendship: Profound Disability, Theological Anthropology and Ethics*. Grand Rapids, MI: Eerdmans Publishing Co.

Robertson, J., Emerson, E., Gregory, M., Hatton, C., Kessissoglou, S., Hallam, A. *et al.* (2001a) Social networks of people with intellectual disabilities in residential settings, *Mental Retardation*, 39: 201–14.

Robertson, J., Emerson, E., Hatton, C., Gregory, N., Kessissoglou, S., Hallam, A. *et al.* (2001b) Environmental opportunities and supports for exercising self-determination in community-based residential settings, *Research in Developmental Disabilities*, 22(6): 487–502.

Robertson, J., Emerson, E., Hatton, C., Elliot, J., McIntosh, B., Swift, P. *et al.* (2007) Person-centred planning: factors associated with successful outcomes for people with intellectual disabilities, *Journal of Intellectual Disability Research*, 51(3): 232–43.

Roeher Institute (1990) *Making Friends: Developing Relationships between People with a Disability and Other Members of the Community*. Ontario: The Roeher Institute.

Rowlands, A. (2002) Circles of support building social networks, *British Journal of Therapy and Rehabilitation*, 9(2): 56–65.

Seebohm Report (1968) *Report of the Committee on Local Authority and Allied Personal Social Services*. London: HMSO.

Stancliffe, R. and Keane, S. (2000) Outcomes and costs of community living: a matched comparison of group homes and semi-independent living, *Journal of Intellectual and Developmental Disability*, 25(4): 281–305.

Taylor, S. (2001) The continuum and current controversies in the USA, *Journal of Intellectual and Developmental Disability*, 26(1): 15–33.

Taylor, S.J. and Bogdan, R. (1989) On accepting relationships between people with mental retardation and nondisabled people: towards an understanding of acceptance, *Disability, Handicap and Society*, 4(1): 21–36.

Taylor, S.J., Racino, J.A., Knoll, J.A. and Lutfiyya, Z. (1987) *The Nonrestrictive Environment: On Community Integration for People with the Most Severe Disabilities*. Syracuse, NY: Human Policy Press.

Taylor, S.J., Bogdan, R. and Lutfiyya, Z. (eds) (1995) *The Variety of Community Experience: Qualitative Studies of Family and Community Life*. Baltimore, MD: Paul H. Brookes.

Weiss, R.S. (1979) The fund of sociality, *Transaction/Society*, 6(9): 36–43.

Weiss, R.S. (1998) A taxonomy of relationships, *Journal of Social and Personal Relationships*, 15(5): 671–83.

Wenger, G.C. (1992) Bangor longitudinal study of ageing, *Generations Review*, 2: 6–8.

Willer, B.S., Allen, K., Anthony, J. and Cowlan, G. (1993) *Circles of Support for Individuals with Acquired Brain Injury*. Buffalo: Rehabilitation Research and Training Center on Community Integration of Persons with Traumatic Brain Injury, State University of New York.

Willmott, P. and Young, M. (1960) *Family and Class in a London Suburb*. London: Routledge and Kegan Paul.

Part Five
Ageing and end-of-life issues

In this final part of the book we consider ageing and end-of-life issues. Not so long ago, three score years and ten was a stage in life that very few people with severe learning disabilities would reach. How things have changed. Indeed, a 'good old age' is something to be enjoyed by increasing numbers of people, but the chapters in this section demonstrate that it is a life stage full of creative challenges for health and social care practitioners.

In common with the previous four parts of the book, Chapter 31 presents more narratives, this time about older people with learning disabilities. The reader should be aware that narrative accounts of older people with learning disabilities are still relatively rare. In the right hands, such narratives offer incredibly important insights into personal histories, telling us much about the ways in which society has moulded people, what people have in turn contributed to the world around them, and how they have made sense of their lives.

Kelley Johnson shows us that life in old age can indeed be a fruitful and rich picking, for some people more meaningful than earlier life stages. It need not be marked by an inexorable physical, psychological and social decline, though losses and disabling consequences do occur. Memories and reminiscences become an increasing part of people's lives, while hopes and dreams are ever present. The experience of later life fuses the past, present and future, as if to remind us not to reduce the complexities of old age to what people are able to utter or to their typical behaviour, important though these may be. There are also reminders in this chapter about not slipping into further stereotypes about ageing. The narratives demonstrate that everyone has a story to tell, and none are the same. They provide the reader with an appreciation of:

- different explanations for reactions to earlier traumatic events in people's lives;

- the importance of mementoes to people as ways of linking the past with the present;
- long-term consequences of losses in people's lives;
- evidence of forms of resistance to challenges and deprivation that can lead to resilience;
- the importance of dreams and aspirations in later life.

Christine Bigby in Chapter 32 tells us about ways in which older people with learning disabilities adapt as they age. She focuses on the active engagement and participation of older people, demonstrating that social inclusion is realizable for people in later life. Drawing on a template from gerontological research, she draws attention to social relationships and subjective perceptions where belonging, continuity and purpose are critical ingredients. The chapter reminds us that an understanding of later life in people with learning disabilities can be improved by knowledge of developments in mainstream gerontology. The chapter will help the reader to understand:

- ageing and diversity in older people with learning disabilities;
- the functions of informal support for older people;
- impacts of retirement policies;
- heuristics for enriching the social relations of older people;
- ways of engaging older people more meaningfully in plans and decision-making about their own lives.

Bereavement and end-of-life issues are the subjects of Chapter 33. Through a series of case studies, Sheila Hollins and Irene Tuffrey-Wijne depict experiences of death, loss and bereavement in the lives of older people with learning disabilities, their families and care workers. Taboos about death and dying, often involving conspiracies of silence, are identified that can prevent older people from securing the help they need. It is shown that with sensitive, timely and co-ordinated support, older people with learning disabilities can be assisted to work through these challenges, as long as they are kept at the centre of decision-making. The chapter helps the reader towards an understanding of:

- the complexities of end-of-life decision-making;
- ethical issues that can arise in relation to consent, risk and quality of life;
- involving and informing people about their personal health and illnesses;
- acting on the presumption of capacity in decision-making;
- issues faced by all those principally involved – people with learning disabilities, families and practitioners.

Chapter 34 addresses the subject of healthy and successful ageing. Taking a cue from Chapter 32, Gordon Grant reviews ideas and theories from the gerontological literature to inform a better understanding of healthy and successful ageing in people with learning disabilities. Paradoxically, it is shown that accessing health services remains problematic for many older people, and that services have much to accomplish in 'getting closer' to older people in everyday practice. Determinants of health in old age and how people make sense of their lives in later life are discussed. The practice implications of supporting healthy and successful ageing are also considered. This edition also summarizes the results of two recent 'state of science' reviews on this theme. The chapter seeks to provide the reader with an appreciation of:

- theories about healthy and successful ageing;
- the importance of life history and life cycle influences on later life adaptation;

- challenges for achieving 'person-centredness' in supporting older people;
- determinants of physical and mental health in later life;
- personal experiences of older people with learning disabilities.

Chapter 35, the last in this book, is quite different from all the others. Deliberately positioned at the very end, it represents an *envoi* or concluding word as well as a watershed. We have therefore left the last word to Jan Walmsley to say something about the evolution of the inclusive research agenda and how this may shape the search for knowledge in the future. It raises big questions about the ways we research the everyday lives of people with learning disabilities, and whether and how inclusive research can help to liberate people. Written at a time when agencies that fund research are seeking more meaningful ways to place research at the service of people with learning disabilities, the chapter can indeed be seen as a kind of watershed between old and new ways of thinking about the relations between research, the production of knowledge and the everyday lives of people with learning disabilities. In this chapter the reader is guided towards an understanding of:

- the genesis and evolution of inclusive research with people with learning disabilities;
- effects of the social model of disability on the development of inclusive research;
- differences between participatory and emancipatory research;
- alliances in research between people with learning disabilities, academics and others.

Enjoy this final part of the book, and leave time to reflect . . .

Where is the Life we have lost in living?
Where is the wisdom we have lost in knowledge?
Where is the knowledge we have lost in information?
(T.S. Eliot, *The Rock*, 1934)

31

A late picking: narratives of older people with learning disabilities

Kelley Johnson

A late picking – the old man sips his wine
And eyes his vineyard flourishing row on row.
Ripe clusters, hanging heavy on the vine,
Catch the sun's afterglow.

(Hope 1975)

Introduction

Sometimes the best wine comes late in the season. And for some older people with learning disabilities life may reach its fullness and its strength later in life (Bigby 2000). Of course this is not always so. It is a mistake to believe that the lives of all people with learning disabilities follow a similar trajectory. For some people increasing age may lead to physical fragility which can disrupt the very foundations of their former lives (Allen *et al.* 2005a, b) and sometimes the responsibilities that come with age, such as caring for parents or the death of family or close friends, can seem overwhelming (Hiscoe and Johnson 2006). However, the narratives in this chapter do suggest that for some people with learning disabilities their later years are indeed experienced as a 'late picking'.

I feel somewhat uncomfortable about writing a chapter which documents the life narratives of people with learning disabilities. Surely they can speak for themselves? Many can. However, access to editors, to publishers and to the written word remain problematic for many people with learning disabilities who have a story to tell. This may be particularly true for older people who have sometimes had less access to formal education and fewer opportunities to be heard. Others find articulating their experience in spoken or written ways very difficult or impossible. This chapter provides a space for some of these voices to be heard. It also provides a place where questions can be asked about people's lives and where the role of a researcher

who works with people with learning disabilities can be explored and made subject to questions.

Where do the narratives come from?

The life narratives which make up a substantial part of this chapter have been contributed by three different people with whom I have worked over the past ten years. It is important to explore how they were written and in what circumstances, and in particular the role which I played in their production. The position of the writer in what are originally largely oral narratives is important because it can shape the way people's stories are told and the way in which they are documented (Goodley *et al.* 2004). Each of these narratives is accompanied by a short commentary and by a series of questions for reflection. One of the narratives in this chapter is essentially a case study while the others are autobiographical accounts or autobiographies (Walmsley and Atkinson 2000). They come from three different research studies which are briefly described below.

Deinstitutionalizing women

'In the early 1990s I spent 20 months in a locked unit in a large Australian institution for people with learning disabilities' (Johnson 1998a, b). Twenty-one women lived in the unit and all had been labelled as having learning disabilities and challenging behaviour. They ranged in age from early twenties to 72 years old and they had had very diverse life experiences. Most were not able to tell their stories directly.

Lena Johnson's narrative, which is included in this chapter, was developed by talking with her over time, reading her files, observing her life in the locked unit and talking with staff about her. Lena found it difficult to talk about her life in any extended way but did make very clear some of the things she had done and the nature of her preferences. I did not show Lena the account I wrote of her life because it was completed after she had left the institution and because it would have been difficult for her to make sense of a narrative presented in this fashion. I continue to feel somewhat uncomfortable about this. The words in Lena's story are mine although I use quotes from her and from her institutional files to develop what is essentially a case study.

Living safer sexual lives

This was a large action research study in which 13 women and 12 men with learning disabilities talked with researchers over an extended period of time about their lives (Johnson *et al.* 2000; Harrison *et al.* 2002; Frawley *et al.* 2003; Walmsley and Johnson 2003). The study had a strong focus on relationships and sexuality but we held the view that this issue should be seen within the context of people's lives. I met with the woman whose narrative is included in this chapter for several hours at her home over three different visits. We talked together about her life and with her permission I taped our discussion, taking the resulting narrative back to her for approval or change.

Life history project in Ireland

In 2006–07 I undertook a national project in the Republic of Ireland as a Marie Curie Research Fellow at Trinity College in Dublin. The project focused on supporting people with learning disabilities to under-take their own research. As part of the project I worked with Patrick Kearney whose life story in an edited form appears in this chapter. Patrick is an older man who has now retired and lives in supported accommodation. Patrick was very keen to tell his life story and to have it published. We met three times at his home to talk about his life and then to finalize the story. Photographs of his earlier life were added and the life history was finally published as a book (Kearney with Johnson 2009). This chapter has a shortened version of Patrick's book to which he has given his consent.

Exercise 31.1

Developing narratives which are not the direct written words of the person concerned is always problematic because the writer's attitudes, views and concerns may determine what is included. Reflect on the two ways in which narratives were gathered for this chapter. What differences might you expect to see in the style and content?

Narratives usually exclude people who are not able to tell their story. What kinds of method can be used so that people who are not able to converse with others can also be heard?

The position of the researcher and writer is important. I am an Anglo-Australian woman in my middle years now working in the UK. I work as an academic and as an advocate with people with disabilities. How might these characteristics influence the way I collaborate with people with learning disabilities who are contributing narratives? Think about yourself. What characteristics might impact on work you might do with people with learning disabilities either in direct service provision or in research?

Some people with learning disabilities feel very strongly about the 'ownership' of information about them. How far do you think these narratives are owned by the people who contributed them? How far do you think that they are really 'my' stories as the writer?

Lena Johnson: 'Lena is all ready'

'Lena's probably always been like this and she's too old to change' (staff member in the locked unit).

Lena lived in a locked unit within a large institution when I met her. She was aged 72. She was a short sturdy woman who was extremely fit. Each day she would arrive in the room where the women spent most of their days, carefully dressed, most often in a pleated skirt and a matching grey and red jumper. Her short grey hair was always carefully combed. She sat primly on the vinyl couch with her feet together and her hands in her lap. Unlike the other women in the unit, her front teeth had not been removed. She was a very sociable woman with a loud voice and a constant flow of conversation that referred to herself always in the third person. ('Lena is all ready. She has her good clothes on.') Until she was 64 she had lived with her mother in the wider community. She spoke often of her mother who was 100 years old and lived in a nursing home where Lena visited her on a fortnightly basis. Sometimes she talked about her former home and the vegetable garden, her visits to the races and the card games with her mother's friends. She was highly skilled, could cook, clean, ride a bicycle and knew the basics of driving a car (though she did not have a licence).

When Lena's mother became ill she was sent to the institution. At first she was in an open unit with other older women. Although staff recorded that she was kind to these women for the first few months, she had little in common with them. All were frail, many could not speak and none had her kinds of skills. After some time there were staff reports that Lena was attacking the other women in the unit and that she had 'dirty habits'. As a result she was moved to the locked unit where she lived for four years. There was little for her to do there, although sometimes she assisted staff in folding the clean clothes. Lena very much enjoyed knitting but staff only allowed her to do this on rare occasions because she had attacked some other women in the unit with the knitting needles. There were no books or magazines in the unit. She could not go outside except on twice-weekly walks in the grounds. She had no friends in the unit.

In the locked unit, she would frequently climb through the windows in an effort to escape. Staff would watch her in amusement and then go out to fetch her back. She collected small items from other women in the unit or from staff and hid them carefully, in her bed, her clothes and her shoes. Sometimes she left a neat pile of faeces behind the couch in the day room.

In the years since her admission to the institution she had been on large doses of largactil and melleril which had been stopped by staff in the locked unit. She was now the only woman there who was not on some form of tranquillizer. During the closure of the institution there was much discussion about Lena's future.

There was general consensus among staff in the locked unit that she should live in the community. However, regional staff, responsible for supporting her there, refused to accept her so she was matched to a large metropolitan institution. Advocacy by one staff member and myself prevented this and she was eventually matched to a community residential unit in the country. The locked unit was closed relatively early in the institutional closure process and Lena was moved to another unit with different staff and additional residents. At this time her mother died unexpectedly.

Lena attended the funeral and then visited her former home for the last time. She was helped to dig up some rhubarb roots as a lasting memory of her former life. She had no photographs and no other mementoes. The house was sold.

Commentary

Becoming older inevitably means loss of many different kinds: relationships, work and sometimes home. In the space of eight years, Lena had lost a whole way of life, her family, the less restricted lifestyle in the open unit and then what passed as her home within the locked unit. Finally her mother died.

Lena's reactions to these traumatic life events were interpreted by those around her in terms of 'challenging behaviour'. Another way of looking at her reactions may be to see them in terms of her grief-filled response to very traumatic life events (Sinason 1992).

Alternatively her behaviour could be seen as one form of resistance to the position in which she had been placed. Her behaviour can then be seen as a way of attempting, unconsciously or consciously, to change the situation in which she found herself and as a way of escaping from it.

For all of us, but particularly for many older people, the memories of a past life, reminiscences and the presence of photographs and mementoes are important ways of linking present and past experience. Lena had nothing. Unlike many other older people with learning disabilities, Lena had spent most of her life in the community. With brief exceptions, when she was admitted to respite care, she had lived with her mother and had had a relatively 'ordinary life'. Once her mother became ill and old, institutional care was seen as the only solution. Other older people with disabilities may find themselves placed in nursing home care or feel at constant risk of reinstitutionalization (West 2000; Allen *et al.* 2005b).

Exercise 31.2

The professional training we receive provides us with ways of seeing the world. Sometimes this can lead us to ignore or neglect important aspects of people's lives that lie outside our professional focus. How do you think the professional training of the people working with Lena may have limited their ability to relate to her?

If you were working with Lena, what changes would you have wanted to make to her life circumstances to give her a better quality of life?

What strategies would you use to work with someone on loss issues, particularly if they found it difficult to tell you about them?

Margaret Crowley: 'I wanted it real nice . . . not sex like that'

I'm 57. I live in Broadmeadows. I live by myself. I do cooking and that. Cleaning up a bit and all that. I do it on my own. Sometimes Tim comes over and helps me.

He lives down at Altona. I've been in this flat since October. Before that I've been all over the place. I couldn't share with anybody any more because things happen. I couldn't share with people because they used to get upset or things like that or eat my food off my plate. And wear my clothes.

I go out to work at the neighbourhood house. Part-time job cleaning. I'm on the committee. I go out and teach about legal rights and I'm on the board of an advocacy group. I do art and I do reading and writing. I'm going to be involved with Stepping Out, a new advocacy group. That will be next year probably. We're going to have a conference. I'm always out.

Dad went to war and mum couldn't look after us. I didn't know she had a disability. He came back from the war. But I thought he went to war and didn't come back. I only remember him when he used to come back from war. He used to lift me up in the air. I was taken away when I was 2 years old. Two years old I was taken away. We all got split up. Tim, me, Pearl, Maree, Jimmy, May. I went into a convent and I was only there for a little while and then I got sent away from my sister and I went to the Manor House. And I went to school there.

It was alright. We used to have dates, Irish dancing, the bishop came. We had parties and all that. We had a holiday house down at the beach. And we used to have stars. Stars, like if you were tidy or things like that or you did it good. You got a star and then you got a prize. And then we used to have church and say the rosary and all that.

I knew I had a mother but I used to cry every night and all that. I had jobs. I couldn't keep jobs. I used to mind children, two children and clean up the place and things like that. I used to come out and go to this lady's place. And the lady said 'Oh you're a good worker.' But I was getting sick, I was getting tired. I used to lay on the bed and go to sleep. I was only a teenager, 16 or 17. I was crying and bumping my head against the wall. And the nuns said, 'Oh you're playing up.' And I used to never go to bed. I used to sleep on the floor and the next morning I used to get up and all that. I used to run down the paddock with no shoes on.

And I was starting to get sick. 'Cause I wanted me mum. She didn't visit me until I was about 14. We all went into this big party and I didn't know my mum was there and two brothers. Big brother and little brother. And I didn't know. And she came over and I remember that it was me mum and all that. And then I went over to one of the nuns, 'That's my mum, that's my mum.' And I threw my arms around her and started to cry. And then dad, my stepfather was there. My stepfather said, 'Come on, come on come and sit by me.' And all the girls were sitting around looking and all that and we were talking and he gave me a kiss on the head. And then it was time to go. So we all went separate ways and I turned back and start looking and all that. They had gone. And then I started to get sick.

At the Manor House I used to work in the kitchen and things like that. The nuns put me away. Because I just wanted me mum. Because I was running away. From the Manor House. Going to people's places. I run to a shop and the lady said, 'Oh where do you come from?' I said I came from the Manor House and so she gave me a drink of water and rang the Manor House up. The nuns came and I went back with them.

They didn't tell me they were going to put me in Hillside [an institution for people with intellectual disabilities]. They put me in this infirmary. And it was small with about four beds. And I used to sleep on the floor. I wouldn't sleep on the bed. I used to sleep on the floor. And the doctor came and said why is she sleeping on the floor. 'Oh she wants to.' And the doctor gave me a needle in the leg so I wouldn't run away and I had to have a shower and they packed my case. Some of the clothes in it wasn't belonging to me. And so they packed my case and didn't tell me where I was going. And we got in, I think it was a taxi. I can't remember. And one nun sat on one side and one on the other side so I wouldn't jump out. How can I jump out because I was all dopey?

I went to Stony Glen [psychiatric hospital] and the two nuns went inside and I was sitting out in reception. The two nuns came out and said, 'Oh good-bye good-bye' and left me. And left me there. And I had to go in this big dormitory and I was crying. I had to get undressed. And they were having supper. And I was crying. And the doctor came and I wouldn't look at him. I was under the blankets and wouldn't look at him. And the doctor asked me a few things.

'Oh what . . . oh do you hear voices?' I said 'No I don't hear no voices. I miss my mum.' So after that he went off. And the next morning I had to have shock treatment. Shock treatment. 'Cause I was doing all these things and that. Laying down and running away and laying on the ground. So after that I had shock treatment, not all at once, now and again. I was getting a lot better.

The nuns only came to see me about twice that's all and then they didn't come back. They didn't want me back. So then the doctors said, 'You're going to a nice ward you're going to Hillside. Going into a nice ward. Going into an open ward.'

And so I went in the bus and that. And they said, 'Look over there. You're going right up on that hill.' So I went there and I had to go and see all these doctors and they asked me questions and things like that and I had to go to the receiving ward. I was there for a couple of months. I can't remember how long. And then I stayed down there and they decided to shift me. To F28. That was up the top [of the hill]. I was upset I wouldn't eat me meals and wouldn't come inside for the staff. I used to lay out in the yard and six or more staff used to drag me inside. I used to go right out in the yard but I wouldn't move and this staff sister said, 'Well get her inside.' I wouldn't come inside. So I didn't have no food. But when the sister came out I used to go in for her. I wouldn't go in for the nurses. And then when she didn't come on duty they used to drag me inside and shove the food in my mouth and things like that. I used to tear my clothes up. Smash windows and all that. Smash windows and tear clothes. And they used to put me, drag me in a single room and no clothes on and there was a bar thing on the window. Then I started to get better. Because me mum started to come. She started visiting me. Because she used to visit Tim, my brother. But I didn't know. I didn't know he was there.

She didn't know that I was up there. And the sisters and nurses didn't tell her, didn't tell me mum. So Pearl me sister was up there too. And she had a boyfriend. And that's how I got to know how my brother was there. Pearl had a boyfriend and over the fence we used to talk to the boys. So that's how I found out. And then I called out, 'Are you really my brother?' And he said 'Yes.' So I had this long dress on; no shoes on.

My hair wasn't done properly and that. Then he went back and told the staff. And the staff must have rung up the ward that I was in. And they said yes there is two Crowleys. And then she started coming.

I was in Hillside for 25 years. I worked there. I worked there, scrubbed floors, made beds, swept floors, scrubbed all the skirting boards. If it wasn't done properly you had to do it again. Things like that. We didn't get paid for work. If you gave someone a meal you got punished. A nurse lost her ring and we all got punished. Weren't allowed to talk in the day room. Weren't allowed to go to bed.

I went and saw the social worker and said I want to get out. I was scared at first. So I had a lot of chances to go out. I didn't take them. Then this lady came and she said do you want to go to Mayberry House and I said, 'Oh yeah I want to go to Mayberry House.' It was a halfway house and all that. So I wanted to go. I was a bit nervous and they said goodbye and all that. Tim was there. He was out. Tim was out at the time. I was sitting there thinking, 'What am I going to do?' Sitting down and me brother came in. 'What am I going to do?' 'Do you want to go out?' And I said, 'Oh yes I want to go out.' Live it all up. I was drinkin'. Tim used to work and things like that. We used to have big jugs of beer and all that.

We used to be upset. We come out of Hillside. I mean we used to drown our sorrows. We used to drink and all that. We hadn't done it before and things like that. And Mayberry House was terrible. Oh I was sick. I had to see what do you call it a psychiatrist. He didn't say much. I was scared of him. I was scared of this lady on the staff. Oh she used to bang on the table and all. Oh she shouted at me. She didn't hit people. She used to dope me up and things like that.

After Mayberry House I went to some people from Hillside. I used to look after them and feed them 'cause they couldn't do that. I thought I wasn't going to look after them. I didn't want to. I said, 'I'm not going to stay here.' So we all went to our separate house. I went by myself. I went by myself with this other girl. She had psych problems. She got this carving knife. She nearly hurt me. I said, 'I'm not going to stay here. I'm not staying here.'

One minute she was all right and the next minute she was orf. So I never used to come home. I used to go out and I didn't come back. I lived in lots of different places. Now I live on my own.

I was in Stony Glen and they had dances and things like that in Stony Glen. And I went over by myself to the dance and met this boy and that and then he took me over to the dance, went behind the tree I was scared. He put his thing, you know his penis, out and I got scared and I ran away. And I said, 'Oh oh' and I ran back and I told the staff and staff said, 'Don't go there any more.' Down to the dance.

I must have been about 18. I didn't really know what he wanted. I was scared 'cause it was my first time 'cause I was in the convent. I knew nothing about sex. Because I came from the convent. And came out and didn't know.

Staff didn't talk to us about sex. But like when I was in Hillside I can't remember now but they showed a video about babies, babies coming out and all that. The staff used to get off with other residents up there. It was awful. Well I was working in the laundry and one of the staff said to me, 'Come on, come into my car and we'll go . . .' But I didn't get into his car.

Well at Hillside I went down the paddock, down the paddock, I went down the paddock. With a bloke who lived in one of the other units. First we went to the dance. At Hillside. You were allowed to dance with him and that. We went down there to the paddock. 'Cause you didn't have any privacy. Weren't allowed to go in people's rooms. He took me clothes off. He took me clothes off and things like that and I said, 'Oh geez.' And I went looking down looking to see if anyone was coming. 'Cause I got scared. So then the bloke was laying on top of me. And he wouldn't get off me. He wouldn't get off. I said, 'Get off me. Get off me.' I started putting me clothes back on. He wouldn't get off me. I wanted it real nice but not sex like that. So I told him you know get off me. But he wouldn't get off me. I saw him after that. I was dancing with him and that. I didn't really want to dance with him.

The other bloke I met. He was quite nice. He lived at Hillside too. He was quite nice. We went into the toilet and we had condoms. He had it on. He went to do it and it snapped. So he said, 'I'm not going to do it again.' So we didn't do it any more. He got scared. And then another time I went into his room we had sex. He got scared of the staff. So I got into bed but we didn't do anything because of the staff. I writ a letter, stupid me writ a letter to him and the staff got it. We weren't allowed to see each other any more. He said to me 'cause he was getting out he said to me, 'Oh can you get out 'cause I'm getting out.' He said, 'Well you don't ask you'll be in there forever.' That's what he said and that. But I didn't go out.

When I got out I met this man in Carlton. We got engaged. And everything was going all right. He used to come to Mayberry House and see me. I had an engagement party. Things like that. I was going to get married. I was looking forward to it. He was going to move out of that place and go to a cleaner place. Then a dreadful thing happened. Part of it was I didn't know what I was doing. It was another bloke, and me boyfriend and they got stuck into me. They didn't rape me. I can't remember now it was so long ago. I got sick and things like that. They didn't beat me up. They did sex to me. I was so upset. I was drunk. They were gentle.

And then the boyfriend said, 'Oh you knew all about that didn't you?' I didn't see him any more. I felt terrible. And I wasn't engaged any more.

Later I got engaged again you know. He was all right. But he went off with me flatmate. I don't think he loved me very much. Well he didn't sit by me he didn't sit next to me at the train. He sat somewhere else. He didn't hang on to me hand.

And things like that. He didn't give me a bed. He made me sleep on the floor. Yeah on the floor, on the couch. He didn't give me his bed. We had intercourse a couple of times. We had a good relationship. He used to come over for weekends and things like that.

I wanted somebody like I've got now, like I've got now. A nice one now. And we go out together and he stays here for weekends and all things like that. He touches me first and things like that. See the blokes I go with you know. They just want sex I think. Dave's all right. But the others yeah.

I met Dave down at Coburg. Near the station and he asked me. To be his you know girlfriend. And I said, 'Yes.' I thought I'd chance it. He was on his bike. I thought I'd give him a chance. I don't want it to be like the others. He cares about me. He helps with housework. Sometimes he'll cook for me. And I'll cook for him and we'll share. We didn't have intercourse straight away. We have intercourse now and again. I won't have it without a condom and he says that's all right. I want to get married. We want to get married in the gardens. I'm just thinking about getting married. We've been together nearly seven weeks I think. He stayed the last week. The weekend. It was all right. He helped me cook and that and those things were good.

I couldn't have children. Too old. Must have been about 39 or something. 'Cause I got out of Hillside then. I didn't have children I didn't have a chance to and I love children. I used to look after children in Hillside. Taught them how to sweep the floor how to make the beds when they were small.

Commentary

Supporting Margaret to tell her story was a very emotional experience for me. At many levels her story is bleak. The losses of relationships and lifestyle that many of us experience as we get older happened for her in early life. The loss of her family, particularly her mother, wounded her deeply and left scars that she still carries. For Margaret this loss explains much of her later behaviour which was interpreted by those around her as either 'mad' or 'challenging'. Like many women with learning disabilities Margaret was denied any of the stereotypical roles of adult women, as worker, lover or mother (Asch and Fine 1988, 1992; Johnson and Traustadottir 2000). Yet in some ways her life was also a distorted mirror of the lives of often poor women in the wider community: hard unpaid (or poorly paid) work, caring for children (though not her own) and those in need, and few opportunities for leisure. However, for her there were not the intimate adult relationships, the links with family and friends that other women may find as part of their lives. For her these came later. Bleak though her story is, she is resilient and resists negative life experiences. She enjoys now, in later life, a flat of her own, peace and meaningful activities. These things are accompanied by a hope that the future may offer a loving relationship. It is as if the expectations of early adulthood have been pushed into older life: a late picking indeed.

Ageing and end-of-life issues

Exercise 31.3

Margaret's story is rich in detail and memory. Yet in many instances we fail to take account of the memories and experiences of people with learning disabilities. What difference does it make to our perceptions of people if we see them as having a past and memories?

How do we balance the understanding of the person that comes from knowing their past, their memories and their dreams with the need for them to have privacy?

How could you have supported Margaret to lead 'an ordinary life' in her younger years?

Patrick Kearney: I'm happy as Larry

Childhood. As poor as a church mouse

We lived for 27 years in Corofin down near the end of the village. It's about eight miles from Ennis. It was a thatched house. It was falling down at the back and we couldn't get a thatcher for love or money. It was a long house. And the back wall was splitting open, spreading out at the back and we were afraid the whole lot would collapse. It was beautiful. You put down a big fire by night and your sins would be burned. It was so hot you couldn't stand in front of it. We used to make lovely sweet cakes at Christmas and buns and that years ago. There was only the kitchen and one room. I slept on the settle bed in the kitchen. My mother and grandmother slept in the other room . . . We had to move because the house in Corofin was falling down . . . My grandmother was working on the railways on the gates of the railway for 40 years and she used to do laundry for the guest houses. And then she had a shilling for the shirt and one and six for a blouse and you had to starch it and iron it. And all she had in her lifetime was ten bob pension . . . Mother was a tall bony woman. A great woman. We used to go to the pictures in Corofin and we go on Wednesday night and Friday night and Sunday night. I like the cowboys. The we wah wahs, the we wah wahs and the big chief.

I worked. I brought timber. I brought 190 bats on my back for my mother in the house. On holidays, I would start at 9 and I wouldn't finish until 6 or 7 o'clock in the evening. The only time I got off would be on a Sunday.

It was very tough, very tough, very tough, very tough [at school]. I was bullied from the first day I went to school till the day I left it. I was called dunce. Kearney the dunce . . . The teacher used to call me Kearney the dunce. I got my own fucking back when she died. I said, 'May she rot down the pits of hell.' I was at school till I was 14 years. And I left it then and I wasn't bloody sorry. I was coming home from school one evening and this is true and the grown-up boys naked me they naked me. They caught me beyond Shannon's Lane and it was the month of October and they hit me with a stick and they beat me with nettles and they put marks across my back. And they tied my hands behind my back and I couldn't free myself. And put my clothes up beside the wall. I couldn't get them. It was desperate. And I was shaking with the cold. The gardai had to get them. The guard dressed me and brought me down . . .

I was bullied and I hate bullying. I hate it. It don't happen now. Because I stand on my own two feet and nobody walks on me. From my point of view it is a good thing that doesn't happen now because I couldn't put up with it. I couldn't really put up with that now . . .

A working life

After I left school I used to clean cabins and I used to bring the hay in with the farmers and I used to dig the market garden out the back and clean it up and sort potatoes and all that . . . All I had was five bob a week to live and get milk on. That was what you called relief.

[Then] we went to the railway gates . . . we had to be up at 8 o'clock in the morning and start opening the gates. Two lots and then you had to put up the signal lamp. And you put that up and you had a light inside and oil or something so it wouldn't blow with the wind. And you closed down the shutter. And that would be for the train. That was my job . . . You worked every day: Sunday and Monday. I did it for 15 years. I didn't get nothing. I didn't get a penny. I didn't get a thing for the gate. All we got was the house. I took it as a cross I couldn't do nothing about it. My mother was there at that time. But she wasn't very well and couldn't very well do it like . . . My grandmother too . . . The trains were all taken away. All taken away. The gates and all were taken away. All gone now.

I [then] worked at the Brothers of Charity workshop in Ennis for 17 years. It was a long time. I did like making the altar bread . . . I worked in the garden at the workshop for a long number of years. Every morning I worked . . . Well you got up in the morning at 8 o'clock and you had your lunch at 11 o'clock and you came in and did chores in the garden . . . Well to a certain extent I was the boss in the garden. I had to see that everything was done to the manager's satisfaction like. One fella wouldn't do a thing. Not as much as an iota. He stood up against like the wall. He stood up against the wall. Leaned against the wall. And I said to him one day I said, 'I'm sorry I have to disturb you', I said, 'I have to see the wall.' [Things changed.] All the good boys left for other jobs and it wasn't the same. The life was gone. All I got a week was a fiver and then I went down to (the garden) and then I got a tenner.

Life now

I like everything about my life now as you know now. I tell you the truth. I like to have company. I like to be talking to people. And having auld chats and thinking about things that have gone by years ago when I was small. I've been in this house in Dormers Lane up from Hogan's shop for three years. Oh it has been grand. It's mighty to be here. And I love it and I wouldn't lose it now. I like the atmosphere of it. I like the people here and the boys and girls who come here. I like it. I have a lovely room. I do, with my television and a beautiful bed, a new bed there. And I have my tape recorder and I have two guitars, two musical guitars . . . I can do anything I like in the kitchen. I sit down and watch the television if I want to or if I don't want to I can play on my banjo. I can have an old talk like I'm having to you now and I think it is very very good to have that. And be broadminded and get what you have to say out.

And I go to Clarecastle every Thursday. Clarecastle has a centre. For old people. And I go there every Thursday. And I bring my banjo . . . We play bingo and I got four euros last week. I am fairly alright at it . . . Well some days I goes out walking. With the people in the house and come back walking . . . I used to look after this garden here. We put down onions. They were very big this year . . . I go to hurling games in Ennis . . .

I get on well with the people here. There's three of them . . . There are house parents . . . They are a nice kind of people in this house . . . I saw my family at Christmas. I was at Michael's house for Christmas and I got my Christmas dinner and I was there for Christmas Eve and for St Stephen's Day . . .

I'm not wealthy but I'm comfortable as the man says. People here look after me. I think myself that if you are happy everyone is happy. If you are sad everyone is sad. And you have to grin and bear it. I am happy. I am as happy as the day goes long. And I'm happy as Larry.

Commentary

Unlike the other people whose life stories are in this chapter, Patrick lived all his life in one community, mostly in a small rural village in Ireland. This experience shaped both the ways he viewed others in his world and himself. A strong theme in both the shortened life story here and in the extended one is the important role his family played in his life: particularly his grandmother and his mother. They were advocates for him and while poor he remembers with great detail and love the good times that he had with them. And this was a reciprocal relationship even from childhood. He worked all his life. While some older people with learning disabilities experienced some form of institutional living, it is important to remember that many people lived with their parents for a large part of their lives and contributed to their family and to the wider community. Patrick's life is also a reminder that life in the community is not always positive. His experiences of bullying, of difficult times at the village school and his difficulty in getting paid work suggest that it was not easy to gain acceptance in this small community. For Patrick, independence and meaningful work were important to him. While he may not have earned (any) or much in wages he talks with great energy and detail of the work on the railways and later in the then sheltered workshop. Of his life now, in retirement, he writes 'I'm as happy as Larry.' With supported housing life has become easier; a bedroom of his own, freedom and opportunities to meet people and to share stories are important themes to him, as is his continuing link with his family.

Exercise 31.4

What differences and similarities do you find between Patrick's experience and that of Margaret and Lena? How important do you think gender and culture are in shaping the way these people have lived their lives?

What lessons can we learn from Patrick's lifelong experience of living in the community? How far do you think things have changed for people with learning disabilities?

What role do you think that services should play in the lives of people with learning disabilities? And how should we support people as the move towards more personalized living gains ground?

Conclusion

A late picking. For some people with learning disabilities later life can be richer and more meaningful than their earlier lives. This is particularly true for those people who are now entering later life, as can be seen in Chapter 34, which provides some theorizing about healthy and successful ageing. The hope is that the dreams and hopes that they are carrying into their older years are ones that can be achieved more readily by younger people now.

The narratives in this chapter reveal how important the personal construction of a life is as we get older. Margaret and Patrick speak from within their lives. There are memories, dreams, hopes and wounds. They see their lives as ordinary. They are not victims to themselves but people who are seeking meaning and love in their lives. In contrast, Lena's narrative comes from the outside. I did not know what motivated her nor what her dreams and fears were. I could make inferences about this; guess between the lines. As a result her narrative is less internal, less real. Yet many of us work with people who find it difficult to articulate their past and their dreams. We need to be aware constantly that 'not being able to say it' does not mean that the person's inner world does not exist, a lesson that emerges with respect to end-of-life care (Chapter 33). We need to act and relate always on the assumption that it is there.

As people grow older their experience of life also extends and memories and reminiscences become increasingly a part of their lives. A failure on the part of those around them to value or to learn about these things reduces the complexity of an individual to a snapshot of current behaviour. Nor should we assume that because people are growing older they are ceasing to dream of what might still be in their lives. For people who have been denied many of the experiences that those without a disability take for granted, such dreams may focus on newly opened possibilities. For others the dreams may be different. To be aware of the reality of dreams for individuals can shift the way we work with them, making our responses more exciting and stimulating and changing the way we see both 'older people' and those with disabilities.

Note

This project was funded by the Victorian Health Promotion Foundation and was undertaken at the Australian Research Centre in Sex, Health and Society at La Trobe University, Melbourne. I would like to acknowledge the other principal researchers on this project: Dr Lynne Hillier and Dr Lyn Harrison.

References

Allen, T., Traustadottir, R. and Spina, L. (2005a) It's never too late, in K. Johnson and R. Traustadottir (eds) *In and Out of Institutions: Deinstitutionalisation and People with Intellectual Disabilities*. London: Jessica Kingsley.

Allen, T., Traustadottir, R. and Spina, L. (2005b) A home before I die? in K. Johnson and R. Traustadottir (eds) *In and Out of Institutions: Deinstitutionalisation and People with Intellectual Disabilities*. London: Jessica Kingsley.

Asch, A. and Fine, M. (1988) Introduction: beyond pedestals, in M. Fine and A. Asch (eds) *Women with Disabilities: Essays in Psychology, Culture and Politics*. Philadelphia, PA: Temple University Press.

Asch, A. and Fine, M. (1992) Beyond pedestals: revisiting the lives of women with disabilities, in M. Fine (ed.) *Disruptive Voices: The Possibilities of Feminist Research*. Ann Arbor, MI: University of Michigan Press.

Bigby, C. (2000) *Moving on Without Parents: Planning, Transitions and Sources of Support for Middle-aged and Older Adults with Intellectual Disability*. Eastgardens: McLennan and Petty.

Frawley, P., Johnson, K., Hillier, L. and Harrison, L. (2003) *Living Safer Sexual Lives: A Training and Resource Pack for People with Learning Disabilities and Those Who Support Them*. Brighton: Pavilion.

Goodley, D., Lawthom, R., Clough, P. and Moore, M. (2004) *Researching Life Stories. Method, Theory and Analyses in a Biographical Age*. London: Routledge and Falmer.

Harrison, L., Johnson, K., Hillier, L. and Strong, R. (2002) Nothing about us without us: the ideals and realities of participatory action research with people with an intellectual disability, *Scandinavian Journal of Intellectual Disability Research*, 5(2): 56–70.

Hiscoe, C. and Johnson, K. (2006) Be there for me. Case management in my life, in C. Bigby, C. Fyffe and E. Ozanne (eds) *Planning and Support for People with Intellectual Disabilities*. London: Jessica Kingsley.

Hope, A.D. (1975) *A Late Picking*. London: Angus & Robertson.

Johnson, K. (1998a) *Deinstitutionalising Women: An Ethnographic Study of Institutional Closure*. Melbourne: Cambridge University Press.

Johnson, K. (1998b) Deinstitutionalisation: the management of rights, *Disability and Society*, 13(3): 375–87.

Johnson, K. and Traustadottir, R. (2000) Finding a place, in R. Traustadottir and K. Johnson (eds) *Women with Intellectual Disabilities: Finding a Place in the World*. London: Jessica Kingsley.

Johnson, K., Hillier, L., Harrison, L. and Frawley, P. (2000) *People with Intellectual Disabilities: Living Safer Sexual Lives*. Melbourne: Australian Research Centre in Sex, Health and Society, La Trobe University.

Kearney, P. with Johnson, K. (2009) *This Was My Life: I'm Here To Tell It. The Life and Times of Patrick Kearney*. Ennis: Brothers of Charity County Clare.

McCarthy, M. (1999) *Sexuality and Women with Learning Disabilities*. London: Jessica Kingsley.

McCarthy, M. (2000) Consent, abuse and choices, in R. Traustadottir and K. Johnson (eds) *Women with Intellectual Disabilities: Finding a Place in the World*. London: Jessica Kingsley.

Nind, M. and Johnson, K. (unpublished manuscript) Listening not labelling: changing the discourse of challenging and stereotyped behaviour.

Sinason, V. (1992) *Mental Handicap and the Human Condition: New Approaches from the Tavistock*. London: Free Association Books.

Walmsley, J. and Atkinson, D. (2000) Oral history and the history of learning disability, in J. Bornat, R. Perks, P. Thompson and J. Walmsley (eds) *Oral History, Health and Welfare*. London: Routledge.

Walmsley, J. and Johnson, K. (2003) *Inclusive Research with People with Learning Disabilities*. London: Jessica Kingsley.

West, R. (2000) Finding a sister, in R. Traustadottir and K. Johnson (eds) *Women with Intellectual Disabilities: Finding a Place in the World*. London: Jessica Kingsley.

32

Growing old: adapting to change and realizing a sense of belonging, continuity and purpose

Christine Bigby

Introduction

Increased life expectancy during the last 50 years means that ageing has become an integral part of the life course for people with intellectual disability. The experience of ageing is shaped by each individual's unique biography, the historic time through which they have lived and their current social context. As knowledge about later life for people with intellectual disability increases, many of the individual changes and the altered social context and expectations should be anticipated. Presently, however, some commentators suggest that old age is more likely to pose threats to an individual's sense of continuity, belonging and purpose rather than being celebrated as a valued achievement (Thompson 2002; Bigby 2004). The aim of this chapter is to consider why this might be so and how these tendencies might be countered.

The theme of this chapter is the continued active engagement of older people with intellectual disabilities in social relationships and the achievement of a lifestyle in which the critical ingredients are a sense of belonging, continuity and purpose. While such domains are found in conceptualizations of the quality of life, the notion of achieving a 'sense of' is drawn from a framework developed by Nolan *et al.* (2001). This framework emphasizes the subjective and perceptual nature of experiences and what might constitute a 'good life' for an older person. I chose to focus on these aspects to draw attention to the importance of social relationships and subjective perceptions in complementing good health in the achievement of well-being in later life.

Individuals derive their sense of belonging from meaningful relationships with family and friends and by being part of communities of interest. A sense of

continuity highlights an individual's connection with his or her past, the pre-existing and sometimes life-long interests, relationships, health and lifestyle that accompany him or her on their journey into old age. A sense of purpose is achieved through opportunities to exercise choice and pursue one's own goals and chosen activities.

Belonging, continuity and purpose are subjective outcomes that stem from the principles of rights, independence, choice/control and inclusion that inform policy and guide a vision of aspirations for the lives of people with intellectual disabilities of all ages (Department of Health 2001, 2009). Interpreting and implementing these principles poses some different dilemmas in later life. This chapter examines these challenges and the changing social contexts – expectations, family roles and composition, service structures and policy directions – that impact on people with intellectual disability as they age.

Ageing and diversity

With the exception of people with Down's syndrome and those with profound and multiple disabilities, the life expectancy of people with intellectual disability is closer to that of the general population than ever before. However, a common stereotypical view is that people with intellectual disability age prematurely. This view stems from the widely acknowledged premature ageing processes experienced by people with Down's syndrome and the use by researchers of younger definitions to ensure that this group is not excluded from studies of ageing.

UK estimates suggest that almost 13 per cent of the population with intellectual disability are 60 years or over, approximately 127,000 people (Emerson and Hatton 2004). In Australia, the proportion is generally smaller, at around 6 per cent (Bigby 2004). Two demographic trends are clear:

- the number and proportion of older people with intellectual disability is increasing and will continue to do so until after the 'baby boomer' generation moves into later life;
- the absolute numbers of older people with intellectual disability are small, and they form a very small proportion of both the general older population and of those with intellectual disability.

If 60 years marks the (arbitrary) start of old age, the years to come might be thought of as categories. For example, the 'younger old' are often differentiated from the 'old old' or the 'frail aged', or the 'third age' from the 'fourth age' (Laslett 1989). The third age, during the sixties and early seventies, is a period when people are more likely to be relatively fit and active and, having retired from work, seek other roles and activities to gain a sense of purpose. The fourth age, during the mid-seventies onwards, is more likely to be characterized by fragility, declining health and consequent restrictions on activity and community participation. The majority of older people with intellectual disabilities are, at the moment, among the younger old rather than the old old group (i.e. the third rather than the fourth age category). Each cohort of older people will have lived through a different historic time and have been influenced by that unique combination of changing attitudes, policies and social conditions that characterizes their generation. The significance of cohort is highlighted for people with intellectual disabilities currently in their sixties, born between 1940 and 1950. They and their families have experienced remarkable shifts in attitudes and responses to disability, from a focus on segregation and protection to one of inclusion and community support. As the narratives in Chapter 31 illustrate, some of the current cohort of older people, unlike those born in the last two decades, will have spent much of their lives in large-scale congregate living, only moving out in mid and later life as institutions have closed. Such experiences have a lasting impact on connections to family, community and to one's own life history. For example, those who have remained at home with parents have stronger

relationships with family members in later life than those who left home at an earlier age (Bigby 1997a; Hatzidimitriadou and Forrester-Jones 2002, cited in Forrester-Jones *et al.* 2006). Moving from an institution can threaten an individual's sense of continuity unless formal and informal institutional records and stories of their past life are captured and transferred with them to the community. Institutional closure can act as a catalyst in reconnecting individuals to their past or in rediscovering family members (West 2000; Bigby 2008).

Older people with an intellectual disability are a diverse group in regard to health, ability, connections with family and friends, service use patterns and the individual impact of the ageing process. Nevertheless, as a group, they have things in common. They:

- age at a similar rate to the general population, and have a slightly reduced lifespan compared to the general population (there are, however, some notable exceptional sub-groups such as people with Down's syndrome; Evenhuis *et al.* 2001);
- have high risk factors associated with ill-health, particularly related to lifestyle such as exercise, diet and socio-economic status (Rimmer and Yamaki 2006);
- have high rates of psychological disturbance, largely accounted for by a high rate of Alzheimer's disease among people with Down's syndrome (Cooper 1997; Strydom *et al.* 2007);
- are less likely to be employed or attend a day service than their younger counterparts (Walker *et al.* 1996; Bigby 2004);
- are more likely to live in shared supported accommodation than in a private home with family members or friends (Emerson *et al.* 2001);
- have reduced access to specialist disability services (Thompson and Wright 2001; Bigby 2004);
- are less likely to have strong advocates and robust informal social networks than their younger counterparts (Bigby 2000, 2008);
- experience substantial discrimination on the basis of age (Walker and Walker 1998);
- are expected by staff to have a lower potential for growth, development and acquisition of skills and greater levels of independence compared to their younger counterparts (Walker and Walker 1998; Bigby *et al.* 2001);

- have fewer choices and opportunities for active programming than their younger peers (Moss and Hogg 1989).

Yet in sharp contrast, older people with intellectual disabilities are the survivors of their generation and also have:

- a continuing ability to learn (Lifshitz 1998);
- less severe disabilities than their younger counterparts, being more skilled in relation to adaptive behaviour and functional skills (Moss 1991);
- greater competence than at any other stage of their lives (Edgerton 1994).

Stereotypes and age discrimination

The profile above reflects systematically low expectations, limited opportunities and poor access to support for older people with intellectual disabilities. Many of these aspects stem from age-related discriminatory societal attitudes and structures, or from ageism, rather than from inherent personal characteristics or from the ageing process itself.

Negative views and low expectations held by workers become self-fulfilling prophecies, contrasting sharply with evidence discussed in this chapter that older people can adapt to community living, become more independent, learn new skills, acquire new interests and lead more active lives.

Exercise 32.1

What images come to mind when you think of 'older people'? Do you think these images reflect negative stereotypes and if so, how?

Think of an older person you know well and consider to what extent they conform to the stereotypical image of an older person.

Spend some time talking to an older person about their life history and their perception of themselves.

Countering ageism does not mean disregarding age but requires a more concerted focus on the individual, their needs and aspirations. The principles of equity and inclusion suggest that older people with intel-

lectual disabilities should have opportunities to mix with people of all abilities and ages; should use generally available community facilities; and should be included in diverse social milieu. This does not ignore the need for age-related specialist support, or negate the legitimacy of groups or friendships based on age. Rather it emphasizes that individual needs, choice or common interest should be the basis of support.

Informal social relationships

Informal relationships are as fundamental to inclusion and citizenship as formal rights (Reinders 2002). Inclusion requires connections to others; relationships with family, friends, neighbours and acquaintances. These relationships can help to foster a sense of continuity and belonging.

However, the majority of older people with learning difficulties do not have a spouse or children which means they do not have roles such as partner, grandparent or mother-in-law, although they might acquire new roles such as great aunt. When parents die, their closest relatives are likely to be siblings or more distant relations such as cousins, nieces, nephews, aunts and uncles. For some people the loss of their parents can signify a shift to an adult rather than child role and the opportunity for new intimate friendships.

As people age their social networks are fluid and particularly vulnerable to shrinkage and disruption due to death, illness, house moves and retirement of network members. Many friendships, particularly those with peers, are specific to a particular context such as accommodation or a day centre, and they seldom meet outside of this setting. The context-specific nature of friendships means that such relationships are vulnerable to disruption. For example, an Australian study found that none of the people who had retired from day services, or who had moved to aged care accommodation, retained contact with friends from previous settings. Neither did they retain contact with neighbours when they moved from the locality (Bigby 2000).

Qualitative research suggests that friendships between people with intellectual disability can have depth, richness and longevity (Knox and Hickson 2001; Bigby and Knox 2009). An emphasis on valued social roles can detract from recognizing or valuing friendships between people with intellectual disabilities (Chappell 1994). What is important, however, is to distinguish friendships from mere groupings of people where individuals, although proximate to each other, have no common bonds.

Those people who have remained at home with parents for much of their lives are often strongly connected to family and share friendships with their parents (Knox and Bigby 2007). There is a danger for them that incidental contact with the extended family will be lost when parents die. Although contact with shared family friends might be retained after the death of parents, such friends are likely to be from an older generation and to predecease them.

Being known in a locality or community of interest can be very important to a person's sense of belonging (see Chapters 24 and 30). Grant *et al.* (1995) found that older people with intellectual disabilities were more likely to have acquaintances than close friends. These might be unnamed individuals or groups of people who they see regularly, neighbours in the local area, supporters of a football club or other patrons at a café.

A defining characteristic of older people's informal networks is reported to be a 'key person' who takes responsibility for oversight of their well-being (Bigby 2000). Key people had a close long-term relationship with the older person, demonstrating considerable commitment to their roles as benefactors. They were likely to be a sibling, more distant relative or long-term family friend who had been informally nominated by a parent to assume responsibility for the person following the parent's death. Key people were the most stable element in older people's networks but as they are from the same or an older generation they may predecease the older person. This loss can leave some older people very vulnerable.

Informal relationships provide diverse types of support that can include:

- 'Caring for' functions or 'direct support':

  - provision of hands-on day-to-day care;
  - development of skills;
  - provision of back-up or short-term replacement of other members;
  - emotional support;

  - listening;
  - advising.

- 'Caring about' or 'indirect support':

  - decision-making;
  - financial management;
  - adoption of formal or legal roles;
  - mediating, negotiating and advocating with service systems;
  - monitoring service quality;
  - supervision of medical needs;
  - co-ordinating support from other network members;
  - visiting and companionship.

  (Bigby 2000)

Clearly, some types of informal support can be replicated by formal support services, and paid relationships can replace informal support without detriment to standards. However, it is particularly difficult for formal organizations or paid relationships to have a long-term commitment to an individual. Yet these tasks are critically important for people dependent on services to meet their day-to-day needs. The inability of formal services to substitute for some of the key roles fulfilled by informal network members emphasizes the vulnerability of those people who lack strong informal networks of support.

The question of retirement

Formal roles, such as paid or volunteer worker, or participation in formal programmes, such as adult training and support centres or colleges of further education, are important in fostering successful engagement and social inclusion. Forced retirement from the workforce at an early or fixed chronological age, though more flexibly applied in recent years, is still common. However, this can create an arbitrary way of excluding people from formal programmes, and withdrawal of specialist support can threaten continued engagement and inclusion. This matter has been subject to much debate. Some have argued that retirement is irrelevant for people with intellectual disabilities who have not been in paid employment and that it will lead to social isolation and further devaluation. Others argue that they should have the same rights as other older people to retire, be it from services or work, and to lead a lifestyle of their choice

(Wolfensberger 1985; Sutton *et al.* 1992; Heller 1999).

Retirement from services is sometimes justified on the basis of changes that occur to people's needs as they age. Factors such as the declining skill level of older people, their reduced abilities, the increased time required to perform tasks, a need for a quieter environment, and incompatibilities with the interests of younger participants have been suggested as possible reasons for programme changes (Bigby *et al.* 2004; Bigby 2005). These assumptions are often without foundation. For example, despite evidence showing that a lower proportion of older than younger participants have high support needs, one study showed that staff still considered increased resources to be required for these older people's higher support needs (Bigby *et al.* 2001).

Arguments are also put forward that day programmes for younger people and the staff who run them have neither the resources nor skills to respond to the needs of older people. Implicit in this idea is the requirement for more flexible funding and specialist knowledge of both the ageing process and service systems to provide appropriate programmes for older people (Department of Health 1997). However, while significant reform of day programmes has continued, issues of retirement and its impacts on this group of older people have been largely neglected by governments in both the UK and Australia (Department of Human Services 2002; Department of Health 2009).

Employment and day programmes can be influential in shaping perceptions of the need to retire. For example, one of the drivers behind the development of retirement programmes in the US was that their strong training/developmental focus was perceived as less appropriate as people aged (Moss 1993). Retirement may of course be used as a discriminatory mechanism for managing demand on other parts of the service system.

It can be argued, however, that if day programmes are based on person-centred planning (see Chapter 25) there is little reason why they should not be sufficiently flexible to adapt to age-related changes. Underpinning this argument is the view that merely reaching a particular chronological age should not be sufficient reason for retirement or for instituting changes to a person's lifestyle and daytime activities.

Aspirations and realities

Studies that have investigated the views and experiences of people with intellectual disabilities suggest that they value continued active engagement with their world, desire to continue working and learning, and wish to participate in more leisure activities or structured activities (Bigby 1992, 1997b; Heller 1999; Buys *et al.* 2008; Bigby and Knox 2009). Bigby's (2000) study highlighted the opportunities relished by some older people who perceived later life as a period when they were free to pursue their own interests unrestricted by parental protectiveness. Older people with disabilities who are working seldom express the desire to retire, being concerned about loss of income and social isolation if they do so (Sutton *et al.* 1992; Bigby and Knox 2009). One US study found that the majority of people who had retired even wanted to return to work (Rogers *et al.* 1998). Edgerton's study (1994) suggested that as people aged they became less dependent on benefactors and more competent than at any other stage of their lives, but they wanted the freedom to choose what suited them, and to exercise control even if this meant opting out of day services.

Despite their aspirations for continuing inclusion, older people with intellectual disabilities experience few opportunities to participate in meaningful day and leisure activities of their choice (Grant *et al.* 1995; Rogers *et al.* 1998; Wilson 1998; Hawkins 1999; Messant *et al.* 1999). There is little evidence, however, to suggest that day programmes developed specifically for older participants lead to better outcomes than age-integrated programmes. Such programmes can run the risk of reinforcing age stereotyping and reducing individual choice instead of addressing issues based on individual preference or interest (Bigby 2005).

Evidence of poor-quality services for older people is found in the UK where considerable variation exists in service provision across different regions (Robertson *et al.* 1996; Department of Health 1997; Fitzgerald 1998).

Substantial disparity between the quality and type of programmes available to older people using care services compared to those in receipt of disability services has been reported. In the study in question, disability services were found to offer more individualized and educational activities and participants were more involved in community and leisure pursuits (Moss *et al.* 1992).

As discussed earlier, older people with intellectual disabilities often have poor informal social networks so they are dependent on paid carers and services to compensate for this.. However, contextual, financial, physical and attitudinal barriers have been reported as undermining such social support (Glausier *et al.* 1995; Hogg 1996; Fitzgerald 1998; Messant *et al.* 1999).

Paid carers or support workers often determine choice of activity based on imperatives such as management of group needs rather than individual preferences (Glausier *et al.* 1995; Rogers *et al.* 1998). The congregate nature of activities can accentuate a lack of individual choice and residential staff may have limited time left after undertaking essential housekeeping and caring tasks (Clement and Bigby 2009a). Transport and cost of activities are common difficulties. Public attitudes and relationship difficulties have been reported to affect opportunities and access to community leisure facilities or generic programmes for older people like day centres (Glausier *et al.* 1995; Grant *et al.* 1995; Heller 1999; Bigby and Balandin 2005). Personal factors such as poor motivation, choice, lack of skills, knowledge or preparedness can also hinder participation in activities but structural and contextual elements such as the absence of staff support are considered to be more important (Hawkins 1999).

Ensuring a sense of purpose

Retirement should not be taken as a given but rather critically appraised and accompanied by the question, 'retirement to what?', with weight given to issues of replacement of support and compensation for roles, social relationships or activities that might be lost or disrupted (Janicki 1990; Bigby 2004). The theory of 'selective optimization with compensation' proposed by Baltes and Baltes (1990) provides a useful framework for responding to the individual and social changes associated with ageing. Selective optimization suggests that successful adaptation involves three core processes, all of which should be based on individual choice:

- greater selection of activity as physical capacity reduces;

- compensation for loss of either skill or function by internal and external adjustments (e.g. changes to behaviour, type of support provided, adaptation of the physical environment or use of aids);
- optimization, making the most of what you have, by engaging in behaviours and activities that maximize reserves and enrich life choices.

Adaptation and compensation highlight ways of responding to or compensating for the change or loss associated with ageing. Individual behaviour or patterns of activities may be altered and the external social or physical environment may be adapted, by increasing opportunities, changing support or introducing assistive technologies. The theory can be used to inform planning processes by putting a focus on external as well as individual adaptations to changes necessary to support individuals to realize goals.

Exercise 32.2

Can you provide examples of adaptations and compensations for loss or change associated with ageing? Think about this for: changes in individual behaviour; changes to physical environment; and changes to formal support.

Lifestyle support

Traditional frameworks for considering retirement support tend to pose questions about whether new or specialized programmes should be designed for older people. Three models are generally considered:

- *Age integration*: including older people in programmes for younger people with disabilities; for example, continued attendance at a day activity centre for people with intellectual disability.
- *Generic integration*: including older people with disabilities in programmes for the general aged population; for example, attendance at senior citizens' centres, day centres for the frail aged.
- *Specialist programmes*: developing specialized activities for older people with disabilities; for example, day centres dedicated to older people with intellectual disabilities.

Another approach is to focus on the outcomes sought and the strategies necessary to achieve these.

Case study: *Maurice*

Maurice is aged 62 and moved out of a large institution to a small shared house in the community several years ago. He has a terrific sense of humour and loves being around other people. During the season he attends football matches that are held at his team's home ground. He understands much of what goes on around him but has limited speech and others find it difficult to understand what he is communicating. He has been attending a full-time day programme together with the four other residents in his house, but staff are suggesting he should start to think about retirement. The house has had several changes of supervisor and none of the current staff have a good sense of Maurice's history or the things he enjoys doing. His mother died several years ago and he continues to maintain regular contact with his father who lives on the family farm.

Exercise 32.3

If you were developing a person-centred plan for Maurice:

What else would you need to know about him? How might you find these things out?

What assumptions might you and others make about Maurice and how can these be avoided?

What age-related changes might Maurice be experiencing and what adaptations might be considered to take account of these?

When you have formulated a plan, what strategies might you use to ensure it is a living document and is used to guide the support provided to Maurice?

Key outcomes of effective lifestyle support to older people with intellectual disabilities discussed in this chapter draw on the work of Nolan *et al.* (2001) and are: a sense of belonging, continuity and purpose. Strategic approaches to achieving these, which can be incorporated into a variety of programme models, are:

- provision of choice and person-centred planning;
- maintenance and strengthening of social networks;
- support for participation in the community;
- maintenance of skills;
- opportunities for self-expression and sense of self;
- promotion of health and a healthy lifestyle.

Somewhat unexpectedly, Bigby's (2005) study found that on these dimensions traditional day centres that practised individualized planning were as successful as more specialized age-specific day programmes. The following sections discuss these strategies further.

Provision of choice and person-centred planning

Person-centred planning focuses attention on the capacity and ability of an older person to pursue chosen goals, and provides a safeguard against a more

global response to ageing that can result in the reduction or limitation of opportunities or activities (Sanderson 2000; Cambridge and Carnaby 2005). Planning reinforces the importance of individuality or a sense of significance: that each individual has his or her own characteristics, needs, wishes and aspirations. Plans should reflect an individual's characteristics; health, abilities, interests and their social context; living situation; co-residents and social networks; and previous life experiences. The three narratives in Chapter 31 illustrate the very individual aspirations of each of the older people concerned.

Person-centred planning and choice are embedded in current policies but the scope and breadth with which they are translated into practice still varies considerably. Even when plans are mandated or drawn up, quality and implementation have been major issues (Felce *et al.* 1998; Mansell and Beadle-Brown 2004; Bigby 2005). In tandem with person-centred plans, organizations must also plan the use of resources, primarily support staff, to ensure that visions encapsulated in the plans are implemented.

Maintenance and strengthening of social networks

Support from social workers, case managers or direct care staff can foster development of informal relationships but also, through neglect and ignorance, the obstruction or disruption of these. A first crucial step is recognition of the value and range of informal relationships of each older person. The initial stage of planning should ensure that each individual's network is actively mapped, and that the history and significance of relationships are understood. A proactive stance is required to take account of relationships and adapt support to deal with potential disruption when lifestyle changes, such as retirement, are proposed. Strategies can range from raising the awareness of staff about the importance of relationships to the reorientation of support to facilitate contact with friends or the implementation of more formal 'network-building programmes'.

Formal network-building programmes are based on the idea that participation in activities becomes a means of developing individual relationships. Person-centered planning techniques are used by a 'community builder' to piece together a picture of the person with a disability and to explore the local community for potential sites and activities, where the person may play a role or contribute to community life. Once an activity is identified the community builder's role is to introduce the person, and seek out and foster the development of natural supports from among other participants. Community builders can be employed as part of a specialist programme or such a role may be fulfilled by a case manager. This can require significant investment of time over extended periods (Kultgen *et al.* 2000; Harlan-Simmons *et al.* 2001). Another formal approach is to develop and support a 'circle of support' around a person, drawing on existing family and friends as well as volunteers (Burke 2006; Wightman 2009).

As people age, maintaining family relationships may need more active support as relatives encounter mobility or health problems. The structure of day-to-day activities creates both opportunities and obstacles to building friendships. Occasional outings in large groups to venues such as shopping centres or the cinema are unlikely to lead to the development of new relationships. Yet it is just these sorts of activity to anonymous public spaces in groups that occupy much of the time that people with intellectual disability spend in the community (Walker 1995; Clement and Bigby 2009b). The location, continuity, regularity, size of group and meaning of the activity to the individual are all key considerations in whether obstacles or opportunities occur.

> ### Exercise 32.4
>
> How would you build up a map of Maurice's informal social relationships? What are the different types of relationship he might have?
>
> What sorts of family relationships might an unmarried person of Maurice's age have? In what ways might the support that Maurice needs to maintain contact with his family and friends change as both he and they get older?
>
> What strategies could be pursued to provide opportunities for Maurice to form new relationships?

Support for participation in the community

Person-centred plans should explore strategies for community participation. Sensitive planning should also lead to an exploration of opportunities for volunteer work or membership of clubs and organizations that offer scope for older people to make contributions. Too often community participation is understood to be the mere use of community facilities, important in its own right (Clement and Bigby 2009b), rather than active social interaction with community members on the basis of shared interests. Hallmarks of participation should rather be the sense of purpose to the individual and their active connection to a community of interest.

> ### Exercise 32.5
>
> How would you describe differences for Maurice between participation in the community and merely being present?
>
> What communities of interest might Maurice belong to?

What questions would you ask to be sure that the activities Maurice participates in are meaningful to him?

What strategies would you use to ensure that Maurice has a sense of continuity in his life?

Maintenance of skills

Support to maintain skills helps towards an older person's continuing sense of autonomy and independence. A first step is the recognition that maintaining or developing skills is an important goal that may require planned strategies and creative adjustments to the environment to compensate for changes such as loss of physical or sensory capacities. For example, a person with Alzheimer's disease may slowly lose their motivation to participate in everyday activities or initiate interaction and will progressively require more frequent prompting and increasing levels of support to exercise their skills. Activities may have to be simplified or broken into smaller steps to compensate for cognitive change but support continued engagement. Action to maintain skills should occur in the informal domestic sphere as well as in the service context. Adaptation of teaching strategies and environmental modifications can compensate for cognitive and sensory changes: for example, allowing the person to proceed at their own pace or using environmental cues such as pictures and symbols to complement labels.

Age-related stereotypes can be particularly disadvantageous to individuals in connection to skill development. For example, an Australian study found that programmes generally had few ambitious goals for individuals in regard to skill development, and they often reflected a shift from active to passive pursuits. In some instances, resistance was found to any individual planning concerning skills or activities as it was seen as irrelevant in later life (Bigby 2005).

Opportunities for self-expression and sense of self

Opportunities for self-expression and connection to one's own life history are important in tackling some of the psychological tasks associated with later life. Erikson (1973), who adopts a stage theory of personality development, suggests that older people are confronted with achieving 'ego integrity versus despair'. This involves the acceptance that one's life has had a meaning, whether or not it has been 'successful', and the acceptance of one's own mortality. Seltzer (1985) conceptualizes some of the developmental tasks of ageing for older people with intellectual disabilities as: adjustment to losses, restructuring of roles, reassessment of self-concept and acceptance of mortality.

Strategies for achieving these tasks include reminiscence and life review – opportunities for individuals to express how they feel about themselves and what is happening in their world. Avenues for self-expression and reflection may occur through drama, art, group or individual opportunities to tell personal stories or reminiscence, and use of photo albums and other memorabilia. Where people have lost contact with families, lived in institutions or moved many times, compiling a record of their life story may be an important task. Life story work (see Chapter 1) can also be key in maintaining a connection with people with Alzheimer's, ensuring continuity of engagement with informal network members. Such a strategy has been used by one of the major UK providers of residential care for people with disabilities (Grundy 2002). Carers of middle-aged adults with intellectual disability have used life story books as a means to engage carers in thinking about the future, adopting a proactive approach to preserving a person's life history to inform those who may become involved in the person's life as they age (for example Magrill et al. 2005).

Exercise 32.6

If you were Maurice's case manager, how important do you think it would be to ensure the staff that supported him every day were aware of his life history and significant events and people in his life? How might you ensure this occurred?

What strategies might you put in place to provide Maurice with opportunities to connect with and reflect on his past?

Promotion of health and a healthy lifestyle

Physical health underpins almost all aspects of a person's life, and for people with intellectual disability it can be optimized by an approach that encompasses health promotion, health surveillance and health care (Moss *et al.* 1998). These issues are addressed in depth in other chapters. It is important to incorporate health promotion into all aspects of a person's life. Of note too is that people with intellectual disability often embark on the ageing process from a very disadvantageous and unhealthy lifestyle, having led sedentary lives, with little exercise, poor diets and accompanying weight problems (Janicki *et al.* 2002; Rimmer and Yamaki 2006).

Stereotypical views that lead to inaction on health-related issues can further disadvantage older people. For example, Bigby *et al.* (2001) found that while day programmes used by older people were sensitive to physical health issues, many accepted reduced fitness and poor health without accurate assessment.

Research has shown that older people with intellectual disabilities enjoy structured exercise programmes (Heller *et al.* 2002). Apparently mundane, but important, details of everyday life can be structured to involve more physical activity, for example by dispensing with the automatic TV channel changer, using stairs instead of lifts, walking to the next rather the nearest bus stop, or using a watering can instead of a hose.

Exercise 32.7

Key questions to ask about Maurice's lifestyle might be:

What exercise does he have in the course of a regular week and how could physical activity be built into his everyday routine?

If Maurice were to be confined to a wheelchair how could he continue to exercise?

What types of food should Maurice have in his diet and what should he be avoiding or eating in small quantities?

Who should take responsibility for ensuring Maurice has a healthy lifestyle?

Now go back through all the exercises. You should now have a series of 'best ideas' to support Maurice. Remember this still raises issues about who decides, who implements and who organizes.

Conclusion

This chapter has provided an overview of some issues associated with ageing for people with intellectual disabilities. It has highlighted the diversity of this population and the discriminatory social attitudes that can impact on older people. An individual sense of belonging, continuity and purpose are seen as central to achieving well-being in this group of older people, as with older people in general. The impact of retirement on an individual's social relationships and sense of purpose has been highlighted. Strategic approaches to supporting a purposeful lifestyle for older people with intellectual disabilities are proposed within an overarching framework that emphasizes the importance of adaptation and compensation for individual and social changes associated with ageing. Finally, students should be mindful that the voice of older people with intellectual disabilities is still largely missing from much published research about the experiences of ageing. The meaning of belonging, continuity and purpose for each individual will reflect their own unique perceptions and interpretation of their activities, experiences and relationships. The challenge lies in finding ways to uncover and bring these into focus, so that dreams and aspirations can be realized.

References

Baltes, P. and Baltes, M. (1990) Psychological perspectives on successful aging: the model of selective optimisation with compensation, in P. Baltes and M. Baltes (eds) *Successful*

Ageing: Perspectives from the Behavioural Sciences. Cambridge: Cambridge University Press.

Bigby, C. (1992) Access and linkage: two critical issues for older people with an intellectual disability, *Australia and New Zealand Journal of Developmental Disabilities*, 18: 95–110.

Bigby, C. (1997a) When parents relinquish care: the informal support networks of older people with intellectual disability, *Journal of Applied Intellectual Disability Research*, 10(4): 333–44.

Bigby, C. (1997b) Later life for adults with intellectual disability: a time of opportunity and vulnerability, *Journal of Intellectual and Developmental Disability*, 22(2): 97–108.

Bigby, C. (1998) Shifting responsibilities: patterns of formal service use by older people with intellectual disability, *Journal of Intellectual and Developmental Disability*, 23: 229–43.

Bigby, C. (2000) *Moving on Without Parents: Planning, Transitions and Sources of Support for Older Adults with Intellectual Disabilities*. New South Wales: McLennan & Petty.

Bigby, C. (2004) *Aging with a Lifelong Disability: Policy, Program and Practice Issues for Professionals*. London: Jessica Kingsley.

Bigby, C. (2005) Comparative programs for older people with intellectual disabilities, *Journal of Policy and Practice in Intellectual Disability*, 2(2): 75–85.

Bigby, C. (2008) Known well by no one. Trends of the informal social networks of people with intellectual disability five years after moving to the community, *Journal of Intellectual and Developmental Disabilities*, 33(2): 148–57.

Bigby, C. and Balandin, S. (2005) Another minority group: a survey of the use of aged care day programs and community leisure services by older people with lifelong disability, *Australasian Journal on Ageing*, 24(1): 14–18.

Bigby, C. and Knox, M. (2009) 'I want to see the Queen': the service experiences of older adults with intellectual disability, *Australian Social Work*, 62(2): 216–31.

Bigby, C., Fyffe, C., Balandin, S., Gordon, M. and McCubbery, J. (2001) *Day Support Services Options for Older Adults with a Disability*. Melbourne: National Disability Administrators Group.

Bigby, C., Balandin, S., Fyffe, C., McCubbery, J. and Gordon, M. (2004) Retirement or just a change of pace: an Australian national survey of disability day services used by older people with disabilities, *Journal of Intellectual and Development Disabilities*, 29(3): 239–54.

Burke, C. (2006) *Building Community through Circles of Friends: A Practical Guide to Making Inclusion a Reality for People with Learning Disabilities*. London: The Mental Health Foundation.

Buys, L., Boulton-Lewis, G., Tedman-Jones, J., Edwards, H., Knox, M. and Bigby, C. (2008) Issues of active ageing: perceptions of older people with lifelong intellectual disability, *Australasian Journal of Ageing*, 27(2): 67–71.

Cambridge, P. and Carnaby, S. (2005) *Person Centred Planning and Care Management with People with Learning Disabilities*. London: Jessica Kingsley.

Chappell, A. (1994) A question of friendship: community care and the relationships of people with learning difficulties, *Disability and Society*, 9(4): 419–33.

Clement, T. and Bigby, C. (2009a) *Group Homes for People with Intellectual Disabilities: Encouraging Inclusion and Participation*. London: Jessica Kingsley.

Clement, T and Bigby, C. (2009b) Breaking out of a distinct social space: reflections on supporting community participation for people with severe and profound intellectual disability, *Journal of Applied Research in Intellectual Disability*, 22: 264–75.

Cooper, S. (1997) Epidemiology of psychiatric disorders in elderly compared with younger people with learning disabilities, *British Journal of Psychiatry*, 170: 375–80.

Department of Health (1997) *Services for Older People with Learning Disabilities*. London: HMSO.

Department of Health (2001) *Valuing People: A New Strategy for Learning Disability for the 21st Century*. London: Department of Health.

Department of Health (2009) *Valuing People Now: A New Three-year Strategy for People with Learning Disabilities*. London: Department of Health.

Department of Human Services (2002) *Victorian State Disability Plan 2002–2012*. Melbourne: Department of Human Services.

Edgerton, R. (1994) Quality of life issues: some people know how to be old, in M. Seltzer, M. Krauss and M. Janicki (eds) *Lifecourse Perspectives on Adulthood and Aging*. Washington: American Association on Mental Retardation.

Emerson, E. and Hatton, C. (2004) *Estimating Future Need/ Demand for Supports for Adults with Learning Disabilities in England*. Lancaster: Institute for Health Research, Lancaster University.

Emerson, E., Hatton, C., Felce, D. and Murphy, G. (2001) *Learning Disabilities: The Fundamental Facts*. London: Foundation for People with Learning Disabilities.

Erikson, E. (1973) *Childhood and Society*. New York: Norton.

Evenhuis, H., Henderson, C., Beange, H., Lennox, N. and Chicoine, B. (2001) Healthy ageing – adults with intellectual disabilities: physical health issues, *Journal of Applied Research in Intellectual Disabilities*, 14(3): 175–94.

Felce, D., Grant, G., Todd, S., Ramcharan, P., Beyer, S., McGrath, M. *et al.* (1998) *Towards a Full Life: Researching Policy Innovation for People with Learning Disabilities*. Oxford: Butterworth Heinemann.

Fitzgerald, J. (1998) *Time for Freedom? Services for Older People with Learning Difficulties*. London: Values in Action.

Forrester-Jones, R., Carpenter, J., Coolen-Schrijner, P., Cambridge, P., Tate, A., Beecham, J. *et al.* (2006) The social networks of people with intellectual disability living in the community 12 years after resettlement from long-stay hospitals, *Journal of Applied Research in Intellectual Disabilities*, 19(4): 285–95.

Glausier, S., Whorton, J. and Knight, H. (1995) Recreation and leisure likes/dislikes of senior citizens with mental retardation, *Activities, Adaptations and Aging*, 19: 43–54.

Grant, G. (2001) Older people with learning disabilities: health, community inclusion and family caregiving, in M. Nolan, S. Davies and G. Grant (eds) *Working with Older People and their Families*. Buckingham: Open University Press.

Grant, G., McGrath, M. and Ramcharan, P. (1995) Community inclusion of older adults with learning disabilities, *Care In Place: International Journal of Networks and Community*, 2(1): 29–44.

Grundy, P. (2002) This is your life, *Community Care*, 7(13): 40.

Harlan-Simmons, J., Holtz, P., Todd, J. and Mooney, M. (2001) Building social relationships through values roles: three adults and the community membership project, *Mental Retardation*, 39(3): 171–80.

Hawkins, B. (1999) Rights, place of residence and retirement: lessons from case studies on aging, in S. Herr and G. Weber (eds) *Aging, Rights and Quality of Life*. Baltimore, MD: Brookes.

Heller, T. (1999) Emerging models, in S. Herr and G. Weber (eds) *Ageing, Rights and Quality of Life*. Baltimore, MD: Brookes.

Heller, T., Hsieh, K. and Rimmer, J. (2002) Barriers and supports for exercise participation among adults with Down syndrome, *Journal of Gerontological Social Work*, 38(1/2): 161–78.

Hogg, J. (1996) Leisure, disability and the third age, *Journal of Practical Approaches to Developmental Handicap*, 18: 1.

Hogg, J. and Lambe, K. (2000) Stability and change in the later years: the impact of service provision on older people with intellectual disabilities, in D. May (ed.) *Transitions in the Lives of People with Learning Disabilities*. London: Jessica Kingsley.

Janicki, M. (1990) Growing old with dignity: on quality of life for older persons with lifelong disability, in R. Schalock (ed.) *Quality of Life: Perspectives and Issues*. Washington, DC: American Association on Mental Retardation.

Janicki, M., Dalton, A., Henderson, C. and Davidson, P. (1999) Mortality and morbidity among older adults with intellectual disability: health services considerations, *Disability and Rehabilitation*, 21(5/6): 284–94.

Janicki, M., Davidson, P., Henderson, C., McCallion, P., Teates, J., Force, L. *et al.* (2002) Health characteristics and health service utilisation in older adults with intellectual disability living in community residences, *Journal of Intellectual Disability Research*, 46(4): 287–98.

Knox, M. and Bigby, C. (2007) Moving towards midlife care as negotiated family business: accounts of people with intellectual disabilities and their families, *International Journal of Disability, Development and Education*, 54(3): 287–304.

Knox, M. and Hickson, F. (2001) The meaning of close friendships: the view of four people with intellectual disabilities, *Journal of Applied Research in Intellectual Disabilities*, 14(3): 276–91.

Kultgen, P., Harlan-Simmons, J. and Todd, J. (2000) Community membership, in M. Janicki and E. Ansello (eds) *Community Supports for Aging Adults with Lifelong Disabilities*. Baltimore, MD: Brookes.

Lambe, L. and Hogg, J. (1995) *Their Face to the Wind: Service Developments for Older People with Learning Difficulties in Grampian Region*. Dundee: Enable.

Laslett, P. (1989) *A Fresh Map of Life: The Emergence of the Third Age*. London: Weidenfeld & Nicolson.

Lifshitz, H. (1998) Instrumental enrichment: a tool for enhancement of cognitive ability in adult and elderly people with mental retardation, *Education and Training in Mental Retardation and Developmental Disabilities*, 33(1): 34–41.

Magrill, D., Sanderson, H. and Short, A. (2005) *Person-centred Approaches and Older Families*. London: The Foundation for People with Learning Disabilities.

Mansell, J. and Beadle-Brown, J. (2004) Person-centred planning or person-centred action? Policy and practice in intellectual disability services, *Journal of Applied Research in Intellectual Disabilities*, 17(1): 1–9.

Messant, P., Cooke, C. and Long, J. (1999) Primary and secondary barriers to physically active healthy lifestyles for adults with learning disabilities, *Disability and Rehabilitation*, 21(9): 409–19.

Moss, S. (1991) Age and functional abilities of people with mental handicap: evidence from the Wessex Mental Handicap Register, *Journal of Mental Deficiency Research*, 35: 430–45.

Moss, S. (1993) *Aging and Developmental Disabilities: Perspectives from Nine Countries*. Durham, NH: The International Exchange of Experts and Information in Rehabilitation.

Moss, S. and Hogg, J. (1989) A cluster analysis of support networks of older people with severe intellectual impairment, *Australia and New Zealand Journal of Developmental Disabilities*, 15: 169–88.

Moss, S., Hogg, J. and Horne, M. (1992) Individual characteristics and service support of older people with moderate, severe and profound learning disability with and without community mental handicap team support, *Mental Handicap Research*, 6(3): 3–17.

Moss, S., Lambe, L. and Hogg, J. (1998) *Aging Matters: Pathways for Older People with a Learning Disability*. Worcestershire: British Institute of Learning Disabilities.

Nolan, M., Davies, S. and Grant, G. (2001) Integrating perspectives, in M. Nolan, S. Davies and G. Grant (eds) *Working with Older People and their Families*. Buckingham: Open University Press.

Reinders, J. (2002) The good life for citizens with intellectual disability, *Journal of Intellectual Disability Research*, 46(1): 1.

Rimmer, J.H. and Yamaki, K. (2006) Obesity and intellectual disability, *Mental Retardation and Developmental Disabilities Research Reviews*, 12: 22–7.

Robertson, J., Moss, S. and Turner, S. (1996) Policy, service and staff training for older people with intellectual disability in the UK, *Journal of Applied Research in Intellectual Disabilities*, 9(2): 91–100.

Rogers, N., Hawkins, B. and Eklund, S. (1998) The nature of leisure in the lives of older adults with intellectual disability, *Journal of Intellectual Disability Research*, 42(2): 122–30.

Sanderson, H. (2000) *Person-centred Planning: Key Features and Approaches*. York: Joseph Rowntree Foundation.

Seltzer, G. (1985) Selected psychological processes and aging among older developmentally disabled persons, in M. Janicki and H. Wisniewski (eds) *Aging and Developmental Disabilities: Issues and Approaches.* Baltimore, MD: Brookes.

Strydom, A., Livingston, G., King, M. and Hassiotis, A. (2007) Prevalence of dementia in intellectual disability using different diagnostic criteria, *British Journal of Psychiatry,* 191: 150–7.

Sutton, E., Sterns, H. and Roberts, R. (1992) Retirement for older persons with developmental disabilities, in E. Ansello and N. Eustis (eds) *Aging and Disabilities: Seeking Common Ground.* Amityville, NY: Baywood.

Thompson, D. (2002) Growing older with learning disabilities: the GOLD programme, *Tizard Learning Disability Review,* 7(2): 19–26.

Thompson, D. and Wright, S. (2001) *Misplaced and Forgotten: People with Learning Disabilities in Residential Services for Older People.* London: The Mental Health Foundation.

Walker, A. and Walker, C. (1998) Normalisation and 'normal' ageing: the social construction of dependency among older people with learning difficulties, *Disability and Society,* 13(1): 125–42.

Walker, A., Walker, C. and Ryan, T. (1996) Older people with learning difficulties leaving institutional care – a case of double jeopardy, *Ageing and Society,* 16: 125–50.

Walker, P. (1995) Community based is not community: the social geography of disability, in S. Taylor, R. Bogdan and Z. Lukfiyya (eds) *The Variety of Community Experiences.* Baltimore, MD: Brookes.

West, R. (2000) Discovering a sister, in R. Traustadottir and K. Johnson (eds) *Women with Intellectual Disabilities: Finding a Place in the World.* London: Jessica Kingsley.

Wightman, C. (2009) *Connecting People: Steps to Making it Happen.* London: Foundation for People with Learning Disabilities.

Wilson, C. (1998) Providing quality services for individuals who are aging in community based support settings: what are the issues for service providers? Paper presented at the 34th Annual Conference of the Australian Society for the Study of Intellectual Disability, Adelaide, South Australia.

Wolfensberger, W. (1985) An overview of social role valorisation and some reflections on elderly mentally retarded persons, in M. Janicki and H. Wisniewski (eds) *Aging and Developmental Disabilities: Issues and Approaches.* Baltimore, MD: Brookes.

End-of-life issues

Sheila Hollins and Irene Tuffrey-Wijne

33

Introduction

Nowadays people with learning disabilities are increasingly likely to live into old age, and develop age-related illnesses such as cancer and Alzheimer's disease, of which they may eventually die (Tuffrey-Wijne *et al.* 2007). However, they still have a much shorter life expectancy overall than other people (Hollins *et al.* 1998; Tyrer *et al.* 2007). It is recognized that poorer health and a shorter lifespan often relates not only to the underlying causes of people's learning disabilities but also to inequality of access to health services (Disability Rights Commission 2006; Michael 2008). Some reports have suggested that this leads to abuse, undiagnosed illness and even avoidable death (Mencap 2007; Parliamentary and Health Service Ombudsman 2009).

The experience of death among their contemporaries is thus much commoner for people with learning disabilities. Most of us associate death with older age, and young adults have typically only experienced death among their grandparents. This can lead to a false sense of one's own predicted longevity. Not so for adults with learning disabilities who are very likely to have lost friends through death in their school and college days and from among their friends in clubs and day centres. The causes of earlier death are well documented and include epilepsy, choking or silent aspiration of food, and accidents. Despite this, people with learning disabilities are more likely to be 'protected' from knowledge of death or impending death. Many carers feel concern about their capacity to understand and cope with the finality of death, or do not recognize their need to be informed and included, and to grieve (Oswin 1991; Blackman 2003).

If people with learning disabilities themselves face a life threatening illness, this 'conspiracy of silence' often persists (Tuffrey-Wijne 2009). The availability of choices around end-of-life issues, such as what treatment or care is to be provided and where, is crucial for the achievement of an optimal quality of life, yet this is difficult to achieve if the person concerned is not informed and involved. Providing appropriate and sensitive end-of-life support, whether this is early or late in life, presents a major challenge to family, support networks and services.

This chapter will explore end-of-life issues and bereavement. Through three case studies, it will highlight pertinent issues and best practice in providing appropriate end-of-life and bereavement care.

End of life issues

Case study: *Jennifer*

Jennifer Thomas was born ten weeks prematurely. She was the much longed-for third child of Joan and Brian Thomas, who already had Christopher, aged 2 and Sarah, aged 1. Jennifer had many health problems, including cerebral palsy, epilepsy and severe learning disabilities. Her parents were initially told that she would probably not survive more than a few weeks. She was in hospital for five months. When it became clear that, given intensive support, she might survive a couple of years, her parents were advised to move her into a long-stay hospital for people with learning disabilities. Joan and Brian were grief-stricken and devastated by the situation. They knew that they could not possibly care for Jennifer themselves. They had Christopher and Sarah to consider, and insufficient community support was available. They felt that the best way to cope was by breaking off all contact with Jennifer. They did not tell their other children about her. They asked only to be contacted about Jennifer if there was a life-threatening situation.

Jennifer was transferred to Hollyfields, a large hospital for people with learning disabilities 350 miles away. For the next 26 years, she lived in a ward with 13 other residents. She was the most severely disabled person on the ward. She was unable to move her limbs and couldn't talk, although she had a lovely smile. She spent her life in a cot in one corner of the room. The nurses gave her intensive physical support, including night checks every 20 minutes. Jennifer had regular seizures day and night, which were promptly dealt with. During these 26 years, Jennifer's parents were telephoned 11 times; reasons for alarm included severe epileptic seizures, pneumonia and unexplained physical deterioration. They rushed to the hospital several times, and were deeply shocked and distressed by the sight of their daughter in an alien-looking environment, surrounded by severely disabled people. Each time, Jennifer pulled through. Brian and Joan did not visit Jennifer between these calls nor did they maintain any other contact with the hospital.

When long-stay hospitals were beginning to close down, it was suggested that Jennifer was moved into a community home. After much negotiation, a potential home was found for her not far from where her parents lived. A social worker and a community psychiatrist went to talk to Joan and Brian, to find out how they felt about their daughter. They spent a number of long, difficult and tearful sessions with them. Joan and Brian felt that their family had never been really complete. They decided that they would like Jennifer to live nearby in an ordinary home, and that it was time to tell their other children about her. Christopher and Sarah were shocked by the news, but wanted to meet their sibling.

The nurses on the ward were extremely upset by the proposal of Jennifer's move. They felt that Jennifer belonged on the ward, it was her home, and although she could not communicate her wishes, she seemed happy enough. They also felt that a community home would not be able to provide Jennifer with the same level of care; their 20-minute night checks had saved Jennifer's life on a number of occasions. They argued that Jennifer should be allowed to stay in the hospital.

Joan, Brian and their grown-up children knew the risks involved. The proposed home would care for six severely disabled adults, but it was homely rather than hospital-like. There would be two sleeping staff at night, one of whom would have a nursing qualification and would be connected to residents' rooms through an intercom. Joan and Brian had always wanted to get to know their daughter, but felt unable to do so while she was in hospital.

The community psychiatrist and the social worker supported Jennifer's move. The hospital managers were keen to move out as many people as possible. The resident doctor thought that although Jennifer's needs were profound, with the right support she could live in a community setting. However, he recognized that this was not without risk: if Jennifer had a major epileptic seizure that was not promptly treated, she could die. In any case, her health could deteriorate at any time.

Exercise 33.1

What do you think is the best way forward in this situation? Should Jennifer stay in the hospital where she has lived all her life, and where her life has been saved on several occasions? Or should she be moved into a more homely environment, where her family could get to know her? If possible, get together with others to debate this issue, each taking on a different professional or parental role. You **must** reach a decision.

Outcome 1

Despite the protestations of the nurses on the ward, Jennifer was settled into her new home. Her parents and siblings visited her regularly, and were happy about the renewed contact. Two months later, Jennifer had a major epileptic seizure during the night and could not be resuscitated. Joan and Brian were sad about this, but felt happy that Jennifer was part of their family at the end of her life. Joan said she finally felt 'whole' as a mother and was grateful that she and her husband had been supported to be parents to Jennifer.

Outcome 2

It was decided that Jennifer would be allowed to stay on the ward. The nurses continued to care for Jennifer in the same way. They felt she was not unhappy, although it was impossible to be sure about this. Joan and Brian still got distressed by the hospital set-up, and never visited again. Neither did her sister Sarah. Jennifer's brother Christopher came to see her three times over the next few years. Jennifer died seven years later of a chest infection.

Exercise 33.2

Having read these outcomes, how do you feel now about the decision you proposed? Do you think future outcomes alter the way decisions are perceived as right or wrong?

What if the outcomes were altogether different? For example:

Outcome 3

As in **Outcome 1**, Jennifer was settled into her new home and was visited regularly by her family. It was difficult to tell whether she was happier than before, but her family was delighted with Jennifer's inclusion. Jennifer died seven years later of a chest infection.

Outcome 4

As in **Outcome 2**, Jennifer remained on the ward, and her family didn't visit. Despite the nurses' dedicated care, she died two months later following an epileptic seizure.

End-of-life decision-making

End-of-life decision-making means making choices that are likely to affect the quality of someone's remaining life, how long someone will live, and where they will live and be cared for. This is hardly ever straightforward, because it is usually difficult to predict exactly what will happen to someone's health, and what the consequences of any choices are. There are often no clear right or wrong answers. As in Jennifer's case, a number of salient issues need to be considered, including quality of life, communication and collaboration.

Quality of life

'Quality of life' is a key consideration in the provision of palliative care, and should inform all end-of-life decision-making. This is not as easy as it sounds. It is not unusual for health professionals to base the decision whether or not to provide active treatment on their own assumptions about the quality of another person's life. However, 'quality of life' is a very personal concept. It is the individual's satisfaction or happiness in life in domains he or she considers important (Flanagan 1978). While a healthy person may feel that their life would not be worth living if they could not walk and talk, someone like Jennifer (who has never known any different) may still be enjoying a good quality of life. When making treatment and care choices, it is therefore important to consider 'quality of life' from the other person's perspective. If the person cannot tell us what they value in their life, it can often still be determined by talking to those who know the person well.

Quality of life is affected by ill-health. Our priorities might change, and illness has an impact on the domains that are important to us for a good quality of life. Various tools have been developed to measure quality of life at the end of life (for example, Cohen 1995; Wilson 1995). Most of these look at a number of domains, such as physical, emotional, social, cognitive and spiritual domains; some include an assessment of symptoms and their impact. While it may not be possible to use such tools directly with people with learning disabilities, it can be useful to keep those domains in mind when thinking about someone's quality of life.

A focus on quality of life becomes particularly important if it is clear that someone's life expectancy is limited, and the personal cost of prolonging life may be considerable. Any proposed course of action that could be detrimental to someone's quality of life needs to be carefully discussed and agreed by all involved. If the person is able to make his or her wishes known, this should be the main consideration in the decision-making process.

There can be a degree of risk involved in allowing someone to enjoy a good quality of life. In Jennifer's case, it could be argued that the risk of being less protective (not having her in her cot at all times, and not observing her every 20 minutes) would be too great: she would probably die sooner. However, for Jennifer to live in a more stimulating environment and enjoy family relationships may be so valuable that it is worth taking the risk. Thinking about risk management, what level of risk would you be comfortable with? What personal reasons in your own life might influence your perspective?

Exercise 33.3

Think about the following questions:

What do you value most in your life? Can you name five things that contribute to your quality of life? (This could be anything, for example family, friends, health, work, skills, hobbies, faith, food, holidays . . .)

Think of one person with learning disabilities you know. What do you think this person values most in life? If you don't know, how could you find out? Could you ask the person? Spend time with him/her? Ask close carers, family, friends?

The complexity of issues at the end of life

When a person with learning disabilities reaches the end of life, those involved are affected in different ways. Let us look at some of the issues. First, those faced by the person with learning disabilities:

- *Changes in health.* The person is likely to notice that they are less able to do things, needing increased help with tasks of daily living. They may experience symptoms such as fatigue, pain, nausea, shortness of breath, or others.

- *Worry and anxiety.* The person will probably be worried, especially if they are not helped to understand their situation. It can be particularly worrying if they receive conflicting messages, where one person says 'you are ill', and another says 'everything is just fine'.

- *Changes in circumstances.* The person may have to go to hospital, or move into a different setting altogether. Their familiar routines may be disrupted.

- *Communication problems.* It is likely that the person has difficulty in communicating their feelings, symptoms, fears or wishes. Their ways of communicating may be misinterpreted or disregarded.

- *Need for relationships.* Many people who are terminally ill want to spend more time with family and friends. People with learning disabilities also may want to be with their family, even if they haven't seen them for a long time.

- *Tendency to protect others.* The person may be acutely aware of the burden they place on others, and may try to protect their family and carers, for example, by not complaining. In addition, people with learning disabilities are often actively encouraged by those around them to be cheerful and keep smiling, even if they have every reason to be sad.

Issues faced by the family include:

- *Involvement.* Families who have not been particularly involved in a person's life may want or need more involvement now (as in Jennifer's case). While many care settings are excellent at including the family as important partners, others may resent the (sometimes sudden) emergence of family wishes. Many families, however, are very involved throughout the person's life, and often know the person better than anyone else. They need to be included in end-of-life care and decision-making.

- *Experience of services.* Some families, particularly of older people, do not have an entirely positive experience of learning disability services. They may have had to struggle in the past to get the best possible care for their relative. Services have changed enormously over the past decades, and the way families have experienced this will affect their way of coping and communicating with the influx of new services at the end of life. Alternatively, if the family has been happy with the services provided, or if they feel that their relative is finally settled happily, it may be difficult to accept that a change of services is now necessary.

- *Anticipatory loss.* The family has to face an imminent bereavement. In addition to the general shock and sadness of loss faced by all of us, families of people with learning disabilities may re-experience feelings of loss and bereavement faced when a disabled child was born, or when their child or sibling left the family home. Some people will have feelings of guilt or anger. Many people with learning disabilities have an important place within their families. Even relatives who haven't seen the person regularly (or even lost contact altogether) can feel deeply bereft when the person dies.

Issues faced by paid carers include:

- *Lack of skills and resources.* Paid caregivers may feel strongly that they do not have the skills and resources to support someone towards the end of life. This can be particularly difficult if the person lives in a residential home rather than with their family. Staff at the home may feel that they don't have enough staff to cope with physical illness; they lack the facilities; or they have a philosophy of enabling independence rather than giving increased support.
- *Involvement.* Many carers, including paid carers at residential homes, are highly committed to the people they support, and go well beyond the call of duty when someone is terminally ill. Such involvement often leads to genuine loving care, and contributes to a good quality of life for the person. However, the cost can be high if carers' commitment and emotional involvement is not recognized and supported by others (in particular, their managers), for example through offering opportunities to debrief, and through recognition of carers' feelings of grief. In some cases, carers'

involvement can be damaging, particularly if they feel that they are the only ones who can support the person properly, to the exclusion of other services.

- *Lack of experience around death.* Many carers in learning disability services are relatively young, and may never have experienced death at close hand, leading to feelings of fear.

Issues faced by services include:

- *The right place of care.* Residential care services have to decide whether the person can continue to be supported in their usual home. This depends largely on the level of support available in the home, either through the home's own staff or with additional support services (such as primary care or community palliative care teams). The person's wishes, and those of the family, need to be taken into account. Sometimes, if the person can no longer be supported at home, there is no other suitable care setting available.
- *Profusion of services.* Towards the end of life, a huge variety of professionals can become involved, including GPs, district nurses, hospital doctors, physiotherapists, chaplains, palliative care (or hospice) doctors and nurses, social workers and learning disability teams. It is not difficult to imagine a damaging lack of co-ordination among all these services.
- *Lack of training.* Staff in mainstream health care services (including hospitals) lack training around the support of people with learning disabilities.

This list of issues is not exhaustive, but gives a flavour of the complexity of issues that may arise towards the end of someone's life. Everybody's experience and viewpoint is valid and needs to be acknowledged. In order to provide optimum support, it is crucial that all parties involved communicate among themselves and with each other. Studies have shown that people were most satisfied with services around life-limiting illness and end of life when there was a good partnership working between the different organizations involved, and a sharing of knowledge and information (Northfield and Turnbull 2001; Brown *et al.* 2005; Tuffrey-Wijne 2009).

All these issues emerged in an in-depth study of the experiences of 13 people with learning disabilities who had cancer, carried out by the authors. They are described vividly, often using the words and viewpoints of people with learning disabilities themselves, in *Living with Learning Disabilities, Dying with Cancer* (Tuffrey-Wijne 2009).

Feelings and emotions often run high when someone with learning disabilities faces a life-limiting situation. If you role-played Jennifer's situation, you may have realized how passionate people can become. It is crucial that any decision is taken with the best interest of the person with learning disabilities in mind. Looking back to the people involved in Jennifer's situation, they would have to ask themselves what their own interest was, and whether this would truly serve Jennifer best. There can often be no easy answers.

Case study: *Charles*

Charles Manning was a 62-year-old man with moderate learning disabilities. He lived in a flat with two friends, where a team of support workers took turns to come in during the day. Having lived in an institution when he was young, Charles was happy to have a degree of independence now, and particularly enjoyed going to the day centre. Charles's only relative was a brother in America who hadn't been in contact for 35 years.

When Charles noticed that he was having difficulty passing urine, he mentioned this to Mohammed, the support worker he was closest to. Mohammed took him to see his GP, who referred him to hospital for investigations. Charles found this difficult as he had a fear of hospitals, but he coped well. Cancer of the prostate was diagnosed, which was still in the early stages and had not spread to any other parts of the body.

The hospital consultant called Mohammed in to discuss the results. He explained that the best course of action was to 'wait and see'. Cancer of the prostate is usually slow growing, and in any case the consultant thought Charles would not be able to cope with the radiotherapy treatments.

Mohammed did not know that prostate cancer in the early stages can often be cured by radiotherapy.

Exercise 33.4

What do you think of the proposed course of action?

What do you think Mohammed should do?

Should Charles be told about his diagnosis and any possible treatments?

Consider what could happen next.

Outcome 1

Mohammed did not know much about cancer, and assumed that the doctor would give him the best possible advice. He reported back to his manager that the hospital had said Charles didn't need any treatment. The team of support workers assured Charles that everything was OK. Charles coped with his urine difficulties as best he could. After three years, he started complaining of painful legs. Mohammed had left by then, and the new support worker didn't think it was anything serious, so initially Charles didn't see a doctor. Over the next six months, the pain got progressively worse. When Charles finally went to the GP, he was sent into hospital immediately, and it was found that the cancer had spread to his bones. Charles was given painkillers. He was never told his diagnosis. He became increasingly weak and died of metastatic prostate cancer a year later.

Outcome 2

Mohammed felt uncomfortable about not telling Charles, but he didn't think he knew enough about cancer to talk to Charles himself. He asked his manager for help, who called the local learning disabilities team for advice.

Dianne, the learning disability nurse, contacted the hospital consultant and questioned him about his decision not to treat Charles. She discovered that the consultant would have treated other people with the same cancer as Charles, but that he didn't think that Charles could give his informed consent to treatment. Dianne called together a case conference, and it was agreed that she would explain everything to Charles, and try to establish his wishes. Using a picture book *(Getting on with Cancer,* see **Resources**, page 471*)*, Dianne talked to Charles about his cancer, and explained the possibility of having curative radiotherapy. Charles understood this, and decided he would have the treatment because he didn't want things to get worse. He went into hospital ten times for radiotherapy treatments. Dianne and Mohammed supported him when his fear of hospitals took over, helping him again and again to understand why he needed to go. They also helped him to take things easy when he was tired from the treatments. Five years later, scans confirmed that the cancer had not returned, and Charles enjoyed a good quality of life for many more years.

Exercise 33.5

With others, role play the following scenarios:

- The consultant tells Mohammed the test results. Mohammed asks questions, and disagrees with the consultant; he thinks Charles should be told.
- Dianne or Mohammed (or both) explain everything to Charles.

What was it like to act out these roles?

If you were in Mohammed's position, what support would you need?

What do you think Charles needs?

This case has highlighted a number of difficult issues that often arise when someone develops a life-threatening illness. These include consent to treatment, talking about the illness, and choice-making. Let us look at these issues more closely.

Consent to treatment

Charles's consultant made the assumption that Charles wouldn't be able to give consent to treatment. It should never be assumed that people are not able to make their own decisions, simply because they have learning disabilities. The laws on consent to treatment vary. Scotland led the way with the Adults with Incapacity (Scotland) Act, which took effect in 2000 (Department for Constitutional Affairs 2000). Under this Act, doctors are ultimately responsible for making health care decisions if a person is not capable of giving consent. It gives them clear guidelines on how to assess capacity, starting from the principle that all adults (including those with learning disabilities) are presumed capable of taking health care decisions. However, it recognizes that capacity of an individual may vary, depending on time, circumstances and types of decision. In England and Wales, the Mental Capacity Act 2005 (Department for Constitutional Affairs 2007) came into effect in 2007. It brings clarity and certainty to the decisions that have to be made by both health and social care workers for the people they support. As in Scotland, the new Act recognizes that adults may be able to take some decisions, even if they are not able to consent to others. Professionals will have to argue clearly why they think someone cannot take a particular decision. Where someone cannot consent to treatment, decisions must be taken in the person's 'best interest'. In other words, professionals have to do 'what is right' for their patient. Such decisions should be discussed in a 'best interested meeting', involving everyone who is involved in the person's support: medical staff as well as those who know the person best. Advice on consent can be found in a guidance document titled *Seeking Consent: Working with People with Learning Disabilities* (Department of Health 2001a).

So let us look more closely at Charles's situation. In order to be able to give valid consent, Charles needs to be competent (in other words: capable of taking that particular decision); he should not be pressured into a decision; and he should be provided with enough information to enable him to make the decision. In order to assess his capacity to decide about having treatment, he must be able to comprehend and retain information material about the treatment, understand the consequences of not having the treatment, and use this information to make his decision.

In this case (**Outcome 2**), Charles was capable to decide about having radiotherapy treatment. But what if he couldn't? Would the consultant then be right not to treat him? It can be argued that the consultant would be denying Charles potentially life-saving treatment, which he would have given if Charles didn't have learning disabilities. This lack of treatment could be seen as negligent. The consultant would have to decide what was in Charles's best interest, and to do this he would have to sit down with Charles's carers, advocate and (if he had any) his family. On the face of it, it seems that Charles's interest would be best served by giving him life-saving treatment. There would need to be a strong consensus to decide the opposite (for example, if Charles's hospital phobia made having treatment more or less impossible).

Talking about the illness

Most people in our culture want to know about their illness. Even if they do not want to know all the details, or are happy to let the doctor decide what treatment is best, they want their questions answered honestly. For many years health care and palliative care professionals have advocated openness and honesty as the best way to help people cope with terminal illness, although they recognize that this needs to be done sensitively (Seale 1991). There is no reason to believe that this should be any different for people with learning disabilities. However, people with learning disabilities are often shielded from knowledge about their diagnosis (Todd 2005; McEnhill 2008). Family and carers are often closest to the person, and have developed effective ways of communicating. While most will probably work from

the principles of choice and respect, they themselves may be unfamiliar with talking openly about illness and death, and feel very anxious about these taboo subjects. Health professionals are used to truth telling, but they may be at a complete loss about how to communicate with people with learning disabilities, or they may think that others will tell the person about their illness. The only way forward is for everyone to work closely together.

People with learning disabilities need to have their illness and any (proposed) medical procedures explained to them in very concrete, practical terms. Exactly what is happening now? What will happen next? Doctors and nurses (for example, a Macmillan nurse) can help family and carers with this. Time needs to be taken to explain, with the help of demonstrations or pictures if necessary. A series of picture books has been designed for this purpose (the *Books Beyond Words* series, see **Resources**, page 471). It is important that everyone involved knows what information has been given, and conflicting messages are avoided. It is not unusual for one person to answer questions honestly, while another person says that everything will get better. This can only add to someone's confusion and distress.

Choice-making

Towards the end of life, and particularly if there is a life-threatening illness that can no longer be cured, any decisions and choices about the person's life should be aimed at achieving the best possible quality of life. We have already considered the many variables that can contribute to someone's quality of life. Choices need to be made, not only about the big issues (treatments, wills and funerals) but also about the day-to-day issues that may be of more immediate importance to the person with learning disabilities. Here are some examples of end-of-life choices:

- My mum is coming to visit, but I get so tired now from the day centre that I won't enjoy her visit. Maybe I can stay at home on the day when she visits?
- I want to be free of pain, but the painkillers make me feel sleepy and I don't like that. Are there any other ways to cope with the pain?

- I know that the chemotherapy makes me live longer, but I hate it so much. Do I have to have it?
- Who do I want to look after me when I get more ill? I like it here at home, but I'm not sure my mum can manage.
- They say that I shouldn't smoke but I like it and I want to.

There are many different ways to help someone make choices, and such help needs to be highly individualized and culturally sensitive. One idea could be to create a life story book, with pointers to the important people, events and values in someone's life. Another is to think carefully about what the person values in life (for example, relationships and activities) and what makes him or her distressed. If the person cannot communicate this clearly, it will be necessary to involve family, friends and carers in this assessment. In the course of her research, one author has attended many funerals of people with learning disabilities. It was surprising how often paid carers were surprised when they listened to the memories of relatives for the first time, and wished they had known this earlier. Understanding of the person's background, including childhood and family relationships, can often throw light on what is important to the person at the end of life.

Religion, culture and end of life

The choices people make around the end of life are strongly influenced by their religion and culture, which will have shaped attitudes and beliefs that are important in their lives. Different faiths usually have a set of practices and rituals, including death rituals. In some cultures it is normal behaviour to express feelings of distress by crying, while in others this would be seen as a sign of weakness and 'not coping'. It is important never to make assumptions, as cultural and religious practices can vary widely. For example, it is not enough to know that someone grew up in the West End of London and belongs to the Muslim faith. You would need to find out what particular elements from a specific culture or religion someone embraced. You can only do this by communicating closely with the person involved, their family and their close friends.

It takes a team to support someone at the end of life. The team consists of the person with learning disabilities themselves, their close friends and family, their carers and advocates; it can include the learning disabilities team, the primary care team, the hospital and specialist teams, the faith community: the list is potentially very long. Working and living with death and dying is never easy, but if everyone works together and the person with learning disabilities is fully included, it can be an enriching life experience for everyone involved.

Bereavement issues

Case study: *Kumar*

Kumar Parikh had Down's syndrome and was the only child of Saroj and Gyan Parikh. His mother, Saroj, was his main carer until her health deteriorated. His father, Gyan, was a businessman who travelled a great deal during his working life until his late sixties, so had relied on his wife to make decisions about family matters. Saroj died of heart failure after a long illness when she was 73, and Kumar was just 40. During her illness, which included many hospital admissions, Gyan began to play a bigger part in supporting Kumar each day. He was now 74 years old and fully retired. He enjoyed quite good health but was aware that Kumar was likely to outlive him.

Kumar had always lived at home and, as an only child with a busy father, had been used to being the centre of his mother's attention. When his father retired there were some upsetting battles as Gyan began to assert more authority at home, and eventually the family requested advice and help from the community learning disability team. When Saroj was admitted to hospital the team arranged for Kumar to have two weeks' respite care. This soon became a pattern, with Kumar having respite, if it was available, whenever his mother was admitted. During her last illness, the period of respite was longer than usual and Kumar was in respite when his mother died.

Exercise 33.6

What do you think is the best way forward in this situation? Should Kumar stay in the respite unit until the funeral is over or should his father be supported to take Kumar home so that he can be involved in the Hindu funeral rituals and grieve with his father and other family and friends (Raji *et al.* 2003)? Should he stay in the respite unit until a decision has been made about where he will live in the future? Or should he be able to go home and make plans for his future over the next few months when he and his father have had time to come to terms with Saroj's death? If possible, get together with others to debate this issue, each taking on a different point of view, e.g. father wants him to stay in respite, Kumar wants to go home, community nurse agrees with Kumar. You must reach a decision. Consider what could happen next:

Outcome 1

It was decided that Kumar should stay in the respite unit and the manager agreed with Gyan that Kumar would not attend the funeral as they thought he would not fully understand what was happening. Although it is traditional for male relatives to participate fully in Hindu funeral rites, children and women do not and people with learning disabilities are also often excluded. Kumar went to the day centre as usual on the day of the funeral and did not see his father for some days, although some of the relatives who came to the funeral did visit him in the unit. The family suggested to Gyan that it would be too difficult for him to have Kumar back home, but they were all worried about what would happen to Kumar. Gyan's sister thought that there was a risk that Gyan would be left to cope on his own and was worried what would happen if he became ill or died. Gyan decided to say that Kumar couldn't come home. The community team social worker started to look for a new home for him, and found an adult family placement for him with a Hindu family in another part of town. His Dad was able to visit him and invited him to come home for a meal once a month. Kumar seemed to settle although he was very quiet and became incontinent, and would become very angry if anyone mentioned his mother. His father died three years later and the family home was left to his sister.

Outcome 2

It was decided that Kumar should go home as soon as possible and social services agreed to pay for a one-to-one worker to provide several hours' support each day. They agreed that the support would be reviewed in six weeks' time, and adjusted if necessary, but the social worker reassured Gyan that it would not be withdrawn until Kumar had his own person-centred plan with the support he needed in place. The social worker also said that he would have the choice of Direct Payments so that he could purchase care that was culturally sensitive and flexible to meet his particular needs. An agency support worker was found who came from the Hindu community and was able to support Kumar in the immediate period after his mother's death. Another worker soon joined him and they took it in turns to support Kumar in his personal care, and in resuming his daytime occupation. Kumar made it clear that he wanted to stay at home with his father, but his behaviour and mood became difficult when it was suggested to him that he should move into a group home. His father was worried that the support being offered now might not be sustained in the longer term and realized that he needed a great deal of financial advice before being able to decide whether to leave his house to Kumar in his will (Harker *et al.* 2002). He was put in touch with a housing adviser and decided to set up a family trust. He decided that he wanted Kumar to stay in the house he had lived in for his whole life. He made arrangements for his care to be managed by the trust and made appropriate provision in his will. Gyan died three years later and Kumar stayed at home with increased support. A friend of Kumar's came to live with him and through the Supporting People finance available in each local authority they were able to afford to have a support worker sleeping in the house every night. Kumar missed his father and initially hid all the photos of his parents. A support worker referred him to the local bereavement counselling service, and he saw a counsellor for several months, which helped him a great deal.

Exercise 33.7

Having read these outcomes, how do you feel now about the decision you proposed? Do you think future outcomes alter the way decisions are perceived as right or wrong?

What if the outcomes were altogether different? For example:

Outcome 3

As in **Outcome 1** Kumar settled into his new home, but one of his new 'family' died suddenly and Kumar was immediately moved back into respite.

Outcome 4

As in **Outcome 2** Kumar stayed at home with his father but the support agency appointed a worker who later exploited Kumar by 'borrowing' money from him when he went with him to the bank.

The impact of a bereavement

Grief following the death of a close relative or friend is a normal and common reaction. The following responses are described by many bereaved people: feeling fear and panic; numbness and disbelief about what has happened; feeling out of control; being under- or over-active; losing an appetite for food; being unable to sleep; having a poor memory; hearing the voice of the dead person; wanting to talk to them; forgetting they have died; being cross with other people; crying a lot; being unable to think or work. For someone with a learning disability the same reactions may be expressed behaviourally rather than in words. Disturbances of sleep and appetite are relatively easy to notice, but unexplained anger towards people or objects or self-harm may be harder to understand (Dodd *et al.* 2005, 2008).

Exercise 33.8

Think about the following questions:

In **Exercise 32.3** you were asked to name five things that contribute to your quality of life. You may have chosen family, health, work, skills, hobbies, faith, food, holidays . . . What would it be like for you to lose one, two or even all of these five things, for example following a bereavement?

Think of one person with learning disabilities you know who has been bereaved. What do you think this person values most in life? How many of these things were lost when they were bereaved? Is there anything anyone could do to restore some of these things to the person now? If you don't know, how could you find out? Could you ask the person? Spend time with him/her? Ask close carers, family and friends?

Communication and collaboration

When a person with learning disabilities is bereaved, those involved are affected in different ways. Let us look at some of the issues.

Issues faced by the person with learning disabilities include:

- *Changes in skills.* Grief can lead us all to lose some skills, usually temporarily, and this may be because of our preoccupation with our loss or because of the unexpected additional skills we need to acquire to cope without the person who has died. For example, people with learning disabilities may become incontinent, become less articulate, or forget the way home from a familiar activity.
- *Worry and anxiety.* The person may not understand about the finality of death. Worry about where the deceased person has gone may lead to searching behaviour. Carers may describe this as wandering or repetitive behaviour, not recognizing what the person is looking for. For example: the person who did not attend her father's funeral, and

was told that Dad had gone away, kept asking 'Where's Dad?' over and over. Staff saw this as inappropriate when it was still being asked three years later, but having missed the opportunity to include her in the funeral rituals, nobody had found a way to explain his death to her. The emotional experience of being a chief mourner, and the way in which the different senses help us to understand the finality of death, had been denied to her.

- *Changes in circumstances.* Sometimes the person who died was the main carer or the only person who really understood the speech or signs used by the bereaved person. Often someone will lose so much more than the person who has died. They may lose their home, their familiar routines, the experience of being understood, their neighbours, visiting tradesmen – the list is endless. Unfamiliar people, places and routines replace these losses, and initial moves are usually temporary. Oswin (1991) described how some people might be moved several times in the months following the death of their last surviving parent.
- *Communication problems.* Just as with the end-of-life issues discussed above, it is likely that the person has difficulty in communicating their feelings, fears or wishes. Their way of communicating may be misinterpreted or disregarded.

Issues faced by the family include:

- *Involvement.* Many families are very involved throughout the person's life, and often know the person better than anyone else. They need to be included in important decision-making at times of transition. Family members including siblings, who have not been recently involved in a person's life, may want or need more involvement now. The bereavement their relative is experiencing may be a shared bereavement, with their own grief affecting their response to the family member with a learning disability. While many care managers and care settings are excellent at including the family as important partners, others may resent the (sometimes sudden) emergence of family wishes. Recent English government White Papers on learning disability recognized that family carers were often not fully involved in decision-making, and strongly advocated more family involvement (Department of Health 2001b, 2009).
- *Experience of services.* Families who have continued to care for their relative at home may find the sudden involvement and influence of social workers or learning disability professionals rather difficult, particularly if they have been used to doing their own problem-solving within their own informal networks. They may be confused by the gap between the reality of the service response to their family bereavement and the aspirations in *Valuing People Now* or the plans being discussed by their local Partnership Board. Alternatively, they may be familiar with more traditional segregated service provision and find newer ideas about person-centred planning bewildering.

Issues faced by carers include:

- *Lack of skills and resources.* Daily caregivers may think that they have the skills and resources to support someone who has been bereaved, but in practice find that it is an area of human experience with which they are unfamiliar. This can be particularly difficult if the person lives in a residential home rather than with their family. Staff at the home may feel that they don't have enough staff to cope with changes in behaviour or mood or to offer any increased support with someone's emotional needs at such a time.
- *Involvement.* Many carers, including paid carers at residential homes, are highly committed to the people they support, perhaps to the extent of not wanting to use other supports which are available to all community members. Sometimes this may still result in a good outcome for the person. However, sometimes if carers feel that they are the only ones who can support the person properly, they miss out when carers do not have all the skills required. One study found that bereaved people with learning disabilities were able to benefit from referral to volunteer bereavement counselling services when their carers had the foresight to recognize the specialist skills of trained bereavement counsellors (Dowling *et al.* 2006).
- *Lack of experience around death.* Many carers in learning disability services are relatively young, and may never have experienced bereavement at

close hand, leading them to avoid talking about the person who has died.

Issues faced by services include:

- *The right place to live.* Services may have to consider how to continue supporting the person in their usual home. This depends on the level of support available at home, which will be particularly pertinent if the person who died was the main carer. The person's wishes, and those of the family, need to be taken into account. There may be pressure on services to make decisions about services immediately after the bereavement. However, it is not a good idea to assess somebody's skills and wishes at this time for reasons discussed above.

- *Profusion of services.* At any time of transition there can be a large number and variety of professionals and others involved, including support workers, GPs, social workers and learning disability teams as well as family members, advocates and concerned neighbours or friends. There is a risk that some of the professionals will communicate well with each other but leave other key people out including both formal and informal supporters and friends. Sometimes despite a relative lack of service availability, responses to bereavement can be over-professionalized, and fail to mobilize more ordinary personal and community support.

Each bereavement is different and the points raised here will not apply in every situation, but they do reflect issues that have recurred many times in the authors' own experiences. It is crucial that the person themselves remains at the centre of any response made by families and professionals, and that they are supported to remember their deceased friend or family member. This may require special attention to their understanding of the meaning of death.

Communication issues

Readers are encouraged to use the bereavement titles in the *Books Beyond Words* series of picture books for adults with learning disabilities, of which one author is the series editor (see **Resources**, below). These are books which tell clear stories in pictures with the dual aim of providing information for non-readers and helping people to explore their feelings.

Conclusion

When people with learning disabilities approach the end of life, they and their family, carers and services face a wide range of complex issues. Many people with learning disabilities are denied access to the same end-of-life care as the rest of the population. Issues around disclosure and consent can be particularly pertinent. Bereavement can be equally complex. Death, loss and bereavement are difficult areas of life, and for many people they are still taboo.

It is possible to provide sensitive and timely support, but this can only be achieved if everyone involved works closely and actively together, and if the person with learning disabilities is kept firmly in the centre of any choice and decision-making.

Resources

Books Beyond Words series. This is a series of picture books written for and with people with learning disabilities, edited by Sheila Hollins and published by RCPsych Publications/St George's, University of London (London).

Online orders: www.rcpsych.ac.uk/publications/booksbeyondwords.

Relevant titles include:

Donagney, V., Bernal, J., Tuffrey-Wijne, I. and Hollins, S. (2002) *Getting On with Cancer*. This book tells the story of a woman who is diagnosed with cancer, and then has surgery, radiotherapy and chemotherapy. The book ends on a positive note.

Hollins, S. and Sireling, L. (both 1994) *When Mum*

Died and *When Dad Died*. Both books take a straightforward and honest approach to death and grief in the family. The pictures tell the story of the death of a parent in a simple but moving way.

Hollins, S. and Tuffrey-Wijne, I. (2009) *Am I Going to Die?* This book tells the story of John, who has a terminal illness. It deals with both physical deterioration and the emotional aspects of dying in an honest and moving way. The book is useful for carers and supporters, health and other professionals who provide support to people with learning disabilities who are terminally ill.

Hollins, S., Blackman, N. and Dowling, S. (2003) *When Somebody Dies*. This book shows people with learning disabilities that they need not be alone when they feel sad about someone's death, and that talking about it to a friend or to a counsellor can help them get through a difficult time.

References

Blackman, N. (2003) *Loss and Learning Disability*. London: Worth Publishing.

Brown, H., Burns, S. and Flynn, M. (2005) *Dying Matters: A Workbook on Caring for People with Learning Disabilities who are Terminally Ill*. London: The Mental Health Foundation.

Cohen, S., Mount, M., Strobel, M. and Bui, F. (1995) The McGill Quality of Life Questionnaire: a measure of quality of life appropriate for people with advanced disease. A preliminary study of validity and acceptability, *Palliative Medicine*, 9: 207–19.

Department for Constitutional Affairs (2000) *Adults with an Incapacity (Scotland) Act 2000*. London: The Stationery Office.

Department for Constitutional Affairs (2007) *Mental Capacity Act 2005: Code of Practice*. London: The Stationery Office.

Department of Health (2001a) *Seeking Consent: Working with People with Learning Disabilities*. London: Department of Health.

Department of Health (2001b) *Valuing People: A New Strategy for Learning Disability for the 21st Century*. A White Paper. London: Department of Health.

Department of Health (2009) *Valuing People Now: A New Three-year Strategy for People with Learning Disabilities*. London: The Stationery Office.

Disability Rights Commission (2006) *Equal Treatment: Closing the Gap. A Formal Investigation into Physical Health Inequalities Experienced by People with Learning Disabilities and/or Mental Health Problems*. London: Disability Rights Commission.

Dodd, P., Dowling, S. and Hollins, S. (2005) A review of the emotional, psychiatric and behavioural responses to bereavement in people with intellectual disabilities, *Journal of Intellectual Disability Research*, 49(7): 537–43.

Dodd, P., Guerin, S., McEvoy, J., Buckley, S., Tyrrell, J. and Hillery, J. (2008) A study of complicated grief symptoms in people with intellectual disabilities, *Journal of Intellectual Disability Research*, 52(5): 415–25.

Dowling, S., Hubert, J. and Hollins, S. (2006) Bereaved adults with intellectual disabilities: a combined randomized controlled trial and qualitative study of two community-based interventions, *Journal of Intellectual Disability Research*, 50(4): 277–87.

Flanagan, J. (1978) A research approach to improving your quality of life, *American Psychology*, 33: 138–47.

Harker, H. and King, N. (2002) *Renting Your Own Home: Housing Options for People with Learning Disabilities*. Kidderminster: British Insitute of Learning Disabilities.

Hollins, S., Attard, M.T., von Fraunhofer, N., McGuigan, S. and Sedgwick, P. (1998) Mortality in people with learning disability: risks, causes, and death certification findings in London, *Developmental Medicine & Child Neurology*, 40(1): 50–6.

McEnhill, L. (2008) Breaking bad news of cancer to people with learning disabilities, *British Journal of Learning Disabilities*, 36(3): 157–64.

Mencap (2007) *Death by Indifference*. London: Mencap.

Michael, J. (2008) *Healthcare for All: Report of the Independent Inquiry into Access to Healthcare for People with Learning Disabilities*. London: Aldrick Press.

Northfield, J. and Turnbull, J. (2001) Experiences from cancer services, in J. Hogg, J. Northfield and J. Turnbull (eds) *Cancer and People with Learning Disabilities: The Evidence from Published Studies and Experiences from Cancer Services*. Kidderminster: BILD Publications.

Oswin, M. (1991) *Am I Allowed to Cry? A Study of Bereavement amongst People who have Learning Disabilities*. London: Souvenir Press.

Parliamentary and Health Service Ombudsman (2009) *Six Lives: The Provision of Public Services to People with Learning Disabilities*, HC 203 I–VIII. London: The Stationery Office.

Raji, O., Hollins, S. and Drinnan, A. (2003) How far are people with learning disabilities involved in funeral rites? *British Journal of Learning Disabilities*, 31(1): 42–5.

Seale, C. (1991) Communication and awareness about death: a study of a random sample of dying people, *Social Science and Medicine*, 32(8): 943–52.

Todd, S. (2005) Surprised endings: the dying of people with learning disabilities in residential services, *International Journal of Palliative Nursing*, 11(2): 80–2.

Tuffrey-Wijne, I. (2009) *Living with Learning Disabilities, Dying with Cancer: Thirteen Personal Stories*. London: Jessica Kingsley.

Tuffrey-Wijne, I., Hogg, J. and Curfs, L. (2007) End-of-life and palliative care for people with intellectual disabilities who have cancer or other life-limiting illness: a review of the literature and available resources, *Journal of Applied Research in Intellectual Disability*, 20(4): 331–44.

Tyrer, F., Smith, L. and McGrother, C. (2007) Mortality in adults with moderate to profound intellectual disability: a population-based study, *Journal of Intellectual Disability Research*, 51(7): 520–7.

Wilson, I. (1995) Linking clinical variables with health-related quality of life: a conceptual model of patient outcomes, *Journal of the American Medical Association*, 273(1): 59–65.

34

Healthy and successful ageing

Gordon Grant

Introduction

Earlier chapters in this last section of the book have illustrated that survival to and beyond national retirement age has become increasingly common among people with learning disabilities, at least in post-industrial societies. Statistics from developed countries like the US, Canada, Australia and the UK suggest that there is now but a handful of years that separate the life expectancy of people with learning disabilities from the population at large (Bigby 2004; Haveman *et al.* 2009). However, life chances are significantly reduced when environmental factors like living conditions, poverty and world region are taken into account in addition to personal factors like gender and degree/complexity of disability. By far the most significant among these are the environmental factors. This is once again a reminder that environmental factors are the source of major inequalities in the lives of people with learning disabilities as they reach old age, something that has been on the agenda of the World Health Organization (2001) for some years now. People with learning disabilities living in the world's poorest regions, for example, have a life expectancy that is just half that of those in more prosperous nations, a situation no doubt fuelled by systems of global economic and political governance that perpetuate a gulf between the world's richer and poorer nations.

This chapter concerns: ideas and theories that help to inform an understanding of healthy and successful ageing in people with learning disabilities; how people with learning disabilities talk about and make sense of ageing; and implications for practice.

Healthy and successful ageing – ideas and theories

Ageing is a process, not an event. How successfully individuals age depends on many factors including lifestyle, life history, informal and formal support from earlier years, genetic dispositions, and environmental constraints and opportunities. Many older people with learning disabilities age in a similar way to the general population so it is worth briefly introducing generic theories of successful ageing as most of these are equally applicable to people with learning disabilities. This applies just as well to their health status in later life. Indeed, healthy ageing is integral to successful ageing, and it is quite difficult to separate the two. In this section, therefore, ideas and theories about successful ageing are introduced before considering some of the exceptional or additional needs and circumstances of older people with learning disabilities, especially with regard to their health, and how these can be understood.

According to Franklin and Tate (2009), there is still a lack of consensus about either an agreed definition or indeed the determinants of successful ageing, largely due to the complex nature of the construct and its many psychosocial and biomedical domains. However, there is no lack of useful theorizing that can aid practice in working with older people.

Brandstadter and Grieve (1994) place an emphasis on the ability of older people to maintain a sense of personal continuity and meaning in the face of different kinds of losses that accompany the ageing process. In order to achieve this they argue that three sets of complementary processes need to be invoked:

- *assimilation*: defines efforts people make to realize their original goals and aspirations; most useful when problems are reversible and can be easily compensated for;
- *accommodation*: when assimilation is not possible, it may be necessary to reshape goals, activities and priorities consistent with available resources;
- *immunization*: this occurs when individuals selectively interpret demands that threaten core

components of an individual's identity that need to be protected, requiring either a reinterpretation of the significance of demands or a readjustment of individual performance.

All three processes are linked and integral to positive adaptation. If goals and aspirations remain consistent with realistic options then successful ageing is likely. People with learning disabilities might be expected to struggle more than most with the types of cognitive coping implied by the above strategies, but this remains a hypothesis yet to be tested.

Atchley's (1999) continuity theory suggests that over time individuals display remarkable consistency in patterns of thinking, living arrangements, social relationships and activity profiles. Similar to Branstadter and Grieve (1994), Atchley also stresses the importance of life history and biography to an understanding of experiences in later life. Reminiscence therapy in people with dementia is premised on such thinking. However, it serves to remind us that the present generation of older people with learning disabilities may have past lives punctuated by gaps and confusions about their identities, family and social relations as a result of the segregated and institutionalized conditions in which they used to live (see Chapters 1, 2, 5 and 31), making later life adjustment more difficult.

In their theory of 'selective optimization with compensation', Baltes and Carstensen (1996) suggest that three core processes are involved in successful ageing: greater selection of activity and function as physical activity reduces; compensation for loss of skill or function by using alternative means to achieve goals; and optimization by making the most of personal reserves to support selection and compensation. This line of thinking is useful in emphasizing that, like their younger counterparts, older people have goals, agency (capacity), the ability to discriminate and make choices, and the prospect of making accommodations and adjustments in the face of demands and challenges.

Meanwhile, in their cross-cultural study involving developed and developing nations, Fry et al. (1997) have shown that a good old age was associated with reliable physical health and functioning, material security, family and kinship networks and 'sociality'. Reliable physical health and functioning includes the capacity to take part in activities of one's choice, together with the energy, strength and vitality to continue in these. Material security refers to money, entitlements and resources sufficient to sustain a given level of living. Family and kinship networks define the immediate social structures to which older people are connected that provide them with support and care, advice and information, reassurance and worth. 'Sociality' has to do with life domains that allow people to receive positive feedback about themselves, as reflected in things like being and feeling part of the community and communities of interest, having the freedom to choose what to do and, by association, the ability to exert a sense of control over things that matter in one's life.

Activity theory proposed long ago by Lawton and Nahemow (1973) suggests that successful ageing depends upon maintaining activity in later life, a readiness to replace old roles with new ones, and a continuing involvement in the community and in social relations. Lawton et al. (1995) subsequently went on to demonstrate that activity alone is not enough and that cognitive challenges are required that allow older people to demonstrate competence and mastery. These are in turn likely to be important to positive self-image. Nahemow's (1990) subsequent ecological theory suggests, however, that in later life people need environments that are neither too demanding nor too devoid of stimulation.

For Coleman (1997), however, further development and empirical testing of theories of ageing is still necessary, especially in regard to:

- the importance of life history and lifespan influences on later life adaptation;
- development in later life with a focus on ordinary as opposed to exceptional ageing;
- understanding individual differences;
- a better appreciation of the existential challenges of frailty.

Coleman reminds us that in concentrating on successful ageing there is of course a danger of overlooking the impairments and chronic illnesses that can accompany the ageing process and how these are experienced. The onset and course of impairments and illnesses, and their implications for individuals, are real and inescapable. Hence, people in later life may be facing significant restrictions and declines in some areas of their lives while continuing to experience development and growth in others.

These generic theories and ideas about successful ageing have some clear implications for practice:

- If personal continuity and meaning are important in understanding how people age successfully, there is a need to be sensitive to factors that can give rise to discontinuities across the lifecourse (see book introduction) and how these can be predicted, prevented or ameliorated.
- Helping people to face and come to terms with biographical gaps or disruptions in their past lives may be difficult and even traumatic for individuals, as for example in the case of people who were previously institutionalized or the many older women with learning disabilities who have had their children taken away from them.
- Resourcefulness and resilience in individuals do not disappear just because they have reached a good old age. Rather, these attributes need to be respected and nurtured since they are integral to helping people to maintain a positive self-image.
- Commitment to the support of successful ageing is likely to require a balanced attention to people's strengths as well as to their needs, including an understanding of the internal processes individuals use to make accommodations as they age.

Exercise 34.1

Think of a close relative, perhaps a parent, that you know well who is aged 60 years or more. Then try to identify examples of assimilation, accommodation and immunization from the way your relative talks about managing things in later life. Consider which if any of these strategies seems to be most important to them.

According to Bigby (2004), some theories of successful ageing appear to be beyond the reach of many older people with learning disabilities. For example, writers such as Jorm *et al.* (1998) and Rowe and Kahn (1998) define successful ageing in terms of criteria that would be hard to reach such as absence of disease and disability, high cognitive skills and productive activity. Crowther *et al.* (2002) revisited Rowe and Kahn's model and suggested that it failed to emphasize not only biological determinants but also social structure and self-efficacy. Importantly, they introduced the notion of 'positive spirituality' into this model to good effect, suggesting the importance of core beliefs and values to individuals.

In relation to people with learning disabilities, Heller (2004) describes a support–outcomes model of successful ageing which emphasizes the importance of the environment and individualized supports in influencing outcomes. Outcomes are considered in relation to independence, quality of life, physical and emotional well-being and community inclusion. Interactions between personal and environmental factors are depicted as influencing these outcomes. Personal factors are described in terms of capabilities such as competence and attributes that help individuals to function in society. Environmental factors comprise the demands and constraints of everyday life. Desirable environments are seen to possess three main characteristics: opportunities for fulfilling people's needs; possibilities for fostering physical, social, material and cognitive well-being; and prospects for realizing a sense of stability, predictability and control. Supports may come from a variety of sources including people, technology and services.

Case study: successful ageing?

Maria is 61 years of age. She lives in a group home with two of her long-standing friends, Freda and Susan. The three women have known each other for decades, dating back to the time when they were all residents in a long stay hospital. The home is managed by a local voluntary organization and the three women all hold tenancies.

Maria's parents died years ago though she had long since lost contact with them when she was a long stay hospital resident. The circumstances surrounding this loss of contact are still rather cloudy. Maria compares her present living situation very favourably to that when she was living in a hospital. She likes the creature comforts of having her own room, a key to come and go when she pleases, and close friends in Freda and Susan with whom she shares much of her life. Maria had to leave the local day centre when she was 60. It is based on the other side of town so she rarely sees friends and companions that she knew there. Her home is based conveniently for local shops and amenities, but though she can walk to most places she has mobility difficulties due to having cerebral palsy. When she has been out on her own she has once or twice fallen and had to be taken to the accident and emergency department at the local hospital.

Because of her appearance and gait, over the years Maria has experienced many jibes and taunts from members of the public, usually gangs of young boys. Though she tries to ignore these comments they still affect her deeply. Maria has limited vocabulary and finds it difficult to defend herself against the offensive behaviour of other people. Like one or two of her friends she has tried to join the local physically handicapped and able bodied (PHAB) club, but been rejected, apparently on the grounds that her learning disability disqualified her. This really hurt her. Her care manager has been trying to resolve this situation with the club, thus far without success.

Maria considers herself to be quite healthy though she admits to not having the energy she once had. Risk of falling and the avoidance of antisocial behaviour from gangs of young people have made her even more wary about being out by herself. Beyond her immediate friends, Freda and Susan, Maria does not really have a wider social circle. Since her retirement from the day centre her life has become even more home-based. As a result, she spends a lot of time listening to the radio or reading magazines in her own room or watching TV with Freda and Susan in the lounge. Maria has conservative expectations for material possessions, probably the by-product of a life lived dependent upon financial support from the state.

Maria seems quite aware of her own mortality and is becoming increasingly concerned about the failing health of her two friends, Freda and Susan, both more frail than her.

Exercise 34.2

Thinking of Maria, consider what features of her environment enhance her well-being and what features undermine it.

Make a note of the features of Maria's social relations that have some influence on her well-being.

Thinking of the successful ageing model described by Heller (2004), what are the consequences for Maria of seeking a more stable and predictable lifestyle?

Accessing health services in later life

We are still a long way from knowing about all the factors that govern the health status of older people with learning disabilities. One of the reasons for this is that we do not know where many older people with learning disabilities are, so little or nothing is known of their circumstances. Older people with mild learning disabilities have probably long since successfully 'disappeared' in mainstream society and are no doubt managing their lives quite adequately, without specialist learning disability services. This is an assumption still in need of testing. Even for those with high support needs, many are 'lost' from specialist learning disability services, having retired from day services, moved into generic or elder care services, or managed somehow to get lost in the system because of a lack of active case finding or integrated case records linked by a 'cradle to grave' philosophy. This also makes it difficult, even impossible, to produce an accurate estimate of the number of older people with learning disabilities in most localities. Because this can leave individuals with less than appropriate support, it can easily result in unnecessarily restricted lifestyles (Foundation for People with Learning Disabilities 2002). Interestingly, *Valuing People Now* (Department of Health 2009a) is strangely silent on these issues.

Even when people are known to services, there are barriers that continue to make it difficult for them to access appropriate health care. Searching reviews about healthy ageing in people with learning disabilities (Evenhuis *et al.* 2001; Haveman *et al.* 2009) has identified many factors that mediate access to health services. These can be split for convenience into two groups: person-specific and environment-specific.

Person-specific

The limited articulacy of people with severe cognitive impairments is one of the main difficulties. This can inevitably lead to a significant masking of the ability of individuals to disclose how they are feeling, placing a high premium on those with close personal knowledge of the individual to make judgements on such matters, with all the risks this can entail. Similar challenges arise in the case of people with multiple or complex disabilities where one condition can confuse or compromise patterns of symptomatology associated with another, thereby increasing the risk of inappropriate diagnosis and treatment. Imagine for example a deaf or hard of hearing person who is also aphasic (unable to understand or express speech because of brain damage) and unable to make use of a recognized signing system. Examples like this are quite common.

Environment-specific

Many more barriers to appropriate health care are created by the very environments in which people find themselves. Medical history-taking can take a long time and can become too dependent on observations of staff, family members or advocates who know the person well. Staff turnover is a complicating factor here, as also is the death, migration or incapacity of family members where important biographical and life history details can quickly disappear. Consent procedures and associated concerns, while necessary to protect the health and welfare of individuals, can protract medical history-taking even further.

Behavioural difficulties constitute an additional potential barrier. Individuals commonly find themselves being assessed in unfamiliar health care environments like surgeries, by people not well known to them. As a consequence they may have difficulty co-operating with examinations, tests and questions, primarily because of their fears and confusion associated with unfamiliar environments and people. Consent to treatment and compliance with treatment may therefore become problematic. There is plenty of evidence suggesting that many health care providers, especially those working in primary health care settings, still lack the skills and sensitivities to deal with these situations in helpful ways (Grant and Ramcharan 2007).

Case complexity represents a further barrier to effective health care. People often require access to a variety of medical and other specialists, placing a high premium on an integrated approach to case management, case co-ordination and person-centred planning (see Chapters 22 and 25). Although the jury is still out on how well such systems work (Mansell and Beadle-Brown 2004), there are some encouraging signs that person-centred planning can and does work for some people (Robertson *et al.* 2007) but still not all.

Exercise 34.3

Think of an older person with learning disabilities well known to you who is at least 50 years of age. In regard to their ability to access generic health services, list all the personal factors that appear to act as barriers, then list all the environmental factors that seem to inhibit or bar access. Consider what should be done to deal with these barriers.

Getting closer to the person in everyday practice

These considerations raise interesting challenges for the types of knowledge likely to be necessary in helping people to negotiate access to services and more particularly in 'getting closer to the person' in professional practice. Drawing on the work of Liaschenko (1997) and Mead and Bower (2000), these can be summarized as follows: case knowledge, patient knowledge, communicative knowledge and person knowledge.

- *Case knowledge* refers to disembodied biomedical knowledge – that is, a knowledge of aetiology, clinical symptoms, prognoses and treatments. It is this knowledge that most clearly differentiates professional and clinical workers (as people with authority and power) from patients, families and others.

- *Patient knowledge* refers to a person's social circumstances and support relevant to contextualizing case knowledge. To some extent, health care workers will have access to such knowledge through case files and medical records.

- *Communicative knowledge* has to do with how people convey intent, meaning and understanding. This is especially important for older people with learning disabilities as for many such people their verbal competencies are severely impaired, making non-verbal communication, assistive communication technologies, allies and advocates important. In the use of these complementary communication systems people with learning disabilities are often more expert than those they are seeking to consult.

- *Person knowledge* comprises dimensions of agency, temporality and space. Agency refers to an individual's capacity to initiate meaningful action; temporality refers to how their life patterns are shaped by developmental, social and cultural clocks; while space here refers to how individuals relate to physical, social and political environments.

Person knowledge and communicative knowledge are domains in which the person with learning disabilities and their family have superior insights and relevant knowledge than professional and clinical workers. It is also the domain in which professionals are least knowledgeable. Patient knowledge, as defined above, is also a domain in which the person will in most circumstances have superior knowledge to other stakeholders, though this may also depend on their 'mental capacity'. Case knowledge, finally, is the most obvious domain in which practitioners will have superior knowledge.

In the present policy climate, where such a great emphasis is placed on the forging of partnerships between doctors, health and social care workers, patients and families (Department of Health 2006), all of these types of knowledge have to be brought into the equation. A dependency on case knowledge simply will not do as it reinforces traditional power relations and fails to capture the other types of knowledge mentioned that are central to understanding and empowering people. Though an oversimplification, Table 34.1 suggests that most of the relevant knowledge lies with the person, and to some extent their families, not the professional worker. This leaves a huge onus of responsibility with professionals to draw upon all these sources of knowledge if they are to stand a chance of 'getting close to the person', thus helping to ensure that the person gets the support and help they need.

It remains ironic that one of the most long-standing barriers directly affecting access to appropriate health care in the UK for people with learning disabilities in general is that many are still not registered with GPs. Bringing registration up to 100 per cent was one of the targets of *Valuing People* (Department of Health 2001) that was to have been achieved by June 2004. Unfortunately it was not achieved; and it was further demonstrated that health facilitation and health action planning arrangements were slow to develop, leaving the service infrastructure wanting in giving people good access to personalized health support (Grant and Ramcharan 2007). It remains to be seen whether the new

Type of knowledge	Person as expert	Family as expert	Practitioner as expert
Case knowledge	Low	Low	High
Patient knowledge	High	Medium	Medium
Communicative knowledge	High	High	Low
Person knowledge	High	High	Low

Table 34.1 Knowledge, the person, the family and the practitioner

arrangements for health action planning or person-centred planning envisaged by *Valuing People Now* (Department of Health 2009a) can deliver in these particular respects.

The *Health Needs Assessment Report* about people with learning disabilities in Scotland (NHS Health Scotland 2004) reaffirms some of these points by suggesting that there is a basic lack of health promotion, under-identification of ill health and a deficit in meeting those health needs specific to people with learning disabilities.

Determinants of health in old age

Physical health

Access to health care services aside, older people with learning disabilities experience rates of common adult and older age-related conditions comparable to the general population. These seem to reflect the same connections between hereditary disposition and environment present in older people. For some conditions, rates are higher in older people with learning disabilities compared to age-related peers without learning disabilities, for example obesity, dental disease, gastro-oesophageal reflux and oesophagitis, constipation and gastrointestinal cancer. Further examples are reported to include heart disease, mobility impairments, thyroid disease, osteoporosis, pneumonia and psychotropic drug problems (Evenhuis *et al.* 2001; Haveman *et al.* 2009).

It is important when considering the physical health of older people with learning disabilities that syndrome-specific conditions and associated conditions arising from central nervous system compromise are taken into account. The weight of evidence about these matters is developing very quickly now but there is insufficient space to detail it here.

It is thought that for people with milder learning disabilities there is the possibility that increased lifestyle choices may result in potential for risky behaviours, for example tobacco and substance abuse, violent behaviour and high-risk sexual behaviour. Poor diet and inappropriate caring practices are thought to have contributed to high rates of periodontal disease in adults with learning disabilities. Sedentary lifestyles, lack of exercise and work

environments that fail to stimulate people are all implicated as environmental factors shaping poor health. Permissive attitudes that have too often led to the exclusion of people with learning disabilities from health screening programmes should no longer be allowed to hold sway.

However, there is no evidence that preventative health practices recommended for the general population should be withheld from people with learning disabilities. Evenhuis *et al.* (2001) in fact suggest that lifestyle issues should be targeted specifically because these may well result in substantial gains in longevity, improved functional capacity and quality of life in old age. In particular it is thought that special programmes targeted at safe sex practices, avoidance of tobacco and other harmful substances, oral hygiene, exercise and diet, and fire safety education are all in need of development and evaluation.

Mental health

Compared to younger adults, older people with learning disabilities are much more likely to have accompanying psychiatric disorders, especially depression, generalized anxiety disorder and dementia (Cooper 1997). Past history of affective disorder is also reported to be present in a larger proportion of the older group. As people with learning disabilities age their need for psychiatric services appears to increase.

The increased prevalence of psychiatric disorders in adults is associated with social, biological and medical factors, life events and specific syndromes (Cooper 1997; Tyrell and Dodd 2003). Among social factors are lack of education, institutionalization at an early age, limited social networks, loss of close and confiding relationships, bereavement, lack of valued roles (e.g. paid work, marriage/partnership, parenthood), low income and relative poverty, service breaks and transitions and shifting patterns of interdependence with parents during the life cycle. All these factors are thought to impact on personality and predispose individuals to mental health problems in later life. Abuse and neglect can have long-term consequences for individuals and their families (O'Callaghan *et al.* 2003) but it is difficult to gauge from the available evidence whether and how this may manifest itself in later life.

Biological factors are also important. The presence of a behavioural phenotype can heighten risk. For example, Down's syndrome can predispose to an increased risk of dementia of the Alzheimer's type. According to Prasher's (1995) findings, for example, dementia in people with Down's syndrome grows from 2 per cent for those aged 30–39 years, to 9.4 per cent for those aged 40–49 years, 36.1 per cent for those aged 50–59 years and 54.5 per cent for those aged 60–69 years. This is substantially higher than in the general population. Conditions associated with compromise to the central nervous system such as cerebral palsy and epilepsy add further layers of dependency as the person ages (see Chapter 12).

With new funding, and its commitment to improved diagnosis, early intervention and more effective services underpinned by 'living well' ideals, the new Dementia Care Strategy (Department of Health 2009b) is likely to offer many adults with learning disabilities at risk of dementia the prospects of improved lives.

Case study: premature ageing

Albert is 47 years old. His parents died several years ago so he now lives with his sister and brother-in-law, Kath and Jim. They live together on a smallholding in the rural hinterland of a popular coastal resort. Albert has Down's syndrome.

Albert used to attend the local day centre where he had many friends but he has not been there for a long time. Consequently he has lost touch with many of them. He was never the most regular attender as his parents were content to look after him at home. Subsequent to his parents' deaths he used to like going out with Jim to the local market, sometimes dropping in to the pub, where they would meet and have a banter with many of Jim's friends, but he now no longer does so. Kath regarded herself as having a close sisterly relationship with Albert and she unquestioningly took over responsibility for his support following her parents' deaths. Earlier in life Albert was sociable, helpful around the house and took an interest in things.

According to Kath and Jim, Albert's behaviour began to change before his parents died, making his parents even more indulgent towards him. Looking back they were unaware of the scenario that was to unfold.

Albert was displaying many of the characteristics of early onset dementia typical of a sizeable proportion of his age-related peers with Down's syndrome. It was some time before the reasons for this were understood. Understandably, Kath and Jim looked initially for environmental factors that may be behind Albert's behaviour changes – anticipation of his parents' deaths, cumulative effects of medication – before coming to realize that there was more to it than that. Albert's behaviour and personality had in fact been changing gradually but increasingly, turning him into an apparently different person. He was becoming withdrawn, taciturn, unresponsive, reclusive but also provocative. During the early stages of these changes, Kath and Jim tended to 'blame' Albert for acting in these ways, presuming his behaviour to be intentional or deliberate. Even now, with the full weight of a clinical diagnosis of his dementia of the Alzheimer's type, it is still difficult for them to accommodate Albert's persistent lack of co-operation.

Kath and Jim have different coping strategies. Kath somehow manages most of the time to displace her frustrations by telling herself that the dementia is masking the real Albert and that things beyond his control, his dementia, are the triggers behind his behaviour. Jim by contrast still personalizes Albert's behaviour and reacts angrily to what he sees as wilfully disruptive displays from Albert. On many occasions the bath water has been switched on and left running, gates have been left open allowing pets and animals to escape, and facial grimaces have been directed at Jim which he thinks are designed to provoke him. Given the chance, Albert wanders off. These difficulties have led Kath and Jim to limit shopping and other trips into the community with Albert. As a result Albert is now virtually a captive in his sister and brother-in-law's house.

Tyrell and Dodd (2003) report that side-effects of medications are more common in older people with learning disabilities because of slower hepatic metabolism and renal excretion, and in some cases because of altered brain anatomy. Medications for epilepsy may, over a period of years, lead to over-sedation and confusion. These authors also suggest that in later life sensory impairments such as hearing loss or cataracts can lead to increased risk of behaviour disturbance. Similarly, physical health problems associated with ageing can predispose to depression and anxiety.

Gender and health

As in earlier life stages it is important to be aware of the gendered nature of conditions that can affect people in later life, and of the particular needs of women and men. After years of neglect this has become a priority for the World Health Organization (1997), which has become increasingly involved in promoting:

- advocacy for women's health and gender-sensitive health care delivery;
- promotion of women's health and prevention of ill health;
- making health care systems more responsive to women's needs;
- gender equality;
- involvement of women in the design, implementation and monitoring of health policies and programmes.

The health needs and circumstances of older women with learning disabilities was the subject of study for the World Health Organization (Walsh *et al.* 2001). In regard to sexual health in later life, people with learning disabilities have been reported as finding their needs and circumstances being ignored both by family members and services. It is easy for people's sexual health needs to be trivialized because of presumptions about incapacity, thresholds for giving consent and even in some cases because of perceptions that older people with learning disabilities are asexual beings able to live a fulfilling life without a sexual appetite. Such misplaced attitudes can lead to people being denied access to advice, education and support about safe sex and about all the range of reproductive health issues. Sadly some men and women with learning disabilities find themselves victims of sexual abuse that can leave them prone to sexually transmitted diseases, HIV and AIDS but these can go unrecognized for lengthy periods. Telling others about such abuse can be complicated because of a lack of knowledge, poor communication skills, fear and confusion.

At the time of writing little is known about the effects of the menopause on women with learning disabilities, though it is recognized that early onset is associated with particular syndromes like Down's and Fragile X.

Arrangements for screening women for breast cancer and cervical cancer, and similarly prostate cancer in men, frequently operate under such economic pressures that the extra time and resources required to explain and implement the procedures become barriers to participation.

Gender issues and health over the lifespan for people with learning disabilities are high on the national and international research agenda at this time. Narrative accounts that throw further light on these issues are now beginning to emerge, as we will see in the next section.

How people make sense of ageing

The narrative chapter in this last section (Chapter 31) of the book sheds important light on the personal and social world of older people. The narratives described there remind us that in later life people do indeed have stories to tell and memories to share, as well as hopes and dreams that they can articulate. However, some people have difficulties accomplishing this in ways that others can understand, which can lead us to think, erroneously, that they do not have important things to share and insights to offer.

Erickson *et al.* (1989) have shown that older people with learning disabilities display considerable insights into age-related changes in their personal and social lives. They were shown to have quite varied perceptions about growing older. Some wished to dissociate themselves from ageing while others had more concrete concerns about it, ranging from sedentary lifestyles, changes in employment status and loss of mobility to reduced social contacts, fears about incipient ill-health and a recognition that ageing ultimately heralds death. Some people were more optimistic than others about their future lives, especially about their anticipated use of leisure time. When considering the aspirations and anxieties of older people with learning disabilities it is clearly important to avoid stereotyping.

Edgerton *et al.* (1994), in their qualitative studies, have similarly shown considerable diversity in reports by older people with learning disabilities about their own health. There were nevertheless some consistent threads in people's experiences. Few attempted to exercise on a regular basis, even when enrolled on rehabilitative programmes. Only one person consistently avoided a high-fat, high-sugar diet. As a consequence many were reported to be overweight. Despite the best advice of relatives and care workers, many smoked cigarettes, possibly a legacy of years spent in institutionalized settings. Little drug or alcohol dependency was in evidence, however. Few had any understanding of the links between smoking, diet, exercise and health. Only a handful of people

could provide basic information about their own ailments or worries. All were reported to have problems determining when they were in need of health care, communicating their needs to others and understanding how to co-operate in treatment plans.

In the same study it was found that doctors often relied on informed guesswork about medications needed by individuals, and they were unaware of the drug hoarding habits of some individuals. Several serious cases came to light where doctors had overlooked medical and surgical procedures that individuals required.

In a recent study involving 18 countries, Walsh and LeRoy (2004) uniquely brought together accounts from 167 older women with learning disabilities about their experiences of ageing. In regard to well-being in later life, it was found that many of the women spoke of issues mirrored by population-wide studies of older women. Health, home, employment and financial security were commonly reported when they talked about their own well-being. For some of the women, religion was important. Pets were a source of comfort and company for others. Although a third of the women claimed that they had no worries, the rest pointed to familiar themes that were a source of anxiety to them: disability, family members, health, finances, the future, global threats and a host of more specific things. Fears about the death and poor health of family members were quite prevalent, and there were some anxieties about just 'getting on' with family members. Interestingly, we can see here that some of the big issues – especially health, family/home and finances – could be sources of well-being *or* of worry and concern. These were mixed blessings, and depended very much on individual circumstances. The case studies described in this chapter reaffirm this in some respects.

The women in Walsh and LeRoy's study were depicted as being relatively happy and composed, but nonetheless aware of lost opportunities. Many still yearned for marriage and intimacy. A few desired wistfully to bear children, despite awareness that this was no longer a realistic option for them. When asked about the worst event of the past year, many pinpointed fearful events such as robbery, falls, injuries and unpleasant health treatments (cervical smears, tooth extraction, ear operations and so on), once again demonstrating an awareness of rather more unpleasant things beyond their personal control. The majority of the women, however, retained realistic hopes and dreams for the future, some modest in nature such as continuing to live in the same familiar surroundings, and others more ambitious, hoping for a safer and more peaceful world.

Overall these women had achieved considerable life satisfaction and resilience (see also Chapter 21), while retaining an awareness of their own mortality and of environmental factors that contribute to or constrain their well-being. Life's 'late pickings' (see Chapter 31) show that people with learning disabilities can have many things to look forward to in later life. Their dreams are the dreams of ordinary people who have often lived extraordinary lives. Helping them to realize those dreams requires, on the part of those in support roles, a commitment to engaging with the constellation of personal and environmental factors that shape them.

Conclusion

Hopefully this chapter has shown that older people with learning disabilities can age successfully and have lots to look forward to in later life. Healthiness is integral to successful ageing and older people with learning disabilities have identified this themselves.

A number of theories about successful ageing have been introduced in order to sensitize the reader to ways of thinking about the psychological processes involved, and how these are shaped by individual and environmental factors. What virtually all these theories share in common is a presumption that older people with learning disabilities will be able to share the 'good life' in old age. While prospects for decline in cognitive and physical functioning may accompany ageing (Strydom *et al.* 2009), much as it does in the general population, there are typically compensations to be found in other domains of people's lives. It remains the case, however, that we know considerably more about cognitive decline in adults with Down's syndrome than we do with other syndromes. This needs to be corrected in order to get to grips with variations in biological determinants affecting healthy and successful ageing.

It is important to emphasize that the theories described in this chapter are yet to be formally tested on populations of older people with learning disabilities. Perhaps the best way to think about them is as possible heuristics for glimpsing and making sense of the personal and social worlds of older people.

At a more pragmatic level it has been shown that older people with learning disabilities face formidable barriers in gaining proper access to health services. With health being so integral to successful ageing, it is high time that the evident defects in the design and delivery of health services that complicate or obscure access to these older people are put right. There are undoubtedly parallel problems for people needing to access social care services too but evidence about that lies beyond the scope of this chapter.

In the review conducted by Haveman *et al.* (2009) it was concluded that while the combination of lifelong disorders and the associated medications used, together with the 'normal' ageing processes, puts people with learning disabilities at a greater risk for ill health and an earlier burden of disease in terms of neurological decline, cardiovascular deterioration and some cancers may be less common. However:

> lack of physical activity combined with dental ill-health and inappropriate nutrition resulting in overweight and obesity are the major preventable, and modifiable, risk factors; and these areas need to be addressed in younger age to enable people to develop healthy lifestyle habits that will ensure they continue to mature and age with a sense of wellbeing.
>
> (Haveman *et al.* 2009: 40–1)

In short, preventive health care work is crucial. The review also highlighted key training implications for professionals working in this context, especially:

- taking time with people with communication difficulties;
- building on the person's understanding of their own bodies and what 'health' means for them;
- recognizing special features of illness in people with lifelong disability; and
- understanding the earlier onset of symptomatology of increasing disability in people as they age.

We already know a lot about the biological, biographical and environmental determinants of health as people with learning disabilities age, and a growing amount about how people themselves make sense of what they experience in the process. Some of that evidence is reported in these pages. It is of some concern then that *Valuing People Now* (Department of Health 2009a) is conspicuously silent about ageing in people with learning disabilities. If politicians and policy-makers have left a void here, it is most certainly time for practitioners to take the lead as ambassadors for this group of older people.

References

Atchley, R. (1999) *Continuity and Adaptation in Aging: Creating Positive Experiences*. Baltimore, MD: Johns Hopkins University Press.

Baltes, M. and Carstensen, L.L. (1996) The process of successful ageing, *Ageing and Society*, 16(4): 397–422.

Bigby, C. (2004) *Ageing with a Lifelong Disability: A Guide to Practice, Program and Policy Issues for Human Service Professionals*. London: Jessica Kingsley.

Brandstadter, J. and Grieve, W. (1994) The aging self: stabilising and protective processes, *Developmental Review*, 14: 52–80.

Coleman, P. (1997) The last scene of all, *Generations Review*, 7(1): 2–5.

Cooper, S.A. (1997) Epidemiology of psychiatric disorders in elderly compared with younger adults with learning disabilities, *British Journal of Psychiatry*, 170: 375–80.

Crowther, M.R., Parker, M.W., Achenbaum, W.A., Larimore, W.L. and Koenig, H.G. (2002) Rowe and Kahn's model of successful ageing revisited: positive spirituality – the forgotten factor, *The Gerontologist*, 42(5): 613–20.

Department of Health (2001) *Valuing People: A New Strategy for Learning Disability for the 21st Century*. London: Department of Health.

Department of Health (2006) *Our Health, Our Care, Our Say: A New Direction for Community Services*. Cm 6737. London: Department of Health.

Department of Health (2009a) *Valuing People Now: A New Three Year Strategy for People with Learning Disabilities*. London: Department of Health.

Department of Health (2009b) *Living Well with Dementia: A National Dementia Strategy*. London: Department of Health.

Edgerton, R.B., Gaston, M.A., Kelly, H. and Ward, T.W. (1994) Health care for aging people with mental retardation, *Mental Retardation*, 32(2): 146–50.

Erickson, M., Krauss, M.W. and Seltzer, M.M. (1989) Perceptions of old age among a sample of ageing people with mental retardation, *Journal of Applied Gerontology*, 8(2): 251–60.

Evenhuis, H., Henderson, C.M., Beange, H., Lennox, N. and

Chicoine, B. (2001) Healthy ageing – adults with intellectual disabilities: physical health issues, *Journal of Applied Research in Intellectual Disabilities*. 14: 175–94.

Franklin, N.C. and Tate, C.A. (2009) Lifestyle and successful aging: an overview, *American Journal of Lifestyle Medicine*, 3(1): 6–11.

Foundation for People with Learning Disabilities (2002) *Today and Tomorrow: The Report of the Growing Older with Learning Disabilities Programme*. London: Mental Health Foundation.

Fry, C.L., Dickerson-Putnam, J., Draper, P., Ikels, C., Keith, J., Glascock, A.P. et al. (1997) Culture and the meaning of old age, in J. Sokolovsky (ed.) *The Cultural Context of Aging: Worldwide Perspectives*. Westport, CT: Bergin & Garvey.

Grant, G. and Ramcharan, P. (2007) *Valuing People and Research: The Learning Disability Research Initiative – Overview Report*. London: Department of Health.

Haveman, M.J., Heller, T., Lee, L.A, Maaskant, M.A, Shooshtari, S. and Strydom, A. (2009) *Report on the State of Science on Health Risks and Ageing in People with Intellectual Disabilities*. IASSID Special Interest Research Group on Ageing and Intellectual Disabilities/Faculty Rehabilitation Sciences, University of Dortmund.

Heller, T. (2004) Aging with developmental disabilities: emerging models for promoting health, independence and quality of life, in B.J. Kemp and L. Mosqueda (eds) *Aging with a Disability: What a Clinician Needs to Know*. Baltimore, MD: Johns Hopkins University Press.

Jorm, A., Christensen, H., Henderson, S., Jacomb, P., Korten, P. and Mackinnon, A. (1998) Factors associated with successful aging, *Australasian Journal on Aging*, 17(1): 33–7.

Lawton, M. and Nahemow, L. (1973) Ecology and the aging process, in C. Eisensdorfer and M. Lawton (eds) *Psychology of Adult Development and Aging*. Washington, DC: American Psychological Association.

Lawton, M., Moss, M. and Dumanel, L. (1995) The quality of life among elderly care receivers, *Journal of Applied Gerontology*, 14(2): 150–71.

Liaschenko, J. (1997) Knowing the patient, in S.E. Thorne and V.E. Harp (eds) *Nursing Praxis: Knowledge and Action*. Thousand Oaks, CA: Sage.

Mansell, J. and Beadle-Brown, J. (2004) Person-centred

planning or person-centred action? Policy and practice in intellectual disability services, *Journal of Applied Research in Intellectual Disabilities*, 17(1): 1–10.

Mead, N. and Bower, P. (2000) Patient-centredness: a conceptual framework and review of literature, *Social Science and Medicine*, 51: 1087–110.

Nahemow, L. (1990) The ecological theory of aging: how has it been used? Paper presented to the American Psychological Association, Boston Symposium on Environment and Aging.

NHS Health Scotland (2004) *Health Needs Assessment Report – Summary: People with Learning Disabilities in Scotland*. Glasgow: NHS Health Scotland.

O'Callaghan, A., Murphy, G. and Clare, I.C.H. (2003) The impact of abuse on men and women with severe learning disabilities and their families, *British Journal of Learning Disabilities*, 31(4): 175–80.

Prasher, V.P. (1995) Age-specific prevalence, thyroid dysfunction and depressive symptomatology in adults with Down syndrome and dementia, *International Journal of Geriatric Psychiatry*, 10: 25–31.

Robertson, J., Emerson, E., Hatton, C., Elliott, J., McIntosh, B., Swift, P. *et al.* (2007) Person-centred planning: factors associated with successful outcomes for people with intellectual disabilities, *Journal of Intellectual Disability Research*, 51(3): 232–43.

Rowe, J. and Kahn, R. (1998) *Successful Aging*. New York: Random House.

Strydom, A., Lee, L.A, Jokinen, N., Shooshtari, S., Raykar, V., Torr, J. *et al.* (2009). *Report on the State of Science on Dementia in People with Intellectual Disabilities*. IASSID Special Interest Research Group on Ageing and Intellectual Disabilities.

Tyrell, J. and Dodd, P. (2003) Psychopathology in older age, in P.W. Davidson, V.P. Prasher and M. Janicki (eds) *Mental Health, Intellectual Disabilities and the Aging Process*. Oxford: Blackwell.

Walsh, P.N. and LeRoy, B. (2004) *Women with Disabilities Aging Well: A Global View*. Baltimore, MD: Paul H. Brookes.

Walsh, P.N., Heller, T., Schupf, N. and van Schrojenstein Lantman-de Valk, H. (2001) Healthy ageing – adults with intellectual disabilities: women's health and related issues, *Journal of Applied Research in Intellectual Disabilities*, 14: 195–217.

World Health Organization (1997) Gender as determinant of health, in *The World Health Report*. Geneva: WHO.

World Health Organization (2001) Healthy ageing – adults with intellectual disabilities: summative report, *Journal of Applied Research in Intellectual Disabilities*, 14: 256–75.

35

Research and emancipation: prospects and problems

Jan Walmsley

Introduction

In this chapter the contribution of disability research to the field of learning disabilities is discussed. This exploration seeks to illuminate the interconnections between developments in disability studies and the evolution of policy, research and practice in learning disability.

The chapter begins by describing developments in thinking about disability, in particular the social model of disability. This is contrasted with what are called more traditional approaches to researching disability (including learning disability). The influence these developments in thinking about disability have had in learning disability is then discussed with a focus on three areas:

- the way policy has developed, using the recent English policy documents *Valuing People* and *Valuing People Now* and their implementation as examples;
- the way research has developed, with particular reference to the degree to which learning disability research follows the principles of 'emancipatory research' as developed in disability studies;
- the extent to which people with learning difficulties acknowledge a disabled identity.

Two recent developments have influenced disability research – the 'social model' of disability and what are loosely called 'social constructionist' approaches (see Chapter 2). There is no question that these ideas, in particular the social model, have been influential in learning disability, but it is by no means a straightforward story, for, as a number of commentators have said, the disabled people's movement has had an uneasy relationship with learning disability, more often than not ignoring its existence. Furthermore, relatively few people involved in learning disability –

whether they are researchers, policy-makers, practitioners or service users themselves – have acknowledged the significance of the influence of disability studies. Only a few people, including the present author, all associated with learning disability, have attempted to theorize connections between the two (Aspis 2000; Chappell *et al.* 2001; Walmsley 2001, Goodley 2002). Had we been writing this book 30 years ago it is highly unlikely that this issue would have been thought worthy of consideration. For until the 1990s, when the term 'learning disability' was adopted by the UK government, the links with the disability movement were relatively insignificant. The word 'mental' in 'mental handicap' linked more directly to the area of mental illness, and indeed the legislative framework of the 1959 Mental Health Act applied both to mental illness and to 'subnormality', as learning disability was then called. It is a connection which lingers in the public mind, but legislators are very clear – the *Valuing People* White Paper (Department of Health 2001) and its revision *Valuing People Now* (Department of Health 2009) could not be more different to their equivalents in mental health. Learning disability policy is increasingly aligned to legislation prompted by disability rights, such as the Disability Discrimination Act 1995. In the past generation the position of learning disability in the pantheon of social policy has shifted, from an alignment with mental illness to an alignment with disability. The realignment is far from perfect – the disability movement continues by and large to conceptualize impairment as physical rather than mental, while learning disability, with its own set of policy papers, sits in a solitary place, as much influenced, I will argue, by normalization/social role valorization as it is by the social model of disability. But links there are, particularly conceptual, and these, along with their implications, will be explored here.

The social model of disability

One could argue that the social model of disability is one of the most significant influences on the philosophical landscape in social policy of the late twentieth century. Its influence on thinking in relation to oppressed and excluded groups is profound. As Mike Oliver commented, with reference to then Prime Minister Tony Blair's stated determination to remove barriers to people fulfilling their potential, 'we are all social modellists now' (Oliver 2004: 7)!

The social model of disability defines disability as the societal response to impairment. As Tom Shakespeare summed it up, 'People are disabled by social barriers and failures of provision, not by their bodies' (Shakespeare 2003: 28). The contrasts with more traditional definitions of disability are sharp. Whereas the social model locates problems in society – barriers to full participation by people with a variety of impairments – the traditional (often called 'medical') model locates the problem in the individual. To put it very crudely, rather than telling someone 'you can't do that job because you are blind' (the traditional or medical model), the social model puts the onus on society – in the case of employment, the employer – to make it possible for a person with visual impairments to carry out the job.

Exercise 35.1

Consider the case of a person with visual impairment applying to do your job. What adaptations would need to be made to make it possible?

Comment

As an academic I had direct experience of this. A woman with a visual impairment did do a very similar job to me. She had a number of aids to assist her – a reading service which put papers onto tape for her, a magnifying glass, a change in our habits to ensure we explained what was on a laptop projector image or handout. However, she also commented that time was a major factor. The common practice of circulating papers just before a meeting often meant she could not use her reading service. The sheer weight of work to do at, for example, exam time, in a very short space of time, really taxed her and made it hard to carry out the job to the same standard a person with adequate sight could do without working ridiculously long hours.

Although the idea of 'barriers' appears quite straightforward, and in some cases is, the example above shows that barriers need not be just physical. Barriers can be physical, such as inaccessible buildings; they can be attitudinal, such as the belief that people with impairments cannot do certain things; they can be environmental, such as the way meetings are carried out; or they can be structural, built into the very fabric of society.

What about learning disability? We come to that later, but here it is worth pausing to note that Tom Shakespeare specifically refers to 'bodies', not 'brains' or 'minds' in his definition. This is not insignificant – people who write about the social model do not always consider impairments which are located in the brain rather than the body. As a consequence, our understanding of the barriers people with learning difficulties experience is far less well developed.

To understand the social model requires a distinction to be made between impairment and disability. Impairment is defined as 'lacking all or part of a limb', or 'having a defective limb, organ or mechanism of the body' (UPIAS 1976: 14). Disability is defined as:

> The disadvantage or restriction of activity caused by a contemporary social organisation which takes little or no account of people who have physical impairments and thus excludes them from participation in the mainstream of social activities. Physical disability is therefore a particular form of social oppression.
>
> (UPIAS 1976: 14)

In order to fully understand the idea of barriers it is helpful to categorize the types of things which are seen as barriers within the social model. French (2001) identifies three categories:

- *Structural barriers*: the underlying norms, practices and ideologies of society which are predicated upon a false notion of normal. The social model posits that the underlying assumptions of most societies are that everyone is an able-bodied autonomous adult – others are therefore at a disadvantage.

- *Environmental barriers*: physical obstacles such as steps and narrow doorways, as well as assumptions – for example, about how meetings are run (with reference to written papers) or the time allowed to carry out particular tasks.
- *Attitudinal barriers*: beliefs that because people have an impairment they are unable to do certain things.

Exercise 35.2

Consider the barriers experienced by people with learning disabilities. Try to think of an example of each of the following:

  Structural barriers
  Environmental barriers
  Attitudinal barriers

Comment

Structural barriers: the time allocated for certain tasks can be regarded as a structural barrier. In my own work, bids for research funding are often given very short timescales which make it impossible to fully include people with learning disabilities and enable them to understand and contribute to the bid.

Environmental barriers: the way bus and train timetables are displayed. They rely on people having good reading skills and good eyesight. Recently introduced voice systems on trains and buses make it more likely that people who cannot read well can travel with confidence.

Attitudinal barriers: have you ever taken someone with rather odd behaviour into a shop or a restaurant? If so, you'll know that at best you get stares and at worst you might be asked to leave.

The social model was a radical paradigm shift, with highly significant impact on individuals, on academic thinking and on policy. At a practical level, it was social model thinking that led to the conceptualization of independent living as a goal for disabled people, to be achieved by employing appropriate personal assistance (Morris 1993). It was, at least in part, campaigning by disabled people that led to legislation which made it mandatory for local authorities to

make Direct Payments available so that assistance was under the direct control of disabled people, rather than mediated through care managers (Shakespeare 2003).

Perhaps as important has been the impact on disabled people's self-confidence. Numerous individuals testify to the importance of the social model as a vehicle for empowerment and liberation. Liz Crow, for example: 'For years now the social model of disability has enabled me to confront, survive and even surmount countless situations of exclusion and discrimination' (Crow 1996: 207). A perception that the impairment itself is not the problem, that it lies in societal structures and attitudes, has been tremendously liberating for many disabled people. It has led to developments like disability arts and music, and to the readoption of particular terms, such as cripple (Mairs 1986), to express defiance at the world. It has also inspired remarkably successful direct action, one factor leading to the passage of anti-discriminatory legislation in the UK during the 1990s (Shakespeare 2003).

It is, however, important to acknowledge that the social model is not adopted by everyone with impairments. Wendell (1996: 70) usefully reminds us that '[it is] important not to assume that people with disabilities identify with all others who have disabilities or share a single perspective on disability (or anything else), or that having a disability is the most important aspect of a person's identity or social position'. Nevertheless, the social model has undoubtedly contributed to a radical shift in the way disability, and disabled people, are viewed.

The social model and learning disability

How far have ideas associated with the social model influenced learning disability? As indicated in the introduction, this is approached through consideration of three areas:

- *implementing policy change*: the example of the UK White Paper *Valuing People* and its 2009 revision *Valuing People Now*;
- *research*: user involvement in learning disability research;
- *practice*: the extent to which people with learning difficulties and the organizations controlled by

them have adopted the social model and the ideas associated with it.

Implementing policy change

In order to consider the influence of disability studies on policy change, I have chosen to focus on the UK where *Valuing People*, published by the Department of Health in 2001, was the first learning disability White Paper (signalling a major policy shift) since *Better Services for the Mentally Handicapped* in 1971 (DHSS 1971). It is a useful benchmark by which to consider how far ideas developed in disability studies had influenced learning disability policy in 2001.

The key principles enunciated in *Valuing People* were:

- rights;
- independence;
- choice;
- inclusion.

All of these ideas, but especially rights and independence, are associated with the social model. We can usefully compare *Valuing People* with ideas developed by people who espouse the social model through considering *The Disability Manifesto*, published in the UK in the year *Valuing People* was published (Campbell and Hasler 2001). The *Manifesto* summarizes the aspirations of the UK disabled people's movement at the beginning of the twenty-first century. It sets out the disability movement's view of independent living, and what is needed to achieve it:

> Independent living means enabling disabled people – regardless of age, impairment or where they live – to achieve the same rights and independence as non-disabled people. Independence is not about doing everything for yourself. Nobody does that. It is about having choices about what happens to you . . . The cornerstone of independent living for the many disabled people who need support with aspects of daily life is personal assistance.
>
> (Campbell and Hasler 2001: 11)

The authors, Jane Campbell and Frances Hasler, set out what this might mean for community services:

- involvement of disabled people in drafting eligibility criteria;
- Direct Payments mandatory;
- end to charging for non-residential services, such as day centres;
- end to charging for social care services.

As Means *et al.* (2003: 163) point out, the *Manifesto*, although not at first sight revolutionary, implied a 'radical challenge to community care as currently organised' because it implied a change to the locus of control of what is provided, and how, from care services to individuals.

Valuing People, although it voiced some of the aspirations implicit in the *Manifesto*, did not go as far as identifying personal assistance as the key to realizing rights, independence, choice and inclusion. Rather, it continued to emphasize the importance of improving both specialist learning disability and mainstream services of all kinds – health, housing, support to carers, education – and of developing the workforce through training and partnership working. The nearest the White Paper approached to social model ideas is in Chapter 4, entitled 'More choice and control for people with learning disabilities', where reference is made to advocacy (including self-advocacy), involvement in decision-making, accessible information and communication, Direct Payments and the role of the Disability Rights Commission in helping individuals enforce their rights.

However, the main emphasis in the White Paper was on service improvement. The key tool for achieving this at an individual level was not personal assistance as such, but person-centred planning (see Chapter 25). Although the need for personal assistance may be the outcome of a person-centred plan, the thrust was a service-based process, rather than an emphasis on the right to the type of assistance an individual needs to achieve his or her goals.

Although at first sight the principles of *Valuing People* seem to owe much to the rights-based approaches developed in disability studies, the mechanisms for achieving the principles were heavily dependent on the type of service development most closely associated with normalization/social role valorization. Barriers were not much mentioned, and the solutions were those developed by people associated with normalization/social role valorization through service improvement.

Partnership Boards became the key tool for

implementation of local improvements to service delivery. Although they have representation from 'users and carers', they remain under the control of the statutory services – a far cry from giving power to people with learning disabilities to determine their own futures. Key issues in *The Disability Manifesto*, particularly control over personal assistance, were minor refrains in *Valuing People*; faith was still placed in the ability of services, albeit modernized and more responsive, to achieve the principles.

In the years between 2001 and 2009, the application of social model ideas about personal assistance was extended to people with learning difficulties who piloted Individual Budgets, an extension of Direct Payments. Individual budgets (see Chapter 22) pool the money people are entitled to from a range of benefits and allowances, and allow them to spend it as they wish, rather than be provided with services. In 2003 the government set up a new system of self-directed support called 'In Control'. An evaluation of In Control's second phase in 2008 showed that most people reported improvements in quality of life, choice and control, spending time with people they like, and personal dignity (Hatton 2008).

In 2009, *Valuing People* was revisited and, after a lengthy consultation, a new policy document, *Valuing People Now* (Department of Health 2009) was issued. The alignment with disability is far more explicit in this new strategy than it was in the original *Valuing People*. It is, symbolically, co-signed by the Minister for Disabled People and the Minister for Social Care. Reference is made to the need to 'deliver equality and independent living for all disabled people as we made clear in our cross-Government Report *Improving the Life Chances of Disabled People* (2005)' (Department of Health 2009: 2). The aspiration is explicitly for everyone to have the support they need to exercise the 'right to lead their lives like any others, with the same opportunities and responsibilities' (Department of Health 2009: 4) and the statement that 'the strategy is written from a human rights approach' (p. 11) reads as if the social model, with its emphasis on rights and accessing citizenship via personal assistance, has been a highly significant influence.

Tracing the development of policy statements from *Valuing People* to *Valuing People Now* indicates an increasing alignment of learning disability policy intention with the principles of the social model – that the task in hand is to provide the right services and supports for people to exercise their 'human rights' to be 'equal citizens in society' (Department of Health 2009: 101).

Research

The impact of the social model of disability on research has been considerable. Here I set out the salient features of both traditional and social model research, and then discuss the extent to which its principles have been applied in learning disability research.

The social model of disability and research

If the social model defines disability as the societal response to impairment, it follows that research should shift from studying the 'problems' created by impairment to changing society in order to increase disabled people's opportunities for full inclusion. People who embrace the social model have been very critical of traditional or medical model research which is characterized as:

- research in which experts set the agenda, and decide what questions to ask;
- research in which disabled people are subjects whose problems are examined by non-disabled experts;
- research which assumes that the problem lies within the individual and his or her impairments, not within society;
- research which claims to be objective;
- research which does little to improve the lives of disabled people.

(Zarb 1992)

In a much-quoted exercise, disabled scholar Mike Oliver critiqued the Office of Population Censuses and Surveys' 1986 *Survey of Disabled Adults*. He turned questions such as 'What complaint causes your difficulty in holding, gripping or turning things?' into 'What defects in the design of everyday equipment like jars, bottles and tins causes you difficulty in holding, gripping or turning them?' This simple exercise completely altered the locus of the problem (Oliver 1990: 7, 8). It demonstrated that a census, an apparently scientific and value-free activity, was actually rooted in a strongly medicalized, individualized perspective on impairment. This made the critique particularly powerful, showing how apparently objective research was actually rooted in a particular way of seeing the world.

Exercise 35.3

Change this traditional research question into one which reflects a social model approach: Does your health problem/disability prevent you from going out as often as you would like?

Social model theorists have pointed to three particular problems with traditional research:

- the focus was on the individual with impairments, not on their social relationships or the construction of society;
- it had failed to engage disabled people, except as passive subjects;
- it had not improved the quality of life of disabled people 'though it might have substantially improved the career prospects of researchers'.

(Oliver 1992: 63)

In arguing for change, leading social model proponents (e.g. Oliver 1992; Zarb 1992) identified 'emancipatory research' as the way forward. This built on the work of Paolo Freire (1986), who championed participatory action research, in which people in disadvantaged communities defined the problem and then took action to address it. Disadvantaged people were thus in charge of the research agenda and how it was carried out. Freire argued that this was the liberating way forward if research was to make a real difference. Like Freire, supporters of the social model saw research as a tool for radical social change rather than merely an exercise in finding out more about particular phenomena. True achievement of emancipatory research requires drastic change in what Zarb called the 'material relations' of research. Key features are:

- research as a tool for improving the lives of disabled people;
- research commissioned and funded by organizations of disabled people;

- research in which disabled people have the opportunity to carry out the research;
- researchers accountable to the democratic organizations of disabled people;
- researchers 'on the side of' disabled people – no claim to objectivity.

Emancipatory research rapidly gained a position as the gold standard to which all right-thinking researchers in the disability rights camp aspired. For example, Mark Priestley, a non-disabled researcher, used the extent to which his work on the implementation of community care was emancipatory as a reference point throughout his account of it (Priestley 1999). It is difficult to point to many examples of research projects which fully meet the criteria 'emancipatory'. However, the aspiration has been immensely important, putting any researchers who are not themselves disabled in the position of needing to justify their stance, as Priestley did, and leading to a number of major funding bodies in the UK requiring that any academics aspiring to disability research must demonstrate how disabled people are engaged and involved – the Joseph Rowntree Foundation and the Big Lottery Fund being prominent examples.

Emancipatory research and learning disability

So, 'emancipatory research' was the model advocated by leading scholars in disability research. This type of thinking is in marked contrast to traditional approaches in learning disability research which are based on experts scrutinizing people with learning disabilities as subjects (Kiernan 1999). A good example is the considerable body of research conducted during the 1980s and 1990s on deinstitutionalization from long-stay hospitals (see e.g. Mansell et al. 1987). On the whole this research relied upon an examination of the degree to which people were enabled to participate in society, using principles like O'Brien's five accomplishments (O'Brien and Lyle 1987) as a guide. There was very little consideration given to the idea that society needed to change to reduce people's barriers to participation. Rather, services were enjoined to try harder, to modify people's behaviour to make them more acceptable, to increase staffing levels so that people could take part in valued social activities (paid work, leisure), and to promote integration with 'valued people' – i.e. not people with learning difficulties (Chappell 1997). Chappell argues that this devalues people with learning disabilities by implying that associating with people with the same label is devaluing them.

The dominant philosophy here was normalization/social role valorization (Wolfensberger and Tullman 1989), a set of ideas which put much more emphasis on people changing to fit in, and on services adopting correct attitudes, than it did on barriers (Brown and Smith 1992; Emerson 1992). From the early 1990s research based on participatory principles began to emerge, in which people with learning disabilities joined with academic researchers as 'junior partners' (Walmsley 1994: 157), and the researchers themselves were sympathetic allies. This began to result in a different emphasis. For example, the book by Tim and Wendy Booth (1994) on parents with learning disabilities argued for a move away from the assumption of deficit to an acknowledgement that people struggle with parenting as much because of poverty, negative and unhelpful staff attitudes and practices, and lack of good role models as because of their impairments. Although the term 'barriers' was not used, this marked a departure from more traditional approaches. In a paper published in 1994 I reflected upon what it would mean to apply emancipatory research thinking to the situation of parents with learning disabilities:

> Perhaps a group of parents getting together, deciding they wanted to find out why people like them were having such a hard time, raising some money, employing interviewers or doing it themselves, supervising the production of the report and finding someone to publish it. It is almost impossible to visualise such a scenario given the way things are at present; yet it is such a vision that application of the social model can create.
>
> (Walmsley 1994: 157)

The specific influence of the social model of disability on developments in research in learning disability were evident from the early 1990s onwards. This led some researchers to struggle to go beyond participation, to try to meet the more stringent demands of emancipatory research. In this form of research the researcher is the expert servant of disabled people who must put their knowledge and skills at the disposal of their research subjects, for them to use in whatever ways they choose (Oliver 1992: 111). This formulation goes beyond participatory research and transforms the long-standing role of the sympathetic ally into something more akin to an expert adviser to people with learning disabilities (Walmsley 2004).

In research terms, the association with the social model of disability increased the demands on those who aspired to conduct research with people with learning disabilities, because true emancipatory research gives power and control of the research to disabled people. This raised the stakes considerably. The type of research characteristic of normalization-inspired models – that the research should demonstrate ways in which a 'normal life' could be promoted – was not enough. Somehow, the researcher was expected to find ways of giving control to people with learning disabilities, and of being accountable to them.

Townsley (1998: 78) cites emancipatory research principles in arguing for research to be made accessible: 'The field of disability research is currently making efforts to move towards a more emancipatory approach where the involvement of disabled researchers and consultants is central to the success of any research project'. Rodgers (1999) published a reflective piece on the extent to which her work with women on health issues met the demands of emancipatory research, and, while she concluded that it did not, indicated by her title, 'Trying to get it right', that it should have done! Williams and Simons (2005) extend this debate, suggesting that the non-disabled researcher's role needs to include teaching about research, as well as support, and liken it to a 'writer in residence' model.

Partly because the disabled people's movement has not embraced issues relating to learning disability (Shakespeare 2006) or indeed mental health problems seriously (Beresford 2000), it has been difficult to explore its implications for people with learning disabilities. For example, the belief that access is vital, something subscribed to by all inclusive learning disability researchers (Townsley 1998), is less pressing in the disability field where it can safely be assumed that at least some physically disabled people can access complex theory. Physically impaired academics do not need plain text versions, Makaton or illustrated reports to be able to understand research, whereas most people with learning disabilities do. Similarly, the assumption that, ideally, disabled people should carry out some research themselves is more difficult to achieve for people with learning disabilities.

Even the ability to access research funds is easier for organizations of disabled people (though not as easy as it should be, perhaps) than it is for people with learning disabilities. These groups are likely to need support in discovering what sources of funding are available, in completing a literature review and in filling in the forms.

Physically impaired scholars have the luxury of debating whether narrative research, the focus on individual experience, is a valid focus for research (Finkelstein 1996). However, if this position were adopted in learning disability, most of what has so far been published would not be permissible. The auto-biography, life history and ethnographic traditions have led the field in inclusive learning disability research. There is little else other than service evaluations (Walmsley and Johnson 2003).

Parallels between people with physical impairments and people with learning disabilities are striking – but differences are also considerable. The equivalent to Braille, guide dogs, ramps and so on is not technological but human. For most research, people with learning disabilities need the assistance of non-disabled allies – and they are less amenable to control than technology.

To date, a wholesale migration to emancipatory research with people with learning disabilities has been considered but not implemented. The slogan 'Nothing about us without us' challenges non-disabled researchers to justify their right even to do research into learning disability, just as disabled activists have done. There is no question that some people with learning disabilities have adopted these ideas from the disabled people's movement (see e.g. Aspis 2000).

Exercise 35.4

Consider what 'emancipatory research' might mean for people with learning disabilities. What problems might there be in adopting this approach? Are there other ways of ensuring research does not exploit people with learning disabilities?

The Learning Disability Research Initiative

A brief examination of the Learning Disability Research Initiative, funded by the English Department of Health in the wake of *Valuing People*, will allow us to estimate how far ideas adopted from the disability movement have infiltrated learning disability research. The process by which research was commissioned is one area where a commitment to the involvement of disabled people is evident. Two people with learning disabilities were part of the commissioning panel. Eve Rank Petruzziello was one of these people. She reflected on the extent to which she and her colleague were able to influence the process to meet four principles:

- the extent to which projects included people with learning disabilities;
- inclusion from the very beginning of the research;
- the value of the research to people with learning disabilities;
- value for money.

(Holman 2003)

The connections with the principles of emancipatory research are evident in the first three of these principles. Rank Petruzziello reckoned that she had been able to influence decisions about what to fund to some extent, though she was critical of some of the practicalities – her involvement only began 'from the middle' (Holman 2003: 148) and the paperwork was late in arriving, giving her limited preparation time.

People with learning difficulties are also contributing to the debate about the type of research that is acceptable, building on, but not uncritically accepting, the principles (or the language) associated with emancipatory research. Carlisle Research Collaborative, a group of researchers with and without learning difficulties, has come up with a definition of 'person-led research' which translates the principles of emancipatory research into a language many people with learning difficulties might understand:

Person-led research is research started and controlled by people who have learning difficulties.

Rejected research is where people with learning difficulties are not part of the research when it is about them . . . Where they are not completely included they are rejected.

(Townson *et al.* 2004: 73)

The idea drawn from emancipatory approaches that non-disabled supporters are there solely to carry out the wishes of people with learning difficulties has also been challenged. The Carlisle Research Collaborative explained that they moved from being a self-advocacy group, in which only the members with intellectual disabilities had a voice, to being a collaborative, where everyone has a voice – including researchers and support workers (Townson *et al.* 2004).

Craig Dearden, non-disabled Director of a Cambridge user organization, expresses this view in relation to self-advocacy work more broadly:

> We believe that a partnership between people with and without learning difficulties is far more effective than a situation in which people with learning difficulties are left to do every-thing on their own . . . In my experience, those types of organisations often struggle to deliver, and hit problems in the medium and long term . . . I think that is an incredibly slow approach in a competitive charity environment.
>
> (Dearden, quoted in Mack 2001)

'User participation' (Nolan *et al.* 2007), or partner-ship as Dearden argues, is perhaps more suitable for learning difficulties research than 'emancipatory' approaches.

We must conclude that in research the influence from disability research has been considerable. But it has not been a one-way process. People with learning difficulties, alongside supporters, are finding a way to express ideas about research that are distinctive to the situation of people with learning difficulties, rather than being borrowed wholesale from the disability movement.

Practice: disabled identity

What is probably a far more significant issue for people with learning disabilities is the degree to which they have been influenced, and convinced, by the social model. Critics of normalization argue that it was imposed on people with learning disabilities by others (Chappell 1997). Arguably, the social model is equally external to people with learning disabilities. It has, however, been explicitly adopted by a leading self-advocacy organization, People First London, whose website in 2009 stated:

People First promotes the social model of disability. This is a way of thinking about disability that says it is society that needs to change to include disabled people. We should not have to change to fit in with society. We are against the medical model of disability, which is the view that being disabled means there is 'something wrong' with you.

> http://www.peoplefirstltd.com/
> accessed 28 November 2008

The extent to which social model ideas have been incorporated into learning disability can be explored using the following principles associated with the social model:

- a distinction between disability (oppression created by society) and impairment (the missing or defective part of the body);
- an emphasis on barriers – environmental, attitu-dinal, physical and structural;
- pride in being disabled, assertion of a positive disabled identity.

The use of language is an area where the two groups have differed. The disability movement has insisted on use of the term 'disabled people' to convey the idea that disability is created by society. However, what has been called 'People First language' (Snow 2002) seeks to put the person first and the disability second. In this thinking, people with disabilities are people, first and foremost. As our society's language changes, as we talk about people first, it is argued that:

- perceptions will change; and
- attitudes will change; and
- society's acceptance and respect for people with disabilities will increase; and
- an inclusive society will become a reality.

> (Snow 2002)

This is reinforced by a number of studies (see e.g. Williams 2002) which show that people with learning disabilities reject labels. Indeed, the People First slogan, 'Label jars, not people', itself emphasizes this anti-labelling position. This position was reiterated by People First London on their website:

> Doctors and teachers and other professionals put labels on us marking us out as different from everyone else. It is these labels which get

in the way and stop us taking part the same as anyone else; for example people labelled as having a learning difficulty get sent to special schools and then on to day centres when what we would really like is to get a job; we get put in group homes to live with other people with the same label, with whom we didn't choose to live, when we would prefer to live on our own with support or with a boyfriend or girlfriend.

http://www.peoplefirstltd.com/
accessed 28 November 2008

There is an obvious tension in establishing a self-advocacy group on the basis of belonging to the social category 'people with learning difficulties' and values which emphasize being part of an inclusive society (Simons 1992). Such a group reinforces the very category that people are seeking to downplay.

While people with learning difficulties and their allies have been trying to establish the principle of a common humanity, groups representing disabled people have been claiming the right to define and name themselves as a group with a distinctive separate identity. The disability movement promoted a much less ambiguous stance towards what some people would term 'segregation', by encouraging peer support, peer advocacy, disability arts, disability pride and disability culture.

The self-organizations of disabled people have challenged prevailing negative stereotypes and put forward the idea that disabled people were taking control of their own identity, confronting oppression and empowering themselves, especially through political activism. The development of disability culture in opposition to popular culture was a key strategy for promoting positive cultural conceptions of disability. The arts have been used as a means of fighting back against the disabling dominant culture (Campbell and Oliver 1996).

Disabled people claim that if they do not define themselves, then others will continue to do it for them. Thus, 'coming out' as a disabled person has important political meaning (Wendell 1996). The extent to which people with learning disabilities have embraced their identity as a distinct social group is questionable. Simons (1992) noted few connections between self-advocacy and disabled people's groups. It is only recently that social model ideas about pride in

a separate identity have begun to impact on the self-advocacy 'movement', as have attempts to include people with learning difficulties in the disability movement. I have argued (Walmsley 1997) that when the social model of disability was being developed by disabled people, services for people with learning difficulties were largely influenced by a different family of ideas: normalization (Wolfensberger 1972); ordinary life (King's Fund 1980); social role valorization (Wolfensberger 1983); and the five accomplishments (O'Brien and Lyle 1987). The chief strategy for change that arises out of these service ideologies is for people with learning difficulties to 'pass' into the non-disabled group, to be 'inserted' into mainstream society (Winance 2007). In contrast, the more politicized lobby of disabled people draws upon the social model of disability to raise the consciousness of all disabled people, with the intention of tackling disadvantage through political action (Oliver 1990).

As noted already, the relationship that people with learning difficulties and self-advocacy organizations have with the disability movement is not straightforward. Aspis (quoted in Campbell and Oliver 1996) draws attention to the discrimination that people with learning difficulties have faced in the disability movement. People with certain impairments, including those with learning difficulties, are not always welcome. There have also been disagreements over language. Goodley (2002), for example, discusses criticisms of the term 'people with learning difficulties' made by those who prefer the term 'disabled people'. A degree of tension between people with learning difficulties and the disability movement is indicated in this statement from Swindon People First:

Disabled people without learning difficulties need to:

- respect us;
- listen to us;
- learn from us;
- not lecture us and tell us what we should think.

(Swindon People First 2002: 100)

At present it is hard to assess what impact the social model of disability has had on people with learning difficulties and their organizations. However, research that explores how individuals perceive themselves suggests a very limited self-identification as 'disabled'. Davies and Jenkins (1997) found that only 28 per cent of their sample of people with learning difficulties included themselves in the social category of people with mental handicap/learning difficulties, and that 13 per cent of those discussed their identity in ways that were partial or unclear. Finlay and Lyons (2000) reported that it was hard to find evidence of a group identity, which they argue needs to be present if people with learning difficulties are to discuss and bring about change for themselves. The common assumption that people with learning difficulties experience a negative identity is hard to verify. There are a number of strategies which people may use to protect a 'threatened identity' (Breakwell 1986). Finlay and Lyons (2000: 47) suggested that

> It is not really possible to know for sure whether people do or do not really think they are group members but we cannot assume that just because researchers think the category is salient that the participants also see things this way.

There is plenty of evidence that people with learning difficulties reject labels (Palmer *et al.* 1999; Williams 2002). Despite adopting the social model, the website of People First London quoted above indicates that it is labels, rather than a wider range of barriers, that get in the way of people achieving what they want in life.

Perhaps what is needed is for people with learning difficulties to have opportunities to learn about the social model and mould it more specifically to their circumstances. Simone Aspis, a self-advocate who acknowledges how she has been influenced by the social model, consciously chooses to describe herself as a 'disabled person with learning difficulties' (Aspis 2000). Louise Townson, a leading self-advocate, acknowledges how much she has learnt about the potential of the performing arts as a means of challenging negative perceptions through reviewing a book. She writes:

> However, the book taught me about the potential of performing arts for self-advocacy

which was something I had no idea about.

(Townson 2003: 836)

This indicates that the power of social model ideas to help people with learning difficulties understand and challenge their situation has yet to be fully realized – exchange of information and the opportunities to learn would appear to be key issues here.

One might argue that people with learning difficulties are subject to internal oppression, in which they absorb the devalued position that they as a group have in society, and try to distance themselves from this negative identity. Recently, some disability scholars have adapted the social model to consider the idea of 'internal oppression': that the attitudes of disabled people may themselves be self-defeating. Eddie, interviewed for a book, recalled how hard it was for him to accept that he was disabled – denial was a strategy both he and his family used to deal with his difference:

> I was brought up believing I was the same as my brothers ... [My family] have come to accept the fact that I'm the same as everyone else, can do as well as anyone else which has its advantages which was not being molly coddled ... I was normal like everyone else and I had the opinion that I was better than disabled people and I wasn't disabled ... I knew I was disabled but I just couldn't accept it.

(Shakespeare *et al.* 1996: 50)

It is not difficult to recognize that attitudes from parents may contribute to this denial of difference for people with learning difficulties also. Todd and Shearn (1997) identified strategies used by parents to shield people from knowing that they were the possessors of a 'toxic identity'. People with learning difficulties may need the opportunity to learn about the social model before one concludes that it is an alien concept, imposed from afar.

Exercise 35.5

How far do you think the idea of 'internalized oppression' explains the failure of people with learning difficulties to develop a pride in being different?

Conclusion

Ideas developed in the disability movement have influenced thinking in learning disability also. Academics, policy-makers, practitioners and some people with learning difficulties have clearly been influenced by the disability movement's big idea. It is perhaps regrettable that the powerful thinking that has revolutionized thinking about physical impairment has not been brought to bear equally on the situation of people with learning difficulties. Although it is arguable that disabled people should be natural allies of people with learning difficulties, given that they share experiences of impairment and oppression, in fact, in the UK at least, relationships have been patchy, and much disability research assumes that impairment is of the body rather than of the mind. A barriers approach has a great deal to offer the learning disability field. It is liberating to think of barriers as being in society rather than as unmovable aspects of an individual. It is, however, necessary to recognize that a direct translation of action developed for people with physical impairments is too crude a tool to deliver real and lasting changes for people with learning difficulties. More hard thinking is needed if policy and practice are usefully to adapt the social model for people with learning difficulties, but an important start has been made.

References

Aspis, S. (2000) Researching our history: who is in charge? in L. Brigham, D. Atkinson, M. Jackson, S. Rolph and J. Walmsley (eds) *Crossing Boundaries: Change and Continuity in the History of Learning Disabilities*. Kidderminster: BILD.

Beresford, P. (2000) What have madness and psychiatric system survivors got to do with disability and disability studies? *Disability and Society*, 15(1): 167–72.

Booth, T. and Booth, W. (1994) *Parenting under Pressure: Mothers and Fathers with Learning Difficulties*. Buckingham: Open University Press.

Breakwell, G.M. (1986) *Coping with Threatened Identities*. London: University Paperbacks.

British Journal of Learning Disabilities (2003) Special issue, *Valuing People – The Interface with Research*, 31(4).

Brown, H. and Smith, H. (eds) (1992) *Normalisation: A Reader for the Nineties*. London: Routledge.

Campbell, J. and Hasler, F. (2001) *The Disability Manifesto*. London: Scope.

Campbell, J. and Oliver, M. (1996) *Disability Politics: Understanding our Past, Changing our Future*. Leeds: Disability Press.

Chappell, A. (1997) From normalization to where? in L. Barton and M. Oliver (eds) *Disability Studies Past, Present and Future*. Leeds: Disability Press.

Chappell, A., Goodley, D. and Lawthorn, R. (2001) Making connections: the relevance of the social model of disability for people with learning difficulties, *British Journal of Learning Disabilities*, 29: 45–50.

Crow, L. (1996) Including all of our lives, in J. Morris (ed.) *Encounters with Strangers: Feminism and Disability*. London: Women's Press.

Davies, C.A. and Jenkins, R. (1997) She has different fits to me: how people with learning difficulties see themselves, *Disability and Society*, 12(1): 95–109.

Department of Health (2001) *Valuing People: A New Strategy for Learning Disability for the 21st Century*. London: Department of Health.

Department of Health (2009) *Valuing People Now*. London: Department of Health.

Department of Health and Social Security (1971) *Better Services for the Mentally Handicapped*. Cm 4683. London: HMSO.

Emerson, E. (1992) What is normalization? in H. Brown and H. Smith (eds) *Normalisation: A Reader for the Nineties*. London: Routledge.

Finkelstein, V. (1996) The disability movement has run out of steam, *Disability Now*, February: 11.

Finkelstein, V. (1999) Doing disability research (extended book review), *Disability and Society*, 14(6): 859–67.

Finlay, W.M.L. and Lyons, E. (2000) Social categorisations, social comparisons and stigma: presentations of self in people with learning difficulties, *British Journal of Social Psychology*, 39: 129–46.

Freire, P. (1986) *Pedagogy of the Oppressed*. Harmondsworth: Penguin.

French, S. (2001) Living in the mainstream, in *K202 Care Welfare and Community, Workbook 2, Theories and Practice*. Milton Keynes: The Open University.

Goodley, D. (2002) What's in a label? *Community Living*, 15(3): 2.

Hatton, C. (2008) *A Report on In Control's Second Phase: Evaluation and Learning 2005–7*. London: In Control.

Holman, A. (2003) In conversation: Eve Rank-Petruziello, *British Journal of Learning Disabilities*, 31(4): 148–9.

Kiernan, C. (1999) Participation in research by people with learning disability: origins and issues, *British Journal of Learning Disabilities*, 27(2): 43–7.

King's Fund (1980) *An Ordinary Life*. London: King's Fund.

Mack, T. (2001) We'll do it our way, *Guardian Weekend*, 14 April.

Mairs, N. (1986) On being a cripple, in *Plaintexts: Essays, 9–20*. Tucson, AZ: University of Arizona Press.

Mansell, J., Felce, D., Jenkins, J., de Kock, U. and Toogood, S. (1987) *Developing Staffed Housing for People with Mental Handicap*. Tunbridge Wells: Costello.

Means, R., Richards, S. and Smith, R. (2003) *Community Care: Policy and Practice*, 3rd edn. London: Palgrave.

Morris, J. (1993) *Community Care or Independent Living*. York: Joseph Rowntree Foundation in association with Community Care.

Nolan, M., Hanson, E., Grant, G. and Keady, J. (eds) (2007) *User Participation in Health and Social Care Research*, London: McGraw-Hill.

Noonan Walsh, P. (2003) A courtly welcome: observations on the research initiative, *British Journal of Learning Disabilities*, 31(4): 190–3.

O'Brien, J. and Lyle, C. (1987) *Framework for Accomplishments: A Workshop for People Developing Better Services*. Decatur, GA: Responsive System Associates.

Oliver, M. (1990) *The Politics of Disability*. London: Macmillan.

Oliver, M. (1992) Changing the social relations of research production, *Disability, Handicap and Society*, 7(2): 101–14.

Oliver, M. (2004) Introduction, in M. Oliver, C. Barnes, J. Swain and S. French (eds) *Disabling Barriers: Enabling Environments*, 2nd edn. London: Sage.

Palmer, N., Peacock, C., Turner, F. and Vasey, B. supported by Williams, V. (1999) Telling people what you think, in J. Swain and S. French (eds) *Therapy and Learning Difficulties*. London: Butterworth Heinemann.

Priestley, M. (1999) *Disabled Politics and Community Care*. London: Jessica Kingsley.

Rodgers, J. (1999) Trying to get it right: undertaking research involving people with learning difficulties, *Disability and Society*, 14(4): 421–33.

Shakespeare, T. (2003) Having come so far, where to now? *Times Higher Education Supplement*, 7 November: 28.

Shakespeare, T. (2006) *Disability Rights and Wrongs*. London: Routledge.

Shakespeare, T., Gillespie-Sells, K. and Davies, D. (1996) *The Sexual Politics of Disability: Untold Desires*. London: Cassell.

Simons, K. (1992) *'Sticking up for Yourself': Self Advocacy and People with Learning Difficulties*. York: Joseph Rowntree Foundation.

Snow, K. (2002) People First language, www.modmh.state.mo.us/Sikeston/people.htm.

Swindon People First Research Team (2002) *Journey to Independence: Direct Payments for People with Learning Difficulties*. Swindon: Swindon People First.

Todd, S. and Shearn, J. (1997) Family dilemmas and secrets: parents' disclosure of information to their adult offspring with learning disabilities, *Disability and Society*, 12(3): 341–66.

Townsley, R. (1998) Information is power: the impact of accessible information on people with learning difficulties, in L. Ward (ed.) *Innovations in Advocacy and Empowerment for People with Intellectual Disabilities*. Chorley: Lisieux Hall.

Townson, L. with Chapman, R. (2003) Review of *Disability Arts Against Exclusion* by D. Goodley and M. Moore, *Disability and Society*, 18(6): 835–6.

Townson, L., Macauley, S., Harkness, E., Chapman, R., Docherty, A. *et al.* (2004) We are all in the same boat: doing people led research, *British Journal of Learning Disabilities* 32(2): 72–6.

UPIAS (Union of the Physically Impaired against Segregation) (1976) *Fundamental Principles of Disability*. London: UPIAS.

Walmsley, J. (1994) Learning disability: overcoming the barriers? in S. French (ed.) *On Equal Terms*. London: Butterworth-Heinemann.

Walmsley, J. (1997) Including people with learning difficulties: theory and practice, in L. Barton and M. Oliver (eds) *Disability Studies: Past, Present and Future*. Leeds: Disability Press.

Walmsley, J. (2001) Normalisation, emancipatory research and learning disability, *Disability and Society*, 16(2): 187–205.

Walmsley, J. and Johnson, K. (2003) *Inclusive Research with People with Learning Disabilities: Past, Present and Futures*. London: Jessica Kingsley.

Walmsley, J. (2004) Inclusive research in learning disability: the (non disabled) researcher's role, *British Journal of Learning Disabilities*, 32(2): 65–71.

Wendell, S. (1996) *The Rejected Body*. London: Routledge.

Williams, V. (2002) Being researchers with the label of learning difficulty: an analysis of talk carried out by a self-advocacy research group. Unpublished PhD thesis, Open University.

Williams, V. and Simons, K. (2005) More researching together: the role of non disabled researchers in working with People First members, *British Journal of Learning Disabilities*, 33(1): 6–14.

Winance, M. (2007) Being normally different? Changes to normalization processes: from alignment to work on the norm, *Disability and Society*, 22(6): 625–38.

Wolfensberger, W. (1972) *The Principle of Normalisation in Human Services*. Toronto: National Institute on Mental Retardation.

Wolfensberger, W. (1983) Social role valorization: a proposed new term for the principle of normalization, *Mental Retardation*, 21(6): 234–9.

Wolfensberger, W. and Tullman, S. (1989) A brief outline of the principle of normalization, in A. Brechin and J. Walmsley (eds) *Making Connections: Reflecting on the Lives and Experiences of People with Learning Difficulties*. Sevenoaks: Hodder & Stoughton.

Zarb, G. (1992) On the road to Damascus: first steps towards changing the relations of disability research production, *Disability, Handicap and Society*, 7: 125–38.

Index

Locators shown in *italics* refer to figures and tables.

...ucture and organization, 96–7
...tion to learning difficulty services, 90–6
...earning disabled
...cteristics and roll, 374
Sell, R., 249
Seltzer, G., 453
senses, human
    influence of impairment of on learning disabled behaviours, 140
    strategies for assisting in child cerebral palsy, 163–4
    see also specific senses eg eyesight, impairment of
services, learning disability
    difficulty of accessing for those with additional mental health problems, 382–3
    history of delivery, 59–70, *64, 66–7*
    link between reality, quality of and quality-of-life, 73–6, *74,* 449–50
    provision supporting family carers, 178–80
    responses in relation to sexuality, 256–7
    salience in the lives of learning disabled children, 110–11
    see also specific types, elements and players eg care, social; healthcare; personalization; protection, learning disabled; self-advocacy; staff, healthcare
sexuality, learning disabled
    adolescent narratives of approaches to, 194–5
    history and characteristics of female, 259–60
    improvements necessary to change female, 260–2
    role of discussion in understanding, 250–2
    role of research in describing, 262–4
    role of stereotyping of, 255–6
    salience of identity and risk in understanding, 252–5
    service responses in relation to, 256–7
    social history of understanding and context of, 248–9
    teaching versus learning about, 249–50
    see also lesbianism
Sexual Offences Act (1956), 270
Sexual Offences Act (1967), 270
Sexual Offences Act (2003), 47, 248
Shakespeare, T., 96, 490, 499
Shaping the Future of Care Together (2009), 294
Sheard, D., 346
Shearer, A., 92
Shearn, J., 204
Sheffield
    example of learning disabled daytime opportunity provision, 377–8
Shirley (case study)
    joys and trials of being learning disabled parent, 320–2
Shotter, J., 253
Shoultz, B., 92
siblings
    salience in the lives of learning disabled children, 107–8
sickness *see* illness
sight, impairment of
    definitions, characteristics and child need, 164–5
    strategies for assisting child health needs, 165
signing (sign language)
    use of as teaching technique for learning disabled, 229–30
Simon, G., 62–3
Simons, K., 88, 498
Sinason, V., 35, 283

skills, interpersonal and personal
    as driver for friendship development among learning disabled, 332–4
    particular need for as learning disabled age, 453
Smith Magenis syndrome, 138, 139, 140
Smull, M., 347–8, 353
Snow, K., 497
social construction
    significance on understanding learning disability, 19–24, *21, 22*
Social Rational Model of Disability (Thomas), 106
society
    impact of on quality-of-life of learning disabled, 78, 79–80
    role in developing learning disabled self protection, 285–6
Song, M., 286
Sourani, T., 285
Special Education Needs and Disability Act (2001), 48
speech and language *see* language and speech
stability, social
    role in nurturing learning disabled friendships, 339
staff, healthcare
    experience of America in relation to learning disabled care, 422–4
    need for education as response to learning disabled behaviours, 243–4
    role clarification when imparting diagnosis of learning disability, 152
    see also qualities required eg professionalism, staff
stages, life *see* lifecourse and lifespan, the
Stancliffe, R., 301
Stansfield, A., 264
statements, police
    extent of reliability of from learning disabled, 274–5
    role and importance of Registered Intermediaries in process of, 275
stereotypying, personal
    role in denial of learning disabled sexuality, 255–6
sterilization
    role of in female learning disabled sexuality, 264
Stern, D., 122
Stevens, A., 301
stories, life *see* narratives, life
Story so Far, The (Greig), 375
strategies, physical and sensory
    in cases of child cerebral palsy, 163–4
    in cases of child hearing impairment, 166–7
    in cases of child visual impairment, 165
strategies, reactive and preventive
    as response to learning disabled behaviours, 236–9
strategies, teaching
    communication for learning disabled, 128–31
    see also specific eg signing; systems, visual
Strauss, A., 203
stress, family carers
    transactional models of coping, 172–3
    see also resilience, personal, family carers
structures, social
    impact of on quality-of-life of learning disabled, 78, 79–80
Sturmey, P., 289, 290
support, for parents
    characteristics, 155–7
    models of, 154–5
    salience of early when coping with newly diagnosed learning disability, 153–4